WITHDRAWN

The Poetical Works of
JOHN GAY

JOHN GAY

From the painting by W. Aikman

The Poetical Works of
JOHN GAY

Including 'POLLY'
'THE BEGGAR'S OPERA'
and Selections from the other
Dramatic Work

Edited by
G. C. FABER, M.A.
Fellow of All Souls College

NEW YORK / RUSSELL & RUSSELL

REPRODUCED FROM A COPY IN THE COLLECTIONS
OF THE BROOKLYN PUBLIC LIBRARY

FIRST PUBLISHED IN 1926
REISSUED, 1969, BY RUSSELL & RUSSELL
A DIVISION OF ATHENEUM PUBLISHERS, INC.
L. C. CATALOG CARD NO: 68-15124
PRINTED IN THE UNITED STATES OF AMERICA

4469

CONTENTS.

(The dates given are those of publication, unless otherwise stated.)

CONTENTS.

CONTENTS.

PAGE

CONTENTS.

CONTENTS.

PAGE

PLAYS AND OPERAS.

APPENDIXES.

INTRODUCTION.

I

LIGHTLY undertaken so long ago as 1913 and interrupted by ' the soldier's trade ', this edition of Gay's poems and some of his plays is completed in an atmosphere unexpectedly indulgent to the poet. *The Beggar's Opera* and *Polly* (though her begetter would hardly have known her!) have enjoyed their respective reincarnations. *Trivia*, magnificently illustrated and upholstered, may be had by book-loving millionaires. The same publisher (Mr. Daniel O'Connor) issues Mr. Lewis Melville's *Life and Letters of John Gay*. But the Poet's resurrection is only partial. Few read his *Fables* ; the rest of his work is all but forgotten.[1]

Yet Gay's achievement was not inconsiderable. Born and educated in Barnstaple and apprenticed to a silk-mercer in London, he was buried with pomp in Westminster Abbey, and honestly mourned by Dukes and Duchesses. Nor was this the reward of ' gentle qualities ' only. His family (it is said) was good ; but there was more than gentility in his veins. The unkindly critics of our own time have labelled him a shiftless, careless, out-at-elbows writer, the amiable satellite of the great wits, living for a while by a reflected splendour, but destined finally to succumb to a deserved obscurity. This was not the opinion of his contemporaries, whether of the great wits or the great world. ' In wit a man ', he endeared himself to Pope and Swift, no less than to the Queensberrys and the Hon. Mrs. Howard. Pope writes his epitaph ; Swift, for days, dare not read the letter which contains the news of his ' dear friend Mr. Gay's death '. Both very great men, and not fond of fools.

Gay has, indeed, the purely lyrical gift denied, in equal measure, to these two. There is, moreover, originality, both of form and matter, in almost all his work.[2] His wit is less shrewd and subtle than Pope's, less gross and forcible than Swift's ; but, like salt in solution, it pervades the whole and preserves it from the expected decay. His craftsmanship, incapable except at rare moments of Pope's extreme felicity or Swift's monstrous vigour, is careful, neat, sustained. He observes, and records ; loves the concrete, the visible and tangible instance, loathes vapidity. Like all the men of his age, he likes to feel his feet on the firm earth ; and if at times the irresistible breath of song lifts him off it, he is not carried far. No counterfeit Olympus

---

[1] Written, and in type, before the reissue of his Plays and some of his Poems in the attractive format of *The Abbey Classics* by Messrs. Chapman and Dodd.

[2] Signally, of course, in *The Beggar's Opera*, which Georgy Calmus calls *eine der originellsten und geistreichsten Erscheinungen auf dem Gebiet der Opern-Parodie.* (Sammelbände der Internationalen Musik-Gesellschaft, VIII, ii, 286.)

for him ; the lower slopes of a friendly Parnassus, where his playful ironic fancy breathes a congenial air—these are his spiritual home.

And yet this child of the ' Age of Reason ' has his face to the light of the nineteenth century. There are, for instance, gleams of a power of expression beyond the normal of his day, as in

> He look'd, and saw the miser's breast,
> A troubled ocean, ne'er at rest. (*Fables*, 2nd series, vii.)

The metaphor, it is true, is not sustained, as it would have been by a nineteenth-century poet, beyond the moment of its inception. Four commonplace lines succeed, before the image is vivified by the concluding lines :

> And never, or in thought or dream,
> His breast admits one happy gleam.

Nevertheless, here and elsewhere Gay is the forerunner of a later age. And not merely in an occasional suggestive phrase. His *Contemplation on Night*, and more than one passage besides, utter a sense of the sublime akin to Wordsworth's.

These ideas cannot be pursued here ; they only serve to measure our surprise at the completeness of the oblivion into which the great bulk of his work has dropped. For long after his death, his place in English letters seemed assured. Editions of the *Fables* and the *Poems* continued to stream from the presses ; the *Beggar's Opera* enchanted successive generations ; the famous songs, *Sweet William*, *'Twas when the seas were roaring*, *Oh ruddier than the Cherry*, remained popular favourites ; collected editions of his poetical works followed each other from 1770 onwards at frequent intervals. Even the harsh verdict of Dr. Johnson (in 1781) did him no harm :

As a poet, he cannot be rated very high. He was, as I once heard a female critic remark, ' of a lower order '. He had not in any great degree the ' mens divinior ', the dignity of genius.

To which, in 1804, the editor of Cooke's Pocket Edition :

With respect to Dr. Johnson's estimate of the poetical character of our Author, the Editor cannot but, in justice to the transcendant merit of Gay, observe, that the great critic animadverts, in some instances, with a degree of asperity that cannot be agreeable to a candid reader.

And indeed, if ' transcendant ' be hardly the *mot juste* for Gay, Dr. Johnson for his part did the poet less than justice. ' Of his little Poems the public judgment seems to be right ; they are neither much esteemed, nor totally despised.' This ' public judgment ' was the Critic's own, projected on the mist which so often conceals popular opinion from great men. Gay was still a ' popular ' author when Johnson wrote, and the lease of his popularity had yet a long time to run—until in fact the ' Age of Reason ' died away in the nineteenth century. And even then Gay's reputation wilted more slowly than might have been expected, in a day when poets no longer walked the streets and sat in coffee-houses, but stood apart, in rapt communion with Nature. In 1884 Austin Dobson, while he denies to the *Fables* permanent literary merit, somewhat grudgingly admits that ' they have given pleasure to several generations of readers, old and young ; and they have enriched the language with more than one indispensable quotation '. But in 1893, when Mr. Underhill published his edition—the only complete modern edition of the poems—Gay is evidently less esteemed by his editor as a poet than as an historical figure. The reader, he thinks, ' will probably marvel at the reputation which Gay enjoyed in his lifetime, and still more at the high position in the hierarchy of English poets that is now accorded to him . . . time has indeed laid a gentle hand upon the literary fame of John Gay '.

II

No really satisfactory text of Gay's collected works exists, and apart from the early editions (by which phrase, here and elsewhere, I mean editions published in Gay's lifetime or soon after his death) there are very few satisfactory texts of any of the poems or plays. The reprints by Mr. O'Connor of *Trivia* and *Polly*, Lovat Fraser's edition of *The Beggar's Opera*, and Mr. MacLeod's earlier edition of the same play are perhaps the only trustworthy texts published since the early editions.[1] A certain disgust lays hold of the spirit, as one grows familiar with the process of modernization to which the early eighteenth-century writers have been submitted. It is a process of vulgarization. All the old typographical beauties disappear— the use of italics, the use of capitals, the old-fashioned spelling and punctuation. Fine shades of meaning are obliterated ; gross and gratuitous errors are not wanting. But there are none to do battle with. Nameless hacks and proof-readers are but poor targets for the just *odium bibliographicum* of an exacter age.

I have recorded the chief collected editions in the *Bibliographical Summary*, and I need only refer to them briefly here. Collected editions were published in Dublin (1770) and in London (1772) ; but these were very far from being complete. In 1773 John Bell is said to have published a four-volume edition, which I have been unable to trace.[2] In 1777 appeared Bell's *Poets of Great Britain* ; Gay's poems occupied three volumes. This edition is evidently based on the 1773 edition ; and I refer to it frequently as *Bell*. In punctuation, spelling, and typography it stands at the beginning of the modern tradition ; and it is much more complete than the editions of 1770 and 1772. In 1779 appeared a new edition, in volumes 41 and 42 of *The Works of the English Poets*, for which Dr. Johnson's Prefaces were written, and published separately in 1781[3] ; the editor added some new

---

[1] Since this Introduction was written, the editions of *The Beggar's Opera* and *Polly* published by Heinemann, and Chapman & Dodd, and Mr. Brett-Smith's edition of *The Shepherd's Week*, as well as the *Abbey Classics* reprint mentioned in a preceding foot-note, must be added to those named above.

[2] See below, pp. xxiv and xxix.

[3] Mr. R. W. Chapman comments : ' To say that Johnson's Prefaces were " published separately in 1781 " is accurate but a trifle misleading. What

pieces and omitted others given by Bell. In 1795 Jeffery published his six-volume edition of the complete works ; of which the first four volumes appear to have been based on Bell's 1773 edition. The text is *not* modernized, but is very carelessly edited. The later editions of Cooke and Park have no textual value. In 1893 Mr. John Underhill published his two-volume edition in *The Muses' Library*.

Underhill's edition is, and has been since its publication, generally accepted as the standard edition of Gay. It is warmly praised by Mr. Melville, who speaks of it as ' admirable '. On the historical side the praise is fully deserved ; the Memoir and Notes are excellent. But it can hardly be a matter for surprise that an editor, who avowedly despises his author, should provide us with a text in many respects even less satisfactory than its predecessors. His interest was directed primarily to the fascinating task of re-setting the early eighteenth-century stage. It was natural that he should accept the traditional text. It was natural that he should rely—in editing the *Fables*—on the guidance of so distinguished a critic as Austin Dobson, who was himself unfortunate in lending his name and his famous preface to a text which he had certainly not edited and probably not even read. It was natural that he should take the Quarto of 1720 as presenting a final text, though it was in fact overhauled by Gay for the 12mo edition of 1731 ; that he should record only a few of the more obvious variants ; that he should attempt no systematic collation ; and that he should lay no re-straining hand upon the imaginative impulses of his printer. But he ought not, in these circumstances, to have claimed that ' every effort has been made to put forward a complete and trustworthy text '.

It is curious, too, to find Mr. Underhill recording, without any apparent remorse, that ' the spelling and the punctuation have in all cases been made to conform to the usage of the present day '. As a matter of fact the spelling and punctuation of his edition are more than a hundred years old. It was Bell's editor who, in 1777, re-punctuated and re-spelt Gay. It was Bell, in short, who poured the old wine into the new bottles, and not, as Mr. Underhill's preface seems to convey, Mr. Underhill. Nor can it be said that where the editor of 1893 differs from the editor of 1777 the difference is for the better. The contrary statement would be nearer to the truth. Such differences are, for the most part, errors which made their way into the text after Bell.

I have some remarks upon Gay's punctuation and spelling to offer below. Here I will but give a single example of the progressive deteriorations of our text.

happened was this. The Prefaces were intended to precede the works of each Poet, and were paged (&c.) accordingly. But in 1779 the 56 volumes of Poets were ready, and Johnson had done only four-tenths of his work. The publishers accordingly " gave directions to the binder " to collect the existing prefaces in 4 volumes. They were too prudent to allow the public to buy the 4 without the 56 ; and when in 1781 4 became 10 the new 6 were issued only " to compleat setts ".'

In Fable I the Lyon boasts :

> These carcasses on either hand,
> Those bones that whiten all the land
> My former deeds and triumphs tell,
> Beneath these jaws what numbers fell.

So the passage is printed in the early editions. The absence of a comma after *land* conforms to Gay's rule not to interpose a stop between the last subject and its verb. *Deeds and triumphs* are the object not the subject of *tell*. The last line explains what they were. Bell puts a comma after *land*. But Dobson's editor, followed by Underhill, completely misreading the passage, inserts a further comma after *triumphs*. This makes *deeds and triumphs* into a third subject, parallel with *carcasses* and *bones* ; the last line becomes directly dependent on the verb. Such a reading is not only unnecessary and destructive of the sense ; but it attributes to Gay the kind of nerveless craftsmanship from which he was remarkably free. It was not his habit so to couple the concrete and the abstract.

The principle of making an old writer conform to modern usage is, indeed, to my thinking, unintelligent. It is certainly dangerous. If it is to be applied in this thoroughgoing manner, it is difficult to exaggerate the degree of care which must be exercised. What pitfalls await the editor, when the brain lags behind the eye (as it too often will !), the example just given sufficiently indicates. But more irritating to a careful reader than even such mistakes as this— which could hardly be suspected by the *most* careful reader—are the inconsistencies which continually affront him. How difficult it is for an editor to be consistent I know only too well. But there is one inconsistency from within (that is, of the author), and another inconsistency from without (that is, of the editor). The kind of inconsistency I mean here is a wilful, habitual, inconsistency, not at all dependent on the author's *ipsissima verba*, but resulting from the careless application of our own rules. We pickle our rods for our own backs. We decide always to print (say) *confined*, and yet constantly let *confin'd* slip past our pen ; or we baffle the expectation of *heaven's* by *heav'n's* or even *heav'ns* ; or we print *mis'ries* where Gay for once wrote and meant *miseries*.[1] We level our author's capitals with the common herd of lower case letters ; yet not only do we leave a few unaccountably standing, but we set up new and quite inappropriate capitals of our own.[2] The ' white lines ', which Gay in the *Fables* most deliberately employed, to separate the ' general ' from the ' particular ', or to mark a natural line of cleavage, we ignore ; but we introduce white lines, without the author's sanction, and cleave his poems into unnatural parts.[3] In one respect, only, has modern usage achieved complete consistency. There are practically no italics in Mr. Underhill's edition.

[1] Fable VII, 2nd series, l. 131.
[2] e.g. Fable XI, l. 34. The *T*urkey or the *G*oose.
[3] e.g. Fable II, between ll. 16 and 17.

III

The present edition aims at providing a complete and, as far as possible, an accurate text of all Gay's *poetical* work. Mr. Underhill's edition, though it included ' Songs from the Plays ', did not contain *Dione,* or *The What d'ye call it,* or *The Captives.* I give these, and I have also thought it desirable to include *The Mohocks* (which is partly in verse), and the three ' Operas ' ; for it is impossible to appreciate the Songs, when they are divorced from their original setting. The fragments of verse from *The Wife of Bath, Three Hours after Marriage, The Distress'd Wife,* and *The Rehearsal at Goatham* are included for the sake of completeness. The *Translations from Ariosto* (from Gay's own manuscript) appear in print for the first time. The *Inscription to Mr. Tommy Potter,* and the lines *My dear Belladine* are minor new-comers. *The Despairing Shepherd,* and (among the ' doubtful ' pieces) *Horace Epod. iv imitated,* the *Ode for the New Year,* and *The Banish'd Beauty* have not, I think, ever been previously reprinted. To each poem or play, or group of poems, a brief account of the early, and sometimes of a few later, editions is prefixed.[1] I have always taken as the basis of my text the last of the editions which I believe Gay to have supervised ; my notes record the variants of the early editions, occasional readings by later editions, and all departures of my own, of spelling or punctuation or what not, from the text of the early editions. What I have here to say on these topics can be most conveniently said under the headings of *Variants, Spelling,* and *Punctuation.* I should add that the typographical detail (capitals, italics, and so forth) is carefully reproduced from the early editions, and is often (perhaps too often) referred to in the notes.

Variants. A great deal of Gay's work was republished several times in his own lifetime ; the differences between such editions are sometimes insignificant, often of great importance. Gay (far from being the lazy scribbler too often portrayed by his biographers) was a very laborious and careful writer. We know from the Preface to *Polly* that the first draft of that play was contained in ' my own first foul blotted papers ' ; from these the poet made his own fair copy. At the Playhouse a second copy was made, which was in its turn copied by another hand (Mr. Stede) for the Lord Chamberlain. This last copy was minutely compared with the first fair copy ; and the latter was also carefully revised by Gay for the press. We know, too, from his correspondence that Gay often composed slowly ; and that he was conscientious in preparing his poems for the press. The fragmentary copy of the *Welcome to Pope* (see Appendix IV) is particularly interesting. It illustrates an intermediate stage. It is itself a fair copy (as the fragments of an earlier rough copy of stanzas 2 and 3 show) ; but it is not the final copy, which was circulated in manuscript and subsequently printed in the *Additions to the Works of Alexander Pope.*[2] All this goes to show that Gay's poems, in their

---

[1] It is as well to say here that these bibliographical details are not intended to be complete.

[2] The fragment of the first draft of *Trivia,* printed in Appendix III, belongs to a similar stage.

earliest printed form, were probably developed from a cruder state ; but his preoccupation with them did not end with their publication. *Trivia* was first published in 1716 ; it is still undergoing revision in 1731. The differences between earlier and later versions of *Rural Sports, The Fan, The Toilette,* and other poems, often amount to re-writing. I do not pretend that this is the first edition to record variants ; Mr. Underhill included a considerable number. But it is certainly the first edition to record all verbal variants, so far as I have been able to discover them.

Spelling. It is in the matter of spelling that I feel myself most open to the charge of inconsistency, which I have brought against Gay's last editor. But if I am inconsistent, so was Gay. It is Gay's own spelling which I have sought to preserve, and which with its antique flavour contributes not a little to the taste of his verses in modern mouths. English spelling during his lifetime was still fluid. By his death the more modern forms had begun to crystallize. His own spelling probably changed. The generation of schoolboys, to which I belonged, began by calling Caesar *Seezer* and ended by trying to call him *Kyzer* ; it is now impossible for me to know beforehand how I shall pronounce any Latin word. So it was with Gay and his generation, in the matter of spelling. One day, *chace, lyon, faithfull, fantastick, ruine* ; the next, these words are spelled as we spell them now. Nevertheless, on the whole, the spelling is of an antique type. I have generally followed the spelling of Gay's middle period—the spelling, that is, of the Quarto of 1720, in those poems which were published in the Quarto. Otherwise I have followed the spelling of the first editions. Changes in spelling, as of punctuation, in the later editions were, I fancy, for the most part due to publisher or printer. They have to be considered on their merits. In the second series of Fables, never seen through the press by Gay, and not published till six years after his death, I have allowed myself a certain latitude, and have restored to some extent the spelling of the first series. The preparation of this edition has occupied me, off and on, for the last ten years ; my own attitude to the question of spelling has altered insensibly in that time, and I fear I have not always applied the same canon. But, in general, the spelling of this edition faithfully reflects the spelling of Gay, and the gradual invasion of modern forms during his life.[1]

Punctuation. This is really a much more important matter than spelling. It is not possible to prepare for the press the poems of an early eighteenth-century writer, without realizing how much simpler and more natural, if less logical, was his punctuation than ours. By what right do we make it ' conform to the usage of the present day ' ? It is as much an integral character of his work as his vocabulary. If we ruthlessly impose our own stopping, we shall repeatedly find that we have either sacrificed the sense or disturbed the balance of the original. But this evil work is not altogether of our

---

[1] To have recorded all variations in the spelling of the early editions would have swollen the already large bulk of my notes. I have referred to a few of the more interesting variations only.

own age. By 1777 most of the alterations have been made; they are continued, and imitated, by subsequent editors. I have already shown how such a process may lead to actual distortion of the meaning. A short example will serve to illustrate its lesser dangers. In the *Introduction to the Fables*, ll. 47-50, Gay wrote :

> The hen, who from the chilly air
> With pious wing protects her care,
> And ev'ry fowl that flies at large
> Instructs me in a parent's charge.

Bell prints :

> The hen, who from the chilly air,
> With pious wing, protects her care,
> And ev'ry fowl that flies at large,
> Instructs me in a parent's charge.

The additional stopping merely encumbers a simple passage ; and it leads to later error. Later editions follow Bell, but omit the comma after *wing*. Thus the final text (as in Underhill) conforms neither to Gay nor to 'modern usage'. Such errors are frequent, and are beneath notice, save in an apology for Gay's own more artless stopping. But is it really so artless as the editors assume ? Take the first ten lines from the same *Introduction*. As printed by most editors they run :

> Remote from cities liv'd a Swain,
> Unvex'd with all the cares of gain ;
> His head was silver'd o'er with age,
> And long experience made him sage ;
> In summer's heat, and winter's cold,
> He fed his flock and penn'd the fold ;
> His hours in cheerful labour flew,
> Nor envy nor ambition knew :
> His wisdom and his honest fame
> Through all the country rais'd his name.

Only the colon in the eighth line suggests (and that too late to affect the run of the passage) that we have here anything but a succession of five similar couplets of equal balance and value. But let the reader turn to p. 235 and read the passage as the author printed it. It falls, surely, into three parts : the first four lines say what the Swain *was*, the next four what he *did* ; the concluding couplet rounds off the sketch by telling us what men thought of him. These things are intended. More than this, the commas before and after *and winter's cold* spoil the poet's meaning.[1]

---

[1] Bell, it is true, prints a third comma after *flock*—which is evidence that his editor understood the passage correctly. But to use three commas, where none are needed, involves the sense and weakens the rhythm.

In 'The Despairing Shepherd' (p. 194, l. 4) the 'Flocks were penn'd within the Fold'. But that is a much more conventional piece of work than the Introduction to the Fables.

The Swain did not ' pen the fold ' in summer. Gay had his clear picture of the shepherd seeking the pastures in summer and penning the flock in winter ; he trusted to the plain antithesis and shunned the awkward complication of stops. But no ! the editors must rush in with their colons and their semi-colons and commas, and dry up the sense with their false lucidity.

These affected niceties of punctuation might be less distressing to a careful reader if they were consistently maintained. But it is to be feared that the disciples of modern usage have seldom read with attention what they punctuate with such generosity. Not twenty, but a thousand times, an editor, after adding the stops which his soul desired, has made a gap in Gay's own punctuation through which all the rest like sheep have gone astray. Here is a single instance from Fable V, 2nd series :

> This in love-vanity transcends ;
> That, smitten with his face and shape,
> By dress distinguishes the ape ;

where Bell, Dobson, and Underhill omit the comma after *That*.

Not content with turning their author's simplicity into nonsense, the editors do their best now and then to make him appear ridiculous. Thus, Gay says, quite simply, in Fable VI, 2nd series :

> A cottage lodg'd the royal guest.

But Dobson and Underhill must needs convert the full stop into an exclamation mark—which makes the line look merely silly.

Is there, then, to be no censorship of stops ? It would be idle to maintain that all Gay's poems are punctuated with such care as the first series of Fables. But in my view it is better, as a general rule, to leave the original stopping, even when corrected by later editions in Gay's own lifetime, unaltered except in cases of necessity. The difficulty is to be sure when it *is* necessary to alter ; and the standard of necessity being subjective, and liable to fluctuation over a long period of years, consistency on the editor's part is improbable. I can only say that I have altered as little as possible, and (to the best of my belief) never without mentioning the alteration in the notes. Time and again I have been on the point of replacing a comma by a stop more natural to modern eyes, or to ' correct ' Gay's punctuation in some other way. How seldom I have persevered in my ' correction ' the notes will show. Almost invariably, on a closer analysis, I have found that my alteration would have destroyed the subtle emphasis which the poet wished to place on this or that word, or phrase, or line, or momentary pause.

The chief feature of Gay's system of stopping, on which a few observations may be profitably offered, is his use of commas. These constantly perform the functions of our own semi-colons, colons, and even full points. The latter kind of stops Gay keeps as a rule for definite purposes—to mark the division between ideas, groups of contrasted characteristics, and the like, rather than a purely grammatical joint. Thus he will use a comma before a demonstrative, where a relative pronoun might be used ; e.g. Fable IX :

> Weigh well his manners, life, and scope,
> On these depend thy future hope.

or where a number of statements, or imperatives, succeed each other, strung upon a single idea, as e.g. in the last seven lines of Fable X ; or before a statement of cause, even when not introduced by a ' for ' or ' because ' ; e.g. Fable XII :

> The man grows jealous, and with cause,
> Nothing can save him but divorce,

Sometimes, especially in the earlier poems, he uses commas where a modern writer would not place any stop—at the end of a line, or even in the middle, to mark a pause in the rhythm. A good example is *The Birth of the Squire*, l. 35 :

> How in one day beneath his furious speed,
> He tir'd seven coursers of the fleetest breed ;

where I have let the comma stand ; but in *The Fan*, Book III, l. 105

> Down drops the martial maid ; the bloody ground,
> Floats with a torrent from the purple wound.

I have treated the comma as accidental. Or, again, he will put a comma after a participle, as in the *True Story of an Apparition*, l. 103 :

> Then mutt'ring hasty pray'rs, he mann'd his heart.

Attention may also, perhaps, be called to Gay's normal stopping of a group of three nouns. Ordinarily one comma does for the lot. As, e.g. :

> Kites, hawks and wolves deserve their fate.

The exceptions show that the rule is seldom departed from without good reason. In the lines quoted above from Fable IX, is it fanciful to think that the comma after *life* emphasizes the ' weightiness ' of the judgement which the parent is invited to make ? Or, to take another example, in *Rural Sports*, 2nd version, i. 188–9, the commas point the parallelism of the two lines.

The treatment of brackets is often awkward. Gay's practice is inconsistent. Sometimes he has a comma before the first bracket and a second comma immediately before the second bracket ; more often there is no second comma ; often there are no commas. I have not felt able to tolerate the second of these three modes. When a comma marks the beginning of the parenthesis, I have inserted a second comma, where Gay would have placed it, immediately before the second bracket.

In re-editing the posthumous volume of *Fables* (2nd series) I have, with great caution, applied Gay's own principles, so far as I felt I had certainly grasped them. But, though indications are not wanting that the punctuation of this volume was not always the author's (e.g. the much more frequent use of the colon), 1 have not ventured on to more uncertain ground.

All variations of punctuation, as of spelling, in the early editions, I have not thought it advisable to record. I have, however, noted all that seemed to be of interest, and many that may be thought of none.

My thanks are due, first and foremost, to Mr. T. J. Wise, who most kindly lent several of his rare specimens for examination and collation. I have recorded my disagreement with his views upon one or two points, as an Editor is bound to do ; but his kindly help has much increased whatever value this edition may possess. I must also thank Mr. I. A. Williams, to whom I owe *My dear Belladine* and the discovery of the original edition of the lines *To the Author of Licentia Poetica Discuss'd.* (*The London Mercury,* April 1923. I had already decided to include the latter in this edition ; but it never occurred to me to look for them in Dr. Coward's book.) To Sir Frank Mackinnon I owe the interesting letter printed in Appendix III. My debt to Mr. Frederick Page, of the Oxford University Press, is too general to be particularized.

Not far from where I wrote the first draft of this Introduction, stands, or rather stood, Amesbury Abbey, where the last few years of Gay's short life were so largely spent, in the intimate society of his delightful Duchess. It was destroyed by re-building in 1840. Its passing may, by a stretch of fancy (pardonable to an editor whose work is completed), be regarded as almost symbolical. So, a little later, passed Gay's fame ; so, a little earlier, passed the age to which he belonged. It would be foolish, in a Preface of this character, to begin the analysis of either. But there are signs of a change, of a revolt against the tyranny of nature. Man, alternately uplifted and dejected by the advances and upheavals of his immediate past, is haunted by the fear lest he be, after all, a creature of no importance. A cure for that disease is to be found in the writers of the Eighteenth Century. For their creation of a kingdom held together in defiance of the brutal environment of nature by its own self-invented laws, we can forgive them much—their artificiality, their triviality, their grossness. Perhaps, indeed, it is our own timidity which fastens so peculiar a reproach upon these qualities. If we believed in ourselves as they did, we might come to think artificiality and triviality less vices than virtues. Some may even be tempted to envy them the licence of speech, as of subject, which they shared with other great ages of the race.

However that may be, it is certain that the Eighteenth Century seems less contemptible now than yesterday. If Gay had (as he had) a place in its literature, his place in English Literature, as a whole, will not be with the lowest. Here he is, at any rate, among the Oxford Poets.

GEOFFREY FABER.

Hampstead, 1925.

THE DOUBTFUL OR DISPUTED
POEMS.

(Pieces named below, and marked with an asterisk, are included by
Mr. Underhill in his edition.)

By far the most embarrassing problem, with which a conscientious
editor of an eighteenth-century poet is confronted, is the problem
of determining what he is to include as his author's. It is an embarrassing problem, and yet the labour spent upon it is for the most
part unremunerative ; for the pieces in doubt are generally of
minor, if not of trifling, importance. However, a decision has to
be made and supported ; and this kind of detective work is not
altogether without interest.

In order to clear the ground, we will begin by excluding from
immediate consideration the following : (1) *Wine* ; (2) pieces not
hitherto printed in any collection of Gay's poems (of which more
below); (3) the 'Gulliver' verses (discussed on p. xxxiv) ; (4) the *Poems
from Gay's Chair*, which I have no doubt are deliberate forgeries ;[1]
(5) the Prologues to the *Three Hours after Marriage* and *Achilles*, which
must needs be printed with the plays for which they were written,
and are there discussed. We are left with a score of poems, long and
short, which have been at one time or another attributed to Gay
by his editors, and which may possibly or probably have been
wrongly so attributed. They fall into four curiously definite groups,
which we will examine in order.

The editions consulted are the late eighteenth- and early nineteenth-century editions, which helped to fix the tradition. They
are : Potts, Dublin, 1770 ; Trade Edition, London, 1772 ; Bell,
1777 ; Trade Edition, London, 1779 (printed by J. Nichols ; part of
the series for which Johnson's *Lives of the Poets* were written, and
published in 1781) ; Jeffery, 1795 ; Cooke, 1804 ; Park, 1808, with
Supplement 1809. These all purport to be complete editions. No
complete edition that I know of was published before 1770. Bell's
edition of 1773 I have never seen ; but I believe its text to be followed
by that of 1777. I refer, in what follows, to all these editions by name,
calling the 1772 edition 'Trade', and the 1779 edition 'Nichols'.
Bell, it should be noticed, was among the publishers for whom the
Trade Edition of 1772 (but not that of 1779) was printed. For fuller
particulars of the above-named editions the reader is referred to the
Bibliographical Summary on p. xlii.

I. The largest group consists of eleven pieces taken from Pope and
Swift's *Miscellanies*. This famous collection of prose and verse by

[1] See Appendix V.

various hands, but mainly by Pope and Swift, appeared in five volumes from 1727 to 1735. We are only concerned with two out of the five; namely, *Miscellanies in Verse*, 1727, and *Miscellanies. The Third Volume*, 1732. The latter volume contained some verse, but more prose. No indication of authorship was given. In 1747 the *Miscellanies* were reissued.[1] The fourth volume of the reissue, ' consisting of verses by Dr. Swift, Dr. Arbuthnot, Mr. Pope, and Mr. Gay . . . 1747 ', is the one which we have to notice. It contains all the verse from the volumes of 1727 and 1732, together with two or three additional poems. As it formed part of a uniform edition of Swift's miscellaneous pieces, Swift's contributions had to be in some way distinguished from the others. Certain pieces are marked, both in the List of Contents and in the text, with a ' star '; and we are told that ' whatever are not mark'd with a star, are Dr. Swift's '. It does not, however, follow, that whatever is marked with a star, is *not* Swift's ; and I own to a strong suspicion that Swift preferred not to recognize the legitimacy of some of his children.[2] The 1747 volume was reprinted in 1754 as volume vi of the fine demy 8vo edition of *The Works of Dr. Jonathan Swift*, issued by the same publisher, Bathurst.

Of these eleven pieces, seven were in the 1727 volume, namely *Molly Mog*, *Nelly*, *Quadrille*, *New Song of New Similies*, *Newgate's Garland*, *The Quidnuncki's*, *Ay and No*. All of these were included as Gay's by Bell, Nichols, Jeffery, Cooke, and Park ; except that Park does not give *Ay and No*. Two more—*Epitaph of Bye-Words* and *Verses for a Picture*—come from the 1732 volume, and are given as Gay's by all five editions. The remaining two—*Bounce to Fop* and *Duke upon Duke*—were not printed in the *Miscellanies* till 1747. The first is given as Gay's by all five editions ; the second only by Nichols and Cooke, and avowedly ' on conjecture only '. It is surprising that out of the mass of unclaimed material in the *Miscellanies* something was not chosen more in Gay's manner than this long and tedious ballad. It is certainly not by Gay, and is not mentioned by Underhill.

Eliminating *Duke upon Duke*, we are left with ten poems traditionally ascribed to Gay. Upon what authority ? On that of John Bell or his editor. It was John Bell's four-volume edition of 1773 which fixed this tradition. I take the following from an apparently well-informed article by J. Yeowell in *Notes and Queries*, 2nd series, viii. 172 :

' In 1773, Isaac Reed having several pieces by Gay not found in his collected *Works*, and wishing to help a necessitous relative named John Bailey, desired him to offer them to Mr. Bell, and turn them to the best use he could. Bell purchased them, and handed them over to the editor of his edition, who, not content with the additional pieces furnished by Isaac Reed, appears to have ransacked the Miscellanies and

---

[1] The first volume of the reissue is called ' The Fifth Edition '.

[2] I am assuming that Swift, who died in 1745, had left indications of his own authorship, e.g. in marked copies of the original volumes. But, of course, the ascriptions may have been made without such direct evidence.

various Collections for others *supposed* to have been written by Gay. Among the doubtful pieces included in this edition may be mentioned the following : 1. An Elegiac Epistle to a Friend. 2. A Ballad on Ale. 3. Gondibert. 4. The Story of Cephisa. 5. The Man-Mountain's Answer to the Lilliputian Verses. . . . All these doubtful pieces, as well as *Molly Mog*, are omitted in the trade edition of Gay's Poems, 2 vols., 12mo, 1775 ; but Bell's edition appears to have been made the text for all the subsequent editions of the poet's works.'

I do not know from what source Mr. Yeowell derived his information ;[1] but it bears the impress of accuracy. His conclusions, however, are obviously unsound. The five pieces he mentions are, in fact, the only entirely new pieces printed by Bell, and must almost certainly have been those ' furnished by Isaac Reed '. We shall return to them below. What does seem to be clear is that Bell's editor chose out of the *Miscellanies* the ten pieces we have now to consider ; and that he had no special clue, denied to other editors, to help him in his search.

We must then, it seems to me, so far as pieces from the *Miscellanies* are concerned, reject the idea that the tradition initiated by Bell has any claim to be regarded as authoritative, and consider each piece purely on its own merits. *Molly Mog* * is certainly, for the most part, Gay's (see p. 188). *Nelly* is usually given to Arbuthnot. He writes to Swift, under date October 14, 1718 : ' Among other things I had the honour to carry an Irish lady to court, that was admired beyond all the ladies in France for her beauty. She had great honours done her. The hussar himself was ordered to bring her the king's cat to kiss. Her name is Bennet.' *Quadrille* is printed by Sir Walter Scott in his edition of Swift's *Works* (vol. xiii, p. 356), with the sub-heading ' Written by Mr. Congreve '. What authority he had for this ascription I do not know ; Congreve is not mentioned in the volume of 1747 as a contributor to the *Miscellanies*. The *New Song of New Similies* * is very possibly Gay's. *Newgate's Garland* * and *The Quidnuncki's* * are discussed at length below. *Ay and No* * may be Gay's ; I doubt it. The style is too rapid, and the addition of an explanatory note in the edition of 1754 suggests a different authorship. The *Epitaph on Bye-Words* * is not at all in Gay's manner ; no more are the *Verses for a Picture*.* The latter is an attack upon Sir Richard Blackmore, who was a physician as well as a copious poetaster. Arbuthnot makes a sneering allusion to his poetic abilities in a letter to Swift (December 11, 1718), and probably wrote this cruel catalogue of his works. Last of the ten, *Bounce to Fop* is now generally supposed to be Pope's. Not only was it not printed till long after Gay's death ; but (as Mr. Underhill points out) the name ' Lord Fanny ' as applied to Lord John Hervey was originated by Pope himself in 1733 in his *Imitation of the First Satire of the Second Book of Horace*. It is an

---

[1] Nichols's *Literary Anecdotes* contain a deal of information about Isaac Reed, one of the most celebrated bibliophiles of the eighteenth century. But there is nothing there to confirm Mr. Yeowell's statement.

odd fact that twelve lines were added to this poem in Nichols's edition (1779) ; the editor perhaps had access to some information that Bell's editor had not. Mr. T. J. Wise has a copy of *Bounce to Fop* published in 1736, with ' by Dr. S—T ' printed on the title-page. Whether Swift's or Pope's, it is certainly not Gay's.

To return to *Newgate's Garland* and *The Quidnuncki's*. I should not have found the two Broadside versions of *Newgate's Garland* (catalogued at the British Museum under ' Blueskin '), nor the Broadside of *The Quidnuncki's* (catalogued under ' Orleans '), without the help of Mr. F. Elrington Ball (*Notes and Queries*, 12th series, xii. 174). Mr. Ball says (*loc. cit.*) that the Broadside of *Newgate's Garland*, dated 1724–5, is ' in a volume of productions of the kind issued at Dublin ' ; and that the second Broadside of the same Ballad appeared ' in a Postscript to the *St. James's Post* of Nov. 28, 1725 '. Starting with these supposed facts he advances with great confidence the theory that both *Newgate's Garland* and *The Quidnuncki's* (which latter piece is also in the volume of Broadsides described) are by Swift and not by Gay.

' The former is redolent of the atmosphere of the deanery at the period, and the latter foreshadows " Gulliver's Travels ". But Swift had no part in the insertion of the " Newgate Garland " in the *St. James's Post*, for in its version as well as in the one in Gay's works, " honest Wild " is changed to " Jonathan ", a name which Swift would naturally have avoided. My suggestion is that in some way Gay got hold of the Dublin broadsides and adopted them, after making alterations, very possibly with Swift's approval, as his own. That Swift helped him there is no question. To what extent is an inquiry on which Gay's admirers have not seen their way to enter.'

But, with all the respect of a pupil for his teacher, I cannot agree that the premises are correct. In the first place, a number of the Broadsides in the volume referred to are, in fact, London Broadsides, printed in London ; and there is nothing to show that these particular Broadsides were not also printed in London. In the second place, the Ballad was not inserted in the *Post* for November 28, 1725, but was printed on the back of a single-sheet supplement to the *Post* for November 28, 1715. (There are two copies of this print in the British Museum.)

Against the hypothesis of Swift's authorship of the Ballad are the following considerations. First, that the incident that gave rise to it occurred in London and not in Dublin, and was a London and not a Dublin sensation. Second, that both pieces are starred in the 1747 edition of the *Miscellanies*. Third, that Wild was the prototype of Peachum in *The Beggar's Opera*.

It will make for clearness to recall briefly the circumstances. Jonathan Wild was the Moriarty of the Eighteenth Century. A master-criminal, a receiver of stolen goods on a huge scale, he posed as the guardian of public order. He had himself effected the arrest of his former tool, Joseph Blake. Blake attacked him during the trial, and succeeded in wounding him in the throat with a penknife.

Blake was hanged on November 11, 1724; five days later the famous Jack Sheppard, who had also fallen foul of Wild, was hanged. Six months later, on May 24, 1725, Wild himself came to the scaffold.

The hypothesis, which I suggest covers all these facts, is this. Gay, soon after the occurrence of the assault on Wild, wrote to Swift, with whom he was in correspondence but whom he had not at that time met, sending him a copy of verses on a theme which was the talk of the town. This copy consisted of the first five stanzas of the Ballad. Swift replied, adding stanzas 6 and 7. Gay published the Ballad anonymously, including the additional stanzas. The Ballad caught on, and was speedily sold out. Later, when Wild himself came to trial, a revised version of the Ballad was hastily struck off on the only paper available at the moment, which happened to be a pile of ten-year-old supplements to the *Post*, printed on one side only.

Stanzas 6 and 7 differ curiously from the rest of the poem. In stanza 6 ' you ' is singular ; elsewhere, it is plural. In stanza 7 ' thy ' and ' thee ' appear for the only time, and replace ' the ' and ' you ' in the original version. Why ? Because, I suggest, in these stanzas Swift is speaking to Gay, his English correspondent, and has not in his mind the ' Gallants of Newgate ' to whom Gay addressed himself in the first five stanzas. Strong colour is given to this view by the fact that stanzas 6 and 7 are omitted in the collected editions of Gay's poems.

As for *The Quidnuncki's*, I feel less certain of their parentage. The piece strikes. me as imitative rather than original—as, indeed, very much the sort of thing that Gay might have written under Swift's powerful influence. But I am content to put it with the doubtfuls.

To sum up : I print *Molly Mog* and *Newgate's Garland* as Gay's ; I omit *Duke upon Duke* and *Bounce to Fop* ; the remainder I print in Appendix I.

II. The next group is a small one, and consists of two pieces only —*The Coquet Mother and Coquet Daughter* * and *The Epistle to a Lady on her fondness for Old China*.* These two pieces are printed by Potts, 1770, among the ' Miscellanies ' in the second volume (which generally corresponds to the second volume of Gay's *Poems upon Several Occasions*). They occupy the same position in the Trade edition of 1772. I find them also in an Edinburgh edition of the *Poems and Fables*, published in 1773. They are *not* in the 1762 edition of the *Poems on Several Occasions*. Every subsequent editor has included them without question. It is strange to find them stealing unannounced into Gay's works at so late a date.

It was only after this edition was in proof that I learned that they had previously been printed. Mr. T. J. Wise has a copy of Tonson's quarto *To a Lady on her passion for old China*, published in 1725. Another copy has been recently found in the British Museum— hitherto catalogued under ' Lady '. Beyond the association between Gay and Tonson, there is no further confirmation in this of Gay's authorship. But it is interesting to know that the piece had been separately published in Gay's lifetime, after the Quarto of 1720. *The Coquet Mother* I have now found in Steele's *Poetical Miscellany*— the Second (not the First) Edition, 1727, also published by Tonson. No author's name is given ; but Gay contributed other pieces, one —*A Thought on Eternity*—unsigned but known certainly to be his, to the same volume.

Both pieces are thoroughly in Gay's manner ; and I include them, without hesitation, in this edition.

III. The third group consists of pieces, other than those already mentioned, which are for the first time printed in Bell's edition. There are five of these ; and all are named in the extract from *Notes and Queries* given above. Nichols and Cooke do not include them ; but they are accepted by Jeffery and Park. A word about each. *Gondibert* is a continuation of Sir William Davenant's unfinished poem, published in 1651. I take the following note from Bell (1777) :

' Though we do not pretend to give the following as the production of Mr. Gay, yet as we had them from a person of undoubted veracity, who assures us that they were found among his papers after his decease ; and as many marks of correction were made in them, so there is little doubt that they have undergone the inspection of that celebrated Author. Considering these things, and that the imitation seemed too good to be lost, we have, on mature deliberation, given these Cantos a place in this Work, and have the greatest hopes that they will prove agreeable to our readers (*Gay's Works*, vol. iv, edit. 1773).'

It is not stated whether the manuscript was in Gay's hand-writing or not. But I think it is reasonable to argue that if it had been in the poet's hand it would undoubtedly have been printed as Gay's without more ado. It is a dull piece of narrative, and is probably no more than an exercise by a friend submitted to Gay for criticism. I do not think it necessary to encumber this edition with its eight hundred and thirty-four lines.

An Elegiac Epistle to a Friend, written by Mr. Gay, when he laboured under a Dejection of Spirits is a different matter. Like the three remaining pieces of this group, it is given by Bell without qualification as Gay's, and with them was undoubtedly printed from the papers supplied by Isaac Reed. Were they—like the *Poems from Gay's Chair*, at a later date—forgeries ? It is entirely unlike any other poem of Gay's ; but this very unlikeness is strong evidence in its favour. I have no doubt that it was written by Gay, either in 1729 or in the last year of his life. He was already suffering from the internal disorder which killed him, and his letters reveal the depression of his spirits. It is in 1729 that he writes to Pope : ' I find myself in such a strange confusion and dejection of spirits, that I have not strength enough to make my will, though I perceive, by many warnings, I have no continuing city here.' He writes to

Swift in May 1732 : ' As for myself, I am often troubled with the colic. I have as much inattention, and have, I think, lower spirits than usual, which I impute to my having no one pursuit in life ' ; and to Pope in October 1732 : ' I am frequently out of order with my colical complaint, so as to make me uneasy and dispirited, though not to any violent degree. . . . I begin to fear the illness I have so long complained of, is inherent in my constitution, and that I have nothing for it but patience.' Pope called his death in December, after a sudden and violent attack, ' unexpected '. But it is clear that Gay was, both in 1729 and in 1732, profoundly uneasy about his condition ; so uneasy, indeed, that he followed Swift's advice and took hard exercise for three months in the summer of 1732, and was deeply disappointed to find himself no better.

The interest of this epistle is not merely biographical. Few would connect the names of Gay and Shelley. Yet these lines written in a dejection of spirits are curiously suggestive of the *Stanzas written in dejection, near Naples*. I cannot help thinking that the greater poet had them in his mind. And, lest this should be thought an utterly fanciful association of ideas, I will suggest, further, that the famous line in the *Ode to the West Wind*,

> I fall upon the thorns of life, I bleed !

was inspired by Gay's

> Full well I know, in life's uncertain road,
> The thorns of mis'ry are profusely sown.

Accepting the *Elegiac Epistle* as genuine, I am the less disposed to reject the *Ballad on Ale** and *Cephisa*. Both stand on the same footing ; and both are quite in Gay's manner. There remains the *Man-Mountain's Answer to the Lilliputian Verses*. I believe this, too—as distinct from the other ' Gulliver ' verses—must be from Gay's hand.[1]

I could write with more assurance upon the authenticity of this group, if I had been able to discover the four-volume edition of 1773, or the authority for Mr. Yeowell's statement quoted above.

An ' Advertisement ' bound up in the wrong place in the British Museum copy of Jeffery's 1795 edition in six volumes is, however, evidently taken from the 1773 edition. It contains the following passage :

With regard to the second volume, it comprises the poetical pieces of Mr. Gay not already inserted in those volumes that generally bear the title of his works. His translations and other little pieces are to be found for the most part dispersed in Garth's Ovid and in Swift's Miscellanies. As to the Poem called Wine, the Editor has already given his reasons for inserting it in a note at the bottom, and the Story of Cephisa, the Elegiac Epistle to a Friend, the Man Mountain's Answer to the Liliputian Ode, and the Ballad on Ale are inserted from no less an authority. As [to] the intrusion of Gondibert in this miscellany, if the apology already offered

---

[1] See below on the ' Gulliver ' verses, p. xxxiv.

for it be not thought sufficient by the Critics, nothing further can be said here to excuse it, than to urge the good intentions of the Compiler, and his repeated hopes that it may prove agreeable to the generality of his readers.

It is curious that in Jeffery's edition these pieces are all printed not in the second but the fourth volume—where they were evidently printed in Bell's 1773 edition. (See the note quoted in Bell's 1777 edition, given above.) All six pieces are marked, in the List of Contents of volume iv, with an asterisk. *Wine* and *Gondibert* stand each on a different footing. But the remaining four rest, so far as external evidence goes, on exactly the same footing ; so that if one be thought genuine, there is no reason for rejecting the others.

It may be noted here that Nichols's edition was the first collected edition of Gay's works to include four undoubtedly genuine small pieces and one important poem which had been already printed elsewhere. The four small pieces are : *The Epigrammatical Petition* (from a letter to Swift printed in Hawkesworth's edition, and also in *Additions to Pope*, 1776) ; *A Receipt for Stewing Veal** (from a letter to Swift, printed by Hawkesworth in 1766) ; *A Motto for an Opera* (from the *Additions to Pope*) ; the *Epigrammatical Expostulation* (from the pamphlet on *Mohocks and Hawkubites* by Pope and Gay, 1712) ; and, last but most important of all, *A Welcome from Greece**, Gay's congratulatory ode to Pope on the completion of his *Iliad*, first printed in the *Additions to Pope*, 1776. Jeffery has none of these ; Park has the *Welcome from Greece*, but not the four short pieces.

We return now to the pieces that we excluded from immediate consideration on p. xxiii.

(1) *Wine**. This poem was first included by Bell, and is given in all the subsequent editions named in this Preface. Bell's editor gives his authority for ascribing the poem to Gay. It is a letter from Aaron Hill to Savage, dated June 23, 1736 (Hill's *Works*, i. 339), in which he gives some particulars of Gay's life. Here is the relevant passage :

that poem you speak of, call'd WINE, he printed in the year 1710, as I remember : I am sure, I have one, among my pamphlets ; but they lie . . . so . . . numerous, and . . . mix'd, that to distinguish any one of them . . . is a task of more labour, than consequence. Yet I will look for it, and send it you, if 'twill be of use, or satisfaction, to any gentleman of your acquaintance.

The date of *Wine* was 1708 not 1710 ; but this slip hardly invalidates Hill's testimony. Unnecessary doubt has been thrown on Gay's authorship of the poem.[1] It is involved and immature ; but ' the minute touch of *Trivia* ', as Austin Dobson well observes, is already evident in its concluding lines.

(2) *Pieces not hitherto printed in any collection of Gay's poems*. There

---

[1] *Notes and Queries*, 2nd series, viii. 145 and 175.

are not many of these.   No doubt hangs over the *Translations from Ariosto*, or the *Inscription to Mr. Tommy Potter*, or *My dear Belladine*, or *The Despairing Shepherd*.   Four other pieces I have included in the Appendix of ' doubtfuls '.

(i) *Horace, Epod. iv. Imitated by Sir James Baker Kt.*   Both the British Museum and Bodleian Catalogues treat Sir James Baker as a pseudonym of Gay's—I do not know on what authority. The piece, a libel on Lord Cadogan, was published as a Broadside together with *An Excellent New Ballad* beginning ' Of all the days in the Year '.   The latter, a coarse and clumsy Jacobite ballad, is certainly not the composition of Gay.   The Broadside can be dated with certainty.   Cadogan received his barony in June 1716, and his earldom in May 1718.   In the summer of 1717 he was maliciously accused of embezzlement by the Jacobites ;   Gay's friend Pulteney was concerned in the attack ;   and in July 1717 Pulteney took Gay with him to Aix.   This combination of circumstances, together with the allusions in ll. 22–4 and 36, and the attribution of the piece to Gay, justify us in supposing that Gay may have written it in 1717 at Pulteney's instance.

(ii) *An Ode for the New Year* was attributed to Gay by a correspondent of *Notes and Queries* (2nd series, x. 1).   Gay and Cibber were enemies; the latter's appointment as Poet Laureate was resented and ridiculed by Gay's circle.   But whether Gay wrote this singularly cruel attack on the Royal Family is perhaps more than doubtful.

(iii) The third piece, *The Banish'd Beauty*, has been maintained to be Gay's by no less an authority than Mr. T. J. Wise.   I cannot myself agree with this view, for the reasons I shall' briefly give ; but—as with the *Poems from Gay's Chair*—I leave the verdict to the reader's judgement.

To my thinking the poem was written not by Gay, but by one of his friends.   Gay would not have written of his own ' pointed numbers ', nor have spoken of himself as ' much envied ', nor have suggested that he might fail in kindness to his patroness, nor have developed an exhortation to himself at such length.   The words ' at large ' do not, surely, refer to this particular poem, but mean that Gay is exhorted to devote his talents generally to the service of the Duchess.   The Macheath allusions, too, seem to me such as Gay neither would nor could have made.   In *Polly* Macheath is, of course, put to death, and not reprieved.   The criticism has often been made that this adds a dash of real tragedy to something essentially farcical.   *The Banish'd Beauty* was, I think, written by one of Gay's friends, who felt this incongruity and thought Gay's satire would be more effective if it were more directly turned on Walpole. Lastly, the obscurity of the piece is alien to Gay's style.

(iv) Mr. Wise has brought to my notice *An Epistle to the most Learned Doctor W**d****d ; from a Prude,* published in 1723.   The Doctor is Dr. Woodward, the geologist, ridiculed by Pope, Arbuthnot, and Gay in *Three Hours after Marriage* (1717).   He was an old butt of Arbuthnot's, who had so far back as 1697 attacked his views on the Deluge.   In 1719 Arbuthnot, with as much coarseness as humour, pulled to pieces poor Dr. Woodward's *State of Physic and of Diseases*. Woodward had advocated the use of emetics.

I am inclined to think that Arbuthnot rather than Gay was the author of this epistle. ' The question of his literary work ', says Aitken, ' is surrounded with difficulties, for he generally published anonymously, and took no trouble to secure fame through his writings . . . he was always ready to help his friends, and much of his work is therefore merged in the humorous writings of Swift, Pope and Gay, and others, and cannot now be distinguished.' But it must be admitted that in 1723 Gay was a good deal in Arbuthnot's company ; and that, while Arbuthnot was undoubtedly the source of all the opprobrium heaped upon Woodward, Gay may have taken his cue from his friend. There is a remarkable parallelism between the opening passage of the *Epistle from a Prude* and lines 19–27 of the *Epistle to a Lady on her passion for old China*, which may be thought to support the theory of Gay's authorship. But, while the sentiment of the two passages is the same, the ideas the same, and the ridicule the same in intention, the expression in the *Old China* piece is infinitely more pointed and capable. The latter reads to me like the work of a professional writer—and by 1723 Gay was an old hand at this sort of thing ; the former like the work of an amateur—such as Arbuthnot was, for all his wit and invention. The coarseness of the *Prude's Epistle* does not, perhaps, prevent it from being considered Gay's. But Gay was far less of an offender in this respect than most of his contemporaries. The indecency of his Tales is artistically necessary ; it is pointed, rather than gross. That can hardly be said of the Prude's metamorphosis !

One more argument is worth mentioning. The simile of Mother Earth suddenly pushing up a Mountain suggests a hidden mock at Woodward's theory of the Deluge. (He held that the centre of the Earth was originally a cavity, full of water, which burst forth at the Flood.) This would be natural from Arbuthnot, but scarcely so probable from Gay.

It may also be noted that, if this piece is by Gay, the Ballad on *Nelly*, believed to be by Arbuthnot, may very well be Gay's. 1 have never felt certain that Gay did not in fact write that Ballad after hearing from Arbuthnot of the incident which it describes. Even if it be held that the Prude's Epistle is Arbuthnot's (as I believe it to be), the parallelism noted above goes to show that Gay did borrow Arbuthnot's ideas.

Of other pieces attributed to Gay, I ought perhaps to mention :

Yarhell's Kitchen : *or, the Dogs of Egypt. An Heroic Poem.* London, Lintott, 1713. This poem, a folio of 24 pages, has among the mottoes on the title-page this from Hudibras

> —Till they're understood, all Tales
> (Like Nonsense) are not true nor false.

The hidden meaning is not very difficult to fathom. Yarhell (the hero, who defeats the dogs of Egypt) is Harley ; Ausan, the ' glorious

Monster ' who ' did invade this Isle ', is William I (Nassau) ; the three Dogs, Haman, Touni, and Onnah are Walpole (who, like Haman, had fallen from his high estate), Godolphin (Touni is perhaps an allusion to Charles II's famous eulogy of G. ' never in the way and never out of the way ' ; but it may simply mean ' in and out of office '), and Marlborough (Onnah = Hanno).

Now Harley was the patron and friend of Prior, and the hand seems to be the hand of Prior rather than of Gay. The opening lines

> I am the Bard ; who whilom did rehearse
> Pathetick Tales of Love in humble Verse :
> Who solemn Hymns compos'd for Raree Shows ;
> And *Ghosts* and *Goblins* feign'd in tuneful Prose :
> Who oft have made judicious Mobs rejoice,
> Attentive to the Ragged *Siren*'s Voice :
> Works gratefull unto Hawking Dames.—
> But now the MUSE bids strike a higher String,
> In peerless Numbers now—*Arms, and the Man I sing.*

seem to allude to Prior's literary record, and in particular to his prose *Dialogues of the Dead*, preserved unpublished at Longleat until Mr. A. R. Waller's Cambridge edition (1907). Mr. Waller does not, however, include *Yarhell's Kitchen* in his edition, nor even refer to it. A modern hand has pencilled ' By M. Prior ' on the British Museum copy of *Yarhell*; and the motto from Hudibras (an author imitated by Prior in his *Alma*) helps to confirm what I should regard as a certain attribution.

The Fair Quakers : A Poem. London, 1713. [Wrenn Library Catalogue, University of Texas, 1920.] According to the Catalogue, however, this was the work of Hildebrand Jacob, on whom Gay pretended to father *The Mad Dog*, when he reprinted it separately in 1730. (See p. 125.)

A Tale of a Bottomless Tub. London, 1723. [Wrenn Library Catalogue.]

The Ball. Stated in a Dialogue between a Prude and a Coquet, Last Masquerade Night, the 12th of May. Printed for J. Roberts. 1724. A very long-winded affair.

A New Ballad. To the Tune of, London is a fine Town, &c. London 1726. [Wrenn Library Catalogue.]

The Pig, and the Mastiff. Two Tales. London, 1727. [Wrenn Library Catalogue.]

The Oak, and the Dunghill. A Fable. London, 1728. [Wrenn Library Catalogue.]

A Tale, being an addition to Mr. Gay's Fables, 1728. A quasi-satirical attack on Gay's hunt for a sinecure.

Ode after the Manner of the First of Horace Inscrib'd to the Right Honourable Horatio Walpole Esq. London, 1732. [Wrenn Library Catalogue.]

So far as I know, there is no evidence for any of these ascriptions.

One other piece is said to have been attributed by Pope to Gay—

the dirty doggerel lines on Ditton and Whiston, from the *Miscellanies*.[1] I should have been inclined to give them to Arbuthnot, who in his Letters is for ever mocking at Whiston and his new method of determining longitude. Could Pope have made a mistake ? I have not included them in this edition. If they are by Gay, there is a further argument for Gay's authorship of *Nelly*—Arbuthnot in each case sowing the seed in his friend's versatile mind. But a good deal of Pope's reported conversation in *Spence's Anecdotes* is known to be inaccurate.

(3) *The ' Gulliver' verses.* There is a pretty puzzle connected with the *Verses on Mr. Gulliver's Travels.* Pope, in a letter to Swift, under date March 8, 1726–7, writes :

You receiv'd, I hope, some commendatory verses from a Horse and a Lilliputian, to Gulliver ; and an heroic Epistle of Mrs. Gulliver.

Pope here refers only to *three* pieces : namely the *Grateful Address of the Unhappy Houyhnhnms*, the *Ode to Quinbus Flestrin*, *the Man-Mountain*, and the *Epistle of Mary Gulliver*. The two latter, together with the *Lamentation of Glumdalclitch*, were published in pamphlet form, by Benj. Motte, with the title *Several Copies of Verses on Occasion of Mr. Gulliver's Travels*, 1727, price six-pence. A copy of this pamphlet is bound up in the Bodleian copy of the *Miscellanies*. The same three pieces (*Ode, Epistle*, and *Lamentation*) were also included in the *Miscellanies in Verse*, 1727. All four pieces were printed by Roscoe.

The *Ode, Epistle*, and *Lamentation* were printed by Bell as Gay's, together with yet another piece, *The Man-Mountain's Answer to the Lilliputian Verses.* Johnson and Cooke give the former three, but omit the *Answer*. Jeffery and Park follow Bell and print the *Answer*, which is a companion piece to the *Ode*.

Where did Bell get his additional poem from ? I incline to the view that it must have been one of the additional pieces ' furnished by Isaac Reed ', and that it was written by Gay in imitation of Pope's *Ode*. Otherwise it seems difficult to account for the facts (*a*) that Pope does not mention it to Swift, (*b*) that it was not printed in the Pamphlet or in the *Miscellanies*, (*c*) that it came into Bell's hands at all. This hypothesis also explains the inclusion by Bell of the other pieces, which were, in fact, by Pope. It is possible that the *Lamentation* was written by Gay ; but I must admit that it is more in the style of Pope, and as it is easily accessible in Pope's works I do not include it in this edition.

(4) *The ' Poems from Gay's Chair '.* These are printed in Appendix V, where their origin is discussed at length.

---

[1] ' The little copy of verses on Ditton and Whiston, in the third volume of the Miscellanies, was written by Gay.' Pope *loquitur*. Spence's *Anecdotes*, p. 201.

BIBLIOGRAPHICAL SUMMARY.

THE following lists do not pretend to form a complete Bibliography.
List A summarizes all the early authorized editions known to the editor, and used by him in the preparation of the text, and names most posthumous editions up to the middle of the eighteenth century. Editions not collated by him, either because inaccessible or of no textual value, are enclosed in square brackets. Fuller details are given under the separate poems. When a volume contains more than one poem the letters (q.v.) indicate where such details are to be looked for. Poems marked * are considered 'doubtful'; those marked † are omitted from this edition.

List B summarizes, with rather more detail, a few of the important collected editions.

List C gives the most important modern editions of single works.

Barnstaple Grammar School (with William Fortescue and Aaron Hill). London (as an apprentice to a silk mercer). Quits shop. Stays some months with his uncle at Barnstaple. Returns to London.

1685. BIRTH OF JOHN GAY. (Christened at Barnstaple, September 16.)

LIST A.

Meets Pope.

1708. (May.) *Wine.* A Poem. Wm. Keble. Folio. Anonymous.

1709. *To the Learned Ingenious Author of Licentia Poetica Discuss'd.*

1711. (May 3.) *The Present State of Wit*, in a Letter to a Friend in the Country. 8vo. Anonymous. (Prose.)

1712. *An Argument proving that the present Mohocks and Hawkubites are the Gog and Magog mention'd in the Revelation*, etc. Lintott. One Penny. Single sheet, folio. Anonymous. (Prose, but contains the verses ' From Mohock ', &c.)
(April 15.) *The Mohocks.* A Tragi-Comical Farce. Lintott. 8vo. (By ' W. B.')
(May.) *Miscellaneous Poems and Translations.* By Several Hands. Lintott. 8vo. Containing *Arachne* (q.v.) and *To Lintott. On a Miscellany of Poems.*

Secretary to Duchess of Monmouth.

1713. (Jan. 13.) *Rural Sports*. A Poem. Inscribed to Mr. Pope. By Mr. Gay. Tonson. Folio. (See Appendix 2.)

The Guardian. March 24, *Reproof and Flattery.* (Prose.) Sept. 21, *Dress.* (Prose.)

(May 12. Produced Drury Lane.) *The Wife of Bath.* A Comedy. 4to. (Prose ; but Prologue, Epilogue, and Fragments in verse.)

(Dec. 8.) *The Fan.* A Poem. In three Books. By Mr. Gay. Tonson. Folio. (Imprint 1714.)

(Dec.) *Poetical Miscellanies*, Consisting of Original Poems and Translations. By the best Hands. Publish'd by Mr. Steele. Tonson. 8vo. Containing *Panthea* (q.v.), *Araminta, A Contemplation on Night*, (' By Mr. Gay '), and *A Thought on Eternity* (Anonymous). (Imprint 1714.)

At Hanover, as secretary to Lord Clarendon. (June–Sept.) In correspondence with Swift.

1714. *Miscellaneous Poems and Translations.* Second Edition. 8vo.

(April 15.) *The Shepherd's Week.* In Six Pastorals. By Mr. J. Gay. Burleigh. 8vo.

The Shepherd's Week. Second Edition. Taylor. 8vo.

(Nov. 20.) *A Letter to A Lady.* Occasion'd by the Arrival of Her Royal Highness, the Princess of Wales. Lintott. Folio.

Visit to Exeter, at Lord Burlington's expense. (Summer.)

1715. (Feb. 23 : Produced at Drury Lane. March 19 : Published.) *The What d'ye call it :* A Tragi-Comi-Pastoral Farce. By Mr. Gay. Lintott. 8vo. (No date.)

The What d'ye call it. Second Edition. 8vo. (No date ; either 1715 or 1716.)

Two Epistles ; One, to the Right Honourable Richard Earl of Burlington (q.v.) ; *The Other, to a Lady.* (Fifth Edition.) By Mr. Gay. Lintott. Price 6d. 8vo. (No date ; the Epistle to Burlington certainly written in 1715.)

Again in Devonshire ; thence to Bath. (July.)

1716. (Jan. 26.) *Trivia : or, the Art of Walking the Streets of London.* By Mr. Gay. Lintott. 8vo.

(March 26.) *Court Poems.* Roberts. Price Six-Pence. 8vo. Containing *The Toilet* (q.v.).

The What d'ye call it. Third Edition. 8vo.

Visits Paris and Aix with the Pulteneys. (June–? Nov.)

1717. (Jan. 16 : Produced at Drury Lane. Jan. 21 : Published.) *Three Hours after Marriage :* a Comedy. By Mr. Gay. Lintott. 8vo. (Prose ; prologue and epilogue in verse.)

Ovid's Metamorphoses. . . . Translated by the most Eminent Hands. Tonson. Folio. Edited by Garth. (Most of the Ninth Book by Gay.)

(? July.) **Horace, Epod. iv.* Imitated by Sir James Baker Kt. To Lord Cad—n. Broad-side. N.d.

Stays with Lord 1718.
Harcourt at
Cockthorpe and
Stanton Har-
court.

On the Con- 1719.
tinent ' rambling
from place to
place '. Has a
fever at Spa.
(? July to Nov.)

Loses the profits 1720. (Probably in the first quarter.) *Poems on Several*
of the *Poems* *Occasions.* By Mr. John Gay. Tonson and Lintot.
(over £1,000)
in the ' South Volume the First.—Volume the Second.—Issued as
Sea Bubble '. a single volume, paged continuously throughout.
(October.)
Pressed by 4to. Containing :
Tonson 'to make Vol. 1. *Rural Sports* (q.v.) ; *The Fan ; The*
up my account '. *Shepherd's Week ; Trivia ; The what d'ye call it.*

Vol. 2. Epistles on Several Occasions (*to a Lady,
Burlington, Pulteney, Methuen*).

Tales (*Answer to the Sompner's Prologue, Work for
a Cooper, The Equivocation, A true Story of an Apparition, The Mad Dog*).

Eclogues (*The Birth of the Squire, The Toilette, The
Tea-Table, The Funeral, The Espousal*).

Miscellanies (*To W— L—, Panthea, Araminta, The
Elegy on a Lap-dog, To a young Lady with some
Lampreys, Prologue for Dione, Sweet William's Fare-
well, The Lady's Lamentation, Damon and Cupid,
Daphnis and Chloe, A Contemplation on Night, A
Thought on Eternity, My own Epitaph*).

Dione, a Pastoral Tragedy.

Miscellaneous Poems and Translations. Third Edition.
12mo. Containing, besides *Arachne* and *To Lintott,
Sweet William's Farewell* and the *Epistles to a Lady*
and *to Burlington*.

Sweet William's Farewell to Black-ey'd Susan.—Musical
Settings by Carey, Leveridge, Hayden, and Sandoni.
Two Broadsides, with music. (? 1720, B.M. Catalogue.)

Pope's *Eloisa to Abelard.* Second Edition. Lintot.
8vo. Containing the Ballad from ' The What-d'ye-
call-it '—'*Twas when the Seas were Roaring.*

Trivia. The Second Edition. 8vo. (No date ; ? 1720,
B.M. Catalogue.)

Daphnis and Cloe. A new Song. Broadside, with music.
(? 1720, B.M. Catalogue.)

Living ' almost 1721. (Feb. 8.) *A Panegyrical Epistle to Mr. Thomas Snow,* etc.
altogether with Lintot. Price Three-Pence. Folio. Anonymous.
Lord Burling-
ton '. (August.) *The Shepherd's Week.* Third Edition. Tonson. 8vo.
At Bath, ' always
with the Duchess
of Queensberry '.
(Sept.)

At Bath 'near eleven weeks for a colic'. (? In the autumn). Lodging 'at present in Burlington House'. (Dec.)

1722. *Miscellaneous Poems and Translations.* Fourth Edition. 12mo. Containing the same pieces as the third edition.

(July 11.) *An Epistle to Her Grace, Henrietta, Dutchess of Marlborough.* By Mr. Gay. Tonson. Folio.

Commissioner of State Lottery, at £150. (Until 1731.) Is granted Lodgings in Whitehall. (Until 1729.) At Tonbridge Wells, with a colic. (July and August.) Reads *The Captives* to the Princess of Wales.

1723. * *An Epistle to the most Learned Doctor W - - d - - - d ; from a Prude, That was unfortunately Metamorphos'd on Saturday December 29, 1722.* J. Roberts, B. Creak, S. Chapman. Folio. Anonymous.

At Bath, taking the waters, with Lord and Lady Fitzwilliam. Returns to London with Lord Scarborough.

1724. (Jan. 15. Produced at Drury Lane.) *The Captives :* a Tragedy. 8vo.
The Captives. Second Edition.
**A Poem address'd to the Quidnunc's, etc.* Broadside. Anonymous.

At work on the *Fables.* (Dec.)

1725. *The What d'ye call it.* Fourth Edition. 8vo.
Blueskin's Ballad. Broadside. 1724-5. Anonymous.
Newgate's Garland. (The above, slightly altered.) Broadside. N.d. Anonymous.
To a Lady on her Passion for old China. Tonson. 4to. Anonymous.
Allan Ramsay's *Tea Table Miscellany,* vol. ii. Containing *The Complaint* (published in ? 1720 as *The Poor Shepherd*).
Daphnis and Cloe. Broadside, with music. (? 1725. B.M. Catalogue.)
Sweet William's Farewell to Black-Ey'd Susan. Broadside, with music. (? 1725. B.M. Catalogue.)

Swift in England ; meets Gay, probably for first time, and lodges with him in Whitehall. (March, or after.) Gay with the Queensberrys ' in Oxfordshire and at Petersham, and wheresoever they would carry me ', but not to Amesbury. (Summer.) In

1726. *Miscellany Poems.* Vol. I. Lintot. 12mo. Containing *Sweet William's Farewell* and '*Twas when the seas were Roaring.* (Vide *Arachne.*)
Molly Mog. Mist's Journal. August 27. Anonymous.
Molly Mogg, A Song set by an Eminent Master. Broadside, with music. N.d.

London or at
Twickenham.
(Autumn and
winter.) 'A
slight fever.'
(October.)

Death of
George I.
(June 11.)
Declines ap-
pointment as
gentleman-
usher to Princess
Louise. (Octo-
ber.)

1727. (March.) *Fables.* By Mr. Gay. Tonson and Watts. 4to.
Miscellany Poems. Vol. II. By several Hands. The
Fifth Edition. Lintot. 12mo. Containing *Arachne*
(q.v.), *Molly Mog,* and the *Epistles to Burlington and
Snow ;* all ' By Mr. Gay '.
Miscellanies in Verse. Motte. 8vo. (Part of the
series of Miscellanies, in five volumes, published by
Pope and Swift from 1727 to 1735.) Containing
*Prologue to the Three Hours after Marriage, Panegyrical
Epistle to Snow* (q.v.), *Newgate's Garland, Molly
Mog,* *Nelly, *Ballad on Quadrille, *New Song of New
Similies, * The Quidnunchi's, *Ay and No.
Molly Mog. Broadside. (? 1727, B.M. Catalogue.)
Poetical Miscellanies. Publish'd by Sir Richard Steele.
Second Edition. Tonson. 8vo. Including *The Coquet
Mother and Coquet Daughter* (anonymous).

Makes
£693 13s. 6d.
out of four
Author's Nights
of *The Beggar's
Opera.*
Sells copyright
of *The Beggar's
Opera* and the
Fables for
90 guineas.
Visits Pulteney
at Canterbury.
(March.)
Thence to
Bathurst and
the Boling-
brokes. At
Bath. (May–
July.) In Here-
fordshire at
Lady Scuda-
more's, Holm
Lacy. (July–
Aug.) A ' very
severe attack of
a fever'. (Nov.)
Polly ' not al-
lowed to be
acted '. (Dec.)

1728. (Jan. 29 : Produced at Lincoln's Inn Fields. Feb. 14 :
Published.) *The Beggar's Opera.* . . . Written by
Mr. Gay. . . . To which is Added, The Musick Engrav'd
on Copper-Plates. Watts. Price 1s. 6d. 8vo.
The Beggar's Opera. The Second Edition : To which is
Added The Overture in Score ; And the Musick
prefix'd to each Song. Watts. 8vo.
Fables. Second Edition. Tonson and Watts. 8vo.
The Shepherd's Week. Fourth Edition. Tonson. 8vo.

The Queens-
berrys quarrel
with the Court
over *Polly.* Gay
loses his apart-
ments in White-
hall. Lives with
the Queens-
berrys.

1729. *The Beggar's Opera.* The Third Edition : With the
Overture in Score, The Songs, and the Basses, . . .
Curiously Engrav'd on Copper Plates. Watts. 4to.
(? March.) *Polly :* An Opera. Being the Second Part
of the Beggar's Opera. Written by Mr. Gay. Printed
for the Author.

Seriously ill with 'fever, asthma, and pleurisy'. (March.) Over 10,500 copies of Polly printed, bringing the author nearly £1,200. With the Queensberrys at Middleton Stoney 'new writing a damned play .. called " The Wife of Bath"'. (Aug.–Nov.) Returns to London with the Queensberrys.

4to. Uniform with the third edition of the *Beggar's Opera*, the Songs and the Basses similarly engraved. Sold at six shillings.

* *The Banish'd Beauty* : *or, a Fair Face in Disgrace.* A. Moore. Folio. Anonymous.

Fables. Third Edition. Tonson and Watts. 8vo.

The Musical Miscellany ; Being a Collection of Choice Songs, Set to the Violin and the Flute, By the most Eminent Masters. John Watts. 8vo. Vol. 1, containing *The Despairing Shepherd.* Vol. 2, containing *Daphnis and Chloe, Molly Mog,* and *The Faithful Maid* (i.e. '*'Twas when the Seas were Roaring '*).

' I cannot bear the town as I could formerly.' (March 3.) With the Queensberrys at Amesbury. (March–Dec.)

1730. (Jan. 19. Produced at Lincoln's Inn Fields.) *The Wife of Bath.* Revised and altered. Lintot.

Trivia. Third Edition. 8vo.

Molly Mogg. Broadside, with music. N.d.

Watts's *Musical Miscellany.* Vol. 4, containing * *A New Song of New Similies,* and *Sweet William's Farewell.*

The Mad Dog, A Tale. By H—— J—— Esq. A. Moore. 8vo. (Reprinted from the Poems, 1720.)

In town [1] after a bashful fit, for having writ something like a love-letter'. (Before April 27.) This affair (with a Mrs. Drelincourt) came to nothing. With the Queensberrys at Amesbury. (Most of the year.) At work ' in the way of those Fables I have already published '. (Dec.) At Twickenham. (Dec.)

1731. *Poems on Several Occasions.* 2 vols. Tonson and Lintot. 12mo. (A second edition of the 4to, with a few alterations, but the same Contents.)

Watts's *Musical Miscellany.* Vol. 5, containing *Newgate's Garland* and * *A Ballad on Quadrille.*

In London. (Jan. and again in May.) At Amesbury, ' finishing the work I intended ', i.e. Fables and Achilles. (July.) Visits Sir William Wyndham at Orchard Wyndham. (Sept.–Oct.) Refuses Pope's suggestion

1732. *Miscellanies.* The Third Volume. Motte and Gilliver. 8vo. Containing *Verses to be placed under the Picture of England's Arch-Poet* (q.v.) and **An Epitaph* (of By-Words).

(May. Produced at the Haymarket.) *Acis and Galatea :* An English Pastoral Opera. . . . Set to Musick By Mr. Handel. Watts. Price Six Pence. 8vo. Anonymous. (The words only.)

Ovid's Metamorphoses. A new edition of Garth's Folio, with the Latin added parallel to the English. Amsterdam. Printed for the Wetsteins and Smith. Folio.

that he should
write 'panegyric'
on Queen Caro-
line's ' hermi-
tage '. In Lon-
don ' before the
family, to
follow my own
inventions '.
(Nov.) Rapid
illness and
death. (Dec. 3.)
Burial in West-
minster Abbey.
(Dec. 23.)
Said to have
left £6,000.

DEATH OF JOHN GAY. (Dec. 3.)

SOME POSTHUMOUS EDITIONS, AND POSTHUMOUS WORKS.

1733. *The Beggar's Opera.* The Third [*sic*] Edition : To which is Added
The Overture in Score ; and the Musick prefix'd to each Song.
Watts. 8vo.
(Feb. 10. Produced at Lincoln's Inn Fields.) *Achilles.* An Opera.
Written by the late Mr. Gay. With the Musick prefix'd to each
Song. Watts. Price One Shilling and Six Pence. 8vo.
Fables. Fourth Edition. 8vo.

1735. *The Beggar's Opera.* Fourth Edition. 8vo.

1736. [*The What d'ye call it.* Fifth Edition.]

1737. [*Poems on Several Occasions.* Third Edition. 12mo.]
[*Fables.* Fifth Edition. 8vo.]

1738. [*Fables.* Sixth Edition. 8vo.]
(Sept. 29.) *Fables.* By the late Mr. Gay. Volume the Second.
Printed for J. and P. Knapton and T. Cox. Containing sixteen
additional Fables, of greater length than the original Fables ;
and published simultaneously in 4to and 8vo, uniform with the
existing editions.

1740. [*Trivia.* Fourth Edition. 8vo.]

1742. [*The Beggar's Opera.* Fifth Edition. 8vo.]
And many later editions, not mentioned here.
[*The Shepherd's Week.* Fifth Edition. 8vo.]
And later editions, not mentioned here.

1743. *The Distress'd Wife.* A Comedy. By the late Mr. Gay. Astley.
8vo.

1745. [*Poems on Several Occasions.* Fourth Edition. 12mo.]
And many later editions, not mentioned here.

1746. [*Fables.* The two volumes in one. 8vo.]
And many later editions, not mentioned here.

1747. *Miscellanies.* The Fourth Volume. Consisting of Verses by Dr. Swift,
Dr. Arbuthnot, Mr. Pope, and Mr. Gay. Bathurst. 8vo. Distinguishing Swift's contributions from the others. A collection of
all the verses in the volumes of 1727 and 1732, with a few more

added. Containing, for the first time, †*Bounce to Fop*, and †*Duke upon Duke*. Vide p. 177.

1750. *The Distress'd Wife.* Second Edition.

1754. *The Rehearsal at Goatham.* Astley. 8vo.

1776. *Additions to the Works of Alexander Pope Esq.* Containing *Mr. Pope's Welcome from Greece, A Motto for an Opera, The Epigrammatical Petition.*

1820. **Gay's Chair*: Poems never before printed. Longman. 8vo. (But printed in Barnstaple.)

LIST B.

SOME COLLECTED EDITIONS.

1760. *Plays written by Mr. John Gay*, viz. The Captives, a Tragedy. The Beggar's Opera. Polly, or, the Second Part of the Beggar's Opera. Achilles, an Opera. The Distress'd Wife, a Comedy. The Rehearsal at Goatham, a Farce. To which is added, An Account of the Life and Writings of the Author. London : Printed for J. and R. Tonson, in the Strand. MDCCLX.

1770. *The Works of Mr. John Gay.* In four volumes. To which is added an Account of the Life and Writings of the Author. *His jocamur, ludimus, amamus, dolemus, querimur, irascimur ; describimus aliquid modò pressius, modò elatius : atque ipsâ varietate tentamus efficere, ut alia aliis, quaedam fortasse omnibus placeant.* Plin. *Epist.* Dublin : Printed by James Potts, at Swift's-Head, in Dane-Street. MDCCLXX.

    Vol. I. The Life (as in Bell).

         The Poems on Several Occasions vol. i.

    Vol. II. The Poems on Several Occasions vol. ii (*plus To a Lady on her passion for old China* and *The Coquet Mother to her Daughter*).

    Vol. III. The Plays (as in the volume of 1760).

    Vol. IV. The Fables.

1772. *The Works of Mr. John Gay.* Complete, In Four Volumes. London : Printed for [thirty-two different firms, including J. Bell]. M.DCC.LXXII.

    Similar to the foregoing, except that Vol. I contains no ' Life ' ; Vol. III is ' Fables ' ; Vol. IV is ' Plays ', and has the ' Life ' from the volume of 1760.

Poems and Fables ; By Mr. John Gay. *His jocamur* [&c.]. Aberdeen : Printed for, and Sold by J. Boyle. M.DCC.LXXVI. Vols. 11 and 12 of *A Collection of the English Poets,* In Twenty Volumes. 12mo.

    Contains the Poems on Several Occasions (without additions) and the Fables.

Plays. A reprint of the Plays of 1760. Printed for W. Strahan, T. Lowndes, T. Caslon, W. Griffin, W. Nicoll, S. Bladon, and G. Kearsley. MDCCLXXII.

1773. [*Gay's Works*. In four volumes. J. Bell.]
This edition is in neither the British Museum nor the Bodleian
Libraries ; and I have failed to obtain a copy.   It is referred to in
Bell's 1777 edition. (See pp. xxiv and xxix.)
Poems on Several Occasions. By the late Mr. John Gay.   *His
jocamur* [&c.].   Edinburgh : Printed for A. Kincaid and W. Creech ;
and J. Balfour.   M, DCC, LXXIII.   In two vols. : being vols. 29
and 30 of ' The British Poets '.   The second volume is entitled
Poems and Fables.
Practically a reissue of the original *Poems on Several Occasions,*
with the addition of the *Epistle to the Dutchess of Marlborough,*
the lines *To a Lady, on her passion for old China, The Coquet
Mother and Daughter,* and the *Fables.*
12mo.

1772–5. [*Gay's Works.* London.   6 vols.   12mo.]
Mentioned in Lowndes' *Bibliographer's Manual.*

1775. [*Gay's Poems.* In two volumes. Trade edition.   12mo.]
Mentioned by Mr. Yeowell (see p. xxv) as omitting the doubtful
additions made by the foregoing.

1777. Bell's *British Theatre.*   Vol. 9 (Beggar's Opera, Polly, and Achilles).
The Poetical Works of John Gay.   Including his Fables.   In three
volumes.   With the Life of the Author.   From the Royal Quarto
Edition of 1720.   [*His jocamur* &c., and part of Pope's Epitaph.]
Vol. I.   Edinburgh : at the Apollo Press, by Jno Martins.   Anno
1777.
12mo.   Each volume has an engraving on the leaf preceding
the title-page ; each engraving bears at the head the inscription
' Bell's Edition.   The Poets of Great Britain Complete from
Chaucer to Churchill ', and at the foot ' Printed for John Bell
near Exeter Exchange Strand London Septr. 16th 1777 '.   The
engraved frontispiece (a portrait of Gay) is dated ' Feby. 21st
1778 '.
This is the edition frequently referred to in my notes as ' Bell '.
Vol. I.   Contains : Life, Rural Sports, Trivia, The Fan, The
Shepherd's Week, Acis and Galatea.
Vol. II.   Epistles, Tales, Eclogues, Songs and Ballads, Elegies,
Gondibert, Miscellanies.   (The additional poems are distributed
among the headings.)
Vol. III.   Fables.

1779. *The Works of the English Poets.*   With Prefaces, Biographical and
Critical, By Samuel Johnson. . . . London : Printed by J. Nichols ;
for [thirty-six firms ;   Bell not included].   M DCC LXXIX.
Vol. 41   Contains all the Poems on Several Occasions with a
number of additional pieces.
Vol. 42   The Tales and the Fables.

1794. *The Poetical Works of John Gay*. . . . Edinburgh : Printed by Mundell and Son, Royal Bank Close. Anno 1794.
Forming part of vol. 8 of *A Complete Edition of the Poets of Great Britain*. . . . London : Printed for John & Arthur Arch, . . . and for Bell & Bradfute and L. Mundell & Co. Edinburgh.
Based on Nichols' edition.
Large 8vo.

1795. *The Poetical, Dramatic, and Miscellaneous Works of John Gay*. In six volumes. To which is prefixed, Dr. Johnson's Biographical and Critical Preface. . . . London : Printed for Edward Jeffery, opposite Carlton House, Pall Mall. M.DCC.XCV. [Price in Boards One Pound Four Shillings.]
This is the nearest approach to a really complete edition of Gay. But it is very unintelligently put together ; for it lacks the additional pieces given by the foregoing—including the important *Mr. Pope's Welcome from Greece*.

Vol. 1. Contains Johnson's Life, and the Fables.
Vol. 2. The Poems on Several Occasions, vol. 1.
Vol. 3. The Poems on Several Occasions, vol. 2.
Vol. 4. Poems and Translations (that is, all the additions made by Bell, which in the 1777 edition are distributed among the Epistles, &c.).
Vol. 5. Plays. (A reprint of *Plays* 1760, ' Life ' and all.)
Vol. 6. Plays and Essays. (Three Hours after Marriage, The Mohocks, The Wife of Bath, and two essays from the Guardian.)

From the ' Advertisement' (quoted on p. xxix) I imagine the first four volumes to be a mere reprint of Bell's four-volume edition of 1773.

1804. Cooke's Pocket Edition of the Original and Complete Works of Select British Poets, or Entertaining Poetical Library, Containing the most Esteemed Poetic Productions Superbly Embellished.
The Poetical Works of John Gay. With the Life of the Author, by Dr. Johnson.
Vol. 1. Contains the Life, the Fables, Acis and Galatea, Dione, Rural Sports, and Tales.
Vol. 2. The Shepherd's Week, Epistles, Eclogues, Elegies, Miscellanies, Translations, and Songs.
This is descended from the edition of 1779.

1808 and 1809. The Works of the British Poets, collated with the Best Editions : by Thomas Park, F.S.A. London. 1808.
The Poetical Works of John Gay. In Three Volumes.
Supplement to the British Poets. London. 1809.
Vol. 1. Contains Fables.
Vol. 2. Poems on Several Occasions, vol. 1 ; Acis and Galatea.
Vol. 3. Poems on Several Occasions, vol. 2, with additions.

The Supplement contains *Mr. Pope's Welcome from Greece,* and three other small poems.

Unlike Jeffery and Cooke, who draw on Bell and Nichols respectively for their additions, Park dips into both sources, but contributes nothing new of his own.

1854. *The Poetical Works of John Gay.* With a Life of the Author, by Dr. Johnson. In Two Volumes. Boston : Little, Brown and Company. New York : Evans and Dickerson. Philadelphia : Lippincott, Grambo and Co. M.DCCC.LIV.

8vo. With a Portrait. The Advertisement says : ' These volumes follow, in most respects, the text of Park, which professes to have been collated with the best editions.'

Vol. 1. Contains Fables, Rural Sports, Trivia.

Vol. 2. Contains The Fan, The Shepherd's Week, Acis and Galatea, Epistles, Eclogues, Songs and Ballads, Elegies, Tales, Gondibert, Miscellanies.

A pleasing, and well-printed edition, with a far better text than Underhill's ; but entirely derivative.

1893. *The Poetical Works of John Gay* edited with a Life and Notes by John Underhill. London : Lawrence & Bullen, 16 Henrietta St., W.C. 1893.

Forming part of ' The Muses' Library '.

8vo. Two Volumes.

Vol. I. Contains Preface, Memoir, Longer Poems, Epistles, and Epistolary Verse, Eclogues, Notes, and Rural Sports (1st Edition) in an Appendix.

Vol. II. Translations, Prologues and Epilogues, Fables, Poems from Gay's Chair, Miscellaneous Pieces in Verse, Songs and Ballads, Notes, and the Tales in an Appendix.

1905. Reprint of the foregoing [without indication of date] for George Routledge & Sons, Ltd.

1923. The Abbey Classics—XIV and XV. *The Plays of John Gay.* In two volumes. Chapman & Dodd. Small 8vo.

Vol. 1. Johnson's Life, Bibliography of the Plays, The Mohocks, The What d'ye call it, The Captives, The Beggar's Opera (with the airs).

Vol. 2. Polly (with the airs, printed separately), Achilles, The Distress'd Wife, The Rehearsal at Goatham.

The Abbey Classics—XVI. *Poems by John Gay.* With an Introduction by Francis Bickley. Chapman & Dodd.

Small 8vo. Containing Rural Sports, The Fan, The Shepherd's Week, Trivia, The Fables, Eclogues, and fourteen minor pieces. The text follows, apart from the Fables, the 1731 edition of the Poems on Several Occasions.

LIST C.

MODERN EDITIONS OF SINGLE WORKS.

(N.B.—This List is confined to Editions used by the Editor.)

Trivia.

 1899. *Trivia and other poems by John Gay.* Edited by J. Potter Briscoe, F.R.H.S. Gay and Bird. 12mo.
  In ' The Bibelots ' Series.

 1922. *Trivia.* Edited by Professor W. H. Williams. O'Connor. Imperial 8vo. Illustrations. A reprint of the First Edition.

Fables. (Mr. Wright's Bibliography records nearly 150 editions in French and English, and is not complete.)

 1779. *Fables.* By John Gay. Newcastle. With cuts by John Bewick. (Many later editions with John and Thomas Bewick's cuts.)

 1793. *Fables.* By John Gay. With a Life of the Author. John Storkdale, Piccadilly. Royal 8vo. Many engravings, including a few small plates by Blake.

 N.d. Cassell's Library Edition of British Poets. Part 51, containing *Gay's Fables*, &c. The text edited by Charles Cowden Clarke.

 1854. *The Fables of John Gay*, with an original memoir, introduction, and annotations, by Octavius Freire Owen, M.A., F.S.A., of Christ Church, Oxford. Routledge. 1854. Dedicated to his children ' with every affectionate desire for their improvement '.

 1884. *Fables by Mr. John Gay*, with a memoir by Austin Dobson. London : Kegan Paul, Trench & Co. MDCCC LXXX IIII.

 1889. *The Fables of John Gay.* With Biographical and Critical Introduction and Bibliographical Appendix. Edited by W. H. Kearley Wright, F.R.H.S., Borough Librarian, Plymouth. A New Edition. Frederick Warne & Co. 1889.
  In ' The Chandos Classics '. More than one subsequent edition. Has a useful bibliography, but is of no value for the text.

The Beggar's Opera.

 N.d. Dicks' Standard Plays. Number 45.

 1905. The King's Library, edited by Professor Gollancz. De La More Press Quartos.
  Number III. *The Beggar's Opera*, edited with a Preface, Notes, and Bibliography by G. Hamilton MacLeod.
  4to.

 1914. *Representative English Dramas from Dryden to Sheridan.* Edited by Frederick and James Tupper. New York : Oxford University Press.

1920. *The Beggar's Opera.* Secker. 8vo.

1921. *The Beggar's Opera.* Heinemann. 4to and 8vo. With the music prefixed to each song, a memoir of Lovat Fraser, a note and illustrations by Fraser.

Polly.

1922. A reprint of the First Edition, with a foreword by Oswald Doughty, M.A. O'Connor. 8vo.

1923. *Polly.* Heinemann. 4to and 8vo. With the music prefixed to each song, and illustrations by William Nicholson.

The Beggar's Opera and Polly.

1923. *The Beggar's Opera and Polly,* by John Gay Together with the Airs of the Music from the original editions of 1728 and 1729. Chapman & Dodd.

(A 4to reprint of the 2nd edition of the Beggar's Opera, and the 1st edition of Polly.)

The Shepherd's Week.

1924. A reprint of the edition published by R. Burleigh. Edited by H. F. B. Brett-Smith. Oxford, Blackwell. 8vo.

W I N E

A

P O E M.

Nulla placere diu, nec vivere carmina possunt,
Quae scribuntur aquae potoribus. Hor. Epist. 19. Lib. 1.

[*Editions* :
1. WINE | A | POEM. | *Nulla placere diu, nec vivere carmina possunt,* | *Quæ Scribuntur aquæ potoribus. Epist.* 19 *Lib.* 1 *Hor.* | *LONDON :* | Printed for WIL-LIAM KEBLE, at the *Black-Spread-* | *Eagle* in *Westminster-Hall*, MDCCVIII.
    Folio. 16 pp. A copy is preserved in the Godwyn Pamphlets at the Bodleian Library, a second is in the possession of Mr. T. J. Wise, a third in the Wrenn Library, University of Texas, U.S.A., and a fourth belongs to Mr. H. T. Butler. The British Museum has no copy. I have not met with any other examples ; nor, to judge from his reliance on the version in Bell's edition (' said to be printed from a copy of the original edition ') had Mr. Underhill.
    2. A pirated edition. ' Printed and Sold by *H. Hills,* in *Black-Fryers,* | near the Water-side. 1708.'
    Small 8vo. A copy is in the British Museum.
    3. A reprint of 2 ' To which is added,—*Old* England's *New Triumph :* Or, | *the Battle of* Audenard. | A SONG '.
    Small 8vo, 1708, reprinted 1709.
The Poem was not included in any edition of Gay's poetical works until John Bell admitted it to his edition of Gay's Works in 1773, giving his authority in a footnote (see p. xxx). His version differs considerably from the original Folio ; I cannot say from what source his alterations are derived. My references, as I have explained on p. xiii, are to Bell's 1777 edition.
I have not attempted to correct the Folio, except in 188 and 244. Underhill takes his text from Bell.]

Of Happiness Terrestrial, and the Source
Whence human pleasures flow, sing *Heavenly* Muse,
Of sparkling juices, of th' enliv'ning Grape,
Whose *quickning* tast adds *vigour* to the Soul,
Whose sov'raign pow'r revives decaying nature,
And thaws the frozen Blood of hoary Age
A kindly warmth diffusing, Youthful fires
Gild his dim Eyes, and paint with ruddy hue
His wrizzled Visage, ghastly wan before :
Cordial restorative, to mortal Man   10
With *copious* Hand by *bounteous* Gods bestow'd.

4 *These, and most of the italicized expressions throughout, are peculiar to the Folio,*
9 wrizzled] wrinkled *Bell*.
10 restorative, to mortal Man] restorative to mortal man, *Bell* (*Hills, without comma after* man).

BACCHUS Divine, aid my *adventrous* Song,
That with no middle flight intends to soar
Inspir'd, *Sublime* on *Pegasean* Wing
By thee upborn, I draw *Miltonic* Air.

When fumy Vapours clog our loaded Brows
With furrow'd Frowns, when stupid downcast Eyes
Th' external Symptoms of remorse within,
Our Grief express, or when in sullen Dumps
With Head Incumbent on *Expanded* Palm,　　　　　20
Moaping we sit in silent sorrow drown'd :
Whether Inviegling *Hymen* has trappand
Th' unwary Youth, and ty'd the *Gordian* Knot
Of jangling Wedlock, *Indissoluble* ;
Worried all Day by loud *Xantippes* Din,
And when the gentle Dew of sleep inclines
With slumbrous weight his Eye-lids, *She* inflam'd
With *Uncloy'd* Lust, and itch Insatiable,
His Stock exhausted, still yells on for *more* ;
Nor fails She to Exalt him to the Stars,　　　　　30
And fix him there among the Branched Crew
(*Taurus*, and *Aries*, and *Capricorn*,)
The greatest Monster of the *Zodiac* ;
Or for the loss of Anxious Worldly Pelf,
Or *Celia's* scornful slights, and cold disdain
Had check'd his Am'rous flame with *coy* repulse,
The worst Events that Mortals can befall :
By cares *depress'd*, in pensive *Hypoish* Mood,
With slowest pace, the tedious Minuits Roll.

Thy charming sight, but much more charming Gust　　40
New Life incites, and warms our *chilly* Blood,
Strait we, with pert Looks, we raise our drooping fronts,
And pour in Chrystal *pure*, thy *purer* juice,
With chearful Countenance, and steady Hand
Raise it *Lip-high*, then fix the spatious Rim
T' expecting Mouth, and now with Grateful tast,
The ebbing Wine glides swiftly o're the Tongue,
The circling *Blood* with quicker motion flies ;
Such is thy pow'rful influence, thou strait
Dispell'st those Clouds that lowring dark eclips'd　　50
The *whilom* Glories of our gladsom Face,
And dimpled Cheeks, and sparkling rolling Eyes,

---

13 soar] soar. *Hills*　　soar : *Bell.*　　　　　　19 Our Grief express] Express
our grief *Bell.*　　　24 *Indissoluble*] not to be dissolved *Bell.*　　　26–9 *These lines
are omitted without indication by Bell.*　　30 Nor fails She] Who fails not *Bell.*
32 *Capricorn*,)] Capricorn, *Bell, who in l.* 33 *prints* monsters *and the bracket after*
Zodiac, *making nonsense of the whole passage.*　　36 Had] Which *Bell, a mistaken
emendation.*　　38 *Hypoish*] hippish *Bell.*　　40 *Bell joins this to the preceding
paragraph.*　　46 *Bell emends to* To the expecting mouth ;—with grateful taste,
51 our] the *Bell.*　　52 And dimpled] White dimpled *Bell.*

Thy chearing Virtues, and thy worth proclaim.
So *Mists* and *Exhalations* that arise
From Hills or steamy Lake, Dusky or Gray
Prevail, till *Phœbus* sheds *Titanian* Rays,
And paints their *Fleecy* skirts with *shining* Gold ;
Unable to resist, the Foggy damps
That veild the surface of the verdant Fields,
At the *Gods* penetrating Beams disperse :   6o
The Earth again in former Beauty smiles,
In gaudiest Livery drest, all *Gay* and *Clear.*

When disappointed *Strephon* meets Repulse,
Scofft at, despis'd, in Melancholic mood
Joyless he wasts in sighs the lazy Hours,
Till *Reinforc't* by thy Almighty aid,
He *Storms* the Breach, and *Wins* the Beauteous Fort

To pay *Thee* Homage, and receive *Thy* Blessings,
The *British* Marriner quits native shore,
And ventures through the tractless vast Abyss,   70
Plowing the Ocean, whilst the *Upheav'd* Oak
With beaked Prow, Rides tilting ore the Waves ;
Shockt by Tempestuous jarring Winds she Rolls
In dangers *Imminent,* till she arrives
At those blest *Climes,* thou favourst with thy presence ;
Whether, at *Lusitanian* sultry Coasts,
Or lofty *Teneriff, Palma, Ferro,*
Provence, Or at the *Celtiberian* Shores ;
With gazing Pleasure, and Astonishment
At *Paradice,* (Seat of our antient sire,)   80
He thinks himself arriv'd, the Purple *Grape*
In largest Clusters Pendant, Grace the *Vines*
Innumerous, in Fields *Grottesque* and *Wild*
They with Implicit Curles the *Oak* entwine,
And load with Fruit Divine Her spreading Boughs ;
Sight most delicious, not an Irksom Thought,
Or of left native *Isle,* or absent *Friends,*
Or dearest *Wife,* or tender sucking *Babe,*
His kindly treach'rous Mem'ry now presents ;
The Jovial *GOD* has left no room for Cares.   90

CELESTIAL Liquor, thou that didst inspire
Maro and *Flaccus,* and the *Grecian* Bard,
With lofty Numbers, and *Heroic* strains
Unparelell'd, with Eloquence profound,
And Arguments *Convincive* didst enforce

66 Almighty] most potent *Bell.*   68 Blessings] blessing *Bell.*   69 The
British seaman quits his native shore, *Bell.*   70 vast] deep *Bell.*   71 whilst]
while *Bell.*   76 Lusitania's sultry coast *Bell.*   81 *Grape*] grapes *Bell.*
85 Her] his *Bell.*   91 thou that] that thou *Folio, corrected in the Errata to* thou that.

Fam'd *Tully*, and *Demosthenes* Renown'd :
Ennius first Fam'd in *Latin* Song, invain
Drew *Heliconian* streams, Ungrateful whet
To *Jaded* Muse, and oft' with vain attempt
Heroic Acts in Flagging Numbers *dull*   100
With pains essay'd, but abject still and low,
His *Unrecruited* Muse could never reach
The mighty Theme, till from the Purple Font
Of bright *Lenæan* fire, Her barren drought
He quench'd, and with inspiring *Nect'rous* Juice
Her drooping Spirits chear'd, aloft she towres
Born on stiff *Pennons*, and of Wars alarms,
And *Trophies* won, in loftiest Numbers sings :
Tis thou the *Hero*'s breast to Martial Acts,
And resolution bold, and ardour brave   110
Excit'st, thou check'st Inglorious lolling ease,
And sluggish Minds with gen'rous fires inflam'st,
O *thou*, that first my quickned Soul engag'd,
Still with thy aid assist me, What is *dark*
Illumin, What is *low* raise and support,
That to the height of this great Argument,
Thy Universal Sway o're all the World,
In everlasting Numbers, like the *Theme*
I may record, and sing thy *Matchless* Worth.

Had the *Oxonian* Bard thy Praise rehears'd,   120
His *Muse* had yet retain'd her wonted height ;
Such as *of late* o're *Blenheims* Field she soard
Aerial, now in *Ariconian* Bogs
She lies Inglorious floundring, like her Theme
Languid and Faint, and on damp Wing immerg'd
In *acid juice*, invain attempts to rise.

With what sublimest Joy from noisy Town,
At *Rural* Seat, *Lucretilis* retir'd,
Flaccus, untainted by perplexing Cares,
Where the white *Poplar*, and the lofty *Pine*   130
Join Neighbouring Boughs, sweet Hospitable shade
Creating, from *Phœbean* Rays secure,
A cool Retreat, with few well chosen Friends
On flowry Mead *Recumbent*, spent the Hours
In Mirth *Innocuous*, and Alternate Verse !
With Roses Interwoven, Poplar wreaths
Their Temples bind, dress of *Sylvestrian* Gods ;
Choicest *Nectarian* juice Crown'd largest Bowles,
And Overlook'd the lid, alluring sight,
Of fragrant Scent *attractive*, tast Divine !   140

103 Font] fount *Bell.*   113 engag'd] didst warm *Bell.*   114 What is *dark*]
that thy praise *Bell, omitting ll.* 115–16.   128 *Lucretilis*] *Lucretelus* Hills and
Bell.   139 lid] brim *Bell.*

Whether from *Formian* Grape depress'd, *Falern*
Or *Setin*, *Massic*, *Gauran* or *Sabine*,
Lesbian or *Cæcuban*, the chearing Bowl
Mov'd briskly round, and spur'd their heightned Wit
To Sing *Mecænas* praise their *Patron* kind.

But *we*, not as our Pristin sires, repair
T' *umbrageous* Grot or Vale, but when the Sun
Faintly from Western Skies his rays oblique
Darts sloping, and to *Thetis* watry Lap
Hastens in Prone Career, with Friends Select   150
Swiftly we hie to Devil *Young* or *Old*
Jocund and Boon, where at the entrance stands
A Stripling, who with Scrapes and *Humil* Cringe,
Greets us in winning Speech and Accent Bland ;
With lightest bound, and safe unerring step
He skips before, and nimbly climbs the Stairs :
Melampus thus, panting with lolling Tongue,
And wagging Tail, Gamboles, and frisks before
His sequel *Lord* from pensive walk return'd,
Whether in *Shady* Wood, or Pastures *Green*,   160
And waits his coming at the well known Gate.
Nigh to the Stairs Ascent, in regal Port
Sits a *Majestic* Dame, whose looks denounce
Command and *Sov'reignty*, with haughty Air,
And *Studied* Mien, in *Semicirc'lar* Throne
Enclos'd, she deals around her dread Commands ;
Behind her (*Dazling* sight) in order Rang'd,
Pile above Pile *Chrystallin* Vessels shine ;
Attendant Slaves with eager stride advance,
And after Homage paid, bawl out aloud   170
Words Unintelligible, *noise* confus'd :
She knows the *Jargon* Sound, and strait describes
In Characters *Mysterious* Words obscure ;
More legible are *Algebraic* Signs,
Or *Mystic* Figures by *Magicians* drawn,
When they Invoke aid *Diabolical*.

Drive hence the Rude and Barb'rous Dissonance
Of Savage *Thracians*, and *Croatian* Boors ;
The loud *Centaurean* Broiles with *Lapithæ*
Sound harsh, and grating to *Lenæan* God :   180
Chase brutal Feuds of *Belgian* skippers hence,
(Amid their Cups, whose *Innate* Tempers shown)
In clumsy Fist wielding *Scymetrian* Knife,
Who slash each others Eyes, and *Blubber'd* Face,

---

159 sequel] sequent *Bell*.　　　160 Pastures] Pasture *Hills*　pasture *Bell*.
169 stride] strides *Bell*.　　172 Sound] Sounds *Hills*　sounds *Bell*.　　176 aid
Diabolical] th' infernal spirits' aid *Bell*.　　182 Tempers] temper's *Bell, not un-
derstanding the intended classicism.*

Prophaning *Bacchanalian* solemn rites :
Musicks Harmonious Numbers better suit
His Festivalls, from Instrument or Voice,
Or *Gasperini*'s Hand the trembling string
Should touch, or from the *Tuscan* Dames,
Or warbling *TOFTS* more soft Melodious Tongue   190
Sweet *Symphonies* should flow, the *Delian* God
For Airy *BACCHUS* is Associate meet.

The Stairs Ascent now gain'd, our Guide unbars
The Door of Spatious Room, and creaking Chairs
(To ear offensive) round the Table sets,
We sit, when thus his Florid *Speech* begins :
Name, Sirs, the *WINE* that most invites your Tast,
Champaign or *Burgundy*, or *Florence* pure,
Or *Hock* Antique, or *Lisbon* New or Old,
Bourdeaux, or neat *French* White, or *Alicant* :   200
For *Bourdeaux* we with Voice Unanimous
Declare, (such Sympathy 's in Boon *Compeers*.)
He quits the Room *Alert*, but soon returns,
One Hand Capacious glist'ring Vessels bore
Resplendant, th' other with a grasp secure,
A Bottle (*mighty charge*) upstaid, full Fraught
With goodly Wine, *He* with extended Hand
Rais'd high, pours forth the Sanguin frothy *Juice*,
O'respread with Bubbles, dissipated soon :
We strait t' our Arms repair, experienc't Chiefs ;   210
Now Glasses clash with Glasses, (*charming sound*,)
And Glorious *ANNA*'s Health the *first* the *best*
Crowns the *full* Glass, at *HER* inspiring Name
The sprightly Wine *Results*, and seems to Smile,
With hearty Zeal, and wish *Unanimous*
The Health we Drink, and in *HER* Health our own.

A Pause ensues, and now with grateful Chat
W' improve the *Interval*, and Joyous Mirth
Engages our *rais'd* Souls, Pat Repartee,
Or Witty Joke our airy *Senses* moves   220
To pleasant *Laughter*, strait the Ecchoing Room
With Universal *Peals* and *Shouts* Resounds.

The *ROYAL DANE*, *blest* Consort of *blest QUEEN*,
Next Crowns the Rubied Nectar, all whose Bliss
In *ANNA*'s plac't, with Sympathetic Flame,
And Mutual Endearments, all *HER* Joys,

---

187 Instrument] instruments *Bell.*   188 *Gasperini*'s] *Gasperini*'s Folio.
189 the *Tuscan* Dames] the dulcet Tuscan dames *Bell.*   190 *TOFTS* more soft]
Tofts' far more *Bell.*   200 White] wine *Bell.*   204 bore] bears *Bell.*   210 t'our
Arms] to arms *Bell.*   214 *Results*] exults *Bell.*   216 The Health] Her health
Bell.   223 *blest QUEEN*] the queen *Bell.*

Like the kind Turtles pure untainted Love,
Center in *HIM*, who shares the grateful Hearts
Of Loyal Subjects, with his Sov'reign *QUEEN* ;
For by *HIS* Prudent Care, united shores 230
Were sav'd from Hostile Fleets Invasion dire.

The Hero *MARLBRO* next, whose vast Exploits
Fames Clarion sounds, fresh Laurels, Triumphs new
We wish, like those *HE* won at *Hockstets* Field.

Next *DEVONSHIRE* Illustrious, who from Race
Of Noblest Patriots sprung, whose Soul's Endow'd,
And is with ev'ry Vertuous gift Adorn'd
That shon in His most worthy Ancestors,
For then distinct in sep'rate Breasts were seen
Virtues distinct, but all in *HIM* Unite. 240

Prudent *GODOLPHIN*, of the Nations weal
Frugal, but free and gen'rous of his own
Next Crowns the Bowl, with Faithful *SUNDERLAND*,
And *HALIFAX*, the Muses darling Son,
In whom *Conspicuous*, with full Lustre shine
The *surest* Judgment, and the *brightest* Wit,
Himself *Mecænas* and a *Flaccus* too,
And all the Worthies of the *British* Realm
In order rang'd succeeded, *Healths* that ting'd
The *Dulcet* Wine with a more charming Gust. 250

Now each the Mistress by whose scorching Eyes
Fir'd, tosts *Cosmelia* Fair, or *Dulcibella*,
Or *Sylvia* Comely Black, with jetty Eyes
Piercing, or Airy *Celia* sprightly Maid.
Insensibly thus flow *Unnumber'd* Hours ;
Glass succeeds Glass, till the *DIRCÆAN GOD*
Shines in our Eyes, and with his Fulgent Rays
Enlightens our glad Looks with lovely Die ;
All Blithe and Jolly that like *Arthurs* Knights,
Of Rotund Table, Fam'd in Pristin Records, 260
Now most we seem'd, such is the Power of Wine.

236 Soul's Endow'd,] worthy soul *Bell.*   237 Is with each fair and virtuous
gift adorn'd, *Bell.*   241 Nations] *nation's* Underhill.   242 his own] *his own*
Underhill.   244 Muses] Muses' *Bell* Muse's *Underhill.*   Son] son *Bell* Song
Folio, Hills, an evident misprint.   249 In order rang'd, succeed ; such healths
as tinge *Bell.*
   251-2   Now each his mistress toasts, by whose bright eye
                He's fir'd ; Cosmelia fair, or Dulcibell', *Bell.*
   251 the] their *Hills.*   252 Fir'd,] *Hills* Fird, *Folio, corrected in Errata.*   tosts]
tost *Hills.*   260 Table] *Hills, Bell* Fable *Folio, corrected in Errata.*
Pristin] old *Bell.*

Thus we the winged Hours in harmless Mirth,
And Joys Unsully'd pass, till Humid Night
Has half her Race perform'd, now all Abroad
Is hush'd and silent, nor the *Rumbling* noise
Of Coach or Cart, or smoaky Link-Boys call
Is heard; but *Universal silence* Reigns :
When we in Merry Plight, Airy and Gay,
Surpriz'd to find the Hours so swiftly flie,
With hasty knock, or *Twang* of *Pendant* Cord   270
Alarm the drowsy Youth from slumb'ring Nod ;
Startled he flies, and stumbles o'er the Stairs
Erroneous, and with busie Knuckles plies
His yet clung Eye-lids, and with stagg'ring Reel
Enters Confus'd, and Mutt'ring asks our Wills ;
When we with *Lib'ral* Hand the *Score* discharge,
And Homeward each his Course with *steady* step
Unerring steer'd, of Cares and Coin bereft.

278 steer'd] steers *Bell*.

THE
F A N.
A
P O E M.
IN THREE BOOKS.

—— ἔνθά τε οἱ θελκτήρια πάντα τέτυκτο·
Ἔνθ᾽ ἔνι μὲν φιλότης, ἐν δ᾽ ἵμερος, ἐν δ᾽ ὀαριστίς
Πάρφασις, ἥτ᾽ ἔκλεψε νόον πύκα περ φρονεόντων·
Τὸν ῥά οἱ ἔμβαλε χερσίν. Homer Iliad. 14.

[*Editions :*
1. THE | FAN. | A | POEM. | In THREE BOOKS. | *By Mr.* GAY. | —*ἔνθά δε*
θελκτήρια πάντα τέτυκτο· | *Ἔνθα ενι μὲν φιλότης, ἐν δ᾽ ἵμερος, ἐν δ᾽ ὀαριστὺς,* | *Πάρφασις*
ἥτ᾽ ἔκλεψε νόον πύκα περ φρονεόντων· | *Τὸν ῥά δι ἔμβαλε χερσὶν.* Homer. Iliad.
14. | *LONDON :* | Printed for *J. Tonson,* at *Shakespear's-Head* over- | against
Catherine-street in the *Strand.* 1714.
Folio.
2. POEMS | ON | SEVERAL OCCASIONS. | By Mr. *JOHN GAY.* | Volume *the*
First. | *His jocamur, ludimus, amamus, dolemus, querimur, irasci-* | *mur ; describimus*
aliquid modò pressius, modò elatius : | *atque ipsá varietate tentamus efficere, ut alia aliis,*
quae- | *dam fortasse omnibus placeant.* Plin. Epist. | *LONDON :* | Printed for Jacob
Tonson, *at Shakespear's-Head* in the | *Strand, and* Bernard Lintot, *between the*
Temple- | *Gates in Fleetstreet.* MDCCXX.
Demy 4to. Two vols. Printed by subscription. For the contents of the two
volumes see *Bibliographical Summary,* p. xxxviii.
3. *Poems on Several Occasions.* London : Tonson and Lintot. 1731.
Post 12mo. Two vols. A revised edition, following the style of 1720, except
for its employment of white lines between paragraphs. The present edition follows
that of 1720 in this respect.
According to Underhill the Folio, though bearing the date 1714, was actually
published on December 8, 1713.
The Folio employs capital letters very freely ; other variations are recorded in
the notes.]

BOOK I.

I sing that graceful toy, whose waving play
With gentle gales relieves the sultry day,
Not the wide fan by *Persian* dames display'd,
Which o'er their beauty casts a grateful shade ;
Nor that long known in *China's* artful land,
Which, while it cools the face, fatigues the hand :
Nor shall the muse in *Asian* climates rove,
To seek in *Indostan* some spicy grove,
Where stretch'd at ease the panting lady lies,
To shun the fervor of meridian skies,   10

Motto. ἔνθά τε οἱ] ἔνθά δε *all early editions.*
2 day,] Day. *1714.*   7 *Asian*] *Indian 1714.*   10 To shun] And shuns *1714.*

While sweating slaves catch ev'ry breeze of air,
And with wide-spreading fans refresh the fair ;
No busie gnats her pleasing dreams molest,
Inflame her cheek, or ravage o'er her breast,
But artificial Zephyrs round her fly,
And mitigate the feaver of the sky.
　Nor shall *Bermudas* long the Muse detain,
Whose fragrant forests bloom in *Waller's* strain,
Where breathing sweets from ev ry field ascend,
And the wild woods with golden apples bend ;　　　20
Yet let me in some od'rous shade repose,
Whilst in my verse the fair *Palmetto* grows :
Like the tall pine it shoots its stately head,
From the broad top depending branches spread ;
No knotty limbs the taper body bears,
Hung on each bough a single leaf appears,
Which shrivell'd in its infancy remains,
Like a clos'd fan, nor stretches wide its veins,
But as the seasons in their circle run,
Opes its ribb'd surface to the nearer sun :　　　30
Beneath this shade the weary peasant lies,
Plucks the broad leaf, and bids the breezes rise.
　Stay, wand'ring Muse, nor rove in foreign climes,
To thy own native shore confine thy rhimes.
Assist, ye Nine, your loftiest notes employ,
Say what celestial skill contriv'd the toy ;
Say how this instrument of Love began,
And in immortal strains display the Fan.
　Strephon had long confess'd his am'rous pain,
Which gay *Corinna* railly'd with disdain :　　　40
Sometimes in broken words he sigh'd his care,
Look'd pale, and trembled when he view'd the fair ;
With bolder freedoms now the youth advanc'd,
He dress'd, he laugh'd, he sung, he rhim'd, he danc'd :
Now call'd more pow'rful presents to his aid,
And, to seduce the mistress, brib'd the maid ;
Smooth flatt'ry in her softer hours apply'd,
The surest charm to bind the force of pride :
But still unmov'd remains the scornful dame,
Insults her captive, and derides his flame.　　　50
When *Strephon* saw his vows dispers'd in air,
He sought in solitude to lose his care ;
Relief in solitude he sought in vain,
It serv'd, like Musick, but to feed his pain.
To *Venus* now the slighted Boy complains,
And calls the Goddess in these tender strains.
　O potent Queen, from *Neptune's* empire sprung,
Whose glorious birth admiring *Nereids* sung,

38 Fan] *Fan* 1714 *and so throughout.*

Who 'midst the fragrant plains of *Cyprus* rove,
Whose radiant presence gilds the *Paphian* grove,   60
Where to thy name a thousand altars rise,
And curling clouds of incense hide the skies :
O beauteous Goddess, teach me how to move,
Inspire my tongue with eloquence of love.
If lost *Adonis* e'er thy bosom warm'd,
If e'er his eyes, or godlike figure charm'd,
Think on those hours when first you felt the dart,
Think on the restless feaver of thy heart ;
Think how you pin'd in absence of the swain :
By those uneasie minutes know my pain.   70
Ev'n while *Cydippe* to *Diana* bows,
And at her shrine renews her virgin vows.
The lover, taught by thee, her pride o'ercame ;
She reads his oaths, and feels an equal flame :
Oh, may my flame, like thine, *Acontius*, prove,
May *Venus* dictate, and reward my love.
When crouds of suitors *Atalanta* try'd,
She wealth, and beauty, wit and fame defy'd ;
Each daring lover with advent'rous pace
Pursu'd his wishes in the dang'rous race ;   80
Like the swift hind, the bounding damsel flies,
Strains to the goal, the distanc'd lover dies.
Hippomenes, O *Venus*, was thy care,
You taught the swain to stay the flying fair,
Thy golden present caught the virgin's eyes,
She stoops ; he rushes on, and gains the prize.
Say, *Cyprian* Deity, what gift, what art,
Shall humble into love *Corinna*'s heart ;
If only some bright toy can charm her sight,
Teach me what present may suspend her flight.   90
Thus the desponding youth his flame declares.
The Goddess with a nod his passion hears.
    Far in *Cythera* stands a spacious grove,
Sacred to *Venus* and the God of love ;

60 And whose bright Presence *1714*.   62 curling] frequent *1714*.   69 swain :]
Swain, *1714*.   70 know] guess *1714*.
70 *here follow in the Folio :*
        Thy Suppliant, O Propitious Goddess, aid,
        Or quench my Flame, or bend the stubborn Maid.
72 renews] renew'd *1714*.
73–4   Her Lover, by thy Present, won the Dame,
        And in a lucky Motto spoke his Flame. *1714*.
82 She gains the Goal, *1714*
86 And while she stoop'd, he won the beauteous Prize. *1714*.
87–8   Say, *Cyprian* Goddess, by what Gift or Art,
        I may subdue *Corinna*'s faithless Heart ; *1714*.
90 may suspend] will prevent *1714*.   92 And melts the Goddess with his
falling Tears. *1714*.

Here the luxuriant myrtle rears her head.
Like the tall oak the fragrant branches spread ;
Here nature all her sweets profusely pours,
And paints th' enamell'd ground with various flow'rs ;
Deep in the gloomy glade a grotto bends,
Wide through the craggy rock an arch extends,   100
The rugged stone is cloath'd with mantling vines,
And round the cave the creeping woodbine twines.
  Here busie *Cupids*, with pernicious art,
Form the stiff bow, and forge the fatal dart ;
All share the toil ; while some the bellows ply,
Others with feathers teach the shafts to fly :
Some with joint force whirl round the stony wheel,
Where streams the sparkling fire from temper'd steel ;
Some point their arrows with the nicest skill,
And with the warlike store their quivers fill.   110
  A different toil another forge employs ;
Here the loud hammer fashions female toys,
Hence is the fair with ornament supply'd,
Hence sprung the glitt'ring implements of pride ;
Each trinket that adorns the modern dame,
First to these little artists ow'd its frame.
Here an unfinish'd di'mond crosslet lay,
To which soft lovers adoration pay ;
There was the polish'd crystal bottle seen,
That with quick scents revives the modish spleen :   120
Here the yet rude unjoynted snuff-box lyes,
Which serves the railly'd fop for smart replies ;
There piles of paper rose in gilded reams,
The future records of the lover's flames ;
Here clouded canes 'midst heaps of toys are found,
And inlaid tweezer-cases strow the ground.
There stands the *Toilette*, nursery of charms,
Compleatly furnish'd with bright beauty's arms ;
The patch, the powder-box, pulville, perfumes,
Pins, paint, a flattr'ing glass, and black-lead combs.   130
  The toilsome hours in diff'rent labour slide,
Some work the file, and some the graver guide ;
From the loud anvil the quick blow rebounds,
And their rais'd arms descend in tuneful sounds.
Thus when *Semiramis*, in ancient days,
Bad *Babylon* her mighty bulwarks raise ;
A swarm of lab'rers diff'rent tasks attend :
Here pullies make the pond'rous oak ascend,
With ecchoing strokes the cragged quarry groans,
While there the chissel forms the shapeless stones ;   140

95 Where the luxuriant Myrtle rears its Head, *1714.*   99 Deep in the gloomy
glade] In the remotest Part *1714.*   100 an] its *1714.*   106 the] their *1714.*
108 Where sparkling Fire streams from the temper'd Steel ; *1714.*   113 Ornaments
1714.   124 future] tender *1714.*   132 work] wear *1714.*   133 From] Now *1714.*

The weighty mallet deals resounding blows,
'Till the proud battlements her tow'rs enclose.
Now *Venus* mounts her car, she shakes the reins,
And steers her turtles to *Cythera's* plains ;
Strait to the grott with graceful step she goes,
Her loose ambrosial hair behind her flows :
The swelling bellows heave for breath no more,
All drop their silent hammers on the floor ;
In deep suspence the mighty labour stands,
While thus the Goddess spoke her mild commands.   150
Industrious *Loves*, your present toils forbear,
A more important task demands your care ;
Long has the scheme employ'd my thoughtful Mind,
By judgment ripen'd, and by time refin'd.
That glorious bird have ye not often seen
Who draws the car of the celestial Queen ?
Have ye not oft survey'd his varying dyes,
His tail all gilded o'er with *Argus'* eyes ?
Have ye not seen him in the sunny day
Unfurle his plumes, and all his pride display,   160
Then suddenly contract his dazling train,
And with long-trailing feathers sweep the plain ?
Learn from this hint, let this instruct your art ;
Thin taper sticks must from one center part :
Let these into the quadrant's form divide,
The spreading ribs with snowy paper hide ;
Here shall the pencil bid its colours flow,
And make a miniature creation grow.
Let the machine in equal foldings close,
And now its plaited surface wide dispose.   170
So shall the fair her idle hand employ,
And grace each motion with the restless toy,
With various play bid grateful *Zephyrs* rise,
While love in ev'ry grateful *Zephyr* flies.
The master *Cupid* traces out the lines,
And with judicious hand the draught designs,
Th' expecting *Loves* with joy the model view,
And the joint labour eagerly pursue.
Some slit their arrows with the nicest art,
And into sticks convert the shiver'd dart ;   180
The breathing bellows wake the sleeping fire,
Blow off the cinders, and the sparks aspire ;
Their arrow's point they soften in the flame,
And sounding hammers break its barbed frame :
Of this, the little pin they neatly mold,
From whence their arms the spreading sticks unfold ;

142 Till the proud Walls the lofty Tow'rs enclose. *1714.*   155 ye] you *1714 and
in ll.* 157–9.   156 Who] Which *1714.*   159 in some sunny Day, *1714.*
166 with] let *1714.*   173 With various Airs bid the soft Zephyrs rise, *1714.*
174 grateful] gentle *1714.*   182 cinders] cindars *1731.*

In equal plaits they now the paper bend,
And at just distance the wide ribs extend,
Then on the frame they mount the limber skreen,
And finish instantly the new machine.   190
    The Goddess pleas'd, the curious work receives,
Remounts her chariot, and the grotto leaves;
With the light fan she moves the yielding air,
And gales, till then unknown, play round the fair.
    Unhappy lovers, how will you withstand,
When these new arms shall grace your charmer's hand ?
In ancient times, when maids in thought were pure,
When eyes were artless, and the look demure,
When the wide ruff the well-turn'd neck enclos'd,
And heaving breasts within the stays repos'd,   200
When the close hood conceal'd the modest ear,
E'er black-lead combs disown'd the virgin's hair ;
Then in the muff unactive fingers lay,
Nor taught the fan in fickle forms to play.
    How are the Sex improv'd in am'rous arts,
What new-found snares they bait for human hearts !
    When kindling war the ravag'd globe ran o'er,
And fatten'd thirsty plains with human gore,
At first, the brandish'd arm the jav'lin threw,
Or sent wing'd arrows from the twanging yew ;   210
In the bright air the dreadful fauchion shone,
Or whistling slings dismiss'd th' uncertain stone.
Now men those less destructive arms despise,
Wide-wastful death from thundring cannon flies,
One hour with more battalions strows the plain,
Than were of yore in weekly battels slain.
So love with fatal airs the nymph supplies,
Her dress disposes, and directs her eyes.
The bosom now its panting beautys shows,
Th' experienc'd eye resistless glances throws ;   220
Now vary'd patches wander o'er the face,
And strike each gazer with a borrow'd grace ;
The fickle head-dress sinks and now aspires
A tow'ry front of lace on branching wires.
The curling hair in tortur'd ringlets flows,
Or round the face in labour'd order grows.

195 lovers,] Lovers ! *1714.*   200 Nor the bare Bosom heaving Breasts expos'd,
1714.   202 Nor was the Forehead crown'd with powder'd Hair ; *1714.*   203
unactive] th' unactive *1714.*   204 fickle] various *1714.*
206 new-found] num'rous *1714. Here follow in the Folio :*

        Each Nymph is deeply vers'd in treach'rous Wiles,
        With Tears she softens, and betrays with Smiles;
        Her Dress, her Hand, her Air, her Glances move,
        And Woman is encompass'd round with Love.

214 And wasteful Death *1714.*   216 of yore] before *1714.*   219 naked
Beauty *1714.*   224 And rears its tow'ry Front on rising Wires : *1714.*

How shall I soar, and on unweary wing
Trace varying habits upward to their spring !
What force of thought, what numbers can express,
Th' inconstant equipage of female dress ?   230
How the strait stays the slender waste constrain,
How to adjust the manteau's sweeping train ?
What fancy can the petticoat surround,
With the capacious hoop of whalebone bound ?
But stay, presumptuous Muse, nor boldly dare
The *Toilette*'s sacred mysteries declare ;
Let a just distance be to beauty paid ;
None here must enter but the trusty maid.
Should you the wardrobe's magazine rehearse,
And glossy manteaus rustle in thy verse ;   240
Should you the rich brocaded suit unfold,
Where rising flow'rs grow stiff with frosted gold,
The dazled Muse would from her subject stray,
And in a maze of fashions lose her way.

BOOK II.

Olympus' gates unfold ; in heav'n's high towers
Appear in council all th' immortal Powers ;
Great *Jove* above the rest exalted sate,
And in his mind revolv'd succeeding fate,
His awful eye with ray superiour shone,
The thunder-grasping eagle guards his throne ;
On silver clouds the great assembly laid,
The whole creation at one view survey'd.
But see, fair *Venus* comes in all her state,
The wanton *Loves* and *Graces* round her wait ;   10
With her loose robe officious *Zephyrs* play,
And strow with odoriferous flowers the way,
In her right hand she waves the flutt'ring fan,
And thus in melting sounds her speech began.
Assembled Powers, who fickle mortals guide,
Who o'er the sea, the skies and earth preside,

227-8 *These lines, with slight differences, in the Folio follow l.* 244 : *see below.*
229 What Thought, what various Numbers can express, *1714.*   237 paid ;] paid,
1714.   242 gold,] gold ; *1714.*
244 *In the Folio these lines follow :*

> How should I soar, and with unwearied Wing,
> Trace varying Habits upward to their Spring !
> The mighty Task my humble Muse declines,
> Which future Bards shall sing in loftier Lines.

1 heav'n's] heav'ns *all early editions.*   5 eye with ray] Eyes with Rays *1714.*
superiour] superior *1714 and 1731.*   10 The *Loves* and *Graces* round the
Goddess wait ; *1714.*   12 way,] Way. *1714.*   16 That o'er the Sea, the
Skies or Earth preside, *1714.*

Ye fountains whence all human blessings flow,
Who pour your bounties on the world below ;
Bacchus first rais'd and prun'd the climbing vine,
And taught the grape to stream with gen'rous wine ;   20
Industrious *Ceres* tam'd the savage ground,
And pregnant fields with golden harvests crown'd ;
Flora with bloomy sweets enrich'd the year,
And fruitful autumn is *Pomona's* care.
I first taught woman to subdue mankind,
And all her native charms with dress refin'd :
Celestial Synod, this machine survey,
That shades the face, or bids cool *Zephyrs* play ;
If conscious blushes on her cheek arise,
With this she veils them from her loyer's eyes ;   30
No levell'd glance betrays her am'rous heart,
From the fan's ambush she directs the dart.
The royal scepter shines in *Juno's* hand,
And twisted thunder speaks great *Jove's* command ;
On *Pallas'* arm the *Gorgon* shield appears,
And *Neptune's* mighty grasp the trident bears :
Ceres is with the bending sickle seen,
And the strung bow points out the *Cynthian* Queen
Henceforth the waving fan my hands shall grace,
The waving fan supply the scepter's place.   40
Who shall, ye Powers, the forming pencil hold ?
What story shall the wide machine unfold ?
Let *Loves* and *Graces* lead the dance around,
With myrtle wreaths and flow'ry chaplets crown'd ;
Let *Cupid's* arrows strow the smiling plains
With unresisting nymphs, and am'rous swains :
May glowing picture o'er the surface shine,
To melt slow virgins with the warm design.
Diana rose ; with silver crescent crown'd,
And fix'd her modest eyes upon the ground ;   50
Then with becoming mien she raised her head,
And thus with graceful voice the virgin said.
Has woman then forgot all former wiles,
The watchful ogle, and delusive smiles ?

17 Ye] The *1714.*   19 'Twas *Bacchus*, first who prun'd the climbing Vine, *1714.*
23 bloomy] blooming *1714.*
28 *In the Folio these lines follow :*

> This with new Graces shall inspire the Fair,
> Her Beauty heighten, and improve her Air ;
35–6   *Minerva* does the *Gorgon's* Terrors bear,
> And her right Hand sustains the glitt'ring Spear, *1714.*

39 my] these *1714.*   41 Say then, ye Pow'rs, who shall the Pencil hold, *1714.*
46–8   With melting Nymphs and their adoring Swains,
> Let glowing Figures o'er the Surface shine,
> And heav'nly Colours speak the great Design. *1714.*
47 pictures *some later editions, perhaps rightly.*

Does man against her charms too pow'rful prove,
Or are the sex grown novices in love ?
Why then these arms ? or why should artful eyes,
From this slight ambush, conquer by surprize ?
No guilty thought the spotless virgin knows,
And o'er her cheek no conscious crimson glows ;   60
Since blushes then from shame alone arise,
Why should we veil them from her lover's eyes ?
Let *Cupid* rather give up his command,
And trust his arrows in a female hand.
Have not the Gods already cherish'd pride,
And women with destructive arms supply'd ?
Neptune on her bestows his choicest stores,
For her the chambers of the deep explores ;
The gaping shell its pearly charge resigns,
And round her neck the lucid bracelet twines :   70
Plutus for her bids earth its wealth unfold,
Where the warm oar is ripen'd into gold ;
Or where the ruby reddens in the soil,
Where the green emerald pays the searcher's toil.
Does not the di'mond sparkle in her ear,
Glow on her hand, and tremble in her hair ?
From the gay nymph the glancing lustre flies,
And imitates the lightning of her eyes.
But yet if *Venus'* wishes must succeed,
And this fantastick engine be decreed,   80
May some chast story from the pencil flow,
To speak the virgin's joy, and *Hymen's* woe.
    Here let the wretched *Ariadne* stand,
Seduc'd by *Theseus* to some desart land,
Her locks dishevell'd waving in the wind,
The crystal tears confess her tortur'd mind ;
The perjur'd youth unfurles his treach'rous sails,
And their white bosoms catch the swelling gales.
Be still, ye winds, she crys, stay, *Theseus*, stay ;
But faithless *Theseus* hears no more than they.   90
All desp'rate, to some craggy cliff she flies,
And spreads a well-known signal in the skies ;
His less'ning vessel plows the foamy main,
She sighs, she calls, she waves the sign in vain.

62 we] She *1714.*
64 *In the Folio these lines follow :*
        This Trinket will be more pernicious found,
        And strike each Gazer with a surer Wound.
66 women] Woman *1714.*
74 green] bright *1714.*   80 be] is *1714.*
81 chast] kind *1714.*   82 joy] Joys *1714.*
85-6   Let her dishevell'd Locks wave in the Wind,
        And streaming Eyes confess her tortur'd Mind ; *1714.*
88 white] wide *1714.*   91 Now desperate, *1714.*

Paint *Dido* there amidst her last distress,
Pale cheeks and blood-shot eyes her grief express :
Deep in her breast the reeking sword is drown'd,
And gushing blood streams purple from the wound :
Her sister *Anna* hov'ring o'er her stands,
Accuses heav'n with lifted eyes and hands,   100
Upbraids the *Trojan* with repeated cries,
And mixes curses with her broken sighs.
View this, ye maids ; and then each swain believe ;
They're *Trojans* all, and vow but to deceive.
    Here draw *OEnone* in the lonely grove,
Where *Paris* first betray'd her into love ;
Let wither'd garlands hand on ev'ry bough,
Which the false youth wove for *OEnone*'s brow,
The garlands lose their sweets, their pride is shed,
And like their odours all his vows are fled ;   110
On her fair arm her pensive head she lays,
And *Xanthus'* waves with mournful look surveys ;
That flood which witness'd his inconstant flame,
When thus he swore, and won the yielding dame :
These streams shall sooner to their fountain move,
Than I forget my dear OEnone's *love.*
Roll back, ye streams, back to your fountain run,
Paris is false, *OEnone* is undone.
Ah wretched maid ! think how the moments flew,
E'er you the pangs of this curs'd passion knew,   120
When groves could please, and when you lov'd the plain,
Without the presence of your perjur'd swain.
    Thus may the nymph, whene'er she spreads the fan,
In his true colours view perfidious man,
Pleas'd with her virgin state in forests rove,
And never trust the dang'rous hopes of love.
    The Goddess ended.   Merry *Momus* rose,
With smiles and grins he waggish glances throws,
Then with a noisie laugh forestalls his joke,
Mirth flashes from his eyes while thus he spoke.   130
    Rather let heav'nly deeds be painted there,
And by your own examples teach the fair.

98 And gushing Blood streams from the fatal Wound ; *1714*.   100 She beats
her Breast, she wrings her lifted Hands, *1714*.   103 Now, ye fond Maids, each
Swain that swears Believe, *1714*.   105 the] some *1714*.   115 *Sooner these Streams*
shall to their Fountain move, 1714.

122 *In the Folio these lines follow* :
How vain were all thy Hopes, how short thy Joy !
A fairer Nymph now holds th' ungrateful Boy :
Thy Face, thy Voice, thy Touch no more invite,
Thy rural Charms are lost in *Helen*'s Light.
    Let *Daphne* there fly lightly o'er the Plains,
While at her Heel impatient *Phoebus* strains ;
See branching Laurel from her Fingers shoot,
Her Feet grow stiff, and wander in the Root.

123 may] shall *1714.*

Let chast *Diana* on the piece be seen,
And the bright crescent own the *Cynthian* Queen ;
On *Latmos'* top see young *Endymion* lies,
Feign'd sleep hath clos'd the bloomy lover's eyes,
See, to his soft embraces how she steals,
And on his lips her warm caresses seals ;
No more her hand the glitt'ring Jav'lin holds,
But round his neck her eager arms she folds.   140
Why are our secrets by our blushes shown ?
Virgins are virgins still—while 'tis unknown.
Here let her on some flow'ry bank be laid,
Where meeting beeches weave a grateful shade,
Her naked bosom wanton tresses grace,
And glowing expectation paints her face,
O'er her fair limbs a thin loose veil is spread,
Stand off, ye shepherds ; fear *Actæon's* head ;
Let vig'rous *Pan* th' unguarded minute seize,
And in a shaggy goat the virgin please.   150
Why are our secrets by our blushes shown ?
Virgins are virgins still—while 'tis unknown.
There with just warmth *Aurora's* passion trace,
Let spreading crimson stain her virgin face ;
See *Cephalus* her wanton airs despise,
While she provokes him with desiring eyes ;
To raise his passion she displays her charms,
His modest hand upon her bosom warms ;
Nor looks, nor pray'rs, nor force his heart persuade,
But with disdain he quits the rosie maid.   160
Here let dissolving *Leda* grace the toy,
Warm cheeks and heaving breasts reveal her joy ;
Beneath the pressing swan she pants for air,
While with his flutt'ring wings he fans the fair.
There let all-conqu'ring gold exert its pow'r,
And soften *Danae* in a glitt'ring show'r.
Would you warn beauty not to cherish pride,
Nor vainly in the treach'rous bloom confide,

134 own] speak *1714*.   135 young] where *1714*.   136 bloomy] youthful *1714*.
139 glitt'ring] dreadful *1714*.   141 Why should our secret Thoughts weak Blushes
own ? *1714*.   144 meeting] friendly *1714*.   148 Stand off, ye Swains, think
of *Actæon's* Head ; *1714*.
151-2   Blush not, Chast Goddess, nor thy Guilt reveal,
          When Maids comply, they should the Slip conceal. *1714*.
154 crimson] Blushes *1714*.
154 *In the Folio these lines follow :*
          Behind her rosie Mantle loosely flows,
          Her blooming Features youthful Health disclose.
156 *In the Folio these lines follow :*
          Now unconstrain'd she will indulge her Flame,
          Prevailing Love hath stifled all her Shame ;
158 And his fair Hand on her soft Bosom warms ; *1714*.
160 rosie] Blushing *1714*.   167 cherish] feed its *1714*.

On the machine the sage *Minerva* place,
With lineaments of wisdom mark her face ;   170
See, where she lies near some transparent flood,
And with her pipe chears the resounding wood :
Her image in the floating glass she spies,
Her bloated cheeks, worn lips, and shrivell'd eyes ;
She breaks the guiltless pipe, and with disdain
Its shatter'd ruins flings upon the plain.
With the loud reed no more her cheek shall swell,
What, spoil her face ! no. Warbling strains, farewell.
Shall arts, shall sciences employ the fair ?
Those trifles are beneath *Minerva's* care.   180
    From *Venus* let her learn the married life,
And all the virtuous duties of a wife.
Here on a couch extend the *Cyprian* dame,
Let her eye sparkle with the growing flame ;
The God of war within her clinging arms,
Sinks on her lips, and kindles all her charms.
Paint limping *Vulcan* with a husband's care,
And let his brow the cuckold's honours wear ;
Beneath the net the captive lovers place,
Their limbs entangled in a close embrace.   190
Let these amours adorn the new machine,
And female nature on the piece be seen ;
So shall the fair, as long as fans shall last,
Learn from your bright examples to be chast.

175 the guiltless] her harmless *1714*.
177–8   No more her Breath the vocal Reed shall swell,
          Musick Adieu, ye warbling Strains farewell. *1714.*
182 And all the Duties of a Virtuous Wife. *1714*.
184 growing] glowing *1731, probably a misprint*.
184–6   Let sparkling Eyes confess her growing Flame ;
          The God of War lock'd in her clinging Arms,
          Her yielding Lips with melting Kisses warms ; *1714.*
186 *In the Folio these lines follow :*
          The prying Sun their am'rous Strife betrays,
          And through the Casement darts his treach'rous Rays.
189 captive] captiv'd *1714*.
190 *In the Folio these lines follow :*
          The summon'd Gods survey the struggling Bride,
          And with contemptuous Smiles the Spouse deride.
194 your] these *1714*.

BOOK III.

THUS *Momus* spoke.   When sage *Minerva* rose,
From her sweet lips smooth elocution flows,
Her skillful hand an iv'ry pallet grac'd,
Where shining colours were in order plac'd.
As Gods are bless'd with a superior skill,
And, swift as mortal thought, perform their will,
Strait she proposes, by her art divine,
To bid the paint express her great design.
Th' assembled Pow'rs consent.   She now began,
And her creating pencil stain'd the fan.   10
  O'er the fair field, trees spread, and rivers flow,
Tow'rs rear their heads, and distant mountains grow ;
Life seems to move within the glowing veins,
And in each face some lively passion reigns.
Thus have I seen woods, hills, and dales appear,
Flocks graze the plains, birds wing the silent air
In darken'd rooms, where light can only pass
Through the small circle of a convex glass ;
On the white sheet the moving figures rise,
The forest waves, clouds float along the skies.   20
  She various fables on the piece design'd,
That spoke the follies of the female kind.
  The fate of pride in *Niobe* she drew :
Be wise, ye nymphs, that scornful vice subdue.
In a wide plain th' imperious mother stood,
Whose distant bounds rose in a winding wood ;
Upon her shoulder flows her mantling hair,
Pride marks her brow, and elevates her air ;
A purple robe behind her sweeps the ground,
Whose spacious border golden flow'rs surround :   30
She made *Latona*'s altars cease to flame,
And of due honours robb'd her sacred name.
To her own charms she bad fresh incense rise,
And adoration own her brighter eyes.
Sev'n daughters from her fruitful loyns were born,
Sev'n graceful sons her nuptial bed adorn,
Who, for a mother's arrogant disdain,
Were by *Latona*'s double offspring slain.
Here *Phœbus* his unerring arrow drew,
And from his rising steed her first-born threw,   40

1 sage] bright *1714*.   19 On the] On a *1714*.   21 fables] Stories *1714*.
22 *In the Folio these lines follow :*
        The moral Stories warn the gazing Dame,
        To shun those Faults that damp a Lover's Flame.
33 bad] bids *1714*.   34 adoration] Adorations *1714*.   37 Who for their
Parent's arrogant Disdain, *1714*.

His op'ning fingers drop the slacken'd rein,
And the pale corse falls headlong to the plain.
Beneath her pencil here two wrestlers bend,
See, to the grasp their swelling nerves distend,
Diana's arrow joins them face to face,
And death unites them in a strict embrace.
Another here flies trembling o'er the plain ;
When heav'n pursues we shun the stroke in vain.
This lifts his supplicating hands and eyes,
And 'midst his humble adoration dies.   50
As from his thigh this tears the barbed dart,
A surer weapon strikes his throbbing heart :
While that to raise his wounded brother tries,
Death blasts his bloom, and locks his frozen eyes.
The tender sisters bath'd in grief appear,
With sable garments and dishevell'd hair,
And o'er their gasping brothers weeping stood ;
Some with their tresses stopt the gushing blood,
They strive to stay the fleeting life too late,
And in the pious action share their fate.   60
Now the proud dame o'ercome by trembling fear,
With her wide robe protects her only care ;
To save her only care in vain she tries,
Close at her feet the latest victim dies.
Down her fair cheek the trickling sorrow flows,
Like dewy spangles on the blushing rose,
Fixt in astonishment she weeping stood,
The plain all purple with her children's blood ;
She stiffens with her woes : no more her hair
In easie ringlets wantons in the air ;   70
Motion forsakes her eyes, her veins are dry'd,
And beat no longer with the sanguine tide ;
All life is fled, firm marble now she grows,
Which still in tears the mother's anguish shows.
    Ye haughty fair, your painted fans display,
And the just fate of lofty pride survey ;
Though lovers oft extoll your beauty's power,
And in celestial similies adore,
Though from your features *Cupid* borrows arms,
And Goddesses confess inferior charms,   80
Do not, vain maid, the flatt'ring tale believe,
Alike thy lovers and thy glass deceive.
    Here lively colours *Procris'* passion tell,
Who to her jealous fears a victim fell.

44 And to the Grasp their stretching Nerves distend, *1714*.   49 To wrathful
Heav'n This lifts his streaming Eyes, *1714*.   53 that] This *1714*.   58 stopt]
stopp'd *1714*.   68 And view'd the Plain dy'd with her Children's Blood ; *1714*.
70 In easie Curles plays in the wanton Air ; *1714*.   82 Alike] For both *1714*.
    84 *In the Folio these lines follow :*
        See where in secret Ambuscade she lies,
        With Jealousie she turns her watchful Eyes ;

Here kneels the trembling hunter o'er his wife,
Who rolls her sick'ning eyes, and gasps for life ;
Her drooping head upon her shoulder lies,
And purple gore her snowy bosom dies.
What guilt, what horror on his face appears !
See, his red eye-lid seems to swell with tears,   90
With agony his wringing hands he strains,
And strong convulsions stretch his branching veins.
    Learn hence, ye wives ; bid vain suspicion cease,
Lose not in sullen discontent your peace.
For when fierce love to jealousie ferments,
A thousand doubts and fears the soul invents,
No more the days in pleasing converse flow,
And nights no more their soft endearments know.
    There on the piece the *Volscian* Queen expir'd,
The love of spoils her female bosom fir'd ;   100
Gay *Chloreus'* arms attract her longing eyes,
And for the painted plume and helm she sighs ;
Fearless she follows, bent on gaudy prey,
Till an ill-fated dart obstructs her way ;
Down drops the martial maid ; the bloody ground
Floats with a torrent from the purple wound.
The mournful nymphs her drooping head sustain,
And try to stop the gushing life in vain.
    Thus the raw maid some tawdry coat surveys,
Where the fop's fancy in embroidery plays ;   110

Now *Cephalus*, hot with pursuit of Spoils,
Invok'd cool Aura to relieve his Toils :
The fatal Sound scarce reach'd her list'ning Ears,
Aurora in th' uncertain Voice she hears;
She starts. The rustling Brake her Spouse deceives,
Who thought some rouzing Prey disturb'd the Leaves ;
Swift as the Wind he flings th' unerring Dart,
The bloody Steel transfix'd his *Procris'* Heart.

85 hunter] Huntsman *1714*.
89–90   The Husband's Brow Surprize and Sorrow wears,
    And his red Eye-lids seem to swell with Tears, *1714*.
93 suspicion] Suspicions *1714*.
94 Nor lose in sullen Discontents your Peace. *1714*.
102 *In the Folio these lines follow :*
    His golden Quiver at his Shoulder shone,
    His scaly Mail glow'd with the dazling Sun :
    Camilla now pursues the glitt'ring Prize,
    From her swift Chase the shining Warrior flies;
105 ground] ground, *all early editions*.   106 the] her *1714*.
107 Her Mourning Nymphs *1714*.
108 *In the Folio these lines follow :*
    These with rude Strokes their naked Bosoms wound
    And throw their useless Jav'lins on the Ground :
    Her Lips no longer boast their crimson Hue,
    From her cold Cheek the blushing Colour flew,
    Her Eye-balls seem with dying Pangs to roll,
    While through the Wound crouds her reluctant Soul.

His snowy feather edg'd with crimson dyes,
And his bright sword-knot lure her wand'ring eyes;
Fring'd gloves and gold brocade conspire to move,
Till the nymph falls a sacrifice to love.
   Here young *Narcissus* o'er the fountain stood,
And view'd his image in the crystal flood;
The crystal flood reflects his lovely charms,
And the pleas'd image strives to meet his arms.
No nymph his unexperienc'd breast subdu'd,
Eccho in vain the flying boy pursu'd,   120
Himself alone the foolish youth admires,
And with fond look the smiling shade desires:
O'er the smooth lake with fruitless tears he grieves,
His spreading fingers shoot in verdant leaves,
Through his pale veins green sap now gently flows,
And in a short-lived flow'r his beauty blows.
   Let vain *Narcissus* warn each female breast,
That beauty's but a transient good at best.
Like flow'rs it withers with th' advancing year,
And age like winter robs the blooming fair.   130
Oh *Araminta*, cease thy wonted pride,
Nor longer in thy faithless charms confide;
Ev'n while the glass reflects thy sparkling eyes,
Their lustre and thy rosie colour flies!
   Thus on the fan the breathing figures shine,
And all the Powers applaud the wise design.
   The *Cyprian* Queen the painted gift receives,
And with a grateful bow the synod leaves.
To the low world she bends her steepy way
Where *Strephon* pass'd the solitary day;   140
She found him in a melancholy grove,
His down-cast eyes betray'd desponding love,
The wounded bark confess'd his slighted flame,
And ev'ry tree bore false *Corinna*'s name;
In a cool shade he lay with folded arms,
Curses his fortune, and upbraids her charms,
When *Venus* to his wond'ring eyes appears,
And with these words relieves his am'rous cares.
   Rise, happy youth, this bright machine survey,
Whose ratt'ling sticks my busie fingers sway,   150
This present shall thy cruel charmer move,
And in her fickle bosom kindle love.
   The fan shall flutter in all female hands,
And various fashions learn from various lands.
For this, shall elephants their ivory shed;
And polish'd sticks the waving engine spread:
His clouded mail the tortoise shall resign,
And round the rivet pearly circles shine.

136 Powers] powers *1720 and 1731, but elsewhere* Powers *or* Pow'rs.   Pow'rs *1714.*
137 *In the Folio this line does not begin a new paragraph.*

On this shall *Indians* all their art employ,
And with bright colours stain the gaudy toy;   160
Their paint shall here in wildest fancies flow,
Their dress, their customs, their religion show,
So shall the *British* fair their minds improve,
And on the fan to distant climates rove.
Here *China*'s ladies shall their pride display,
And silver figures gild their loose array;
This boasts her little feet and winking eyes;
That tunes the fife, or tinkling cymbal plies:
Here cross-leg'd nobles in rich state shall dine,
There in bright mail distorted heroes shine.   170
The peeping fan in modern times shall rise,
Through which unseen the female ogle flies;
This shall in temples the sly maid conceal,
And shelter love beneath devotion's veil.
Gay *France* shall make the fan her artist's care,
And with the costly trinket arm the fair.
As learned Orators that touch the heart,
With various action raise their soothing art,
Both head and hand affect the list'ning throng,
And humour each expression of the tongue.   180
So shall each passion by the fan be seen,
From noisie anger to the sullen spleen.
    While *Venus* spoke, joy shone in *Strephon*'s eyes,
Proud of the gift, he to *Corinna* flies.
But *Cupid* (who delights in am'rous ill,
Wounds hearts, and leaves them to a woman's will)
With certain aim a golden arrow drew,
Which to *Leander*'s panting bosom flew:

165 Here shall the *Chinese* Dame her Pride display, *1714*.   166 their] her *1714*.
167 This] She *1714*.   168 That] And *1714*.   170 Where on the Floor large
painted Vessels shine, *1714*.
In the Folio these lines follow :
            For These, O *China*, shall thy Realms be sought,
            With These shall *Europe*'s mighty Ships be fraught,
            Thy glitt'ring Earth shall tempt their Ladies Eyes,
            Who for thy brittle Jars shall Gold despise.
171–4 *These lines in the Folio follow l.* 182.   181 Thus ev'ry Passion by the
Fan is seen, *1714*.   182 noisie] chatt'ring *1714*.
In the Folio ll. 171–4 *occur here, followed by these lines :*
            While Widows seek once more the Nuptial State,
            And wrinkled Maids repent their Scorn too late,
            As long as youthful Swains shall Nymphs deceive,
            And easie Nymphs those youthful Swains believe,
            While Beaus in Dress consume the tedious Morn,
            So long the *Fan* shall female Hands adorn.
185–6 *Commas instead of brackets, 1714.*
186 *In the Folio these lines follow :*
            An unsuspected Artifice employs,
            And in a Moment *Strephon's* Hope destroys:
187 A golden Shaft the waggish Archer threw, *1714*.

Leander lov'd ; and to the sprightly dame
In gentle sighs reveal'd his growing flame ;   190
Sweet smiles *Corinna* to his sighs returns,
And for the fop in equal passion burns.
　Lo *Strephon* comes ! and with a suppliant bow,
Offers the present, and renews his vow.
When she the fate of *Niobe* beheld,
Why has my pride against my heart rebell'd ?
She sighing cry'd.　Disdain forsook her breast,
And *Strephon* now was thought a worthy guest.
　In *Procris'* bosom when she saw the dart,
She justly blames her own suspicious heart,   200
Imputes her discontent to jealous fear,
And knows her *Strephon's* constancy sincere.
　When on *Camilla's* fate her eye she turns,
No more for show and equipage she burns :
She learns *Leander's* passion to despise,
And looks on merit with discerning eyes.
　Narcissus' change to the vain virgin shows,
Who trusts to beauty, trusts the fading rose.
Youth flies apace, with youth your beauty flies,
Love then, ye virgins, e'er the blossom dies.   210
　Thus *Pallas* taught her.　*Strephon* weds the dame,
And *Hymen's* torch diffus'd the brightest flame.

191 With Smiles *Corinna* his soft Sighs returns, *1714.*
193 Now *Strephon* comes, *1714.*
194 *In the Folio these four lines here conclude the poem :*
　　The gay *Coquette*, of her last Conquest vain,
　　Snatches the Trinket from the trembling Swain,
　　Then turns around with a disdainful Mien,
　　Smiles on the Fop, and flirts the new Machine.
195–end. *So 1720 and subsequent editions.*
197 cry'd.] cry'd : *all early editions.*　199 dart,] dart ; *all early editions.*

THE
SHEPHERD's WEEK.
IN
SIX PASTORALS.

——Libeat mihi sordida rura,
*Atque humiles habitare casas.——*Virg.

[*Editions :*
1. THE | *SHEPHERD'S WEEK.* | IN SIX | PASTORALS. | *By Mr.* J. GAY. | *——Libeat mihi sordida rura,* | *Atque humiles habitare Casas.——*Virg. | *LONDON,* | Printed : And Sold by FERD. BURLEIGH in | *Amen-Corner.* MDCCXIV.
Post 8vo. With a frontispiece and a full-page illustration before each Pastoral, drawn and engraved by Du Guernier. [Ref. 1714[1].]
2. 'The Second Edition.' Printed for *J. T.* and Sold by *W. Taylor* at the | *Ship* in *Pater-noster-Row.* MDCCXIV.
Post 8vo. Same illustrations and pagination as 1. [Ref. 1714[2].]
3. *Poems on Several Occasions.* 1720. 4to. [Ref. 1720.]
Underhill says there is ' one engraving ' in this edition. My copy contains none.
4. A third edition. (No mention of this on title-page.) Printed for JACOB TONSON at *Shakespear's-Head*| over-against *Katharine-street* in the *Strand.* 1721.
Post 8vo. Same illustrations and pagination as 1. [Ref. 1721.]
5. 'The Fourth Edition.' Printed for JACOB TONSON in the *Strand.* | MDCCXXVIII.
Post 8vo. Same illustrations and pagination as 1. [Ref. 1728.]
6. *Poems on Several Occasions.* 1731. With a frontispiece to ' The Shepherd's Week ', engraved by Fourdrinier. 12mo. [Ref. 1731.]

The versions (though the differences are unimportant) divide themselves typographically into two classes. The 1st and 2nd 8vo editions, and the 4to and 12mo editions of the *Poems on Several Occasions,* on the one side ; on the other the 3rd and 4th 8vo editions. The latter use roman letters in the Proeme for quotations only, and italics elsewhere only for the foot-notes. (But the 4th 8vo edition occasionally has italics in the text.) The former print the work as it is here reproduced, except that the 1st and 2nd 8vo editions make free use of capital letters throughout. The 8vo editions all divide paragraphs by white lines in the Proeme and in the text ; the 12mo uses white lines in the text but not in the Proeme ; the 4to does not use them at all. There are indications of revision by the author in the 3rd and 4th 8vo editions, and of separate revision in the 12mo edition.

Another edition, to which I refer in the notes as *17*—, must be mentioned. The title-page is that of the first edition, but has R. BURLEIGH instead of FERD. BURLEIGH. The date is the same—MDCCXIV. Supposing it to be the First Edition (as which it was sold to me) I was puzzled by the fact that typographically it corresponds to the modernized editions of 1721 and 1728. Comparison with the genuine First Edition showed that it was probably published much later. It has the passage in the First Pastoral, which is not given by the first and second editions ; and it has some of the corrections made in 1721. On the other hand, in some readings it agrees with the first and second editions.

I take it that all the 8vo editions were, in fact, printed by the same business ; the 2nd and later editions were printed for Tonson, whereas the 1st edition was printed *and sold* by Ferd. Burleigh. R. Burleigh, succeeding to the business, and finding his stock of the 1st edition exhausted, set up the Poem again, including the passage added in 1720, with some corrections adopted in Tonson's 3rd edition. Whether this edition was in any way authorized it is not easy to say—probably not, since otherwise the title-page would not have borne the date of the original edition. This is hypothesis only ; but it fits the facts. Mr. Brett-Smith, in his introduction to a pleasing reprint of the R. BURLEIGH edition (Oxford, Blackwell, 1924), published since the above was in type, assumes, I think mistakenly, that it is ' of the first year, but not the first, though it is considerably the rarer of the two '.]

THE

PROEME

To the Courteous

READER.

GREAT marvell hath it been (and that not unworthily) to diverse worthy wits, *that in this our Island of* Britain, *in all rare sciences so greatly abounding, more* *especially in all kinds of Poesie highly flourishing, no Poet (though otherways of* *notable cunning in roundelays) hath hit on the right simple Eclogue after the true* *ancient guise of* Theocritus, *before this mine attempt.*   5
Other Poet travailing in this plain high-way of Pastoral know I none. Yet, *certes, such it behoveth a Pastoral to be, as nature in the country affordeth ; and* *the manners also meetly copied from the rustical folk therein. In this also my* *love to my native country* Britain *much pricketh me forward, to describe aright* *the manners of our own honest and laborious plough-men, in no wise sure more* *unworthy a* British *Poet's imitation, than those of* Sicily *or* Arcadie ; *albeit, not* *ignorant I am, what a rout and rabblement of critical gallimawfry hath been made* *of late days by certain young men of insipid delicacy, concerning, I wist not what,* Golden Age, *and other outragious conceits, to which they would confine Pastoral.* *Whereof, I avow, I account nought at all, knowing no age so justly to be instiled* Golden, *as this of our* Soveraign Lady Queen ANNE.   16
This idle trumpery (only fit for schools and schoolboys) unto that ancient Dorick Shepherd Theocritus, *or his mates, was never known ; he rightly, throughout* *his fifth* Idyll, *maketh his louts give foul language, and behold their goats at rut* *in all simplicity.*   20

Ὠπόλος ὅκκ' ἐσορῇ τὰς μηκάδας οἷα βατεῦνται,
Τάκεται ὀφθαλμώς, ὅτι οὐ τράγος αὐτὸς ἔγεντο. Theoc.

Verily, as little pleasance receiveth a true homebred tast, from all the fine finical *new-fangled fooleries of this gay Gothic garniture, wherewith they so nicely bedeck* *their court clowns, or clown courtiers, (for, which to call them rightly, I wot not)* *as would a prudent citizen journeying to his country farms, should he find them* *occupied by people of this motley make, instead of plain downright hearty cleanly* *folk, such as be now tenants to the* Burgesses *of this realme.*   28

1 *been*] been, all early editions.
21–22 *The lines are from Idyll I, 87–8, and are printed with varying inaccuracy in* *early editions.*   28 Burgesses] *wealthy burgesses* 1714[1] and [2].

Furthermore, it is my purpose, gentle reader, to set before thee, as it were a picture, or rather lively landschape of thy own country, just as thou mightest see it, didest thou take a walk into the fields at the proper season : even as maister Milton *hath elegantly set forth the same.*   32

As one who long in populous city pent,
Where houses thick and sewers annoy the air
Forth issuing on a summer's morn to breathe
Among the pleasant villages and farms
Adjoin'd, from each thing met conceives delight ;
The smell of grain or tedded grass or kine
Or dairie, each rural sight, each rural sound.   39

Thou wilt not find my shepherdesses idly piping on oaten reeds, but milking the kine, tying up the sheaves, or if the hogs are astray driving them to their styes. My shepherd gathereth none other nosegays but what are the growth of our own fields, he sleepeth not under myrtle shades, but under a hedge, nor doth he vigilantly defend his flocks from wolves, because there are none, as maister Spencer *well observeth.*

Well is known that since the *Saxon* King
Never was wolf seen, many or some
Nor in all *Kent* nor in christendom.   48

For as much, as I have mentioned maister Spencer, *soothly I must acknowledge him a bard of sweetest memorial. Yet hath his shepherd's boy at some times raised his rustick reed to rhimes more rumbling than rural. Diverse grave points also hath he handled of churchly matter and doubts in religion daily arising, to great clerks only appertaining. What liketh me best are his names, indeed right simple and meet for the country, such as Lobbin, Cuddy, Hobbinol, Diggon, and others, some of which I have made bold to borrow. Moreover, as he called his Eclogues, the* shepherd's *calendar, and divided the same into the twelve months, I have chosen (paradventure not over-rashly) to name mine by the days of the week, omitting Sunday or the Sabbath, ours being supposed to be christian shepherds, and to be then at church worship. Yet further of many of maister* Spencer's *eclogues it may be observed ; though months they be called, of the said months therein, nothing is specified ; wherein I have also esteemed him worthy mine imitation.*   62

That principally, courteous reader, whereof I would have thee to be advised, (seeing I depart from the vulgar usage) is touching the language of my shepherds ; which is, soothly to say, such as is neither spoken by the country maiden nor the courtly dame ; nay, not only such as in the present times is not uttered, but was never uttered in times past ; and, if I judge aright, will never be uttered in times future. It having too much of the country to be fit for the court, too much of the court to be fit for the country ; too much of the language of old times to be fit for the present, too much of the present to have been fit for the old, and too much of both to be fit for any time to come. Granted also it is, that in this my language, I seem unto my self, as a London *mason, who calculateth his work for a term of years, when he buildeth with old materials upon a ground-rent that is not his own, which soon turneth to rubbish and ruins. For this point, no reason can I alledge, only deep learned ensamples having led me thereunto.*   75

57 *paradventure*] peradventure *17—, 1721, and 1728.*   63 *advised*] 1721 and 1728 *advertised* remainder.   65 *nor*] or 1720 and 1731.

But here again, much comfort ariseth in me, from the hopes, in that I conceive, when these words in the course of transitory things shall decay, it may so hap, in meet time that some lover of Simplicity *shall arise, who shall have the hardiness to render these mine eclogues into such more modern dialect as shall be then understood, to which end, glosses and explications of uncouth pastoral terms are annexed.*

Gentle Reader, turn over the leaf, and entertain thyself with the prospect of thine own country, limned by the painful hand of 82

thy Loving Countryman,

J O H N. G A Y.

P R O L O G U E.

To the Right Honourable the

Lord Viscount B O L I N G B R O K E.

Lo, I who erst beneath a tree
Sung *Bumkinet* and *Bowzybee*,
And *Blouzelind* and *Marian* bright,
In apron blue or apron white,
Now write my sonnets in a book,
For my good lord of *Bolingbroke.*

As lads and lasses stood around
To hear my boxen haut-boy sound,
Our *Clerk* came posting o'er the green
With doleful tidings of the *Queen* ; 10
That *Queen*, he said, to whom we owe
Sweet *Peace that maketh riches flow* ;
That *Queen* who eas'd our tax of late,
Was dead, alas !—and lay in state.

At this, in tears was *Cic'ly* seen,
Buxoma tore her pinners clean,
In doleful dumps stood ev'ry clown,
The parson rent his band and gown.

For me, when as I heard that death
Had snatch'd *Queen ANNE* to
Elzabeth, 20
I broke my reed, and sighing swore
I'd weep for *Blouzelind* no more.

While thus we stood as in a stound,
And wet with tears, like dew, the ground,

Full soon by bonefire and by bell
We learnt our Liege was passing well.
A skilful leach (so God him speed)
They said had wrought this blessed deed.
This leach *Arbuthnot* was yclept,
Who many a night not once had slept ;
But watch'd our gracious Sov'raign still : 31
For who could rest when she was ill ?
Oh, may'st thou henceforth sweetly sleep !
Sheer, swains, oh sheer your softest sheep
To swell his couch ; for well I ween,
He sav'd the realm who sav'd the Queen.

Quoth I, please God, I'll hye with glee
To court, this *Arbuthnot* to see.
I sold my sheep and lambkins too,
For silver loops and garment blue : 40
My boxen haut-boy sweet of sound,
For lace that edg'd mine hat around ;
For *Lightfoot* and my scrip I got
A gorgeous sword, and eke a knot.

So forth I far'd to court with speed,
Of soldier's drum withouten dreed ;
For Peace allays the shepherd's fear
Of wearing cap of Granadier.
There saw I ladies all a-row
Before their Queen in seemly show. 50
No more I'll sing *Buxoma* brown,
Like goldfinch in her *Sunday* gown ;
Nor *Clumsilis*, nor *Marian* bright,
Nor damsel that *Hobnelia* hight.
But *Lansdown* fresh as flow'r of *May*,
And *Berkely* lady blithe and gay,
And *Anglesey* whose speech exceeds
The voice of pipe, or oaten reeds ;
And blooming *Hyde*, with eyes so rare,
And *Montague* beyond compare.   60
Such ladies fair wou'd I depaint
In roundelay or sonnet quaint.
There many a worthy wight I've
seen
In ribbon blue and ribbon green.
As *Oxford*, who a wand doth bear,
Like *Moses*, in our Bibles fair ;
Who for our traffick forms designs,
And gives to *Britain Indian* mines.
Now, shepherds, clip your fleecy care,
Ye maids, your spinning-wheels pre-
pare,   70
Ye weavers, all your shuttles throw,
And bid broad-cloths and serges grow,

For trading free shall thrive again,
Nor leasings leud affright the swain.
There saw I *St. John*, sweet of mien,
Full stedfast both to Church and
Queen.
With whose fair name I'll deck my
strain,
St. John, right courteous to the swain ;
For thus he told me on a day,
Trim are thy sonnets, gentle *Gay*,   80
And certes, mirth it were to see
Thy joyous madrigals twice three,
With preface meet, and notes pro-
found.
Imprinted fair, and well y-bound.
All suddenly then home I sped,
And did ev'n as my Lord had said.
Lo here, thou hast mine Eclogues
fair,
But let not these detain thine ear.
Let not affairs of States and Kings
Wait, while our *Bowzybeus* sings.   90
Rather than verse of simple swain
Should stay the trade of *France* or
Spain,
Or for the plaint of Parson's maid,
Yon' Emp'ror's packets be delay'd ;
In sooth, I swear by holy *Paul*,
I'd burn book, preface, notes and all.
April, 1714.

89 affairs *1728 and 1731*   th' affairs *remainder*.
96 *The date, oddly enough, is only printed in 1721 and 1728.*

M O N D A Y;

O R, T H E

S Q U A B B L E.

Lobbin Clout, Cuddy, Cloddipole.

LOBBIN CLOUT.
THY younglings, Cuddy, are but just awake;
No thrustles shrill the bramble-bush forsake,
No chirping lark the welkin sheen invokes;
No damsel yet the swelling udder strokes;
O'er yonder hill does scant the dawn appear,
Then why does *Cuddy* leave his cott so rear?
CUDDY.
Ah *Lobbin Clout!* I ween, my plight is guest,
For *he that loves, a stranger is to rest*;
If swains belye not, thou hast prov'd the smart,
And *Blouzelinda* 's mistress of thy heart.   10
This rising rear betokeneth well thy mind,
Those arms are folded for thy *Blouzelind.*
And well, I trow, our piteous plights agree,
Thee *Blouselinda* smites, *Buxoma* me.
LOBBIN CLOUT.
Ah *Blouzelind!* I love thee more by half,
Than does their fawns, or cows the new-fall'n calf:
Woe worth the tongue! may blisters sore it gall,
That names *Buxoma, Blouzelind* withal.
CUDDY.
Hold, witless *Lobbin Clout,* I thee advise,
Lest blisters sore on thy own tongue arise.   20
Lo yonder *Cloddipole,* the blithesome swain,
The wisest lout of all the neighbouring plain!

Line
3. Welkin *the same as* Welken, *an old* Saxon *word signifying a* Cloud; *by poetical licence it is frequently taken for* the Element *or* Sky, *as may appear by this verse in the* Dream *of* Chaucer.
          Ne in all the Welkin was no Cloud.
   Sheen *or* Shine, *an old word for* shining *or* bright.
5. Scant, *used by ancient* British *authors for* scarce.
6. Rear, *an expression in several counties of* England, *for* early in the morning.
7. To ween, *derived from the* Saxon, *to* think *or* conceive.

2 forsake,] forsake. *1731.*   5, n. *by]* 1728 *in the* 1731 *in* remainder.
18-19 *CUDDY.] LOBBIN CLOUT. 1720.*

From *Cloddipole* we learnt to read the skies,
To know when hail will fall, or winds arise.
He taught us erst the heifer's tail to view,
When stuck aloft, that show'rs would strait ensue ;
He first that useful secret did explain,
That pricking corns foretold the gath'ring rain.
When swallows fleet soar high and sport in air,
He told us that the welkin would be clear.   30
Let *Cloddipole* then hear us twain rehearse,
And praise his sweetheart in alternate verse.
I'll wager this same oaken staff with thee,
That *Cloddipole* shall give the prize to me.

LOBBIN CLOUT.

See this tobacco-pouch that 's lin'd with hair,
Made of the skin of sleekest fallow deer.
This pouch, that 's ty'd with tape of reddest hue,
I'll wager, that the prize shall be my due.

CUDDY.

Begin thy carrols then, thou vaunting slouch,
Be thine the oaken staff, or mine the pouch.   40

LOBBIN CLOUT.

My *Blouzelinda* is the blithest lass,
Than primrose sweeter, or the clover-grass.
Fair is the king-cup that in meadow blows,
Fair is the daisie that beside her grows,
Fair is the gillyflow'r, of gardens sweet,
Fair is the mary-gold, for pottage meet.
But *Blouzelind*'s than gillyflow'r more fair,
Than daisie, mary-gold, or king-cup rare.

CUDDY.

My brown *Buxoma* is the featest maid,
That e'er at Wake delightsome gambol play'd.   50
Clean as young lambkins or the goose's down,
And like the goldfinch in her Sunday gown.
The witless lamb may sport upon the plain,
The frisking kid delight the gaping swain,
The wanton calf may skip with many a bound,
And my cur *Tray* play deftest feats around ;
But neither lamb nor kid, nor calf nor *Tray*,
Dance like *Buxoma* on the first of *May*.

LOBBIN CLOUT.

Sweet is my toil when *Blouzelind* is near,
Of her bereft 'tis winter all the year.   60

Line
25. erst, *a contraction of* ere this, *it signifies* sometime ago *or* formerly.
56. Deft, *an old word signifying* brisk *or* nimble.

---

25 heifer's tail] *1720 and 1731*   heifers tails *1714*[1] and [2] *and 17—*   heifers tail *1721
and 1728.*   34–5 LOBBIN CLOUT.] CUDDY. *1720.*
38 wager,] wager *1721 and 1728.*

* C

With her no sultry summer's heat I know;
In winter, when she's nigh, with love I glow.
Come *Blouzelinda*, ease thy swain's desire,
My summer's shadow and my winter's fire !
CUDDY.
As with *Buxoma* once I work'd at hay,
Ev'n noon-tide labour seem'd an holiday ;
And holidays, if haply she were gone,
Like worky-days I wish'd would soon be done.
Eftsoons, O sweet-heart kind, my love repay,
And all the year shall then be holiday.   70
LOBBIN CLOUT.
As *Blouzelinda* in a gamesome mood,
Behind a haycock loudly laughing stood,
I slily ran, and snatch'd a hasty kiss,
She wip'd her lips, nor took it much amiss.
Believe me, *Cuddy*, while I'm bold to say,
Her breath was sweeter than the ripen'd hay.
CUDDY.
As my *Buxoma* in a morning fair,
With gentle finger stroak'd her milky care,
I queintly stole a kiss ; at first, 'tis true,
She frown'd, yet after granted one or two.   80
Lobbin, I swear, believe who will my vows,
Her breath by far excell'd the breathing cows.
LOBBIN CLOUT.
Leek to the *Welch*, to *Dutchmen* butter's dear,
Of *Irish* swains potatoe is the chear ;
Oats for their feasts, the *Scottish* shepherds grind,
Sweet turnips are the food of *Blouzelind*.
While she loves turnips, butter I'll despise,
Nor leeks nor oatmeal nor potatoe prize.
CUDDY.
In good roast-beef my landlord sticks his knife,
The capon fat delights his dainty wife,   90
Pudding our Parson eats, the Squire loves hare,
But white-pot thick is my *Buxoma*'s fare.
While she loves white-pot, capon ne'er shall be,
Nor hare, nor beef, nor pudding, food for me.

Line
69. Eftsoons *from* eft *an ancient* British *word signifying* soon. *So that* eftsoons
    is a doubling of the word soon, *which is, as it were, to say* twice soon, *or* very
    soon.
79. Queint *has various significations in the ancient* English *authors. I have used it
    in this place in the same sense as* Chaucer *hath done in his* Miller's Tale. *As*
    Clerkes been full subtil and queint, *(by which he means* arch *or* waggish)
    and not in that obscene sense wherein he useth it in the line immediately following.
83.   *Populus Alcidæ gratissima, vitis Iaccho,
           Formosæ Myrtus Veneri, sua Laurea Phœbo.
           Phillis amat Corylos. Illas dum Phillis amabit,
           Nec Myrtus vincet Corylos nec Laurea Phœbi. &c.*   Virg.

79 true,] true *all early editions.*   83–94 *The foods are italicized by* 1714[1] and [2].

LOBBIN CLOUT.
As once I play'd at *Blindman's-buff*, it hapt
About my eyes the towel thick was wrapt.
I miss'd the swains, and seiz'd on *Blouzelind*.
True speaks that ancient proverb, *Love is blind.*

CUDDY.
As at *Hot-cockles* once I laid me down,
And felt the weighty hand of many a clown ;   100
Buxoma gave a gentle tap, and I
Quick rose, and read soft mischief in her eye.

LOBBIN CLOUT.
On two near elms, the slacken'd cord I hung,
Now high, now low my *Blouzelinda* swung.
With the rude wind her rumpled garment rose,
And show'd her taper leg, and scarlet hose.

CUDDY.
Across the fallen oak the plank I laid,
And my self pois'd against the tott'ring maid,
High leapt the plank ; adown *Buxoma* fell ;
I spy'd—but faithful sweethearts never tell.   110

LOBBIN CLOUT.
This riddle, *Cuddy*, if thou can'st, explain,
This wily riddle puzzles ev'ry swain.
What flower is that which bears the Virgin's *name,*
The richest metal joined with the same ?

CUDDY.
Answer, thou Carle, and judge this riddle right,
I'll frankly own thee for a cunning wight.
*What flower is that which royal honour craves,
Adjoin the Virgin, *and 'tis strown on graves.*

CLODDIPOLE.
Forbear, contending louts, give o'er your strains,
An oaken staff each merits for his pains.   120
But see the sun-beams bright to labour warn,
And gild the thatch of goodman *Hodges'* barn.
Your herds for want of water stand adry,
They're weary of your songs—and so am I.

Line   † *Marygold.*   * *Rosemary.*
117. *Dic quibus in terris inscripti nomina Regum*
     Nascantur Flores.   Virg.
120. *Et vitula tu dignus & hic.* Virg.

103-10 *First printed in 1720, and in all subsequent editions, including 17—.*
108 maid,] maid; *17—, 1721, and 1728.*   110 I spy'd.—But *17—, 1721, and 1728.*
117 *flower*] 1720 *Flower* 1731 Flow'r *or* flow'r *remainder.*   118 *Later editions*
print with a question-mark, but it is best to leave the clumsy sentence as Gay printed it.
122 Hodges'] *some editors, including Underhill, alter to* Hodge's. *But the Index*
confirms Hodges'.

T U E S D A Y;

OR, THE

D I T T Y.

MARIAN.

YOUNG *Colin Clout*, a lad of peerless meed,
Full well could dance, and deftly tune the reed ;
In ev'ry wood his carrols sweet were known,
At ev'ry wake his nimble feats were shown.
When in the ring the rustick routs he threw,
The damsels pleasures with his conquests grew ;
Or when aslant the cudgel threats his head,
His danger smites the breast of ev'ry maid,
But chief of *Marian*. *Marian* lov'd the swain,
The Parson's maid, and neatest of the plain.   10
Marian, that soft could stroke the udder'd cow,
Or lessen with her sieve the barley mow ;
Marbled with sage the hardn'ing cheese she press'd,
And yellow butter *Marian*'s skill confess'd ;
But *Marian* now devoid of country cares,
Nor yellow butter nor sage cheese prepares.
For yearning love the witless maid employs,
And *Love*, say swains, *all busie heed destroys.*
Colin makes mock at all her piteous smart,
A lass, who *Cic'ly* hight, had won his heart,   20
Cic'ly the western lass who tends the kee,
The rival of the Parson's maid was she.
In dreary shade now *Marian* lyes along,
And mixt with sighs thus wails in plaining song.
  Ah woful day ! ah woful noon and morn !
When first by thee my younglings white were shorn,
Then first, I ween, I cast a lover's eye,
My sheep were silly, but more silly I.
Beneath the shears they felt no lasting smart,
They lost but fleeces while I lost a heart.   30
  Ah *Colin* ! canst thou leave thy Sweetheart true !
What I have done for thee will *Cic'ly* do ?

Line
21. Kee, *a West-Country Word for* Kine *or* Cows.

4 At] In *1714*[1] and [2] *and 17—*.   12 Or with her Winnow ease the Barly Mow;
1714 [1 and 2] *and 17—*.   20 lass, who] *1728*   lass that *remainder*.   21 who] *1728*
that *remainder*.   31 Sweetheart] sweetheart *17—*, *1721, and 1728.*

Will she thy linnen wash or hosen darn,
And knit thee gloves made of her own-spun yarn ?
Will she with huswife's hand provide thy meat,
And ev'ry *Sunday* morn thy neckcloth plait ?
Which o'er thy kersey doublet spreading wide,
In service-time drew *Cic'ly*'s eyes aside.
　Where-e'er I gad I cannot hide my care,
My new disasters in my look appear.　　40
White as the curd my ruddy cheek is grown,
So thin my features that I'm hardly known ;
Our neighbours tell me oft in joking talk
Of ashes, leather, oatmeal, bran and chalk ;
Unwittingly of *Marian* they devine,
And wist not that with thoughtful love I pine.
Yet *Colin Clout*, untoward shepherd swain,
Walks whistling blithe, while pitiful I plain,
　Whilom with thee 'twas *Marian*'s dear delight
To moil all day, and merry-make at night.　　50
If in the soil you guide the crooked share,
Your early breakfast is my constant care.
And when with even hand you strow the grain,
I fright the thievish rooks from off the plain,
In misling days when I my thresher heard,
With nappy beer I to the barn repair'd ;
Lost in the musick of the whirling flail,
To gaze on thee I left the smoking pail ;
In harvest when the Sun was mounted high,
My leathern bottle did thy drought supply ;　　60
When-e'er you mow'd I follow'd with the rake,
And have full oft been sun-burnt for thy sake ;
When in the welkin gath'ring show'rs were seen,
I lagg'd the last with *Colin* on the green ;
And when at eve returning with thy carr,
Awaiting heard the gingling bells from far ;
Strait on the fire the sooty pot I plac't,
To warm thy broth I burnt my hands for haste.
When hungry thou stood'st *staring, like an Oaf*,
I slic'd the luncheon from the barly loaf,　　70
With crumbled bread I thicken'd well thy mess.
Ah, love me more, or love thy pottage less !
　Last *Friday*'s eve, when as the sun was set,
I, near yon stile, three sallow gypsies met.
Upon my hand they cast a poring look,
Bid me beware, and thrice their heads they shook,
They said that many crosses I must prove,
Some in my worldly gain, but most in love.
Next morn I miss'd three hens and our old cock,
And off the hedge two pinners and a smock.　　80

　45 devine] divine *1714* [1] and [2], *17—, and 1721.*

I bore these losses with a christian mind,
And no mishaps could feel, while thou wert kind.
But since, alas! I grew my *Colin's* scorn,
I've known no pleasure, night, or noon, or morn.
Help me, ye gypsies, bring him home again,
And to a constant lass give back her swain.

Have I not sate with thee full many a night,
When dying embers were our only light,
When ev'ry creature did in slumbers lye,
Besides our cat, my *Colin Clout,* and I ?   90
No troublous thoughts the cat or *Colin* move,
While I alone am kept awake by love.

Remember, *Colin,* when at last year's wake,
I bought the costly present for thy sake,
Couldst thou spell o'er the posie on thy knife,
And with another change thy state of life ?
If thou forget'st, I wot, I can repeat,
My memory can tell the verse so sweet.
As this is grav'd upon this knife of thine,
So is thy image on this heart of mine.   100
But woe is me ! Such presents luckless prove,
For *Knives,* they tell me, *always sever Love.*

Thus *Marian* wail'd, her eyes with tears brimfull,
When Goody *Dobbins* brought her cow to bull.
With apron blue to dry her tears she sought,
Then saw the cow well serv'd, and took a groat.

99-100 *Printed in roman letters 17— and 1721.*

W E D N E S D A Y;

OR, THE

*D U M P S.

SPARABELLA.

THE wailings of a maiden I recite,
A maiden fair, that *Sparabella* hight.
Such strains ne'er warble in the linnet's throat,
Nor the gay goldfinch chaunts so sweet a note.
No magpye chatter'd, nor the painted jay,
No ox was heard to low, nor ass to bray.
No rusling breezes play'd the leaves among,
While thus her madrigal the damsel sung.
  A while, O *D'Urfey*, lend an ear or twain,
Nor, though in homely guise, my verse disdain;   10
Whether thou seek'st new kingdoms in the sun,
Whether thy muse does at *New-market* run,
Or does with gossips at a feast regale,
And heighten her conceits with sack and ale,
Or else at wakes with *Joan* and *Hodge* rejoice,
Where *D'Urfey's* lyricks swell in every voice;
Yet suffer me, thou bard of wond'rous meed,
Amid thy bays to weave this rural weed.

---

* Dumps, *or* Dumbs, *made use of to express a fit of the* Sullens. *Some have pretended that it is derived from* Dumops, *a King of* Egypt, *who built a Pyramid, and dy'd of Melancholy. So* Mopes *after the same manner is thought to have come from* Merops, *another* Egyptian *King who dy'd of the same distemper; but our* English *Antiquaries have conjectured that* Dumps, *which is,* a grievous heaviness of spirits, *comes from the word* Dumplin, *the heaviest kind of pudding that is eaten in this country, much used in* Norfolk, *and other counties of* England.

Line
5. *Immemor Herbarum quos est mirata juvenca*
   Certantes quorum stupefactæ carmine Lynces:
   Et mutata suos requierunt flumina cursus.   Virg.
9. *Tu mihi seu magni superas jam saxa Timavi,*
   Sive oram Illyrici legis æquoris——
11. *An Opera written by this Author, called the* World in the Sun, *or the* Kingdom of Birds; *he is also famous for his Song on the* New-market Horse Race, *and several others that are sung by the* British Swains.
17. Meed, *an old word for* Fame *or* Renown.

Dumps, n., ll. 2 and 4 *who*] 1728 *that* remainder.   4 note.] *1731* note, *re-mainder.*   9 and 16 *D'Urfey*] D——y *1714*[1] and [2] *and 17—.*

Now the Sun drove adown the western road,
And oxen laid at rest forget the goad,   20
The clown fatigu'd trudg'd homeward with his spade,
Across the meadows stretch'd the lengthen'd shade :
When *Sparabella* pensive and forlorn,
Alike with yearning love and labour worn,
Lean'd on her rake, and strait with doleful guise
Did this sad plaint in moanful notes devise.
Come night as dark as pitch, surround my head,
From *Sparabella Bumkinet* is fled ;
The ribbon that his val'rous cudgel won,
Last *Sunday* happier *Clumsilis* put on.   30
Sure if he'd eyes (*but Love*, they say, *has none*)
I whilome by that ribbon had been known.
Ah, well-a-day ! I'm shent with baneful smart,
For with the ribbon he bestow'd his heart.
My plaint, ye lasses, with this burthen aid
'Tis hard so true a damsel dies a maid.
Shall heavy *Clumsilis* with me compare ?
View this, ye lovers, and like me despair.
Her blubber'd lip by smutty pipes is worn,
And in her breath tobacco whiffs are born ;   40
The cleanly cheese-press she could never turn,
Her aukward fist did ne'er employ the churn ;
If e'er she brew'd, the drink would strait go sour,
Before it ever felt the thunder's power :
No huswifry the dowdy creature knew ;
To sum up all, her tongue confess'd the shrew.
My plaint, ye lasses, with this burthen aid,
'Tis hard so true a damsel dies a maid.
I've often seen my visage in yon lake,
Nor are my features of the homeliest make.   50
Though *Clumsilis* may boast a whiter dye,
Yet the black sloe turns in my rolling eye ;
And fairest blossoms drop with ev'ry blast,
But the brown beauty will like hollies last.
Her wan complexion's like the wither'd leek,
While *Katherine* pears adorn my ruddy cheek.
Yet she, alas ! the witless lout hath won,
And by her gain, poor *Sparabell's* undone !

Line
18.   ——*Hanc sine tempora circum*
         Inter victrices ederam tibi serpere lauros.
25.   *Incumbens tereti Damon sic cœpit Olivæ.*
33. Shent, *an old word signifying* Hurt *or* harmed.
37. *Mopso Nisa datur : quid non speremus Amantes ?* Virg.
49. *Nec sum adeo informis, nuper me in Littore vidi.* Virg.
53. *Alba ligustra cadunt, vaccinia nigra leguntur.* Virg.

26 moanful] *Cooke and Underhill have* mournful.
31 they say] *italicized by the editions using italics : but this must be a mistake :*
vide Tuesday, l. 102.   42 aukward] *1728 and 1731* awkward *remainder.*

Let hares and hounds in coupling straps unite,
The clocking hen make friendship with the kite,   60
Let the fox simply wear the nuptial noose,
And join in wedlock with the wadling goose ;
For love hath brought a stranger thing to pass,
The fairest shepherd weds the foulest lass.
  My plaint, ye lasses, with this burthen aid,
'Tis hard so true a damsel dies a maid.
Sooner shall cats disport in waters clear,
And speckled mackrels graze the meadows fair,
Sooner shall scriech-owls bask in sunny day,
And the slow ass on trees, like squirrels, play,   70
Sooner shall snails on insect pinions rove,
Than I forget my shepherd's wonted love.
  My plaint, ye lasses, with this burthen aid,
'Tis hard so true a damsel dies a maid.
Ah ! didst thou know what proffers I withstood,
When late I met the *Squire* in yonder wood !
To me he sped, regardless of his game,
While all my cheek was glowing red with shame ;
My lip he kiss'd, and prais'd my healthful look,
Then from his purse of silk a *Guinea* took,   80
Into my hand he forc'd the tempting gold,
While I with modest struggling broke his hold.
He swore that *Dick* in liv'ry strip'd with lace,
Should wed me soon, to keep me from disgrace
But I nor footman priz'd nor golden fee,
For what is lace or gold compar'd to thee ?
  My plaint, ye lasses, with this burthen aid,
'Tis hard so true a damsel dies a maid.
Now plain I ken whence *Love* his rise begun.
Sure he was born some bloody butcher's son,   90
Bred up in shambles, where our younglings slain,
Erst taught him mischief and to sport with pain.

Line
59. *Jungentur jam Gryphes equis ; ævoque sequenti*
   Cum canibus timidi venient ad pocula Damæ. Virg.
67. *Ante leves ergo pascentur in æthere Cervi*
   Et freta destituent nudos in littore Pisces——
   Quam nostro illius labatur pectore vultus. Virg.
89. To ken, *scire.* Chaucero, *to ken ;* and kende *notus.* A.S. cunnan. Goth.
  kunnan. Germanis kennen. Danis kiende. Islandis kunna. Belgis kennen.
  This word is of general use, but not very common, though not unknown to the
  vulgar. Ken *for* prospicere *is well known and used* to discover by the eye.
  Ray. F.R.S.
  Nunc scio quid sit Amor, &c.
  Crudelis mater magis an puer improbus ille ?
  Improbus ille puer, crudelis tu quoque mater. Virg.

---

68 mackrels] Mackrel *1714*[1] and [2] and *17*—.
72 love.] *1728* love *1731* love ! *remainder.*
78 While] Whilst *1714*[1] and [2] and *17*—.

The father only silly sheep annoys,
The son the sillier shepherdess destroys.
Does son or father greater mischief do ?
The sire is cruel, so the son is too.
My plaint, ye lasses, with this burthen aid,
'Tis hard so true a damsel dies a maid.
Farewell ye woods, ye meads, ye streams that flow ;
A sudden death shall rid me of my woe.   100
This penknife keen my windpipe shall divide.
What, shall I fall as squeaking pigs have dy'd !
No——To some tree this carcass I'll suspend.
But worrying curs find such untimely end !
I'll speed me to the pond, where the high stool
On the long plank hangs o'er the muddy pool,
That stool, the dread of ev'ry scolding quean ;
Yet, sure a lover should not dye so mean !
There plac'd aloft, I'll rave and rail by fits,
Though all the parish say I've lost my wits ;   110
And thence, if courage holds, myself I'll throw,
And quench my passion in the lake below.
Ye lasses, cease your burthen, cease to moan,
And, by my case forewarn'd, go mind your own.
The sun was set ; the night came on a-pace,
And falling dews bewet around the place,
The bat takes airy rounds on leathern wings,
And the hoarse owl his woful dirges sings ;
The prudent maiden deems it now too late,
And 'till to-morrow comes defers her fate.   120

Line
99.   ——————————————————— *vivite Sylvæ.*
          Præceps aerii specula de montis in undas
          Deferar. Virg.

---

101 divide.] divide.—— *1714*[1] and *2*, *17*—, and *1721*.
103 No——To] No. To *1728*.   suspend.] suspend.—— *1714*[1] and *2* and *17*—.
suspend—— *1721*.
107 quean;] *1731* Quean.—— *1714*[1] and *2* and *17*— Quean—— *1721* Quean. *1728*
quean *1720*.

T H U R S D A Y;

O R, T H E

S P E L L.

HOBNELIA.

Hobnelia, seated in a dreary vale,
In pensive mood rehears'd her piteous tale,
Her piteous tale the winds in sighs bemoan,
And pining eccho answers groan for groan.
    I rue the day, a rueful day, I trow,
The woful day, a day indeed of woe !
When *Lubberkin* to town his cattle drove,
A maiden fine bedight he hapt to love ;
The maiden fine bedight his love retains,
And for the village he forsakes the plains.   10
Return my *Lubberkin,* these ditties hear ;
Spells will I try, and spells shall ease my care.
    With my sharp heel I three times mark the ground,
And turn me thrice around, around, around.
    When first the year, I heard the cuckow sing,
And call with welcome note the budding spring,
I straitway set a running with such haste,
Deb'rah, who won the smock, scarce ran so fast.
'Till spent for lack of breath, quite weary grown,
Upon a rising bank I sat adown,   20
Then doff'd my shoe, and by my troth, I swear,
Therein I spy'd this yellow frizled hair,
As like to *Lubberkin's* in curl and hue,
As if upon his comely pate it grew.
    With my sharp heel I three times mark the ground,
And turn me thrice around, around, around.
    At eve last *Midsummer* no sleep I sought,
But to the field a bag of hemp-seed brought,
I scatter'd round the seed on ev'ry side,
And three times in a trembling accent cry'd,   30
This hemp-seed with my virgin hand I sow,
Who shall my true-love be, the crop shall mow.
I strait look'd back, and if my eyes speak truth,
With his keen scythe behind me came the youth.

Line
  8. Dight *or* bedight, *from the* Saxon *word* dightan, *which signifies* to set in order.
  21. Doff *and* don, *contracted from the words* do off *and* do on.

8 n. to set in order] *italicized by all early editions.*
18 *So 1728.* Deb'rah that won the smock scarce ran so fast. *remainder.*
31 *hand*] hands 1714[1] and [2] and 17—.

With my sharp heel I three times mark the ground,
And turn me thrice around, around, around.
   Last *Valentine*, the day when birds of kind
Their paramours with mutual chirpings find ;
I rearly rose, just at the break of day,
Before the sun had chas'd the stars away ;   40
A-field I went, amid the morning dew
To milk my kine (for so should huswives do ;)
Thee first I spy'd, and the first swain we see,
In spite of fortune shall our true-love be ;
See, *Lubberkin*, each bird his partner take,
And canst thou then thy sweatheart dear forsake ?
With my sharp heel I three times mark the ground,
And turn me thrice around, around, around.
   Last *May-day* fair I search'd to find a snail
That might my secret lover's name reveal ;   50
Upon a gooseberry bush a snail I found,
For always snails near sweetest fruit abound.
I seiz'd the vermine, home I quickly sped,
And on the hearth the milk-white embers spread.
Slow crawl'd the snail, and if I right can spell,
In the soft ashes mark'd a curious *L* :
Oh, may this wondrous omen lucky prove !
For *L* is found in *Lubberkin* and *Love*.
With my sharp heel I three times mark the ground,
And turn me thrice around, around, around.   60
   Two hazel-nuts I threw into the flame,
And to each nut I gave a sweet-heart's name.
This with the loudest bounce me sore amaz'd,
That in a flame of brightest colour blaz'd.
As blaz'd the nut so may thy passion grow,
For 'twas thy nut that did so brightly glow.
With my sharp heel I three times mark the ground,
And turn me thrice around, around, around.
   As peascods once I pluck'd, I chanc'd to see
One that was closely fill'd with three times three,   70
Which when I cropp'd I safely home convey'd,
And o'er my door the spell in secret laid.
My wheel I turn'd, and sung a ballad new,
While from the spindle I the fleeces drew
The latch mov'd up, when who should first come in,
But in his proper person,—*Lubberkin*.

Line
64. ————ἐγὼ δ' ἐπὶ Δέλφιδι δάφναν
Αἴθω· χ' ὡς αὐτὰ λακέει μέγα καππυρίσασα.   Theoc.
66. *Daphnis me malus urit, ego hanc in Daphnide.*

42 do ;)] do) *all early editions.*   44 spite] spight *1728.*   72 laid.] laid,
1720 and 1731.   76 person,] person *17—, 1721, and 1728.*

I broke my yarn surpriz'd the sight to see,
Sure sign that he would break his word with me.
Eftsoons I join'd it with my wonted slight,
So may again his love with mine unite !
With my sharp heel I three times mark the ground,   8ɔ
And turn me thrice around, around, around.
This *Lady-fly* I take from off the grass,
Whose spotted back might scarlet red surpass.
Fly, Lady-Bird, *North, South, or East or West,*
Fly where the Man is found that I love best.
He leaves my hand, see, to the *West* he 's flown,
To call my true-love from the faithless town.
With my sharp heel I three times mark the ground.
And turn me thrice around, around, around.   9ɔ
I pare this pippin round and round again,
My shepherd's name to flourish on the plain.
I fling th' unbroken paring o'er my head,
Upon the grass a perfect *L* is read ;
Yet on my heart a fairer *L* is seen
Than what the paring marks upon the green.
With my sharp heel I three times mark the ground,
And turn me thrice around, around, around.
This pippin shall another tryal make,
See from the core two kernels brown I take ;   1oo
This on my cheek for *Lubberkin* is worn,
And *Boobyclod* on t' other side is born.
But *Boobyclod* soon drops upon the ground,
A certain token that his love 's unsound,
While *Lubberkin* sticks firmly to the last ;
Oh were his lips to mine but join'd so fast !
With my sharp heel I three times mark the ground,
And turn me thrice around, around, around.
As *Lubberkin* once slept beneath a tree,
I twitch'd his dangling garter from his knee ;   11o
He wist not when the hempen string I drew,
Now mine I quickly doff of inkle blue ;
Together fast I tye the garters twain,
And while I knit the knot repeat this strain.
Three times a true-love's knot I tye secure,
Firm be the knot, firm may his love endure.
With my sharp heel I three times mark the ground,
And turn me thrice around, around, around.

Line
93. *Transque Caput jace : ne respexeris.*   Virg.
109. *Necte tribus nodis ternos, Amarylli, colores*
      Necte, Amarylli, modo : & Veneris dic vincula necto.   **Virg.**

91-2 *So 1731. The remainder have*
                    This mellow pippin, which I pare around,
                    My shepherd's name shall flourish on the ground.
94-5 *L*] L *all early editions ; but vide l. 56.*
96 marks] *all early editions ;* makes *Underhill with the odd note* ' 1 Ed. marks '.

As I was wont, I trudg'd last market-day
To town, with new-laid eggs preserv'd in hay.   120
I made my market long before 'twas night,
My purse grew heavy and my basket light.
Strait to the pothecary's shop I went,
And in love-powder all my mony spent ;
Behap what will, next *Sunday* after prayers,
When to the ale-house *Lubberkin* repairs,
These *golden flies* into his mug I'll throw,
And soon the swain with fervent love shall glow.
With my sharp heel I three times mark the ground,
And turn me thrice around, around, around.   130
But hold—our *Light-foot* barks, and cocks his ears,
O'er yonder stile see *Lubberkin* appears.
He comes, he comes, *Hobnelia*'s not bewray'd,
Nor shall she crown'd with willow die a maid.
He vows, he swears, he'll give me a green gown,
Oh dear ! I fall adown, adown, adown !

Line
123. Has *herbas, atque hæc Ponto mihi lecta venena*
    Ipse dedit Mæris.   Virg.
127. ——Ποτὸν κακὸν ἄυριον οἰσῶ.   Theoc.
131. *Nescio quid certe est : & Hylax in limine latrat.*

124 mony] money *1731*.   125 *Sunday*] sunday *1720*.

F R I D A Y;

O R, T H E

*D I R G E.

B U M K I N E T, G R U B B I N O L.

B U M K I N E T.

WHY, *Grubbinol*, dost thou so wistful seem ?
There 's sorrow in thy look, if right I deem.
'Tis true, yon oaks with yellow tops appear,
And chilly blasts begin to nip the year ;
From the tall elm a show'r of leaves is born,
And their lost beauty riven beeches mourn.

* Dirge, *or* Dyrge, *a mournful Ditty or Song of Lamentation over the dead ; not*
a contraction of the Latin Dirige *in the popish Hymn* Dirige Gressus meos,
as some pretend. But from the Teutonic Dyrke, Laudare, *to praise and extol.*
Whence it is possible their Dyrke *and our* Dirge *was a laudatory Song to*
commemorate and applaud the Dead. Cowell's Interpreter.

Yet ev'n this season pleasance blithe affords,
Now the squeez'd press foams with our apple hoards.
Come, let us hye, and quaff a cheary bowl,
Let cyder new *wash sorrow from thy soul.*   10

GRUBBINOL.

Ah *Bumkinet* ! since thou from hence wert gone,
From these sad plains all merriment is flown ;
Should I reveal my grief 'twould spoil thy chear,
And make thine eye o'erflow with many a tear.

BUMKINET.

Hang sorrow ! Let 's to yonder hutt repair,
And with trim sonnets *cast away our care.*
Gillian of Croydon well thy pipe can play,
Thou sing'st most sweet, *o'er hills and far away.*
Of *Patient Grissel* I devise to sing,
And catches quaint shall make the vallies ring.   20
Come, *Grubbinol*, beneath this shelter, come,
From hence we view our flocks securely roam.

GRUBBINOL.

Yes, blithesome lad, a tale I mean to sing,
But with my woe shall distant vallies ring,
The tale shall make our kidlings droop their head,
For woe is me !—our *Blouzelind* is dead.

BUMKINET.

Is *Blouzelinda* dead ? farewel my glee !
No happiness is now reserv'd for me.
As the wood pigeon cooes without his mate,
So shall my doleful dirge bewail her fate.   30
Of *Blouzelinda* fair I mean to tell,
The peerless maid that did all maids excell.

Henceforth the morn shall dewy sorrow shed,
And ev'ning tears upon the grass be spread ;
The rolling streams with watry grief shall flow,
And winds shall moan aloud—when loud they blow.
Henceforth, as oft as autumn shall return,
The dropping trees, when'er it rains, shall mourn ;
This season quite shall strip the country's pride,
For 'twas in autumn *Blouzelinda* dy'd.   40

Where-e'er I gad, I *Blouzelind* shall view,
Woods, dairy, barn and mows our passion knew.
When I direct my eyes to yonder wood,
Fresh rising sorrow curdles in my blood.
Thither I've often been the damsel's guide,
When rotten sticks our fuel have supply'd ;

Line
15. *Incipe Mopse prior si quos aut Phyllidis ignes*
Aut Alconis habes Laudes, aut jurgia Codri.

27. Glee, *Joy* ; *from the* Dutch, Glooren, *to* recreate.

7 ev'n] even *1731.*

There I remember how her faggots large,
Were frequently these happy shoulders charge.
Sometimes this crook drew hazel boughs adown,
And stuff'd her apron wide with nuts so brown ;   50
Or when her feeding hogs had miss'd their way,
Or wallowing 'mid a feast of acorns lay ;
Th' untoward creatures to the stye I drove,
And whistled all the way—or told my love.
  If by the dairy's hatch I chance to hie,
I shall her goodly countenance espie,
For there her goodly countenance I've seen,
Set off with kerchief starch'd and pinners clean.
Sometimes, like wax, she rolls the butter round,
Or with the wooden lilly prints the pound.   60
Whilome I've seen her skim the clouted cream,
And press from spongy curds the milky stream.
But now, alas ! these ears shall hear no more
The whining swine surround the dairy door,
No more her care shall fill the hollow tray,
To fat the guzzling hogs with floods of whey.
Lament, ye swine, in grunting spend your grief,
For you, like me, have lost your sole relief.
  When in the barn the sounding flail I ply,
Where from her sieve the chaff was wont to fly,   70
The poultry there will seem around to stand,
Waiting upon her charitable hand.
No succour meet the poultry now can find,
For they, like me, have lost their *Blouzelind.*
  Whenever by yon barley mow I pass,
Before my eyes will trip the tidy lass.
I pitch'd the sheaves (oh could I do so now)
Which she in rows pil'd on the growing mow.
There ev'ry deale my heart by love was gain'd,
There the sweet kiss my courtship has explain'd.   80
Ah, *Blouzelind* ! that mow I ne'er shall see,
But thy memorial will revive in me.
  Lament, ye fields, and rueful symptoms show,
Henceforth let not the smelling primrose grow ;
Let weeds instead of butter-flow'rs appear,
And meads, instead of daisies, hemlock bear ;
For cowslips sweet let dandelions spread,
For *Blouzelinda*, blithesome maid, is dead !
Lament ye swains, and o'er her grave bemoan,
And spell ye right this verse upon her stone.   90

Line
84. *Pro molli viola, pro parpureo Narcisso
   Carduus, & spinis surgit Paliurus acutis.*   Virg.
90. *Et Tumulum facite, & tumulo superaddite Carmen.*

76 my] mine *17—.*
88 blithesome] *17–, 1721, and 1728* blithsome *remainder, but vide l.* **23.**

Here Blouzelinda *lyes—Alas, alas !*
Weep shepherds—and remember flesh is grass.
        G R U B B I N O L.
  Albeit thy songs are sweeter to mine ear,
Than to the thirsty cattle rivers clear ;
Or winter porridge to the lab'ring youth,
Or bunns and sugar to the damsel's tooth ;
Yet *Blouzelinda*'s name shall tune my lay,
Of her I'll sing for ever and for aye.
  When *Blouzelind* expir'd, the weather's bell
Before the drooping flock toll'd forth her knell ;   100
The solemn death-watch click'd the hour she dy'd,
And shrilling crickets in the chimney cry'd ;
The boding raven on her cottage sate,
And with hoarse croaking warn'd us of her fate ;
The lambkin, which her wonted tendance bred,
Dropp'd on the plains that fatal instant dead ;
Swarm'd on a rotten stick the bees I spy'd,
Which erst I saw when goody *Dobson* dy'd.
  How shall I, void of tears, her death relate,
While on her dearling's bed her mother sate !   110
These words the dying *Blouzelinda* spoke,
And *of the dead let none the will revoke.*
  Mother, quoth she, let not the poultry need,
And give the goose wherewith to raise her breed,
Be these my sister's care—and ev'ry morn
Amid the ducklings let her scatter corn ;
The sickly calf that 's hous'd, be sure to tend,
Feed him with milk, and from bleak colds defend.
Yet e'er I die—see, mother, yonder shelf,
There secretly I've hid my worldly pelf.   120
Twenty good shillings in a rag I laid,
Be ten the Parson's, for my sermon paid.
The rest is yours—my spinning-wheel and rake,
Let *Susan* keep for her dear sister's sake ;
My new straw-hat that 's trimly lin'd with green,
Let *Peggy* wear, for she 's a damsel clean.
My leathern bottle, long in harvests try'd,
Be *Grubbinol*'s—this silver ring beside :
Three silver pennies, and a ninepence bent,
A token kind, to *Bumkinet* is sent.   130

Line
93. *Tale tuum Carmen nobis, Divine Poeta,*
    Quale sopor fessis in gramine : quale per æstum
    Dulcis aquæ saliente sitim restinguere rivo.
    Nos tamen hæc quocumque modo tibi nostra vicissim
    Dicemus, Daphninque tuum tollemus ad astra.   Virg.
96. Κρέσσον μελπομένῳ τεῦ ἀκουέμεν ἢ μέλι λείχειν.   Theoc.

91-2 *Printed in roman letters 17— and 1721.*   96, n. *The accents are given correctly in 1728.*   110 dearling] darling *17—, 1721, and 1728.*

Thus spoke the maiden, while her mother cry'd,
And peaceful, like the harmless lamb, she dy'd.
To show their love, the neighbours far and near,
Follow'd with wistful look the damsel's bier.
Sprigg'd rosemary the lads and lasses bore,
While dismally the Parson walk'd before.
Upon her grave the rosemary they threw,
The daisie, butter-flow'r and endive blue.
After the good man warn'd us from his text,
That none could tell whose turn would be the next ;   140
He said, that heaven would take her soul, no doubt,
And spoke the hour-glass in her praise—quite out.
To her sweet mem'ry flow'ry garlands strung,
O'er her now empty seat aloft were hung.
With wicker rods we fenc'd her tomb around,
To ward from man and beast the hallow'd ground,
Lest her new grave the Parson's cattle raze,
For both his horse and cow the church-yard graze.
Now we trudg'd homeward to her mother's farm,
To drink new cyder mull'd, with ginger warm.   150
For gaffer *Tread-well* told us by the by,
Excessive sorrow is exceeding dry.
While bulls bear horns upon their curled brow,
Or lasses with soft stroakings milk the cow ;
While padling ducks the standing lake desire,
Or batt'ning hogs roll in the sinking mire ;
While moles the crumbled earth in hillocks raise,
So long shall swains tell *Blouzelinda*'s praise.
Thus wail'd the louts in melancholy strain,
'Till bonny *Susan* sped a-cross the plain ;   160
They seiz'd the lass in apron clean array'd,
And to the ale-house forc'd the willing maid ;
In ale and kisses they forget their cares,
And *Susan Blouzelinda*'s loss repairs.

Line
153.   *Dum juga montis Aper, fluvios dum Piscis amabit,*
          Dumque Thymo pascentur apes, dum rore cicadæ,
          Semper honos nomenque tuum, laudesque manebunt.

137 the] their *all 8vos.*
151 *Tread-well*] Tread-well *17*— Treadwell *1721 and 1728.*
153, n. *amabit,*] amabit *all early editions. The odd use of capital letters is common to all.*

S A T U R D A Y;

O R, T H E

F L I G H T S.

BOWZYBEUS.

SUBLIMER strains, O rustick Muse, prepare;
Forget a-while the barn and dairy's care;
Thy homely voice to loftier numbers raise,
The drunkard's flights require sonorous lays,
With *Bowzybeus'* songs exalt thy verse,
While rocks and woods the various notes rehearse.
   'Twas in the season when the reapers toil
Of the ripe harvest 'gan to rid the soil;
Wide through the field was seen a goodly rout,
Clean damsels bound the gather'd sheaves about,   10
The lads with sharpen'd hook and sweating brow
Cut down the labours of the winter plow.
To the near hedge young *Susan* steps aside,
She feign'd her coat or garter was unty'd,
What-e'er she did, she stoop'd adown unseen,
And merry reapers, what they list, will ween.
Soon she rose up, and cry'd with voice so shrill
That eccho answer'd from the distant hill;
The youths and damsels ran to *Susan's* aid,
Who thought some adder had the lass dismay'd.   20
   There fast asleep they *Bowzybeus* spy'd,
His hat and oaken staff lay close beside.
That *Bowzybeus* who could sweetly sing,
Or with the rozin'd bow torment the string;
That *Bowzybeus* who with finger's speed
Could call soft warblings from the breathing reed;
That *Bowzybeus* who with jocond tongue,
Ballads and roundelays and catches sung.
They loudly laugh to see the damsel's fright,
And in disport surround the drunken wight.   30
   Ah *Bowzybee*, why didst thou stay so long?
The mugs were large, the drink was wondrous strong!
Thou should'st have left the Fair before 'twas night,
But thou sat'st toping 'till the morning light.

Line
22. *Serta procul tantum capiti delapsa jacebant.*   Virg.

---

7 reapers] reaper's *all 8vos.*   21 There] *1728* When *remainder.*
31 *Bowzybee*] *Bowzybeé* 1714[1] [and 2]   Bowzybeé 17—   Bowzybée *1721 and 1728.*

Cic'ly, brisk maid, steps forth before the rout,
And kiss'd with smacking lip the snoring lout.
For custom says, *Whoe'er this venture proves,*
For such a kiss demands a pair of gloves.
By her example *Dorcas* bolder grows,
And plays a tickling straw within his nose.   40
He rubs his nostril, and in wonted joke
The sneering swains with stamm'ring speech bespoke.
To you, my lads, I'll sing my carrol's o'er,
As for the maids,—I've something else in store.
  No sooner 'gan he raise his tuneful song,
But lads and lasses round about him throng.
Not ballad-singer plac'd above the croud
Sings with a note so shrilling sweet and loud,
Nor parish-clerk who calls the psalm so clear,
Like *Bowzybeus* sooths th' attentive ear.   50
  Of nature's laws his carrols first begun,
Why the grave owle can never face the sun.
For owles, as swains observe, detest the light,
And only sing and seek their prey by night.
How turnips hide their swelling heads below,
And how the closing colworts upwards grow ;
How *Will-a-Wisp* mis-leads night-faring clowns,
O'er hills, and sinking bogs, and pathless downs.
Of stars he told that shoot with shining trail,
And of the glow-worm's light that gilds his tail.   60
He sung where wood-cocks in the summer feed,
And in what climates they renew their breed ;
Some think to northern coasts their flight they tend,
Or to the moon in midnight hours ascend.
Where swallows in the winter's season keep,
And how the drowsie bat and dormouse sleep.
How nature does the puppy's eyelid close,
'Till the bright sun has nine times set and rose.
For huntsmen by their long experience find,
That puppys still nine rolling suns are blind.   70
  Now he goes on, and sings of Fairs and shows,
For still new fairs before his eyes arose.
How pedlars stalls with glitt'ring toys are laid,
The various fairings of the country maid.

Line
40. *Sanguineis frontem moris & tempora pingit.*   Virg.
43. *Carmina quæ vultis, cognoscite : carmina vobis.*
  Huic aliud mercedis erit.   Virg.
47. *Nec tantum Phœbo gaudet Parnasia rupes*
  Nec tantum Rhodope mirantur & Ismarus Orphea.   Virg.
51. *Our swain had possibly read* Tusser, *from whence he might have collected these*
  philosophical observations.
  Namque canebat uti magnum per inane coacta &c.   Virg.

51, n. *possibly*] 1731 *probably* remainder.

Long silken laces hang upon the twine,
And rows of pins and amber bracelets shine ;
How the tight lass, knives, combs, and scissars spys,
And looks on thimbles with desiring eyes.
Of lott'ries next with tuneful note he told,
Where silver spoons are won and rings of gold.   80
The lads and lasses trudge the street along,
And all the fair is crouded in his song.
The mountebank now treads the stage, and sells
His pills, his balsams, and his ague-spells ;
Now o'er and o'er the nimble tumbler springs,
And on the rope the ventrous maiden swings ;
Jack Pudding in his parti-colour'd jacket
Tosses the glove, and jokes at ev'ry packet.
Of *Raree-shows* he sung, and *Punch's* feats,
Of pockets pick'd in crowds, and various cheats.   90
    Then sad he sung *the Children in the Wood.*
Ah barb'rous uncle, stain'd with infant blood !
How blackberrys they pluck'd in desarts wild,
And fearless at the glittering fauchion smil'd ;
Their little corps the robin-red-breasts found,
And strow'd with pious bill the leaves around.
Ah gentle birds ! if this verse lasts so long,
Your names shall live for ever in my song.
    For buxom *Joan* he sung the doubtful strife,
How the sly sailor made the maid a wife.   100
    To louder strains he rais'd his voice, to tell
What woeful wars in *Chevy-chace* befell,
When *Piercy drove the deer with hound and horn,*
Wars to be wept by children yet unborn !
Ah *With'rington*, more years thy life had crown'd,
If thou hadst never heard the horn or hound !
Yet shall the Squire who fought on bloody stumps,
By future bards be wail'd in doleful dumps.
    All in the land of Essex next he chaunts,
How to sleek mares starch quakers turn gallants ;   110
How the grave brother stood on bank so green.
Happy for him if mares had never been !
    Then he was seiz'd with a religious qualm,
And on a sudden, sung the hundredth psalm.

Line
97. *Fortunati ambo, si quid mea carmina possunt,*
    Nulla dies unquam memori vos eximet ævo.   Virg.
99. *A Song in the Comedy of* Love for Love, *beginning* A Soldier and a Sailor, *&c.*
109. *A Song of Sir* J. Denham's. *See his Poems.*
112. *Et fortunatam si nunquam Armenta fuissent*
    Pasiphaen.

81 street] streets *17—.*
87 *Jack Pudding*] 1731 *Jack pudding* 1720 *Jack-pudding or* Jack-pudding *8vos.*

THE SHEPHERD'S WEEK.

He sung of *Taffey Welch*, and *Sawney Scot*,
Lilly-bullero and the *Irish Trot*.
Why should I tell of *Bateman* or of *Shore*,
Or *Wantley's Dragon* slain by valiant *Moore*,
The bow'r of Rosamond, or *Robin Hood*,
And how the *grass now grows where* Troy town *stood* ?   120
  His carrols ceas'd : the list'ning maids and swains
Seem still to hear some soft imperfect strains.
Sudden he rose ; and as he reels along
Swears kisses sweet should well reward his song.
The damsels laughing fly : the giddy clown
Again upon a wheat-sheaf drops adown ;
The pow'r that guards the drunk, his sleep attends,
'Till, ruddy, like his face, the sun descends.

Line
117. *Quid loquar aut Scyllam Nisi, &c.*   Virg.
117. *Old English Ballads.*

115 *Taffey Welch*] *Taffey-Welch or* Taffey-Welch *8vos.*   *Sawney Scot*] Sawncy
Scot *17—*   Sawney-Scot *1728.*

A N
ALPHABETICAL CATALOGUE
OF

Names, Plants, Flowers, Fruits, Birds, Beasts, Insects, and other material things mentioned in these Pastorals.

A
Acorns	Past. 5, v. 52
Adder		6, 20
Ale-House		5, 8
Apple		4, 126
Apron	2, 105.	5, 50
Ass	3, 6.	3, 70
Autumn	5, 3.	5, 37

B
Barley	2, 70.	5, 78
Ballad-singer		6, 47
Bat		3, 117
Bateman		6, 117
Bays		3, 18
Barn	1, 122.	5, 69
Beech		5, 6
Bee		5, 107
Bran		2, 44
Blackberry		6, 93
Blind-man's buff		1, 95
Bramble		1, 2
Blouzelind	1, 10.	5, 26
Breakfast		2, 52
Bull		2, 104
Bumkinet		3, 28
Bun		5, 96
Boobyclod		4, 102
Butter		1, 33
Bowzybeus		6
Butcher		3, 90
Butterflower		5, 85
Buxoma		1, 14

C
Calf	1, 16.	1, 55
Capon		1, 90
Carr		2, 65
Cat	2, 90.	3, 67
Cicily	2, 20.	6, 35
Clover-grass		1, 42
Cloddipole		1

Churn	3, 42
Colworts	6, 56
Clumsilis	3, 30
Cock	2, 79
Comb	6, 77
Cow 1, 16. 1, 82.	2, 104
Colin Clout	2, 1
Clouted Cream	5, 61
Cowslips	5, 87
Chalk	2, 44
Cricket	5, 102
Curd	5, 62
Cuddy	1
Church-yard	5, 148
Cuckow	4, 15
Cur	1, 56
Cyder	5, 150
Corns	1, 28

D
Dairy	5, 42
Daisie	1, 44
Dandelion	5, 87
Deborah	4, 18
Death-watch	5, 101
D'Urfey	3, 9
Goody *Dobbins*	2, 104
Deer	1, 36
Dick	3, 83
Doe	1, 16
Dorcas	6, 39
Dragon	6, 118
Drink	3, 43
Goody *Dobson*	5, 108
Duck	5, 155
Duckling	5, 116
Duckingstool	3, 105

E
Eggs	4, 120
Elm	5, 5

Endive	5, 138
Epitaph	5, 90

F
Fair	6, 71
Fawn	1, 16
Fox	3, 61
Fuel	5, 46

G
Gilly-flower	1, 45
Gloves	6, 38
Glow-worm	6, 6c
Garter	4, 110
Goldfinch	1, 52
Ginger	5, 150
Goose	5, 114
Gillian of Croydon	5, 17
Gooseberry	4, 51
Green Gown	4, 135
Grass	4, 94
Grubbinol	5
Gypsy	2, 74

H
Hare	3, 59
Holyday	1, 66
Haycock	1, 72
Hazel-Nut	4, 61
Harvest	6, 8
Hemlock	5, 86
Hempseed,	4, 28
Heifer	1, 25
Hen	3, 60
Hour-glass	5, 142
Holly	3, 54
Hosen	2, 33
Hobnelia	4
Hot-cockles	1, 99
Hog	5, 51
Hodge	3, 15
Horse	5, 148

Catalogue heading. *in these Pastorals.*] by this Author. *1714*[1] and [2] *and 17—.*
References in 1714[1 and 2] *and 17— are by page. The 'Catalogue' is omitted in the 4th 8vo edition*   *D'Urfey*] not in *1714*[1] and [2] and *17—.*

Goodman *Hodges*	1, 122	
Hound	3, 59	

J

Jack-Pudding	6, 87
Jay	3, 5
Joan	6, 99
Irish Trott	6, 116

K

Katherine Pear	3, 56
Kid	1, 54
Kerchief	5, 58
Kidling	5, 25
Kiss	1, 73
Kite	3, 60
Kersey Doublet	2, 37
Knife	1, 89
Kingcup	1, 43

L

Lady-bird	4, 85
Leather	2, 44
Lamb	1, 53
Lobbin Clout	1,
Love Powder	4, 124
Lambkin	5, 105
Lottery	6, 79
Lark	1, 3
Leathern Bottle	5, 127
Lubberkin	4, 7
Lilly	5, 60
Leek	3, 55
Lilly-bullero	6, 116
Linnet	3, 3

M

Mackerell	3, 68
May-Day	1, 58
Mag-pye	3, 5
Milk-pail	2, 58
Mare	6, 110
Mug	6, 32
Marian	2, 9
Moore	6, 118
Marygold	1, 46
Midsummer-Eve	4, 27
Mole	5, 157
Mountebank	6, 83
Mow	5, 75

N

Neckcloth	2, 36
Nuts	5, 50
Ninepence	5, 129

O

Oak	5, 3
Oatmeal	2, 44
Owl	6, 52
Oxen	3, 20

P

Ploughing	2, 51
Pease-cod	4, 69
Penny	5, 129
Peggy	5, 126
Penknife	3, 101
Pidgeon	5, 29
Pedlar	6, 73
Pig	3, 102
Pinner	5, 58
Pippin	4, 91
Pottage	5, 95
Potatoe	1, 84
Pudding	1, 91
Primrose	5, 84
Patient Grissel	5, 19
Poultry	5, 113
Parish Clerk	6, 49
Puppy	6, 67

R

Rake	5, 123
Raven	5, 103
Robin-hood	6, 119
Robin-red-breast	6, 95
Ring	6, 80
Rook	2, 54
Rosamond	6, 119
Roast Beef	1, 89
Ribbon	3, 29
Rosemary	5, 137
Riddle	1, 111

S

Swinging	1, 103
Spring	4, 1C
Sawney	6, 115
Sage	2, 13
Scissars	6, 77
Sheep	2, 28

Straw-Hat	5, 125
Sloe	3, 52
Smock	4, 18
Snail	3, 71
Spinning Wheel	5, 123
Squirrel	3, 70
Sugar	5, 96
Susan	5, 124
Squire	3, 76
Sowing	2, 53
Swallow	1, 29
Shore	6, 117
Swine	5, 64
Summer	1, 61
Silver Spoon	6, 80
Sparabella	3
See-sawing	1, 107

T

Thimble	6, 79
Throstle	1, 2
Tobacco	3, 40
Gaffer *Treadwell*	5, 151
Troy Town	6, 120
Turnip	1, 86
Threshing	2, 55
True-love's Knot	4, 115

V

Valentine's Day	4, 37
Udder	1, 4

W

Wake	2, 4
Weather	5, 99
Winter	1, 60
Weed	5, 85
Will a Whisp	6, 57
Wheat-sheaf	6, 126
Whey	5, 6
Whitepot	1, 92
Wood	5, 43
Worky Day	1, 63
Woodcock	6, 61
Whistling	5, 54

Y

Yarn	4, 77
Youngling	2, 26

Swinging] *not in 1714*[1] and [2] *and 17—*.   See-sawing] *not in 1714*[1] and [2] *and 17—*.
Wheat-sheaf] Wheat *1714*[1] and [2] *and 17—*.

T R I V I A;

OR, THE

ART of *WALKING*

the Streets of

L O N D O N.

Quo te Mœri pedes ? An, quo via ducit, in Urbem ?—Virg.

[*Editions :*
    1. TRIVIA : | OR, THE | *ART* of *WALKING* | THE | Streets of London. | By Mr. *GAY.* | *Quo te Mœri pedes ? An, quo via ducit, in Urbem ?* Virg. | *LONDON* | Printed for *Bernard Lintott,* at the *Cross-Keys* | between the *Temple* Gates in *Fleet-street.*
    Demy 8vo. Published January 26, 1716.
    2. The same as 1, but in Post 8vo, and with less elaborate cuts at the beginning of each Book.
    3. ' The Second Edition.' Small Post 8vo. No date. The cuts resemble those in 2 ; but the street-scene depicted in 1 at the beginning of Book I is reproduced on the title-page in place of the usual sign of the Cross-keys.
    4. *Poems on Several Occasions.* 1720. 4to.
    5. ' The Third Edition.' Small Post 8vo. 1730. Price One Shilling. The street-scene returns to the head of Book I. In the British Museum copy a quite irrelevant frontispiece by Kirkall is bound up.
    6. *Poems on Several Occasions.* 1731. 12mo.
    Of modern editions, besides Underhill, must be mentioned :
    7. *Trivia* and other poems by John Gay, edited by J. Potter Briscoe, F.R.H.S.,in ' The Bibelots '. Pott 12mo. London, Gay and Bird. 1899.
    8. A very sumptuous Imperial 8vo edition of *Trivia,* with illustrations, edited by Professor W. H. Williams, and published by Daniel O'Connor in 1922. A reprint of the first edition, down to the very errata. Professor Williams in a preliminary note observes that the Quarto of 1720 sometimes differs from the first and second editions, and gives a few instances. He has not consulted the versions of 1730 and 1731.
    It is probable that the version of 1730 was actually corrected later than that of 1731. See, for example, Book I, l. 56.
    The various editions differ considerably in typographical detail. Side-headings are given only in the first and second editions. White lines between paragraphs are

used in these and in 1731, but not in 1720 nor in the third edition (1730). Italics are used in all editions except the second, but more freely in the first. The first edition also employs initial capitals very freely; these are removed in the later editions, and are not reproduced here. The second edition contains two or three obvious misprints which I have not recorded. In the first and second editions the lines are not numbered, and the index references are to the page. The punctuation in the third edition (1730) is, as a rule, better than in the other editions; and the spelling is more modern. I have (vide p. xvii), with some inconsistency perhaps, generally followed it in the former and not in the latter respect. I do not record the numerous instances of modernized spelling in the third edition, unless they are shared by the edition of 1731, or serve to explain the older spelling.

The notes refer to the early editions by date; whenever the date 1716 is given, the undated second edition is to be understood to agree with the first (apart from purely typographical differences). Where there is disagreement between the first and second editions, the note refers to the edition and not to the date. For example, in Book II, l. 282, the reading *that* for *who* is common to both editions, while the second edition differs from the first in printing a comma instead of a full stop after *Drury-lane.* The word ' remainder ' does not refer to editions later than 1731.

The interesting letter printed on p. 666 shows that at the end of 1714 Gay had not composed beyond the first hundred lines or so of Book II. In the short passage quoted in the letter (I, 83–104) there are four substantial variants from the printed version.]

ADVERTISEMENT.

The world, I believe, will take so little notice of me, that I need not take much of it. The criticks may see by this poem, that I walk on foot, which probably may save me from their envy. I should be sorry to raise that passion in men whom I am so much obliged to, since they allowed me an honour hitherto only shown to better writers : That of denying me to be the author of my own works.   5

Gentlemen, if there be any thing in this poem good enough to displease you, and if it be any advantage to you to ascribe it to some person of greater merit ; I shall acquaint you, for your comfort, that among many other obligations, I owe several hints of it to Dr. Swift. And if you will so far continue your favour as to write against it, I beg you to oblige me in accepting the following motto.

——Non tu, in *Triviis,* indocte, solebas
Stridenti, miserum, stipulâ, disperdere carmen ?   12

5 In the first edition only, this sentence follows : *I am sensible this must be done in pure Generosity ; because whoever writ them, provided they did not themselves, they are still in the same Condition.*

T R I V I A.

BOOK I.

Of the Implements for walking the Streets, and Signs of the Weather.

THROUGH winter streets to steer your course aright,
How to walk clean by day, and safe by night,
How jostling crouds, with prudence to decline,
When to assert the wall, and when resign,
I sing : Thou, *Trivia*, Goddess, aid my song,
Thro' spacious streets conduct thy bard along ;
By thee transported, I securely stray
Where winding alleys lead the doubtful way,
The silent court, and op'ning square explore,
And long perplexing lanes untrod before.   10
To pave thy realm, and smooth the broken ways,
Earth from her womb a flinty tribute pays ;
For thee, the sturdy paver thumps the ground,
Whilst ev'ry stroke his lab'ring lungs resound ;
For thee the scavinger bids kennels glide
Within their bounds, and heaps of dirt subside.
My youthful bosom burns with thirst of fame,
From the great theme to build a glorious name,
To tread in paths to ancient bards unknown,
And bind my temples with a Civic crown ;   20
But more, my country's love demands the lays,
My country's be the profit, mine the praise.
    When the black youth at chosen stands rejoice,
And *clean your shoes* resounds from ev'ry voice ;
When late their miry sides stage-coaches show,
And their stiff horses through the town move slow ;
When all the *Mall* in leafy ruin lies,
And damsels first renew their oyster cries :
Of Shoes.   Then let the prudent walker shoes provide,
Not of the *Spanish* or *Morocco* hide ;   30
The wooden heel may raise the dancer's bound,
And with the scallop'd top his step be crown'd :
Let firm, well hammer'd soles protect thy feet
Thro' freezing snows, and rains, and soaking sleet.

13 paver] Pavior *first edition.*   32 scallop'd] 'scalloped *1716.*

Should the big laste extend the shoe too wide,
Each stone will wrench th' unwary step aside :
The sudden turn may stretch the swelling vein,
Thy cracking joint unhinge, or ankle sprain ;
And when too short the modish shoes are worn,
You'll judge the seasons by your shooting corn.   40

Of Coats.   Nor should it prove thy less important care,
To chuse a proper coat for winter's wear.
Now in thy trunk thy *D'oily* habit fold,
The silken drugget ill can fence the cold ;
The frieze's spongy nap is soak'd with rain,
And show'rs soon drench the camlet's cockled grain.
True * *Witney* broad-cloth with its shag unshorn,
Unpierc'd is in the lasting tempest worn :
Be this the horse-man's fence ; for who would wear
Amid the town the spoils of *Russia*'s bear ?   50
Within the *Roquelaure*'s clasp thy hands are pent,
Hands, that stretch'd forth invading harms prevent.
Let the loop'd *Bavaroy* the fop embrace,
Or his deep cloak be spatter'd o'er with lace.
That garment best the winter's rage defends,
Which from the shoulders full and low depends ;
By † various names in various counties known,
Yet held in all the true *Surtout* alone :
Be thine of *Kersey* firm, tho' small the cost,
Then brave unwet the rain, unchill'd the frost.   60

Of Canes.   If the strong cane support thy walking hand,
Chairmen no longer shall the wall command ;
Ev'n sturdy carr-men shall thy nod obey,
And rattling coaches stop to make thee way :
This shall direct thy cautious tread aright,
Though not one glaring lamp enliven night.
Let beaus their canes with amber tipt produce,
Be theirs for empty show, but thine for use.
In gilded chariots while they loll at ease,
And lazily insure a life's disease ;   70
While softer chairs the tawdry load convey
To Court, to ‡ *White*'s, Assemblies, or the Play ;
Rosie-complexion'd health thy steps attends,
And exercise thy lasting youth defends.
Imprudent men heav'n's choicest gifts prophane.
Thus some beneath their arm support the cane ;

* *A Town in* Oxfordshire.
† *A* Joseph, *Wrap-rascal,* &c.
‡ White's *Chocolate-house in* St. James's *Street.*

39 shoes] shooes *1720 and 1731, but in ii.* 56 shoes.   43 D'oily] Doily first edition.
56 *So 1730*
          Whose shapeless form in ample plaits depends ; *1716 and 1720.*
          Whose ample form without one plait depends ; *1731.*
75 heav'n's] heaven's *1731*   Heav'ns *or* heav'ns *remainder.*   prophane] profane
1730 and 1731.

The dirty point oft checks the careless pace,
And miry spots thy clean cravat disgrace :
O ! may I never such misfortune meet,
May no such vicious walkers croud the street,   80
May Providence o'er-shade me with her wings,
While the bold Muse experienc'd dangers sings.
    Not that I wander from my native home,
And (tempting perils) foreign cities roam.
Let *Paris* be the theme of *Gallia*'s muse,
Where slav'ry treads the street in wooden shoes ;
Nor do I rove in *Belgia*'s frozen clime,
And teach the clumsy boor to skate in rhyme,
Where, if the warmer clouds in rain descend,
No miry ways industrious steps offend,   90
The rushing flood from sloping pavements pours,
And blackens the canals with dirty show'rs.
Let others *Naples'* smoother streets rehearse,
And with proud *Roman* structures grace their verse,
Where frequent murders wake the night with groans,
And blood in purple torrents dies the stones ;
Nor shall the Muse thro' narrow *Venice* stray,
Where *Gondolas* their painted oars display.
O happy streets, to rumbling wheels unknown,
No carts, no coaches shake the floating town !   100
Thus was of old *Britannia*'s city bless'd,
E'er pride and luxury her sons possess'd :
Coaches and chariots yet unfashion'd lay,
Nor late-invented chairs perplex'd the way :
Then the proud lady trip'd along the town,
And tuck'd up petticoats secur'd her gown,
Her rosie cheek with distant visits glow'd,
And exercise unartful charms bestow'd ;
But since in braided gold her foot is bound,
And a long trailing manteau sweeps the ground,   110
Her shoe disdains the street ; the lazy fair
With narrow step affects a limping air.
Now gaudy pride corrupts the lavish age,
And the streets flame with glaring equipage ;
The tricking gamester insolently rides,
With *Loves* and *Graces* on his chariot's sides ;
In sawcy state the griping broker sits,
And laughs at honesty, and trudging wits :
For you, O honest men, these useful lays
The Muse prepares ; I seek no other praise.   120
Of the   When sleep is first disturb'd by morning cries ;
Weather.   From sure prognosticks learn to know the skies,
Lest you of rheums and coughs at night complain ;
Surpriz'd in dreary fogs or driving rain.

78 thy] the *Underhill.*   83-104 *Compare the version in the letter to Mr. Ford:*
Appendix III, p. 666.   84 *No brackets, 1716.*   88 clumsy] clumzy *1730.*

When suffocating mists obscure the morn,
Let thy worst wig, long us'd to storms, be worn;
Or like the powder'd footman, with due care
Beneath the flapping hat secure thy hair.
Be thou, for ev'ry season, justly drest,
Nor brave the piercing frost with open breast;   130
And when the bursting clouds a deluge pour,
Let thy *Surtout* defend the drenching show'r.

Signs of cold   The changing weather certain signs reveal.
Weather.   E'er winter sheds her snow, or frosts congeal,
You'll see the coals in brighter flame aspire,
And sulphur tinge with blue the rising fire :
Your tender shins the scorching heat decline,
And at the dearth of coals the poor repine ;
Before her kitchen hearth, the nodding dame
In flannel mantle wrapt, enjoys the flame ;   140
Hov'ring, upon her feeble knees she bends,
And all around the grateful warmth ascends.

Signs of fair   Nor do less certain signs the town advise,
Weather.   Of milder weather, and serener skies.
The ladies gayly dress'd, the *Mall* adorn
With various dyes, and paint the sunny morn ;
The wanton fawns with frisking pleasure range,
And chirping sparrows greet the welcome change :
* Not that their minds with greater skill are fraught,
Endu'd by instinct, or by reason taught,   150
The seasons operate on ev'ry breast ;
'Tis hence that fawns are brisk, and ladies drest.
When on his box the nodding coachman snores,
And dreams of fancy'd fares ; when tavern doors
The chairmen idly croud ; then ne'er refuse
To trust thy busie steps in thinner shoes.

Signs of rainy   But when the swinging signs your ears offend
Weather.   With creaking noise, then rainy floods impend ;
Soon shall the kennels swell with rapid streams,
And rush in muddy torrents to the *Thames.*   160
The bookseller, whose shop 's an open square,
Foresees the tempest, and with early care
Of learning strips the rails ; the rowing crew
To tempt a fare, cloath all their tilts in blue :
On hosiers poles depending stockings ty'd,
Flag with the slacken'd gale, from side to side ;

* *Haud equidem credo quia sit divinitus illis,*
  Ingenium, aut rerum fato prudentia major.   Virg. Georg. 1.

127–8 So *1730.*
          This knows the powder'd Footman, and with Care,
          Beneath his flapping Hat, secures his Hair. *1716, followed by 1720*
and 1731 : both the latter omit the comma after hat.
165 hosiers] hosier's *all early editions. The error is repeated in the Index.*

Church-monuments foretell the changing air ;
Then *Niobe* dissolves into a tear
And sweats with secret grief : you 'll hear the sounds
Of whistling winds, e'er kennels break their bounds ;   170
Ungrateful odours common-shores diffuse,
And dropping vaults distill unwholesome dews,
E'er the tiles rattle with the smoaking show'r,
And spouts on heedless men their torrents pour.

Superstition   All superstition from thy breast repel.
to be avoided. Let cred'lous boys, and prattling nurses tell,
How, if the festival of *Paul* be clear,
Plenty from lib'ral horn shall strow the year ;
When the dark skies dissolve in snow or rain,
The lab'ring hind shall yoke the steer in vain ;   180
But if the threat'ning winds in tempests roar,
Then war shall bathe her wasteful sword in gore.
How, if on *Swithin*'s feast the welkin lours,
And ev'ry penthouse streams with hasty show'rs,
Twice twenty days shall clouds their fleeces drain
And wash the pavement with incessant rain.
Let not such vulgar tales debase thy mind ;
Nor *Paul* nor *Swithin* rule the clouds and wind.

If you the precepts of the Muse despise,
And slight the faithful warning of the skies,   190
Others you 'll see, when all the town's afloat,
Wrapt in th' embraces of a kersey coat,
Or double-button'd frieze ; their guarded feet
Defie the muddy dangers of the street,
While you, with hat unloop'd, the fury dread
Of spouts high-streaming, and with cautious tread
Shun ev'ry dashing pool ; or idly stop,
To seek the kind protection of a shop.
But bus'ness summons ; now with hasty scud
You jostle for the wall ; the spatter'd mud   200
Hides all thy hose behind ; in vain you scow'r,
Thy wig alas ! uncurl'd, admits the show'r.
So fierce *Alecto*'s snaky tresses fell,
When *Orpheus* charm'd the rig'rous pow'rs of hell,
Or thus hung *Glaucus*' beard, with briny dew
Clotted and strait, when first his am'rous view
Surpriz'd the bathing fair ; the frighted maid
Now stands a rock, transform'd by *Circe*'s aid.

Implements   Good houswives all the winter's rage despise,
proper for   Defended by the riding-hood's disguise :   210
female   Or underneath th' umbrella's oily shed,
Walkers.   Safe thro' the wet, on clinking pattens tread.

---

168 tear] *1730* tear, *remainder.*   171 common-shores] common sewers *1730 and
so throughout.*   172 dews,] *1716* dews *remainder.*   186 pavement] *1730* pavements *remainder.*   201 scow'r] scour *1730.*   209 houswives] *2nd edition, 1720,
1731* Huswives *1st edition*   housewives *1730.*   212 wet,] *1730*   wet *remainder.*

Let *Persian* dames th' umbrella's ribs display,
To guard their beauties from the sunny ray;
Or sweating slaves support the shady load,
When eastern Monarchs show their state abroad;
Britain in winter only knows its aid,
To guard from chilly show'rs the walking maid.
But, O! forget not, Muse, the patten's praise,
That female implement shall grace thy lays;   220
Say from what art divine th' invention came,
And from its origine deduce the name.

An Episode   Where *Lincoln* wide extends her fenny soil,
of the Inven-   A goodly yeoman liv'd grown white with toil;
tion of Pattens. One only daughter bless'd his nuptial bed,
Who from her infant hand the poultry fed:
Martha (her careful mother's name) she bore,
But now her careful mother was no more.
Whilst on her father's knee the damsel play'd,
Patty he fondly call'd the smiling maid;   230
As years encreased, her ruddy beauty grew,
And *Patty*'s fame o'er all the village flew.

Soon as the gray-ey'd morning streaks the skies,
And in the doubtful day the woodcock flies,
Her cleanly pail the pretty houswife bears,
And singing, to the distant field repairs:
And when the plains with ev'ning dews are spread,
The milky burthen smoaks upon her head,
Deep, thro' a miry lane she pick'd her way,
Above her ankle rose the chalky clay.   240

Vulcan by chance the bloomy maiden spies,
With innocence and beauty in her eyes,
He saw, he lov'd; for yet he ne'er had known
Sweet innocence and beauty meet in one.
Ah *Mulciber*! recal thy nuptial vows,
Think on the graces of thy *Paphian* spouse,
Think how her eyes dart inexhausted charms,
And canst thou leave her bed for *Patty*'s arms?

The *Lemnian* Pow'r forsakes the realms above,
His bosom glowing with terrestrial love: 250
Far in the lane a lonely hut he found,
No tenant ventur'd on th' unwholesome ground.
Here smoaks his forge, he bares his sinewy arm,
And early strokes the sounding anvil warm;
Around his shop the steely sparkles flew,
As for the steed he shap'd the bending shoe.

When blue-ey'd *Patty* near his window came,
His anvil rests, his forge forgets to flame.
To hear his soothing tales she feigns delays;
What woman can resist the force of praise?   260

At first she coyly ev'ry kiss withstood,
And all her cheek was flush'd with modest blood
With headless nails he now surrounds her shoes,
To save her steps from rains and piercing dews ;
She lik'd his soothing tales, his presents wore,
And granted kisses, but would grant no more.
Yet winter chill'd her feet, with cold she pines,
And on her cheek the fading rose declines ;
No more her humid eyes their lustre boast,
And in hoarse sounds her melting voice is lost.   270
This *Vulcan* saw, and in his heav'nly thought,
A new machine mechanick fancy wrought,
Above the mire her shelter'd steps to raise,
And bear her safely through the wintry ways.
Strait the new engine on his anvil glows,
And the pale virgin on the patten rose.
No more her lungs are shook with drooping rheums,
And on her cheek reviving beauty blooms.
The God obtain'd his suit ; tho' flatt'ry fail,
Presents with female virtue must prevail.   280
The patten now supports each frugal dame,
Which from the blue-ey'd *Patty* takes the name.

BOOK II.

Of walking the Streets by Day.

THUS far the Muse has trac'd in useful lays,
The proper implements for wintry ways ;
Has taught the walker, with judicious eyes,
To read the various warnings of the skies.
Now venture, Muse, from home, to range the town,
And for the publick safety risque thy own.
The Morning.   For ease and for dispatch the morning 's best ;
No tides of passengers the street molest.
You'll see a draggled damsel, here and there,
From *Billingsgate* her fishy traffick bear ;   10
On doors the sallow milk-maid chalks her gains ;
Ah ! how unlike the milk-maid of the plains !
Before proud gates attending asses bray,
Or arrogate with solemn pace the way ;
These grave physicians with their milky chear
The love-sick maid and dwindling beau repair ;
Here rows of drummers stand in martial file,
And with their vellom thunder shake the pile,
To greet the new-made bride.   Are sounds like these
The proper prelude to a state of peace ?   20

5 home,] *1730*   home *remainder.*   7 dispatch] *1730*   dispatch, *remainder.*
15 chear] *1730*   chear, *remainder.*   18 vellom thunder] Vellom-Thunder *first*
edition only.

* D

Now industry awakes her busie sons,
Full charg'd with news the breathless hawker runs
Shops open, coaches roll, carts shake the ground,
And all the streets with passing cries resound.

What Trades   If cloath'd in black you tread the busy town,
prejudicial to Or if distinguish'd by the rev'rend gown,
Walkers.   Three trades avoid ; oft in the mingling press
The barber's apron soils the sable dress ;
Shun the perfumer's touch with cautious eye,
Nor let the baker's step advance too nigh.   30
Ye walkers too that youthful colours wear,
Three sullying trades avoid with equal care ;
The little chimney-sweeper skulks along,
And marks with sooty stains the heedless throng ;
When small-coal murmurs in the hoarser throat,
From smutty dangers guard thy threaten'd coat :
The dust-man's cart offends thy cloaths and eyes,
When through the street a cloud of ashes flies ;
But whether black or lighter dyes are worn,
The chandler's basket, on his shoulder born,   40
With tallow spots thy coat ; resign the way,
To shun the surly butcher's greasy tray,
Butchers, whose hands are dy'd with blood's foul stain,
And always foremost in the hangman's train.

To whom to   Let due civilities be strictly paid.
give the Wall. The wall surrender to the hooded maid ;
Nor let thy sturdy elbow's hasty rage
Jostle the feeble steps of trembling age :
And when the porter bends beneath his load,
And pants for breath ; clear thou the crouded road.   50
But, above all, the groping blind direct,
And from the pressing throng the lame protect.
You'll sometimes meet a fop, of nicest tread,
Whose mantling peruke veils his empty head,
At ev'ry step he dreads the wall to lose,
And risques, to save a coach, his red-heel'd shoes ;
Him, like the miller, pass with caution by,
Lest from his shoulder clouds of powder fly.

To whom to But when the bully, with assuming pace,
refuse the Cocks his broad hat, edg'd round with tarnish'd lace,   60
Wall. Yield not the way ; defie his strutting pride,
And thrust him to the muddy kennel's side ;
He never turns again, nor dares oppose,
But mutters coward curses as he goes.

Of whom to   If drawn by bus'ness to a street unknown,
enquire the Let the sworn porter point thee through the town ;
Way. Be sure observe the signs, for signs remain,
Like faithful land-marks to the walking train.

---

25 black] *1730*   black, *remainder.*   27 press] *1730*   press, *remainder.*
43 Butchers] Butcher's *Underhill.*   51 groping] groaping *first edition only.*
56 shoes ;] *first and third editions only*   shoes, *remainder.*

Seek not from prentices to learn the way,
Those fabling boys will turn thy steps astray;   70
Ask the grave tradesman to direct thee right,
He ne'er deceives, but when he profits by't.
    Where famed *St. Giles*'s ancient limits spread,
An inrail'd column rears its lofty head,
Here to sev'n streets sev'n dials count the day,
And from each other catch the circling ray.
Here oft the peasant, with enquiring face,
Bewilder'd, trudges on from place to place;
He dwells on ev'ry sign with stupid gaze,
Enters the narrow alley's doubtful maze,   80
Tries ev'ry winding court and street in vain,
And doubles o'er his weary steps again.
Thus hardy *Theseus*, with intrepid feet,
Travers'd the dang'rous labyrinth of *Crete*;
But still the wandring passes forc'd his stay,
Till *Ariadne*'s clue unwinds the way.
But do not thou, like that bold chief, confide
Thy ventrous footsteps to a female guide;
She'll lead thee with delusive smiles along,
Dive in thy fob, and drop thee in the throng.   90
Useful   When waggish boys the stunted beesom ply
Precepts.   To rid the slabby pavement; pass not by
E'er thou hast held their hands; some heedless flirt
Will over-spread thy calves with spatt'ring dirt.
Where porters hogsheads roll from carts aslope,
Or brewers down steep cellars stretch the rope,
Where counted billets are by carmen tost;
Stay thy rash step, and walk without the post.
    What though the gath'ring mire thy feet besmear,
The voice of industry is always near.   100
Hark! the boy calls thee to his destin'd stand,
And the shoe shines beneath his oily hand.
Here let the Muse, fatigu'd amid the throng,
Adorn her precepts with digressive song;
Of shirtless youths the secret rise to trace,
And show the parent of the sable race.
    Like mortal man, great *Jove* (grown fond of change)
Of old was wont this nether world to range
To seek amours; the vice the monarch lov'd
Soon through the wide etherial court improv'd,   110
And ev'n the proudest Goddess now and then
Would lodge a night among the sons of men;
To vulgar Deitys descends the fashion,
Each, like her betters, had her earthly passion.

75 streets] streets, *1716*.   79 sign] sign, *1716*.   83 *Theseus,*] 1716 *Theseus* remainder.   89 thee] thee, *1716.*   91 ply] ply, *1716.*   97 tost;] *1716* tost *1720*   tost, *1730 and 1731*.   99–220 *added in 1720, and retained in subsequent editions.*

Then *Cloaeina* (Goddess of the tide
Whose sable streams beneath the city glide)
Indulg'd the modish flame ; the town she rov'd,
A mortal scavenger she saw, she lov'd ;
The muddy spots that dry'd upon his face,
Like female patches, heighten'd ev'ry grace :   120
She gaz'd ; she sigh'd. For love can beauties spy
In what seems faults to every common eye.
   Now had the watchman walk'd his second round ;
When *Cloacina* hears the rumbling sound
Of her brown lover's cart, for well she knows
That pleasing thunder : swift the Goddess rose,
And through the streets pursu'd the distant noise,
Her bosom panting with expected joys.
With the night-wandring harlot's airs she past,
Brush'd near his side, and wanton glances cast ;   130
In the black form of cinder-wench she came,
When love, the hour, the place had banish'd shame ;
To the dark alley, arm in arm they move :
O may no link-boy interrupt their love !
   When the pale moon had nine times fill'd her space,
The pregnant Goddess (cautious of disgrace)
Descends to earth ; but sought no midwife's aid,
Nor midst her anguish to *Lucina* pray'd ;
No cheerful gossip wish'd the mother joy,
Alone, beneath a bulk, she dropt the boy.   140
   The child through various risques in years improv'd,
At first a beggar's brat, compassion mov'd ;
His infant tongue soon learnt the canting art,
Knew all the pray'rs and whines to touch the heart.
   Oh happy unown'd youths, your limbs can bear
The scorching dog-star, and the winter's air,
While the rich infant, nurs'd with care and pain,
Thirsts with each heat, and coughs with ev'ry rain !
   The Goddess long had mark'd the child's distress,
And long had sought his suff'rings to redress ;   150
She prays the Gods to take the fondling's part,
To teach his hands some beneficial art
Practis'd in streets : the Gods her suit allow'd,
And made him useful to the walking croud,
To cleanse the miry feet, and o'er the shoe
With nimble skill the glossy black renew :
Each Power contributes to relieve the poor :
With the strong bristles of the mighty boar

---

* Cloacina *was a Goddess whose image* Tatius (*a King of the* Sabines) *found in the
common-shore, and not knowing what Goddess it was, he called it* Cloacina *from
the place in which it was found, and paid to it divine honours.* Lactant. 1, 20.
Minuc. Fel. Oct. *p.* 232.

---

133 alley,] *1730* alley *remainder.*   140 bulk,] *1730* bulk *remainder.*

Diana forms his brush ; the God of day
A tripod gives, amid the crouded way   160
To raise the dirty foot, and ease his toil :
Kind *Neptune* fills his vase with fetid oil
Prest from th' enormous whale ; The God of fire,
From whose dominions smoaky clouds aspire,
Among these gen'rous presents joins his part,
And aids with soot the new japanning art :
Pleas'd she receives the gifts ; she downward glides,
Lights in *Fleet-ditch*, and shoots beneath the tides.
    Now dawns the morn, the sturdy lad awakes,
Leaps from his stall, his tangled hair he shakes,   173
Then leaning o'er the rails, he musing stood,
And view'd below the black canal of mud,
Where common-shores a lulling murmur keep,
Whose torrents rush from *Holborn*'s fatal steep :
Pensive through idleness, tears flow'd apace,
Which eas'd his loaded heart, and wash'd his face ;
At length he sighing cry'd ;   That boy was blest,
Whose infant lips have drain'd a mother's breast ;
But happier far are those, (if such be known)
Whom both a father and a mother own :   180
But I, alas ! hard fortune's utmost scorn,
Who ne'er knew parent, was an orphan born !
Some boys are rich by birth beyond all wants,
Belov'd by uncles, and kind good old aunts ;
When time comes round, a Christmas-box they bear,
And one day makes them rich for all the year.
Had I the precepts of a Father learn'd,
Perhaps I then the coach-man's fare had earn'd,
For lesser boys can drive ; I thirsty stand
And see the double flaggon charge their hand,   190
See them puff off the froth, and gulp amain,
While with dry tongue I lick my lips in vain.
    While thus he fervent prays, the heaving tide
In widen'd circles beats on either side ;
The Goddess rose amid the inmost round,
With wither'd turnip tops her temples crown'd ;
Low reach'd her dripping tresses, lank, and black
As the smooth jet, or glossy raven's back ;
Around her waste a circling eel was twin'd,
Which bound her robe that hung in rags behind.   200
Now beck'ning to the boy ; she thus begun,
Thy prayers are granted ; weep no more, my son :
Go thrive.   At some frequented corner stand,
This brush I give thee, grasp it in thy hand,
Temper the foot within this vase of oil,
And let the little tripod aid thy toil ;

206 the] thy *Underhill*.

On this methinks I see the walking crew
At thy request support the miry shoe,
The foot grows black that was with dirt imbrown'd,
And in thy pocket gingling halfpence sound.   210
The Goddess plunges swift beneath the flood,
And dashes all around her show'rs of mud :
The youth strait chose his post ; the labour ply'd
Where branching streets from *Charing-cross* divide ;
His treble voice resounds along the *Meuse*,
And *White-hall* echoes—*Clean your Honour's shoes.*

Useful
Precepts
(continued).

Like the sweet ballad, this amusing lay
Too long detains the walker on his way ;
While he attends, new dangers round him throng ;
The busy city asks instructive song.   220
    Where elevated o'er the gaping croud,
Clasp'd in the board the perjur'd head is bow'd,
Betimes retreat ; here, thick as hailstones pour
Turnips, and half-hatch'd eggs, (a mingled show'r)
Among the rabble rain : Some random throw
May with the trickling yolk thy cheek o'erflow.

Of narrow
Streets.

Though expedition bids, yet never stray
Where no rang'd posts defend the rugged way.
Here laden carts with thundring waggons meet,
Wheels clash with wheels, and bar the narrow street ;   230
The lashing whip resounds, the horses strain,
And blood in anguish bursts the swelling vein.
O barb'rous men, your cruel breasts asswage,
Why vent ye on the gen'rous steed your rage ?
Does not his service earn your daily bread ?
Your wives, your children by his labours fed !
If, as the *Samian* taught, the soul revives,
And, shifting seats, in other bodies lives ;
Severe shall be the brutal coachman's change,
Doom'd in a hackney horse the town to range :   240
Carmen, transform'd, the groaning load shall draw,
Whom other tyrants with the lash shall awe.

The most
inconvenient
Streets to
Walkers.

Who would of *Watling-street* the dangers share,
When the broad pavement of *Cheap-side* is near ?
Or who * that rugged street would traverse o'er,
That stretches, O *Fleet-ditch*, from thy black shore
To the *Tow'r's* moated walls ?   Here steams ascend
That, in mix'd fumes, the wrinkled nose offend.
Where chandlers cauldrons boil ; where fishy prey
Hide the wet stall, long absent from the sea ;   250
And where the cleaver chops the heifer's spoil,
And where huge hogsheads sweat with trainy oil,

----

* *Thames-street.*

223 pour] *1730* pour, *remainder.*   240 Doom'd, in a *Hackney* horse, the Town
to range : *1st edition.*   Doom'd, in a hackney horse the town to range : *2nd edition.*
242 Tyrants, with the lash, shall awe. *1716.*

Thy breathing nostril hold ; but how shall I
Pass, where in piles † *Cornavian* cheeses lye ;
Cheese, that the table's closing rites denies,
And bids me with th' unwilling chaplain rise.

The Pell-mell celebrated.

   O bear me to the paths of fair *Pell-mell*,
Safe are thy pavements, grateful is thy smell !
At distance rolls along the gilded coach,
Nor sturdy carmen on thy walks encroach ;   260
No lets would bar thy ways were chairs deny'd
The soft supports of laziness and pride ;
Shops breathe perfumes, thro' sashes ribbons glow,
The mutual arms of ladies, and the beau.
Yet still ev'n here, when rains the passage hide,
Oft' the loose stone spirts up a muddy tide
Beneath thy careless foot ; and from on high,
Where masons mount the ladder, fragments fly ;
Mortar, and crumbled lime in show'rs descend,
And o'er thy head destructive tiles impend.   270

The Pleasure of walking through an Alley.

   But sometimes let me leave the noisie roads,
And silent wander in the close abodes
Where wheels ne'er shake the ground ; there pensive stray,
In studious thought, the long uncrouded way.
Here I remark each walker's diff'rent face,
And in their look their various bus'ness trace.
The broker here his spacious beaver wears,
Upon his brow sit jealousies and cares ;
Bent on some mortgage (to avoid reproach)
He seeks bye streets, and saves th' expensive coach.   280
Soft, at low doors, old letchers tap their cane,
For fair recluse, who travels *Drury-lane* ;
Here roams uncomb'd the lavish rake, to shun
His *Fleet-street* draper's everlasting dun.

Inconveniences that attend those who are unacquainted with the Town.

   Careful observers, studious of the town,
Shun the misfortunes that disgrace the clown ;
Untempted, they contemn the jugler's feats,
Pass by the *Meuse*, nor try the * thimble's cheats.
When drays bound high, they never cross behind,
Where bubbling yest is blown by gusts of wind :   290
And when up *Ludgate-hill* huge carts move slow,
Far from the straining steeds securely go,
Whose dashing hoofs behind them fling the mire,
And mark with muddy blots the gazing 'squire.
The *Parthian* thus his jav'lin backward throws,
And as he flies infests pursuing foes.

† Cheshire *anciently so called.*
* *A Cheat commonly practis'd in the streets with three thimbles and a little ball.*

257 *Pell-mell*] Pall-mall *1730.*   282 who] that *1716.* *Drury-lane* ;] *Drury-lane.*
first edition Drury-lane, *second edition.*   283 uncomb'd] uncomb'd, *1716.*   292
steeds] Steeds, *1716.*   294 And mark, with muddy Blots, the gazing 'Squire.
1716.   296 flies] flies, *1716.*

The thoughtless wits shall frequent forfeits pay,
Who 'gainst the centry's box discharge their tea.
Do thou some court, or secret corner seek,
Nor flush with shame the passing virgin's cheek.   300

Precepts
vulgarly
known.

Yet let me not descend to trivial song,
Nor vulgar circumstance my verse prolong;
Why should I teach the maid when torrents pour,
Her head to shelter from the sudden show'r?
Nature will best her ready hand inform,
With her spread petticoat to fence the storm.
Does not each walker know the warning sign,
When wisps of straw depend upon the twine
Cross the close street; that then the paver's art
Renews the ways, deny'd to coach and cart?   310
Who knows not that the coachman lashing by,
Oft' with his flourish cuts the heedless eye;
And when he takes his stand, to wait a fare,
His horses foreheads shun the winter's air?
Nor will I roam when summer's sultry rays
Parch the dry ground, and spread with dust the ways;
With whirling gusts the rapid atoms rise,
Smoak o'er the pavement, and involve the skies.

Frosty
Weather.

Winter my theme confines; whose nitry wind
Shall crust the slabby mire, and kennels bind;   320
She bids the snow descend in flaky sheets,
And in her hoary mantle cloath the streets.
Let not the virgin tread these slipp'ry roads,
The gath'ring fleece the hollow patten loads;
But if thy footsteps slide with clotted frost,
Strike off the breaking balls against the post.
On silent wheel the passing coaches roll;
Oft' look behind, and ward the threatning pole.
In harden'd orbs the school-boy moulds the snow,
To mark the coachman with a dext'rous throw.   330
Why do ye, boys, the kennel's surface spread,
To tempt with faithless pass the matron's tread?
How can ye laugh to see the damsel spurn,
Sink in your frauds, and her green stocking mourn?
At *White*'s the harness'd chairman idly stands,
And swings around his waste his tingling hands:
The sempstress speeds to '*Change* with red-tipt nose:
The *Belgian* stove beneath her footstool glows;
In half-whipt muslin needles useless lie,
And shuttle-cocks across the counter fly.   340

302 Nor] Not *first edition only.*   311 not] not, *1716.*   312 Oft', with his
flourish, cuts *1716.*   315 roam] *1730* roam, *remainder.*   317 gusts] gusts, *1716.*
319 *Frosty weather.* This side-heading is omitted from the second edition.   333
laugh] laugh, *1716.*   334 frauds,] frauds *1716.*   335 *White*'s] White's, *1716.*
336 And swings, around his Waste, his tingling Hands: *1716.*   338 glows;] glows,
1716.

These sports warm harmless ; why then will ye prove,
Deluded maids, the dang'rous flame of love ?

The Dangers   Where *Covent-Garden's* famous temple stands,
of Foot-ball. That boasts the work of *Jones'* immortal hands ;
Columns with plain magnificence appear,
And graceful porches lead along the square :
Here oft' my course I bend, when lo ! from far
I spy the furies of the foot-ball war :
The 'prentice quits his shop, to join the crew,
Encreasing crouds the flying game pursue.   350
Thus, as you roll the ball o'er snowy ground,
The gath'ring globe augments with ev'ry round.
But whither shall I run ? the throng draws nigh,
The ball now skims the street, now soars on high ;
The dext'rous glazier strong returns the bound,
And gingling sashes on the pent-house sound.

An Episode   O roving Muse, recal that wond'rous year,
of the great When winter reign'd in bleak *Britannia's* air ;
Frost.   When hoary *Thames*, with frosted oziers crown'd,
Was three long moons in icy fetters bound.   360
The waterman, forlorn along the shore,
Pensive reclines upon his useless oar,
Sees harness'd steeds desert the stony town,
And wander roads unstable, not their own :
Wheels o'er the harden'd waters smoothly glide,
And rase with whiten'd tracks the slipp'ry tide.
Here the fat cook piles high the blazing fire,
And scarce the spit can turn the steer entire.
Booths sudden hide the *Thames*, long streets appear,
And num'rous games proclaim the crouded fair.   370
So when a gen'ral bids the martial train
Spread their encampment o'er the spacious plain ;
Thick-rising tents a canvas city build,
And the loud dice resound thro' all the field.
'Twas here the matron found a doleful fate :
Let elegiac lay the woe relate,
Soft as the breath of distant flutes, at hours
When silent evening closes up the flow'rs ;
Lulling as falling water's hollow noise ;
Indulging grief, like *Philomela's* voice.   380
Doll ev'ry day had walk'd these treach'rous roads ;
Her neck grew warpt beneath autumnal loads
Of various fruit ; she now a basket bore,
That head, alas ! shall basket bear no more.

345 Columns, with plain magnificence, appear, *1716*.   346 along] around *first edition only, corrected in the Errata to* along.   347 far] *1730*   far, *remainder*. 363 town,] *1730*   town ; *remainder*.   375 *So printed in second and subsequent editions. In the first edition this line does not begin a new paragraph.*   377 Soft, as the breath of distant flutes, at hours, *1716*.   379 Lulling,] *1716*.

*   D 3

Each booth she frequent past, in quest of gain,
And boys with pleasure heard her shrilling strain.
Ah *Doll* ! all mortals must resign their breath,
And industry it self submit to death !
The cracking crystal yields, she sinks, she dyes,
Her head, chopt off, from her lost shoulders flies ;   390
Pippins she cry'd, but death her voice confounds,
And pip-pip-pip along the ice resounds.
So when the *Thracian* furies *Orpheus* tore,
And left his bleeding trunk deform'd with gore,
His sever'd head floats down the silver tide,
His yet warm tongue for his lost consort cry'd ;
Eurydice with quiv'ring voice he mourn'd,
And *Heber*'s banks *Eurydice* return'd.

A Thaw.
But now the western gale the flood unbinds,
And black'ning clouds move on with warmer winds.   400
The wooden town its frail foundation leaves,
And *Thames*' full urn rolls down his plenteous waves ;
From ev'ry penthouse streams the fleeting snow,
And with dissolving frost the pavements flow.

How to know
the Days of
the Week.
Experienc'd men, inur'd to city ways,
Need not the Calendar to count their days.
When through the town with slow and solemn air,
Led by the nostril, walks the muzled bear ;
Behind him moves majestically dull,
The pride of *Hockley-hole*, the surly bull ;   410
Learn hence the periods of the week to name,
Mondays and *Thursdays* are the days of game.
When fishy stalls with double store are laid ;
The golden-belly'd carp, the broad-finn'd maid,
Red-speckled trouts, the salmon's silver joul,
The joynted lobster, and unscaly soale,
And luscious 'scallops, to allure the tastes
Of rigid zealots to delicious fasts ;
Wednesdays and *Fridays* you 'll observe from hence,
Days, when our sires were doom'd to abstinence.   420
When dirty waters from balconies drop,
And dext'rous damsels twirle the sprinkling mop,
And cleanse the spatter'd sash, and scrub the stairs ;
Know *Saturday*'s conclusive morn appears.

Remarks on
the Crys of
the Town.
Successive crys the seasons' change declare,
And mark the monthly progress of the year.
Hark, how the streets with treble voices ring,
To sell the bounteous product of the spring !
Sweet-smelling flow'rs, and elder's early bud,
With nettle's tender shoots, to cleanse the blood :   430

393 *This line in 1731 begins a paragraph.*   397 *Eurydice,* with quiv'ring Voice,
he mourn'd, *1716.*   400 move] roll *first edition only, corrected in the Errata to* move.
406 Calendar] *Calendar* first edition   calendar *second edition*   Kalendar *1730.*
407 town] town, *first edition only.*   429 elder's] elders *1716.*

And when *June*'s thunder cools the sultry skies,
Ev'n *Sundays* are prophan'd by mackrell cries.
   Wallnuts the fruit'rer's hand, in autumn, stain,
Blue plumbs and juicy pears augment his gain ;
Next oranges the longing boys entice,
To trust their copper fortunes to the dice.

Of Christmas.   When rosemary, and bays, the Poet's crown,
Are bawl'd, in frequent cries, through all the town,
Then judge the festival of *Christmas* near,
Christmas, the joyous period of the year.   440
Now with bright holly all your temples strow,
With lawrel green, and sacred misletoe.
Now, heav'n-born Charity, thy blessings shed ;
Bid meagre Want uprear her sickly head :
Bid shiv'ring limbs be warm ; let plenty's bowle
In humble roofs make glad the needy soul.
See, see, the heav'n-born maid her blessings shed ;
Lo ! meagre Want uprears her sickly head ;
Cloath'd are the naked, and the needy glad,
While selfish Avarice alone is sad.   450

Precepts of   Proud coaches pass, regardless of the moan
Charity.   Of infant orphans, and the widow's groan ;
While Charity still moves the walker's mind,
His lib'ral purse relieves the lame and blind.
Judiciously thy half-pence are bestow'd,
Where the laborious beggar sweeps the road.
Whate'er you give, give ever at demand,
Nor let old-age long stretch his palsy'd hand.
Those who give late, are importun'd each day,
And still are teaz'd because they still delay.   460
If e'er the miser durst his farthings spare,
He thinly spreads them through the publick square,
Where, all beside the rail, rang'd beggars lie,
And from each other catch the doleful cry ;
With heav'n, for two-pence, cheaply wipes his score,
Lifts up his eyes, and hasts to beggar more.
   Where the brass knocker, wrapt in flannel band,
Forbids the thunder of the footman's hand ;
Th' upholder, rueful harbinger of death,
Waits with impatience for the dying breath ;   470
As vultures, o'er a camp, with hov'ring flight,
Snuff up the future carnage of the fight.
Here canst thou pass, unmindful of a pray'r,
That heav'n in mercy may thy brother spare ?
   Come, F***, sincere, experienc'd friend,
Thy briefs, thy deeds, and ev'n thy fees suspend ;

---

434 plumbs] Plumbs, *1716.*   445-6 let Plenty's Bowle, | In humble Roofs, *1716.*
460 teaz'd] *1730 and 1731*   teaz'd, *remainder.*   470 Waits, with Impatience, *1716.*
475 F***] i.e. *Fortescue.*

Come let us leave the *Temple*'s silent walls,
Me bus'ness to my distant lodging calls :
Through the long *Strand* together let us stray :
With thee conversing, I forget the way.   480
Behold that narrow street which steep descends,
Whose building to the slimy shore extends ;
Here *Arundel*'s fam'd structure rear'd its frame,
The street alone retains an empty name :
Where *Titian*'s glowing paint the canvas warm'd,
And *Raphael*'s fair design, with judgment, charm'd,
Now hangs the bell'man's song, and pasted here
The colour'd prints of *Overton* appear.
Where statues breath'd, the work of *Phidias*' hands,
A wooden pump, or lonely watch-house stands.   490
There *Essex*' stately pile adorn'd the shore,
There *Cecil*'s, *Bedford*'s, *Villers*', now no more.
Yet *Burlington*'s fair palace still remains ;
Beauty within, without proportion reigns.
Beneath his eye declining art revives,
The wall with animated picture lives ;
There *Hendel* strikes the strings, the melting strain
Transports the soul, and thrills through ev'ry vein;
There oft' I enter (but with cleaner shoes)
For *Burlington* 's belov'd by ev'ry Muse.   500

The   O ye associate walkers, O my friends,
Happiness of Upon your state what happiness attends !
Walkers.   What, though no coach to frequent visit rolls,
Nor for your shilling chairmen sling their poles ;
Yet still your nerves rheumatic pains defye,
Nor lazy jaundice dulls your saffron eye ;
No wasting cough discharges sounds of death,
Nor wheezing asthma heaves in vain for breath ;
Nor from your restless couch is heard the groan
Of burning gout, or sedentary stone.   510
Let others in the jolting coach confide,
Or in the leaky boat the *Thames* divide ;
Or, box'd within the chair, contemn the street,
And trust their safety to another's feet,
Still let me walk ; for oft' the sudden gale
Ruffles the tide, and shifts the dang'rous sail.
Then shall the passenger too late deplore
The whelming billow, and the faithless oar ;
The drunken chairman in the kennel spurns,
The glasses shatters, and his charge o'erturns.   520
Who can recount the coach's various harms,
The legs disjointed, and the broken arms ?

---

477 Come] Come, *1716*.   479 stray :] stray, *1716*.   480 conversing,] *1716*
and 1730 conversing *remainder*.   481 street] Street, *1716*.   487 here] here,
1716.   492 *Villers*'] *Viller*'s 1716.   516 sail.] sail, *first edition only*.

I've seen a beau, in some ill-fated hour,
When o'er the stones choak'd kennels swell the show'r
In gilded chariot loll ; he with disdain
Views spatter'd passengers all drench'd in rain ;
With mud fill'd high, the rumbling cart draws near,
Now rule thy prancing steeds, lac'd charioteer !
The dust-man lashes on with spiteful rage,
His pond'rous spokes thy painted wheel engage,.   530
Crush'd is thy pride, down falls the shrieking beau,
The slabby pavement crystal fragments strow,
Black floods of mire th' embroider'd coat disgrace,
And mud enwraps the honours of his face.
So when dread *Jove* the son of *Phœbus* hurl'd,
Scarr'd with dark thunder, to the nether world ;
The headstrong coursers tore the silver reins,
And the sun's beamy ruin gilds the plains.
    If the pale walker pant with weak'ning ills,
His sickly hand is stor'd with friendly bills :   540
From hence he learns the seventh-born doctor's fame,
From hence he learns the cheapest tailor's name.
    Shall the large mutton smoak upon your boards ?
Such, *Newgate*'s copious market best affords.
Would'st thou with mighty beef augment thy meal ?
Seek *Leaden-hall* ; *St. James*'s sends thee veal.
Thames-street gives cheeses ; *Covent-garden* fruits ;
Moor-fields old books ; and *Monmouth-street* old suits.
Hence may'st thou well supply the wants of life,
Support thy family, and cloath thy wife.   550
    Volumes on shelter'd stalls expanded lye,
And various science lures the learned eye ;
The bending shelves with pond'rous scholiasts groan,
And deep divines to modern shops unknown :
Here, like the bee, that on industrious wing
Collects the various odours of the spring,
Walkers, at leisure, learning's flow'rs may spoil,
Nor watch the wasting of the midnight oil,
May morals snatch from *Plutarch*'s tatter'd page,
A mildew'd *Bacon*, or *Stagyra*'s sage.   560
Here saunt'ring prentices o'er *Otway* weep,
O'er *Congreve* smile, or over *D* * * sleep ;
Pleas'd sempstresses the *Lock*'s fam'd *Rape* unfold,
And * *Squirts* read *Garth*, 'till apozems grow cold.
    O *Lintot*, let my labours obvious lie,
Rang'd on thy stall, for ev'ry curious eye ;

* *The name of an Apothecary's boy, in the Poem of the* Dispensary.

---

525 disdain] Disdain, *1716*.   526 passengers] Passengers, *1716*.   535 *Jove*]
Jove, first edition only.   541 From hence] From hence, *first edition only*.   551
Volumes] *1730* Volumes, *remainder*.   stalls] Stalls, *first edition only*.   555 wing]
Wing, *1716*.   562 *D***] i.e. *Dennis. Briscoe reads* D'Urfey.

So shall the poor these precepts *gratis* know,
And to my verse their future safeties owe.
   What walker shall his mean ambition fix
On the false lustre of a coach and six ?   570
Let the vain virgin, lur'd by glaring show,
Sigh for the liv'ries of th' embroider'd beau.
   See yon bright chariot on its braces swing,
With *Flanders* mares, and on an arched spring ;
That wretch, to gain an equipage and place,
Betray'd his sister to a lewd embrace.
This coach, that with the blazon'd 'scutcheon glows,
Vain of his unknown race, the coxcomb shows.
Here the brib'd lawyer, sunk in velvet, sleeps ;
The starving orphan, as he passes, weeps ;   580
There flames a fool, begirt with tinsell'd slaves,
Who wastes the wealth of a whole race of knaves.
That other, with a clustring train behind,
Owes his new honours to a sordid mind.
This next in court-fidelity excells,
The publick rifles, and his country sells.
May the proud chariot never be my fate,
If purchas'd at so mean, so dear a rate ;
O rather give me sweet content on foot,
Wrapt in my virtue, and a good *Surtout* !   590

567 *gratis*] *first edition only*   gratis *remainder.*   569 fix] fix, *1716.*   573
braces] *1730 and 1731*   harness *the earlier editions.*   574 spring ;] spring, *first edition
only.*   575 wretch,] *first edition only*   wretch *remainder.*   577 coach,] *1716*
coach *remainder.*   585 court-fidelity] Court Fidelity *1716.*

BOOK III.

Of walking the Streets by Night.

O *TRIVIA*, Goddess, leave these low abodes,
And traverse o'er the wide ethereal roads,
Celestial Queen, put on thy robes of light,
Now *Cynthia* nam'd, fair regent of the Night.
At sight of thee the villain sheaths his sword,
Nor scales the wall, to steal the wealthy hoard.
O may thy silver lamp from heav'n's high bow'r
Direct my footsteps in the midnight hour !
The Evening.   When night first bids the twinkling stars appear,
Or with her cloudy vest inwraps the air,   10
Then swarms the busie street ; with caution tread,
Where the shop-windows falling threat thy head ;

1 *Trivia*,] 1716   *Trivia remainder.*   5 thee] thee, *1716.*   7 O] Oh ! *1716.*
from] in *1716.*   8 hour !] Hour. *1716.*

Now lab'rers home return, and join their strength
To bear the tott'ring plank, or ladder's length ;
Still fix thy eyes intent upon the throng,
And as the passes open, wind along.

Of the Pass
of St. Cle-
ment's.

Where the fair columns of *St. Clement* stand,
Whose straiten'd bounds encroach upon the *Strand* ;
Where the low penthouse bows the walker's head,
And the rough pavement wounds the yielding tread ;   20
Where not a post protects the narrow space,
And strung in twines, combs dangle in thy face ;
Summon at once thy courage, rouze thy care,
Stand firm, look back, be resolute, beware.
Forth issuing from steep lanes, the collier's steeds
Drag the black load ; another cart succeeds,
Team follows team, crouds heap'd on crouds appear,
And wait impatient, 'till the road grow clear.
Now all the pavement sounds with trampling feet,
And the mixt hurry barricades the street.   30
Entangled here, the waggon's lengthen'd team
Cracks the tough harness ; here a pond'rous beam
Lies over-turn'd athwart ; for slaughter fed
Here lowing bullocks raise their horned head.
Now oaths grow loud, with coaches coaches jar,
And the smart blow provokes the sturdy war ;
From the high box they whirl the thong around,
And with the twining lash their shins resound :
Their rage ferments, more dang'rous wounds they try,
And the blood gushes down their painful eye.   40
And now on foot the frowning warriors light,
And with their pond'rous fists renew the fight ;
Blow answers blow, their cheeks are smear'd with blood,
'Till down they fall, and grappling roll in mud.
So when two boars, in wild * *Ytene* bred,
Or on *Westphalia's* fatt'ning chest-nuts fed,
Gnash their sharp tusks, and rous'd with equal fire,
Dispute the reign of some luxurious mire ;
In the black flood they wallow o'er and o'er,
'Till their arm'd jaws distil with foam and gore.   50

Of Pick-
Pockets.

Where the mob gathers, swiftly shoot along,
Nor idly mingle in the noisy throng.
Lur'd by the silver hilt, amid the swarm,
The subtil artist will thy side disarm.
Nor is thy flaxen wigg with safety worn ;
High on the shoulder, in a basket born,
Lurks the sly boy ; whose hand to rapine bred,
Plucks off the curling honours of thy head.

* New Forest *in* Hampshire, *antiently so called.*

---

32 Cracks] Crack *first edition only.*   33 fed] fed, *first edition only.*   56 a] the
1716.   born,] *1716* born *remainder.*   58 thy] the *1716.*

Here dives the skulking thief with practis'd slight,
And unfelt fingers make thy pocket light.   60
Where 's now thy watch, with all its trinkets, flown ?
And thy late snuff-box is no more thy own.
But lo ! his bolder theft some tradesman spies,
Swift from his prey the scudding lurcher flies ;
Dext'rous he 'scapes the coach with nimble bounds,
Whilst ev'ry honest tongue *stop thief* resounds.
So speeds the wily fox, alarm'd by fear,
Who lately filch'd the turkey's callow care ;
Hounds following hounds grow louder as he flies,
And injur'd tenants joyn the hunter's cries.   70
Breathless he stumbling falls : Ill-fated boy !
Why did not honest work thy youth employ ?
Seiz'd by rough hands, he 's dragg'd amid the rout,
And stretch'd beneath the pump's incessant spout :
Or plung'd in miry ponds, he gasping lies,
Mud choaks his mouth, and plaisters o'er his eyes.

Of Ballad-   Let not the ballad-singer's shrilling strain
Singers.   Amid the swarm thy list'ning ear detain :
Guard well thy pocket ; for these *Syrens* stand
To aid the labours of the diving hand ;   80
Confed'rate in the cheat, they draw the throng,
And cambrick handkerchiefs reward the song.
But soon as coach or cart drives rattling on,
The rabble part, in shoals they backward run.
So *Jove's* loud bolts the mingled war divide,
And *Greece* and *Troy* retreat on either side.

Of walking   If the rude throng pour on with furious pace,
with a Friend. And hap to break thee from a friend's embrace,
Stop short ; nor struggle through the croud in vain,
But watch with careful eye the passing train.   90
Yet I (perhaps too fond) if chance the tide
Tumultuous bear my partner from my side,
Impatient venture back ; despising harm,
I force my passage where the thickest swarm.
Thus his lost bride the *Trojan* sought in vain
Through night, and arms, and flames, and hills of slain.
Thus *Nisus* wander'd o'er the pathless grove,
To find the brave companion of his love,
The pathless grove in vain he wanders o'er :
Euryalus, alas ! is now no more.   100

Of inadvertent   That walker, who regardless of his pace,
Walkers.   Turns oft' to pore upon the damsel's face,
From side to side by thrusting elbows tost,
Shall strike his aking breast against the post ;

59 thief] *1730* thief, *remainder.*   63 theft] *1730* thefts *remainder.*   65
coach] coach, *1716.*   69 hounds] *1730* hounds, *remainder.*   79 stand] *1730*
stand, *remainder.*   92 Tumultuous] *1730* Tumultuous, *remainder.*   bear] bears
1716.   100 *Euryalus,*] *Euryalus* 1716.

Or water, dash'd from fishy stalls, shall stain
His hapless coat with spirts of scaly rain.
But if unwarily he chance to stray,
Where twirling turnstiles intercept the way,
The thwarting passenger shall force them round,
And beat the wretch half breathless to the ground.   110

*Useful
Precepts.*
 Let constant vigilance thy footsteps guide,
And wary circumspection guard thy side ;
Then shalt thou walk unharm'd the dang'rous night,
Nor need th' officious link-boy's smoaky light.
Thou never wilt attempt to cross the road,
Where alehouse benches rest the porter's load,
Grievous to heedless shins ; no barrow's wheel,
That bruises oft' the truant school-boy's heel,
Behind thee rolling, with insidious pace,
Shall mark thy stocking with a miry trace.   120
Let not thy vent'rous steps approach too nigh,
Where gaping wide, low steepy cellars lie ;
Should thy shoe wrench aside, down, down you fall,
And overturn the scolding huckster's stall,
The scolding huckster shall not o'er thee moan,
But pence exact for nuts and pears o'erthrown.

*Safety first
of all to be
consider'd.*
 Though you through cleanlier allies wind by day,
To shun the hurries of the publick way,
Yet ne'er to those dark paths by night retire ;
Mind only safety, and contemn the mire.   130
Then no impervious courts thy haste detain,
Nor sneering ale-wives bid thee turn again.

*The Danger
of crossing
a Square by
Night.*
 Where *Lincoln's-Inn*, wide space, is rail'd around,
Cross not with vent'rous step ; there oft' is found
The lurking thief, who while the day-light shone,
Made the walls eccho with his begging tone :
That crutch which late compassion mov'd, shall wound
Thy bleeding head, and fell thee to the ground.
Though thou art tempted by the link-man's call,
Yet trust him not along the lonely wall ;   140
In the mid-way he 'll quench the flaming brand,
And share the booty with the pilf'ring band.
Still keep the publick streets, where oily rays
Shot from the crystal lamp, o'erspread the ways.

*The Happi-
ness of
London.*
 Happy *Augusta* ! law-defended town !
Here no dark lanthorns shade the villain's frown ;
No *Spanish* jealousies thy lanes infest,
Nor *Roman* vengeance stabs th' unwary breast ;
Here tyranny ne'er lifts her purple hand,
But liberty and justice guard the land ;   150
No bravos here profess the bloody trade,
Nor is the church the murd'rer's refuge made.

Of Chairmen.
 Let not the chairman, with assuming stride,
Press near the wall, and rudely thrust thy side :

The laws have set him bounds ; his servile feet
Should ne'er encroach where posts defend the street.
Yet who the footman's arrogance can quell,
Whose flambeau gilds the sashes of *Pell-mell*,
When in long rank a train of torches flame,
To light the midnight visits of the dame ?   160
Others, perhaps, by happier guidance led,
May where the chairman rests, with safety tread ;
Whene'er I pass, their poles unseen below,
Make my knee tremble with the jarring blow.

Of crossing the Street.
    If wheels bar up the road, where streets are crost,
With gentle words the coachman's ear accost :
He ne'er the threat, or harsh command obeys,
But with contempt the spatter'd shoe surveys.
Now man with utmost fortitude thy soul,
To cross the way where carts and coaches roll ;   170
Yet do not in thy hardy skill confide,
Nor rashly risque the kennel's spacious stride ;
Stay till afar the distant wheel you hear,
Like dying thunder in the breaking air ;
Thy foot will slide upon the miry stone,
And passing coaches crush thy tortur'd bone,
Or wheels enclose the road ; on either hand
Pent round with perils, in the midst you stand,
And call for aid in vain ; the coachman swears,
And car-men drive, unmindful of thy prayers.   180
Where wilt thou turn ? ah ! whither wilt thou fly ?
On ev'ry side the pressing spokes are nigh.
So sailors, while *Carybdis'* gulph they shun,
Amaz'd, on *Scylla's* craggy dangers run.

Of Oysters.
    Be sure observe where brown *Ostrea* stands,
Who boasts her shelly ware from *Wallfleet* sands ;
There may'st thou pass, with safe unmiry feet,
Where the rais'd pavement leads athwart the street.
If where *Fleet-ditch* with muddy current flows,
You chance to roam ; where oyster-tubs in rows   190
Are rang'd beside the posts ; there stay thy haste,
And with the sav'ry fish indulge thy taste :
The damsel's knife the gaping shell commands,
While the salt liquor streams between her hands.
    The man had sure a palate cover'd o'er
With brass or steel, that on the rocky shore
First broke the oozy oyster's pearly coat,
And risqu'd the living morsel down his throat.
What will not lux'ry taste ? Earth, sea, and air
Are daily ransack'd for the bill of fare.   200
Blood stuff'd in skins is *British* christians food,
And *France* robs marshes of the croaking brood ;

158 *Pell-mell*,] *Pell-mell* ? 1716 *Pall-mall*, 1730.   183 *Carybdis'* gulph] *Charybdis'* Gulphs *first edition only.*   201 christians] christian's *all early editions* christians' *Underhill.*

Spongy morells in strong ragousts are found,
And in the soupe the slimy snail is drown'd.

Observations concerning keeping the Wall.

When from high spouts the dashing torrents fall,
Ever be watchful to maintain the wall;
For should'st thou quit thy ground, the rushing throng
Will with impetuous fury drive along;
All press to gain those honours thou hast lost,
And rudely shove thee far without the post.   210
Then to retrieve the shed you strive in vain,
Draggled all o'er, and soak'd in floods of rain.
Yet rather bear the show'r, and toils of mud,
Than in the doubtful quarrel risque thy blood.
O think on *OEdipus'* detested state,
And by his woes be warn'd to shun thy fate.
Where three roads join'd, he met his sire unknown;
(Unhappy sire, but more unhappy son !)
Each claim'd the way, their swords the strife decide,
The hoary monarch fell, he groan'd and dy'd !   220
Hence sprung the fatal plague that thin'd thy reign,
Thy cursed incest ! and thy children slain !
Hence wert thou doom'd in endless night to stray
Through *Theban* streets, and cheerless groap thy way.

Of a Funeral.

Contemplate, mortal, on thy fleeting years;
See, with black train the funeral pomp appears!
Whether some heir attends in sable state,
And mourns with outward grief a parent's fate;
Or the fair virgin, nipt in beauty's bloom,
A croud of lovers follow to her tomb.   230
Why is the herse with 'scutcheons blazon'd round,
And with the nodding plume of Ostrich crown'd ?
No : The dead know it not, nor profit gain;
It only serves to prove the living vain.
How short is life ! how frail is human trust !
Is all this pomp for laying dust to dust ?

Of avoiding Paint.

Where the nail'd hoop defends the painted stall,
Brush not thy sweeping skirt too near the wall;
Thy heedless sleeve will drink the colour'd oil,
And spot indelible thy pocket soil.   240
Has not wise nature strung the legs and feet
With firmest nerves, design'd to walk the street ?
Has she not given us hands, to groap aright,
Amidst the frequent dangers of the night ?
And think'st thou not the double nostril meant,

Of various Cheats formerly in practice.

To warn from oily woes by previous scent ?
Who can the various city frauds recite,
With all the petty rapines of the night ?

203 morells . . . ragousts] *Morells . . . Ragousts* first edition only.
215 *In 1730 this line begins the new paragraph, instead of l.* 217.
243 groap] *first edition only* grope *remainder.   But see l.* 224.
247 In the editions without side-headings is the foot-note *Various cheats formerly in practice.*

Who now the Guinea-dropper's bait regards,
Trick'd by the sharper's dice, or juggler's cards ?   250
Why should I warn thee ne'er to join the fray,
Where the sham-quarrel interrupts the way ?
Lives there in these our days so soft a clown,
Brav'd by the bully's oaths, or threat'ning frown ?
I need not strict enjoyn the pocket's care,
When from the crouded play thou lead'st the fair ;
Who has not here, or watch, or snuff-box lost,
Or handkerchiefs that *India*'s shuttle boast ?

An Admoni-   O ! may thy virtue guard thee through the roads
tion to Virtue. Of *Drury*'s mazy courts, and dark abodes,   260
The harlots guileful paths, who nightly stand,
Where *Katherine-street* descends into the *Strand*.
Say, vagrant Muse, their wiles and subtil arts,
To lure the strangers unsuspecting hearts ;
So shall our youth on healthful sinews tread,
And city cheeks grow warm with rural red.

How to know   'Tis she who nightly strowls with saunt'ring pace,
a Whore. No stubborn stays her yielding shape embrace ;
Beneath the lamp her tawdry ribbons glare,
The new-scower'd manteau, and the slattern air ;   270
High-draggled petticoats her travels show,
And hollow cheeks with artful blushes glow ;
With flatt'ring sounds she sooths the cred'lous ear,
My noble captain ! charmer ! love ! my dear !
In riding-hood near tavern-doors she plies,
Or muffled pinners hide her livid eyes.
With empty bandbox she delights to range,
And feigns a distant errand from the *'Change* ;
Nay, she will oft' the Quaker's hood prophane,
And trudge demure the rounds of *Drury-lane*.   280
She darts from sarsnet ambush wily leers,
Twitches thy sleeve, or with familiar airs
Her fan will pat thy cheek ; these snares disdain,
Nor gaze behind thee, when she turns again.

A dreadful   I knew a yeoman, who for thirst of gain,
Example. To the great city drove from *Devon*'s plain
His num'rous lowing herd ; his herds he sold,
And his deep leathern pocket bagg'd with gold ;
Drawn by a fraudful nymph, he gaz'd, he sigh'd ;
Unmindful of his home, and distant bride,   290
She leads the willing victim to his doom,
Through winding alleys to her cobweb room.
Thence thro' the street he reels from post to post,
Valiant with wine, nor knows his treasure lost.

---

261 harlots] Harlots' *first edition only*   harlot's *remainder*.   264 strangers]
1730 stranger's *remainder*.   275 riding-hood] riding-hood, *first edition only*.
282 airs] airs, *1716*.   293 reels] *1730* reels, *remainder*.

The vagrant wretch th' assembled watchmen spies,
He waves his hanger, and their poles defies ;
Deep in the Round-house pent, all night he snores,
And the next morn in vain his fate deplores.
Ah hapless swain, unus'd to pains and ills !
Canst thou forego roast-beef for nauseous pills ?   300
How wilt thou lift to Heav'n thy eyes and hands,
When the long scroll the surgeon's fees demands !
Or else (ye Gods avert that worst disgrace)
Thy ruin'd nose falls level with thy face,
Then shall thy wife thy loathsome kiss disdain,
And wholesome neighbours from thy mug refrain.

Of Watchmen.   Yet there are watchmen, who with friendly light
Will teach thy reeling steps to tread aright ;
For sixpence will support thy helpless arm,
And home conduct thee, safe from nightly harm ;   310
But if they shake their lanthorns, from afar
To call their breth'ren to confed'rate war
When rakes resist their pow'r ; if hapless you
Should chance to wander with the scow'ring crew ;
Though fortune yield thee captive, ne'er despair,
But seek the constable's consid'rate ear ;
He will reverse the watchman's harsh decree,
Moved by the rhet'rick of a silver fee.
Thus would you gain some fav'rite courtier's word ;
Fee not the petty clarks, but bribe my Lord.   320

Of Rakes.   Now is the time that rakes their revells keep ;
Kindlers of riot, enemies of sleep.
His scatter'd pence the flying * *Nicker* flings,
And with the copper show'r the casement rings.
Who has not heard the *Scowrer*'s midnight fame ?
Who has not trembled at the *Mohock*'s name ?
Was there a watchman took his hourly rounds,
Safe from their blows, or new-invented wounds ?
I pass their desp'rate deeds, and mischiefs done
Where from *Snow-hill* black steepy torrents run ;   330
How matrons, hoop'd within the hoghead's womb,
Were tumbled furious thence, the rolling tomb
O'er the stones thunders, bounds from side to side.
So *Regulus* to save his country dy'd.

A necessary   Where a dim gleam the paly lanthorn throws
Caution in   O'er the mid pavement, heapy rubbish grows ;
a dark Night. Or arched vaults their gaping jaws extend,
Or the dark caves to common-shores descend.
Oft' by the winds extinct the signal lies,
Or smother'd in the glimmering socket dies,   340

* *Gentlemen, who delighted to break windows with half-pence.*

307 light] light, *1716*.   311 afar] afar, *1716*.   312 war] War, *1716*.   329
done] done, *1716*.   333 side.] side, *1730*.   336 O'er the mid' Pavement; heapy
Rubbish grows, *1716*.   339 winds] Winds, *1716*.   340 dies,] *1716* dies *remainder*.

E'er night has half roll'd round her ebon throne ;
In the wide gulph the shatter'd coach o'erthrown
Sinks with the snorting steeds ; the reins are broke,
And from the crackling axle flies the spoke.
So when fam'd *Eddystone*'s far-shooting ray,
That led the sailor through the stormy way,
Was from its rocky roots by billows torn,
And the high turret in the whirlewind born,
Fleets bulg'd their sides against the craggy land,
And pitchy ruines blacken'd all the strand.   350
    Who then through night would hire the harness'd steed,
And who would choose the rattling wheel for speed ?

A Fire.
    But hark ! distress with screaming voice draws nigh'r,
And wakes the slumb'ring street with cries of fire.
At first a glowing red enwraps the skies,
And born by winds the scatt'ring sparks arise ;
From beam to beam the fierce contagion spreads ;
The spiry flames now lift aloft their heads,
Through the burst sash a blazing deluge pours,
And splitting tiles descend in rattling show'rs.   360
Now with thick crouds th' enlighten'd pavement swarms,
The fire-man sweats beneath his crooked arms,
A leathern casque his vent'rous head defends,
Boldly he climbs where thickest smoak ascends ;
Mov'd by the mother's streaming eyes and pray'rs,
The helpless infant through the flame he bears,
With no less virtue, than through hostile fire
The *Dardan* hero bore his aged sire.
See forceful engines spout their levell'd streams,
To quench the blaze that runs along the beams ;   370
The grappling hook plucks rafters from the walls,
And heaps on heaps the smoaky ruine falls.
Blown by strong winds the fiery tempest roars,
Bears down new walls, and pours along the floors ;
The Heav'ns are all a-blaze, the face of night
Is cover'd with a sanguine dreadful light :
'Twas such a light involv'd thy tow'rs, O *Rome*,
The dire presage of mighty *Cæsar*'s doom,
When the sun veil'd in rust his mourning head,
And frightful prodigies the skies o'erspread.   380
Hark ! the drum thunders ! far, ye crouds, retire :
Behold ! the ready match is tipt with fire,
The nitrous store is laid, the smutty train
With running blaze awakes the barrell'd grain ;
Flames sudden wrap the walls ; with sullen sound
The shatter'd pile sinks on the smoaky ground.

342 o'erthrown] o'erthrown, *1716*.   344 crackling] cracking *1716*.   357
to beam] to Beam, *1716*.   367 fire] Fire, *1716*.   385 sound] Sound,
1716.

So when the years shall have revolv'd the date,
Th' inevitable hour of *Naples'* fate,
Her sapp'd foundations shall with thunders shake,
And heave and toss upon the sulph'rous lake ;   390
Earth's womb at once the fiery flood shall rend,
And in th' abyss her plunging tow'rs descend.
  Consider, reader, what fatigues I've known,
The toils, the perils of the wintry town ;
What riots seen, what bustling crouds I bor'd,
How oft' I cross'd where carts and coaches roar'd ;
Yet shall I bless my labours, if mankind
Their future safety from my dangers find.
Thus the bold traveller, (inur'd to toil,
Whose steps have printed *Asia*'s desert soil,   400
The barb'rous *Arabs* haunt ; or shiv'ring crost
Dark *Greenland*'s mountains of eternal frost ;
Whom providence in length of years restores
To the wish'd harbour of his native shores ;)
Sets forth his journals to the publick view,
To caution, by his woes, the wandring crew.
  And now compleat my gen'rous labours lye,
Finish'd, and ripe for immortality.
Death shall entomb in dust this mould'ring frame,
But never reach th' eternal part, my fame.   410
When *W** and *G***, mighty names, are dead ;
Or but at *Chelsea* under custards read ;
When Criticks crazy bandboxes repair,
And Tragedies, turn'd rockets, bounce in air ;
High-rais'd on *Fleet-street* posts, consign'd to fame,
This work shall shine, and walkers bless my name.

399–404 *No brackets in first and second editions.*   411 *W** and *G***] i.e. *Ward*
and *Gibbon.*

THE
STORY OF ARACHNE,
FROM
The Beginning of the Sixth Book of Ovid's Metamorphoses.

[*Editions* :
1. MISCELLANEOUS | POEMS | AND | *TRANSLATIONS.* | BY | SEVERAL HANDS. | —*Multa Poetarum veniet manus, auxilio quæ* | *Sit mihi*—— Hor. *LONDON* : | Printed for *Bernard Lintott* at the *Cross-Keys* be- | tween the Two *Temple* Gates in *Fleetstreet.* 1712. | Cr. 8vo.
2. The Second Edition. 1714. Cr. 8vo.
3. The Third Edition. 1720. Post 12mo.
4. The Fourth Edition. 1722. Post 12mo.
5. MISCELLANY | POEMS. | VOL. II. | By several Hands. | The FIFTH EDITION.| *LONDON* : | Printed for BERNARD LINTOT, at the *Cross-Keys,* | between the *Temple-*Gates in *Fleet-street,* 1727.
Post 12mo. This volume contains four pieces of Gay's : *Arachne*, the *Epistle to Burlington*, the *Epistle to Snow*, and *Molly Mog*.
Vol. I also contains the two ballads, *'Twas when the seas were roaring* and *Sweet William's farewell to Black-ey'd Susan.* It is dated 1726.
The two volumes appear to be a much expanded fifth edition of the *Miscellaneous Poems and Translations.*]

> PAllas, attentive heard the Muses song,
> Pleas'd that so well they had reveng'd their wrong ;
> Reflecting thus,—A vulgar soul can praise,
> My fame let glorious emulation raise,
> Swift vengeance shall pursue th' audacious pride
> That dares my sacred Deity deride.
> Revenge the Goddess in her breast revolves,
> And strait the bold *Arachne*'s fate resolves.
> Her haughty mind to heav'n disdain'd to bend,
> And durst with *Pallas* in her art contend.
> No famous town she boasts, or noble name ;
> But to her skillful hand owes all her fame ;

10

Sub-title. *Metamorphoses*] *Metamorphosis* 1712 and **1714.**
11 name ;] name, *1712 and 1714.*
12 So *1727 : remainder have*
> But to her work alone owes all her fame;

Idmon her father on his trade rely'd,
And thirsty wool in purple juices dy'd ;
Her mother, whom the shades of death confine,
Was, like her husband, born of vulgar line.
At small *Hypæpæ* though she did reside,
Yet industry proclaim'd what birth deny'd,
All *Lydia* to her name due honour pays,
And ev'ry city speaks *Arachne*'s praise.   20
Nymphs of *Timolus* quit their shady woods,
Nymphs of *Pactolus* leave their golden floods,
And oft' with pleasure round her gazing stand,
Admire her work, and praise her artful hand,
They view'd each motion, with new wonder seiz'd ;
More than the work her graceful manner pleas'd.
    Whether raw wool in its first orbs she wound,
Or with swift fingers twirl'd the spindle round,
Whether she pick'd with care the knotty piece,
Or comb'd like streaky clouds the stretching fleece,   30
Whether her needle play'd the pencil's part ;
'Twas plain from *Pallas* she derived her art.
But she, unable to sustain her pride,
The very mistress of her art defy'd.
Pallas obscures her bright celestial grace,
And takes an old decrepid beldam's face.
Her head is scatter'd o'er with silver hairs,
Which seems to bend beneath a load of years.
Her trembling hand, emboss'd with livid veins,
On trusty staff her feeble limbs sustains.   40
    She thus accosts the nymph, " Be timely wise,
" Do not the wholesome words of age despise,
" For in the hoary head experience lies :
" On earth contend the greatest name to gain ;
" To *Pallas* yield ; with heav'n you strive in vain."
    Contempt contracts her brow, her passions rise,
Wrath and disdain inflame her rolling eyes :
At once the tangling thread away she throws,
And scarce can curb her threatning hands from blows.
" Worn out with age, and by disease declin'd,   50
" (She cries) thy carcase has surviv'd thy mind ;
" These lectures might thy servile daughters move,
" And wary doctrines for thy neices prove ;
" My counsel 's from my self, my will commands,
" And my first resolution always stands :

33 she,] she *1727*.   36 decrepid] decrepit *1727*.   44 gain ;] *1712 and 1714* gain, *remainder*.   45 you strive] *1727* thou striv'st *remainder*.
47 So *1727* : *remainder have*
                        And proud disdain glares in her rolling eyes :
48 At once] *1727* Enrag'd, *remainder*.   53 neices] neeces, *1727*.   54 my self,] *1727* my self ; *remainder*.

" Let her contend ; or does her fear impart
" That conquest waits on my superior art ? "
 The goddess strait throws off her old disguise,
And heav'nly beauty sparkles in her eyes,
A youthful bloom fills up each wrinkled trace,   60
And *Pallas* smiles with ev'ry wonted grace.
The nymphs surpriz'd the deity adore,
And *Lydian* dames confess her matchless pow'r ;
The rival maid alone unmov'd remains,
Yet a swift blush her guilty feature stains ;
In her unwilling cheek the crimson glows,
And her check'd pride a short confusion knows.
So when *Aurora* first unveils her eyes,
A purple dawn invests the blushing skies ;
But soon bright *Phœbus* gains th' horizon's height,   70
And gilds the hemisphere with spreading light.
 Desire of conquest sways the giddy maid,
To certain ruin by vain hopes betray'd,
The goddess with her stubborn will comply'd,
And deign'd by trial to convince her pride.
Both take their stations, and the piece prepare,
And order ev'ry slender thread with care ;
The web inwraps the beam ; the reed divides,
While through the wid'ning space the shuttle glides,
Which their swift hands receive ; then pois'd with lead,   80
The swinging weight strikes close th' inserted thread.
They gird their flowing garments round their wast,
And ply their feet and arms with dext'rous haste.
Here each inweaves the richest *Tyrian* dye,
There fainter shades in soften'd order lye ;
Such various mixtures in the texture shine,
Set off the work, and brighten each design.
As when the sun his piercing rays extends,
When from thin clouds some drisly show'r descends ;
We see the spacious humid arch appear,   90
Whose transient colours paint the splendid air ;
By such degrees the deep'ning shadows rise
As pleasingly deceive our dazled eyes ;
And though the same th' adjoining colour seems,
Yet hues of diff'rent natures die th' extremes.
Here height'ning gold they midst the woof dispose,
And in the web this antique story rose.
 Pallas the lofty mount of *Mars* designs,
Celestial judgment guides th' unerring lines ;

56 impart] *1727* impart, *remainder.*   59 eyes,] *1727* eyes ; *remainder.*
82–3 *So 1727 : remainder have*
     Each girds her flowing garments round her waste,
     And plies her feet and arms with dextrous haste.

85 soften'd] *1727* beauteous *remainder.*   87 design.] *1722* design : *remainder.*
89 descends ;] *1722* descends. *remainder.*

Here, in just view, the *Athenian* structures stand, 100
And there, the Gods contend to name the land ;
Twelve deities she frames with stately mien,
And in the midst superior *Jove* is seen ;
A glowing warmth the blended colours give,
The figures in the picture seem to live.
Heav'n's thundring monarch sits with awful grace,
And dread omnipotence imprints his face :
There *Neptune* stood, disdainfully he frown'd,
And with his trident smote the trembling ground,
The parting rocks a spacious chasm disclose, 110
From whence a fiery prancing steed arose ;
And on that useful gift he founds his claim,
To grace the city with his honour'd name.
See her own figure next with martial air,
A shining helmet decks her flowing hair ;
Her thoughtful breast her well-pois'd shield defends,
And her bare arm a glitt'ring spear extends,
With which she wounds the plain ; from thence arose
A spreading Tree, green olives load the boughs ;
The Pow'rs her gift behold with wondring eyes, 120
And to the goddess give the rightful prize.
　　Such mercy checks her wrath, that to dissuade
By others fate the too presumptuous maid,
With miniature she fills each corner space,
To curb her pride, and save her from disgrace.
　　Hæmus and *Rhodope* in this she wrought,
The beauteous colours spoke her lively thought ;
With arrogance and fierce ambition fir'd,
They to the sacred names of Gods aspir'd ;
To mountains chang'd their lofty heads arise, 130
And lose their less'ning summits in the skies.
　　In that, in all the strength of art was seen
The wretched fate of the *Pygmæan* queen ;
Juno enrag'd, resents th' audacious aim,
And to a crane transforms the vanquish'd dame ;
In that voracious shape she still appears,
And plagues her people with perpetual wars.

105 *So 1727 : remainder have*
　　　　And in the piece each Figure seems to live.
114 *So 1727 : remainder have*
　　　　In her own shape a warlike port appears,
115 hair ;] *1727* hairs, *remainder.*
124–5 *So 1727 : remainder have*
　　　　A small design each corner-space supply'd,
　　　　Of the just downfal of contending pride.
127 The] *1727* And *remainder.*
132 *So 1727 : remainder have*
　　　　In that, in curious miniature was seen

  In this, *Antigone* for beauty strove
With the bright consort of imperial *Jove* :
Juno incens'd, her royal pow'r display'd,   140
And to a bird converts the haughty maid.
Laomedon his daughter's fate bewails,
Nor his, nor *Ilion*'s fervent pray'r prevails,
But on her lovely skin white feathers rise,
Chang'd to a clam'rous stork she mounts the skies.
  In the remaining orb, the heav'nly maid
The tale of childless *Cynaras* display'd,
A settled anguish in his look appears,
And from his bloodshot eyes flow streams of tears ;
On the cold ground, no more a father, thrown ;   150
He, for his daughters, clasp'd the polish'd stone.
And when he sought to hold their wonted charms,
The temple's steps deceiv'd his eager arms.
Wreaths of green olive round the border twine,
And her own tree incloses the design.
  Arachne paints th' amours of mighty *Jove*,
How in a bull the God disguis'd his love,
A real bull seems in the piece to roar,
And real billows breaking on the shore :
In fair *Europa*'s face appears surprize,   160
To the retreating land she turns her eyes,
And seems to call her maids, who wond'ring stood,
And with their tears increas'd the briny flood ;
Her trembling feet she by contraction saves
From the rude insult of the rising waves.
  Here am'rous *Jove* dissolving *Leda* trod,
And in the vig'rous swan conceal'd the God.
Love lends him now an eagle's new disguise,
Beneath his flutt'ring wings *Asteria* lies.
Th' enliv'ning colours here with force express'd   170
How *Jove* the fair *Antiope* caress'd.
In a strong satyr's muscled form he came
Instilling love, transports the glowing dame,
And lusty twins reward his nervous flame.
Here how he sooth'd the bright *Alcmena*'s love,
Who for *Amphitryon* took th' impostor *Jove*,

---

138 In this, Antigone] *1727*   In this Antigone, *remainder.*
147 childless] childish *1727*   152 to hold] *1727*   t' embrace *remainder.*
155 *So 1727 : remainder have*

  And her own peaceful tree adorns the fair design.
165 insult] *1727*   insults *remainder.*
170 *So 1727 : remainder have*

  Here her enliv'ning colours well express'd
172 muscled] *1727*   rough-hewn *remainder.*
172-3 *So 1720 and 1722*   he came, Instilling Love *1712 and 1714*   he came
Instilling love *1727.*   175 Here] Hear *1722 only.*

And how the God, in golden show'r, allur'd
The guarded nymph, in brazen walls immur'd.
How, in a swain, *Mnemosyne* he charms ;
How lambent flame the fair *Ægina* warms : 180
And how with various glitt'ring hues inlaid
In serpent's form *Deöis* he betray'd.
Here you, great *Neptune*, with a short-liv'd flame
In a young bull enjoy th' *Æolian* dame.
Then in *Enipeus'* shape intrigues pursue.
'Tis thus th' *Aloïds* boast descent from you.
Here to *Bisaltis* was thy love convey'd,
When a rough ram deceiv'd the yielding maid.
 Ceres, kind mother of the bounteous year,
Whose golden locks a sheafy garland bear ; 190
And the dread dame, with hissing serpents hung,
(From whom the *Pegasæan* courser sprung,)
Thee in a snuffling stallion's form enjoy,
Exhaust thy strength, and ev'ry nerve employ ;
Melantho as a dolphin you betray,
And sport in pleasures on the rolling sea ;
Such just proportion graces ev'ry part,
Nature her self appears improv'd by art.
Here in disguise was mighty *Phœbus* seen,
With clownish aspect, and a rustick mien ; 200
Again transform'd, he 's dress'd in faulcon's plumes,
And now the lion's noble shape assumes ;
Now, in a shepherd's form, with treach'rous smiles,
He *Macareian Isse's* heart beguiles.
Here his plump shape enamour'd *Bacchus* leaves,
And in the grape *Erigone* deceives.
There *Saturn*, in a neighing horse, she wove,
And *Chiron's* double form rewards his love.
Festoons of flow'rs inwove with ivy shine,
Border the wond'rous piece, and round the texture twine. 210
 Not *Pallas*, nor ev'n spleen it self could blame,
The wond'rous work of the *Mæonian* dame ;
With grief her vast success the goddess bore,
And of celestial crimes the story tore.
Her boxen shuttle, now enrag'd, she took,
And thrice the proud *Idmonian* artist struck :
Th' unhappy maid, to see her labours vain,
Grew resolute with pride, and shame, and pain :

177 *So 1727 : remainder have*
    And how the God in golden show'rs allured
 178 nymph,] *1727* nymph *remainder.* 179 charms ;] *1727* charms, *remainder.*
180 How lambent flame] *1727* In lambent flames *remainder.* 184 enjoy] *1727*
enjoy'd *remainder.* 187 was thy] *1727* you your *remainder.* 188 When a
rough] *1727* And as a *remainder.* 191 with hissing] *1727* whose head's with
remainder. 192 *Brackets in 1727 only.* 212 wond'rous] *1727* skilful
remainder. 214 the story tore.] *1727* th' upbraiding hist'ry tore. *remainder.*
217 to see] *1727* who found *remainder.*

Around her neck a fatal noose she ty'd,
And sought by sudden death her guilt to hide.   220
Pallas with pity saw the desp'rate deed,
And thus the virgin's milder fate decreed.
" Live, impious rival, mindful of thy crime,
" Suspended thus to waste thy future time,
" Thy punishment involves thy num'rous race,
" Who, for thy fault, shall share in thy disgrace : "
Her incantation magick juices aid,
With sprinkling drops she bath'd the pendent maid,
And thus the charm its noxious power display'd.
Like leaves in autumn drop her falling hairs,   230
With these her nose, and next her rising ears.
Her head to the minutest substance shrunk,
The potent juice contracts her changing trunk ;
Close to her sides her slender fingers clung,
There chang'd to nimble feet in order hung.;
Her bloated belly swells to larger size,
Which now with smallest threads her work supplies ;
The virgin in the spider still remains ;
And in that shape her former art retains.

219 ty'd] *1727* ties *remainder*.
220 So *1727* : *remainder have*

  And in despair to death for shelter flies.

221 desp'rate] *1727* sudden *remainder*.
225 Thy] *1727* This *remainder*.   226 shall share in] *1727* inherit *remainder*.
228 So *1727* : *remainder have*

  With which she sprinkles o'er the pendent maid,

230 So *1727* : *remainder have*

  Like autumn leaves she sheds her falling hairs,

233 The potent] *1727* And the strong *remainder*.
234 Close to her sides] *1727* Strait to her sides, *remainder*.
235 There chang'd to] *1727* And there, her *remainder*.

OVID'S
METAMORPHOSES.
BOOK IX.

The Story of A C H E L O Ü S
and H E R C U L E S.

[*Editions :*
1. OVID's | *METAMORPHOSES* | IN | FIFTEEN BOOKS. | *Translated by the most Eminent* HANDS. | Adorn'd with SCULPTURES. | *LONDON* : | Printed for JACOB TONSON at *Shakespear's-Head* | over-against *Katharine-Street* in the *Strand.* | M DCC XVII. A magnificent Folio, edited by Garth; the 'sculptures' by Vertue, Smith, Kirkall and Du Guernier; the translations by Dryden, Addison, Eusden, Maynwaring, Croxall, Tate, Stonestreet, Vernon, Gay, Pope, Harvey, Congreve, Ozell, Stanyan, Catcott, Rowe, Garth, and Welsted.
2. The same, with the Latin added in parallel to the English, ' with Historical Explications of the Fables, written in French by the Abbot Banier . . . translated into English. Adorned with Sculptures, by B. Picart, and other able Masters. Amsterdam, Printed for the Wetsteins and Smith. MDCCXXXII.' The arrangement of the Episodes is somewhat altered.
An enormous Book !]

THeseus requests the God to tell his Woes,
Whence his maim'd Brow, and whence his Groans arose :
When thus the *Calydonian* Stream reply'd,
With twining Reeds his careless Tresses ty'd.
Ungrateful is the Tale ; for who can bear,
When conquer'd, to rehearse the shameful War ?
Yet I 'll the melancholy Story trace ;
So great a Conqu'ror softens the Disgrace :
Nor was it still so mean the Prize to yield,
As great and glorious to dispute the Field.　　　　10
　Perhaps you 've heard of *Deïanira's* Name,
For all the Country spoke her Beauty's Fame.
Long was the Nymph by num'rous Suiters woo'd,
Each with Address his envy'd Hopes pursu'd :
I joyn'd the loving Band ; to gain the Fair,
Reveal'd my Passion to her Father's Ear.
Their vain Pretensions all the Rest resign,
Alcides only strove to equal mine ;
He boasts his Birth from *Jove*, recounts his Spoils,
His Step-dame's Hate subdu'd, and finish'd Toils.　　20

10 As great] As great, *1732.*

Can Mortals then (said I) with Gods compare ?
Behold a God ; mine is the watry Care :
Through your wide Realms I take my mazy Way,
Branch into Streams, and o'er the Region stray :
No foreign Guest your Daughter's Charms adores,
But one who rises in your native Shores.
Let not his Punishment your Pity move ;
Is *Juno*'s Hate an Argument for Love ?
Though you your Life from fair *Alcmena* drew,
Jove's a feign'd Father, or by Fraud a true.   30
Chuse then ; confess thy Mother's Honour lost,
Or thy Descent from *Jove* no longer boast.
    While thus I spoke, he look'd with stern Disdain,
Nor could the Sallies of his Wrath restrain,
Which thus break forth. This Arm decides our Right ;
Vanquish in Words, be mine the Prize in Fight.
    Bold he rush'd on. My Honour to maintain,
I fling my verdant Garments on the Plain,
My Arms stretch forth, my pliant Limbs prepare,
And with bent Hands expect the furious War.   40
O'er my sleek Skin now gather'd Dust he throws,
And yellow Sand his mighty Muscles strows.
Oft he my Neck and nimble Legs assails,
He seems to grasp me, but as often fails.
Each Part he now invades with eager Hand ;
Safe in my Bulk, immoveable I stand.
So when loud Storms brea high, and foam and roar
Against some Mole, that stretches from the Shore ;
The firm Foundation lasting Tempests braves,
Defies the warring Winds, and driving Waves.   50
    Awhile we breathe, then forward rush amain,
Renew the Combat, and our Ground maintain ;
Foot strove with Foot, I prone extend my Breast,
Hands war with Hands, and Forehead Forehead prest.
Thus have I seen two furious Bulls engage,
Inflam'd with equal Love, and equal Rage ;
Each claims the fairest Heifer of the Grove,
And Conquest only can decide their Love :
The trembling Herds survey the Fight from far,
Till Victory decides th' important War.   60
Three times in vain he strove my Joints to wrest,
To force my Hold, and throw me from his Breast ;
The fourth he broke my Gripe, that clasp'd him round,
Then with new Force he stretch'd me on the Ground ;
Close to my Back the mighty Burthen clung,
As if a Mountain o'er my Limbs were flung.
Believe my Tale ; nor do I, boastful, aim
By feign'd Narration to extol my Fame.

35 break] broke *Underhill*.   59 Fight] *1732* Sight *1717*.

No sooner from his Grasp I Freedom get,
Unlock my Arms, that flow'd with trickling Sweat,   70
But quick he seiz'd me, and renew'd the Strife,
As my exhausted Bosom pants for Life:
My Neck he gripes, my Knee to Earth he strains ;
I fall, and bite the Sand with Shame and Pains.
  O'er-match'd in Strength, to Wiles and Arts I take,
And slip his Hold, in Form of speckled Snake ;
Who, when I wreath'd in Spires my Body round,
Or show'd my forky Tongue with hissing Sound,
Smiles at my Threats ; Such Foes my Cradle knew,
He cries, dire Snakes my Infant Hand o'erthrew ;   80
A Dragon's Form might other Conquests gain,
To war with me you take that Shape in vain.
Art thou proportion'd to the *Hydra*'s Length,
Who by his Wounds receiv'd augmented Strength ?
He rais'd a hundred hissing Heads in Air,
When one I lopt, up-sprung a dreadful Pair.
By his Wounds fertile, and with Slaughter strong,
Singly I quell'd him, and stretch'd dead along.
What can'st thou do, a Form precarious, prone,
To rouse my Rage with Terrors not thy own ?   90
He said ; and round my Neck his Hands he cast,
And with his straining Fingers wrung me fast ;
My Throat he tortur'd, close as Pincers clasp,
In vain I strove to loose the forceful Grasp.
  Thus vanquish'd too, a third Form still remains,
Chang'd to a Bull, my Lowing fills the Plains.
Strait on the Left his nervous Arms were thrown
Upon my brindled Neck, and tugg'd it down ;
Then deep he struck my Horn into the Sand,
And fell'd my Bulk along the dusty Land.   100
Nor yet his Fury cool'd ; 'twixt Rage and Scorn,
From my maim'd Front he tore the stubborn Horn :
This, heap'd with Flowers and Fruits, the *Naiads* bear,
Sacred to Plenty, and the bounteous Year.
  He spoke ; when lo, a beauteous Nymph appears,
Girt like *Diana*'s Train, with flowing Hairs ;
The Horn she brings in which all Autumn's stor'd,
And ruddy Apples for the second Board.
  Now Morn begins to dawn, the Sun's bright Fire
Gilds the high Mountains, and the Youths retire ;   110
Nor stay'd they, till the troubled Stream subsides,
And in its Bounds with peaceful Current glides.
But *Acheloüs* in his oozy Bed
Deep hides his Brow deform'd, and rustick Head :

70 Sweat,] *1717* Sweat ; *1732.*   74 Shame] *1717* Shame, *1732.*   75 Wiles] *1717* Wiles, *1732.*   80 cries,] *1717* cries ; *1732.*   95 *It is tempting to emend* too *to* two *: but the Latin* Sic quoque devicto restabat tertia tauri | Forma trucis *confirms the English text.*   110 Mountains,] *1717* Mountains *1732.*

No real Wound the Victor's Triumph show'd,
But his lost Honours griev'd the watry God ;
Yet ev'n that Loss the Willow's Leaves o'erspread,
And verdant Reeds, in Garlands, bind his Head.

The Death of NESSUS *the Centaur.*

THIS Virgin, too, thy Love, O *Nessus*, found
To her alone you owe the fatal Wound.
As the strong Son of *Jove* his Bride conveys,
Where his Paternal Lands their Bulwarks raise ;
Where from her slopy Urn *Evenus* póurs
Her rapid Current, swell'd by wintry Show'rs,
He came.   The frequent Eddies whirl'd the Tide,
And the deep rolling Waves all Pass deny'd.
As for himself, he stood unmov'd by Fears,
For now his Bridal Charge employ'd his Cares,   10
The strong-limb'd *Nessus* thus officious cry'd,
(For he the Shallows of the Stream had try'd)
Swim thou, *Alcides*, all thy Strength prepare,
On yonder Bank I'll lodge thy Nuptial Care.
   Th' *Aonian* Chief to *Nessus* trusts his Wife,
All pale, and trembling for her Heroe's Life :
Cloath'd as he stood in the fierce Lion's Hide,
The laden Quiver o'er his Shoulder ty'd,
(For cross the Stream his Bow and Club were cast),
Swift he plung'd in ;   These Billows shall be past,   20
He said, nor sought where smoother Waters glide,
But stem'd the rapid Dangers of the Tide.
The Bank he reach'd ;   again the Bow he bears ;
When, hark !   his Bride's known Voice alarms his Ears.
Nessus, to thee I call (aloud he cries)
Vain is thy Trust in Flight, be timely wise :
Thou Monster double-shap'd, my Right set free ;
If thou no Rev'rence owe my Fame and me,
Yet Kindred shou'd thy lawless Lust deny:
Think not, perfidious Wretch, from me to fly,   30
Tho' wing'd with Horse's Speed ;   Wounds shall pursue ;
Swift as his Words the fatal Arrow flew :
The Centaur's Back admits the feather'd Wood,
And thro' his Breast the barbed Weapon stood ;
Which, when in Anguish, thro' the Flesh he tore,
From both the Wounds gush'd forth the spumy Gore
Mix'd with *Lernæan* Venom ;   this he took,
Nor dire Revenge his dying Breast forsook.
His Garment, in the reeking Purple dy'd,
To rouse Love's Passion, he presents the Bride.   40

5 Urn] *1732*   Urn, *1717*.   9 As for himself,] As, for himself, *1717*.
16 pale,] *1732*   pale *1717*.
35 *So 1717.   In the edition of 1732 ‘ Fables III and IV ’ begin here,*
          The Dart, in Anguish, thro’ the Flesh he tore,

The Death of HERCULES.

Now a long Interval of Time succeeds,
When the great Son of *Jove*'s immortal Deeds,
And Stepdame's Hate, had fill'd Earth's utmost Round ;
He from *OEchalia*, with new Lawrels crown'd,
In Triumph was return'd.   He Rites prepares,
And to the King of Gods directs his Pray'rs ;
When Fame (who Falshood cloaths in Truth's Disguise,
And swells her little Bulk with growing Lies)
Thy tender Ear, O *Deianira*, mov'd,
That *Hercules* the fair *Iole* lov'd.   10
Her Love believes the Tale ; the Truth she fears
Of his new Passion, and gives way to Tears.
The flowing Tears diffus'd her wretched Grief.
Why seek I thus, from streaming Eyes, Relief ?
She cries ; indulge not thus these fruitless Cares,
The Harlot will but triumph in thy Tears :
Let something be resolv'd, while yet there 's Time ;
My Bed not conscious of a Rival's Crime.
In Silence shall I mourn, or loud complain ?
Shall I seek *Calydon*, or here remain ?   20
What tho', ally'd to *Meleager*'s Fame,
I boast the Honours of a Sister's Name ?
My Wrongs, perhaps, now urge me to pursue
Some desp'rate Deed, by which the World shall view
How far Revenge and Woman's Rage can rise,
When weltring in her Blood the Harlot dies.
    Thus various Passions rul'd by turns her Breast.
She now resolves to send the fatal Vest,
Dy'd with *Lernæan* Gore, whose Pow'r might move
His Soul anew, and rouse declining Love.   30
Nor knew she what her sudden Rage bestows,
When she to *Lychas* trusts her future Woes ;
With soft Endearments she the Boy commands,
To bear the Garment to her Husband's Hands.
    Th' unwitting Heroe takes the Gift in haste,
And o'er his Shoulders *Lerna*'s Poyson cast,
As first the Fire with Frankincense he strows,
And utters to the Gods his holy Vows ;
And on the Marble Altar's polish'd Frame
Pours forth the grapy Stream ; the rising Flame   40
Sudden dissolves the subtle pois'nous Juice,
Which taints his Blood, and all his Nerves bedews.
With wonted Fortitude he bore the Smart,
And not a Groan confess'd his burning Heart.
At length his Patience was subdu'd by Pain,
He rends the sacred Altar from the Plain ;
OEte's wide Forests eccho with his Cries :
Now to rip off the deathful Robe he tries,

Where-e'er he plucks the Vest, the Skin he tears,
The mangled Muscles and huge Bones he bares,   50
(A ghastful Sight!) or raging with his Pain,
To rend the sticking Plague he tugs in vain.
As the red Iron hisses in the Flood,
So boils the Venom in his curdling Blood.
Now with the greedy Flame his Entrails glow,
And livid Sweats down all his Body flow;
The cracking Nerves burnt up are burst in twain,
The lurking Venom melts his swimming Brain.

    Then, lifting both his Hands aloft, he cries,
Glut thy Revenge, dread Empress of the Skies;   60
Sate with my Death the Rancour of thy Heart,
Look down with Pleasure, and enjoy my Smart.
Or, if e'er Pity mov'd a hostile Breast,
(For here I stand thy Enemy profest)
Take hence this hateful Life with Tortures torn,
Inur'd to Trouble, and to Labours born.
Death is the Gift most welcome to my Woe,
And such a Gift a Stepdame may bestow.
Was it for this *Busiris* was subdu'd,
Whose barb'rous Temples reek'd with Strangers Blood?   70
Press'd in these Arms his Fate *Antæus* found,
Nor gain'd recruited Vigour from the Ground.
Did I not triple-form'd *Geryon* fell?
Or did I fear the triple Dog of Hell?
Did not these Hands the Bull's arm'd Forehead hold?
Are not our mighty Toils in *Elis* told?
Do not *Stymphalian* Lakes proclaim thy Fame?
And fair *Parthenian* Woods resound thy Name?
Who seiz'd the golden Belt of *Thermodon*?
And who the Dragon-guarded Apples won?   80
Could the fierce Centaur's Strength my Force withstand
Or the fell Boar that spoil'd th' *Arcadian* Land?
Did not these Arms the *Hydra*'s Rage subdue,
Who from his Wounds to double Fury grew?
What if the *Thracian* Horses, fat with Gore,
Who human Bodies in their Mangers tore,
I saw, and with their barb'rous Lord o'erthrew?
What if these Hands *Nemæa*'s Lion slew?
Did not this Neck the heav'nly Globe sustain?
The female Partner of the Thund'rer's Reign   90
Fatigu'd, at length suspends her harsh Commands,
Yet no Fatigue hath slack'd these valiant Hands.
But now new Plagues pursue me; neither Force,
Nor Arms, nor Darts can stop their raging Course.

50 Muscles] *1717* Muscles, *1732*.
53 *In the edition of 1732 a new paragraph begins here.*
63 a] *1732* an *1717*.   70 Strangers] Stranger's *1717 and 1732*.
77 Do] *1732* Did *1717*.   91 Fatigu'd,] *1717* Fatigu'd *1732*.

Devouring Flame thro' my rack'd Entrails strays,
And on my Lungs and shrivell'd Muscles preys.
Yet still *Eurystheus* breathes the vital Air.
What Mortal now shall seek the Gods with Pray'r ?

The Transformation of LYCHAS *into a Rock.*

THE Hero said ; and with the Torture stung,
Furious o'er *OEte*'s lofty Hills he sprung.
Stuck with the Shaft, thus scours the Tyger round,
And seeks the flying Author of his Wound.
Now might you see him trembling, now he vents
His anguish'd Soul in Groans and loud Laments ;
He strives to tear the clinging Vest in vain,
And with up-rooted Forests strows the Plain ;
Now kindling into Rage, his Hands he rears,
And to his kindred Gods directs his Pray'rs.   10
When *Lychas*, lo, he spies ; who trembling flew,
And in a hollow Rock conceal'd from View,
Had shun'd his Wrath.   Now Grief renew'd his Pain,
His Madness chaf'd, and thus he raves again.
     Lychas, to thee alone my Fate I owe.
Who bore the Gift, the Cause of all my Woe.
The Youth all pale, with shiv'ring Fear was stung,
And vain Excuses faulter'd on his Tongue.
Alcides snatch'd him, as with suppliant Face
He strove to clasp his Knees, and beg for Grace :   20
He toss'd him o'er his Head with airy Course,
And hurl'd with more than with an Engine's Force ;
Far o'er the *Eubœan* Main aloof he flies,
And hardens by Degrees amid the Skies.
So show'ry Drops, when chilly Tempests blow,
Thicken at first, then whiten into Snow,
In Balls congeal'd the rolling Fleeces bound
In solid Hail result upon the Ground.
Thus, whirl'd with nervous Force thro' distant Air,
The Purple Tide forsook his Veins, with Fear ;   30
All Moisture left his Limbs.   Transform'd to Stone,
In ancient Days the craggy Flint was known ;
Still in th' *Eubœan* Waves his Front he rears,
Still the small Rock in human Form appears,
And still the Name of hapless *Lychas* bears.

The Apotheosis of HERCULES.

BUT now the Hero of immortal Birth
Fells *OEte*'s Forests on the groaning Earth ;
A Pile he builds ; to *Philoctetes'* Care
He leaves his deathful Instruments of War ;
To him commits those Arrows, which again
Shall see the Bulwarks of the *Trojan* Reign.
The Son of *Pæan* lights the lofty Pyre,
High round the Structure climbs the greedy Fire ;
Plac'd on the Top, thy nervous Shoulders spread
With the *Nemæan* Spoils, thy careless Head   10
Rais'd on the knotty Club, with Look Divine,
Here thou, dread Hero, of Celestial Line,
Wert stretch'd at Ease ; as when a chearful Guest,
Wine crown'd thy Bowls, and Flow'rs thy Temples drest.
    Now on all Sides the potent Flames aspire,
And crackle round those Limbs that mock the Fire :
A sudden Terror seiz'd th' immortal Host,
Who thought the World's profess'd Defender lost.
This when the Thund'rer saw, with Smiles he cries,
'Tis from your Fears, ye Gods, my Pleasures rise ;   20
Joy swells my Breast, that my all-ruling Hand
O'er such a grateful People boasts Command,
That you my suff'ring Progeny wou'd aid ;
Tho' to his Deeds this just Respect be paid,
Me you've oblig'd.   Be all your Fears forborn,
Th' *OEtean* Fires do thou, great Hero, scorn.
Who vanquish'd all things, shall subdue the Flame.
That Part alone of gross maternal Frame
Fire shall devour ; while what from me he drew
Shall live immortal, and its Force subdue ;   30
That, when he 's dead, I'll raise to Realms above ;
May all the Pow'rs the righteous Act approve.
If any God dissent, and judge too great
The sacred Honours of the heav'nly Seat,
Ev'n he shall own his Deeds deserve the Sky,
Ev'n he, reluctant, shall at length comply.
Th' assembled Pow'rs assent.   No Frown till now
Had mark'd with Passion vengeful *Juno*'s Brow.
Mean while whate'er was in the Pow'r of Flame
Was all consum'd ; his Body's nervous Frame   40
No more was known, of human Form bereft,
Th' eternal Part of *Jove* alone was left.

1 *No break in the edition of 1732.*   3 *Quaere, for* Pile *read* Pyre ?   6 Shall]
Must *Underhill.*   7 *Pæan*] P\was *Underhill.*   13 Wert] Was *Underhill.*
17 Terror] tremor *Underhill.*   36 he,] he *1717.*

As an old Serpent casts his scaly Vest,
Wreathes in the Sun, in youthful Glory drest ;
So when *Alcides* mortal Mold resign'd,
His better Part enlarg'd, and grew refin'd ;
August his Visage shone ; Almighty *Jove*
In his swift Carr his honour'd Offspring drove ;
High o'er the hollow Clouds the Coursers fly,
And lodge the Hero in the starry Sky.   50

The *Transformation* of GALANTHIS.

ATLAS perceiv'd the Load of Heav'n's new Guest.
Revenge still rancour'd in *Eurystheus'* Breast
Against *Alcides'* Race. *Alcmena* goes
To *Iolè*, to vent maternal Woes ;
Here she pours forth her Grief, recounts the Spoils
Her Son had bravely reap'd in glorious Toils.
This *Iolè*, by *Hercules'* Commands,
Hyllus had lov'd, and joyn'd in nuptial Bands.
Her swelling Womb the teeming Birth confess'd,
To whom *Alcmena* thus her Speech address'd.   10
    O, may the Gods protect thee, in that Hour,
When, 'midst thy Throws, thou call'st th' *Ilithyian* Pow'r !
May no Delays prolong thy racking Pain,
As when I su'd for *Juno's* Aid in vain.
    When now *Alcides'* mighty Birth drew nigh,
And the tenth Sign roll'd forward on the Sky,
My Womb extends with such a mighty Load,
As *Jove* the Parent of the Burthen show'd.
I could no more th' encreasing Smart sustain :
My Horror kindles to recount the Pain ;   20
Cold chills my Limbs while I the Tale pursue,
And now methinks I feel my Pangs anew.
Sev'n Days and Nights amidst incessant Throws,
Fatigu'd with Ills I lay, nor knew Repose ;
When lifting high my Hands, in Shrieks I pray'd,
Implor'd the Gods, and call'd *Lucina's* Aid.
She came, but prejudic'd, to give my Fate
A Sacrifice to vengeful *Juno's* Hate.
She hears the groaning Anguish of my Fits,
And on the Altar at my Door she sits.   30
O'er her left Knee her crossing Leg she cast,
Then knits her Fingers close, and wrings them fast :
This stay'd the Birth ; in mutt'ring Verse she pray'd,
The mutt'ring Verse th' unfinish'd Birth delay'd.
Now with fierce Struggles, raging with my Pain,

4 *Iolè*] 1717 Iole 1732.

At *Jove*'s Ingratitude I rave in vain.
How did I wish for Death ! such Groans I sent,
As might have made the flinty Heart relent.
  Now the *Cadmeian* Matrons round me press,
Offer their Vows, and seek to bring Redress ;   40
Among the *Theban* Dames *Galanthis* stands,
Strong limb'd, red hair'd, and just to my Commands :
She first perceiv'd that all these racking Woes
From the persisting Hate of *Juno* rose.
As here and there she pass'd, by chance she sees
The seated Goddess ; on her close-press'd Knees
Her fast-knit Hands she leans ; with chearful Voice
Galanthis cries, Whoe'er thou art, rejoice,
Congratulate the Dame, she lies at Rest,
At length the Gods *Alcmena*'s Womb have blest.   50
Swift from her Seat the startled Goddess springs,
No more conceal'd, her Hands abroad she flings ;
The Charm unloos'd, the Birth my Pangs reliev'd ;
Galanthis' Laughter vex'd the Pow'r deceiv'd.
Fame says, the Goddess dragg'd the laughing Maid
Fast by the Hair ; in vain her Force essay'd
Her grov'ling Body from the Ground to rear ;
Changed to Fore-feet her shrinking Arms appear :
Her hairy Back her former Hue retains,
The Form alone is lost ; her Strength remains ;   60
Who, since the Lye did from her Mouth proceed,
Shall from her pregnant Mouth bring forth her **Breed**
Nor shall she quit her long frequented Home,
But haunt those Houses where she lov'd to roam.

    57 grov'ling] *1717*   groveling *1732*.

I OLAUS *restor'd to* Youth.

WHILE *Iolè* the fatal Change declares,
Alcmena's pitying Hand oft wip'd her Tears.
Grief too stream'd down her Cheeks ; soon Sorrow flies,
And rising Joy the trickling Moisture dries,
Lo *Iolaus* stands before their Eyes.
A Youth he stood ; and the soft Down began
O'er his smooth Chin to spread, and promise Man.
Hebe submitted to her Husband's Pray'rs,
Instill'd new Vigour, and restor'd his Years.

The Prophecy of THEMIS.

Now from her Lips a solemn Oath had past,
That *Iolaus* this Gift alone shou'd taste,
Had not just *Themis* thus maturely said,
(Which check'd her Vow, and aw'd the blooming Maid.)
    Thebes is embroil'd in War. *Capaneus* stands
Invincible, but by the Thund'rer's Hands.
Ambition shall the guilty *Brothers fire,
Both rush to mutual Wounds, and both expire.
The reeling Earth shall ope her gloomy Womb,
Where the † yet breathing Bard shall find his Tomb.   10.
The §Son shall bathe his Hands in Parent's Blood,
And in one Act be both unjust and good.
Of Home and Sense depriv'd, where-e'er he flies,
The Furies and his Mother's Ghost he spies.
His Wife the fatal Bracelet shall implore,
And *Phegeus* stain his Sword in Kindred Gore.
Callirhoë shall then with suppliant Pray'r
Prevail on *Jupiter's* relenting Ear.
Jove shall with Youth her Infant Sons inspire
And bid their Bosoms glow with manly Fire.   20

   * Eteocles *and* Polynices.   † Amphiaraus.   § Alcmæon.

  12 unjust] *1717* unjust, *1732.*   13 Home] *1717* Home, *1732.*   14 Furies]
1717 Furies, *1732.*

The Debate of the GODS.

WHEN *Themis* thus with prescient Voice had spoke,
Among the Gods a various Murmur broke ;
Dissention rose in each immortal Breast,
That one should grant what was deny'd the rest.
Aurora for her aged Spouse complains,
And *Ceres* grieves for *Jason's* freezing Veins ;
Vulcan would *Erichthonius'* Years renew,
Her future Race the Care of *Venus* drew,
She would *Anchises'* blooming Age restore ;
A diff'rent Care employ'd each heav'nly Pow'r.   10
Thus various Int'rests did their Jars encrease,
Till *Jove* arose ; he spoke, their Tumults cease.
    Is any Rev'rence to our Presence giv'n,
Then why this Discord 'mong the Pow'rs of Heav'n ?
Who can the settled Will of Fate subdue ?
'Twas by the Fates that *Iolaus* knew

    4 grant] *1717* have *1732.*

A second youth. The Fates determin'd Doom
Shall give *Callirhoe*'s Race a youthful Bloom.
Arms nor Ambition can this Pow'r obtain ;
Quell your Desires ; ev'n me the Fates restrain.   20
Could I their Will controul, no rolling Years
Had *Æacus* bent down with Silver Hairs ;
Then *Rhadamanthus* still had Youth possess'd,
And *Minos* with eternal Bloom been bless'd.
Jove's Words the Synod mov'd ; the Pow'rs give o'er,
And urge in vain unjust Complaint no more.
Since *Rhadamanthus*' Veins now slowly flow'd,
And *Æacus* and *Minos* bore the Load ;
Minos, who in the Flow'r of Youth and Fame,
Made mighty Nations tremble at his Name,   30
Infirm with Age, the proud *Miletus* fears,
Vain of his Birth, and in the Strength of Years,
And now regarding all his Realms as lost,
He durst not force him fron his native Coast.
But you by choice, *Miletus*, fled his Reign,
And thy swift Vessel plow'd th' *Ægean* Main ;
On *Asiatick* Shores a Town you frame,
Which still is honour'd with the Founder's Name.
Here you *Cyanëe* knew, the beauteous Maid,
As on her *Father's winding Banks she stray'd :   40
Caunus and *Byblis* hence their Lineage trace,
The double Offspring of your warm Embrace.

* Mæander.

---

17 Fates] Fate's *1717 and 1732*.   19 Arms] *1717* Arms, *1732*.   23 Then]
1717 Then, *1732*.   29 Youth] *1717* Youth, *1732*.

RURAL SPORTS.

A

G E O R G I C.

INSCRIBED

To Mr. *P O P E.*

———*Securi Prœlia ruris*
Pandimus.   Nemesian.

[*Editions :*
  1. RURAL SPORTS. | A | POEM. | INSCRIBED | To Mr. *POPE.* | By Mr. *GAY* | *Aegrestem tenui Musam meditabor Avenâ.*   Virg. | *LONDON :* | Printed for *J. Tonson,* at *Shakespear's-Head* over- | against *Catherine-street* in the *Strand.*   1713.
      Folio.   Underhill cites a letter from Gay to Maurice Johnson in Nichols' Literary Anecdotes as evidence that the date of publication was January 13, 1713.
  2. *Poems on Several Occasions,* 1720.
  3. Ditto, 1731.
The version of 1720 and 1731, given here, is practically a new poem.   The version of 1713 is given in Appendix II.]

YOU, who the sweets of rural life have known,
Despise th' ungrateful hurry of the town ;
In *Windsor* groves your easie hours employ,
And, undisturb'd, your self and Muse enjoy.
Thames listens to thy strains, and silent flows,
And no rude wind through rustling osiers blows,
While all his wond'ring Nymphs around thee throng,
To hear the *Syrens* warble in thy song.
  But I, who ne'er was bless'd by Fortune's hand,
Nor brighten'd plough-shares in paternal land,   10
Long in the noisie town have been immur'd,
Respir'd its smoak, and all its cares endur'd,
Where news and politicks divide mankind,
And schemes of state involve th' uneasie mind ;
Faction embroils the world ; and ev'ry tongue
Is moved by flatt'ry, or with scandal hung

1 life] *1720*   Life *1731.*   15 tongue] *1720*   Tongue *1731.*

Friendship, for sylvan shades, the palace flies,
Where all must yield to int'rest's dearer ties ;
Each rival *Machiavel* with envy burns,
And honesty forsakes them all by turns ;   20
While calumny upon each party 's thrown,
Which both promote, and both alike disown.
Fatigu'd at last ; a calm retreat I chose,
And sooth'd my harrass'd mind with sweet repose,
Where fields, and shades, and the refreshing clime,
Inspire the sylvan song, and prompt my rhime.
My muse shall rove through flow'ry meads and plains,
And deck with Rural Sports her native strains,
And the same road ambitiously pursue,
Frequented by the *Mantuan* swain, and you.   30
   'Tis not that rural sports alone invite,
But all the grateful country breaths delight :
Here blooming health exerts her gentle reign,
And strings the sinews of th' industrious swain.
Soon as the morning lark salutes the day,
Through dewy fields I take my frequent way,
Where I behold the farmer's early care,
In the revolving labours of the year.
   When the fresh spring in all her state is crown'd,
And high luxuriant grass o'erspreads the ground,   40
The lab'rer with the bending scythe is seen,
Shaving the surface of the waving green,
Of all her native pride disrobes the land,
And meads lays waste before his sweeping hand :
While with the mounting sun the meadow glows,
The fading herbage round he loosely throws ;
But if some sign portend a lasting show'r,
Th' experienc'd swain foresees the coming hour,
His sun-burnt hands the scatt'ring fork forsake,
And ruddy damsels ply the saving rake ;   50
In rising hills the fragrant harvest grows,
And spreads along the field in equal rows.
   Now when the height of heav'n bright *Phœbus* gains,
And level rays cleave wide the thirsty plains,
When heifers seek the shade and cooling lake,
And in the middle path-way basks the snake ;
O lead me, guard me from the sultry hours,
Hide me, ye forests, in your closest bowers :
Where the tall oak his spreading arms entwines,
And with the beech a mutual shade combines ;   60
Where flows the murm'ring brook, inviting dreams,
Where bord'ring hazle overhangs the streams
Whose rolling current winding round and round,
With frequent falls makes all the wood resound ;
Upon the mossy couch my limbs I cast,
And ev'n at noon the sweets of ev'ning taste.

Here I peruse the *Mantuan*'s Georgic strains,
And learn the labours of *Italian* swains ;
In ev'ry page I see new landschapes rise,
And all *Hesperia* opens to my eyes.   70
I wander o'er the various rural toil,
And know the nature of each different soil :
This waving field is gilded o'er with corn,
That spreading trees with blushing fruit adorn :
Here I survey the purple vintage grow,
Climb round the poles, and rise in graceful row :
Now I behold the steed curvet and bound,
And paw with restless hoof the smoaking ground :
The dewlap'd bull now chases along the plain,
While burning love ferments in ev'ry vein ;   80
His well-arm'd front against his rival aims,
And by the dint of war his mistress claims :
The careful insect 'midst his works I view,
Now from the flow'rs exhaust the fragrant dew ;
With golden treasures load his little thighs,
And steer his distant journey through the skies ;
Some against hostile drones the hive defend ;
Others with sweets the waxen cells distend :
Each in the toil his destin'd office bears,
And in the little bulk a mighty soul appears.   90
    Or when the ploughman leaves the task of day,
And trudging homeward whistles on the way ;
When the big-udder'd cows with patience stand,
Waiting the stroakings of the damsel's hand ;
No warbling chears the woods ; the feather'd choir
To court kind slumbers to their sprays retire ;
When no rude gale disturbs the sleeping trees,
Nor aspen leaves confess the gentlest breeze ;
Engag'd in thought, to *Neptune*'s bounds I stray,
To take my farewel of the parting day ;   100
Far in the deep the sun his glory hides,
A streak of gold the sea and sky divides ;
The purple clouds their amber linings show,
And edg'd with flame rolls ev'ry wave below :
Here pensive I behold the fading light,
And o'er the distant billow lose my sight.
    Now night in silent state begins to rise,
And twinkling orbs bestrow th' uncloudy skies ;
Her borrow'd lustre growing *Cynthia* lends,
And on the main a glitt'ring path extends ;   110
Millions of worlds hang in the spacious air,
Which round their suns their annual circles steer.
Sweet contemplation elevates my sense,
While I survey the works of providence.

    85 treasures] *1720*   Treasures *1731*.

O could the muse in loftier strains rehearse,
The glorious author of the universe,
Who reins the winds, gives the vast ocean bounds,
And circumscribes the floating worlds their rounds,
My soul should overflow in songs of praise,
And my Creator's name inspire my lays!   120
   As in successive course the seasons roll,
So circling pleasures recreate the soul.
When genial spring a living warmth bestows,
And o'er the year her verdant mantle throws,
No swelling inundation hides the grounds,
But crystal currents glide within their bounds;
The finny brood their wonted haunts forsake,
Float in the sun, and skim along the lake,
With frequent leap they range the shallow streams,
Their silver coats reflect the dazling beams.   130
Now let the fisherman his toils prepare,
And arm himself with ev'ry watry snare;
His hooks, his lines peruse with careful eye,
Encrease his tackle, and his rod retye.
   When floating clouds their spongy fleeces drain,
Troubling the streams with swift-descending rain,
And waters tumbling down the mountain's side,
Bear the loose soil into the swelling tide;
Then, soon as vernal gales begin to rise,
And drive the liquid burthen thro' the skies,   140
The fisher to the neighb'ring current speeds,
Whose rapid surface purles unknown to weeds;
Upon a rising border of the brook
He sits him down, and ties the treach'rous hook;
Now expectation chears his eager thought,
His bosom glows with treasures yet uncaught,
Before his eyes a banquet seems to stand,
Where ev'ry guest applauds his skilful hand.
   Far up the stream the twisted hair he throws,
Which down the murm'ring curren gently flows;   150
When if or chance or hunger's pow'rful sway
Directs the roving trout this fatal way,
He greedily sucks in the twining bait,
And tugs and nibbles the fallacious meat:
Now, happy fisherman, now twitch the line!
How thy rod bends! behold, the prize is thine!
Cast on the bank, he dies with gasping pains,
And trickling blood his silver mail distains.
   You must not ev'ry worm promiscuous use,
Judgment will tell thee proper bait to chuse;   160
The worm that draws a long immod'rate size
The trout abhors, and the rank morsel flies;

136 swift-descending] *1720* swift descending *1731*.
140 burthen] *1720* Burthen *1731*.   142 purles] *1731* purles, *1720*.

And if too small, the naked fraud's in sight,
And fear forbids, while hunger does invite.
Those baits will best reward the fisher's pains,
Whose polish'd tails a shining yellow stains :
Cleanse them from filth, to give a tempting gloss,
Cherish the sully'd reptile race with moss ;
Amid the verdant bed they twine, they toil,
And from their bodies wipe their native soil.   170
  But when the sun displays his glorious beams,
And shallow rivers flow with silver streams,
Then the deceit the scaly breed survey,
Bask in the sun, and look into the day.
You now a more delusive art must try,
And tempt their hunger with the curious fly.
  To frame the little animal, provide
All the gay hues that wait on female pride,
Let nature guide thee ; sometimes golden wire
The shining bellies of the fly require ;   180
The peacock's plumes thy tackle must not fail,
Nor the dear purchase of the sable's tail.
Each gaudy bird some slender tribute brings,
And lends the growing insect proper wings :
Silks of all colours must their aid impart,
And ev'ry fur promote the fisher's art.
So the gay lady, with expensive care,
Borrows the pride of land, of sea, and air ;
Furs, pearls, and plumes, the glittering thing displays,
Dazles our eyes, and easie hearts betrays.   190
  Mark well the various seasons of the year,
How the succeeding insect race appear ;
In this revolving moon one colour reigns,
Which in the next the fickle trout disdains.
Oft' have I seen a skilful angler try
The various colours of the treach'rous fly ;
When he with fruitless pain hath skim'd the brook,
And the coy fish rejects the skipping hook,
He shakes the boughs that on the margin grow,
Which o'er the stream a waving forrest throw ;   200
When if an insect fall (his certain guide)
He gently takes him from the whirling tide ;
Examines well his form with curious eyes,
His gaudy vest, his wings, his horns and size.
Then round his hook the chosen fur he winds,
And on the back a speckled feather binds,
So just the colours shine thro' ev'ry part,
That nature seems to live again in art.
Let not thy wary step advance too near,
While all thy hope hangs on a single hair ;   210

170 soil] *1731* Soil *1720*.   171 sun] *1720* Sun *1731*.

The new-form'd insect on the water moves,
The speckled trout the curious snare approves ;
Upon the curling surface let it glide,
With nat'ral motion from thy hand supply'd,
Against the stream now gently let it play,
Now in the rapid eddy roll away.
The scaly shoals float by, and seiz'd with fear
Behold their fellows tost in thinner air ;
But soon they leap, and catch the swimming bait,
Plunge on the hook, and share an equal fate.   220
    When a brisk gale against the current blows,
And all the watry plain in wrinkles flows,
Then let the fisherman his art repeat,
Where bubbling eddys favour the deceit.
If an enormous salmon chance to spy
The wanton errors of the floating fly,
He lifts his silver gills above the flood,
And greedily sucks in th' unfaithful food ;
Then downward plunges with the fraudful prey,
And bears with joy the little spoil away.   230
Soon in smart pain he feels the dire mistake,
Lashes the wave, and beats the foamy lake,
With sudden rage he now aloft appears,
And in his eye convulsive anguish bears ;
And now again, impatient of the wound,
He rolls and wreaths his shining body round ;
Then headlong shoots beneath the dashing tide,
The trembling fins the boiling wave divide ;
Now hope exalts the fisher's beating heart,
Now he turns pale, and fears his dubious art ;   240
He views the tumbling fish with longing eyes,
While the line stretches with th' unwieldy prize ;
Each motion humours with his steady hands,
And one slight hair the mighty bulk commands :
'Till tir'd at last, despoil'd of all his strength,
The game athwart the stream unfolds his length.
He now, with pleasure, views the gasping prize
Gnash his sharp teeth, and roll his blood-shot eyes ;
Then draws him to the shore, with artful care,
And lifts his nostrils in the sick'ning air :   250
Upon the burthen'd stream he floating lies,
Stretches his quivering fins, and gasping dies.
    Would you preserve a num'rous finny race ?
Let your fierce dogs the rav'nous otter chase ;
Th' amphibious monster ranges all the shores,
Darts through the waves, and ev'ry haunt explores :
Or let the gin his roving steps betray,
And save from hostile jaws the scaly prey.

      215 gently let it] *1731*   let it gently *1720.*

I never wander where the bord'ring reeds
O'erlook the muddy stream, whose tangling weeds   260
Perplex the fisher ; I, nor chuse to bear
The thievish nightly net, nor barbed spear ;
Nor drain I ponds the golden carp to take,
Nor trowle for pikes, dispeoplers of the lake.
Around the steel no tortur'd worm shall twine,
No blood of living insect stain my line ;
Let me, less cruel, cast the feather'd hook,
With pliant rod athwart the pebbled brook,
Silent along the mazy margin stray,
And with the fur-wrought fly delude the prey.   270

CANTO II.

Now, sporting Muse, draw in the flowing reins,
Leave the clear streams awhile for sunny plains.
Should you the various arms and toils rehearse,
And all the fisherman adorn thy verse ;
Should you the wide-encircling net display,
And in its spacious arch enclose the sea,
Then haul the plunging load upon the land,
And with the soale and turbet hide the sand ;
It would extend the growing theme too long,
And tire the reader with the watry song.   280
   Let the keen hunter from the chase refrain,
Nor render all the plowman's labour vain,
When *Ceres* pours out plenty from her horn,
And cloaths the fields with golden ears of corn.
Now, now, ye reapers, to your task repair,
Haste, save the product of the bounteous year :
To the wide-gathering hook long furrows yield,
And rising sheaves extend through all the field.
   Yet if for silvan sport thy bosom glow,
Let thy fleet greyhound urge his flying foe.   290
With what delight the rapid course I view !
How does my eye the circling race pursue !
He snaps deceitful air with empty jaws,
The subtle hare darts swift beneath his paws ;
She flies, he stretches, now with nimble bound
Eager he presses on, but overshoots his ground ;
She turns, he winds, and soon regains the way,
Then tears with goary mouth the screaming prey
What various sport does rural life afford !
What unbought dainties heap the wholesome board !   300

266 stain] *1720*   stains *1731.*

Nor less the spaniel, skilful to betray,
Rewards the fowler with the feather'd prey.
Soon as the lab'ring horse with swelling veins,
Hath safely hous'd the farmer's doubtful gains,
To sweet repast th' unwary partridge flies,
With joy amid the scatter'd harvest lies ;
Wandring in plenty, danger he forgets,
Nor dreads the slav'ry of entangling nets.
The subtle dog scowrs with sagacious nose
Along the field, and snuffs each breeze that blows,   310
Against the wind he takes his prudent way,
While the strong gale directs him to the prey ;
Now the warm scent assures the covey near,
He treads with caution, and he points with fear ;
Then (lest some sentry fowl the fraud descry,
And bid his fellows from the danger fly)
Close to the ground in expectation lies,
Till in the snare the flutt'ring covey rise.
Soon as the blushing light begins to spread,
And glancing *Phœbus* gilds the mountain's head,   320
His early flight th' ill-fated partridge takes,
And quits the friendly shelter of the brakes :
Or when the sun casts a declining ray,
And drives his chariot down the western way,
Let your obsequious ranger search around,
Where yellow stubble withers on the ground :
Nor will the roving spy direct in vain,
But numerous coveys gratifie thy pain.
When the meridian sun contracts the shade,
And frisking heifers seek the cooling glade ;   330
Or when the country floats with sudden rains,
Or driving mists deface the moist'ned plains ;
In vain his toils th' unskilful fowler tries,
While in thick woods the feeding partridge lies.
  Nor must the sporting verse the gun forbear,
But what's the fowler's be the muse's care.
See how the well-taught pointer leads the way :
The scent grows warm ; he stops ; he springs the prey ;
The flutt'ring coveys from the stubble rise,
And on swift wing divide the sounding skies ;   340
The scatt'ring lead pursues the certain sight,
And death in thunder overtakes their flight.
Cool breathes the morning air, and winter's hand
Spreads wide her hoary mantle o'er the land ;
Now to the copse thy lesser spaniel take,
Teach him to range the ditch and force the brake ;
Not closest coverts can protect the game :
Hark ! the dog opens ; take thy certain aim ;
The woodcock flutters ; how he wav'ring flies !
The wood resounds : he wheels, he drops, he dies.   350

   The tow'ring hawk let future poets sing,
Who terror bears upon his soaring wing :
Let them on high the frighted hern survey,
And lofty numbers paint their airy fray.
Nor shall the mountain lark the muse detain,
That greets the morning with his early strain ;
When, midst his song, the twinkling glass betrays ;
While from each angle flash the glancing rays,
And in the sun the transient colours blaze,
Pride lures the little warbler from the skies :   360
The light-enamour'd bird deluded dies.
   But still the chase, a pleasing task, remains ;
The hound must open in these rural strains.
Soon as *Aurora* drives away the night,
And edges eastern clouds with rosie light,
The healthy huntsman, with the chearful horn,
Summons the dogs, and greets the dappled morn ;
The jocund thunder wakes th' enliven'd hounds,
They rouze from sleep, and answer sounds for sounds ;
Wide through the furzy field their route they take,   370
Their bleeding bosoms force the thorny brake :
The flying game their smoaking nostrils trace,
No bounding hedge obstructs their eager pace ;
The distant mountains eccho from afar,
And hanging woods resound the flying war :
The tuneful noise the sprightly courser hears,
Paws the green turf, and pricks his trembling ears ;
The slacken'd rein now gives him all his speed,
Back flies the rapid ground beneath the steed ;
Hills, dales and forests far behind remain,   380
While the warm scent draws on the deep-mouth'd train
Where shall the trembling hare a shelter find ?
Hark ! death advances in each gust of wind !
New stratagems and doubling wiles she tries,
Now circling turns, and now at large she flies ;
Till spent at last, she pants, and heaves for breath,
Then lays her down, and waits devouring death.
   But stay, advent'rous muse, hast thou the force
To wind the twisted horn, to guide the horse ?
To keep thy seat unmov'd hast thou the skill   390
O'er the high gate, and down the headlong hill ?
Can'st thou the stag's laborious chace direct,
Or the strong fox through all his arts detect ?
The theme demands a more experienc'd lay :
Ye mighty hunters, spare this weak essay.
   O happy plains, remote from war's alarms,
And all the ravages of hostile arms !
And happy shepherds, who secure from fear,
On open downs preserve your fleecy care !
Whose spacious barns groan with encreasing store,   400
And whirling flails disjoint the cracking floor :

No barb'rous soldier, bent on cruel spoil,
Spreads desolation o'er your fertile soil ;
No trampling steed lays waste the ripen'd grain,
Nor crackling fires devour the promis'd gain :
No flaming beacons cast their blaze afar,
The dreadful signal of invasive war ;
No trumpet's clangor wounds the mother's ear,
And calls the lover from his swooning fair.
    What happiness the rural maid attends,   410
In chearful labour while each day she spends !
She gratefully receives what heav'n has sent,
And, rich in poverty, enjoys content:
(Such happiness, and such unblemish'd fame
Ne'er glad the bosom of the courtly dame.)
She never feels the spleen's imagin'd pains,
Nor melancholy stagnates in her veins ;
She never loses life in thoughtless ease,
Nor on the velvet couch invites disease ;
Her home-spun dress in simple neatness lies,   420
And for no glaring equipage she sighs :
Her reputation, which is all her boast,
In a malicious visit ne'er was lost :
No midnight masquerade her beauty wears,
And health, not paint, the fading bloom repairs.
If love's soft passion in her bosom reign,
An equal passion warms her happy swain ;
No homebred jars her quiet state controul,
Nor watchful jealousie torments her soul ;
With secret joy she sees her little race   430
Hang on her breast, and her small cottage grace ;
The fleecy ball their busy fingers cull,
Or from the spindle draw the length'ning wool :
Thus flow her hours with constant peace of mind,
Till Age the latest thread of life unwind.
    Ye happy fields, unknown to noise and strife,
The kind rewarders of industrious life ;
Ye shady woods, where once I us'd to rove;
Alike indulgent to the muse and love ;
Ye murm'ring streams that in *Mæanders* roll,   440
The sweet composers of the pensive soul,
Farewel.—The city calls me from your bow'rs :
Farewel amusing thoughts and peaceful hours.

415 dame.)] Dame.) *1713*   dame) *1720 and 1731*.   432 busy] *1731*   little *1720*.

T A L E S.

An Answer to the Sompner's *Prologue of* Chaucer.

In imitation of Chaucer's *style.*

[From *Poems on Several Occasions*, 1720 and 1731. Printed by Underhill in an Appendix, presumably because of ' the indecency . . . which is [their] distinguishing characteristic '.]

THE *Sompner* leudly hath his Prologue told,
And saine on the Freers his tale japing and bold ;
How that in Hell they searchen near and wide,
And ne one Freer in all thilke place espyde,
But lo ! the devil turned his erse about,
And twenty thousand Freers wend in and out.
By which in *Jeoffrys* rhyming it appears,
The devil's belly is the hive of Freers.
　Now listneth lordings ! forthwith ye shall hear,
What happend at a house in *Lancashire*.　　　　　　10
A misere that had londs and tenement,
Who raketh from his villaines taxes and rent,
Owned a house which emptye long y-stood,
Full deeply sited in a derkning wood,
Murmring a shallow brook runneth along,
Mong the round stones it maken doleful song.
　Now there spreaden a rumour that everich night
The rooms ihaunted been by many a sprite,
The miller avoucheth, and all there about,
That they full oft' hearen the hellish rout ;　　　　　20
Some saine they hear the jingling of chains,
And some hath yheard the psautries straines,
At midnight some the headless horse imeet,
And some espien a corse in a white sheet,
And oother things, faye, elfin and elfe,
And shapes that fear createn to it selfe.
　Now it so hapt, there was not ferre away,
Of grey Freers a faire and rich Abbaye,
Where liven a Freer ycleped *Pere Thomas*,
Who daren alone in derke through church-yerds pass.　　30

28 faire] *1720*　fair *1731*.

This Freer would lye in thilke house all night,
In hope he might espyen a dreadful sprite.
He taketh candle, beades, and holy watere,
And legends eke of Saintes, and bookes of prayere.
He entreth the room, and looketh round about,
And haspen the door to haspen the goblin out.
The candle hath he put close by the bed,
And in low tone his *ave marye* said.
With water now besprinkled hath the floore,
And maken cross on key-hole of the doore.   40
Ne was there not a mouse-hole in thilke place,
But he y-crossed hath by God his grace ;
He crossed hath this, and eke he crossed that,
With *benedicite* and God knows what.
    Now he goeth to bed and lieth adown,
When the clock had just stricken the twelfth soun.
Bethinketh hem now what the cause had ibeen,
Why many sprites by mortals have been seen.
Hem remembreth how *Dan Plutarch* hath y-sed
That *Cæsar*'s sprite came to *Brute* his bed ;   50
Of chains that frighten erst *Artemidore*,
The tales of *Pline*, *Valere*, and many more.
Hem thinketh that some murdere here been done,
And he mought see some bloodye ghost anone,
Or that some orphlines writings here be stor'd,
Or pot of gold laine deep beneath a board :
Or thinketh hem, if he might see no sprite,
The Abbaye mought buy this house cheape outright.
    As hem thus thinketh, anone asleep he lies.
Up starten *Sathanas* with saucer eyes.   60
He turned the Freer upon his face downright,
Displaying his nether cheeks ful broad and white.
Then quoth *Dan Sathanas* as he thwacked him sore,
Thou didst forget to guard thy postern-door.
There is an hole which hath not crossed been :
Farewel, from whence I came, I creepen in.
    Now plain it is ytellen in my verse,
If Devils in Hell bear Freers in their erse,
On earth the Devil in Freers doth y-dwell ;
Were there no Freers, the Devil mought keep in hell.   70

WORK *for a* COOPER.

A *T A L E.*

A MAN may lead a happy life,
Without that needful thing, a wife :
This long have lusty Abbots known,
Who ne'er knew spouses—of their
    own.
  What, though your house be clean
    and neat,
With couches, chairs, and beds com-
    pleat ;
Though you each day invite a friend,
Though he should ev'ry dish com-,
    mend,
On *Bagshot-heath* your mutton fed,
Your fowls at *Brandford* born and
    bred ;   10
Though purest wine your cellars
    boast,
Wine worthy of the fairest Toast ;
Yet there are other things requir'd :
Ring, and let 's see the maid you
    hir'd—
Bless me ! those hands might hold
    a broom,
Twirle round a mop, and wash a
    room :
A batchelor his maid should keep,
Not for that servile use to sweep,
Let her his humour understand,
And turn to ev'ry thing her hand. 20
Get you a lass that 's young and tight,
Whose arms are, like her apron, white;
What though her shift be seldom seen ?
Let that though coarse be always
    clean ;
She might each morn your tea attend,
And on your wrist your ruffle mend ;
Then if you break a roguish jest,
Or squeeze her hand, or pat her breast,

She crys, oh dear Sir, don't be naught!
And blushes speak her last night's
    fault.   30
To her your houshold cares confide,
Let your keys gingle at her side,
A footman's blunders teaze and fret
    ye,
Ev'n while you chide, you smile on
    Betty.
Discharge him then, if he 's too
    spruce,
For *Betty*'s for his master's use.
  Will you your am'rous fancy baulk,
For fear some prudish neighbour talk?
But you 'll object, that you 're afraid
Of the pert freedoms of a maid ;   40
Besides your wiser heads will say,
That she who turns her hand this way,
From one vice to another drawn,
Will lodge your silver spoons in pawn.
Has not the homely wrinkled jade
More need to learn the pilf'ring trade ?
For Love all *Betty*'s wants supplys,
Laces her shoes, her manteau dyes,
All her stuff suits she flings away,
And wears thread sattin every day. 50
  Who then a dirty drab would
    hire,
Brown as the hearth of kitchin fire ?
When all must own, were *Betty* put
To the black dutys of the slut,
As well she scowers or scrubs a floor,
And still is good for something more.
  Thus, to avoid the greater vice,
I knew a Priest, of conscience nice,
To quell his lust for neighbour's
    spouse,
Keep fornication in his house.   60

47 Love] *1720* love *1731*.

55 scowers] *1720* scow'rs *1731*.

But you're impatient all this time,
Fret at my counsel, curse my rhyme,
Be satisfy'd. I'll talk no more,
For thus my tale begins—Of yore
There dwelt at *Blois* a Priest full fair,
With rolling eye and crisped hair,
His chin hung low, his brow was sleek,
Plenty lay basking on his cheek,
Whole days at cloyster grates he sat,
Ogled, and talk'd of this and that 70
So feelingly ; the Nuns lamented
That double barrs were e'er invented.
If he the wanton wife confest
With downcast eye, and heaving
        breast ;
He stroak'd her cheek to still her fear,
And talk'd of sins *en Cavalier.*
Each time enjoyn'd her pennance
        mild,
And fondled on her like his child.
At ev'ry jovial gossip's feast
Pere Bernard was a welcome guest, 80
Mirth suffer'd not the least restraint,
He could at will shake off the saint ;
Nor frown'd he when they freely
        spoke,
But shook his sides, and took the joke;
Nor fail'd he to promote the jest,
And shar'd the sins which they confest.
Yet that he might not always roam,
He kept conveniencies at home.
His maid was in the bloom of beauty,
Well-limb'd for ev'ry social duty ; 90
He meddled with no houshold cares,
To her consign'd his whole affairs ;
She of his Study kept the keys,
For he was studious—of his ease :
She had the power of all his locks,
Could rummage ev'ry chest and box,
Her honesty such credit gain'd,
Not ev'n the cellar was restrain'd.
   In troth it was a goodly show,
Lin'd with full hogsheads all a-row ;
One vessel, from the rank remov'd, 101
Far dearer than the rest he lov'd.
Pour la bonne bouche 'twas set aside,
To all but choicest friends deny'd.

He now and then would send a quart,
To warm some wife's retentive heart,
Against confession's sullen hour :
Wine has all secrets in its power.
At common feasts it had been waste.
Nor was it fit for layman's taste ; 110
If monk or friar were his guest,
They drank it, for they know the
        best.
Nay, he at length so fond was grown,
He always drank it when—alone.
   Who shall recount his civil labours,
In pious visits to his neighbours ?
Whene'er weak husbands went astray,
He guest their wives were in the
        way,
'Twas then his charity was shown,
He chose to see them when alone. 120
   Now was he bent on cuckoldom :
He knew friend *Dennis* was from
        home ;
His wife (a poor neglected beauty,
Defrauded of a husband's duty)
Had often told him at confession,
How hard she struggled 'gainst trans-
        gression.
He now resolves, in heat of blood,
To try how firm her virtue stood.
He knew that wine (to love best aid)
Has oft' made bold the shamefac'd
        maid, 130
Taught her to romp, and take more
        freedoms,
Than nymphs train'd up at *Smith*'s
        or *Needham*'s.
   A mighty bottle strait he chose,
Such as might give two Friars their
        dose :
Nannette he call'd : the cellar door
She strait unlocks, descends before,
He follow'd close. But when he spys
His fav'rite cask ; with lifted eyes
And lifted hands aloud he crys. 139
Heigh day ! my darling wine astoop !
It must, alas ! have sprung a hoop ;
That there's a leak is past all doubt,
(Reply'd the maid)—I'll find it out.

103 *Pour la bonne bouche*] 1731, Underhill   *Pour faire bon bouche* 1720   *Pour faire bonne bouche* Bell.   110 taste ;] *1720*   taste, *1731.*

She sets the candle down in haste,
Tucks her white apron round her waste,
The hogshead's mouldy side ascends,
She straddles wide, and downward bends ;
So low she stoops to seek the flaw,
Her coats rose high, her master saw—
I·see—he crys—(then claspt her fast)
The leak through which my wine has past. 151
   Then all in haste the maid descended,

And in a trice the leak was mended.
He found in *Nannette* all he wanted.
So *Dennis'* brows remain'd unplanted.
   E'er since this time all lusty Friars
(Warm'd with predominant desires,
Whene'er the flesh with spirit quarrels)
Look on the sex as leaky barrels.
Beware of these, ye jealous spouses,
From such like coopers guard your houses ; 161
For if they find not work at home,
For jobs through all the town they roam.

The EQUIVOCATION.

A *TALE*.

An Abbot rich (whose taste was good
Alike in science and in food)
His Bishop had resolv'd to treat ;
The Bishop came, the Bishop eat ;
'Twas silence, 'till their stomachs fail'd ;
And now at Hereticks they rail'd ;
What Heresy (the Prelate said)
Is in that Church where Priests may wed !
Do not we take the Church for life ?
But those divorce her for a wife, 10
Like laymen keep her in their houses,
And own the children of their spouses.
Vile practices ! the Abbot cry'd,
For pious use we're set aside !
Shall we take wives ? marriage at best
Is but carnality profest.
Now as the Bishop took his glass,
He spy'd our Abbot's buxom lass
Who cross'd the room ; he mark'd her eye
That glow'd with love ; his pulse beat high. 20

Fye, father, fye, (the Prelate crys)
A maid so young ! for shame, be wise.
These indiscretions lend a handle
To lewd lay tongues, to give us scandal ;
For your vows sake, this rule I give t' ye,
Let all your maids be turn'd of fifty.
   The Priest reply'd, I have not swerv'd,
But your chast precept well observ'd ;
That lass full twenty five has told,
I've yet another who's as old ; 30
Into one sum their ages cast ;
So both my maids have fifty past.
   The Prelate smil'd, but durst not blame ;
For why ? his Lordship did the same.
   Let those who reprimand their brothers
First mend the faults they find in others.

14 we're] *1731* were *1720*.

32 have] are *Underhill*.

A true STORY *of an* APPARITION.

SCEPTICKS (whose strength of argument makes out
That wisdom's deep enquirys end in doubt)
Hold this assertion positive and clear,
That sprites are pure delusions rais'd by fear.
Not that fam'd ghost, which in presaging sound
Call'd *Brutus* to *Philippi*'s fatal ground ;
Nor can *Tiberius Gracchus*' goary shade
These ever-doubting disputants persuade.
Strait they with smiles reply ; those tales of old
By visionary Priests were made and told :   10
Oh might some ghost at dead of night appear,
And make you own conviction by your fear !
I know your sneers my easy faith accuse,
Which with such idle legends scares the Muse :
But think not that I tell those vulgar sprites,
Which frighted boys relate on winter nights ;
How cleanly milk-maids meet the fairy train,
How headless horses drag the clinking chain,
Night-roaming ghosts, by saucer eye-balls known,
The common spectres of each country town.   20
No, I such fables can like you despise,
And laugh to hear these nurse-invented lies.
Yet has not oft the fraudful guardian's fright
Compell'd him to restore an orphan's right ?
And can we doubt that horrid ghosts ascend,
Which on the conscious murd'rer's steps attend ?
Hear then, and let attested truth prevail,
From faithful lips I learnt the dreadful tale.
    Where *Arden*'s forest spreads its limits wide,
Whose branching paths the doubtful road divide,   30
A trav'ler took his solitary way ;
When low beneath the hills was sunk the day.
And now the skies with gath'ring darkness lour,
The branches rustle with the threaten'd shower ;
With sudden blasts the forest murmurs loud,
Indented lightnings cleave the sable cloud,
Thunder on thunder breaks, the tempest roars,
And heav'n discharges all its watry stores.
The wand'ring trav'ler shelter seeks in vain,
And shrinks and shivers with the beating rain ;   40
On his steed's neck the slacken'd bridle lay,
Who chose with cautious step th' uncertain way ;
And now he checks the rein, and halts to hear
If any noise foretold a village near.
At length from far a stream of light he sees
Extend its level ray between the trees ;

14 scares] *1731* frights *1720* (*corrected to* scares *in Errata*).
15 sprites] *1720* sprights *1731*.

Thither he speeds, and as he nearer came
Joyfull he knew the lamp's domestick flame
That trembled through the window ; cross the way
Darts forth the barking cur, and stands at bay.   50
    It was an ancient lonely house, that stood
Upon the borders of the spacious wood ;
Here towers and antique battlements arise,
And there in heaps the moulder'd ruine lyes ;
Some Lord this mansion held in days of yore,
To chase the wolf, and pierce the foaming boar :
How chang'd, alas, from what it once had been !
'Tis now degraded to a publick Inn.
    Strait he dismounts, repeats his loud commands ;
Swift at the gate the ready landlord stands ;   60
With frequent cringe he bows, and begs excuse.
His house was full, and ev'ry bed in use.
What not a garret, and no straw to spare ?
Why, then, the kitchin fire and elbow-chair
Shall serve for once to nod away the night.
The kitchin ever is the servant's right,
Replys the host ; there, all the fire around,
The Count's tir'd footmen snore upon the ground.
    The maid, who listen'd to this whole debate,
With pity learnt the weary stranger's fate.   70
Be brave, she crys, you still may be our guest,
Our haunted room was ever held the best ;
If then your valour can the fright sustain
Of rattling curtains, and the clinking chain,
If your couragious tongue have power to talk,
When round your bed the horrid ghost shall walk ;
If you dare ask it, why it leaves its tomb,
I'll see your sheets well-air'd, and show the room.
Soon as the frighted maid her tale had told,
The stranger enter'd, for his heart was bold.   80
    The damsel led him through a spacious hall,
Where Ivy hung the half-demolish'd wall ;
She frequent look'd behind, and chang'd her hue,
While fancy tipt the candle's flame with blue.
And now they gain'd the winding stairs ascent,
And to the lonesome room of terrors went.
When all was ready, swift retir'd the maid,
The watch-lights burn, tuckt warm in bed was laid
The hardy stranger, and attends the sprite
Till his accustom'd walk at dead of night.   90
    At first he hears the wind with hollow roar
Shake the loose lock, and swing the creaking door
Nearer and nearer draws the dreadful sound
Of rattling chains, that dragg'd upon the ground :
When lo, the spectre came with horrid stride,
Approach'd the bed, and drew the curtains wide !

64 fire] *1731* fire, *1720*.   85 stairs] stair's *Underhill*.

In human form the ghastful Phantom stood,
Expos'd his mangled bosom dy'd with blood.
Then silent pointing to his wounded breast,
Thrice wav'd his hand. Beneath the frighted guest   100
The bed-cords trembled, and with shudd'ring fear
Sweat chill'd his limbs, high rose his bristled hair;
Then mutt'ring hasty pray'rs, he mann'd his heart,
And cry'd aloud ; Say, whence and who thou art.
The stalking ghost with hollow voice replys,
Three years are counted, since with mortal eyes
I saw the sun, and vital air respir'd.
Like thee benighted, and with travel tir'd,
Within these walls I slept.   O thirst of gain !
See, still the planks the bloody mark retain ;   110
Stretch'd on this very bed, from sleep I start,
And see the steel impending o'er my heart ;
The barb'rous hostess held the lifted knife,
The floor ran purple with my gushing life.
My treasure now they seize, the golden spoil
They bury deep beneath the grass-grown soil,
Far in the common field.   Be bold, arise,
My steps shall lead thee to the secret prize ;
There dig and find ; let that thy care reward :
Call loud on justice, bid her not retard   120
To punish murder ; lay my ghost at rest,
So shall with peace secure thy nights be blest ;
And when beneath these boards my bones are found,
Decent interr them in some sacred ground.
     Here ceas'd the ghost.   The stranger springs from bed,
And boldly follows where the Phantom led ;
The half-worn stony stairs they now descend,
Where passages obscure their arches bend
Silent they walk ; and now through groves they pass,
Now through wet meads their steps imprint the grass ;   130
At length amidst a spacious field they came :
There stops the spectre, and ascends in flame.
Amaz'd he stood, no bush, no briar was found,
To teach his morning search to find the ground ;
What could he do ? the night was hideous dark,
Fear shook his joints, and nature dropt the mark :
With that he starting wak'd, and rais'd his head,
But found the golden mark was left in bed.
     What is the statesman's vast ambitious scheme,
But a short vision, and a golden dream ?   140
Power, wealth, and title elevate his hope ;
He wakes.   But for a garter finds a rope.

---

    101 fear] fear, *1720 and 1731.*   128 bend] *1720 and 1731*   bend. *Bell, Cooke,*
Underhill.   133 no bush, no briar] *1720 and 1731*   no bush or briar *Bell, Cooke,*
Underhill.

The M A D - D O G.

A T A L E.

[Editions :
1. *Poems on Several Occasions.* 1720.
2. THE | MAD DOG, | A | TALE. | By *H——— J———*, Esq ; |
    When once too potent Flesh and Blood
    Gain Empire o'er frail Woman's Soul,
    What Confessor can do her Good ?
    What Art the dear Disease controul ?
    Soon as her Fancy learns to stray
    Where Love's soft Extasy invites,
    Back she but seldom finds her Way,
    Or wants Excuse for what delights.

LONDON : | Printed for A. Moore, and sold by the Book- | sellers of *London* and *Westminster*, 1730. | (Price, Six-pence.)
    Folio. A copy is in Mr. T. J. Wise's Library ; another in the British Museum, catalogued under J———, H———.
3. *Poems on Several Occasions,* 1731.
The version of 1730 is a distinct improvement. I follow it (except in its use of capital letters) and give the readings of 1720 and 1731 in the notes.]

A Prude, at morn and ev'ning pray'r,
Had worn her velvet cushion bare ;
Upwards she taught her eyes to roll,
As if with them she wing'd her soul ;
And when devotion warm'd the croud,
None sung, or smote their breasts, so loud.
Pale Penitence had mark'd her face
With all the meagre signs of grace ;
Her mass-book was compleatly lin'd
With painted Saints of ev'ry kind :
But when in ev'ry page she view'd 11
Fine Ladys who the flesh subdu'd,
As quick her beads she counted o'er,
And cry'd—Such wonders are no more !
She chose not to delay confession,
To bear at once a year's transgression,
But ev'ry week set all things even,
And ballanc'd her accounts with heaven.
  Behold her now in humble guise,
Upon her knees, with downcast eyes 20

Before the Priest : She thus begins,
And sobbing, blubbers forth her sins ;
  " Who could that tempting man resist ?
" My virtue languish'd, as he kiss'd ;
"I strove,—till I could strive no longer,
" How can the weak resist the stronger ? "
  The Father ask'd her, where and when ?
How many times ? What sort of men ?
By what degrees her blood was heated ?
How oft' the failing was repeated ? 30
  Thus have I seen a pregnant wench
All flush'd with guilt, before the bench ;
The Judges (wak'd by wanton thought)
Dive to the bottom of her fault ;
They leer, they simper at her shame,
And make her call all things by name.
  And now to sentence he proceeds,
Prescribes how oft' to tell her beads,

1 pray'r] prayer   3 Upwards] upward   4 As if she watch'd her soaring soul ;   6 breasts] breast   10 ev'ry] various   12 subdu'd,] subdu'd ;
14 And] She   18 heaven] heav'n   26 resist] subdue   28 How many ? and what sort of men ?   30 failing] frailty   31 *This line does not begin a new paragraph in 1720 and 1731.*

Shows her what Saints could do her
good,
Doubles her fasts to cool her blood. 40
Eas'd of her sins, and light as air,
Away she trips ; perhaps to pray'r.
'Twas no such thing.——Why then
this haste ?
The clock has struck, the hour is past,
And on the spur of inclination,
She scorn'd to bilk her assignation.

Whate'er she did, next week she
came,
And piously confess'd the same ;
The Priest, who female frailties pity'd,
First chid her, then her crimes re-
mitted.

But did she now her crimes bemoan
In penitential sheets alone ? 52
And was no bold, no beastly fellow
The nightly partner of her pillow ?
No, none,——for next time, in the
grove,
A bank was conscious of her love.
Confession day was come about,
And now again it all must out;
She seems to wipe her twinkling eyes ;
What now, my child, the father crys ;
Again, says she !—with threatning
looks, 61
He thus the prostrate dame rebukes.
 " Madam, I own there 's something
in it,
 " That virtue has th' unguarded
minute ;
 " But pray now tell me, what are
whores,
 " But women of unguarded hours ?
 " Then you must sure have lost all
shame ;
 " What ! ev'ry day, and still the same !
 " And no fault else ! 'Tis strange to
find
 " A woman to one sin confin'd ! 70
 " Pride is this day her darling passion,
 " The next day slander is in fashion ;

"Gaming succeeds; if fortune crosses,
 " Then virtue 's mortgaged for her
losses ;
 " By use her fav'rite vice she loaths,
 " And loves new follies like new
cloaths:
 " But you ! beyond all thought un-
chaste,
 " Have all sin center'd near your
waste !
 " Whence is this appetite so strong ?
 " Say, Madam, did your mother long ?
 " Or is it lux'ry or high diet 81
 " That won't let virtue sleep in
quiet ? "
 She tells him now with meekest
voice,
That she had never err'd by choice ;
Nor was there known a virgin chaster,
'Till ruin'd by a sad disaster.

That she a fav'rite lap-dog had,
Which, (as she stroak'd and kiss'd)
grew mad,
And on her lip a wound indenting,
First set her youthful blood fer-
menting. 90
 The Priest reply'd with zealous
strain,
 " You should have sought the means
to gain ;
 " Doctors by various ways, we find,
 " Treat these distempers of the mind.
 " Let gaudy ribbands be deny'd
 " To her, who raves with scornful
pride ;
 " And if religion rack her notions,
 " Lock up her volumes of devotions ;
 " But if for man her rage prevail, 99
 " Barr her the sight of creatures male.
 " Or else to cure such venom'd bites,
 " And set the shatter'd thoughts to
rights,
 " They send you to the ocean's shore,
 " And plunge the Patient o'er and
o'er.

50 crimes] sins　　　51 crimes] crime　　　55 for next] for the next　　　57 *This*
line begins a new paragraph in 1720 and 1731.　　　63 own] grant　　　81 or] and
83 *This line does not begin a new paragraph in 1720 and 1731.*　　　91 strain] fury
92 gain] cure ye　　　97 rack] crack　　　102 to rights,] arights ;

" The dame reply'd, Alas ! in vain
"My kindred forc'd me to the *Main* ;
" Naked, and in the face of day ;
" (Look not, ye fishermen, this way !)
" What virgin had not done as I did ?
" My modest hand, by nature guided,
" Debarr'd at once from human
   eyes   111
" The place where female honour lyes,
" And tho' thrice dipt from top to toe,
" I still secur'd the post below ;
" And cover'd it with Gripe so fast
" Not one drop through my fingers
   past ;
" Thus owe I to my bashful care,
" That all the rage is settled *there.*"
   [Weigh well the projects of man-
   kind ;   119
Then tell me, Reader, canst thou find
The man from madness wholly free ?
They all are mad—save you and me.
Do not the statesman, fop and wit
By daily follies prove they 're bit ?
And when the briny cure they try'd,
Some part still kept above the tide ?

Some men (when drench'd beneath
   the wave)
High o'er their heads their fingers
   save :
Those hands by mean extortion thrive
Or in the pocket lightly dive :   130
Or more expert in pilf'ring vice,
They burn and itch to cog the dice.
   Plunge in a courtier ; strait his
   fears
Direct his hands to stop his ears.
And now truth seems a grating noise,
He loves the sland'rer's whisp'ring
   voice :
He hangs on flatt'ry with delight,
And thinks all fulsome praise is right.
   All women dread a watry death :
They shut their lips to hold their
   breath,   140
And though you duck them ne'er so
   long,
Not one salt drop e'er wets their
   tongue ;
'Tis hence they scandal have at will,
And that this member ne'er lyes still.]

111 human] humane *1730.*   112 place] seat   115 And guarded it with
grasp so fast   119-44 *These lines are omitted in 1730.*

THE

STORY of *CEPHISA.*

[Text from *The Poetical, Dramatic and Miscellaneous Works of John Gay* 1795.
Also given by *Bell* 1777, and *Park* 1808.]

IN western climes where the bright God of day
Darts on the gladsome earth a warmer ray,
While smiling Spring led on the jocund hours,
And early months bestrew'd the fields with flow'rs,
In bloom of youth *Cephisa*, lovely maid,
Trac'd the wide lawns, and thro' the forests stray'd ;
Not all the nymphs who swell *Diana's* train
From *Cynthus'* top, when issuing on the plain,
With hound and horn they raise the chearful cry,
And the rocks echo and the floods reply :   10

1 day] day, *1795.*   5 maid,] maid *1795*   maid ! *Bell.*

Not all their train for beauty could compare
Their goddess' self scarce like *Cephisa* fair.—
Struck with the sight of such transcendant charms,
With gifts the shepherds woo'd her to their arms.
The am'rous toys no grace nor favour gain'd ;
The gifts, and givers she alike disdain'd ;
Resolv'd in happy solitude to rove
A sylvan huntress thro' the leafy grove.
   But envious Fate the nymph no respite gives,
In ev'ry heart her lov'd idea lives :   20
E'en *Pan* himself, with ardent passion fir'd,
The God of woods, the woodland nymph desir'd ;
Still as he views, he pants to clasp the maid,
And softly sighing to himself he said :
" O happy winds, which kiss that snowy breast,
" O happy garments, which those limbs invest,
" But, happier he who gains so rich a prize,
" Pants in those arms, and on that bosom dies ! "
   Thus he ;—the Nymph far other loves employ,
The chace her glory, and the woods her joy ;   30
Oft' as the God is present to her sight,
So oft' the nymph prepares for sudden flight,
Eludes his search, swift skimming o'er the lawn,
As from the beagle flies the bounding fawn.
   A bow'r there was, a close sequester'd shade,
By poplar boughs and twining osiers made,
Fast by whose side a chrystal fountain flow'd,
(The banks with flow'rs of various colours glow'd ;)
Here oft' at noon the weary fair reclin'd
To court the coolness of the gentle wind,   40
For here soft Zephyr with a grateful breeze,
Kiss'd the young plants, and whisper'd thro' the trees.
   It chanc'd that *Pan* had mark'd the pebbled bed
Where the stream issu'd from its fountain-head,
Thence pouring on, through mossy windings roll'd,
O'er fertile tracks and sands that glow'd with gold ;
Its course the God with curious search pursu'd,
Till pleas'd, at length, the fragrant bow'r he view'd ;
But far more pleas'd the beauteous nymph survey'd,
Stretch'd at her ease beneath the cooling shade.   50
His near approach the pensive nymph alarms,
Who rises hasty, with disorder'd charms,
Springs from her covert like the tim'rous hare,
And, flying, fills with shrieks the ambient air.
With wings of love *Pan* urges on the course,
Fear lends her strength, while Love supplies his force.
Yet oft' the god, in the mid' chase, delays,
Stops short of conquest and submissive prays,

" O thou," he cries, " the loveliest of thy kind,
" Why fly'st thou thus, and leav'st thy love behind ?   60
" No savage foe, no plunderer is near,
" Nor mountain-robber with his dreadful spear,
" Nor mean am I tho' woods my lineage claim,
" My sire immortal, and myself the same ;
" Nor on the crook, nor plough do I depend,
" Nor on the mountain's top a scanty flock attend ;—
" *PAN* is my name ;—the herds on yonder plains,
" My herbage fattens and my care sustains ;
" To me the woodland empire is decreed,
" I claim th' invention of the vocal reed ;   70
" Yet vain these arts, these gifts in vain bestow'd,
" Great as I am, and worshipp'd as a God,
" If thou bright nymph with coyness and disdain,
" Repay thy lover, and deride his pain."
    Thus urg'd the sylvan God his am'rous pray'r,
But all his words were lost in empty air.
With double speed the nymph her course renew'd,
With double speed the ravisher pursu'd,
O'er hills and dales they hold the rapid race,
Till, spent at length, and weary'd with the chace,   80
With secret dread she views the sun descend,
And twilight o'er the earth her veil extend ;
For now the swift pursuer nearer drew,
And almost touch'd her garments as she flew ;
Wheel'd as she wheel'd, on ev'ry footstep gain'd,
And no relief nor glimpse of hope remain'd.
Fast by a stream, an ancient altar stood,
And close behind it rose a wavy wood,
Whose twining boughs exclude the parting light,
And dusky shades anticipate the night,   90
Thither, collecting all her force, she flies,
And, " Oh ! whatever god (the damsel cries)
" Protects this altar, may that gen'rous pow'r
" Hear and relieve me in this dang'rous hour,
" Give me at least to save my spotless fame,
" And still in death preserve a virgin's name."
    While thus to unknown pow'rs *Cephisa* pray'd,
Victorious *Pan* o'ertook the fainting maid.
Around her waste his eager arms he throws,
With love and joy his throbbing bosom glows ;   100
When, wonderful to tell, her form receives
A verdant cov'ring of expanded leaves ;
Then shooting downward trembling to the ground
A fibrous root her slender ancles bound.
Strange to herself, as yet, aghast she stands,
And to high Heav'n she rears her spotless hands ;

60 behiud ?] *Bell* behind ; *1795.*   63 woods] *Bell* words *1795.*

These while she spreads them still in spires extend,
Till in small leaves her taper fingers end ;
Her voice she tries ; but utt'rance is deny'd,
The smother'd sounds in hollow murmurs dy'd ;   110
At length, quite chang'd, the God with wonder view'd
A beauteous plant arising where she stood ;
This from his touch with human sense inspir'd,
Indignant shrinking, of itself retir'd ;
Yet *Pan* attends it with a lover's cares,
And fost'ring aid with tender hand prepares ;
The new form'd plant reluctant seems to yield,
And lives the grace and glory of the field.
But still, as mindful of her former state,
The nymph's perfections on her change await,   120
And tho' transform'd, her virtue still remains,
No touch impure her sacred plant sustains,
From whence the name of SENSITIVE it gains.
This oft' the nymphs approach with secret dread,
While crimson blushes o'er their cheeks are spread ;
Yet the true virgin has no cause for fear,
The test is equal if the maid's sincere.
This in thy walks O —— is found,
Thy walks for virgins fair and chaste renown'd.
This from the mild Hesperian clime convey'd,   130
Shall ever bloom, O *W*—— in thy shade ;
Yet *Western* nymphs thy wondrous tree avoid,
Lest all their hopes be by a touch destroy'd.
Britannia's daughters no such terrors know,
With no lewd flames their spotless bosoms glow ;
Tho' ev'ry shrub our cultur'd gardens boast,
And all of foreign stock, a countless host ;
Should all at once the precious gift receive,
And ev'ry plant become a SENSITIVE,
Yet should *their* fame the dreadful trial stand,   140
And add new honours to their native land ;
Honours their latest progeny shall share,
For ever virtuous, as for ever fair.

128 O ——] i. e. *Montague.*   131 O *W*——] i. e. *Wortley.*
128 found,] *Bell* found *1795.*   143 For] *Bell* Nor *1795.*

ECLOGUES.

THE

BIRTH of the *SQUIRE.*

An ECLOGUE.

In Imitation of the POLLIO *of* VIRGIL.

[All five 'Eclogues' appeared in *Poems on Several Occasions* (1720 and 1731).
One, *The Toilette* (q.v.), had been previously published. *The Espousal* was the result
of a suggestion by Swift in 1716.]

YE sylvan Muses, loftier strains recite,
Not all in shades, and humble cotts delight.
Hark! the bells ring; along the distant grounds
The driving gales convey the swelling sounds;
Th' attentive swain, forgetful of his work,
With gaping wonder, leans upon his fork.
What sudden news alarms the waking morn?
To the glad Squire a hopeful heir is born.
Mourn, mourn, ye stags; and all ye beasts of chase,
This hour destruction brings on all your race: 10
See the pleas'd tenants duteous off'rings bear,
Turkeys and geese and grocer's sweetest ware;
With the new health the pond'rous tankard flows,
And old *October* reddens ev'ry nose.
Beagles and spaniels round his cradle stand,
Kiss his moist lip and gently lick his hand;
He joys to hear the shrill horn's ecchoing sounds,
And learns to lisp the names of all the hounds.
With frothy ale to make his cup o'er-flow,
Barley shall in paternal acres grow;   20
The bee shall sip the fragrant dew from flow'rs,
To give metheglin for his morning hours;
For him the clustring hop shall climb the poles,
And his own orchard sparkle in his bowles.
   His Sire's exploits he now with wonder hears,
The monstrous tales indulge his greedy ears;

How when youth strung his nerves and warm'd his veins,
He rode the mighty *Nimrod* of the plains :
He leads the staring infant through the hall,
Points out the horny spoils that grace the wall ;   30
Tells, how this stag thro' three whole Countys fled,
What rivers swam, where bay'd, and where he bled.
Now he the wonders of the fox repeats,
Describes the desp'rate chase, and all his cheats ;
How in one day beneath his furious speed,
He tir'd seven coursers of the fleetest breed ;
How high the pale he leapt, how wide the ditch,
When the hound tore the haunches of the * witch !
These stories which descend from son to son,
The forward boy shall one day make his own.   40
    Ah, too fond mother, think the time draws nigh,
That calls the darling from thy tender eye ;
How shall his spirit brook the rigid rules,
And the long tyranny of grammar schools ?
Let younger brothers o'er dull authors plod,
Lash'd into *Latin* by the tingling rod ;
No, let him never feel that smart disgrace :
Why should he wiser prove than all his race ?
    When rip'ning youth with down o'ershades his chin,
And ev'ry female eye incites to sin ;   50
The milk-maid (thoughtless of her future shame)
With smacking lip shall raise his guilty flame ;
The dairy, barn, the hay-loft and the grove
Shall oft' be conscious of their stolen love.
But think, *Priscilla*, on that dreadful time,
When pangs and watry qualms shall own thy crime ;
How wilt thou tremble when thy nipple 's prest,
To see the white drops bathe thy swelling breast !
Nine moons shall publickly divulge thy shame,
And the young Squire forestall a father's name.   60
    When twice twelve times the reaper's sweeping hand
With levell'd harvests has bestrown the land,
On fam'd *St. Hubert*'s feast, his winding horn
Shall cheer the joyful hound and wake the morn :
This memorable day his eager speed
Shall urge with bloody heel the rising steed.
O check the foamy bit, nor tempt thy fate,
Think on the murders of a five-bar gate !
Yet prodigal of life, the leap he tries,
Low in the dust his groveling honour lies,   70
Headlong he falls, and on the rugged stone
Distorts his neck, and cracks the collar bone ;

* *The most common accident to sportsmen ; to hunt a witch in the shape of a hare.*

59 thy] *1731* her *1720 (corrected to* thy *in Errata)*, Underhill.

O ventr'ous youth, thy thirst of game allay,
Mayst thou survive the perils of this day !
He shall survive ; and in late years be sent
To snore away Debates in *Parliament.*
   The time shall come, when his more solid sense
With nod important shall the laws dispense ;
A Justice with grave Justices shall sit,
He praise their wisdom, they admire his wit.   80
No greyhound shall attend the tenant's pace,
No rusty gun the farmer's chimney grace ;
Salmons shall leave their covers void of fear,
Nor dread the thievish net or triple spear ;
Poachers shall tremble at his awful name,
Whom vengeance now o'ertakes for murder'd game.
   Assist me, *Bacchus*, and ye drunken Pow'rs,
To sing his friendships and his midnight hours !
   Why dost thou glory in thy strength of beer,
Firm-cork'd, and mellow'd till the twentieth year ;   90
Brew'd or when *Phœbus* warms the fleecy sign,
Or when his languid rays in *Scorpio* shine.
Think on the mischiefs which from hence have sprung !
It arms with curses dire the wrathful tongue ;
Foul scandal to the lying lip affords,
And prompts the mem'ry with injurious words.
O where is wisdom, when by this o'erpower'd ?
The State is censur'd, and the maid deflower'd !
And wilt thou still, O Squire, brew ale so strong ?
Hear then the dictates of prophetic song.   100
   Methinks I see him in his hall appear,
Where the long table floats in clammy beer,
'Midst mugs and glasses shatter'd o'er the floor,
Dead-drunk his servile crew supinely snore ;
Triumphant, o'er the prostrate brutes he stands,
The mighty bumper trembles in his hands ;
Boldly he drinks, and like his glorious Sires,
In copious gulps of potent ale expires.

THE

TOILETTE.

A Town ECLOGUE.

LYDIA.

[*Editions:*
1. COURT | POEMS. | *VIZ* ; | I. The *Basset-Table*. An ECLOGUE. | II. The DRAWING-ROOM. | III. The TOILET. | *Publish'd faithfully, as they were found in a* | *Pocket-Book taken up in* Westminster-Hall, | *the Last Day of the Lord* Winton's *Tryal.* | *LONDON :* | Printed for J. ROBERTS, near the *Oxford-* | *Arms* in *Warwick-Lane.* MDCCVI. | Price Six-Pence.
     The date is a misprint. The volume appeared on March 26, 1716.
     8vo. Capital letters freely used.
The Basset-Table was by Pope, *The Drawing-Room* by Lady Mary Wortley Montague, to whom *The Toilet* has also been wrongly attributed. Gay claimed it as his own in the *Poems on Several Occasions*. Moreover, Pope spoke of it as Gay's with the exception of ' only five or six lines new set in it ' by Lady M. W. M. *Spence's Anecdotes.*
     2. *Poems on Several Occasions* 1720.
     3. Ditto 1731.
I follow the much-amended version of 1720 and 1731, and do not record trifling differences of punctuation or spelling.]

Now twenty springs had cloath'd the Park with green,
Since *Lydia* knew the blossom of fifteen ;
No lovers now her morning hours molest,
And catch her at her Toilette half undrest ;
The thund'ring knocker wakes the street no more,
No chairs, no coaches croud her silent door ;
Her midnights once at cards and *Hazard* fled,
Which now, alas ! she dreams away in bed.
Around her wait Shocks, monkeys and mockaws,
To fill the place of Fops, and perjur'd Beaus ;   10
In these she views the mimickry of man,
And smiles when grinning *Pug* gallants her fan ;
When *Poll* repeats, the sounds deceive her ear,
For sounds, like his, once told her *Damon*'s care.
With these alone her tedious mornings pass ;
Or at the dumb devotion of her glass,

The only heading in the first edition is THE | TOILET.
1 had] has *1716*.   2 blossom] Blosoms *1716*.
6 No . . . no] Nor . . . nor *1716*.   her] the *1716*.
7-20 *These lines are not in the first edition, which has instead the couplet :*
          Now at the Window all the Mornings pass,
          Or at the dumb Devotion of the Glass ;

She smooths her brow, and frizles forth her hairs,
And fancys youthful dress gives youthful airs ;
With crimson wooll she fixes ev'ry grace,
That not a blush can discompose her face.　　20
Reclin'd upon her arm she pensive sate,
And curs'd th' inconstancy of youth too late.
　O Youth ! O spring of life ! for ever lost !
No more my name shall reign the fav'rite Toast,
On glass no more the di'mond grave my name,
And rhymes mispell'd record a lover's flame :
Nor shall side-boxes watch my restless eyes,
And as they catch the glance in rows arise
With humble bows ; nor white-glov'd Beaus encroach
In crouds behind, to guard me to my coach.　　30
Ah hapless nymph ! such conquests are no more,
For *Chloe*'s now what *Lydia* was before !
　'Tis true, this *Chloe* boasts the peach's bloom.
But does her nearer whisper breathe perfume ?
I own her taper shape is form'd to please.
Yet if you saw her unconfin'd by stays !
She doubly to fifteen may make pretence,
Alike we read it in her face and sense.
Her reputation ! but that never yet
Could check the freedoms of a young Coquet.　　40
Why will ye then, vain Fops, her eyes believe ?
Her eyes can, like your perjur'd tongues, deceive.
　What shall I do ? how spend the hateful day ?
At chappel shall I wear the morn away ?
Who there frequents at these unmodish hours,
But ancient matrons with their frizled tow'rs,
And gray religious maids ? my presence there
Amid that sober train wou'd own despair ;
Nor am I yet so old ; nor is my glance
As yet fixt wholy to devotion's trance.　　50
　Strait then I'll dress, and take my wonted range
Through ev'ry *Indian* shop, through all the *Change* ;
Where the tall jarr erects his costly pride,
With antic shapes in *China*'s azure dy'd ;
There careless lies the rich brocade unroll'd,
Here shines a cabinet with burnish'd gold ;
But then remembrance will my grief renew,
'Twas there the raffling dice false *Damon* threw ;

22 youth] Men *1716*.　　24 reign] ring *1716*.　　25 the di'mond] shall Diamond
1716.　　26 a] my *1716*.　　27 restless] wand'ring *1716*.　　31–42 *These lines are
not in the first edition, but ll.* 33–8 *in a slightly different form followed l.* 78 (*see below*).
43 What shall I do to spend the hateful Day ? *1716*.　　45 frequents] appears
1716.　　these] those *1716*.　　48 own] cause *1716*.　　52 To *Indian* Shops,
Motteux's, or the *Change* ; *1716*.　　56 with] of *1716*.　　57–70 *These lines are
not in the first edition, which ends the paragraph with the couplet :*
　　　But then, alas ! I must be forc'd to Pay,
　　　Or bring no Penny-worths, or Fan away.

The raffling dice to him decide the prize.
'Twas there he first convers'd with *Chloe*'s eyes ;   60
Hence sprung th' ill-fated cause of all my smart,
To me the toy he gave, to her his heart.
But soon thy perj'ry in the gift was found,
The shiver'd *China* dropt upon the ground ;
Sure omen that thy vows would faithless prove ;
Frail was thy present, frailer is thy love.
  O happy *Poll*, in wiry prison pent ;
Thou ne'er hast known what love or rivals meant,
And *Pug* with pleasure can his fetters bear,
Who ne'er believ'd the vows that lovers swear   70
How am I curst ! (unhappy and forlorn)
With perjury, with love, and rival's scorn !
False are the loose Coquet's inveigling airs,
False is the pompous grief of youthful heirs,
False is the cringing courtier's plighted word,
False are the dice when gamesters stamp the board,
False is the sprightly widow's publick tear ;
Yet these to *Damon*'s oaths are all sincere.
  Fly from perfidious man, the sex disdain ;
Let servile *Chloe* wear the nuptial chain.   80
Damon is practis'd in the modish life,
Can hate, and yet be civil to a wife.
He games ; he swears ; he drinks ; he fights ; he roves ;
Yet *Chloe* can believe he fondly loves.
Mistress and wife can well supply his need,
A miss for pleasure, and a wife for breed.
But *Chloe*'s air is unconfin'd and gay,
And can perhaps an injur'd bed repay ;
Perhaps her patient temper can behold
The rival of her love adorn'd with gold,   90

71-4   How am I curs'd, unhappy, and forlorn ;
  My Lover's Triumph, and my Sex's Scorn ?
  False is the Pompous Grief of Youthful Heirs ;
  False are the Loose *Coquet*'s Inveig'ling Airs : *1716*

75 cringing] Crafty *1716*.
79-80 *These lines are not in the first edition, which has instead the following :*

  For what Young Flirt, Base Man, am I abus'd ?
  To please your Wife, am I unkindly us'd ?
  'Tis true, her Face may boast the Peach's Bloom ;
  But does her nearer whisp'ring Breath perfume ?
  I own, her Taper-Shape is made to please ;
  Yet when you see her unconfin'd by Stays,
  She doubly to Fifteen may claim Pretence ;
  Alike we read it in her Wit and Sense.
  Insipid, Servile Thing, that I disdain,
  Whose Phlegm can best support the Marriage Chain.

82 a] his *1716*.   85 can well] by Turns *1716*.
87-90 *These lines are not in the first edition.*

Powder'd with di'monds ; free from thought and care,
A husband's sullen humours she can bear.
  Why are these sobs ? and why these streaming eyes ?
Is love the cause ? no, I the sex despise ;
I hate, I loath his base perfidious name.
Yet if he should but feign a rival flame ?
But *Chloe* boasts and triumphs in my pains,
To her he's faithful, 'tis to me he feigns.
  Thus love-sick *Lydia* rav'd.   Her maid appears
A band-box in her steady hand she bears.   100
How well this ribband's gloss becomes your face,
She crys, in raptures ! then, so sweet a lace !
How charmingly you look ! so bright ! so fair !
'Tis to your eyes the head-dress owes its air.
Strait *Lydia* smil'd ; the comb adjusts her locks,
And at the Play-house *Harry* keeps her box.

91-2   Tower'd with Diamonds, free from Thought or Care,
        She can a sullen Husband's Humour bear. *1716*.
93-8   *These lines take the place of the following, which were in the first edition :*
        Her cred'lous Friendship, and her stupid Ease,
        Has often been my Jest in happier Days.
        Now CHLOE Boasts and Triumphs in my Pains ;
        To her he's Faithful, 'tis to me he Feigns.
        Am I that senseless Thing to bear Neglect,
        And force a Smile not daring to suspect.
        No,—Perjur'd Man ! A Wife may be content ;
        But you shall find a Mistress can resent.
100-2   With steddy Hand the Band-box-Charge She bears.
        How well those Ribbands-Gloss becomes your Face,
        She cries in Raptures,—Then so sweet a Grace ; *1716*
103 bright] strait *1716*.   104 the] your *1716*.   105 locks] Looks *1716*.

THE

TEA-TABLE.

A Town ECLOGUE.

DORIS and *MELANTHE*.

SAINT *James*'s noon-day bell for prayers had toll'd,
And coaches to the Patron's *Levée* roll'd,
When *Doris* rose. And now through all the room
From flow'ry Tea exhales a fragrant fume.
Cup after cup they sipt, and talk'd by fits,
For *Doris* here, and there *Melanthe* sits.
Doris was young, a laughter-loving dame,
Nice of her own alike and others fame ;
Melanthe's tongue could well a tale advance,
And sooner gave than sunk a circumstance ;   10
Lock'd in her mem'ry secrets never dy'd ;
Doris begun, *Melanthe* thus reply'd.

DORIS.

Sylvia the vain fantastic Fop admires,
The Rake's loose gallantry her bosom fires ;
Sylvia like that is vain, like this she roves,
In liking them she but her self approves.

MELANTHE.

Laura rails on at men, the sex reviles,
Their vice condemns, or at their folly smiles.
Why should her tongue in just resentment fail,
Since men at her with equal freedom rail ?   20

DORIS.

Last *Masquerade* was *Sylvia* nymphlike seen,
Her hand a crook sustain'd, her dress was green ;
An am'rous shepherd led her through the croud,
The nymph was innocent, the shepherd vow'd ;
But nymphs their innocence with shepherds trust ;
So both withdrew, as nymph and shepherd must.

MELANTHE.

Name but the licence of the modern stage,
Laura takes fire, and kindles into rage ;

The whining Tragic love she scarce can bear,
But nauseous Comedy ne'er shock'd her ear : 30
Yet in the gall'ry mob'd, she sits secure,
And laughs at jests that turn the Box demure.

DORIS.

Trust not, ye Ladys, to your beauty's pow'r,
For beauty withers, like a shrivell'd flow'r ;
Yet those fair flowers that *Sylvia*'s temples bind,
Fade not with sudden blights or winter's wind ;
Like those her face defys the rolling years,
For art her roses and her charms repairs.

MELANTHE.

Laura despises ev'ry outward grace,
The wanton sparkling eye, the blooming face 40
The beauties of the soul are all her pride,
For other beauties Nature has deny'd ;
If affectation show a beauteous mind,
Lives there a man to *Laura*'s merits blind ?

DORIS.

Sylvia be sure defies the town's reproach,
Whose *Deshabille* is soil'd in hackney coach ;
What though the sash was clos'd ? must we conclude,
That she was yielding, when her Fop was rude ?

MELANTHE.

Laura learnt caution at too dear a cost.
What Fair could e'er retrieve her honour lost ? 50
Secret she loves ; and who the nymph can blame,
Who durst not own a footman's vulgar flame ?

DORIS.

Though *Laura*'s homely taste descends so low ;
Her footman well may vye with *Sylvia*'s Beau.

MELANTHE.

Yet why should *Laura* think it a disgrace,
When proud *Miranda*'s groom wears *Flanders* lace ?

DORIS.

What, though for musick *Cynthio* boasts an ear ?
Robin perhaps can hum an *Opera* air.
Cynthio can bow, takes snuff, and dances well,
Robin talks common sense, can write and spell ; 60
Sylvia's vain fancy dress and shows admires,
But 'tis the man alone who *Laura* fires.

MELANTHE.

Plato's wise morals *Laura*'s soul improve :
And this no doubt must be *Platonic* love !
Her soul to gen'rous acts was still inclin'd ;
What shows more virtue than an humble mind ?

47 clos'd ?] *1720* clos'd, *1731* closed, *Underhill.* 56 *Flanders*] *Flander*'s 1720
and 1731 62 who] *1720* whom *1731, wrongly.*

DORIS.

What, though young *Sylvia* love the Park's cool shade,
And wander in the dusk the secret glade ?
Masqu'd and alone (by chance) she met her Spark,
That innocence is weak which shuns the dark.   70

MELANTHE.

But *Laura* for her flame has no pretence
Her footman is a footman too in sense.
All Prudes I hate, and those are rightly curst
With scandal's double load, who censure first.

DORIS.

And what if *Cynthio Sylvia*'s garter ty'd !
Who such a foot and such a leg would hide ;
When crook-knee'd *Phillis* can expose to view
Her gold-clock'd stocking, and her tawdry shoe ?

MELANTHE.

If pure Devotion center in the face,
If cens'ring others show intrinsick grace,   80
If guilt to publick freedoms be confin'd,
Prudes (all must own) are of the holy kind !

DORIS.

Sylvia disdains reserve, and flys constraint :
She neither is, nor would be thought a Saint.

MELANTHE.

Love is a trivial passion, *Laura* crys,
May I be blest with friendship's stricter tyes ;
To such a breast all secrets we commend ;
Sure the whole *Drawing-room* is *Laura*'s friend.

DORIS.

At marriage *Sylvia* rails ; who men would trust ?
Yet husband's jealousies are sometimes just.   90
Her favours *Sylvia* shares among mankind,
Such gen'rous love should never be confin'd.

As thus alternate chat employ'd their tongue,
With thund'ring raps the brazen knocker rung.
Laura with *Sylvia* came ; the nymphs arise :
This unexpected visit, *Doris* crys,
Is doubly kind ! *Melanthe Laura* led,
Since I was last so blest, my dear, she said,
Sure 'tis an age ! they sate ; the hour was set
And all again that night at *Ombre* met.   100

THE

FUNERAL.

A Town ECLOGUE.

SABINA. LUCY.

TWICE had the moon perform'd her monthly race,
Since first the veil o'ercast *Sabina*'s face.
Then dy'd the tender partner of her bed.
And lives *Sabina* when *Fidelio*'s dead ?
Fidelio's dead, and yet *Sabina* lives.
But see the tribute of her tears she gives ;
Their absent Lord her rooms in sable mourn,
And all the day the glimmering tapers burn ;
Stretch'd on the couch of state she pensive lies,
While oft' the snowy Cambric wipes her eyes.   10
Now enter'd *Lucy*, trusty *Lucy* knew
To roll a sleeve, or bear a *Billet-doux* ;
Her ready tongue, in secret service try'd,
With equal fluency spoke truth or ly'd,
She well could flush, or humble a gallant,
And serve at once as maid and confidant ;
A letter from her faithful stays she took :
Sabina snatch'd it with an angry look,
And thus in hasty words her grief confest,
While *Lucy* strove to sooth her troubled breast.   20

SABINA.

What, still *Myrtillo*'s hand ! his flame I scorn,
Give back his passion with the seal untorn.
To break our soft repose has man a right,
And are we doom'd to read whate'er they write ?
Not all the sex my firm resolves shall move ;
My life 's a life of sorrow, not of love.
May *Lydia*'s wrinkles all my forehead trace,
And *Celia*'s paleness sicken o'er my face,
May Fops of mine, as *Flavia*'s, favours boast,
And Coquets triumph in my honour lost ;   30
May cards employ my nights, and never more
May these curst eyes behold a Matadore !
Break *China*, perish *Shock*, die *Perroquet* !
When I *Fidelio*'s dearer love forget.
Fidelio's judgment scorn'd the foppish train,
His air was easy, and his dress was plain,

His words sincere, respect his presence drew,
And on his lips sweet conversation grew.
Where 's wit, where 's beauty, where is virtue fled ?
Alas ! they're now no more ; *Fidelio*'s dead !   40

LUCY.

Yet when he liv'd, he wanted ev'ry grace ;
That easy air was then an aukward pace :
Have not your sighs in whispers often said,
His dress was slovenly, his speech ill-bred ?
Have not I heard you, with a secret tear,
Call that sweet converse sullen and severe ?
Think not I come to take *Myrtillo*'s part,
Let *Chloe, Daphne, Doris* share his heart.
Let *Chloe*'s love in ev'ry ear express
His graceful person and genteel address.   50
All well may judge, what shaft has *Daphne* hit,
Who suffers silence to admire his wit.
His equipage and liv'ries *Doris* move,
But *Chloe, Daphne, Doris* fondly love.
Sooner shall Cits in fashions guide the Court,
And Beaus upon the busy *Change* resort ;
Sooner the nation shall from snuff be freed,
And Fops apartments smoke with *India*'s weed,
Sooner I'd wish and sigh through nunn'ry grates,
Than recommend the flame *Sabina* hates.   60

SABINA.

Because some widows are in haste subdued
Shall ev'ry Fop upon our tears intrude ?
Can I forget my lov'd *Fidelio*'s tongue,
Soft as the warbling of *Italian* song ?
Did not his rosy lips breathe forth perfume,
Fragrant as steams from Tea's imperial bloom ?

LUCY.

Yet once you thought that tongue a greater curse
Than squawles of children for an absent nurse.
Have you not fancy'd in his frequent kiss
Th' ungrateful leavings of a filthy Miss ?   70

SABINA.

Love, I thy pow'r defie ; no second flame
Shall ever raze my dear *Fidelio*'s name.
Fannia without a tear might lose her Lord,
Who ne'er enjoy'd his presence but at board.
And why should sorrow sit on *Lesbia*'s face ?
Are there such comforts in a sot's embrace ?
No friend, no lover is to *Lesbia* dead,
For *Lesbia* long had known a sep'rate bed.

52 suffers silence] *1731* can be silent *1720*
   58 Fops] Fop's *1720* fop's *1731* fops' *Bell, Underhill. The correction seems*
necessary.   71 flame] *Bell, Underhill* flame, *1720 and 1731.*

Gush forth, ye tears ; waste, waste, ye sighs, my breast ;
My days, my nights were by *Fidelio* blest !   80

L U C Y.

You cannot sure forget how oft' you said
His teazing fondness jealousy betray'd !
When at the Play the neighb'ring box he took,
You thought you read suspicion in his look ;
When cards and counters flew around the board,
Have you not wish'd the absence of your Lord ?
His company was then a poor pretence,
To check the freedoms of a wife's expence !

S A B I N A.

But why should I *Myrtillo*'s passion blame,
Since Love 's a fierce involuntary flame ?   90

L U C Y.

Could he the sallys of his heart withstand,
Why should he not to *Chloe* give his hand ?
For *Chloe*'s handsome, yet he slights her flame ;
Last night she fainted at *Sabina*'s name.
Why, *Daphne*, dost thou blast *Sabina*'s charms ?
Sabina keeps no lover from thy arms.
At *Crimp Myrtillo* play'd, in kind regards
Doris dealt love ; he only dealt the cards ;
Doris was touch'd with spleen ; her fan she rent,
Flew from the table and to tears gave vent.   100
Why, *Doris*, dost thou curse *Sabina*'s eyes ?
To her *Myrtillo* is a vulgar prize.

S A B I N A.

Yet say, I lov'd ; how loud would censure rail !
So soon to quit the duties of the veil !
No, sooner Plays and Op'ras I'd forswear,
And change these *China* jars for *Tunbridge* ware
Or trust my mother as a Confidant,
Or fix a friendship with my maiden aunt ;
Than till—tomorrow throw my Weeds away.
Yet let me see him, if he comes to-day !   110

[Hasty she snatch'd the letter, tore the seal ;
She read, and blushes glow'd beneath the veil.]

98 *So 1731.* Doris threw love, unmindful of the cards ; *1720.*   99 she] he
all editions cited. The correction is obvious.   109 away.] *1731* away, *1720.*
111–12 *These lines are omitted in 1731.*

THE

ESPOUSAL.

A Sober ECLOGUE.

Between two of the People called Quakers.

CALEB. TABITHA.

BENEATH the shadow of a beaver hat,
Meek *Caleb* at a silent meeting sate ;
His eye-balls oft' forgot the holy trance,
While *Tabitha* demure, return'd the glance.
The Meeting ended, *Caleb* silence broke,
And *Tabitha* her inward yearnings spoke.

CALEB.

Beloved, see how all things follow love,
Lamb fondleth lamb, and dove disports with dove ;
Yet fondled lambs their innocence secure,
And none can call the turtle's bill impure ;   10
O fairest of our sisters, let me be
The billing dove, and fondling lamb to thee.

TABITHA.

But, *Caleb*, know that birds of gentle mind
Elect a mate among the sober kind,
Not the mockaws, all deck'd in scarlet pride,
Entice their mild and modest hearts aside ;
But thou, vain man, beguil'd by Popish shows,
Dotest on ribbands, flounces, furbelows.
If thy false heart be fond of tawdry dyes,
Go, wed the painted arch in summer skies ;   20
Such love will like the rainbow's hue decay,
Strong at the first, but passeth soon away.

CALEB.

Name not the frailtys of my youthful days,
When vice mis-led me through the harlot's ways ;
When I with wanton look thy sex beheld,
And nature with each wanton look rebell'd ;

Portions of *The Espousal* were set to music—without the author's knowledge,
no doubt. See the British Museum Catalogue for the following entry.
    ' On Monday next the 14th of August, at the Marlborough Bowling-Green, will
be perform'd ... in the 3rd Act, the following ode by ... John Gay, etc. [Commencing:
" Beneath the shadow of a Beaver's Hat ", etc.] Dublin ? 1720 ? s. sh. fol.'

Then parti-colour'd pride my heart might move
With lace ; the net to catch unhallow'd love.
All such-like love is fading as the flower,
Springs in a day, and withereth in an hour :   30
But now I feel the spousal love within,
And spousal love no sister holds a sin.

TABITHA.

I know thou longest for the flaunting maid,
Thy falsehood own, and say I am betray'd ;
The tongue of man is blister'd o'er with lies,
But truth is ever read in woman's eyes ;
O that my lip obey'd a tongue like thine !
Or that thine eye bewray'd a love like mine !

CALEB.

How bitter are thy words ! forbear to teaze,
I too might blame—but love delights to please.   40
Why should I tell thee, that when last the sun
Painted the downy peach of *Newington*,
Josiah led thee through the garden's walk,
And mingled melting kisses with his talk ?
Ah Jealousy ! turn, turn thine eyes aside,
How can I see that watch adorn thy side ?
For verily no gift the sisters take
For lust of gain, but for the giver's sake.

TABITHA.

I own, *Josiah* gave the golden toy,
Which did the righteous hand of *Quare* employ ;   50
When *Caleb* hath assign'd some happy day,
I look on this and chide the hour's delay :
And when *Josiah* would his love pursue,
On this I look and shun his wanton view.
Man but in vain with trinkets trys to move,
The only present love demands is love.

CALEB.

Ah *Tabitha*, to hear these words of thine,
My pulse beats high, as if inflam'd with wine !
When to the brethren first with fervent zeal
The spirit mov'd thy yearnings to reveal,   60
How did I joy thy trembling lip to see
Red as the cherry from the *Kentish* tree ;
When Ecstasie had warm'd thy look so meek,
Gardens of roses blushed on thy cheek.
With what sweet transport didst thou roll thine eyes,
How did thy words provoke the brethren's sighs !
Words that with holy sighs might others move,
But, *Tabitha*, my sighs were sighs of love.

TABITHA.

Is *Tabitha* beyond her wishes blest ?
Does no proud worldly dame divide thy breast ?   70

Then hear me, *Caleb*, witness what I speak,
This solemn promise death alone can break ;
Sooner I would bedeck my brow with lace,
And with immodest fav'rites shade my face,
Sooner like *Babylon*'s lewd whore be drest
In flaring di'monds and a scarlet vest,
Or make a curtsie in Cathedral pew,
Than prove inconstant, while my *Caleb*'s true.

         CALEB.
When I prove false, and *Tabitha* forsake,
Teachers shall dance a jig at country wake ;   80
Brethren unbeaver'd then shall bow their head,
And with prophane mince-pies our babes be fed.

         TABITHA.
If that *Josiah* were with passion fir'd,
Warm as the zeal of youth when first inspir'd ;
In steady love though he might persevere,
Unchanging as the decent garb we wear,
And thou wert fickle as the wind that blows,
Light as the feather on the head of Beaus ;
Yet I for thee would all thy sex resign,
Sisters, take all the rest—be *Caleb* mine.   90

         CALEB.
Though I had all that sinful love affords,
And all the concubines of all the Lords,
Whose couches creak with whoredom's sinful shame,
Whose velvet chairs are with adult'ry lame ;
Ev'n in the harlot's hall, I would not sip
The dew of lewdness from her lying lip ;
I'd shun her paths, upon thy mouth to dwell,
More sweet than powder which the merchants sell ;
O solace me with kisses pure like thine !
Enjoy, ye Lords, the wanton concubine.   100
The spring now calls us forth ; come, sister, come,
To see the primrose, and the daisie bloom.
Let ceremony bind the worldly pair,
Sisters esteem the brethren's words sincere.

         TABITHA.
Espousals are but forms. O lead me hence,
For secret love can never give offence.

Then hand in hand the loving mates withdraw.
True love is nature unrestrain'd by law.
This tenet all the holy sect allows.
So *Tabitha* took earnest of a spouse.   110

89 thy] the *Underhill*.   104 brethren's] *Bell, Underhill* breth'rens *1720*
and 1731.   109 tenet] *1731* tenent *1720.*

EPISTLES ON SEVERAL OCCASIONS.

AN

EPISTLE

TO A

LADY.

OCCASION'D BY THE ARRIVAL OF HER ROYAL HIGHNESS.

[*Editions :*
1. First edition. (Title-page missing from the copy collated.) Published in November 1714.
    Folio.
2. ' Fifth Edition '. Published together with the Epistle to Burlington. See p. 152. 8vo.
3. *Poems on Several Occasions.* 1720.
4. *Miscellaneous Poems and Translations.* Third edition. 1720. See pp. xxxvii and 88. [Ref. 1720 misc.]
    The first two editions do not contain this Epistle.
5. *Miscellaneous Poems and Translations.* Fourth edition. 1722.
6. *Poems on Several Occasions.* 1731.
    Capital letters are freely used by 1 and 2 ; white lines are used by 1, 2, and 6.]

MADAM, to all your censures I submit,
And frankly own I should long since have writ :
You told me, silence would be thought a crime,
And kindly strove to teaze me into rhyme :
No more let trifling themes your Muse employ,
Nor lavish verse to paint a female toy ;
No more on plains with rural damsels sport,
But sing the glories of the *British* court.
    By your commands and inclination sway'd,
I call'd th' unwilling Muses to my aid ;   10

The heading in the first edition has A LETTER *for* AN EPISTLE *and adds* THE PRINCESS OF WALES.
9 *In the versions of 1720 misc. and 1722 this line does not begin a new paragraph.*

Resolved to write, the noble theme I chose,
And to the Princess thus the poem rose.
   Aid me, bright Phœbus; *aid, ye sacred Nine;*
Exalt my Genius, and my verse refine.
My strains with Carolina's *name I grace,*
The lovely parent of our royal race.
Breathe soft, ye winds, ye waves in silence sleep;
Let prosp'rous breezes wanton o'er the deep,
Swell the white sails, and with the streamers play,
To waft her gently o'er the watry way.   20
   Here I to *Neptune* form'd a pompous pray'r,
To rein the winds, and guard the royal Fair ;
Bid the blue *Tritons* sound their twisted shells,
And call the *Nereids* from their pearly cells.
   Thus my warm zeal had drawn the Muse along,
Yet knew no method to conduct her song :
I then resolv'd some model to pursue,
Perus'd *French* Criticks, and began anew.
Long open panegyrick drags at best,
And praise is only praise when well address'd.   30
   Strait, *Horace* for some lucky Ode I sought :
And all along I trac'd him thought by thought :
This new performance to a friend I show'd ;
For shame, says he, what, imitate an Ode !
I'd rather ballads write, and *Grubstreet* lays,
Than pillage *Cæsar* for my patron's praise :
One common fate all imitators share,
To save mince-pies, and cap the grocer's ware.
Vex'd at the charge, I to the flames commit
Rhymes, similies, Lords names, and ends of wit ;   40
In blotted stanzas scraps of Odes expire,
And fustian mounts in Pyramids of fire.
   Ladies, to you I next inscrib'd my lay,
And writ a letter in familiar way :
For still impatient till the Princess came,
You from description wish'd to know the dame.
Each day my pleasing labour larger grew,
For still new graces open'd to my view.
Twelve lines ran on to introduce the theme,
And then I thus pursu'd the growing scheme.   50

12 In the first edition here follows the couplet :
    Muse, *fly the Shades, the sylvan Song forbear,*
    And pipe no more to please the Shepherd's Ear.
14 In the first edition here follows the couplet :
    Accept, illustrious Fair, my grateful Song :
    To you my Duty and my Lays belong :
15 Carolina's] CAROLINA's *1714, and so throughout with Royal Names.*
19 *Swell the white sails,*] *Just swell the sails, 1714.*   24 call] *1731* call'd
remainder.   31 Strait,] Strait *1731.*   41 stanzas] *1720 and 1731* Stanza's
(*or* stanza's) *remainder.*

Beauty and wit were sure by nature join'd,
And charms are emanations of the mind;
The soul transpiercing through the shining frame,
Forms all the graces of the Princely Dame:
Benevolence her conversation guides,
Smiles on her cheek, and in her eye resides.
Such harmony upon her tongue is found,
As softens English *to* Italian *sound:*
Yet in those sounds such sentiments appear,
As charm the Judgment, while they sooth the ear. 60
Religion's chearful flame her bosom warms,
Calms all her hours, and brightens all her charms.
Henceforth, ye Fair, at chappel mind your pray'rs,
Nor catch your lovers eyes with artful airs;
Restrain your looks, kneel more, and whisper less,
Nor most devoutly criticize on dress.
From her form all your characters of life,
The tender mother, and the faithful wife.
Oft have I seen her little infant train,
The lovely promise of a future reign; 70
Observ'd with pleasure ev'ry dawning grace,
And all the mother op'ning in their face:
The son shall add new honours to the line,
And early with paternal virtues shine;
When he the tale of Audenard *repeats,*
His little heart with emulation beats;
With conquests yet to come his bosom glows,
He dreams of triumphs and of vanquish'd foes.
Each year with arts shall store his rip'ning brain,
And from his Grandsire he shall learn to reign. 80
Thus far I'd gone: Propitious rising gales
Now bid the sailor hoist the swelling sails.
Fair *Carolina* lands; the cannons roar,
White *Albion's* cliffs resound from shore to shore,
Behold the bright original appear,
All praise is faint when *Carolina* 's near.
Thus to the nation's joy, but Poet's cost,
The Princess came, and my new plan was lost.

56 *eye*] *Eyes* 1714.
60 In the first edition here follows the couplet :
Such pure Religion in her Bosom reign'd,
For that, Imperial Crowns she once disdain'd ;
61 *The chearful Flame her Heart with Transport warms,* 1714.
64 *lovers*] *lover's* 1720 *and* 1731.   72 *face :*] *face,* 1720 *and* 1731.
81 Propitious rising gales] *1720 and 1731* The Wind with prosp'rous Gales, *remainder.*
82 bid] *1720 and 1731* bids *remainder.*
83 the cannons roar] *1720 and 1731* the Cannons Sound *1714* the cannon's sound *remainder.*
84 resound from shore to shore,] *1720 and 1731* from shore to shore rebound. *remainder.*

Since all my schemes were baulk'd, my last resort,
I left the Muses to frequent the Court;   90
Pensive each night, from room to room I walk'd,
To one I bow'd, and with another talk'd;
Enquir'd what news, or such a Lady's name,
And did the next day, and the next, the same.
Places, I found, were daily giv'n away,
And yet no friendly Gazette mention'd *Gay*.
I ask'd a friend what method to pursue;
He cry'd, I want a place as well as you.
Another ask'd me, why I had not writ:
A Poet owes his fortune to his wit.   100
Strait I reply'd, With what a courtly grace
Flows easy verse from him that has a place!
Had *Virgil* ne'er at court improv'd his strains,
He still had sung of flocks and homely swains;
And had not *Horace* sweet preferment found,
The *Roman* lyre had never learnt to sound.
    Once Ladies fair in homely guise I sung,
And with their names wild woods and mountains rung.
Oh, teach me now to strike a softer strain!
The Court refines the language of the plain.   110
    You must, cries one, the Ministry rehearse,
And with each Patriot's name prolong your verse.
But sure this truth to Poets should be known,
That praising all alike, is praising none.
    Another told me, if I wish'd success,
To some distinguish'd Lord I must address;
One whose high virtues speak his noble blood,
One always zealous for his country's good;
Where valour and strong eloquence unite,
In council cautious, resolute in fight;   120
Whose gen'rous temper prompts him to defend,
And patronize the man that wants a friend.
You have, 'tis true, the noble Patron shown,
But I, alas! am to *Argyle* unknown.
    Still ev'ry one I met in this agreed,
That writing was my method to succeed;
But now preferments so possess'd my brain,
That scarce I could produce a single strain:
Indeed I sometimes hammer'd out a line,
Without connection as without design.   130
One morn upon the Princess this I writ,
An Epigram that boasts more truth than wit.
    The pomp of titles easy faith might shake,
She scorn'd an empire for religion's sake:
For this, on earth, the British *crown is giv'n,*
And an immortal crown decreed in heav'n.

91 Pensive, each night from room to room I walk'd, *1714.*
101 grace] grace, *all early editions.*

Again, while *GEORGE*'s virtues raised my thought,
The following lines prophetick fancy wrought.

Methinks I see some Bard, whose heav'nly rage
Shall rise in song, and warm a future age;
Look back through time, and, rapt in wonder, trace
The glorious series of the Brunswick *race.*

From the first George *these godlike kings descend,*
A line which only with the world shall end.
The next a gen'rous Prince renown'd in arms,
And bless'd, long bless'd in Carolina's *charms;*
From these the rest. 'Tis thus secure in peace
We plow the fields, and reap the year's increase:
Now Commerce, *wealthy Goddess, rears her head,*
And bids Britannia's *fleets their canvas spread;*
Unnumber'd ships the peopled ocean hide,
And wealth returns with each revolving tide.

Here paus'd the sullen Muse, in haste I dress'd,
And through the croud of needy courtiers press'd
Though unsuccessful, happy whilst I see,
Those eyes that glad a nation, shine on me.

147 peace] *1714* peace, *remainder.*
148 In the first edition here follows the couplet :
  Rescu'd from Debts, the Land no longer groans
  Beneath the Canker of devouring Loans.

An EPISTLE

to the Right Honourable the

Earl of BURLINGTON.

A Journey to EXETER.

[*Editions :*
1. TWO | EPISTLES ; | One, to the | Right Honourable | *RICHARD*   Earl of *BURLINGTON* ; | The Other, to a | LADY. | By Mr. *GAY* | *LONDON,* | Printed for BERNARD LINTOT, between the | *Temple-Gates.* Price 6d.
    8vo. Date, according to Mr. Underhill, 1715; marked in the British Museum Catalogue [?] 1720 ; Mr. T. J. Wise says ' published in 1720 '.   [Ref. ? 1715.]
2. *Poems on Several Occasions.* 1720.   [Ref. 1720]
3. *Miscellaneous Poems and Translations.* The Third Edition. 1720.
                                                                                      [Ref. 1720 misc.]
    See pp. xxxvii and 88. The first two editions do not contain this Epistle.
4. *Miscellaneous Poems and Translations.* The Fourth Edition. 1722.
5. *Miscellany Poems.* Vol. II. 1727. See p. 88.
6. *Poems on Several Occasions.* 1731.

Of the above versions 1 alone uses capital letters freely ; 1 and 6 alone use white lines between paragraphs.]

> WHILE you, my Lord, bid stately piles ascend,
> Or in your *Chiswick* bow'rs enjoy your friend ;
> Where *Pope* unloads the boughs within his reach,
> Of purple vine, blue plumb, and blushing peach ;
> I journey far—You knew fat Bards might tire,
> And, mounted, sent me forth your trusty Squire.
>   'Twas on the day that city dames repair
> To take their weekly dose of *Hide-Park* air ;
> When forth we trot : no carts the road infest,
> For still on *Sundays* country horses rest.   10
> Thy gardens, *Kensington,* we leave unseen ;
> Through *Hammersmith* jog on to *Turnham-green* :
> That *Turnham-green,* which dainty pidgeons fed,
> But feeds no more : for * *Solomon* is dead.
> Three dusty miles reach *Brandford*'s tedious town,
> For dirty streets, and white-leg'd chickens known :

    * *A man lately famous for feeding pidgeons at* Turnham-green.

---

4 Of] *1727* The *remainder.*   5 far—] far.— ? *1715, 1720 misc., and 1722.*
15 *Brandford*] *Branford 1731.*

Thence o'er wide shrubby heaths, and furrow'd lanes,
We come, where *Thames* divides the meads of *Stanes*.
We ferry'd o'er ; for late the winter's flood
Shook her frail bridge, and tore her piles of wood.   20
Prepar'd for war, now *Bagshot-Heath* we cross,
Where broken gamesters oft' repair their loss.
At *Hartley-Row* the foaming bit we prest,
While the fat landlord welcom'd ev'ry guest.
Supper was ended, healths the glasses crown'd,
Our host extoll'd his wine at ev'ry round,
Relates the Justices late meeting there,
How many bottles drank, and what their cheer ;
What lords had been his guests in days of yore,
And prais'd their wisdom much, their drinking more.   30
     Let travellers the morning vigils keep :
The morning rose ; but we lay fast asleep.
Twelve tedious miles we bore the sultry sun,
And *Popham-Lane* was scarce in sight by one :
The straggling village harbour'd thieves of old,
'Twas here the stage-coach'd lass resign'd her gold ;
That gold which had in *London* purchas'd gowns,
And sent her home a *Belle* to country towns.
But robbers haunt no more the neighbouring wood :
Here unown'd infants find their daily food ;   40
For should the maiden mother nurse her son,
'Twould spoil her match when her good name is gone.
Our jolly hostess nineteen children bore,
Nor fail'd her breast to suckle nineteen more.
Be just, ye Prudes, wipe off the long arrear ;
Be virgins still in town, but mothers here.
     Sutton we pass, and leave her spacious down,
And with the setting sun reach *Stockbridge* town.
O'er our parch'd tongue the rich metheglin glides,
And the red dainty trout our knife divides.   50
Sad melancholy ev'ry visage wears ;
What, no Election come in seven long years !
Of all our race of Mayors, shall *Snow* alone
Be by Sir *Richard*'s dedication known ?
Our streets no more with tides of ale shall float,
Nor coblers feast three years upon one vote.
     Next morn, twelve miles led o'er th' unbounded plain,
Where the cloak'd shepherd guides his fleecy train.
No leafy bow'rs a noonday shelter lend,
Nor from the chilly dews at night defend ;   60
With wondrous art he counts the straggling flock,
And by the sun informs you what 's a clock.

39 neighbouring] neighb'ring *1720 misc.*, *1722, and 1727.*
53 *The edition of 1727 only has the following footnote to* Snow :
A man to whom Sir Rich. Steele *dedicated a political work : not that* Snow, *to whom
the following piece of our author is addressed.*

How are our shepherds fall'n from ancient days !
No *Amaryllis* chaunts alternate lays ;
From her no list'ning ecchos learn to sing,
Nor with his reed the jocund valleys ring.
   Here sheep the pasture hide, there harvests bend,
See *Sarum*'s steeple o'er yon hill ascend ;
Our horses faintly trot beneath the heat,
And our keen stomachs know the hour to eat.   70
Who can forsake thy walls, and not admire
The proud Cathedral, and the lofty spire ?
What sempstress has not prov'd thy scissars good ?
From hence first came th' intriguing ridinghood.
Amid * three boarding-schools well stock'd with misses,
Shall three knights errant starve for want of kisses ?
   O'er the green turf the miles slide swift away,
And *Blandford* ends the labours of the day.
The morning rose ; the supper reck'ning paid,
And our due fees discharg'd to man and maid,   80
The ready ostler near the stirrup stands,
And as we mount, our half-pence load his hands.
   Now the steep hill fair *Dorchester* o'erlooks,
Border'd by meads, and wash'd by silver brooks.
Here sleep my two companions eyes supprest,
And propt in elbow chairs they snoring rest :
I wakeful sit, and with my pencil trace
Their painful postures, and their eyeless face ;
Then dedicate each glass to some fair name,
And on the sash the diamond scrawls my flame.   90
Now o'er true *Roman* way our horses sound,
Grævius would kneel, and kiss the sacred ground.
On either side low fertile valleys lye,
The distant prospects tire the trav'ling eye.
Through *Bridport*'s stony lanes our rout we take,
And the proud steep descend to *Morcombe*'s lake.
As herses pass'd, our landlord robb'd the pall,
And with the mournful scutcheon hung his hall.
On unadulterate wine we here regale,
And strip the lobster of his scarlet mail.   100
   We climb'd the hills, when starry night arose,
And *Axminster* affords a kind repose.
The maid, subdued by fees, her trunk unlocks,
And gives the cleanly aid of dowlas smocks.
Mean time our shirts her busy fingers rub,
While the soap lathers o'er the foaming tub.
If women's geer such pleasing dreams incite,
Lend us your smocks, ye damsels, ev'ry night !

        * *There are three boarding-schools in this town.*

_____

64 lays ;] *1720 and 1731*   lays ! *remainder.*   72 spire ?] *1720, 1727, 1731*
Spire. *remainder.*   81 ostler] ostly *1731.*   87 wakeful] weary *1720 and 1731.*
90 diamond] di'mond *1727.*   103 maid,] maid *1720 and 1731.*

We rise ; our beards demand the barber's art ;
A female enters, and performs the part.   110
The weighty golden chain adorns her neck,
And three gold rings her skilful hand bedeck :
Smooth o'er our chin her easy fingers move,
Soft as when *Venus* stroak'd the beard of *Jove.*
   Now from the steep, midst scatter'd farms and groves,
Our eye through *Honiton*'s fair valley roves.
Behind us soon the busy town we leave,
Where finest lace industrious lasses weave.
Now swelling clouds roll'd on ; the rainy load
Stream'd down our hats, and smoaked along the road ;   120
When (O blest sight !) a friendly sign we spy'd,
Our spurs are slacken'd from the horses side ;
For sure a civil host the house commands,
Upon whose sign this courteous motto stands.
This is the ancient hand, and eke the pen ;
Here is for horses hay, and meat for men.
How rhyme would flourish, did each son of fame
Know his own genius, and direct his flame !
Then he, that could not Epic flights rehearse,
Might sweetly mourn in Elegiac verse.   130
But were his Muse for Elegy unfit,
Perhaps a Distich might not strain his wit ;
If Epigram offend, his harmless lines
Might in gold letters swing on ale-house signs.
Then *Hobbinol* might propagate his bays,
And *Tuttle-fields* record his simple lays ;
Where rhymes like these might lure the nurses eyes,
While gaping infants squawl for farthing pies.
Treat here, ye shepherds blithe, your damsels sweet,
For pies and cheesecakes are for damsels meet.   140
Then *Maurus* in his proper sphere might shine,
And these proud numbers grace great *William*'s sign.
* *This is the man, this the* Nassovian, *whom*
I nam'd the brave deliverer to come.
But now the driving gales suspend the rain,
We mount our steeds, and *Devon*'s city gain.
Hail, happy native land !—but I forbear,
What other counties must with envy hear.

* *Prince* Arthur, *Book* 5.

---

109 rise ;] rise, *1720 and 1731.*   115 farms] *1731*   cotts *remainder.*
125 *hand . . . pen*] hand . . . pen *1727.*
143 *man*] Man *? 1715.*

An *EPISTLE*

To the Right Honourable

WILLIAM   PULTENEY, Esq ;

[*Poems on Several Occasions* 1720 and 1731.]

PULT'NEY, methinks you blame my breach of word
What, cannot *Paris* one poor page afford ?
Yes, I can sagely, when the times are past,
Laugh at those follys which I strove to taste,
And each amusement, which we shar'd, review,
Pleas'd with meer talking, since I talk to you.
But how shall I describe in humble prose,
Their Balls, Assemblies, Operas and Beaus ?
In prose, you cry ! Oh no, the Muse must aid,
And leave *Parnassus* for the *Tuillerie*'s shade ;   10
Shall he (who late *Britannia*'s city trod,
And led the draggled Muse, with pattens shod,
Through dirty lanes, and alleys doubtful ways)
Refuse to write, when *Paris* asks his lays !
    Well then, I'll try. Descend, ye beauteous Nine,
In all the colours of the rainbow shine,
Let sparkling stars your neck and ear adorn,
Lay on the blushes of the crimson morn,
So may ye Balls and gay Assemblies grace,
And at the Opera claim the foremost place.   20
    Trav'lers should ever fit expression chuse,
Nor with low phrase the lofty theme abuse.
When they describe the state of eastern Lords,
Pomp and magnificence should swell their words ;
And when they paint the serpent's scaly pride,
Their lines should hiss, their numbers smoothly slide ;
But they, unmindful of Poetick rules,
Describe alike Mockaws, and great *Moguls*.
Dampier would thus, without ill-meaning satyr,
Dress forth in simple style the *Petit-maitre*.   30
    In Paris, there's a race of animals,
(I've seen them at their Operas and Balls)
They stand erect, they dance when-e'er they walk,
Monkeys in action, perroquets in talk ;

6 you.] *1720* you, *1731*.   13 alleys] alley's *all editions consulted.*

They're crown'd with feathers, like the cockatoo,
And, like camelions, daily change their hue;
From patches justly plac'd they borrow graces,
And with vermillion lacker o'er their faces,
This custom, as we visibly discern,
They, by frequenting Ladies toilettes, learn.   40
Thus might the trav'ler easy truth impart.
Into the subject let me nobly start !
  How happy lives the man, how sure to charm,
Whose knot embroider'd flutters down his arm !
On him the Ladies cast the yielding glance,
Sigh in his songs, and languish in his dance ;
While wretched is the Wit, contemn'd, forlorn,
Whose gummy hat no scarlet plumes adorn ;
No broider'd flowers his worsted ankle grace,
Nor cane emboss'd with gold directs his pace ;   50
No Lady's favour on his sword is hung.
What, though *Apollo* dictate from his tongue,
His wit is spiritless and void of grace,
Who wants th' assurance of brocade and lace.
While the gay fop genteely talks of weather,
The fair in raptures doat upon his feather ;
Like a Court Lady though he write and spell,
His minuet step was fashion'd by * *Marcell* ;
He dresses, fences. What avails to know ?
For women chuse their men, like silks, for show.   60
Is this the thing, you cry, that *Paris* boasts ?
Is this the thing renown'd among our Toasts ?
For such a flutt'ring sight we need not roam ;
Our own Assemblys shine with these at home.
  Let us into the field of Beauty start ;
Beauty 's a theme that ever warm'd my heart.
Think not, ye Fair, that I the Sex accuse :
How shall I spare you, prompted by the Muse ?
(The Muses all are *Prudes*) she rails, she frets,
Amidst this sprightly nation of *Coquettes* ;   70
Yet let not us their loose coquett'ry blame ;
Women of ev'ry nation are the same.
  You ask me, if *Parisian* dames, like ours,
With rattling dice prophane the *Sunday*'s hours ;
If they the gamester's pale-ey'd vigils keep,
And stake their honour while their husbands sleep.
Yes, Sir ; like *English* Toasts, the dames of *France*
Will risque their income on a single chance.
Nannette last night at tricking *Pharaon* play'd,
The cards the Taillier's sliding hand obey'd,   80
To-day her neck no brilliant circle wears,
Nor the ray-darting pendant loads her ears.

          * *A famous dancing-master.*

Why does old *Chloris* an Assembly hold ?
Chloris each night divides the sharper's gold.
Corinna's cheek with frequent losses burns,
And no bold *Trente le va* her fortune turns.
Ah, too rash virgin ! where 's thy virtue flown ?
She pawns her person for the sharper's loan.
Yet who with justice can the fair upbraid,
Whose debts of honour are so duly paid ?   90
    But let me not forget the *Toilette*'s cares,
Where art each morn the languid cheek repairs :
This red 's too pale, nor gives a distant grace ;
Madame to-day puts on her Opera face ;
From this we scarce extract the milkmaid's bloom,
Bring the deep dye that warms across the room :
Now flames her cheek, so strong her charms prevail,
That on her gown the silken rose looks pale !
Not but that *France* some native beauty boasts,
Clermont and *Charolois* might grace our Toasts.   100
    When the sweet-breathing spring unfolds the buds,
Love flys the dusty town for shady woods.
Then *Totenham* fields with roving beauty swarm,
And *Hampstead* Balls the city virgin warm ;
Then *Chelsea*'s meads o'erhear perfidious vows,
And the prest grass defrauds the grazing cows.
'Tis here the same ; but in a higher sphere,
For ev'n Court Ladies sin in open air.
What Cit with a gallant would trust his spouse
Beneath the tempting shade of *Greenwich* boughs ?   110
What Peer of *France* would let his Dutchess rove,
Where *Boulogne*'s closest woods invite to love ?
But here no wife can blast her husband's fame,
Cuckold is grown an honourable name.
Stretch'd on the grass the shepherd sighs his pain,
And on the grass what shepherd sighs in vain ?
On *Chloe*'s lap here *Damon* lay'd along,
Melts with the languish of her am'rous song ;
There *Iris* flies *Palæmon* through the glade,
Nor trips by chance—'till in the thickest shade ;   120
Here *Celimene* defends her lips and breast,
For kisses are by struggling closer prest ;
Alexis there with eager flame grows bold,
Nor can the nymph his wanton fingers hold ;
Be wise, *Alexis* ; what, so near the road !
Hark, a coach rolls, and husbands are abroad !
Such were our pleasures in the days of yore,
When am'rous *Charles Britannia*'s scepter bore ;
The nightly scene of joy the *Park* was made,
And Love in couples peopled ev'ry shade.   130
But since at Court the rural taste is lost,
What mighty summs have velvet couches cost !

Sometimes the *Tuillerie*'s gawdy walk I love,
Where I through crouds of rustling manteaus rove ;
As here from side to side my eyes I cast,
And gaz'd on all the glitt'ring train that past,
Sudden a fop steps forth before the rest ;
I knew the bold embroidery of his vest.
He thus accosts me with familiar air,
Parbleu ! on a fait cet habit en Angleterre !   140
Quelle manche ! ce galon est grossièrement rangé ;
Voila quelque chose de fort beau et degagé !
This said : On his red heel he turns, and then
Hums a soft minuet, and proceeds agen :
Well ; now you've Paris *seen, you'll frankly own*
Your boasted London *seems a country town ;*
Has Christianity yet reach'd your nation ?
Are churches built ?   Are Masquerades in fashion ?
Do daily Soups your dinners introduce ?
Are musick, snuff, and coaches yet in use ?   150
Pardon me, Sir ; we know the *Paris* mode,
And gather *Politesse* from Courts abroad.
Like you, our Courtiers keep a num'rous train
To load their coach ; and tradesmen dun in vain.
Nor has Religion left us in the lurch,
And, as in France, our vulgar croud the Church ;
Our Ladys too support the Masquerade,
The sex by nature love th' intriguing trade.
Strait the vain fop in ign'rant rapture crys,
Paris *the barbarous world will civilize !*   160
Pray, Sir, point out among the passing band
The present Beauties who the town command.
See yonder dame ; strict virtue chills her breast,
Mark in her eye demure the Prude profest ;
That frozen bosom native fire must want,
Which boasts of constancy to one Gallant !
This next the spoils of fifty lovers wears,
Rich Dandin's *brilliant favours grace her ears ;*
The necklace Florio's *gen'rous flame bestow'd,*
Clitander's *sparkling gems her finger load ;*   170
But now, her charms grown cheap by constant use,
She sins for scarfs, clock'd stockings, knots, and shoes.
This next, with sober gait and serious leer,
Wearies her knees with morn and ev'ning prayer ;
She scorns th' ignoble love of feeble pages,
But with three Abbots in one night engages.
This with the Cardinal her nights employs,
Where holy sinews consecrate her joys.
Why have I promised things beyond my power !
Five assignations wait me at this hour,   180

134 manteaus] manteau's *all editions consulted.*
141 *grossièrement*] *grossiérement* 1720 *and* 1731.

The sprightly Countess first my visit claims,
To-morrow shall indulge inferior dames.
Pardon me, Sir, that thus I take my leave,
Gay Florimella *slily twitch'd my sleeve.*
Adieu, Monsieur—The Opera hour draws near.
Not see the Opera! all the world is there;
Where on the stage th' embroider'd youth of *France*
In bright array attract the female glance :
This languishes, this struts, to show his mien,
And not a gold-clock'd stocking moves unseen.   190
   But hark! the full *Orchestra* strike the strings ;
The Hero strutts, and the whole audience sings.
   My jarring ear harsh grating murmurs wound,
Hoarse and confus'd, like *Babel*'s mingled sound.
Hard chance had plac'd me near a noisie throat,
That in rough quavers bellow'd ev'ry note.
Pray Sir, says I, suspend a-while your song,
The Opera 's drown'd ; your lungs are wondrous strong ;
I wish to hear your *Roland*'s ranting strain,
While he with rooted forests strows the plain.   200
Sudden he shrugs surprize, and answers quick,
Monsieur apparemment n'aime pas la musique.
Then turning round, he join'd th' ungrateful noise ;
And the loud Chorus thunder'd with his voice.
   O sooth me with some soft *Italian* air,
Let harmony compose my tortured ear !
When *Anastasia*'s voice commands the strain,
The melting warble thrills through ev'ry vein ;
Thought stands suspense, and silence pleas'd attends,
While in her notes the heav'nly Choir descends.   210
   But you'll imagine I'm a *Frenchman* grown,
Pleas'd and content with nothing but my own,
So strongly with this prejudice possest,
He thinks *French* musick and *French* painting best.
Mention the force of learn'd *Corelli*'s notes,
Some scraping fidler of their Ball he quotes ;
Talk of the spirit *Raphael*'s pencil gives,
Yet warm with life whose speaking picture lives ;
Yes Sir, says he, in colour and design,
Rigaud and *Raphael* are extreamly fine !   220
   'Tis true, his country's love transports his breast
With warmer zeal, than your old *Greeks* profest.
Ulysses lov'd his *Ithaca* of yore,
Yet that sage trav'ler left his native shore ;
What stronger vertue in the *Frenchman* shines !
He to dear *Paris* all his life confines.
I 'm not so fond.   There are, I must confess,
Things which might make me love my country less.
I should not think my *Britain* had such charms,
If lost to learning, if enslav'd by arms ;   230

France has her *Richlieus* and her *Colberts* known,
And then, I grant it, *France* in science shone :
We too, I own, without such aids may chance
In ignorance and pride to rival France.
~ But let me not forget *Corneille, Racine,*
Boileau's strong sense, and *Moliere*'s hum'rous Scene.
Let *Cambray*'s name be sung above the rest,
Whose maxims, *Pult'ney*, warm thy patriot breast ;
In *Mentor*'s precepts wisdom strong and clear
Dictates sublime, and distant nations hear.   240
Hear all ye Princes, who the world controul,
What cares, what terrors haunt the tyrant's soul ;
His constant train are anger, fear, distrust.
To be a King, is to be good and just ;
His people he protects, their rights he saves,
And scorns to rule a wretched race of slaves.
    Happy, thrice happy shall the monarch reign,
Where guardian laws despotic power restrain !
There shall the ploughshare break the stubborn land,
And bending harvests tire the peasant's hand :   250
There liberty her settled mansion boasts,
There commerce plenty brings from foreign coasts.
O *Britain*, guard thy laws, thy rights defend,
So shall these blessings to thy sons descend !
    You'll think 'tis time some other theme to chuse,
And not with Beaus and Fops fatigue the Muse :
Should I let Satyr loose on *English* ground,
There fools of various character abound ;
But here my verse is to one race confin'd,
All *Frenchmen* are of *Petit-maitre* kind.   260

An *EPISTLE*

To the Right Honourable

PAUL METHUEN Esq ;

[*Poems on Several Occasions* 1720 and 1731.]

THAT, 'tis encouragement makes Science spread,
Is rarely practis'd, though 'tis often said ;
When learning droops and sickens in the land,
What Patron 's found to lend a saving hand ?
True gen'rous Spirits prosp'rous vice detest,
And love to cherish vertue when distrest :

1-4 *Substituted in 1731 for the original opening lines :*
    YES, I'll maintain what you have often said,
    That 'tis encouragement makes science spread.

* G

But e'er our mighty Lords this scheme pursue,
Our mighty Lords must think and act like you.
    Why must we climb the *Alpine* mountain's sides
To find the seat where Harmony resides ?   10
Why touch we not so soft the silver lute,
The cheerful haut-boy, and the mellow flute ?
'Tis not th' *Italian* clime improves the sound,
But there the Patrons of her sons are found.
    Why flourish'd verse in great *Augustus'* reign ?
He and *Mecænas* lov'd the Muse's strain.
But now that wight in poverty must mourn
Who was (O cruel stars !) a Poet born.
Yet there are ways for authors to be great ;
Write ranc'rous libels to reform the State :   20
Or if you chuse more sure and ready ways,
Spatter a Minister with fulsome praise :
Launch out with freedom, flatter him enough ;
Fear not, all men are dedication-proof.
Be bolder yet, you must go farther still,
Dip deep in gall thy mercenary quill.
He who his pen in party quarrels draws,
Lists an hir'd bravo to support the cause ;
He must indulge his Patron's hate and spleen,
And stab the fame of those he ne'er has seen.   30
Why then should authors mourn their desp'rate case ?
Be brave, do this, and then demand a place.
Why art thou poor ? exert the gifts to rise,
And banish tim'rous vertue from thy eyes.
    All this seems modern preface, where we're told
That wit is prais'd, but hungry lives and cold :
Against th' ungrateful age these authors roar,
And fancy learning starves because they're poor.
Yet why should learning hope success at Court ?
Why should our Patriots vertue's cause support ?   40
Why to true merit should they have regard ?
They know that vertue is its own reward.
Yet let not me of grievances complain,
Who (though the meanest of the Muse's train)
Can boast subscriptions to my humble lays,
And mingle profit with my little praise.
    Ask Painting, why she loves *Hesperian* air.
Go view, she crys, my glorious labours there ;
There in rich palaces I reign in state,
And on the temple's lofty domes create.   50
The Nobles view my works with knowing eyes,
They love the science, and the painter prize.
    Why didst thou, *Kent*, forgo thy native land,
To emulate in picture *Raphael's* hand ?

9 mountain's] mountains' *Bell, Underhill.*   21 ready] *1731* readier *1720.*
               28 an] a *1720.*

Think'st thou for this to raise thy name at home ?
Go back, adorn the palaces of *Rome* ;
There on the walls let thy just labours shine,
And *Raphael* live again in thy design.
Yet stay awhile ; call all thy genius forth,
For *Burlington* unbyass'd knows thy worth ;   60
His judgment in thy master-strokes can trace
Titian's strong fire and *Guido*'s softer grace ;
But, oh consider, e'er thy works appear,
Canst thou unhurt the tongue of envy hear ?
Censure will blame, her breath was ever spent
To blast the laurels of the Eminent.
While *Burlington*'s proportion'd columns rise,
Does not he stand the gaze of envious eyes ?
Doors, windows are condemn'd by passing fools,
Who know not that they damn *Palladio*'s rules.   70
If *Chandois* with a lib'ral hand bestow,
Censure imputes it all to pomp and show ;
When, if the motive right were understood,
His daily pleasure is in doing good.

Had *Pope* with groveling numbers fill'd his page,
Dennis had never kindled into rage.
'Tis the sublime that hurts the Critic's ease ;
Write nonsense and he reads and sleeps in peace.
Were *Prior*, *Congreve*, *Swift* and *Pope* unknown,
Poor slander-selling *Curll* would be undone.   80
He who would free from malice pass his days,
Must live obscure, and never merit praise.
But let this tale to valiant virtue tell
The daily perils of deserving well.

A crow was strutting o'er the stubbled plain,
Just as a lark descending closed his strain.
The crow bespoke him thus with solemn grace,
Thou most accomplish'd of the feather'd race,
What force of lungs ! how clear ! how sweet you sing !
And no bird soars upon a stronger wing.   90
The lark, who scorn'd soft flatt'ry, thus replys,
True, I sing sweet, and on strong pinion rise ;
Yet let me pass my life from envy free,
For what advantage are these gifts to me ?
My song confines me to the wiry· cage,
My flight provokes the faulcon's fatal rage.
But as you pass, I hear the fowlers say,
To shoot at crows is powder flung away.

MR. POPE's WELCOME FROM GREECE.

A Copy of VERSES *written by Mr.* GAY, *upon Mr.* POPE's *having finished his Translation of* HOMER's ILIAD.

[It is curious that this 'pretty poem', which was thought well of by Gay's circle of friends, was not printed until the appearance of Stevens' *Additions to the Works of Alexander Pope Esq.*, 1776. It is not included in Bell's three-volume edition, 1777, nor in that of Jeffery (1795). Nichols's edition, 1779, has it ; and so, of course, have the later editions of Cooke (1804) and Park (*Supplement to the British Poets*, 1809). A portion of what must have been a complete draft, in Gay's neat hand-writing, is in the British Museum [Brit. Mus. Add. 6419 (53)]. It covers the first eleven and the fourteenth stanzas, and differs from the printed version in several details besides adding a further stanza after the fourteenth. I give an exact transcript in Appendix IV, p. 667. The date of composition was probably 1720. The italics are used on the responsibility of the present editor.]

I.

LONG hast thou, friend ! been absent from thy soil,
   Like patient *Ithacus* at siege of *Troy* ;
I have been witness of thy six years toil,
   Thy daily labours, and thy night's annoy,
Lost to thy native land, with great turmoil,
   On the wide sea, oft threat'ning to destroy :
Methinks with thee I 've trod *Sigæan* ground,
And heard the shores of *Hellespont* resound.

II.

Did I not see thee when thou first sett'st sail
   To seek adventures fair in *Homer*'s land ?   10
Did I not see thy sinking spirits fail,
   And wish thy bark had never left the strand ?
Ev'n in mid ocean often didst thou quail,
   And oft lift up thy holy eye and hand,
Praying the Virgin dear, and saintly choir,
Back to the port to bring thy bark entire.

III.

Chear up, my friend, thy dangers now are o'er ;
   Methinks—nay, sure the rising coasts appear ;
Hark how the guns salute from either shore,
   As thy trim vessel cuts the *Thames* so fair :   20
Shouts answ'ring shouts, from *Kent* and *Essex* roar,
   And bells break loud thro' ev'ry gust of air :
Bonfires do blaze, and bones and cleavers ring,
As at the coming of some mighty king.

1 thy] my *1779*.   22 thro'] from *Underhill.*

IV.

Now pass we *Gravesend* with a friendly wind,
   And *Tilbury's* white fort, and long *Blackwall* ;
Greenwich, where dwells the friend of human kind,
   More visited than or her park or hall,
Withers the good, and (with him ever join'd)
   Facetious *Disney*, greet thee first of all :   30
I see his chimney smoke, and hear him say,
Duke ! that 's the room for *Pope*, and that for *Gay*.

V.

Come in, my friends, here shall ye dine and lie,
   And here shall breakfast, and here dine again ;
And sup, and breakfast on, (if ye comply)
   For I have still some dozens of champaign :
His voice still lessens as the ship sails by ;
   He waves his hand to bring us back in vain ;
For now I see, I see proud *London's* spires ;
Greenwich is lost, and *Deptford* dock retires.   40

VI.

Oh, what a concourse swarms on yonder key !
   The sky re-echoes with new shouts of joy :
By all this show, I ween, 'tis Lord May'r's day ;
   I hear the voice of trumpet and hautboy :—
No, now I see them near—oh, these are they
   Who come in crowds to welcome thee from *Troy*.
Hail to the bard whom long as lost we mourn'd,
From siege, from battle, and from storm return'd !

VII.

Of goodly dames, and courteous knights, I view
   The silken petticoat, and broider'd vest ;   50
Yea Peers, and mighty Dukes, with ribbands blue,
   (True blue, fair emblem of unstained breast.)
Others I see, as noble, and more true,
   By no court-badge distinguish'd from the rest :
First see I *Methuen*, of sincerest mind,
As *Arthur* grave, as soft as woman-kind.

VIII.

What lady 's that, to whom he gently bends ?
   Who knows not her ? ah ! those are *Wortley's* eyes :
How art thou honour'd, number'd with her friends ?
   For she distinguishes the good and wise.   60
The sweet-tongu'd *Murray* near her side attends.
   Now to my heart the glance of *Howard* flies ;
Now *Harvey*, fair of face, I mark full well,
With thee, youth's youngest daughter, sweet *Lepell*.

28 or her] either *Underhill*.   44 hautboy] Hautboy *1776*.

IX.

I see two lovely sisters, hand in hand,
  The fair-hair'd *Martha*, and *Teresa* brown ;
Madge Bellenden, the tallest of the land ;
  And smiling *Mary*, soft and fair as down.
Yonder I see the chearful Duchess stand,
  For friendship, zeal, and blithsome humours known :   70
Whence that loud shout in such a hearty strain ?
Why, all the *Hamiltons* are in her train.

X.

See next the decent *Scudamore* advance,
  With *Winchelsea*, still meditating song :
With her perhaps Miss *Howe* came there by chance,
  Nor knows with whom, nor why she comes along.
Far off from these see *Santlow*, fam'd for dance ;
  And frolick *Bicknell*, and her sister young ;
With other names, by me not to be nam'd,
Much lov'd in private, not in publick fam'd !   80

XI.

But now behold the female band retire,
  And the shrill musick of their voice is still'd !
Methinks I see fam'd *Buckingham* admire,
  That in *Troy*'s ruins thou hast not been kill'd ;
Sheffield, who knows to strike the living lyre,
  With hand judicious, like thy *Homer* skill'd.
Bathurst impetuous hastens to the coast,
Whom you and I strive who shall love the most.

XII.

See generous *Burlington*, with goodly *Bruce*,
  (But *Bruce* comes wafted in a soft sedan,)   90
Dan Prior next, belov'd by every muse,
  And friendly *Congreve*, unreproachful man !
(*Oxford* by *Cunningham* hath sent excuse.)
  See hearty *Watkins* come with cup and cann ;
And *Lewis*, who has never friend forsaken ;
And *Laughton* whisp'ring asks—Is *Troy* town taken ?

XIII.

Earl *Warwick* comes, of free and honest mind ;
  Bold, gen'rous *Craggs*, whose heart was ne'er disguis'd :
Ah why, sweet *St. John*, cannot I thee find ?
  St. John for ev'ry social virtue priz'd.—   100
Alas ! to foreign climates he 's confin'd,
  Or else to see thee here I well surmiz'd :
Thou too, my *Swift*, dost breathe *Bœotian* air ;
When wilt thou bring back wit and humour here ?

90 wafted] *can this be a mistake for* wasted ?   sedan,)] sedan) *1776*.
                    93 excuse.)] excuse) *1776*.

XIV.

Harcourt I see for eloquence renown'd,
    The mouth of justice, oracle of law !
Another *Simon* is beside him found,
    Another *Simon*, like as straw to straw.
How *Lansdown* smiles, with lasting laurel crown'd !
    What mitred prelate there commands our awe ?   110
See *Rochester* approving nods his head,
And ranks one modern with the mighty dead.

XV.

Carlton and *Chandois* thy arrival grace ;
    Hanmer, whose eloquence th' unbiass'd sways ;
Harley, whose goodness opens in his face,
    And shews his heart the seat where virtue stays.
Ned Blount advances next, with busy pace,
    In haste, but sauntring, hearty in his ways :
I see the friendly *Carylls* come by dozens,
Their wives, their uncles, daughters, sons, and cousins.   120

XVI.

Arbuthnot there I see, in physicks art,
    As *Galen* learn'd, or famed *Hippocrate* ;
Whose company drives sorrow from the heart,
    As all disease his med'cines dissipate :
Kneller amid the triumph bears his part,
    Who could (were mankind lost) anew create :
What can th' extent of his vast soul confine ?
A painter, critick, engineer, divine !

XVII.

Thee *Jervas* hails, robust and debonair,
    Now have [we] conquer'd *Homer*, friends, he cries :   130
Dartneuf, grave joker, joyous *Ford* is there,
    And wond'ring *Maine*, so fat with laughing eyes :
(*Gay*, *Maine*, and *Cheney*, boon companions dear,
    Gay fat, *Maine* fatter, *Cheney* huge of size,)
Yea *Dennis*, *Gildon*, (hearing thou hast riches,)
And honest, hatless *Cromwell*, with red breeches.

XVIII.

O *Wanley*, whence com'st thou with shorten'd hair,
    And visage from thy shelves with dust besprent ?
" Forsooth (quoth he) from placing *Homer* there,
    " For ancients to compyle is myne entente :   140
" Of ancients only hath Lord *Harley* care ;

111 his] the *Underhill*.   117 busy] hasty *Underhill*.   122 learn'd] learnèd
Underhill.   124 med'cines] medicines *1776*.   130 *So printed in 1776 and 1779*.
131 grave] gay *Underhill*.   134 size,)] size) *1776*.   135 riches,)] riches) *1776*.
140 For] As *Underhill*.

"But hither me hath my meeke lady sent :—
"In manuscript of *Greeke* rede we thilke same,
"But book yprint best plesyth myn gude dame."

XIX.

Yonder I see, among th' expecting croud,
  Evans with laugh jocose, and tragick *Young* ;
High-buskin'd *Booth*, grave *Mawbert*, wand'ring *Frowd*,
  And *Titcomb*'s belly waddles slow along.
See *Digby* faints at *Southern* talking loud,
  Yea *Steele* and *Tickell* mingle in the throng ;   150
Tickell whose skiff (in partnership they say)
Set forth for *Greece*, but founder'd in the way.

XX.

Lo the two *Doncastles* in *Berkshire* known !
  Lo *Bickford, Fortescue*, of *Devon* land !
Lo *Tooker, Eckershall, Sykes, Rawlinson* !
  See hearty *Morley* takes thee by the hand !
Ayrs, Graham, Buckridge, joy thy voyage done ;
  But who can count the leaves, the stars, the sand ?
Lo *Stonor, Fenton, Caldwell, Ward* and *Broome* !
Lo thousands more, but I want rhyme and room !   160

XXI.

How lov'd ! how honour'd thou ! yet be not vain ;
  And sure thou art not, for I hear thee say,
All this, my friends, I owe to *Homer*'s strain,
  On whose strong pinions I exalt my lay.
What from contending cities did he gain ;
  And what rewards his grateful country pay ?
None, none were paid—why then all this for me ?
These honours, *Homer*, had been just to thee.

144 yprint] reprint *Underhill.*   152 in] on *Underhill.*
    156 takes] take *Underhill.*

AN

EPISTLE

TO HER GRACE,

HENRIETTA,

Dutchess *OF MARLBOROUGH.*

[*Edition :*
AN | *EPISTLE* | TO HER GRACE | HENRIETTA, | Dutchess of *MARL-BOROUGH.* | By Mr. *GAY.* | *LONDON :* | Printed for Jacob Tonson, at *Shake-spear's-Head,* over-against | *Katharine-street* in the *Strand.* MDCCXXII.
Folio.]

Excuse me, Madam, if amidst your tears
A Muse intrudes, a Muse who feels your cares ;
Numbers, like Musick, can ev'n Grief controul,
And lull to peace the tumults of the soul.
    If Partners in our woes the mind relieve,
Consider for your Loss ten thousands grieve,
Th' Affliction burthens not your heart alone ;
When *Marlbro'* dy'd a Nation gave a groan.
    Could I recite the dang'rous toils he chose,
To bless his Country with a fixt repose,   10
Could I recount the Labours he o'ercame
To raise his Country to the pitch of fame,
His councils, sieges, his victorious fights,
To save his Country's Laws and native rights,
No father (ev'ry gen'rous heart must own)
Has stronger fondness to his darling shown.
Britannia's sighs a double loss deplore,
Her Father and her Hero is no more.
    Does *Britain* only pay her debt of tears ?
Yes. *Holland* sighs, and for her freedom fears.   20
When *Gallia*'s Monarch pour'd his wasteful bands,
Like a wide deluge, o'er her level lands,
She saw her frontier tow'rs in ruin lie,
Ev'n Liberty had prun'd her wings to fly ;
Then *Marlbro'* came, defeated *Gallia* fled,
And shatter'd *Belgia* rais'd her languid head,
In him secure, as in her strongest mound
That keeps the raging Sea within its bound.
    O *Germany,* remember *Hockstet*'s plain,
Where prostrate *Gallia* bled at every vein,   30

Think on the rescue of th' Imperial throne,
Then think on *Marlbro*'s death without a groan !
  Apollo kindly whispers me. ' Be wise,
' How to his glory shall thy numbers rise ?
' The force of verse another theme might raise,
' But here the merit must transcend the praise.
' Hast thou, presumptuous Bard, that godlike flame
' Which with the Sun shall last, and *Marlbro*'s fame ?
' Then sing the Man. But who can boast this fire ?
' Resign the task, and silently admire.   40
  Yet, shall he not in worthy lays be read ?
Raise *Homer*, call up *Virgil* from the dead.
But he requires not the strong glare of verse,
Let punctual History his deeds rehearse,
Let Truth in native purity appear,
You'll find *Achilles* and *Æneas* there.
  Is this the comfort which the Muse bestows ?
I but indulge and aggravate your woes.
A prudent friend, who seeks to give relief,
Ne'er touches on the spring that mov'd the grief.   50
Is it not barb'rous to the sighing maid
To mention broken vows and Nymphs betray'd ?
Would you the ruin'd merchant's soul appease,
With talk of sands and rocks and stormy seas ?
Ev'n while I strive on *Marlbro*'s fame to rise,
I call up sorrow in a Daughter's eyes.
  Think on the laurels that his temples shade,
Laurels that (spite of time) shall never fade ;
Immortal Honour has enroll'd his name,
Detraction 's dumb, and Envy put to shame ;   60
Say, who can soar beyond his eagle flight ?
Has he not reach'd to glory's utmost height ?
What could he more, had Heaven prolong'd his date ?
All human power is limited by Fate.
  Forbear. 'Tis cruel further to commend ;
I wake your sorrow, and again offend.
Yet sure your goodness must forgive a crime,
Which will be spread through ev'ry age and clime ;
Though in your life ten thousand summers roll,
And though you compass earth from Pole to Pole, 70
Where-e'er men talk of war and martial fame,
They'll mention *Marlborough*'s and *Cæsar*'s name.
  But vain are all the counsels of the Muse,
A Soul, like yours, cou'd not a tear refuse :
Could you your birth and filial love forego,
Still sighs must rise and gen'rous sorrow flow ;
For when from earth such matchless worth removes,
A great Mind suffers. Virtue Virtue loves.

77 removes,] removes *1722*.

LESSER EPISTLES.

ON A

Miscellany of POEMS

TO

BERNARD LINTOTT.

Ipsa varietate tentamus efficere ut alia aliis ; quædam
fortasse omnibus placeant.
Plin. Epist.

[From *Miscellaneous Poems and Translations*, 1712, 1714, 1720, and 1722.
See pp. xxxv, xxxvii, and 88.
The editions of 1712 and 1714 use capital letters freely, and white lines between
paragraphs ; the editions of 1720 and 1722 do not. The motto from Pliny is only
given in 1712 and 1714.
There is, I think, sufficient though indirect evidence that this poem is by Gay.
In all four editions of the *Miscellaneous Poems and Translations* it is printed anonymously. In the editions of 1712 and 1714 it is, besides *Arachne*, Gay's sole contribu-
tion ; but in the editions of 1721 and 1722 three other poems, with Gay's name
attached, were added (The *Epistle to Burlington, Epistle to a Lady*, and *Sweet*
William's Farewell). *Arachne* was then transposed from its place in the earlier
editions, and printed with the last-named pieces. Between the *Epistles* and *Sweet*
William this poem is printed, followed by the "Verses design'd to be prefix'd to
Mr. Lintott's Miscellany" now generally attributed to Pope. Nichols's edition of
1779 includes our poem ; and the style is very evidently Gay's. There is, in my
judgement, no force in Mr. I. A. Williams's contention that, if this poem is by Gay,
so must be the verses following it and beginning ' Some *Colinaeus* praise, some
Bleau '. Identity of subject, not of authorship, is the reason for their juxtaposition.]

As when some skilful cook, to please each guest,
Would in one mixture comprehend a feast,
With due proportion and judicious care
He fills each dish with diff'rent sorts of fare,
Fishes and fowl deliciously unite,
To feast at once the taste, the smell, and sight.
　So, *Bernard*, must a miscellany be
Compounded of all kinds of poetry ;
The muses *O'lio*, which all tastes may fit,
And treat each reader with his darling wit.　　　　　10

Wouldst thou for miscellanies raise thy fame;
And bravely rival *Jacob*'s mighty name,
Let all the muses in the piece conspire,
The lyrick bard must strike th' harmonious lyre;
Heroick strains must here and there be found,
And nervous sense be sung in lofty sound;
Let elegy in moving numbers flow,
And fill some pages with melodious woe;
Let not your am'rous songs too num'rous prove,
Nor glut thy reader with abundant love;   20
Satyr must interfere, whose pointed rage
May lash the madness of a vicious age;
Satyr, the muse that never fails to hit,
For if there 's scandal, to be sure there 's wit.
Tire not our patience with pindarick lays,
Those swell the piece, but very rarely please:
Let short-breath'd epigram its force confine,
And strike at follies in a single line.
Translations should throughout the work be sown,
And *Homer*'s godlike muse be made our own;   30
Horace in useful numbers should be sung,
And *Virgil*'s thoughts adorn the *British* tongue;
Let *Ovid* tell *Corinna*'s hard disdain,
And at her door in melting notes complain:
His tender accents pitying virgins move,
And charm the list'ning ear with tales of love.
Let ev'ry classick in the volume shine,
And each contribute to thy great design:
Through various subjects let the reader range,
And raise his fancy with a grateful change;   40
Variety 's the source of joy below,
From whence still fresh revolving pleasures flow.
In books and love, the mind one end pursues,
And only change th' expiring flame renews.
Where *Buckingham* will condescend to give,
That honour'd piece to distant times must live;
When noble *Sheffield* strikes the trembling strings,
The little loves rejoyce, and clap their wings,
Anacreon lives, they cry, th' harmonious swain
Retunes the lyre, and tries his wonted strain,   50
'Tis he,—our lost *Anacreon* lives again.
But when th' illustrious poet soars above
The sportive revels of the god of love,
Like *Maro*'s muse he takes a loftier flight,
And towres beyond the wond'ring *Cupid*'s sight.
If thou wouldst have thy volume stand the test,
And of all others be reputed best,
Let *Congreve* teach the list'ning groves to mourn,
As when he wept o'er fair *Pastora*'s urn.
Let *Prior*'s muse with soft'ning accents move,   60
Soft as the strains of constant *Emma*'s love:

Or let his fancy chuse some jovial theme,
As when he told *Hans Carvel*'s jealous dream ;
Prior th' admiring reader entertains,
With *Chaucer*'s humour, and with *Spencer*'s strains.
  Waller in *Granville* lives ; when *Mira* sings
With *Waller*'s hand he strikes the sounding strings,
With sprightly turns his noble genius shines,
And manly sense adorns his easie lines.
  On *Addison*'s sweet lays attention waits,   70
And silence guards the place while he repeats ;
His muse alike on ev'ry subject charms,
Whether she paints the god of love, or arms :
In him, pathetick *Ovid* sings again,
And *Homer*'s *Iliad* shines in his *Campaign*.
  Whenever *Garth* shall raise his sprightly song,
Sense flows in easie numbers from his tongue ;
Great *Phœbus* in his learned son we see,
Alike in physick, as in poetry.
  When *Pope*'s harmonious muse with pleasure roves,   80
Amidst the plains, the murm'ring streams, and groves,
Attentive Eccho pleas'd to hear his songs,
Thro' the glad shade each warbling note prolongs ;
His various numbers charm our ravish'd ears,
His steady judgment far out-shoots his years,
And early in the youth the God appears.
  From these successful bards collect thy strains,
And praise with profit shall reward thy pains :
Then, while calves-leather binding bears the sway,
And sheep-skin to its sleeker gloss gives way ;   90
While neat old *Elzevir* is reckon'd better
Than *Pirate Hill*'s brown sheets, and scurvy letter ;
While print-admirers careful *Aldus* chuse
Before *John Morphew*, or the weekly news :
So long shall live thy praise in books of fame,
And *Tonson* yield to *Lintott*'s lofty name.

To my ingenious and worthy Friend
W — L — Esq ;

*Author of that celebrated treatise in folio,
called the* LAND-TAX BILL.

[*Poems on Several Occasions* 1720 and 1731.]

WHEN Poets print their works, the scribbling crew
Stick the Bard o'er with Bays, like Christmas pew :
Can meagre Poetry such fame deserve ?
Can Poetry ; that only writes to starve ?
And shall no laurel deck that famous head,
In which the Senate's annual law is bred ?
That hoary head, which greater glory fires,
By nobler *ways* and *means* true fame acquires.
O had I *Virgil's* force to sing the man,
Whose learned lines can millions raise *per ann.*   10
Great *L——* his praise should swell the trump of fame,
And *Rapes* and *Wapentakes* resound his name.
    If the blind *Poet* gain'd a long renown
By singing ev'ry *Grecian* chief and town ;
Sure *L——* his prose much greater fame requires, ⎫
Which sweetly counts five thousand Knights and Squires, ⎬.
Their seats, their citys, parishes and shires. ⎭
    Thy copious Preamble so smoothly runs
Taxes no more appear like legal duns,
Lords, Knights, and Squires th' Assessor's power obey,   20
We read with pleasure, though with pain we pay.
    Ah why did *C——* thy works defame !
That author's long harangue betrays his name ;
After his speeches can his pen succeed ?
Though forc'd to hear, we're not oblig'd to read.
    Under what science shall thy works be read ?
All know thou wert not Poet born and bred ;
Or dost thou boast th' Historian's lasting pen,
Whose annals are the *Acts* of worthy men ?
No.   Satyr is thy talent ; and each lash   30
Makes the rich Miser tremble o'er his cash ;
What on the Drunkard can be more severe,
Than direful taxes on his ale and beer ?
    Ev'n *Button's* Wits are nought compar'd to thee,
Who ne'er were known or prais'd but o'er his Tea,
While Thou through *Britain's* distant isle shalt spread,
In ev'ry *Hundred* and *Division* read.

       Title. W—— L——] i.e. *William Lowndes.*
     22 *C——*] i.e. *Coningsby.*

Criticks in *Classicks* oft' interpolate,
But ev'ry word of thine is fix'd as Fate.
Some works come forth at morn, but die at night   40
In blazing fringes round a tallow light,
Some may perhaps to a whole week extend,
Like *S——* (when unassisted by a friend,)
But thou shalt live a year in spite of fate :
And where 's your author boasts a longer date ?
Poets of old had such a wondrous power,
That with their verses they could raise a tower ;
But in thy Prose a greater force is found ;
What Poet ever rais'd ten thousand pound ?
Cadmus, by sowing dragon's teeth, we read,   50
Rais'd a vast army from the poys'nous seed.
Thy labours, *L——*, can greater wonders do,
Thou raisest armys, and canst pay them too.
Truce with thy dreaded pen ; thy Annals cease ;
Why need we armys when the land 's in peace ?
Soldiers are pefect devils in their way,
When once they're rais'd, they're cursed hard to lay.

43 *S——*] i.e. *Steele.* friend,)] friend) *all editions consulted.*
   50 dragon's] dragons' *Bell, Underhill.*

To

A young Lady, with some LAMPREYS.

[*Poems on Several Occasions* 1720 and 1731.]

WITH lovers 'twas of old the fashion
By presents to convey their passion ;
No matter what the gift they sent,
The Lady saw that love was meant.
Fair *Atalanta*, as a favour,
Took the boar's head her Hero gave
  her ;
Nor could the bristly thing affront
  her,
'Twas a fit present from a hunter.
When Squires send woodcocks to the
  dame,
It serves to show their absent flame :
Some by a snip of woven hair,   11
In posied lockets bribe the fair ;

How many mercenary matches
Have sprung from Di'mond-rings and
  watches !
But hold—a ring, a watch, a locket,
Would drain at once a Poet's pocket ;
He should send songs that cost him
  nought,
Nor ev'n be prodigal of thought.
  Why then send Lampreys ? fye,
    for shame !   19
'Twill set a virgin's blood on flame.
This to fifteen a proper gift !
It might lend sixty five a lift.
  I know your maiden Aunt will
    scold,

And think my present somewhat bold.
I see her lift her hands and eyes.
  'What eat it, Niece ; eat *Spanish*
    flies !
'Lamprey 's a most immodest diet :
'You'll neither wake nor sleep in
    quiet.
'Should I to-night eat Sago cream,
''Twould make me blush to tell my
    dream ;   30
'If I eat Lobster, 'tis so warming,
'That ev'ry man I see looks charm-
    ing ;
'Wherefore had not the filthy fellow
'Laid *Rochester* upon your pillow ?
'I vow and swear, I think the present
'Had been as modest and as decent.
  'Who has her virtue in her power ?
'Each day has its unguarded hour ;
'Always in danger of undoing,
'A prawn, a shrimp may prove our
    ruin !   40

'The shepherdess, who lives on
    sallad,
'To cool her youth, controuls her
    palate ;
'Should *Dian*'s Maids turn liqu'rish
    livers,
'And of huge lampreys rob the rivers,
'Then all beside each glade and Visto,
'You'd see Nymphs lying like *Calisto*.
  'The man who meant to heat your
    blood,
'Needs not himself such vicious
    food——
  In this, I own, your Aunt is clear,
I sent you what I well might spare : 50
For when I see you (without joking),
Your eyes, lips, breasts are so pro-
    voking,
They set my heart more cock-a-hoop,
Than could whole seas of craw-fish
    soupe.

26 et seq. *Inverted commas from 1731.*
43 Maids] *Omitted in 1720 : the lacuna is not noticed in the Errata.*

A Panegyrical
EPISTLE
TO
*M*ʀ. THOMAS SNOW.

Goldsmith, *near* Temple-Bar ;

Occasion'd by his Buying and Selling the Third South-Sea *Subscriptions, taken in by the* Directors *at a* Thousand per Cent.

[*Editions :*
1. A | PANEGYRICAL | EPISTLE | TO | Mr. *THOMAS SNOW,* | Goldsmith, near *Temple-Barr :* | Occasion'd by his Buying and Selling of the Third | Subscriptions, taken in by the Directors | of the *SOUTH-SEA* Company, at a Thousand | *per Cent.* | *LONDON* : | Printed for Bernard Lintot, at the *Cross-Keys* between | the Two *Temple-Gates.* MDCCXXI. | Price Three-Pence.
Folio. Anonymous.
2. MISCELLANIES | IN | VERSE. | *LONDON* : | Printed for Benjamin Motte, at the *Middle-Temple Gate* in *Fleet-Street.* M.DCC.XXVII.
Post 8vo.
This was one of the volumes forming the series of Miscellanies published by Pope and Swift. For other pieces contained in it, see p. xxxix.
I follow this version.   [Ref. 1727.]
3. *Miscellany Poems.* Vol. II. 1727.   [Ref. M.P. 1727.]
(See p. 88.)
This agrees very nearly with the version of 1721 ; but does not use white lines or capital letters, as do both the other versions. ' By Mr. Gay ' (in Index).
4. MISCELLANIES. | THE | FOURTH VOLUME. | Consisting of | VERSES | BY Dr. *SWIFT,* Dr. *ARBUTHNOT,* | Mr. *POPE,* and Mr. *GAY.* | *LONDON :* | Printed for Charles Bathurst, at the | *Cross Keys* opposite St. *Dunstan*'s Church, | *Fleet street,* MDCCXLVII.
Small 8vo. An enlarged edition of the *Miscellanies in Verse.*]

    Disdain not, Snow, my humble Verse to hear :
    Stick thy black Pen awhile behind thy Ear.
    Whether thy Compter shine with Sums untold,
    And thy wide-grasping Hand grow black with Gold :
    Whether thy Mien erect, and sable Locks,
    In Crowds of Brokers over-awe the *Stocks* :
    Suspend the worldly Business of the Day ;
    And to enrich thy Mind, attend my Lay.
      O thou, whose penetrative Wisdom found
    The *South-Sea* Rocks and Shelves where Thousands drown'd. 10

4 grow] grows *1747.*

When Credit sunk, and Commerce gasping lay,
Thou stood'st : No Bill was sent unpaid away.
When not a Guinea chink'd on † *Martin*'s Boards,
And † *Atwill*'s self was drain'd of all his Hoards,
Thou stood'st ; (an *Indian* King in Size and Hue)
Thy unexhausted Shop was our *Peru*.
Why did '*Change-Alley* waste thy precious Hours,
Among the Fools who gap'd for golden Show'rs ?
No wonder, if we found some *Poets* there,
Who live on Fancy, and can feed on Air ;   20
No wonder, *they* were caught by *South-Sea* Schemes,
Who ne'er enjoy'd a Guinea, but in Dreams ;
No wonder, *they* their Third Subscriptions sold,
For Millions of imaginary Gold :
No wonder, that *their* Fancies wild can frame
Strange Reasons, that a Thing is still the same,   }
Though chang'd throughout in Substance and in Name.   }
But *you* (whose Judgment scorns Poetick Flights)
With Contracts furnish Boys for Paper Kites.
Let Vulture *H——ns* stretch his rusty Throat,   30
Who ruins Thousands for a single Groat.
I know thou scorn'st his mean, his sordid Mind :
Nor, with Ideal Debts, would'st plague Mankind.
Madmen alone their empty Dreams pursue,
And still believe the fleeting Vision true ;
They sell the Treasures which their Slumbers get,
Then wake, and fancy all the World in Debt.
If to instruct thee all my Reasons fail,
Yet be diverted by this Moral Tale.
Through fam'd *Moor-Fields* extends a spacious Seat,   40
Where Mortals of exalted Wit retreat ;
Where wrapp'd in Contemplation and in Straw,
The wiser Few from the mad World withdraw.
There in full Opulence a *Banker* dwelt,
Who all the Joys and Pangs of Riches felt :
His Side-board glitter'd with imagin'd Plate ;
And his proud Fancy held a vast Estate.
As, on a Time, he pass'd the vacant Hours
In raising Piles of Straw and twisted Bowers ;

† *Names of eminent* Goldsmiths.

12 nor sent one Bill unpaid away. *1721 and M.P. 1727.*   13, 14, n. *Not given
in 1721.*   14 *Atwill's*] *Atwell's M.P 1727.*   17 thy] *thy M.P. 1727.*   19 found]
find *1747.*   21 et seqq. *they*] they *1721 and M.P. 1727.*   25 can] could *M.P.
1727.*   28 *you*] you *1721 and M.P. 1727.*   30 *H——ns*] i.e. *Hopkins.*   31 Who
ruins] Who'd ruin *1721 and M.P. 1727.*   32 scorn'st] spurn'st *1721 and M.P.
1727.*   33 *In the version of 1721 and M.P. 1727 this couplet follows :*
          Why strive his greedy Hands to grasp at more ?
          The Wretch was born to want, whose Soul is poor.
36 Treasures] treasure *M.P. 1727.*
48 As, on a time,] As on a Time *1721 and M.P. 1727.*

A *Poet* enter'd of the neighb'ring Cell,   50
And with fix'd Eye observ'd the Structure well.
A sharpen'd Skew'r cross his bare Shoulders bound
A tatter'd Rug, which dragg'd upon the Ground.
   The banker cry'd, " Behold my Castle Walls,
" My Statues, Gardens, Fountains, and Canals ;
" With Land of twenty thousand Acres round !
" All these I sell thee for ten thousand Pound.
   The Bard with Wonder the cheap Purchase saw,
So sign'd the Contract (as ordains the Law.)
   The Banker's Brain was cool'd, the Mist grew clear ;   60
The Visionary Scene was lost in Air.
He now the vanish'd Prospect understood,
And fear'd the fancy'd Bargain was not good :
Yet loth the Sum entire should be destroy'd ;
" Give me a Penny and thy Contract 's void.
   The startled Bard with Eye indignant frown'd.
" Shall I, ye Gods (he cries) my Debts compound !
So saying, from his Rug the Skew'r he takes,
And on the Stick Ten equal Notches makes :
With just Resentment flings it on the Ground ;   70
" There, take my Tally of Ten Thousand Pound.

     52 Skew'r] Skewer *1721* and *M.P. 1727.*

TO A
L A D Y
ON HER
PASSION FOR *OLD CHINA.*

[*Editions :*
  1. TO A | LADY | ON HER | PASSION | FOR | *OLD CHINA.* | *LONDON* :
Printed for J. TONSON in the *Strand.* 1725.
   Small 4to. Since the appearance of Mr. T. J. Wise's Catalogue of the Ashley
Library the British Museum copy has come to light ; this and Mr. Wise's copy are
the only known examples. *Vide* pp. xxvii–xxviii.
  2. *The Works of Mr. John Gay.* 1772.]

WHAT ecstasies her bosom fire !
How her eyes languish with desire !
How blest, how happy should I be,
Were that fond glance bestow'd on
   me !
New doubts and fears within me war :
What rival 's near ? a *China* Jar.

China 's the passion of her soul ;
A cup, a plate, a dish, a bowl
Can kindle wishes in her breast,
Inflame with joy, or break her rest.
   Some gems collect ; some medals
    prize,   11
And view the rust with lovers eyes ;

Some court the stars at midnight
    hours ;
Some doat on Nature's charms in
    flowers !
But ev'ry beauty I can trace
In *Laura*'s mind, in *Laura*'s face ;
My stars are in this brighter sphere,
My lilly and my rose is here.

Philosophers more grave than wise
Hunt science down in Butterflies ; 20
Or fondly poring on a Spider,
Stretch human contemplation wider ;
Fossiles give joy to *Galen*'s soul,
He digs for knowledge, like a Mole ;
In shells so learn'd, that all agree
No fish that swims knows more than
    he !
In such pursuits if wisdom lies,
Who, *Laura*, shall thy taste despise ?
    Whe1 I some antique Jar behold,
Or white, or blue, or speck'd with
    gold,   30
Vessels so pure, and so refin'd
Appear the types of woman-kind :
Are they not valu'd for their beauty,
Too fair, too fine for household duty ?
With flowers and gold and azure
    dy'd,
Of ev'ry house the grace and pride ?
How white, how polish'd is their skin,
And valu'd most when only seen !
She who before was highest priz'd,
Is for a crack or flaw despis'd ;   40
I grant they're frail, yet they're so
    rare,
The treasure cannot cost too dear !
But Man is made of courser stuff,

And serves convenience well enough ;
He 's a strong earthen vessel, made
For drudging, labour, toil and trade ;
And when wives lose their other self,
With ease they bear the loss of *Delf*.

Husbands more covetous than sage
Condemn this *China*-buying rage ; 50
They count that woman's prudence
    little,
Who sets her heart on things so
    brittle.
But are those wise-men's inclinations
Fixt on more strong, more sure
    foundations ?
If all that 's frail we must despise,
No human view or scheme is wise.
Are not Ambition's hopes as weak ?
They swell like bubbles, shine and
    break.
A Courtier's promise is so slight,   59
'Tis made at noon, and broke at night.
What pleasure 's sure ? The Miss you
    keep
Breaks both your fortune and your
    sleep.
The man who loves a country life,
Breaks all the comforts of his wife ;
And if he quit his farm and plough,
His wife in town may break her vow.
Love, *Laura*, love, while youth is
    warm,
For each new winter breaks a charm ;
And woman 's not like *China* sold,
But cheaper grows in growing old ; 70
Then quickly chuse the prudent part,
Or else you break a faithful heart.

45 vessel, made] vessel made, *all editions consulted.*

SONGS AND BALLADS.

Sweet WILLIAM's Farewell
to Black-ey'd SUSAN.

A BALLAD.

[*Editions :*
  1. A setting 'The Tune by Mr. Carey', giving also 'Mr. Leveridge's tune', 'Mr. Haydon's tune', and 'Sign^r. Sandonis tune'. (Brit. Mus. H. 1601, no. 24.) ? 1720.
  2. The setting by Sandoni, with 'Mr. Leveridge's tune' for the flute, on the back. (Brit. Mus. G. 305 (209).) ? 1720. (A manuscript note, by the way, says : 'This volume contains most of the original Songs and beautiful airs which were selected by Pepusch, Arne and Linley—for "The Beggar's Opera", Love in a Village—and Duenna.')
  3. *Poems on Several Occasions.* 1720.
  4. *Miscellaneous Poems and Translations.* Third edition. 1720.
    See pp. xxxvii and 88. (The Ballad was not included in the first two editions.)
  5. *Miscellaneous Poems and Translations.* Fourth edition. 1722.
    See pp. xxxvii and 88.
  6. The Setting to Carey's Tune: also giving Mr. Leveridge's tune. (Brit. Mus. G. 316. g (2).) ? 1725.
  7. Pope's *Miscellany Poems.* Vol. I. 1726.
    See p. 88.
  8. *Poems on Several Occasions.* 1731.
  9. Watts's *Musical Miscellany*, vol. 4, 1730.
    Mr. Underhill says 'originally published in separate form '—I suppose he means the musical settings, which appear not to be earlier than 1720.]

I.

ALL in the *Downs* the fleet was moor'd,
  The streamers waving in the wind,
When black-ey'd *Susan* came aboard.
  Oh ! where shall I my true love find !
Tell me, ye jovial sailors, tell me true,
If my sweet *William* sails among the crew.

3 aboard.] *1, 2, 3, 6, 8, 9* on board. *4*   on board, *5, 7*.
4 find !] *1, 2, 3, 6, 8* find ? *remainder.*
5 me, . . . sailors,] *3, 8, 9* me . . . sailors *remainder.*
6 If my sweet *William*, if my sweet *William*, sails among the crew *4, 5 and 9 only.*

II.

William, who high upon the yard,
  Rock'd with the billow to and fro,
Soon as her well-known voice he heard,
  He sigh'd and cast his eyes below :   10
The cord slides swiftly through his glowing hands,
And, (quick as lightning,) on the deck he stands.

III.

So the sweet lark, high-pois'd in air,
  Shuts close his pinions to his breast,
(If, chance, his mate's shrill call he hear)
  And drops at once into her nest.
The noblest Captain in the *British* fleet,
Might envy *William*'s lip those kisses sweet.

IV.

O *Susan*, *Susan*, lovely dear,
  My vows shall ever true remain ;   20
Let me kiss off that falling tear,
  We only part to meet again.
Change, as ye list, ye winds ; my heart shall be
The faithful compass that still points to thee.

V.

Believe not what the landmen say,
  Who tempt with doubts thy constant mind :
They'll tell thee, sailors, when away,
  In ev'ry port a mistress find.
Yes, yes, believe them when they tell thee so,
For thou art present wheresoe'er I go.   30

VI.

If to far *India*'s coast we sail,
  Thy eyes are seen in di'monds bright,
Thy breath is *Africk*'s spicy gale,
  Thy skin is ivory, so white.
Thus ev'ry beauteous object that I view,
Wakes in my soul some charm of lovely *Sue*.

VII.

Though battel call me from thy arms,
  Let not my pretty *Susan* mourn ;
Though cannons roar, yet safe from harms,
  William shall to his Dear return.   40

8 billow] *3, 8,* **9** billows *remainder.*   10 sigh'd] *1, 8* sigh'd, *remainder.*   11
through] *3, 8* thro' *remainder*   12 *Brackets from 3, 8 and 9 only.*   15 If,
chance,] *3, 8, 9* If chance *remainder.*   16 nest.] *2, 3, 6, 8* nest, *1, 4* nest : *5, 7, 9.*
17 Captain] *1, 2, 3, 6, 8, 9* captain *remainder.*   18 lip] *3, 8, 9* lips *remainder.*
31 far] **1**, *2, 3, 6, 8, 9* fair *remainder.*   37 Though] *1, 2, 3, 6, 8* Tho' *remainder.*
call] *3, 8, 9* calls *remainder.*   39 Though] *1, 2, 3, 6, 8* Tho' *remainder.*   40
Dear] *2, 3, 6, 8, 9* dear *remainder.*

Love turns aside the balls that round me fly,
Lest precious tears should drop from *Susan*'s eye.

VIII.

The boatswain gave the dreadful word,
    The sails their swelling bosom spread,
No longer must she stay aboard :
    They kiss'd, she sigh'd, he hung his head ;
Her less'ning boat, unwilling rows to land :
Adieu, she cries ! and wav'd her lilly hand.

43 boatswain] *3, 8* Boatswain *remainder.*   46 head ;] *8* Head, *1* head *remainder.*   48 cries !] *3, 8* Cries *1*   cries ; *remainder.*

THE

LADY's LAMENTATION.

A BALLAD.

[*Poems on Several Occasions* 1720 and 1731.]

I.

PHYLLIDA, that lov'd to dream
In the grove, or by the stream ;
    Sigh'd on velvet pillow.
What, alas ! should fill her head
But a fountain or a mead,
    Water and a willow ?

II.

Love in citys never dwells,
He delights in rural cells
    Which sweet wood-bine covers.
What are your *Assemblys* then ?   10
There, 'tis true, we see more men ;
    But much fewer lovers.

III.

Oh, how chang'd the prospect grows !
Flocks and herds to Fops and Beaus,
    Coxcombs without number !
Moon and stars that shone so bright,
To the torch and waxen light,
    And whole nights at *Ombre.*

IV.

Pleasant as it is, to hear
Scandal tickling in our ear,   20
    Ev'n of our own mothers ;
In the chit-chat of the day,
To us is pay'd, when we're away,
    What we lent to others.

V.

Though the fav'rite *Toast* I reign ;
Wine, they say, that prompts the vain,
    Heightens defamation.
Must I live 'twixt spite and fear,
Ev'ry day grow handsomer,
    And lose my reputation ?   30

VI.

Thus the Fair to sighs gave way,
Her empty purse beside her lay.
    Nymph, ah cease thy sorrow.
Though curst fortune frown to-night;
This odious town can give delight
    If you win to-morrow.

DAMON *and* CUPID.

A *SONG*.

[*Poems on Several Occasions* 1720 and 1731.]

I.

THE sun was now withdrawn,
  The shepherds home were sped ;
The moon wide o'er the lawn
  Her silver mantle spread ;
When *Damon* stay'd behind,
  And saunter'd in the grove.
Will ne'er a nymph be kind,
  And give me love for love ?

II.

Oh ! those were golden hours,
  When Love, devoid of cares,   10
In all *Arcadia*'s bow'rs
  Lodg'd swains and nymphs by
    pairs !
But now from wood and plain
  Flys ev'ry sprightly lass,
No joys for me remain,
  In shades, or on the grass.

III.

The winged boy draws near,
  And thus the swain reproves.
While beauty revell'd here,
  My game lay in the groves ;   20
At Court I never fail
  To scatter round my arrows,
Men fall as thick as hail ;
  And maidens love like sparrows.

IV.

Then, swain, if me you need,
  Strait lay your sheep-hook down ;
Throw by your oaten reed,
  And haste away to town.
So well I'm known at Court,
  None asks where *Cupid* dwells ;   30
But readily resort
  To B——n's or L——ll's.

32 *B——n*] i.e. *Bellenden.*   *L——ll*] i.e. *Lepell.*   Vide *Mr. Pope's Welcome from Greece* ll. 64 and 67, pp. 165 and 166.

DAPHNIS *and* CHLOE.

A *SONG*.

[*Editions* :
  1. *Poems on Several Occasions.*   1720.
  2. (Daphnis *and* Cloe) *A new SONG.*   A single-sheet folio, with music, in the British Museum.   ? 1720.
  3. (Daphnis *and* Cloe) *A New SONG.*   Another single-sheet folio, with music, in the British Museum.   ? 1725.
  4. Watts's *Musical Miscellany,* vol. 2.   1729.
  5. *Poems on Several Occasions.*   1731.]

DAPHNIS stood pensive in the
    shade,
  With arms a-cross, and head re-
    clin'd ;
Pale looks accus'd the cruel maid,
  And sighs reliev'd his love-sick
    mind :
His tuneful pipe all broken lay,
Looks, sighs, and actions seem'd to say,
  My *Chloe* is unkind.

II.

Why ring the woods with warbling
    throats ?
Ye larks, ye linnets, cease your
    strains :
I faintly hear in your sweet notes, 10
My *Chloe*'s voice that wakes my
    pains :
Yet why should you your song for-
    bear ?
Your mates delight your song to hear,
    But *Chloe* mine disdains.

III.

As thus he melancholy stood,
    Dejected as the lonely dove ;
Sweet sounds broke gently through
    the wood.
I feel the sound ; my heart-strings
    move.
'Twas not the nightingale that sung ;
No. 'Tis my *Chloe*'s sweeter tongue.
    Hark, hark, what says my love ! 21

IV.

How foolish is the nymph (she crys)
    Who trifles with her lover's pain !
Nature still speaks in woman's eyes,
    Our artful lips were made to feign.
O *Daphnis, Daphnis*, 'twas my pride,
'Twas not my heart thy love deny'd.
    Come back, dear youth, again.

V.

As t'other day my hand he seiz'd,
    My blood with thrilling motion
    flew ;   30

Sudden I put on looks displeas'd,
    And hasty from his hold withdrew.
'Twas fear alone, thou simple swain.
Then hadst thou prest my hand again,
    My heart had yielded too !

VI.

'Tis true, thy tuneful reed I blam'd,
    That swell'd thy lip and rosie
    cheek ;
Think not thy skill in song defam'd ;
    That lip should other pleasures
    seek :
Much, much thy musick I approve ; 40
Yet break thy pipe, for more I love,
    Much more, to hear thee speak.

VII.

My heart forebodes that I'm be-
    tray'd,
    Daphnis I fear is ever gone ;
Last night with *Delia*'s dog he play'd;
    Love by such trifles first comes on.
Now, now, dear shepherd, come away,
My tongue would now my heart obey.
    Ah *Chloe*, thou art won !

VIII.

The youth step'd forth with hasty
    pace,   50
    And found where wishing *Chloe* lay;
Shame sudden lighten'd in her face,
    Confus'd, she knew not what to say.
At last in broken words, she cry'd ;
To-morrow you in vain had try'd,
    But I am lost to-day !

17 wood.] Wood, *1729*.   38 defam'd;] defam'd, *1720 and 1731*   defam'd:
1729.   42 more,] *1729* more *remainder*.   45 play'd;] 1729 play'd, *remainder*.

Newgate's GARLAND:

BEING

A *NEW BALLAD.*

SHEWING

How Mr. *Jonathan Wild*'s Throat was cut from Ear to Ear
with a Penknife, by Mr. *Blake,* alias *Blueskin,* the bold
Highwayman, as he stood at his Tryal in the *Old-Bailey.*
1725.

To the Tune of The Cut-purse.

[*Editions :*
1. BLUE-SKIN'S | BALLAD | *To the Tune of Packington's Pound.* . . . [Follows the
Ballad] . . . Printed in the Year 1724–5.
Broad-side ; single-sheet folio.   [Ref. 1725.]
2. The Ballad, almost in the form here given, is to be found printed on the back
of a Postscript to the St. James's Post, No. 133, Monday, November 28, 1715.
There are two copies in the British Museum; it would appear that a certain
number of old sheets (which had the ' Postscript ' on one side only) were used up ten
years later for the Ballad.   [Ref. *S.J.P.*]
3. *Miscellanies in Verse,* 1727. See p. 177.
4. Watts's *Musical Miscellany,* vol. 5, 1731.
5. *Miscellanies.* The Fourth Volume, 1747. See p. 177.
The text follows that of the *Miscellanies.*
For the question of authorship, see pp. xxvi–xxvii.   Stanzas VI and VII are,
I think, Swift's.   They were omitted in. 1727 and 1747.]

I.

YE Gallants of *Newgate,* whose Fingers are nice,
In diving in Pockets, or cogging of Dice.
Ye Sharpers so rich, who can buy off the Noose,
Ye honester poor Rogues, who die in your Shoes,
    Attend and draw near,
    Good News ye shall hear,
    How *Jonathan*'s Throat was cut from Ear to Ear ;
How *Blueskin*'s sharp Penknife hath set you at Ease,
And every Man round me may rob, if he please,

Heading. Not given in 1725 or 1731.
in the *Old-Bailey.*   1725.] *1727, 1747*   at the Old-Bailey *S.J.P.*
1 Gallants] Fellows *1725, S.J.P.*   2 or] and *1725.*   6 ye] you *1725.*
7 How Honest *Wild*'s Throat *etc. 1725.*   8 How] Nŏw *1725.*   hath] has
1725. And so throughout.   9 he] they *S.J.P. And so throughout.*

II.

When to the *Old-Bailey* this *Blueskin* was led,   10
He held up his Hand, his Indictment was read,
Loud rattled his Chains, near him *Jonathan* stood,
For full Forty Pounds was the Price of his Blood.
    Then hopeless of Life,
    He drew his Penknife,
And made a sad Widow of *Jonathan*'s Wife.
But Forty Pounds paid her, her Grief shall appease,
And every Man round me may rob, if he please.

III.

Some say there are Courtiers of highest Renown,
Who steal the King's Gold, and leave him but a *Crown* ;   20
Some say there are Peers, and some Parliament Men,
Who meet once a Year to rob Courtiers agen :
    Let them all take their Swing,
    To pillage the King,
And get a Blue Ribbon instead of a String.
Now *Blueskin*'s sharp Penknife hath set you at Ease,
And every Man round me may rob, if he please.

IV.

Knaves of old, to hide Guilt by their cunning Inventions,
Call'd Briberies Grants, and plain Robberies Pensions ;
Physicians and Lawyers (who take their Degrees   30
To be Learned Rogues) call'd their Pilfering, Fees ;
    Since this happy Day,
    Now ev'ry Man may
Rob (as safe as in Office) upon the Highway.
For *Blueskin*'s sharp Penknife hath set you at Ease,
And every Man round me may rob, if he please.

V.

Some cheat in the Customs, some rob the Excise,
But he who robs both is esteemed most wise.
Church-Wardens, too prudent to hazard the Halter,
As yet only venture to steal from the Altar :   40
    But now to get Gold,
    They may be more bold,
And rob on the Highway, since *Jonathan*'s cold.
For *Blueskin*'s sharp Penknife hath set you at Ease,
And every man round me may rob, if he please.

---

10 *Old-Bailey*] Old Baily *1725*   Old-Bailey *S.J.P.*   *Old-Baily 1731.*   12 *Jonathan*] honest *Wild 1725.   And so throughout.*   22 agen] again *1725, S.J.P.*
23 But let them have their Swing *1725.*   26 Now] For *1725.*   29 and plain
Robberies] and plain Robbery *1725*   and . . . plain Robberies *S.J.P.*   30–1 *No
brackets, 1725.*   31 call their pilferings Fees. *1725*   call'd their Pilfering . . . Fees ;
S.J.P.   37 Some Rob in the *Customs*, some Cheat in the '*xcise 1725.*   39 who
always have dreaded the Halter *1725, S.J.P.*

[VI.

Some by publick Revenues, which pass'd through their Hands,
Have purchas'd clean Houses, and bought dirty Lands,
Some to steal from a Charity think it no Sin,
Which, at Home (says the Proverb) does always begin;
    But, if ever you be   10
    Assign'd a Trustee,
Treat not Orphans like Masters of the Chancery.
But take the Highway, and more honestly seise,
For every Man round me may rob, if he please.]

[VII.

What a Pother has here been with *Wood* and his Brass,
Who would modestly make a few Half-pennies pass!
The Patent is good, and the Precedent's old.
For *Diomede* changed his Copper for Gold:
    But if *Ireland* despise
    Thy new Half-pennies,   60
With more Safety to rob on the Road I advise.
For *Blueskin*'s sharp Penknife hath set thee at Ease,
And every Man round me may rob, if he please.]

46–7   Some by *Publick Revenues* which pass tho' their Hands
       Have purchas'd *Clean Houses* and bought *Dirty Lands*; *1725.*
50 But, if] If *1725.*   52 of] in *1725.*   54 For ev'ry Man round, &c. *1725.*
55 What a Pother is here with *Woods* and his Brass *1725.*
56 pass!] pass? *1727, 1731, and 1747* pass; *remainder.*
60 Thy] The *1725.*   61 With more Safety] More safely *1725.*
62 hath set thee] hath set you *1725* has set you *S.J.P.*

MOLLY MOG:

OR, THE

FAIR MAID *of the Inn.*

A BALLAD.

[*Editions:*
  1. *Mist's Weekly Journal,* August 27, 1726.   [Ref. M.W.J.]
  2. Molly Mogg, A *SONG Set by an Eminent Master.* A Broadside, in Mr. T. J. Wise's possession. Text, with music, engraved upon one side of a single sheet. No place or date. The last line of music is headed *For the Flute.*
    For a description and reproduction see *Catalogue of the Ashley Library*; and for the reasons which compel me to disagree with Mr. Wise's suggestion that this is an earlier publication than *Mist's Journal* for August 27 see below. It is, however, certainly earlier than No. 4.   [Ref. BS.¹]
  3. Another Broadside, with music, dated by Mr. Wise 1727, and also in his possession. The last line of music is headed *Flute.*   [Ref. BS.²]
  4. *Molly Mog: or, the Fair Maid of the Inn.* A Ballad. A Broadside, without music, preserved in the British Museum.

A manuscript note on this reads, 'in or after 1727 since the alterations agree closely with the copy printed in the *Miscellanies* of Swift and Pope, 1727.' I take it to be slightly earlier than the *Miscellanies*, since in l. 3 it has the earlier reading *That.* [Ref. BS.²]

5. *Miscellany Poems*, Vol. II, 1727. (See p. 88.)

This version agrees generally with the following, except that it numbers the verses, and does not use capital letters. It also has the earlier reading in l. 3. [Ref. M.P.]

6. *Miscellanies in Verse*, 1727. (See p. 177.)

This is evidently the final version, and is followed here, except that I have retained the numbering of the verses, which it omits. [Ref. M.V.]

7. Watts's *Musical Miscellany*, vol. 2, 1729. [Ref. M.M.]

8. *Miscellanies.* The Fourth Volume. 1747. (See p. 177.)

For a full discussion of the authorship of Molly Mog, and of the history of the Ballad, see *Notes and Queries*, 2nd Series, viii. 84, 129, 172, 175.

On its first appearance, in *Mist's Journal*, it was accompanied by the following editorial note : ' In our last we presented our Readers with a short Poem upon Molly Mog ; as few have seen that which occasion'd it, it having never been printed, we shall give it the Publick now, which will make the other better understood.— We shall only observe, it was writ by two or three Men of Wit, (who have diverted the Publick both in Prose and Verse) upon the Occasion of their lying at a certain Inn at Ockingham, where the Daughter of the House was remarkably pretty, and whose Name is MOLLY MOG.'

The Ballad became popular, and was much imitated. Several contributors wrote to *Mist's Journal* to suggest additional verses. Two of these, taken from a letter printed in the *Journal* for September 10, 1726, were subsequently incorporated in the poem ; and this fact might be taken to indicate a composite authorship of the whole ballad. Pope, Swift, and Gay were together in the summer of 1726. It is possible that all three had a hand in it. But Swift, only three years later, in *The History of the Second Solomon*, wrote : ' Solomon had published a humourous ballad, called *Ballyspellin*, whither he had gone to drink the waters, with a new favourite lady. The ballad was in the manner of Mr. *Gay*'s on *Molly Mogg*, pretending to contain all the rhymes of *Ballyspellin*.' Moreover, in Pope's *Miscellany Poems*, vol. ii, 1727, the poem is explicitly assigned to Gay. This proves that Gay at least conceived the Ballad, and probably made up the most of it.

The first and final versions differ considerably. Mr. Wise's Broadside gives us an interesting intermediate version, nearer to the earlier than to the later version, and having some peculiarities of its own. Of the two interpolated verses (VIII and XIII) it has the former, but not the latter. It employs the spelling *Mogg* (revived in the 1747 edition of the *Miscellanies*), whereas both the earlier and the later versions spell *Mog*. It divides the Ballad into seven eight-line verses, whereas all the other versions use four-line verses. This division is for the sake of the tune, which is in twenty bars, two and a half bars to a line. It was, no doubt, in order to make up an even number of verses that Verse VIII was borrowed from the letter in *Mist's Journal* for September 10. Some of the alterations seem to be made for easier singing. This gradual process of correction is thoroughly characteristic of Gay.

The second Broadside (BS.²) differs in some unimportant details of spelling and punctuation from BS.¹ The two are otherwise identical, except for a variant in l. 36. I have not recorded all the many differences of spelling and punctuation between the various versions.

It should be said, to avoid misunderstanding, that the text of the engraved Broadsides (BS.¹ and ²) is, as is usual, in italics ('copper-plate') ; the proper names and words, which would in ordinary printing have been italicized, being engraved in roman lettering. For the sake of clearness I have, in quoting from the Broadsides in the notes, substituted italics for romans, and vice versa.

The varying order of the verses in the three chief versions is a little difficult to grasp. The following table gives the order of verses in each version, the numbers being those of the version as here printed :

M.W.J. 1, 2, 4, 5, 6, 7, 3, 10, 9, 11, 12, 14, 15.
BS.¹ and ². 1, 2, 4, 5, 6, 3, 8, 7, 9, 10, 11, 12, 14, 15.
BS.², M.P., M.V. 1 to 15.]

I.

Says my Uncle, I pray you discover
What hath been the Cause of your Woes,
Why you pine, and you whine, like a Lover ?
I have seen *Molly Mog* of the *Rose*.

II.

O Nephew ! your Grief is but Folly,
In Town you may find better Prog ;
Half a Crown there will get you a *Molly*,
A *Molly* much better than *Mog*.

III.

I know that by Wits 'tis recited,
That Women at best are a Clog ;   10
But I am not so easily frighted,
From loving of sweet *Molly Mog*.

IV.

The School-Boy's desire is a Play-Day,
The School-Master's joy is to flog ;
The Milk-Maid's delight is on *May-Day*,
But mine is on sweet *Molly Mog*.

V.

Will-a-wisp leads the Trav'ler a gadding
Thro' Ditch, and thro' Quagmire and Bog ;
But no Light can set me a madding,
Like the Eyes of my sweet *Molly Mog*.   20

VI.

For Guineas in other Men's Breeches
Your Gamesters will palm and will cog ;
But I envy them none of their Riches,
So I may win sweet *Molly Mog*.

2 hath] has *M.W.J.*, *BS.* ¹ and ². 3 Why] *M.V.* That *remainder.* pine...
whine] whine... pine *BS.* ¹ and ². 4 I have] I've *M.W.J.*, *BS.* ¹ and ². *M.M.* 6 find]
have *BS.* ¹ and ². III. *Follows* VII *in M.W.J.; follows* VI *in BS.* ¹ and ². 11 I am]
I'm *M.W.J.*, *BS.* ¹ and ². *M.M.* (*N.B.—The 1747 and later editions of the* Miscellanies
revert to the earlier I'm.) 12 of] my *M.W.J.*, *BS.* ¹ and ². 13 The School Boys
delight in a Play-Day, *M.W.J.* The School Boys delight is a play day *BS.* ¹ and ².
14 The Masters delight is to Flogg *BS.* ¹ and ² (flogg *BS.* ²). 15 Fop is the Delight of
a Lady, *M.W.J.* Milk-Maid's] Milk-maids *BS.* ¹ Milk Maids *BS.* ². 16 on] in
M.W.J., *BS.* ¹ and ². 17 *Will-a-wisp*] Will a Wisp *M.W.J.* Will a Wisp *BS.* ¹ and ².
(Later editions of the *Miscellanies* print *Will-o'-wisp*.) Trav'ler] Traveller *M.W.J.*
Trav'ller *BS.* ¹ 18 Thro'... thro'] Through... thro' *BS.* ¹ and ². 19 No Light
can e'er set me a padding *M.W.J.* But no light can e'er set me a madding *BS.* ¹ and ²
(Light *BS.* ²). 20 Like] But *M.W.J.* 24 May win] palm my *M.W.J.*, *BS.* ²
Palm my *BS.*

VII.

The Heart, when half-wounded, is changing,
　　It here and there leaps like a Frog ;
But my Heart can never be ranging,
　　'Tis so fix'd upon sweet *Molly Mog.*

VIII.

[Who follows all Ladies of Pleasure,
　　In Pleasure is thought but a Hog :　　　　30
All the Sex cannot give so good measure
　　Of Joys, as my sweet *Molly Mog.*]

IX.

I feel I'm in Love to Distraction,
　　My Senses all lost in a Fog ;
And nothing can give Satisfaction
　　But thinking of sweet *Molly Mog.*

X.

A Letter when I am inditing,
　　Comes *Cupid* and gives me a Jog,
And I fill all the Paper with writing
　　Of nothing but sweet *Molly Mog.*　　　　40

XI.

If I would not give up the three *Graces*
　　I wish I were hang'd like a Dog,
And at Court all the Drawing-Room Faces,
　　For a Glance of my sweet *Molly Mog.*

XII.

Those Faces want Nature and Spirit,
　　And seem as cut out of a Log ;
Juno, Venus, and *Pallas*'s Merit
　　Unite in my sweet *Molly Mog.*

VII. *Follows* VIII *in BS.*[1 and 2].
25 The Hart that 's half wounded, is ranging, *M.W.J.*　　27 ranging] changing
M.W.J.　　28 'Tis] It's *M.W.J.*　　fix'd] fix't *BS.*[1], fixt *BS.*[2], *M.M.*　　upon] on
my *M.W.J.*
VIII. *The version of this verse, as contributed to M.W.J. for September 10, 1726, is :*
Who follows all Women of Pleasure
In Love, has a Taste like a Hog ;
For no Girl can give better Measure
Of Joys, than my sweet Molly Mog.
30 thought but] counted *BS.*[1 and 2].
IX. *Follows* X. *in M.W.J.*　　34 all] are *M.W.J.*　　quite *BS.*[1 and 2].
35 And in nothing can find Satisfaction, *M.W.J.*　　Now there 's nothing can give
Satisfaction *BS.*[2], *M.M.*
36 But thinking of] But in Thoughts of *MWJ.*　　Like thinking on *BS.*[1]　　Like
thinking of *BS.*[2]
39 the] my *M.W.J.*, *BS.*[1 and 2]　　40 Of nothing] Of nothing, *M.P.*, *M.M.*, *BS.*[2]
44 Glance of] Glance at *M.W.J.*　　glimpse of *BS.*[1]　　Glimpse of *BS.*[2]
45 Those] For those *M.W.J.*　　47 *Pallas*'s] *Palas*'s, *BS.*[1]

XIII.

[Those who toast all the Family Royal,
  In Bumpers of *Hogan* and *Nog*,
Have Hearts not more true or more loyal   50
  Than mine to my sweet *Molly Mog*.]

XIV.

Were *Virgil* alive with his *Phillis*,
  And writing another Eclogue ;
Both his *Phillis* and fair *Amaryllis*
  He'd give up for sweet *Molly Mog*.

XV.

When she smiles on each Guest, like her Liquor,
  Then Jealousy sets me agog.
To be sure she's a Bit for the *Vicar*,
  And so I shall lose *Molly Mog*.   60

XIII. *The version of this verse, as contributed to M.W.J. for September 10, 1726, is :*
    Those who toast all the Family Royal
      In Bumpers of Hogan and Nog,
    Can't have Hearts more true, nor more loyal,
      Than mine is for sweet Molly Mog.

51 loyal] loyal, *M.P.*   55 *Amaryllis*] Amarillis *M.W.J., BS.*[1 and 2].   56 give up for] give for my *M.W.J.* give up for my *BS.*[1, 2, 3].   57 When Molly comes up with the Liquor, *M.W.J.* 58 sets] set *BS.*[1] agog] a Gog *M.W.J.* a Gogg *BS.*[1] a gogg *BS.*[2] 60 So I shall loose sweet *Molly Mogg* BS.[1 and 2].

The COQUET MOTHER *and* COQUET DAUGHTER.

A *SONG*.

[From Steele's *Poetical Miscellanies*, the second edition, 1727. Not included in the First Edition. The name of the author is not given. See pp. xxvii–xxviii for the question of authorship.
  A single-sheet folio, with a musical setting by Th. Jno. Worgan, is in the British Museum, and is dated ? 1750.]

I.

AT the close of the Day,
When the Bean-flow'r and Hay
  Breath'd Odours in ev'ry Wind :
Love enliven'd the Veins
Of the Damsels and Swains ;
  Each glance and each action was
    kind.

II.

Molly, wanton and free,
Kiss'd, and sat on each Knee,
  Fond ecstasy swam in her Eyes.
See, thy Mother is near,   10
Hark ! She calls thee to hear
  What Age and Experience advise.

III.

Hast thou seen the blithe Dove
Stretch her Neck to her Love,
 All glossy with Purple and Gold ?
If a Kiss he obtain,
She returns it again :
 What follows, you need not be told.

IV.

Look ye, Mother, she cry'd,
You instruct me in Pride,
 And Men by Good-manners are won.
She who trifles with all
Is less likely to fall
 Than she who but trifles with one.

V.

Pr'ythee, *Molly*, be wise,
Lest by sudden surprize
 Love should tingle in ev'ry Vein :
Take a Shepherd for Life,
And when once you 're a Wife,
 You safely may trifle again. 30

VI.

Molly smiling reply'd,
Then I'll soon be a Bride ;
 Old *Roger* has Gold in his Chest.
But I thought all you Wives
Chose a Man for your Lives,
 And trifled no more with the rest.

A BALLAD *on* ALE.

[Text from *The Poetical Dramatic and Miscellaneous Works of John Gay* 1795.
in which it appears less modernized than in *Bell*'s three-volume edition, 1777. The
italics are without the authority of either edition, but follow Gay's usual practice.]

I.

WHILST some in Epic strains delight,
Whilst others Pastorals invite,
 As taste or whim prevail ;
Assist me, all ye tuneful Nine,
Support me in the great design,
 To sing of nappy Ale.

II.

Some folks of Cyder make a rout,
And Cyder's well enough, no doubt,
 When better liquors fail ;
But Wine, that's richer, better still, 10
Ev'n Wine itself (deny't who will)
 Must yield to nappy Ale.

III.

Rum, Brandy, Gin with choicest
 smack
From *Holland* brought, *Batavia*
 Arrack,
 All these will nought avail
To chear a truly *British* heart,
And lively spirits to impart,
 Like humming, nappy Ale.

IV.

Oh ! whether thee I closely hug
In honest can, or nut-brown jug, 20
 Or in the tankard hail ;
In barrel, or in bottle pent,
I give the gen'rous spirit vent,
 Still may I feast on Ale.

V.

But chief, when to the chearful glass
From vessel pure thy streamlets pass
 Then most thy charms prevail ;
Then, then, I'll bett, and take
 odds,
That nectar, drink of heathen gods,
 Was poor, compar'd to Ale. 30

VI.

Give me a bumper, fill it up.
See how it sparkles in the cup,
 O how shall I regale !
Can any taste this drink divine,
And then compare Rum, Brandy,
 Wine,
 Or aught with nappy Ale ?

1 strains] streams *Underhill*. 14 *Arrack*] 'Arrack, *1795* 'rack *Bell*.

* H

VII.

Inspir'd by thee, the warrior fights,
The lover wooes, the poet writes,
  And pens the pleasing tale ;
And still in *Britain*'s isle confess'd   40
Nought animates the patriot's breast
  Like gen'rous, nappy Ale.

VIII.

High Church and Low oft raise a
  strife,
And oft endanger limb and life,
  Each studious to prevail ;
Yet *Whig* and *Tory* opposite
In all things else, do both unite
  In praise of nappy Ale.

IX.

Inspir'd by thee. shall *Crispin* sing,
Or talk of freedom, church, and king,
  And balance *Europe*'s scale ;   51

While his rich landlord lays out
  schemes
Of wealth, in golden *South Sea*
  dreams,
  Th' effects of nappy Ale.

X.

O blest potation ! still by thee,
And thy companion Liberty,
  Do health and mirth prevail ;
Then let us crown the can, the glass,
And sportive bid the minutes pass
  In quaffing nappy Ale.   60

XI.

Ev'n while these stanzas I indite,
The bar-bell's grateful sounds invite
  Where joy can never fail !
Adieu ! my Muse, adieu ! I haste
To gratify my longing taste
  With copious draughts of ALE.

52 lays out schemes] lays out his schemes *Underhill.*

The DESPAIRING SHEPHERD.

[*Editions :*
  1. (The Poor Shepherd) *The Words by* Mr. Gay.
    A single-sheet folio, with music, in the British Museum.   ? 1720.   [Ref. BS.[1]]
  2. Watts's *Musical Miscellany,* Vol. I, 1729, as ' The despairing Shepherd, by
Mr. Gay '. (See p. xl.)   A different setting.   [Ref. 1729.]
  3. Allan Ramsay's *Tea Table Miscellany,* Vol. II, ninth edition, 1733 (? in first
edition, 1725), as ' The Complaint ', signed ' X '.   [Ref. T.T.M.]
  4. The Poor Shepherd. *Set by* Mr. M. C. Festing.
    A single-sheet folio, with music (a different setting from 1 or 2), in the British
Museum.   ? 1730]   [Ref. BS.[2]]

I.

THE Sun was sunk beneath the Hill,
  The Western Clouds were edg'd with Gold,
The Sky was clear, the Winds were still ;
  The Flocks were penn'd within the Fold,
When from the Silence of the Grove
Poor *Damon* thus despair'd of love ; .

1 Hill] Hills *1729.*   2 edg'd] *1729* lin'd *remainder.*   Clouds were] cloud
was *T.T.M.*   3 Clear was the sky, the wind was still *T.T.M.*   4 penn'd]
1729 and T.T.M.   pent *remainder.*   5 from] in *T.T.M.*

II.

Who seeks to pluck the fragrant Rose
　From the bare Rock, or oozy Beach;
Who, from each barren Weed that grows,
　Expects the Grape and blushing Peach;　　　　10
With equal Faith may hope to find
The Truth of Love in Womankind.

III.

I have no Flocks, nor Fleecy care,
　No Fields that shine with golden Grain,
Nor Meadows green, nor Gardens fair,
　Of Virgins venal Hearts to gain;
Then all in vain my Sighs must prove,
For I, alas! am nought but Love.

IV.

How wretched is the faithful Youth,
　Since Women's Hearts are bought and sold;　　　20
They ask not Vows of sacred Truth,
　Whene'er they sigh, they sigh for Gold.
Gold can the Frowns of Scorn remove;
But I, alas! am nought but Love.

V.

To buy the Gems of *India*'s Coast,
　What Wealth, what Riches can suffice?
But all their Fire can never boast
　The living Lustre of her Eyes:
For there the World too cheap would prove,
But I, alas! am nought but Love.　　　　30

13–16　　I have no Herds no Fleecy care
　　　　No Feilds that Wave with Golden Grain.
　　　　Nor Pastures Green nor Garden Fair
　　　　A Damsells Venal Heart to gain
　　　　　　　BS.[1] *and BS.*[2] (*with trifling variations*)

　　　　No flocks have I, or fleecy care,
　　　　　No fields that wave with golden grain,
　　　　No pastures green, or gardens fair,
　　　　　A woman's venal heart to gain,　　*T.T.M.*

18　　For I alass have nought but Love
　　　　　　BS.[1] *and BS.*[2] (*reading* alass!). *And so in ll.* 24 *and* 30.
　　　　Whose whole estate, alas! is love. *T.T.M.*

20 Women's] Women *BS.*[1]　　　21 not] no *T.T.M.*　　　22 for] to *T.T.M.*
24 Thus I am scorn'd,—who have but love *T.T.M.*　　26 Riches] Treasure *BS.*[1]
treasure *BS.*[2]　　27 Not all their Fire can ever boast *BS.*[1 and 2].　　Yet *India*'s shore
could never boast *T.T.M.*　　28 The lustre of thy rival eyes: *T.T.M.*　　29
there] these *BS.*[1]　　these, *BS.*[2]　　30 Can I then buy?—who have but love.
T.T.M.

VI.

Oh, *Sylvia*, since nor Gems, nor Oar,
　Can with thy brighter Charms compare,
Consider, that I proffer more,
　(More seldom found) a Heart sincere.
Let Treasure meaner Beauties move;
Who pays thy Worth, must pay with Love.

31 Oh, *Sylvia*] Then, *Mary, T.T.M.*　　　32 charms]self *T.T.M.*
33-4　　　Be just, as fair, and value more,
　　　　Than gems or ore, a heart sincere : *T.T.M.*
34 *Brackets in 1729 only.*　　35 move] prove *T.T.M.*　　36 with] *1729*
in *remainder.*

MISCELLANIES.

P A N T H E A.

An E L E G Y.

[*Editions :*
1. POETICAL | MISCELLANIES, | Consisting of | *ORIGINAL POEMS* | AND |TRANSLATIONS. | *By the best Hands.* | Publish'd by Mr. *STEELE.* | *LONDON* : | Printed for JACOB TONSON at *Shake-* | *spear's Head* over-against *Catherine-street* | in the *Strand.* MDDCXIV. (According to Mr. Underhill, published on December 29, 1713.)
    Small 8vo. Containing the four pieces which follow ; of these *A Thought on Eternity* was the only one not printed under the author's name.
    2. *Poems on Several Occasions.* 1720.
    3. *Poetical Miscellanies* [etc.]. Published by Sir Richard Steele. The Second Edition. 1727.
    Small 8vo. The text is identical with that of 1714, and is therefore not referred to in the Notes.
    4. POETICAL | MISCELLANIES : | Consisting of | *Original* Poems | AND | TRANSLATIONS. | *By the best Hands.* | *Publish'd by Mr.* J. GAY. | *DUBLIN :* | Printed for J. THOMPSON, Bookseller, | on *Cork-Hill.* MDCCXXIX.
    Small 8vo. A small collection, probably unauthorized, of pieces by Swift, King, Gay, and others, including *Panthea, A Thought on Eternity,* and *A Contemplation on Night.*
    5. *Poems on Several Occasions.* 1731.
References by date. White lines between paragraphs are used in the editions of 1714 and 1731 only and in the 1729 edition of *A Contemplation on Night.* The version of 1714 and 1729 uses Capital Letters freely for initials.]

      LONG had *Panthea* felt Love's secret smart,
      And hope and fear alternate rul'd her heart ;
      Consenting glances had her flame confest.
      (In woman's eyes her very soul's exprest.)
      Perjur'd *Alexis* saw the blushing maid,
      He saw, he swore, he conquer'd and betray'd :
      Another love now calls him from her arms,
      His fickle heart another beauty warms ;
      Those oaths oft' whisper'd in *Panthea's* ears,
      He now again to *Galatea* swears.   10

An ELEGY] *No sub-title in 1714 and 1729.*
1–2   *PANTHEA* long had felt Love's pleasing Smart,
           And the strong Passion rul'd her tender Heart ; *1714 and 1729.*
4 And told the secret Anguish of her Breast ; *1714 and 1729 (the latter has* Breast). exprest.)] exprest) *1720 and 1731.*

Beneath a beech th' abandon'd virgin laid,
In grateful solitude enjoys the shade ;
There with faint voice she breathed these moving strains,
While fighting Zephyrs shar'd her am'rous pains.
    Pale settled sorrow hangs upon my brow,
Dead are my charms ; *Alexis* breaks his vow !
Think, think, dear shepherd, on the days you knew,
When I was happy, when my swain was true ;
Think how thy looks and tongue are form'd to move,
And think yet more—that all my fault was love.   20
Ah, could you view me in this wretched state !
You might not love me, but you could not hate.
Could you behold me in this conscious shade,
Where first thy vows, where first my love was paid,
Worn out with watching, sullen with despair,
And see each eye swell with a gushing tear ?
Could you behold me on this mossy bed,
From my pale cheek the lively crimson fled,
Which in my softer hours you oft' have sworn,
With rosie beauty far out-blush'd the morn ;   30
Could you untouch'd this wretched object bear,
And would not lost *Panthea* claim a tear ?
You could not sure—tears from your eyes would steal,
And unawares thy tender soul reveal.
Ah, no !—thy soul with cruelty is fraught,
No tenderness disturbs thy savage thought ;
Sooner shall tygers spare the trembling lambs,
And wolves with pity hear their bleating dams ;
Sooner shall vultures from their quarry fly,
Than false *Alexis* for *Panthea* sigh.   40
Thy bosom ne'er a tender thought confest,
Sure stubborn flint has arm'd thy cruel breast ;
But hardest flints are worn by frequent rains,
And the soft drops dissolve their solid veins ;
While thy relentless heart more hard appears,
And is not soften'd by a flood of tears.
    Ah, what is love ! *Panthea's* joys are gone,
Her liberty, her peace, her reason flown !
And when I view me in the watry glass,
I find *Panthea* now, not what she was.   50
As northern winds the new-blown roses blast,
And on the ground their fading ruins cast ;

15-18   Ah cruel Youth ! tho' Love thy Bosom flies,
         And now no Charms reign in *Panthea's* Eyes ;
         Yet think, *Alexis*, that thou once hast known,
         A wretched Virgin by thy Vows undone ; *1714 and 1729.*
16 *Alexis*] 1731   *Alexis,* 1720.   25 sullen] stupid *1714 and 1729.*
26 *Here follows in the version of 1714 and 1729 the couplet*
         Those Eyes, which oft you said were to your Sight
         Grateful as Day, and welcome as the Light :
42 has] hath *1714 and 1729.*   51 northern] *Northern* 1714 and 1729.

As sudden blights corrupt the ripen'd grain,
And of its verdure spoil the mournful plain ;
So hapless love on blooming features preys,
So hapless love destroys our peaceful days.
 Come, gentle sleep, relieve these weary'd eyes,
All sorrow in thy soft embraces dies :
There, spite of all thy perjur'd vows, I find
Faithless *Alexis* languishingly kind ;   60
Sometimes he leads me by the mazy stream,
And pleasingly deludes me in my dream ;
Sometimes he guides me to the secret grove,
Where all our looks, and all our talk is love.
Oh, could I thus consume each tedious day,
And in sweet slumbers dream my life away ;
But sleep, which now no more relieves these eyes,
To my sad soul the dear deceit denies.
 Why does the sun dart forth its chearful rays ?
Why do the woods resound with warbling lays ?   70
Why does the rose her grateful fragrance yield,
And yellow cowslips paint the smiling field ?
Why do the streams with murm'ring musick flow,
And why do groves their friendly shade bestow ?
Let sable clouds the chearful sun deface,
Let mournful silence seize the feather'd race ;
No more, ye roses, grateful fragrance yield,
Droop, droop, ye cowslips, in the blasted field ;
No more, ye streams, with murm'ring music flow,
And let not groves a friendly shade bestow :   80
With sympathizing grief let nature mourn,
And never know the youthful spring's return :
And shall I never more *Alexis* see ?
Then what is spring, or grove or stream to me ?
 Why sport the skipping lambs on yonder plain ?
Why do the birds their tuneful voices strain ?
Why frisk those heifers in the cooling grove ?
Their happier life is ignorant of love.
 Oh ! lead me to some melancholy cave,
To lull my sorrows in a living grave ;   90
From the dark rock where dashing waters fall,
And creeping ivy hangs the craggy wall,
Where I may waste in tears my hours away,
And never know the seasons or the day.
Dye, dye, *Panthea*—flie this hateful grove,
For what is life without the Swain I love ?

53 ripen'd] rip'ning *1714 and 1729.*
55-6   So tort'ring Love preys on the youthful Face,
       And Beauty strips of ev'ry Blooming Grace.
                 1714 and 1729 (the latter has blooming).
79 Stand still, ye murm'ring streams, no longer flow, *1714 and 1729.*
83-4   For my *Alexis* from the Plains is gone,
       And with him all *Panthea*'s Joys are flown. *1714 and 172*
85 on] in *1714 and 1729.*

ARAMINTA.

An ELEGY.

[*Editions : as of the foregoing, except for 1729.*]

Now *Phœbus* rose ; and with his early beams
Wak'd slumb'ring *Delia* from her pleasing dreams ;
Her wishes by her fancy were supply'd,
And in her sleep the nuptial knot was ty'd.
With secret joy she saw the morning ray
Chequer the floor, and through the curtains play ;
The happy morn that shall her bliss compleat,
And all her rivals envious hopes defeat.
In haste she rose ; forgetful of her pray'rs,
Flew to the glass, and practis'd o'er her airs :   10
Her new-set jewels round her robe are plac'd,
Some in a brilliant buckle bind her waist :
Some round her neck a circling light display,
Some in her hair diffuse a trembling ray;
The silver knot o'erlooks the *Mechlen* lace,
And adds becoming beauties to her face :
Brocaded flow'rs o'er the gay manteau shine,
And the rich stays her taper shape confine;
Thus all her dress exerts a graceful pride,
And sporting Loves surround th' expecting bride,   20
For *Daphnis* now attends the blushing maid,
Before the Priest their solemn vows are paid ;
This day which ends at once all *Delia*'s cares,
Shall swell a thousand eyes with secret tears.
Cease, *Araminta*, 'tis in vain to grieve,
Canst thou from *Hymen*'s bonds the youth retrieve ?
Disdain his perj'ries, and no longer mourn:
Recall thy love, and find a sure return.
      But still the wretched maid no comfort knows,
And with resentment cherishes her woes ;   30

An ELEGY] A TOWN ECLOGUE *1714*.   9 forgetful] unmindful *1714*.
17 manteau] Mantoe *1714*.
22 *Here follows in the version of 1714 the couplet*
            Daphnis, for whom so many Ladies sigh,
            Wish of each Heart ; Delight of ev'ry Eye ;
25-8   Cease, *Araminta,* now no longer Grieve,
            Thou ne'er from *Hymen* can'st the Youth retrieve.
            Why then in vain will *Araminta* mourn ?
            Bestow thy Love where thou may'st hope Return.   *1714.*
28 thy] my *all editions consulted.   An obvious misprint.*
29 and **33** *In the version of 1714 these lines do not begin new paragraphs.*

Alone she pines, and in these mournful strains,
Of *Daphnis'* vows, and her own fate complains.
    Was it for this I sparkled at the *Play*,
And loiter'd in the *Ring* whole hours away ?
When if thy chariot in the circle shone,
Our mutual passion by our looks was known :
Through the gay crowd my watchful glances flew,
Where-e'er I pass thy grateful eyes pursue.
    Ah faithless youth ! too well you saw my pain ;
For eyes the language of the soul explain.   40
    Think, *Daphnis*, think that scarce five days are fled,
Since (O false tongue !) those treach'rous things you said
How did you praise my shape and graceful air !
And woman thinks all compliments sincere.
Didst thou not then in rapture speak thy flame,
And in soft sighs breath *Araminta*'s name ?
Didst thou not then with oaths thy passion prove,
And with an awful trembling, say—I love ?
    Ah faithless youth ! too well you saw my pain ;
For eyes the language of the soul explain.   50
    How could'st thou thus, ungrateful youth, deceive ?
How could I thus, unguarded maid, believe ?
Sure thou canst well recall that fatal night,
When subtle love first enter'd at my sight :
When in the dance I was thy partner chose,
Gods ! what a rapture in my bosom rose !
My trembling hand my sudden joy confess'd,
My glowing cheeks a wounded heart express'd ;
My looks spoke love ; while you with answ'ring eyes,
In killing glances made as kind replies.   60
Think, *Daphnis*, think, what tender things you said,
Think what confusion all my soul betray'd ;
You call'd my graceful presence *Cynthia*'s air,
And when I sung, the *Syrens* charm'd your ear ;
My flame blown up by flatt'ry stronger grew,
A gale of love in ev'ry whisper flew.
    Ah faithless youth ! too well you saw my pain ;
For eyes the language of the soul explain.
    Whene'er I dress'd, my maid, who knew my flame,
Cherish'd my passion with thy lovely name ;   70
Thy picture in her talk so lively grew,
That thy dear image rose before my view ;

39–40 *In the version of 1714 this couplet is not italicized. So throughout.*
42 (O false tongue !)] in mine Ears *1714.*
45 Did not thy Tongue in Raptures speak thy Flame, *1714.*
57 joy] Flame *1714.*
65–6 *The version of 1714 has the following four lines here :*
    How did thy Flatt'ry my weak Bosom move,
    When in each Whisper flew a Gale of Love !
    But *Daphnis* now hath forfeited his Truth,
    And Marriage Bonds confine the perjur'd Youth.

She dwelt whole hours upon thy shape and mien,
And wounded *Delia*'s fame to sooth my spleen :
When she beheld me at the name grow pale,
Strait to thy charms she chang'd her artful tale ;
And when thy matchless charms were quite run o'er,
I bid her tell the pleasing tale once more.
Oh, *Daphnis* ! from thy *Araminta* fled !
Oh, to my love for ever, ever dead !   80
Like death, his nuptials all my hope remove,
And ever part me from the man I love.
   Ah faithless youth ! too well you saw my pain
For eyes the language of the soul explain.
O might I by my cruel fate be thrown,
In some retreat far from this hateful town !
Vain dress and glaring equipage, adieu !
Let happier nymphs those empty shows pursue,
Me, let some melancholy shade surround,
Where not the print of human step is found.   90
In the gay dance my feet no more shall move,
But bear me faintly through the lonely grove ;
No more these hands shall o'er the spinnet bound,
And from the sleeping strings call forth the sound ;
Musick adieu, farewel *Italian* airs !
The croaking raven now shall sooth my cares.
On some old ruine lost in thought I rest,
And think how *Araminta* once was blest ;
There o'er and o'er thy letters I peruse,
And all my grief in one kind sentence lose,   100
Some tender line by chance my woe beguiles,
And on my cheek a short-liv'd pleasure smiles ;
Why is this dawn of joy ? flow tears again ;
Vain are these oaths, and all these vows are vain ;
Daphnis, alas ! the *Gordian* knot has ty'd,
Nor force nor cunning can the band divide.
   Ah faithless youth ! since eyes the soul explain,
Why knew I not that artful tongue could feign ?

81 hope] Hopes *1714*.   87 adieu !] Adieu, *1714*.   95 airs !] Airs, *1714*.
96 raven] Ravens *1714*.
97 Involv'd in Thought on some old Trunk I rest, *1714*.
103–5 But Sorrow soon my Bosom will regain,
     And tell me all those Oaths and Vows were vain,
     For *Daphnis* now the *Gordian* Knot hath ty'd, *1714*.
107–8 *The version of 1714 repeats the previous refrain, italicizing it for the first and only time.*

A

CONTEMPLATION

ON

N I G H T.

[*Editions : as of Panthea.*]

WHETHER amid the gloom of night I stray,
Or my glad eyes enjoy revolving day,
Still Nature's various face informs my sense,
Of an all-wise, all pow'rful Providence.
    When the gay sun first breaks the shades of night,
And strikes the distant eastern hills with light,
Colour returns, the plains their liv'ry wear,
And a bright verdure cloaths the smiling year ;
The blooming flow'rs with op'ning beauties glow,
And grazing flocks their milky fleeces show,   10
The barren cliffs with chalky fronts arise,
And a pure azure arches o'er the skies.
But when the gloomy reign of night returns,
Stript of her fading pride all nature mourns :
The trees no more their wonted verdure boast,
But weep in dewy tears their beauty lost ;
No distant landskips draw our curious eyes,
Wrapt in night's robe the whole creation lies.
Yet still, ev'n now, while darkness cloaths the land,
We view the traces of th' almighty hand ;   20
Millions of stars in heav'n's wide vault appear,
And with new glories hang the boundless sphere :
The silver moon her western couch forsakes,
And o'er the skies her nightly circle makes,
Her solid globe beats back the sunny rays,
And to the world her borrow'd light repays.
    Whether those stars that twinkling lustre send,
Are suns, and rolling worlds those suns attend,
Man may conjecture, and new schemes declare,
Yet all his systems but conjectures are ;   30
But this we know, that heav'n's eternal King,
Who bid this universe from nothing spring,

1 amid] amidst *1714 and 1729.*   5 dissolves the breaking night, *1714 and 1729.*
6 strikes] paints *1714 and 1729.*   11 cliffs] Clifts *1714 and 1729.*
23 western] *Western* 1729.

Can at his *Word* bid num'rous worlds appear,
And rising worlds th' all-pow'rful *Word* shall hear.
　When to the western main the sun descends,
To other lands a rising day he lends,
The spreading dawn another shepherd spies,
The wakeful flocks from their warm folds arise,
Refresh'd, the peasant seeks his early toil,
And bids the plough correct the fallow soil.　　　　40
While we in sleep's embraces waste the night,
The climes oppos'd enjoy meridian light ;
And when those lands the busie sun forsakes,
With us again the rosie morning wakes ;
In lazy sleep the night rolls swift away,
And neither clime laments his absent ray.
　When the pure soul is from the body flown,
No more shall night's alternate reign be known :
The sun no more shall rolling light bestow,
But from th' Almighty streams of glory flow.　　　　50
Oh, may some nobler thought my soul employ,
Than empty, transient, sublunary joy !
The stars shall drop, the sun shall lose his flame,
But Thou, O God, for ever shine the same.

34 *Here follow in the versions of 1714 and 1729 these lines :*
　　　　All human Nature nightly Sleep repairs,
　　　　Unbends the Mind, and softens all its Cares ;
　　　　With Sleep the wearied Hind his Strength renews,
　　　　And the next Morn his constant Task pursues.
35 *In the version of 1714 and 1729 this line does not begin a new paragraph.*
　western] *Western 1729.*
37 another] the watchful *1714.*　　　43 those lands] their Clime *1714.*
45 Each sleeps in healthful Ease dull Night away, *1714.*
47 *Here follows in the version of 1714 and 1729 the couplet*
　　　　To blest Abodes she swiftly shoots away,
　　　　And in those Regions drinks Eternal Day ;

A

T H O U G H T

O N

E T E R N I T Y.

[*Editions : as of Panthea.*]

E'ER the foundations of the world were laid,
E'er kindling light th' Almighty word obey'd,
Thou wert ; and when the subterraneous flame
Shall burst its prison, and devour this frame,
From angry heav'n when the keen lightning flies,
When fervent heat dissolves the melting skies,
Thou still shalt be ; still, as thou wert before,
And know no change, when time shall be no more.
O endless thought ! divine eternity !
Th' immortal soul shares but a part of thee ;   10
For thou wert present when our life began,
When the warm dust shot up in breathing man.
    Ah ! what is life ? with ills encompass'd round,
Amidst our hopes, Fate strikes the sudden wound :
To-day the statesman of new honour dreams,
To-morrow death destroys his airy schemes ;
Is mouldy treasure in thy chest confin'd ?
Think all that treasure thou must leave behind ;
Thy heir with smiles shall view thy blazon'd herse,
And all thy hoards with lavish hand disperse.   20
Should certain fate th' impending blow delay,
Thy mirth will sicken and thy bloom decay ;

8 *Here follows in the versions of 1714 and 1729 the couplet*
        As a small Drop in the wide Ocean 's tost,
        So Time shall in Eternity be lost.
14 Amidst our hopes,] 'Midst our vast Hopes, *1714 and 1729.*
15 the statesman] th' Ambitious *1714 and 1729.*
17–20   Does hoarded Treasure moulder in thy Chest ?
        Or, art thou with a beauteous Consort blest ?
        Thy lavish Heir shall soon thy Wealth disperse,
        And with feign'd Tears attend thy blazon'd Herse ; *1714 and 1729.*
20 *Here follows in the versions of 1714 and 1729 the couplet*
        Thy lovely Wife resign her balmy Breath,
        And stiffen in the frozen Arms of Death.
21 certain] dreadful *1714 and 1729.*

Then feeble age will all thy nerves disarm,
No more thy blood its narrow channels warm.
Who then would wish to stretch this narrow span,
To suffer life beyond the date of man ?
 The virtuous soul pursues a nobler aim,
And life regards but as a fleeting dream :
She longs to wake, and wishes to get free,
To launch from earth into eternity.   30
For while the boundless theme extends our thought,
Ten thousand thousand rolling years are nought.

24 No more] Nor can *1714 and 1729.*
 Here follows in the versions of 1714 and 1729 the couplet
   Who would vain Life on such Conditions bear,
   To groan beneath the load of Fourscore Year ;
25 Who then would] Or meanly *1714 and 1729.*
28 And life regards] And looks on Life *1714 and 1729.*
30 To launch from earth] That she may launch *1714 and 1729.*
31 For while to Thee she lifts her soaring Thought, *1714 and 1729.*

AN

ELEGY *on a* LAP-DOG.

[*Poems on Several Occasions* 1720 and 1731.]

SHOCK's fate I mourn ; poor *Shock* is now no more,
Ye Muses mourn, ye chamber-maids deplore.
Unhappy *Shock* ! yet more unhappy Fair,
Doom'd to survive thy joy and only care !
Thy wretched fingers now no more shall deck,
And tye the fav'rite ribband round his neck ;
No more thy hand shall smooth his glossy hair,
And comb the wavings of his pendent ear.
Yet cease thy flowing grief, forsaken maid ;
All mortal pleasures in a moment fade :   10
Our surest hope is in an hour destroy'd,
And love, best gift of heav'n, not long enjoy'd.
 Methinks I see her frantick with despair,
Her streaming eyes, wrung hands, and flowing hair
Her *Mechlen* pinners rent the floor bestrow,
And her torn fan gives real signs of woe.
Hence Superstition, that tormenting guest,
That haunts with fancy'd fears the coward breast;
No dread events upon this fate attend,
Stream eyes no more, no more thy tresses rend.   20
Tho' certain omens oft forewarn a state,
And dying lyons show the monarch's fate;

Why should such fears bid *Celia*'s sorrow rise ?
For when a Lap-dog falls no lover dyes.
  Cease, *Celia*, cease ; restrain thy flowing tears,
Some warmer passion will dispell thy cares.
In man you 'll find a more substantial bliss,
More grateful toying, and a sweeter kiss.
  He 's dead. Oh lay him gently in the ground !
And may his tomb be by this verse renown'd.   30
Here Shock, *the pride, of all his kind, is laid ;*
Who fawn'd like man, but ne'er like man betray'd.

   24 falls] *1731* falls, *1720*   dyes.] *1731* dyes, *1720*.

A N

E L E G I A C   E P I S T L E

T O

A   F R I E N D.

Written by Mr. GAY, when he laboured under a Dejection of Spirits.

[*The Poetical, Dramatic, and Miscellaneous Works of John Gay* 1795.]

I.

FRIEND of my youth, shedd'st thou the pitying tear
  O'er the sad relics of my happier days,
Of nature tender, as of soul sincere,
  Pour'st thou for me the melancholy lays ?

II.

Oh ! truly said !—the distant landscape bright,
  Whose vivid colours glitter'd on the eye
Is faded now, and sunk in shades of night,
  As, on some chilly eve, the closing flow'rets die.

III.

Yet had I hop'd, when first, in happier times,
  I trod the magic paths where Fancy led,   10
The Muse to foster in more friendly climes,
  Where never Mis'ry rear'd its hated head.

IV.

How vain the thought ! Hope after hope expires !
  Friend after friend, joy after joy is lost ;
My dearest wishes feed the fun'ral fires,
  And life is purchas'd at too dear a cost.

V.

Yet, could my heart the selfish comfort know,
  That not alone I murmur and complain ;
Well might I find companions in my woe,
  All born to Grief, the family of Pain !   20

VI.

Full well I know, in life's uncertain road,
  The thorns of mis'ry are profusely sown ;
Full well I know, in this low vile abode,
  Beneath the chast'ning rod what numbers groan.

VII.

Born to a happier state, how many pine
  Beneath th' oppressor's pow'r, or feel the smart
Of bitter want, or foreign evils join
  To the sad symptoms of a broken heart !

VIII.

How many, fated from their birth to view
  Misfortunes growing with their rip'ning years ;   30
The same sad track, through various scenes, pursue,
  Still journeying onward through a vale of tears.

IX.

To them, alas ! what boots the light of heav'n,
  While still new mis'ries mark their destin'd way,
Whether to their unhappy lot be giv'n
  Death's long, sad night, or life's short busy day !

X.

Me not such themes delight ;—I more rejoice,
  When chance some happier, better change I see,
Though no such change await *my* luckless choice,
  And mountains rise between my hopes and me.   40

XI.

For why should he who roves the dreary waste,
  Still joy on ev'ry side to view the gloom,
Or when upon the couch of sickness plac'd,
  Well pleas'd survey a hapless neighbour's tomb ?

39 *my*] my *Bell*   44 tomb ?] *Bell* tomb ; *1795.*

XII.

If e'er a gleam of comfort glads my soul,
  If e'er my brow to wonted smiles unbends,
'Tis when the fleeting minutes, as they roll,
  Can add one gleam of pleasure to my friends.

XIII.

Ev'n in these shades, the last retreat of grief,
  Some transient blessings will that thought bestow ;   50
To Melancholy's self yield some relief,
  And ease the breast surcharg'd with mortal woe.

XIV.

Long has my bark in rudest tempests toss'd,
  Buffetted seas, and stemm'd life's hostile wave ;
Suffice it now, in all my wishes cross'd,
  To seek a peaceful harbour in the grave.

XV.

And when that hour shall come, (as come it must,)
  Ere many moons their waning horns increase,
When this frail frame shall mix with kindred dust,
  And all its fond pursuits and troubles cease :   60

XVI.

When those black gates that ever open stand,
  Receive me on th' irremeable shore,
When Life's frail glass has run its latest sand,
  And the dull jest repeated charms no more :

XVII.

Then may my friend weep o'er the fun'ral hearse,
  Then may his presence gild the awful gloom,
And his last tribute be some mournful verse,
  To mark the spot that holds my silent tomb.—

XVIII.

This—and no more :—the rest let Heav'n provide,
  To which, resign'd, I trust my weal or woe,   70
Assur'd howe'er its justice shall decide,
  To find nought worse than I have left below.

49 grief,] *Bell* grief *1795*.   53 tempests] tempest *Bell*.
60 cease : *Bell* cease. *1795*.   64 more :] *Bell* more. *1795*.
70 *So Bell*
     To which resign'd, I must my weal or woe, *1795*.
I am not sure that Bell's text is not an emendation of what Gay actually wrote.

MINOR MISCELLANEOUS PIECES.

To the Learned Ingenious Author of *Licentia Poetica Discuss'd*, &c.

[Prefixed, together with verses by Aaron Hill and Samuel Barklay, to *Licentia Poetica discuss'd* : or, the True Test of Poetry. *Without which It is Difficult to Judge of, or Compose, A Correct English Poem. Etc.* By W. Coward, Coll. Med. Lond. M.D. 1709. The lines are signed J. Gay.

Not printed by Bell, or by Jeffrey, or by Underhill; but included in Nichols's *The Works of the English Poets* in 1779, in Cooke's Pocket Edition 1804, and Park's *Supplement to the British Poets* 1809. The latter editor says, not quite correctly, 'This is the earliest known poem written by Gay.'

The later editions abolished the italics and many of the capitals.

It was, no doubt, through his association with Aaron Hill (see p. xxx), that Gay came to write these lines.]

> THE Vulgar Notion of Poetic fire,
> Is, *that laborious Art can ne'er aspire,*
> *Nor Constant Studies the bright Bays acquire.*
> *And that high Flights the unborn Bard receives,*
> *And only Nature the due Laurel gives* ;
> But *You*, with innate shining Flames endow'd,
> To wide *Castalian* Springs point out the ⓑⓞⓨ.
> Thro' *your Perspective* we can plainly see,
> The *New Discover'd* Road of Poetry,
> To steep *Parnassus* you direct the way   10
> So smooth, that vent'rous Travellers cannot stray,
> But with unerring steps, rough ways disdain,
> And by *you* led, the beauteous *Summit* gain,
> Where polish'd Lays shall raise their *growing* Fames,
> And with their *tuneful Guide*, enrol their *Honour'd Names*

14 Fames] flames *Park 1809.*

From *MOHOCK* and from
HAWKUBITE.

[*From* AN | ARGUMENT | Proving from | HISTORY, REASON, and SCRIP-
TURE, | That the Present | *MOHOCKS* and *HAWKUBITES* | ARE THE | *GOG*
and *MAGOG* mention'd in the REVELATIONS, | AND THEREFORE | That this vain
and transitory World will shortly be brought to its final Dissolution. | Written by
a Reverend DIVINE, who took it from the Mouth of the SPIRIT of | a PERSON
who was lately slain by one of the *MOHOCKS.*
    Published as a single-sheet by Lintott in 1712.   Price One Penny.
    The Argument is in the form of a Biblical Prophecy, and was reprinted in the
Miscellanies in Prose and Verse ; the verses here given were omitted from the reprint.
    A contemporary hand has added, on the British Museum copy [816 m. 19 (73)], the
words *By Gay.* (The same hand ascribes the *Ode to Lord Cadogan* to Gay. See p. 638.)
    I have no doubt that Gay wrote these verses about the same time as his first farce,
The Mohocks. (See p. 310.)]

From *MOHOCK* and from *HAWKUBITE,*
    Good Lord deliver me,
Who wander through the Streets by Night,
    Committing Cruelty.

They slash our Sons with bloody Knives,
    And on our Daughters fall,
And if they ravish not our Wives,
    We have good Luck withal.

Coaches and Chairs they overturn,
    Nay Carts most easily,
Therefore from *GOG* and eke *MAGOG,*
    Good Lord deliver me.

To the most Honourable the Earl of OXFORD, The Lord High Treasurer.

The Epigrammatical Petition of your Lordship's most humble servant,

JOHN GAY.

[*From* Additions to the Works of Alexander Pope Esq. London 1776. *Also communicated by Gay in a letter to Swift dated* London, June 8, 1714. (Swift's Letters, ed. Hawkesworth, 6th edition, vol. ii. London, 1777.) *Lord Clarendon had 'accepted' Gay 'for his secretary' on his own appointment as 'envoy extraordinary to Hanover'. The petition, Gay tells Swift, was successful.*]

> I'M no more to converse with the swains,
>   But go where fine people resort ;
> One can live without money on plains,
>   But never without it at court.
>
> Yet if when with swains I did gambol,
>   I array'd me in silver and blue,
> When abroad and in courts I shall ramble,
>   Pray, my Lord, how much money will do ?

5 If, when with the swains] *Letter to Swift. So Underhill.*

My own EPITAPH.

[*Poems on Several Occasions*, 1720 and 1731. Also quoted by Gay himself in a letter to Pope in the last year of his life.]

> LIFE is a jest ; and all things show it.
> I thought so once ; but now I know it.

1 it.] it, *1720 and 1731.*

A Receipt for S T E W I N G   V E A L.

[*From a letter to Swift, dated* Whitehall, October 22, 1726.   (Swift's Letters, ed. Hawkesworth, vol. ii.   London 1766.)   *After a postscript Gay writes :* As we cannot enjoy any good things without your partaking of it, accept of the following receipt for stewing veal.]

TAKE a knuckle of veal ;
You may buy it, or steal.
In a few pieces cut it :
In a stewing-pan put it.
Salt, pepper, and mace
Must season this knuckle ;
Then * what 's join'd to a place ;
With other herbs muckle ;
That, which killed king Will † :
And what never ‡ stands still.   10
Some § sprigs of that bed
Where children are bred,
Which much you will mend, if
Both spinnage and endive,
And lettuce, and beet,

With marygold meet.
Put no water at all ;
For it maketh things small.
Which, lest it should happen,
A close cover clap on.   20
Put this pot of ‖ *Wood's* mettle
In a hot boiling kettle,
And there let it be
(Mark the doctrine I teach)
About—let me see,—
Thrice as long as you preach ¶ :
So skimming the fat off,
Say grace with your hat off.
O, then ! with what rapture
Will it fill dean and chapter !   30

   * Vulgo, salary.   † Supposed sorril.
   ‡ This is by Dr. *Bentley* thought to be time, or thyme.
   § Parsley.   Vide *Chamberlayne.*   ‖ Copper.
   ¶ ' Which we suppose to be near four hours.'

   21, n. *In Pope's Works, ed. Elwin, vii. 80, this note is given thus :* Of this composition see the works of the copper-farthing dean.

THE

MAN-MOUNTAIN'S ANSWER

TO THE

LILLIPUTIAN VERSES

[*The Poetical, Dramatic, and Miscellaneous Works of John Gay*, 1795. Given also
by *Bell* 1777 and *Park* 1808.   Not by *Nichols*, who gives the other Gulliver
verses.   See p. xxxiv.]

LITTLE thing!
I would sing,
Lofty song,
Measure long;
But I fear,
That thine ear
Such a poem could not bear.
Therefore I
Mean to try
Humbler lays   10
Worthy praise,
If my strains,
Work'd thee pains,
'Tis not mine,
To divine,
Whether cost,
Labour lost,
May on Lilliput be toss'd.
Horse and foot
Would you put,   20
In the way,
Who could say,
I had blame,
If they came
Near my stride
And beside
My huge foot gigantic dy'd?
But, while here
I appear
Mountain-size,   30
To little eyes;
All that strain,

Seek in vain,
Whilst I climb,
Heights sublime,
To keep pace,
And to trace
My footsteps, as I move with martial
    grace.
Though; 'tis true,
Praise is due,   40
To your lay,
Yet I pray,
You'll attend,
To a friend.
On my hand,
Should you stand;
If those that soar,
Fall the low'r,
All Lilliput would yours deplore.
Humbly then,   50
With little men,
Take your stand,
On firm land,
Lest your place,
Bring disgrace:
High in air,
Great the care,
To be free
From jeopardy,
Careless found,   60
You might bound,
Little poet! to the ground.

27 dy'd?] *Bell*   dy'd. *1795*.

A MOTTO *for the opera of* Mutius Scaevola.

[*From* Additions to the Works of Alexander Pope Esq. London 1776.]

WHO here blames words, or verses, songs, or singers,
Like *Mutius Scaevola* will burn his fingers.

Presentation Inscription.

[Inscribed in Mr. T. J. Wise's large-paper copy of the second issue of the first edition of *The Beggar's Opera* (see p. 474) 'in the florid hand of a professional scribe'.]

To Mr. Tommy Potter JACKY GAY **sendeth Greeting, together with these his unworthy Performances.**

ACCEPT 'em Tommy as they're meant
And you make Jacky Gay content.
If Tommy like his Jacky's Quill,
Let Robin hate him if he will.

' *My dear Belladine.*'

[Sold at SOTHEBY's, December, 5 or 6, 1921. Compare the postscript to Gay's letter to Mrs. Howard from Dijon, September 8, 1719: ' I beg you, madam, to assure Miss Lepell and Miss Bellenden, that I am their humble servant.']

MY Dear Belladine ⎫
O're a Glass of Wine ⎬
We send you this line. ⎭

On Purpose to tell ⎫
You Miss Lepell ⎬
We are all very well. ⎭

If news we should send you from Canterbury
That news to be sure you would think is a lye
And therefore we'll say what before you did know
That we are your Servants wherever we go.

Ann Pulteney.
Wm. Pulteney.
J. Gay.

Canterbury, Saturday.

TRANSLATIONS from ARIOSTO.

The Story of ZERBIN *and* ISABELLA.

From Ariosto. Canto 24th the 28th and 29th.

[Brit. Mus. Add. 6419, folios 55–65 (inclusive). The footnotes preceded by a line number show the readings cancelled in the MS.]

Zerbin, the brave Orlando's steps to find,
Left lawns, vales, mountains and long woods behind
And Isabella fair with equal speed
Spurr'd her fleet Palfrey by her Hero's steed.
  At length afar they spy'd a glitt'ring ray
That from the plain threw back the dazling day;
But when they nearer to the lustre drew
Orlando's arms, and burnish'd helme they knew:
They saw his Horse, they saw the sword he wore,
Then sighing cry'd, Orlando is no more!   10
  Now with swift strides advanc'd along the vale
Beside the stream, a Swain aghast and pale;
That very Swain who from the mountain's height,
Had seen the raging fury of the knight,
How far and wide his shining Arms he threw,
How tore, how rav'd, and how the Shepherds slew!
  Zerbin demands. Whence are these arms? The Swain
Describ'd the frantick knight, the Shepherds slain.
  The Story touch'd his soul. he sought around,
And gather'd up the spoils that strow'd the ground,   20
Then on a Pine in gracefull Order rais'd
Against the Sun the glorious Trophy blaz'd;
And on the bark he grav'd in letters fair,
THE PALADIN ORLANDO'S ARMS I BEAR.
Which thus defys. That bold presumptuous knight
Who takes these Arms shall with Orlando fight.
  When lo! intrepid Mandricard drew nigh
And on the Trophy fixt his haughty eye.
Zerbin with tears Orlando's Story told.
Beware, proud Saracin, be not too bold!   30
  This Menace nought dismay'd the Pagan Lord,
But to the Pine he sprung and snatch'd the Sword.
  Lives there a man (he cryd) whose valour vain
Shall dare attempt this Armor to regain?
Throughout the world I seek that vent'rous knight,
Perpetual Conquest shall support my right.
Orlando fear'd the dangers of that day,
And in feign'd madness flung the spoils away;

13 very] self same

As Cowardice, his Madness I despise
Reason and valour bid me seise the prize.   40
   Zerbin incens'd replyd.   Rash Prince, forbear
Nor think without dispute these arms to wear:
If you the Mail of Hector thus obtain'd
It was by fraud and not by reason gain'd.
   So saying.   Each pours on to meet his foe,
With equal might impends the desp'rate blow ;
Now with a hundred strokes resounds the air,
The horrid prelude of the doubtfull war.
When * Durindana fells with fatal aim ;
Swift as keen lightning shoots its waving flame,   50
Zerbin avoids the stroke ; and like the Doe,
Alert, his nimble steed bounds to and fro :
And it behov'd him well to turn the rein
For that enchanted sword neer smote invain,
One blow had sent his pale enamor'd Ghost,
A fleeting wand'rer to the Stygian Coast.
As the swift Dog amid a spacious plain
Upon the furious boar pours on amain
When near advanc'd stops short, then winds around,
While the tusk'd foe prepares one deadly wound.   60
Thus if the sword hung low, or wav'd on high
Zerbin each motion watch'd with cautious eye,
To save his fame and life at once he trys,
In the same instant stands, wheels, fights, and flys.
But when the Pagan monarch wav'd his blade
And in the whizzing Air bright circles made,
It seem'd, as when march winds with fury blow,
The lofty forrest nods his leafy brow
Proud Oaks to earth their stubborn bodys bend,
And whirl'd in Air the shatter'd boughs ascend.   70
Zerbin with watchfull guard each stroke defends
Till wing'd with rage a mighty blow descends,
Between his sword and shield it swiftly fell,
Nor Mail nor breast-plate could the wound repell,
The trenchant blade his steely vest divides
And to the saddle down his Cuirass glides,
Had not aslant the thirsty weapon past,
It, (like a reed) had cleft him to the waste
The shallow razing wound scarce gives him pain,
Rills of warm blood his burnish'd Armor stain.   80
So when the beauty who commands my heart
On some rich work employs her curious art
I've seen her iv'ry hand the needle guide,
And purple streaks the silver ground divide.
   Nought in this combat Zerbin's arm prevail'd,
Here skill and strength and hardy prowess fail'd ;

* Orlando's sword so called.

45 pours] rushes   49 fells] smote   52 Alert,] Dextrous   54 smote] fell

With greater force the Tartar's nerves were strung,
And on his keener blade enchantment hung,
The wound was slight, yet Isabella's heart
With icy shiv'rings felt the deepest smart.   90
Now Zerbin, (burning with despite and ire,
While from his eye-balls shot resentfull fire)
Rais'd with both hands his sword, his sword fell strong,
And on the fated Helme the fauchion rung,
The haughty Tartar felt the stunning blow,
And bow'd his helmet to the saddle-bow ;
Had not enchanted fire the metal try'd
His cloven skull had fell on either side.
Now hung the Pagan's fauchion o'er his Crest,
And aim'd at once to cleave him to the breast ;   100
Zerbin the threaten'd death with caution ey'd,
His Steed obey'd the rein and sprung aside
Yet fell not now the pond'rous sword invain,
But edg'd with fury, split the shield in twain
And pierc'd his Arm ; thence glancing to his side,
Drove through the steel, forth gush'd the sanguine tide.
But in no part could Zerbin's arm prevail
For not one dent imprest the Pagan's Mail
While many a gash had Zerbin's armor stain'd
His helme was split, no shield his arm sustain'd,   110
His less'ning strength pour'd forth at ev'ry wound,
And ebbing Life impurpled all the ground,
Though scarce his spirits could his limbs uphold,
In undiminish'd force his heart was bold.
   The trembling Isabella pale & wan
Now wing'd with fear to Doralice ran,
Fair Doralice's love the Pagan rul'd,
And as she will'd his anger burn'd or cool'd ;
The tim'rous Dame with tears her aid implor'd,
To part the fight and stay the hanging sword,   120
The courteous Doralice gave consent,
For she too trembled for the dread event ;
Peace she commanded, & a peace was made
And Isabella sheath'd her hero's blade ;
So Zerbin follow'd where she led the way,
And undetermin'd left the dang'rous fray.
No life-preserving cares employ'd his mind,
He burn'd for Durindana left behind,
Till time allayd the feaver of his heart ;
Then of each wound he felt the bitter Smart   130
And each wound rack'd him with such raging pain
That scarce his limbs could feeble life sustain.
Weak, pale and fainting now the rein he stays,
And on the ground his drooping body lays
Near a cool fountain's side. O ruefull maid,
All Comfort's vain, invain you call for aid ;

130 bitter] burning

Far many a league the busy city lyes,
Remote from human skill, forlorn he dyes ;
No learn'd Physician shall his death retard,
Mov'd by kind pity, or more kind reward !   140
What shall she do ? the tears a passage find
She curses fortune, calls the stars unkind.
' When my toss'd ship (she crys) the storm obeyd
' Why was I not beneath the billows laid ?
  Zerbin at this his languid head uprears,
His feeble eyes beheld her gushing tears,
And in those tears more tender pain he found,
Than in the torture of his deadly wound.
  ' And will my Love her Zerbin's fate deplore
' When these weak eyes shall see thy charms no more ?   150
' What's the last pang of death to that I prove
' To leave without a Guardian her I love
' Thus in these dang'rous wilds ? my latest breath
' I could resign in peace, and smile on death
' Wert thou but safe ; far from this savage place,
' And dye with joy thus gazing on thy face.
' But how can this severer fate be born,
' To leave my Treasure thus expos'd, forlorn,
' To leave thee thus ? By those bright eyes I swear,
' By those sweet lips, and by that gracefull hair   160
' Which first engag'd my heart, o'erwhelm'd with woe
' I sink into the dreary realms below,
' Where when I think thee left to grief, to fear
' Not Hell's worst pains will equal my despair.
  These his fond words her heaving bosom stung,
With look enamour'd o'er her Lord she hung,
Then clasp'd him fainting to her throbbing breast,
And fervent kisses on his lips imprest,
Upon those lips where now no crimson glows,
All pale and faded like the gather'd rose,   170
The rose that never knew the Season's pride,
But sickned on his stalk and op'ning dy'd.
  ' Think not, my Love, (she cryd) I here will stay
' When my dear Zerbin's Spirit flits away
' Fear not for me, with thee I'll take my flight
' To the clear realms of day, or depths of Night.
' Dart forth, my Soul ; together let us soar
' Together mount to Joys, to part no more !
' Soon as thy closing eyes be barr'd from day,
' My Life in gusts of grief will force its way ;   180
' If sorrow fail ; this Sword my Soul shall free
' To mingle in immortal Love with thee.
' O may some pious stranger tread these plains,
' And view with weeping eye our cold remains,
' One grave perhaps these bodys shall confine
' And ev'n my smallest dust be mixt with thine !

143 storm] waves

So saying, o'er her dying Love she hangs,
Warms him with kisses in his latest pangs,
Upon his trembling lips in transport lyes,
And drinks his vital Spirit as it flys.   190
  Collecting all at once his fault'ring breath,
Zerbin thus spoke before the gasp of Death.
  ' O Let my Angell hear this last request;
' By all the sacred vows you first profest
' When for my sake you left your native land,
' (Nay, I command you, if I may command)
' That no rash insult to thy life be giv'n,
' But with firm patience wait the will of Heav'n
' And never, never from thy thought remove
' Thy faithfull Zerbin, and his matchless Love.   200
' Heav'n will protect thee.—Further speech he try'd
But on his tongue the broken accents dy'd.
As oer the wax-spent torch with doubtfull rays
The glimm'ring light now swells and now decays,
If some new taper touch the hov'ring fires
It kindles as the trembling flame expires.
  How Isabella shall thy grief be told
When Zerbin lay extended, pale and cold
Lock'd in thy clasping arms?   Herself she throws
On her dead Lord; a stream of sorrow flows   210
And baths the purple wounds; woods, hills & skys
Resound her bitter groans and piercing crys;
She beats her breast her glowing cheeks she tears,
Plucks up and scatters wide her golden hairs,
O Spare thy locks, thy savage hands restrain;
Nor fondly call thy Zerbin's name invain!
  Now mad with grief she drew the pointed Sword,
In this one deed forgetfull of her Lord;
Deep in her bosom had the steel been drown'd,
Had not a holy hermit stay'd the wound;   220
Who at his wonted hour his thirst to slake,
Sought the refreshment of thy crystal lake.
She heard the doctrine of the reverend guide,
Heav'n with persuasive power his words supplyd,
Faith taught her patience and a soul resign'd,
And to celestial hope improv'd her mind
She saw the vanity of earthly joy,
A passing Shadow, and a fading toy,
And strait resolv'd (such faith, such hope was given)
To dedicate her lifes remains to Heaven.   230
  But could she Zerbin from her heart remove?
Alive or dead, she could not quit her Love.
Wher'ere her lot is cast, she'll Zerbin bear,
And on his ashes drop a daily tear.

203 doubtfull] glimm'ring   205 hov'ring fires] dying fire
206 Upon another point the blaze aspires *alt.*   226 improv'd] exalts

The holy Hermit lent his pious aid,
And the lank body cross the Palfrey laid ;
Then march'd they on with solemn pace & slow
Through the long desart wood in silent woe.
The cautious Father turn'd not to his cell ;
Such charms might make the coolest blood rebell ;   240
He knew his power, who had his virtue try'd,
Nor dares in prudence nor in Age confide.
    Where the brown mountains thymy odours breathe,
And overlook Marsilia's shores beneath
A stately Monast'ry its turret's rears
Where Dames devote their life to Priests & prayers
Thither they journey'd but through ways untrod
For with adventures swarm'd the common road.
At length advancing with full speed, from far
They spyd a furious knight that menac'd war,   250
Nearer and nearer still the Terror drew,
And now insulting Rhodomont they knew.
In pensive beauty when he saw the Dame,
Soften'd to love in courteous guise he came,
And in his gentlest voice address'd the Fair,
Enquir'd her State, and why that sad despair.
She told him how she past a life of cares,
And how she vow'd to heav'n her future years.
    The haughty Pagan who all Faith defy'd
Thus with vain mock and scornfull smile reply'd.   260
' With justice is the Miser sinfull found
' Who hides his golden treasure in the ground
' Not his own pleasures are from thence supplyd
' And its just use to all mankind denyd.
' In Dens are monsters bears and Lions pent
' But why confine the Fair and innocent ?
    The pious Hermit trembled while he spoke
Lest his fair Novice should her Vow revoke
And like a Pilot kept her in the way ;
Lest adverse tempests blow her faith astray   270
He places heavenly banquets in her sight,
The Joys of Angells and the realms of light.
    The Pagan who despis'd his Christian Schemes
As idle legends and Monastic dreams
Attempts to still the Father's zealous tongue,
The Father prov'd his Lungs and zeal were strong,
Louder and louder the good end pursu'd,
'Till the proud Pagan's patience was subdu'd.
    Now burn'd his fury, on the Priest he flew,
And by the beard his hoary reverence drew,   280
Rage gives him strength, he tuggs his silver hairs
And from his chin a grasp of wisdom tears.

241 knew] knows   245 its] her   279 burn'd] rag'd

Then, close as pincers join, his throat he strains,
And lifts the sprawling Preacher from the Plains,
High oer his head in rapid wheel he 's tost
And flung aloft in middle ocean lost.
   The Priest remov'd, no more his Fury burn'd
With courteous eye he to the Lady turn'd
Who stood dismay'd and pale ; he bow'd, address'd
And thus in Courtier's phrase his Love profess'd.   290
   ' My Joy, my Hope, my Charmer, Angell fair,
' Life of my life, and all my Soul holds dear !
   Disdain and wonted pride his heart forsook,
And his eye languish'd with imploring look,
No ruffling Force shall discompose her charms.
Who meets a willing Beauty in his arms
Heightens his transport. Still with tender Art
He strove to gain on Isabella's heart.
When the chast Dame the horrid place survey'd
Desart and wild, remote from human aid   300
Not the young Lamb more dreadfull dangers awe,
When underneath the sportive Tyger's paw.
Lest brutal rape her spotless vertue stain
She casts her cautious eye around the plain
And meditates escape ; resolv'd to dye
And never with his base desires comply.
   O hapless Zerbin, couldst thou see her now,
Her Love sincere, her unrepented vow,
How would it glad thy soul ? She'll force despise
And with unsully'd Virtue mount the skys   310
   Now with desire the Pagan's Looks rebell,
How shall weak Woman stronger man repell !
He glows he burns her honour to destroy :
To grasp by violence the secret joy.
How shall she save her fame, what arts invent
What wile shall guard her from the foul intent ?
Thus boldly resolute she sav'd her Fame,
And latest Ages shall adore her name.
   Soon as his civil continence gave way
And his eye menac'd with enamour'd ray,   320
When looks and Actions spoke his inward fire,
And Force prepar'd to gratifye desire,
Thus spoke the pensive Dame. ' My honour spare,
' May my chast Vow no sudden insult fear,
' So shall the Curtesie be doubly paid,
' And lasting gratitude my guardian aid,
' Resolve the transient moment to despise,
' Protect me, and accept a solid prize ;
' Think, courteous knight, the world with Beauty swarms,
' Think, thou mayst satiate Love with willing charms,   330
' A thousand Eyes with keener radiance glow,
' But I alone this secret can bestow.

     305 resolv'd] prepar'd   306 And] Nor

'A Plant I know ; I saw it in the vale
'As I past by ; with rue, & ivy pale
'Let it be mingled ; burn a Cypress brand,
'And let it o'er the blaze fermenting stand,
'Then let unblemish'd fingers press the juice.
'Great are its virtues, wonderfull its use ;
'Who three times in it baths shall fire endure,
'And from the sword his harden'd skin secure.   340
'Let each revolving moon a Bath supply,
'For in one moon its secret virtues dye :
'May I this day the wondrous charm provide,
'So shall the liquor and my faith be try'd,
'Nor let my Lord the proffer'd boon despise,
'For Europe's conquest is a meaner prize.
'But in return, swear by thy Faith profest
'Nor word nor deed my Honour shall molest.

He longs to brave unhurt the hottest wars
Like Cygnus and Achilles proof from scars ;   350
Intent upon the Gift the Pagan swore
To keep with strictness all she ask'd & more,
And he with strictness will his passions rein,
And keep his Oath, 'till he the gift obtain,
But that obtain'd, no more his Oaths shall bind,
No conscience checks an unbeliever's mind ;
A thousand times he promis'd, swore, and ly'd,
For he the saints and King of Heaven defy'd.

O'er the brown mountains and green vales they pass ;
She culls with curious eye each tuft of grass   360
The Pagan followd close his lovely guide.
Her search with various roots and herbs supply'd,
Backward to seek the humble shed she fares,
And for the perils of the night prepares ;
Around the boiling herbs the Cypress flame
Ascends, still Rhodomont observes the Dame.
To speed the hours, he calls his trusty Squires.
The heat, the steam, the smoke, the smoth'ring fires
Awake their thirst, they drink, they joke, they laugh,
And Grecian wine in mighty Goblets quaff.   370
(Two Casks his Squires had seiz'd as lawfull prey,
From certain Merchants trav'ling on the way)
Soon ev'ry object doubles to their eyes,
The reeling Cave in rapid circle flys
For by their Prophet Africk's Sons are taught
Never to taste the grape's inflaming draught.

Meanwhile with carefull hand the busy dame,
The boiling Cauldron lifts from off the flame,
'Bespeaking thus the knight ; Let proof ensue,
'Let proof demonstrate that thy Servant's true   380
'Let the strong virtues of the Charm appear
'Nor let Suspicion banefull poyson fear,

360 culls] cull'd

'But lest my Lord in guilefull words confide,
'May my anointed neck the test abide,
'With this I bath me, lift thy sword on high,
'I dare secure the heaviest blow defye.
  So saying on her head the juice she throws,
The streaming liquor down her bosom flows.
She stretch'd her naked neck, as undismay'd ;
The drunken Saracen the wine obey'd,   390
Wine that can render wit & wisdom vain,
And banish caution from the prudent brain.
  High blaz'd his sword, swift fell the fatal wound,
The sever'd head dropt gasping on the ground,
That gracefull head, where Love & beauty reign'd
Lept from its bounding trunk with blood distain'd
Warm Life still gurgled in the rattling throat,
And Zerbin's name was her last dying note.
To meet her Lord thus fled she to the Skies,
The Pagan stood amaz'd in fixt surprise.   400
  O spotless soul, who to support thy truth
Could life forgo, and all the spring of youth,
Go hence in peace, ascend to realms above,
Seize thy reward of everlasting love,
O may my verse thy virtuous deed record,
And be thy name in future times ador'd,
Go hence in peace, and ev'n in latest days
May emulating Dames thy virtue praise.

               391 wit] strength

The Story of F I O R D I S P I N A.

Ricciardetto relates the Story to Ruggiero, who had sav'd
  him from being burnt. from the 25th Book of Ariosto.

            As on a time my warlike Sister strayd
            Pensive, along a neighb'ring forest's shade,
            A Band of Saracens the wand'rer found,
            And on her unarm'd head descends the wound.
            To stanch the gushing blood the Surgeon's care
            Clip short the tresses of her mantling hair.
              Soon as the wound was heal'd ; the Martial Maid
            Her tender limbs in shining Mail array'd ;
            Then forth she rode, to brave the bold in .fight,
            And seek Adventures fair like hardy knight.   10
            Sunk with labour of the sultry day
            As by a fountain's side she takes her way,

  4 descends] drove deep   5 gushing blood] gaping smart   6 the tresses
of her] her graceful length of   11 Wearied with toil beneath a *false start.*
12 takes] took

The Shade's sweet cool, the stream, that murm'ring flows,
Invite her drooping soul to sweet repose ;
No more the helmet's weight fatigues her head,
And in kind sleep she prints the grassy bed.
    It chanc'd, a Princess of the blood of Spain,
Diana-like, with all her hunting train,
Pass'd near the slumb'ring Maid, in quest of Game,
(Fiordispina was her Royal Name).   **20**
When she the sleeping Bradamante spyd
With the broad sword depending at her side,
Her Limbs in steel encas'd ; Her cheated Sight
Believ'd her, (what she wish'd) a youthfull knight.
O'er her fair face her eyes with pleasure rove,
Till in her breast she feels the dart of Love.
Rise, rise (she calls) the chase forbids delay.
(Yet if all Spys were gone, she fain would stay)
But she no more the Horn's shrill voice obey'd,
Intent on other Game, far off they strayd ;   **30**
The distant Hunters crys were spent in air,
Close was the twilight wood, no witness near.
Soft Speeches, tender Actions spoke her flame,
And Looks that hinted what she fear'd to name
Her burning sighs, her eyes that glow'd with fire
Own'd how her heart consum'd with strong desire ;
Now she look'd pale, then blushes warm'd her look,
And bold with Love a hasty kiss she took.
    My Sister well devin'd the thing she meant.
But how shall Woman Woman's wish content ?   **40**
Then thus she reason'd. 'Tis a gen'rous part
To show her the mistake to cure her heart
Tis better far be found a courteous Maid,
Than thought a coward Man, of Love afraid ;
And well she might that wise conclusion draw.
For he 's a coward, a meer man of Straw
Who, nigh his Lady ripe with nect'rous juice,
Insipid sits, forgetfull of her use ;
And like the Cuckow, niggard of the Spring,
Talks his dull lesson o'er with dangling wing.   **50**
    In courteous guise she strait the Fair addrest,
And to restrain her flame, her sex confest.
That, like Hippolita she fame acquir'd,
Or by Camilla's brave example fir'd,
By war she glory sought in foreign lands,
And pois'd the Shield and spear in infant hands ;
Arzilla gave her Birth whose Towers command
The winding Seas that wash the Afric sand.
But nought avails this tale. Th' enamour'd Dame
Still in her bosom feels the former flame,   **60**

15 The helmets weight no more *alt.*   **26** feels] felt   **28** Yet if no spies
were near *alt.*   *Between* **30, 31** Close was the twilight wood, no witness near *del.*
49 niggard] dotard   **60** the former] an equal

To deep Love's arrow pierc'd ; my Sister's face
Lost not by this confession one sweet grace,
But still her Air and Mien new charms reveal.
No sudden cure the Wounds of Love can heal.
When she beheld her in that manly vest,
Imagination told her all the rest ;
But when she thought her Woman, Sighs ensu'd,
Groans swell'd her breast, and tears her cheek bedew'd.
What harden'd heart could hear her thus complain
Whose pity had not wish'd to share her pain ?   70
     Was ever grief like mine ! O wretched Maid !
All other Love can be with Love repay'd,
Whether a licenc'd, or a guilty flame,
All gain their ends with honour or with shame,
They know to crop the rose from off the Thorn ;
Without reward my Torment must be born.
If at my happy State, O Love, you pin'd,
And to my heart some desp'rate ill design'd,
Whence is thy cruelty so furious grown.
To give me pangs to wretched Nymphs unknown ?   80
It never among Man or Beast was found
That female e'er for female felt the Wound
Woman was never fair in Woman's Eyes
Ewes seek not Ewes, and Does sleek Does despise.
Am I alone, in earth, in Sea, or Air,
Destin'd the Wretch these burning pains to bear ?
Or dost thou this unhappy flame foment,
To show thy Tyranny in full extent ?
The wife of Ninus gain'd her impious Aim
Who with her son indulg'd th' incestuous flame   90
Myrrha her father's Love by stealth enjoy'd,
The Cretan Dame a dewlapt Bull employ'd ;
They by disguises could their wish obtain.
My Love is Madness, for my Love is vain.
In a carv'd Cow Pasiphae hid her shame,
Others try'd diff'rent Arts, their end the same.
Though Skillfull Dædalus should hither fly
Not all his Power could this strong knot untye
By the more potent hand of nature wrought
And against Nature, human fòrce is nought.   100
     Thus wails the beauteous Dame, and in despair
Her bosom beats, and rends her flowing hair,
To see her grief, my Sister shares her pain
And trys to cool her rage, but trys invain
No tender speech her ardent heart relieves
The more she sooths, the more the Princess grieves.
     Now glow'd the western sky with streaks of fire,
And falling Dews persuade them to retire.

65 manly vest] bold attire   92 dewlapt Bull] a Bull's strong nerves
95 carv'd Cow] wrought Bull   96 end] view   106 The more she
sooths her Woe, the more she grieves *alt.*

Come then, Fair Maid, (she crys) not far away
My castle stands ; there ease the Toils of Day.   110
Onward they past, 'till to those Gates they came
Where you preserv'd me from th' expecting flame.
They Enter, She to all presents her Guest,
And all with kind salute the Fair carest.
In female robes she strait her shape array'd
Lest other hearts might be, like hers, betray'd ;
For since her Mien no real Joys could grant,
Who would chuse Scandal, and the Pleasure want ?
And if a Man's disguise had rais'd the flame,
Perhaps her native dress might quench the same !   120
As Partner of her Bed, her Guest she chose,
But longing sighs, and Plaints deny'd repose
If a short slumber chance to close her Eyes,
Fancy awake her utmost wish supplys
She then experienc'd joys neer tryd before
And Bradamante seem'd a Man all oer.
Thus as in broken rest the sickman turns,
When on his tongue the droughty feaver burns
Imagination cools his thirsty dreams
With rills, brooks, rivers, and abundant Streams.   130
She wak'd, and soft her hand she gently laid,
But found it all a dream. Unhappy Maid !
How fervent were her prayers that tedious night
How did she call the Gods to do her right !
By Tokens palpable, O grant my Prayer
Into the better Sex convert the Fair.
Then soft she stretch'd her curious hand again
But found alas that all her Prayers were vain.
    Thus past the Night, 'till Phœbus waken'd Day,
And rais'd his silver head above the Sea,   140
They rose. Who now her mighty griefs shall tell,
When the Fair Maid prepar'd to bid farewell ?
Her ready Groom a prancing Gennet brought,
With Gold the furniture & trappings wrought,
A Garment which with richest art she wove,
All these she gave, as witness of her Love.
The Courteous Dame conducts her on the way,
Adieu, she cryd ; yet prest her still to stay ;
They part. Awhile she pensive stands & mourns
Then to her Palace wishfully returns.   150
My Sister Valleys, Hills & forests crost
Retiring Mountains in the clouds were lost
Thus her swift Palfrey, fleet as rapid wind
Reach'd Montalbano e'er the day declin'd.
What gladness in our mother's bosom sprung !
What shouts of joy through all the Castle rung !

113 They Enter] These entering   115 robes . . . shape] dress. . . limbs
121 As] The   125 She then] Then she
130 abundant] overflowing   135 By palpable strong Tokens grant *alt.*

Long in her absence we her Death deplor'd,
A Daughter, Sister, is to Life restor'd!
Her Helm unlac'd, we wonder to behold
Her shorten'd hair, which whilom round was roll'd   160
In ribband braided; some with curious eyes
Survey her robe enriched with foreign Dyes.
We learn with pleasure her adventures rare,
The desp'rate wound that caus'd her loss of Hair,
And how beside the murm'ring fountain laid,
Her martial Dress deceived the Royal Maid
How mid the secret wood they stray'd alone
And how the Princess made her passion known,
How when the Partner of her Bed she griev'd,
Tis pity such warm Love should be deceiv'd!   170
     In Saragossa I the Dame had seen
And then her beauteous Eyes, her face, her mien,
With Joy with pleasure fill'd my captive mind,
But all Desire was not to sight confin'd,
He who his Love can without hopes foment
May with a dream or shadow be content *

          [The following twelve lines appear in the margin.]

*So strong her image in the tale was found
It reach'd my heart, & touch'd my former wound
With hopes at first Love fed the kindling fire,
And now again Hope waken'd with desire.   180
Desire now taught me to supply my want
To gain all I could ask & she could grant
How can Success on open minds attend?
'Tis well dissembling fraud that gains its end.
So like my Sister were my face, my make
The most discerning Eye might well mistake,
Why should th' enamour'd Dame more knowing prove?
O favour the disguise, kind God of Love!

Shall I or shall I not attempt her charms?
Fortune assists the Bold in Love & arms,   190
I ask'd no counsell, for I sought no aid
But the strong dictates of my soul obey'd.
Sudden in Bradamante's armour drest
Her well-known robe, her shining helme & crest,
Her steed I mounted, prick'd it oer the Lawn
Nor waited 'till the rosy morning's dawn.
Along the darksome night Love leads the way,
When Beauty calls a moment is delay.
Impatient to her Palace Gate I came
Eer in the Deep the Sun had quench'd his flame,   200
How did each servant fly the news to bear!
Who with it first shall greet the Royal fair?

          166 deceived] deceives   185 were] was

Who tells it first a due reward shall gain,
And grace & favour in her sight obtain.
They saw the self-same Steed the day before
They knew the Garment, & the Helme I wore
Like you deceiv'd, each hasty Servant spys
In my smooth feature Bradamante's eyes.
   Fiordispina wing'd with pleasure came
Her sparkling Eye confest her inward flame.   210
In ev'ry action was her soul exprest :
How did she greet me ! how my hand she prest
Then round my neck her eager arms she flings,
With sweet embrace, and to my Lips she clings.
Then, then Love's arrow took the surest aim,
Through ev'ry vein shot quick the tingling flame.
Now hand in hand she to my chamber leads,
Nor calls the Duty of officious maids,
Pleas'd with the Labour, she forgets her pride,
Disarms my Legs, & lays my helme aside.   220
From her own ward-robe a rich Gown was brought,
With all the cost of proud embroid'ry wrought,
With this she gave my Shape a female Air
And in a golden wreath confind my Hair.
My Eyes I turn'd with coy & modest Art
And ev'ry gesture play'd a woman's part ;
My Voice (which had perhaps the fraud reveal'd)
Was in affected shriller tone conceal'd.
And now into the publick Hall we came
Where many a knight, & many a courteous Dame   230
Paid us all honours due to royal State,
The due Civilitys return'd ; we sate.
The frequent glance of gallant knights I caught,
Whose Eye lascivious spoke their wanton thought
On me, alas ! your glance is idly thrown
All is not, as ye wist, beneath the Gown.
The Night was far advanc'd ; they clear'd the Board,
Which all the Daintys of the Season stor'd.
How joy'd I when the ready Dame propos'd,
What I with fear & trembling had disclos'd !   240
Come let's retire, with tender voice, she said
Once more repose the Partner of my Bed.
Her Ladys, Maids, & Pages now were gone
And I with all my wishes left alone,
Undrest, in bed ; The Taper's blaz'd like day ;
Wert thou prepar'd ? why then this cold delay ?
But lest Surprise (to find the Signs of Man)
With shrieks might wake the house, I thus began.
   Wonder not, Princess at this sudden view,
That I who lately bid a long Adieu,   250

204 sight] eyes   209-10 pleasure . . . Eye] joy advanc'd From every Look
231 Receiv'd us with the honours *alt*.

So soon return. Had I the Power, the Art
To cure the love-sick feaver of thy heart
I ne'er had left these hospitable Towers
But to thy Joys devoted all my hours,
But when I found my presence give you pain,
I parted, ne'er to see these Walls again.
But chance or thought misled me as I past
Amidst a wood whose paths thick shrubs oercast,
A female scream from out the Thicket came.
With hasty stride I sprung to save the Dame.   260
Lo on a Bank a furious Fawn I spyd
Below clear waters form'd a spatious tide.
The Savage Fisherman a Naiad took
Who with smart anguish flounder'd on his hook
Near to the shore he drew the dying prize
And view'd the dainty feast with greedy eyes.
Thither I sped, & aim'd a fatal wound,
The Brutal Monster fell & bit the ground.
Freed from the snare, the Nymph with sudden glide
In the mid Lake arose, and thus she cry'd.   270
O valiant knight, this Deed shall be repay'd
Invain thou hast not lent the wretched aid.
Know then, the Nymph of all this Lake I reign,
Ask all thy wishes and thy will obtain.
Oer ev'ry Element my Power extends
And wond'ring Nature on my Nod attends,
With freedom make demand, I grant the Boon
From the pale Sky I'll draw the list'ning Moon
Fire freezes at my charms, the Sun I stay,
Air hardens, and the reeling Earth gives way.   280
    I ask not mighty Nations to command,
Nor to grasp treasure in a Miser-hand,
I ask nor Strength, nor virtue, nor Renown,
From ev'ry war to bear the laurell Crown.
All obstacle, sayd I, Fair Nymph, remove
And teach me gratitude to her I Love ;
I dare no farther my Desires explain
O may not now thy Skill, thy Power be vain ;
I ask no more. The Nymph no answer gave,
But sudden dips beneath the crystal Wave   290
Then spirting oer my face th' enchanted stream
I found myself quite chang'd (as in a dream)
I see, I feel, invain my sex explore,
Signs gave me proof I Woman was no more.
And could I not even now the Truth produce,
I grant Suspicion might my words accuse.
As in the weaker Sex I felt the flame,
My duteous Zeal unchang'd, still burns the same.
This instant then my ready power employ
Give the sweet signal I obey with joy.   300

262 Below] Where

Then oer my side her glowing hand she threw
And fully was convinc'd that all was true.
As one whose heart is check'd by strong despair
Of eer possessing what his soul holds dear
The more he sigh'd, and groan'd & wept, & pin'd,
If he by chance his utmost wishes find
Still more he grieves, he cannot Time regain ;
For all his former life was spent invain.
Thus lay the Dame confus'd in deep suspense
Though often try'd, yet scarce believ'd her sense   310
And though her touch & sight the truth explore,
Dreams had deceiv'd her touch & sight before.
But still the Dame sincerer proof requir'd,
That all was real which her Soul desir'd.
If these be dreams, O God of Sleep, she crys,
From the dear vision may I never rise.
The Lady not too nice, her passion strong,
I know, like her ; you think the story long.
Nor Drum nor Trumpet did the prelude play
To the warm onset of our am'rous fray,   320
But murm'ring kisses, like the billing Dove,
Mark'd ev'ry action in this field of Love.
If sighs and plaints last night her bed possest
'Twas now all joyous talk & pleasing jest ;
Close as Acanthus leaves wreath'd Columns bind,
So arms with Arms & Legs with Legs entwin'd.
    So secret were our joys, Moons roll'd away
And lost in pleasure ev'ry night we lay
At length our close intrigue was learnt by Fame
It spread, & to her royal Father came.   330
You whose strong Prowess made the croud retire,
And sav'd me from the rage of piles of fire,
Well know the rest. But let me never know
The dreadfull Torments she must undergo !

303 check'd] rein'd   306 wishes] wish should   313 Dame sincerer]
wishing Dame more   317 Lady not too] Dame not over   318 the] my
325 leaves] the

F A B L E S.

By Mr. G A Y.

L O N D O N:
Printed for J. Tonson and J. Watts.
M DCC XXVII.

TO

HIS HIGHNESS

WILLIAM

Duke of *CUMBERLAND.*

THESE NEW FABLES,
INVENTED FOR HIS AMUSEMENT,

Are humbly Dedicated, by

HIS HIGHNESS's

Most Faithful and

Most Obedient Servant

JOHN GAY.

[The *Fables* were published in 1727, in Post 4to. The title-page is here reproduced. Each Fable is headed by a small woodcut from the design of William Kent or John Wootton, engraved by Fourdrinier, Baron, or Van der Gucht. A second edition was published by Tonson and Watts in 1728, and a third edition in 1729. These are Demy 8vo, but contain the original plates. Three more editions were issued after Gay's death before the posthumous appearance in 1738 of a second series of Fables, published by J. and P. Knapton and T. Cox, on September 29, in two forms—Post 4to and Demy 8vo—to correspond with the existing editions of the first series. The title-page of the 8vo edition is here reproduced. There is a frontispiece depicting Gay's tomb in Westminster Abbey, and a full-page illustration to each Fable. These, as well as the portrait on the title-page, are engraved by Scotin from the designs of H. Gravelot.

Subsequent editions are innumerable; a careful bibliography is given by Wright in his edition of 1889. In addition to the early editions I have used Bell, Cooke, and Underhill, their several editions of Gay's works, and Austin Dobson's edition of the Fables. Some remarks upon these editions will be found in the Introduction. I have once or twice referred to an edition published at York in 1806 illustrated by Bewick (the first issue of the Fables with Bewick's cuts was in 1779, but this I do not possess), and to Clarke's edition of the Fables in Cassell's Library of British Poets. Stockdale's ' large edition of 1793, which includes, *inter alia*, no less than nine plates, both designed and engraved by William Blake ' (so Austin Dobson) is much valued by collectors, but is textually as worthless as the rest.]

F A B L E S.

First Series.

I N T R O D U C T I O N

T O   T H E

F A B L E S.

The SHEPHERD *and the* PHILOSOPHER.

REMOTE from citys liv'd a Swain,
Unvex'd with all the cares of gain,
His head was silver'd o'er with age,
And long experience made him sage ;
In summer's heat and winter's cold
He fed his flock and pen'd the fold,
His hours in cheerful labour flew,
Nor envy nor ambition knew ;
His wisdom and his honest fame
Through all the country rais'd his
  name.   10
  A deep Philosopher (whose rules
Of moral life were drawn from schools)
The Shepherd's homely cottage
  sought,
And thus explor'd his reach of
  thought.
    Whence is thy learning ? Hath
    thy toil
O'er books consum'd the midnight
  oil ?
Hast thou old *Greece* and *Rome*
  survey'd,
And the vast sense of *Plato* weigh'd ?

Hath *Socrates* thy soul refin'd,
And hast thou fathom'd *Tully's*
  mind ?   20
Or, like the wise *Ulysses* thrown
By various fates on realms unknown,
Hast thou through many citys stray'd,
Their customs, laws and manners
  weigh'd ?
  The Shepherd modestly reply'd.
I ne'er the paths of learning try'd,
Nor have I roam'd in foreign parts
To read mankind, their laws and
  arts ;
For man is practis'd in disguise,   29
He cheats the most discerning eyes :
Who by that search shall wiser grow,
When we ourselves can never know ?
The little knowledge, I have gain'd,
Was all from simple nature drain'd ;
Hence my life's maxims took their
  rise,
Hence grew my settled hate to vice.
  The daily labours of the bee
Awake my soul to industry.

  1 citys] *1727* cities *1728. I give the spelling of the first edition throughout. It is
interesting to note the transition to a more modern form beginning in Fable XXIX, and
to preserve the inconsistencies, which were removed from the second edition. The Fables
were long in writing.*
  1 10 *See Introduction, p. xviii.*

Who can observe the careful ant,
And not provide for future want ? 40
My dog (the trustiest of his kind)
With gratitude inflames my mind ;
I mark his true, his faithful way,
And in my service copy *Tray.*
In constancy, and nuptial love
I learn my duty from the dove.
The hen, who from the chilly air
With pious wing protects her care,
And ev'ry fowl that flies at large
Instructs me in a parent's charge. 50
  From nature too I take my rule
To shun contempt and ridicule.
I never with important air
In conversation overbear ;
Can grave and formal pass for wise,
When men the solemn owl despise ?
My tongue within my lips I rein,
For who talks much must talk in
    vain ;
We from the wordy torrent fly : 59
Who listens to the chatt'ring pye ?

Nor would I with felonious slight
By stealth invade my neighbour's
    right ;
Rapacious animals we hate :
Kites, hawks and wolves deserve their
    fate.
Do not we just abhorrence find
Against the toad and serpent kind ?
But envy, calumny and spite
Bear stronger venom in their bite.
Thus ev'ry object of creation   69
Can furnish hints to contemplation,
And from the most minute and mean
A virtuous mind can morals glean.
  Thy fame is just, the Sage replys,
Thy virtue proves thee truly wise ;
Pride often guides the author's pen,
Books as affected are as men,
But he who studys nature's laws
From certain truth his maxims draws,
And those, without our schools,
    suffice   79
To make men moral, good and wise.

47–50 *See Introduction, p. xviii.*

TO HIS HIGHNESS
WILLIAM, *Duke of* CUMBERLAND.
FABLE I.
The LYON, *the* TYGER, *and the* TRAVELLER.

ACCEPT, young P R I N C E, the moral
    lay,
And in these tales mankind survey ;
With early virtues plant your breast,
The specious arts of vice detest.
Princes, like Beautys, from their
    youth
Are strangers to the voice of truth :
Learn to contemn all praise betimes ;
For flattery's the nurse of crimes ;
Friendship by sweet reproof is shown,
(A virtue never near a throne ;)   10
In courts such freedom must offend,
There none presumes to be a friend.

To those of your exalted station
Each courtier is a dedication ;
Must I too flatter like the rest,
And turn my morals to a jest ?
The muse disdains to steal from those,
Who thrive in courts by fulsome prose.
  But shall I hide your real praise,
Or tell you what a nation says ?   20
They in your infant bosom trace
The virtues of your Royal race,
In the fair dawning of your mind
Discern you gen'rous, mild and kind,
They see you grieve to hear distress,
And pant already to redress.

8 crimes ;] *1729* crimes. *1727 and 1728.*

Go on, the height of good attain,
Nor let a nation hope in vain.
For hence we justly may presage
The virtues of a riper age.   30
True courage shall your bosom fire,
And future actions own your Sire.
Cowards are cruel ; but the brave
Love mercy, and delight to save.

A Tyger, roaming for his prey,
Sprung on a Trav'ler in the way ;
The prostrate game a Lyon spys,
And on the greedy tyrant flys :
With mingled roar resounds the wood,
Their teeth, their claws distill with
    blood,   40
'Till, vanquish'd by the Lyon's
    strength,
The spotted foe extends his length.
The Man besought the shaggy lord,
And on his knees for life implor'd,
His life the gen'rous hero gave.
Together walking to his Cave,
The Lyon thus bespoke his guest.
    What hardy beast shall dare con-
        test
My matchless strength ?   You saw
    the fight,   49
And must attest my pow'r and right.
Forc'd to forego their native home
My starving slaves at distance
    roam,
Within these woods I reign alone,
The boundless forest is my own ;

Bears, wolves, and all the savage
    brood
Have dy'd the regal den with blood ;
These carcasses on either hand,
Those bones that whiten all the land
My former deeds and triumphs tell,
Beneath these jaws what numbers fell.
    True, says the Man, the strength
        I saw   61
Might well the brutal nation awe ;
But shall a monarch, brave like you,
Place glory in so false a view ?
Robbers invade their neighbour's
    right.
Be lov'd.   Let justice bound your
    might.
Mean are ambitious heroes boasts
Of wasted lands and slaughter'd
    hosts ;
Pyrates their power by murders gain,
Wise kings by love and mercy reign ;
To me your clemency hath shown   71
The virtue worthy of a throne ;
Heav'n gives you power above the
    rest,
Like Heav'n to succour the distrest.
    The case is plain, the Monarch said ;
False glory hath my youth mis-led,
For beasts of prey, a servile train,
Have been the flatt'rers of my reign.
You reason well.   Yet tell me, friend,
Did ever you in courts attend ?   80
For all my fawning rogues agree
That human heroes rule like me.

32 your] *It is tempting to conjecture* you, *as does Clarke (Cassell's Library Edition of British Poets), but Gay is here flattering the Prince of Wales.*

50 pow'r]. *In the First Series of Fables* power *is the normal spelling. The exceptions, as here, and in Fables X. 40 and XXXI. 43, are possibly intentional. In the Second Series* pow'r *is the normal spelling, and is probably attributable to the publisher's reader.*

57-60. *See Introduction, p. xv.*

FABLE II.

The SPANIEL *and the* CAMELEON.

A SPANIEL, bred with all the care
That waits upon a fav'rite heir,
Ne'er felt correction's rigid hand ;
Indulg'd to disobey command,
In pamper'd ease his hours were
 spent ;
He never knew what learning meant ;
Such forward airs, so pert, so smart,
Were sure to win his lady's heart,
Each little mischief gain'd him praise;
How pretty were his fawning ways ! 10

 The wind was south, the morning
 fair,
He ventures forth to take the air ;
He ranges all the meadow round,
And rolls upon the softest ground ;
When near him a Cameleon seen
Was scarce distinguish'd from the
 green.
 Dear emblem of the flatt'ring host,
What live with clowns, a genius lost !
To citys and the court repair,
A fortune cannot fail thee there ; 20

Preferment shall thy talents crown.
Believe me, friend ; I know the town.
 Sir, says the sycophant, like you,
Of old, politer life I knew ;
Like you, a courtier born and bred,
Kings lean'd their ear to what I said,
My whisper always met success,
The ladys prais'd me for address,
I knew to hit each courtier's passion,
And flatter'd ev'ry vice in fashion.
But *Jove*, who hates the lyar's ways,
At once cut short my prosp'rous days,
And, sentenc'd to retain my nature,
Transform'd me to this crawling
 creature ;
Doom'd to a life obscure and mean,
I wander in the sylvan scene.
For *Jove* the heart alone regards,
He punishes what man rewards.
How diff'rent is thy case and mine !
With men at least you sup and dine,
While I, condemn'd to thinnest fare
Like those I flatter'd, feed on air. 42

10–11 *So printed in the Second and Third Editions. The First Edition has no white line here.*

FABLE III.

The MOTHER, *the* NURSE, *and the* FAIRY.

GIVE me a son. The blessing sent,
Were ever Parents more content ?
How partial are their doating eyes !
No child is half so fair and wise.

 Wak'd to the morning's pleasing
 care,
The Mother rose, and sought her
 heir ;
She saw the Nurse, like one possest,
With wringing hands and sobbing
 breast.

 Sure some disaster has befel,
Speak Nurse ; I hope the boy is well.
 Dear Madam, think not me to
 blame,   11
Invisible the Fairy came,
Your precious babe is hence convey'd,
And in the place a changeling laid ;
Where are the father's mouth and
 nose,
The mother's eyes, as black as sloes ?
See here, a shocking aukward creature,
That speaks a fool in ev'ry feature.

9 has] *Dobson and Underhill print* hath

The woman's blind, the Mother crys,
I see wit sparkle in his eyes.   20
  Lord! Madam, what a squinting leer!
No doubt the Fairy hath been here.
Just as she spoke, a pigmy sprite
Pops through the key-hole, swift as light,
Perch'd on the cradle's top he stands,
And thus her folly reprimands.

Whence sprung the vain conceited lye
That we the world with fools supply?
What! give our sprightly race away,
For the dull helpless sons of clay!   30
Besides, by partial fondness shown,
Like you we doat upon our own.
Where yet was ever found a mother,
Who'd give her booby for another?
And should we change with human breed,
Well might we pass for fools indeed.

32 you] *1728 and 1729* you, *1727.*

FABLE IV.

The EAGLE, *and the Assembly of* ANIMALS.

As *Jupiter's* all-seeing eye
Survey'd the worlds beneath the sky,
From this small speck of earth were sent
Murmurs and sounds of discontent;
For ev'ry thing alive complain'd
That he the hardest life sustain'd.
  Jove calls his Eagle. At the word
Before him stands the royal bird.
The Bird, obedient, from heav'n's height
Downward directs his rapid flight;   10
Then cited ev'ry living thing,
To hear the mandates of his king.
  Ungrateful creatures, whence arise
These murmurs which offend the skies;
Why this disorder? say the cause:
For just are *Jove's* eternal Laws.
Let each his discontent reveal.
To yon sour dog I first appeal.
  Hard is my lot, the hound replys.
On what fleet nerves the greyhound flys!   20

While I with weary step and slow
O'er plains and vales and mountains go;
The morning sees my chase begun,
Nor ends it 'till the setting sun.
  When (says the greyhound) I pursue,
My game is lost, or caught in view,
Beyond my sight the prey's secure:
The hound is slow but always sure.
And, had I his sagacious scent,   29
Jove ne'er had heard my discontent.
  The lyon crav'd the foxe's art;
The fox, the lyon's force and heart;
The cock implor'd the pidgeon's flight,
Whose wings were rapid, strong and light;
The pidgeon strength of wing despis'd,
And the cock's matchless valour priz'd:
The fishes wish'd to graze the plain,
The beasts to skim beneath the main.
Thus, envious of another's state,
Each blam'd the partial hand of Fate.

9 *The Rev. Octavius Freire Owen rightly observes: ' This is a bad line, and forms an exception to Gay's usual accuracy.' Should we omit* The Bird?
19 replys.] replies. *1729* replys, *1727* replies, *1728.*
31 foxe's] *1727 and 1728* fox's *1729.*

The bird of heav'n then cry'd
aloud.   41
Jove bids disperse the murm'ring
croud :
The God rejects your idle prayers.
Would ye, rebellious mutineers,

Entirely change your name and
nature,
And be the very envy'd creature ?
What, silent all, and none consent !
Be happy then, and learn content.
Nor imitate the restless mind,
And proud ambition of mankind. 50

FABLE V.

The WILD BOAR *and the* RAM.

AGAINST an elm a sheep was ty'd,
The butcher's knife in blood was dy'd;
The patient flock, in silent fright,
From far beheld the horrid sight ;
A savage Boar, who near them stood,
Thus mock'd to scorn the fleecy
brood.
  All cowards should be serv'd like
  you.
See, see, your murd'rer is in view ;
With purple hands and reeking knife
He strips the skin yet warm with life :
Your quarter'd sires, your bleeding
dams,   11
The dying bleat of harmless lambs
Call for revenge. O stupid race !
The heart that wants revenge is base.

  I grant, an ancient Ram replys,
We bear no terror in our eyes,
Yet think us not of soul so tame,
Which no repeated wrongs inflame ;
Insensible of ev'ry ill,
Because we want thy tusks to kill: 20
Know, Those who violence pursue
Give to themselves the vengeance due,
For in these massacres they find
The two chief plagues that waste
mankind.
Our skin supplys the wrangling bar,
It wakes their slumbring sons to war,
And well revenge may rest contented,
Since drums and parchment were
invented.

FABLE VI.

The MISER *and* PLUTUS.

THE wind was high ; the window
shakes,
With sudden start the Miser wakes,
Along the silent room he stalks,
Looks back and trembles as he walks,
Each lock and ev'ry bolt he trys,
In ev'ry creek and corner prys,
Then opes the chest with treasure
stor'd,
And stands in rapture o'er his hoard.
But now, with sudden qualms possest,

He wrings his hands, he beats his
breast,   10
By conscience stung he wildly stares,
And thus his guilty soul declares.
  Had the deep earth her stores con-
  fin'd,
This heart had known sweet peace of
mind.
But virtue 's sold. Good Gods, what
price
Can recompense the pangs of vice !

O bane of good ! seducing cheat !
Can man, weak man, thy power de-
    feat ?
Gold banish'd honour from the mind,
And only left the name behind ;   20
Gold sow'd the world with ev'ry ill ;
Gold taught the murd'rer's sword to
    kill ;
'Twas gold instructed coward hearts
In treach'ry's more pernicious arts :
Who can recount the mischiefs o'er ?
Virtue resides on earth no more !
    He spoke, and sigh'd. In angry
        mood
Plutus, his God, before him stood ;
The Miser trembling lock'd his chest,
The Vision frown'd, and thus addrest.
    Whence is this vile ungrateful rant ?
Each sordid rascal's daily cant :   32
Did I, base wretch, corrupt mankind ?
The fault 's in thy rapacious mind.
Because my blessings are abus'd,

Must I be censur'd, curs't, accus'd?
Ev'n virtue's self by knaves is made
A cloak to carry on the trade,
And power (when lodg'd in their
    possession)   39
Grows tyranny, and rank oppression.
Thus when the villain crams his chest,
Gold is the canker of the breast ;
'Tis av'rice, insolence, and pride,
And ev'ry shocking vice beside.
But when to virtuous hands 'tis
    given,
It blesses, like the dews of Heaven,
Like Heav'n, it hears the orphan's
    cries,
And wipes the tears from widows
    eyes.
Their crimes on gold shall misers lay,
Who pawn'd their sordid souls for
    pay ?   50
Let bravos then (when blood is spilt)
Upbraid the passive sword with guilt.

47 orphan's] orphans' *Cooke, Dobson, Underhill.*

FABLE VII.

The LYON, *the* FOX, *and the* GEESE.

A LYON, tir'd with State affairs,
Quite sick of pomp, and worn with
    cares,
Resolv'd (remote from noise and
    strife)
In peace to pass his latter life.
    It was proclaim'd ; the day was set;
Behold the gen'ral council met.
The Fox was Viceroy nam'd. The
    croud
To the new Regent humbly bow'd :
Wolves, bears and mighty tygers
    bend,
And strive who most shall condescend.
He strait assumes a solemn grace,   11
Collects his wisdom in his face,
The croud admire his wit, his sense :

Each word hath weight and conse-
    quence ;
The flatt'rer all his art displays :
He who hath power is sure of praise.
A fox stept forth before the rest,
And thus the servile throng addrest.
    How vast his talents, born to rule,
And train'd in virtue's honest school !
What clemency his temper sways !   21
How uncorrupt are all his ways !
Beneath his conduct and command
Rapine shall cease to waste the land;
His brain hath stratagem and art,
Prudence and mercy rule his heart.
What blessings must attend the
    nation
Under this good administration !

22 ways !] *1727* ways ? *1728 and 1729.*
28-9 *The second and third editions show a white line here*

He said. A Goose, who distant
  stood,   29
Harangu'd apart the cackling brood.
  Whene'er I hear a knave commend,
He bids me shun his worthy friend.
What praise ! what mighty commen-
  dation !
But 'twas a fox who spoke th' ora-
  tion.

Foxes this government may prize
As gentle, plentiful and wise ;
If they enjoy these sweets, 'tis plain,
We geese must feel a tyrant reign.
What havock now shall thin our race !
When ev'ry petty clerk in place, 40
To prove his taste, and seem polite,
Will feed on geese both noon and
  night.

FABLE VIII.

The LADY *and the* WASP.

WHAT whispers must the Beauty bear!
What hourly nonsense haunts her ear!
Where-e'er her eyes dispense their
  charms
Impertinence around her swarms.
Did not the tender nonsense strike,
Contempt and scorn might look dis-
  like,
Forbidding airs might thin the place,
The slightest flap a fly can chase.
But who can drive the num'rous
  breed ?
Chase one, another will succeed. 10
Who knows a fool, must know his
  brother ;
One fop will recommend another ;
And with this plague she 's rightly
  curst,
Because she listen'd to the first.

  As *Doris*, at her toilette's duty,
Sate meditating on her beauty,
She now was pensive, now was gay,
And loll'd the sultry hours away.
  As thus in indolence she lyes,
A giddy wasp around her flies, 20
He now advances, now retires,
Now to her neck and cheek aspires ;
Her fan in vain defends her charms,
Swift he returns, again alarms,
For by repulse he bolder grew,
Perch'd on her lip and sipt the dew.
  She frowns, she frets. Good Gods,
    she crys,

Protect me from these teazing flys !
Of all the plagues that heav'n hath
  sent
A wasp is most impertinent. 30
  The hov'ring insect thus com-
    plain'd.
Am I then slighted, scorn'd, disdain'd ?
Can such offence your anger wake ?
'Twas beauty caus'd the bold
  mistake.
Those cherry lips that breathe
  perfume,
That cheek so ripe with youthful
  bloom
Made me with strong desire pursue
The fairest peach that ever grew.
  Strike him not, *Jenny, Doris* crys,
Nor murder wasps, like vulgar flys,
For though he 's free (to do him right)
The creature 's civil and polite. 42
  In ecstasies away he posts,
Where-e'er he came the favour boasts,
Brags how her sweetest tea he sips,
And shows the sugar on his lips.
  The hint alarm'd the forward crew.
Sure of success, away they flew ;
They share the daintys of the day,
Round her with airy musick play, 50
And now they flutter, now they rest,
Now soar again, and skim her breast,
Nor were they banish'd, 'till she found
That wasps have stings, and felt the
  wound.

    · 23 charms,] *1727 and 1728* charms. *1729.*

FABLE IX.

The BULL *and the* MASTIFF.

SEEK you to train your fav'rite boy ?
Each caution, ev'ry care employ,
And ere you venture to confide,
Let his preceptor's heart be try'd ;
Weigh well his manners, life, and
    scope,
On these depends thy future hope.

As on a time, in peaceful reign,
A Bull enjoy'd the flow'ry plain,
A Mastiff pass'd ; inflam'd with ire,
His eye-balls shot indignant fire,   10
He foam'd, he rag'd with thirst of
    blood.
    Spurning the ground the monarch
    stood,
And roar'd aloud. Suspend the fight,
In a whole skin, go, sleep to-night ;
Or tell me, ere the battel rage,
What wrongs provoke thee to engage ?
Is it ambition fires thy breast,
Or avarice that ne'er can rest ?

From these alone unjustly springs
The world-destroying wrath of Kings.
    The surly Mastiff thus returns. 21
Within my bosom glory burns.
Like heroes of eternal name,
Whom poets sing, I fight for fame :
The butcher's spirit-stirring mind
To daily war my youth inclin'd,
He train'd me to heroic deed,
Taught me to conquer or to bleed.
    Curst dog, the Bull reply'd, no more
I wonder at thy thirst of gore,   30
For thou (beneath a butcher train'd,
Whose hands with cruelty are stain'd,
His daily murders in thy view,)
Must, like thy tutor, blood pursue.
Take then thy fate. With goring
    wound
At once he lifts him from the ground,
Aloft the sprawling hero flys,
Mangled he falls, he howls, and dyes.

12 *Dobson and Underhill disallow the new paragraph.*

FABLE X.

The ELEPHANT *and the* BOOKSELLER.

THE man, who with undaunted toils
Sails unknown seas to unknown soils,
With various wonders feasts his sight :
What stranger wonders does he write !
We read, and in description view
Creatures which *Adam* never knew ;
For, when we risque no contradiction,
It prompts the tongue to deal in
    fiction.
Those things that startle me or you,
I grant are strange ; yet may be
    true.   10
Who doubts that elephants are found
For science and for sense renown'd ?
Borri records their strength of parts,

Extent of thought, and skill in arts ;
How they perform the law's decrees,
And save the state the hang-man's
    fees,
And how by travel understand
The language of another land.
Let those, who question this report,
To *Pliny's* ancient page resort. 20
How learn'd was that sagacious
    breed !
Who now (like them) the *greek* can
    read !

    As one of these, in days of yore,
Rummag'd a shop of learning o'er,

Not like our modern dealers, minding
Only the margin's breadth and bind-
    ing ;
A book his curious eye detains,
Where, with exactest care and pains,
Were ev'ry beast and bird portray'd,
That e'er the search of man survey'd.
Their natures and their powers were
    writ   31
With all the pride of human wit ;
The page he with attention spread,
And thus remark'd on what he read.
    Man with strong reason is endow'd ;
A Beast scarce is allow'd :
But let this author's worth be try'd,
'Tis plain that neither was his guide.
Can he discern the diffrent natures,
And weigh the pow'r of other crea-
    tures,   40
Who by the partial work hath shown
He knows so little of his own ?
How falsely is the spaniel drawn !
Did Man from him first learn to fawn ?
A dog proficient in the trade !
He, the chief flatt'rer nature made !
Go, man, the ways of courts discern,
You'll find a spaniel still might learn.
How can the foxe's theft and plunder
Provoke his censure, or his wonder ?
From courtiers tricks, and lawyers
    arts   51

The fox might well improve his parts.
The lyon, wolf, and tyger's brood
He curses, for their thirst of blood ;
But is not man to man a prey ?
Beasts kill for hunger, men for pay.
    The Bookseller, who heard him
        speak,
And saw him turn a page of *Greek*,
Thought, what a genius have I found !
Then thus addrest with bow pro-
    found.   60
    Learn'd Sir, if you'd employ your
        pen
Against the senseless sons of men,
Or write the history of *Siam*,
No man is better pay than I am ;
Or, since you're learn'd in *Greek*, let 's
    see
Something against the Trinity.
    When wrinkling with a sneer his
        trunk,
Friend, quoth the Elephant, you're
    drunk ;
E'en keep your money, and be wise ;
Leave man on man to criticise,   70
For that you ne'er can want a pen
Among the senseless sons of men,
They unprovok'd will court the fray,
Envy 's a sharper spur than pay,
No author ever spar'd a brother,
Wits are game-cocks to one another.

40 pow'r] *See Fable I, 50, note.*   44 Man] *1728 and 1729* man *1727.*
58 *Greek*] but in l. 22 *greek*, where the definite article is responsible for the small *g*.

FABLE XI.

The PEACOCK, *the* TURKEY, *and the* GOOSE.

In beauty faults conspicuous grow,
The smallest speck is seen on snow.

    As near a barn, by hunger led,
A Peacock with the poultry fed ;
All view'd him with an envious eye,
And mock'd his gaudy pageantry :
He, conscious of superior merit,

Contemns their base reviling spirit,
His state and dignity assumes,   9
And to the sun displays his plumes,
Which, like the heav'n's o'er-arching
    skies,
Are spangled with a thousand eyes ;
The circling rays and varied light
At once confound their dazled sight,

Title. the GOOSE] GOOSE *early editions.*

On ev'ry tongue detraction burns,
And malice prompts their spleen by
      turns.
   Mark, with what insolence and
      pride
The creature takes his haughty stride,
The Turkey crys. Can spleen con-
      tain ?
Sure never bird was half so vain ! 20
But were intrinsic merit seen,
We turkeys have the whiter skin.
   From tongue to tongue they caught
      abuse ;
And next was heard the hissing Goose.
What hideous legs ! what filthy
      claws !
I scorn to censure little flaws.
Then what a horrid squawling throat !
Ev'n owls are frighted at the note.
   True. Those are faults, the Pea-
      cock crys,

My scream, my shanks you may de-
      spise :   30
But such blind critics rail in vain.
What, overlook my radiant train !
Know, did my legs (your scorn and
      sport)
The turkey or the goose support,
And did ye scream with harsher
      sound,
Those faults in you had ne'er been
      found ;
To all apparent beautys blind,
Each blemish strikes an envious
      mind.

   Thus in Assemblys have I seen
A nymph of brightest charms and
      mien   40
Wake envy in each ugly face ;
And buzzing scandal fills the place.

28–9 *The second and third editions have a white line here.*
40 mien] *1727*   mein *1728 and 1729.*

FABLE XII.

Cupid, Hymen, *and* Plutus.

As *Cupid* in *Cythera's* grove
Employ'd the lesser powers of love,
Some shape the bow, or fit the string,
Some give the taper shaft its wing,
Or turn the polish'd quiver's mold,
Or head the darts with temper'd gold.
   Amidst their toil and various care,
Thus *Hymen*, with assuming air,
Addrest the God. Thou purblind
      chit,
Of aukward and ill-judging wit, 10
If matches are no better made,
At once I must forswear my trade.
You send me such ill-coupled folks,
That 'tis a shame to sell them yokes.
They squabble for a pin, a feather,
And wonder how they came together.
The husband' s sullen, dogged, shy,
The wife grows flippant in reply ;

He loves command and due restric-
      tion,   19
And she as well likes contradiction ;
She never slavishly submits,
She'll have her will, or have her
      fits ;
He this way tugs, she t'other draws,
The man grows jealous, and with
      cause,
Nothing can save him but divorce,
And here the wife complys of course.
   When, says the Boy, had I to do
With either your affairs or you ?
I never idly spend my darts ;
You trade in mercenary hearts : 30
For settlements the lawyer 's fee'd ;
Is my hand witness to the Deed ?
If they like cat and dog agree,
Go rail at *Plutus*, not at me.

29 spend] *Dobson and Underhill have* spent

Plutus appear'd, and said ; 'Tis true,
In marriage, gold is all their view ;
They seek not beauty, wit or sense,
And love is seldom the pretence.
All offer incense at my shrine,
And I alone the bargain sign.   40
How can *Belinda* blame her fate ?

She only ask'd a great estate.
Doris was rich enough, 'tis true,
Her Lord must give her title too :
And ev'ry man, or rich or poor,
A fortune asks, and asks no more.

Av'rice, whatever shape it bears,
Must still be coupled with its cares.

FABLE XIII.

The tame STAG.

As a young Stag the thicket past,
The branches held his antlers fast,
A clown, who saw the captive hung,
Across the horns his halter flung.
  Now, safely hamper'd in the cord,
He bore the present to his lord :
His lord was pleas'd : as was the clown,
When he was tipt with half-a-crown.
The Stag was brought before his wife,
The tender lady begg'd his life.   10
How sleek' s the skin ! how speck'd
    like ermine !
Sure never creature was so charming !
  At first within the yard confin'd,
He flys and hides from all mankind ;
Now bolder grown, with fixt amaze
And distant awe presumes to gaze,
Munches the linnen on the lines,
And on a hood or apron dines ;
He steals my little master's bread,

Follows the servants to be fed,   20
Nearer and nearer now he stands,
To feel the praise of patting hands,
Examines ev'ry fist for meat,
And though repulsed disdains retreat,
Attacks again with levell'd horns,
And man, that was his terror, scorns.

  Such is the country maiden's fright,
When first a red-coat is in sight,
Behind the door she hides her face,
Next time at distance eyes the lace,   30
She now can all his terrors stand,
Nor from his squeeze withdraws her
    hand ;
She plays familiar in his arms,
And ev'ry soldier hath his charms ;
From tent to tent she spreads her
    flame :
For custom conquers fear and shame.

FABLE XIV.

The MONKEY *who had seen the* WORLD.

A MONKEY, to reform the times,
Resolv'd to visit foreign climes ;
For men in distant regions roam
To bring politer manners home :
So forth he fares, all toil defys ;
Misfortune serves to make us wise.

At length the treach'rous snare was laid,
Poor *Pug* was caught, to town convey'd,
There sold ; (How envy'd was his doom,

9-10 *Dobson omits brackets. Underhill prints inverted commas in their place.*

Made captive in a lady's room !)   10
Proud as a lover of his chains,
He day by day her favour gains.
Whene'er the duty of the day,
The toilette calls ; with mimic play
He twirles her knots, he cracks her
    fan,
Like any other gentleman.
In visits too his parts and wit,
When jests grew dull, were sure to hit.
Proud with applause, he thought his
    mind
In ev'ry courtly art refin'd,   20
Like *Orpheus* burnt with publick zeal,
To civilize the monkey weal ;
So watch'd occasion, broke his chain,
And sought his native woods again.
    The hairy sylvans round him press,
Astonish'd at his strut and dress,
Some praise his sleeve, and others
    glote
Upon his rich embroider'd coat,
His dapper perriwig commending
With the black tail behind depending,
His powder'd back, above, below,   31
Like hoary frosts, or fleecy snow ;
But all, with envy and desire,
His flutt'ring shoulder-knot admire.
    Hear and improve, he pertly crys,
I come to make a nation wise ;
Weigh your own worth ;   support
    your place,
The next in rank to human race.

In citys long I pass'd my days,
Convers'd with men, and learnt their
    ways :   40
Their dress, their courtly manners see;
Reform your state, and copy me.
Seek ye to thrive ?   In flatt'ry deal,
Your scorn, your hate, with that con-
    ceal ;
Seem only to regard your friends,
But use them for your private ends,
Stint not to truth the flow of wit,
Be prompt to lye, whene'er 'tis fit ;
Bend all your force to spatter merit ;
Scandal is conversation's spirit ;   50
Boldly to ev'ry thing pretend,
And men your talents shall commend ;
I knew the Great.   Observe me right,
So shall you grow like man polite.
    He spoke and bow'd.   With mut-
    t'ring jaws
The wondring circle grinn'd applause.
    Now, warm with malice, envy, spite,
Their most obliging friends they bite,
And fond to copy human ways,   59
Practise new mischiefs all their days.

    Thus the dull lad, too tall for school,
With travel finishes the fool,
Studious of ev'ry coxcomb's airs,
He drinks, games, dresses, whores and
    swears,
O'erlooks with scorn all virtuous arts,
For vice is fitted to his parts.

32 frosts] *Dobson and Underhill, following some late editions, print* frost
37 worth] *Dobson and Underhill print* words

FABLE XV.

The PHILOSOPHER *and the* PHEASANT.

THE Sage, awak'd at early day,
Through the deep forest took his way ;
Drawn by the musick of the groves,
Along the winding gloom he roves ;
From tree to tree, the warbling
    throats
Prolong the sweet alternate notes.

But where he past he terror threw,
The song broke short, the warblers
    flew,
The thrushes chatter'd with affright,
And nightingales abhorr'd his sight ;
All animals before him ran   11
To shun the hateful sight of man.

Title. PHEASANT] PHEASANTS *early and most late editions.   Underhill's correction is probably right.   Compare Fable XXXIV.*

Whence is this dread of ev'ry
    creature ?
Fly they our figure or our nature ?
    As thus he walk'd in musing
        thought,
His ear imperfect accents caught ;
With cautious step he nearer drew,
By the thick shade conceal'd from
    view :
High on the branch a Pheasant stood,
Around her all her list'ning brood, 20
Proud of the blessings of her nest,
She thus a mother's care exprest.
    No dangers here shall circumvent,
Within the woods enjoy content.
Sooner the hawk or vulture trust
Than man ; of animals the worst ;
In him ingratitude you find,
A vice peculiar to the kind.
The sheep, whose annual fleece is
    dy'd,

To guard his health, and serve his
    pride,   30
Forc'd from his fold and native plain,
Is in the cruel shambles slain.
The swarms, who, with industrious
    skill,
His hives with wax and honey fill,
In vain whole summer days employ'd,
Their stores are sold, the race
    destroy'd.
What tribute from the goose is paid !
Does not her wing all science aid ?
Does it not lovers hearts explain,
And drudge to raise the merchant's
    gain ?   40
What now rewards this general use ?
He takes the quills and eats the goose.
Man then avoid, detest his ways,
So safely shall prolong your days.
When services are thus acquitted,
Be sure we pheasants must be spitted.

36 the] *Dobson and Underhill, following some late editions, print* their

FABLE XVI.

The PIN *and the* NEEDLE.

A PIN who long had serv'd a Beauty,
Proficient in the toilette's duty,
Had form'd her sleeve, confin'd her
    hair,
Or giv'n her knot a smarter air,
Now nearest to her heart was plac'd,
Now in her manteau's tail disgrac'd ;
But could she partial fortune blame,
Who saw her lovers serv'd the same ?
    At length from all her honours cast,
Through various turns of life she past ;
Now glitter'd on a taylor's arm,   11
Now kept a beggar's infant warm,
Now, rang'd within a miser's coat,
Now, Contributes to his yearly groat,
Now, rais'd again from low approach,
She visits in the doctor's coach ;
Here, there, by various fortune tost,
At last in *Gresham* hall was lost.

Charm'd with the wonders of the
    show,
On ev'ry side, above, below,   20
She now of this or that enquires,
What least was understood admires ;
'Tis plain, each thing so struck her
    mind,
Her head 's of virtuoso kind.
    And pray what 's this and this,
        dear sir ?
A needle, says th' interpreter.
She knew the name. And thus the fool
Addrest her as a taylor's tool.
    A needle with that filthy stone,
Quite idle, all with rust o'ergrown ! 30
You better might employ your parts,
And aid the sempstress in her arts.
But tell me how the friendship grew
Between that paultry flint and you ?

18 *Gresham* hall] *A museum.*

Friend, says the Needle, cease to blame ;
I follow real worth and fame.
Know'st thou the loadstone's power and art,
That virtue virtues can impart ?
Of all his talents I partake.
Who then can such a friend forsake ?
'Tis I direct the pilot's hand   41
To shun the rocks and treach'rous sand ;
By me the distant world is known,
And either *India* is our own.
Had I with milliners been bred,
What had I been ? the guide of thread,
And drudg'd as vulgar needles do,
Of no more consequence than you.

FABLE XVII.

The Shepherd's D o g *and the* W o l f.

A W OLF, with hunger fierce and bold,
Ravag'd the plains and thinn'd the fold :
Deep in the wood secure he lay,
The thefts of night regal'd the day ;
In vain the shepherd's wakeful care
Had spread the toils and watch'd the snare,
In vain the dog pursu'd his pace,
The fleeter robber mock'd the chase.
As *Lightfoot* rang'd the forest round,
By chance his foe's retreat he found.
Let us awhile the war suspend,   11
And reason as from friend to friend.
A truce, replys the Wolf ? 'Tis done.
The Dog the parley thus begun.
How can that strong intrepid mind
Attack a weak defenceless kind ?
Those jaws should prey on nobler food,
And drink the boar's and lyon's blood ;
Great souls with gen'rous pity melt,
Which coward tyrants never felt : 20
How harmless is our fleecy care !
Be brave, and let thy mercy spare.
    Friend, says the Wolf, the matter weigh.
Nature design'd us beasts of prey,
As such, when hunger finds a treat,
'Tis necessary wolves should eat.
If mindful of the bleating weal,
Thy bosom burn with real zeal,
Hence, and thy tyrant lord beseech,
To him repeat the moving speech ; 30
A wolf eats sheep but now and then,
Ten thousands are devour'd by men.
An open foe may prove a curse,
But a pretended friend is worse.

13 *For the punctuation compare Fable XIX, l. 33.*

FABLE XVIII.

The P A I N T E R *who pleased No body and Every body.*

L EST men suspect your tale untrue,
Keep probability in view.
The trav'ler leaping o'er those bounds,
The credit of his book confounds ;
Who with his tongue hath armies routed
Makes ev'n his real courage doubted.
But flatt'ry never seems absurd,
The flatter'd always takes your word,
Impossibilities seem just,
They take the strongest praise on trust ;   10
Hyperboles, though ne'er so great,
Will still come short of self-conceit.

So very like a Painter drew,
That ev'ry eye the picture knew
He hit complexion, feature, air,
So just, the life itself was there.
No flatt'ry, with his colours laid,
To bloom restor'd the faded maid,
He gave each muscle all its strength,
The mouth, the chin, the nose's length
His honest pencil touch'd with truth,
And mark'd the date of age and
    youth.   22
    He lost his friends, his practice
    fail'd,
Truth should not always be reveal'd ;
In dusty piles his pictures lay,
For no one sent the second pay.
    Two bustos, fraught with ev'ry
    grace,
A *Venus'* and *Apollo*'s face,
He plac'd in view ; resol'vd to please,
Whoever sate, he drew from these, 30
From these corrected ev'ry feature,
And spirited each aukward creature.
    All things were set ; the hour was
    come,
His pallet ready o'er his thumb,
My lord appear'd, and seated right
In proper attitude and light,
The Painter look'd, he sketch'd the
    piece,
Then dipt his pencil, talk'd of *Greece*,
Of *Titian*'s tints, of *Guido*'s air ; 39
Those eyes, my lord, the spirit there

Might well a *Raphael*'s hand require,
To give them all the native fire;
The features fraught with sense and
    wit
You'll grant are very hard to hit,
But yet with patience you shall view
As much as paint and art can do.
    Observe the work. My lord reply'd,
'Till now I thought my mouth was
    wide,
Besides, my nose is somewhat long,
Dear sir, for me, 'tis far too young. 50
    Oh, pardon me, the artist cry'd,
In this we painters must decide.
The piece ev'n common eyes must
    strike,
I warrant it extreamly like.
    My lord examin'd it anew ;
No looking-glass seem'd half so true.
    A lady came, with borrow'd grace
He from his *Venus* form'd her face
Her lover prais'd the painter's art
So like the picture in his heart !   60
To ev'ry age some charm he lent,
Ev'n Beautys were almost content.
    Through all the town his art they
    prais'd,
His custom grew, his price was rais'd.
Had he the real likeness shown,
Would any man the picture own ?
But when thus happily he wrought,
Each found the likeness in his thought.

57. *This line does not begin a paragraph in the early editions. Rightly corrected by
Bell.*

FABLE XIX.

The LYON *and the* CUB.

How fond are men of rule and place,
Who court it from the mean and base!
These cannot bear an equal nigh,
But from superior merit fly ;
They love the cellar's vulgar joke,
And lose their hours in ale and smoak;
There o'er some petty club preside,
So poor, so paultry is their pride !

Nay, ev'n with fools whole nights will
    sit,
In hopes to be supream in wit.   10
If these can read, to these I write,
To set their worth in truest light.

    A Lyon-cub, of sordid mind,
Avoided all the lyon kind ;

Fond of applause, he sought the feasts
Of vulgar and ignoble beasts,
With asses all his time he spent,
Their club's perpetual president.
He caught their manners, looks and
airs :
An ass in ev'ry thing, but ears ! 20
If e'er his highness meant a joke,
They grinn'd applause before he
spoke ;
But at each word what shouts of
praise !
Good Gods ! how natural he brays !
Elate with flatt'ry and conceit,

He seeks his royal sire's retreat ;
Forward, and fond to show his parts,
His highness brays, the Lyon starts.
Puppy, that curst vociferation
Betrays thy life and conversation ;
Coxcombs, an ever-noisy race, 31
Are trumpets of their own disgrace.
Why so severe, the Cub replys ?
Our senate always held me wise.
How weak is pride, returns the
Sire,
All fools are vain, when fools admire !
But know, what stupid asses prize,
Lyons and noble beasts despise.

FABLE XX.

The Old HEN *and the* COCK.

RESTRAIN your child ; you'll soon
believe
The text, which says, we sprung from
Eve.

As an old Hen led forth her train,
And seem'd to peck to show the grain;
She rak'd the chaff, she scratch'd the
ground,
And glean'd the spacious yard around.
A giddy chick, to try her wings,
On the well's narrow margin springs,
And prone she drops. The mother's
breast
All day with sorrow was possest. 10
A Cock she met ; her son she knew ;
And in her heart affection grew.
My son, says she, I grant your years
Have reach'd beyond a mother's
cares ;
I see you vig'rous, strong and bold,
I hear with joy your triumphs told ;
'Tis not from cocks thy fate I dread :
But let thy ever-wary tread
Avoid yon well ; that fatal place
Is sure perdition to our race. 20
Print this my counsel on thy breast ;
To the just Gods I leave the rest.
He thank'd her care ; yet day by day

His bosom burn'd to disobey,
And ev'ry time the well he saw
Scorn'd in his heart the foolish law ;
Near and more near each day he drew,
And long'd to try the dang'rous view.
Why was this idle charge ? he crys :
Let courage female fears despise. 30
Or did she doubt my heart was brave,
And therefore this injunction gave ?
Or does her harvest store the place,
A treasure for her younger race ?
And would she thus my search pre-
vent ?
I stand resolv'd, and dare th' event.
Thus said. He mounts the margin's
round,
And prys into the depth profound.
He stretch'd his neck ; and from
below
With stretching neck advanc'd a foe ;
With wrath his ruffled plumes he
rears, 41
The foe with ruffled plumes appears ;
Threat answer'd threat, his fury grew,
Headlong to meet the war he flew ;
But when the watry death he found,
He thus lamented, as he drown'd.
I ne'er had been in this condition
But for my mother's prohibition.

11 knew ;] *1728 and 1729* knew, *1727.*

25 ev'ry] *the early editions print* every

FABLE XXI.

The RAT-CATCHER and CATS.

THE rats by night such mischief did,
Betty was ev'ry morning chid :
They undermin'd whole sides of
    bacon,
Her cheese was sapp'd, her tarts were
    taken,
Her pastys, fenc'd with thickest paste,
Were all demolish'd and laid waste.
She curst the cat for want of duty,
Who left her foes a constant booty.
    An Engineer, of noted skill,
Engag'd to stop the growing ill.   10
    From room to room he now surveys
Their haunts, their works, their secret
    ways,
Finds where they 'scape an ambus-
    cade,
And whence the nightly sally 's made.
    An envious Cat, from place to place,
Unseen, attends his silent pace,
She saw that, if his trade went on,
The purring race must be undone,
So, secretly removes his baits,
And ev'ry stratagem defeats.   20
    Again he sets the poyson'd toils,
And puss again the labour foils.
    What foe (to frustrate my designs)
My schemes thus nightly counter-
    mines ?
Incens'd, he crys : this very hour
The wretch shall bleed beneath my
    power.
    So said. A pond'rous trap he
    brought,

And in the fact poor puss was caught.
    Smuggler, says he, thou shalt be
    made
A victim to our loss of trade.   30
    The captive Cat with piteous mews
For pardon, life and freedom sues.
A sister of the science spare,
One int'rest is our common care.
    What insolence ! the man reply'd,
Shall cats with us the game divide ?
Were all your interloping band
Extinguish'd, or expell'd the land,
We rat-catchers might raise our fees,
Sole guardians of a nation's cheese !   40
    A Cat, who saw the lifted knife,
Thus spoke, and sav'd her sister's life.
    In ev'ry age and clime we see,
Two of a trade can ne'er agree,
Each hates his neighbour for en-
    croaching ;
Squire stigmatizes squire for poach-
    ing ;
Beautys with beautys are in arms,
And scandal pelts each other's
    charms ;
Kings too their neighbour kings
    dethrone,
In hope to make the world their own.
But let us limit our desires,   51
Not war like beautys, kings and
    squires,
For though we both one prey pursue,
There 's game enough for us and you.

FABLE XXII.

The GOAT without a Beard.

'TIS certain, that the modish passions
Descend among the croud, like
    fashions.
Excuse me, then ; if pride, conceit,
(The manners of the fair and great)
I give to monkeys, asses, dogs,
Fleas, owls, goats, butterflys and
    hogs.

I say, that these are proud. What
    then ?
I never said, they equal men.

    A Goat (as vain as goat can be)
Affected singularity :   10
Whene'er a thymy bank he found,
He roll'd upon the fragrant ground,

And then with fond attention stood,
Fix'd, o'er his image in the flood.

I hate my frowzy beard, he crys ;
My youth is lost in this disguise.
Did not the females know my vigour,
Well might they loath this rev'rend
    figure.

Resolv'd to smooth his shaggy face,
He sought the barber of the place. 20
A flippant monkey, spruce and smart,
Hard by, profest the dapper art ;
His pole with pewter basons hung,
Black rotten teeth in order strung,
Rang'd cups, that in the window
    stcod,
Lin'd with red rags, to look like blood,
Did well his threefold trade explain,
Who shav'd, drew teeth, and breath'd
    a vein.

The Goat he welcomes with an air,
And seats him in his wooden chair, 30
Mouth, nose and cheek the lather
    hides,
Light, smooth and swift the razor
    glides.

I hope your custom, Sir, says Pug.
Sure never face was half so smug !

The Goat, impatient for applause,
Swift to the neighb'ring hill withdraws
The shaggy people grinn'd and star'd.

Heighday ! what 's here ? without
    a beard !
Say, brother, whence the dire dis-
    grace ?
What envious hand hath robb'd your
    face ?   40
When thus the fop with smiles of
    scorn.
Are beards by civil nations worn ?
Ev'n *Muscovites* have mow'd their
    chins.
Shall we, like formal *Capucins*,
Stubborn in pride, retain the mode,
And bear about the hairy load ?
Whene'er we through the village
    stray,
Are we not mock'd along the way,
Insulted with loud shouts of scorn,
By boys our beards disgrac'd and
    torn ?   50
Were you no more with goats to
    dwell,
Brother, I grant you reason well,
Replys a bearded chief.   Beside,
If boys can mortify thy pride,
How wilt thou stand the ridicule
Of our whole flock ? affected fool !
Coxcombs, distinguish'd from the
    rest,
To all but coxcombs are a jest.

33 Pug] pug *early editions, but elsewhere in the Fables always* Pug

FABLE XXIII.

The Old WOMAN *and her* CATS.

WHO friendship with a knave hath
    made
Is judg'd a partner in the trade.
The matron, who conducts abroad
A willing nymph, is thought a bawd ;
And if a modest girl is seen
With one who cures a lover's spleen,
We guess her, not extreamly nice,
And only wish to know her price.
'Tis thus, that on the choice of friends
Our good or evil name depends.   10

A wrinkled hag, of wicked fame,
Beside a little smoaky flame

Sate hov'ring, pinch'd with age and
    frost ;
Her shrivell'd hands, with veins
    embost,
Upon her knees her weight sustains,
While palsie shook her crazy brains ;
She mumbles forth her backward
    prayers,
An untam'd scold of fourscore years.
About her swarm'd a num'rous brood
Of Cats, who lank with hunger
    mew'd.   20
Teaz'd with their crys her choler
    grew,

And thus she sputter'd.   Hence ye
    crew.
Fool that I was, to entertain
Such imps, such fiends, a hellish
    train !
Had ye been never hous'd and nurst,
I, for a witch, had ne'er been curst.
To you I owe, that crouds of boys
Worry me with eternal noise ;
Straws laid across my pace retard,
The horse-shoe's nail'd (each thres-
    hold's guard ;)   30
The stunted broom the wenches hide,
For fear that I should up and ride ;

They stick with pins my bleeding seat,
And bid me show my secret· teat.
    To hear you prate would vex a saint,
Who hath most reason of complaint ?
Replys a Cat.   Let 's come to proof.
Had we ne'er starv'd beneath your
    roof,
We had, like others of our race,
In credit liv'd, as beasts of chace. 40
'Tis infamy to serve a hag ;
Cats are thought imps, her broom a
    nag ;
And boys against our lives combine,
Because, 'tis said, your cats have nine.

30 guard ;)] guard) *early editions* guard), *some later editions* guard) ; *Dobson
and Underhill. As some stop is clearly needed, I choose the semi-colon, and follow the
model of Fable I, l.* 10. *See Introduction, p. xx.*

FABLE XXIV.

The BUTTERFLY *and the* SNAIL.

ALL upstarts, insolent in place,
Remind us of their vulgar race.

    As, in the sun-shine of the morn,
A Butterfly (but newly born)
Sate proudly perking on a rose ;
With pert conceit his bosom glows,
His wings (all glorious to behold)
Bedropt with azure, jet and gold,
Wide he displays ; the spangled dew
Reflects his eyes and various hue. 10
His now forgotten friend, a Snail,
Beneath his house, with slimy trail
Crawles o'er the grass ; whom when
    he spys,
In wrath he to the gard'ner crys :
    What means yon peasant's daily
    toil,
From choaking weeds to rid the soil ?
Why wake you to the morning's care ?
Why with new arts correct the year ?
Why glows the peach with crimson
    hue ?   19
And why the plum's inviting blue ?
Were they to feast his taste design'd,
That vermine of voracious kind ?

Crush then the slow, the pilfring race,
So purge thy garden from disgrace.
    What arrogance ! the Snail reply'd;
How insolent is upstart pride !
Hadst thou not thus, with insult vain,
Provok'd my patience to complain ;
I had conceal'd thy meaner birth,
Nor trac'd thee to the scum of earth.
For scarce nine suns have wak'd the
    hours,   31
To swell the fruit and paint the
    flowers,
Since I thy humbler life survey'd,
In base, in sordid guise array'd ;
A hideous insect, vile, unclean,
You dragg'd a slow and noisome
    train,
And from your spider bowels drew
Foul film, and spun the dirty clue.
I own my humble life, good friend ;
Snail was I born, and snail shall end.
And what 's a butterfly ? At best, 41
He 's but a caterpillar, drest :
And all thy race (a num'rous seed)
Shall prove of caterpillar breed.

14 gard'ner] gard'ners *Underhill.*

20 plum's] plums *Underhill.*

FABLE XXV.

The SCOLD *and the* PARROT.

THE husband thus reprov'd his wife.
Who deals in slander, lives in strife.
Art thou the herald of disgrace,
Denouncing war to all thy race ?
Can nothing quell thy thunder's rage,
Which spares nor friend, nor sex, nor age ?
That vixen tongue of yours, my dear,
Alarms our neighbours far and near ;
Good Gods ! 'tis like a rolling river,
That murm'ring flows, and flows for ever !   10
Ne'er tir'd, perpetual discord sowing !
Like fame, it gathers strength by going.
   Heighday ! the flippant tongue replys,
How solemn is the fool ! how wise !
Is nature's choicest gift debarr'd ?
Nay, frown not ; for I will be heard.
Women of late are finely ridden,
A parrot's privilege forbidden !
You praise his talk, his squawling song,   19
But wives are always in the wrong.
   Now reputations flew in pieces
Of mothers, daughters, aunts and nieces,

She ran the parrot's language o'er ;
Bawd, hussy, drunkard, slattern, whore,
On all the sex she vents her fury,
Trys and condemns without a jury.
   At once the torrent of her words
Alarm'd cat, monkey, dogs and birds ;
All join their forces to confound her,
Puss spits, the monkey chatters round her,   30
The yelping cur her heels assaults,
The magpye blabs out all her faults ;
Poll, in the uproar, from his cage,
With this rebuke out-scream'd her rage.

   A parrot is for talking priz'd,
But prattling women are despis'd ;
She, who attacks another's honour,
Draws ev'ry living thing upon her.
Think, madam, when you stretch your lungs,
That all your neighbours too have tongues ;   40
One slander must ten thousand get,
The world with interest pays the debt.

19 song,] *1728 and 1729* song ; *1727.*
34-5 *So printed in the second and third editions. First edition has no white line here.*

FABLE XXVI.

The CUR *and the* MASTIFF.

A SNEAKING Cur, the master's spy,
Rewarded for his daily lye,
With secret jealousies and fears
Set all together by the ears.
Poor puss to-day was in disgrace,
Another cat supply'd her place ;

The hound was beat, the mastiff chid,
The monkey was the room forbid,
Each to his dearest friend grew shy,
And none could tell the reason why. 10
   A plan to rob the house was laid ;
The thief with love seduc'd the maid,

Cajol'd the Cur, and strok'd his head,
And bought his secresy with bread.
He next the Mastiff's honour try'd,
Whose honest jaws the bribe defy'd ;
He stretch'd his hand to proffer more ;
The surly dog his fingers tore.
  Swift ran the Cur ; with indigna-
        tion
The master took his information. 20
Hang him, the villain 's curst, he crys,
And round his neck the halter tyes.
  The Dog his humble suit preferr'd
And begg'd in justice to be heard.
The master sat. On either hand

The cited dogs confronting stand ;
The Cur the bloody tale relates,
And, like a lawyer, aggravates.
  Judge not unheard, the Mastiff
      cry'd,
But weigh the cause of either side. 30
Think not that treach'ry can be just,
Take not informers words on trust ;
They ope their hand to ev'ry pay ;
And you and me by turns betray.
  He spoke. And all the truth
      appear'd.
The Cur was hang'd, the Mastiff
      clear'd.

16 bribe] *1728*   bride *1727*.

FABLE XXVII.

The SICK MAN *and the* ANGEL.

Is there no hope ? the sick Man said.
The silent doctor shook his head,
And took his leave, with signs of
      sorrow,
Despairing of his fee to-morrow.
  When thus the Man, with gasping
      breath.
I feel the chilling wound of death.
Since I must bid the world adieu ;
Let me my former life review.
I grant, my bargains well were made,
But all men over-reach in trade ; 10
'Tis self-defence in each profession,
Sure self-defence is no transgression.
The little portion in my hands,
By good security on lands,
Is well encreas'd. If, unawares,
My justice to my self and heirs
Hath let my debtor rot in jail,
For want of good sufficient bail ;
If I by writ, or bond, or deed
Reduc'd a family to need, 20
My will hath made the world amends ;
My hope on charity depends.

When I am number'd with the dead,
And all my pious gifts are read,
By heav'n and earth 'twill then be
      known
My charitys were amply shown.
  An Angel came. Ah friend, he
      cry'd,
No more in flatt'ring hope confide.
Can thy good deeds in former times
Outweigh the ballance of thy crimes ?
What widow or what orphan prays 31
To crown thy life with length of
      days ?
A pious action 's in thy power,
Embrace with joy the happy hour ;
Now, while you draw the vital air,
Prove your intention is sincere :
This instant give a hundred pound ;
Your neighbours want, and you
      abound.
  But why such haste, the sick Man
      whines,
Who knows as yet what Heav'n
      designs ? 40

  1 Man] *1727*   man *1728 and 1729.*
  9 made,] *1729*   made. *1727 and 1728.*
  15, 16 If, unawares, . . . heirs] *Bell*   If unawares, . . . heirs, *early and most subsequent editions, including Dobson and Underhill.*

Perhaps I may recover still.
That sum and more are in my will.
  Fool, says the Vision, now 'tis plain,
Your life, your soul, your heav'n was gain ;
From ev'ry side, with all your might,
You scrap'd, and scrap'd beyond your right,
And after death would fain attone,
By giving what is not your own.
  Where there is life, there 's hope, he cry'd ;
Then why such haste ? so groan'd and dy'd.

FABLE XXVIII.

The PERSIAN, *the* SUN *and the* CLOUD.

Is there a bard whom genius fires,
Whose ev'ry thought the God in-
  spires ?
When Envy reads the nervous lines,
She frets, she rails, she raves, she
  pines,
Her hissing snakes with venom swell,
She calls her venal train from hell,
The servile fiends her nod obey,
And all *Curl*'s authors are in pay.
Fame calls up calumny and spite.
Thus shadow owes its birth to light. 10

  As prostrate to the God of day
With heart devout a *Persian* lay ;
His invocation thus begun.
  Parent of light, all-seeing Sun,
Prolific beam, whose rays dispense
The various gifts of Providence,
Accept our praise, our daily prayer,
Smile on our fields and bless the year.
  A Cloud, who mock'd his grateful
  tongue,   19
The day with sudden darkness hung,
With pride and envy swell'd, aloud
A voice thus thunder'd from the cloud.
  Weak is this gawdy God of thine,
Whom I at will forbid to shine ;
Shall I nor vows, nor incense know ?
Where praise is due, the praise be-
  stow.
  With fervent zeal the *Persian*
  mov'd
Thus the proud calumny reprov'd.
  It was that God, who claims my
  prayer,
Who gave thee birth and rais'd thee
  there :   30
When o'er his beams the veil is
  thrown
Thy substance is but plainer shown.
A passing gale, a puff of wind
Dispells thy thickest troops combin'd.
  The gale arose ; the vapor tost
(The sport of winds) in air was lost ;
The glorious orb the day refines.
Thus Envy breaks, thus Merit shines.

FABLE XXIX.

The FOX *at the point of death.*

A Fox, in life's extream decay,
Weak, sick and faint, expiring lay ;
All appetite had left his maw,
And age disarm'd his mumbling jaw.
His num'rous race around him stand
To learn their dying sire's command ;
He rais'd his head with whining moan,
And thus was heard the feeble tone.
  Ah sons, from evil ways depart,
My crimes lye heavy on my heart. 10
See, see, the murder'd geese appear !
Why are those bleeding turkeys there?

* K

Why all around this cackling train,
Who haunt my ears for chicken slain ?
  The hungry foxes round them
    star'd,
And for the promis'd feast prepar'd.
  Where, Sir, is all this dainty cheer ?
Nor turkey, goose, nor hen is here :
These are the phantoms of your brain,
And your sons lick their lips in vain. 20
  O gluttons, says the drooping sire,
Restrain inordinate desire ;
Your liqu'rish taste you shall deplore,
When peace of conscience is no more.
Does not the hound betray our pace,
And gins and guns destroy our race ?
Thieves dread the searching eye of
    power,
And never feel the quiet hour.
Old-age, (which few of us shall know,)
Now puts a period to my woe.   30
Would you true happiness attain,

Let honesty your passions rein ;
So live in credit and esteem,
And, the good name you lost, redeem.
  The counsel 's good, a fox replies,
Could we perform what you advise.
Think, what our ancestors have done ;
A line of thieves from son to son ;
To us descends the long disgrace,
And infamy hath mark'd our race. 40
Though we, like harmless sheep,
    should feed,
Honest in thought, in word, and deed,
Whatever hen-roost is decreas'd,
We shall be thought to share the
    feast.
The change shall never be believ'd,
A lost good name is ne'er retriev'd.
  Nay then, replys the feeble Fox,
(But, hark ! I hear a hen that clocks)
Go, but be mod'rate in your food ;
A chicken too might do me good. 50

21 sire,] *1729*   sire ; *1727 and 1728.*
29 know,)] know) *early editions. See Fable XXIII, l.* 30, *n.*
35 replies] *see Introduction to the Fables, l.* 1, *n.*   47 Fox] *1727* fox *1728 and 1729.*

FABLE XXX.

The SETTING-DOG *and the* PARTRIDGE.

THE ranging Dog the stubble tries,
And searches ev'ry breeze that flies ;
The scent grows warm ; with cautious
    fear
He creeps, and points the covey near.
The men in silence, far behind,
Conscious of game, the net unbind.
  A Partridge, with experience wise,
The fraudful preparation spies,
She mocks their toils, alarms her
    brood,
The covey springs, and seeks the
    wood ;   10
But ere her certain wing she tries,
Thus to the creeping spaniel cries.
  Thou fawning slave to man's deceit,
Thou pimp of lux'ry, sneaking cheat,
Of thy whole species thou disgrace,

Dogs should disown thee of their
    race !
For if I judge their native parts,
They're born with honest open hearts,
And, ere they serv'd man's wicked
    ends,
Were gen'rous foes or real friends. 20
  When thus the Dog with scornful
    smile.
Secure of wing, thou dar'st revile.
Clowns are to polish'd manners blind ;
How ign'rant is the rustick mind !
My worth sagacious courtiers see,
And to preferment rise like me.
The thriving pimp, who beauty sets,
Hath oft enhanced a nation's debts ;
Friend sets his friend, without regard ;
And ministers his skill reward.   30

Thus train'd by man, I learnt his ways,
And growing favour feasts my days.
  I might have guess'd, the Partridge said,

The place where you were train'd and fed ;
Servants are apt, and in a trice
Ape to a hair their master's vice.
You came from court, you say. Adieu.
She said, and to the covey flew.

FABLE XXXI.

The Universal APPARITION.

A RAKE, by ev'ry passion rul'd,
With ev'ry vice his youth had cool'd ;
Disease his tainted blood assails,
His spirits droop, his vigor fails,
With secret ills at home he pines,
And, like infirm old-age, declines.
  As, twing'd with pain, he pensive sits,
And raves, and prays, and swears by fits,
A ghastly phantome, lean and wan,
Before him rose, and thus began. 10
  My name perhaps hath reach'd your ear ;
Attend, and be advis'd by Care.
Nor love, nor honour, wealth nor power
Can give the heart a cheerful hour,
When health is lost. Be timely wise :
With health all taste of pleasure flies.
  Thus said, the phantome disappears.
The wary counsel wak'd his fears ;
He now from all excess abstains,
With physick purifies his veins ; 20
And to procure a sober life
Resolves to venture on a wife.
  But now again the sprite ascends,
Where'er he walks his ear attends,
Insinuates that beauty 's frail,
That perseverance must prevail,
With jealousies his brain inflames,
And whispers all her lovers names ;
In other hours she represents
His houshold charge, his annual rents,
Encreasing debts, perplexing duns, 31
And nothing for his younger sons.
  Strait all his thought to gain he turns.

And with the thirst of lucre burns ;
But when possest of fortune's store,
The spectre haunts him more and more,
Sets want and misery in view,
Bold thieves and all the murd'ring crew,
Alarms him with eternal frights,
Infests his dream, or wakes his nights.
  How shall he chase this hideous guest ? 41
Power may perhaps protect his rest ;
To pow'r he rose. Again the sprite
Besets him morning, noon and night,
Talks of ambition's tott'ring seat,
How envy persecutes the great,
Of rival hate, of treach'rous friends,
And what disgrace his fall attends.
  The court he quits to fly from Care,
And seeks the peace of rural air ; 50
His groves, his fields amus'd his hours,
He prun'd his trees, he rais'd his flowers ;
But Care again his steps pursues,
Warns him of blasts, of blighting dews,
Of plund'ring insects, snails and rains,
And droughts that starve the labour'd plains.
Abroad, at home, the spectre 's there :
In vain we seek to fly from Care.
  At length he thus the ghost addrest.
Since thou must be my constant guest, 60
Be kind, and follow me no more,
For Care by right should go before.

43 pow'r]. *See Fable I, 50, note.*

FABLE XXXII.

The two OWLS *and the* SPARROW.

Two formal Owls together sate,
Conferring thus in solemn chat.
　How is the modern taste decay'd !
Where 's the respect to wisdom paid ?
Our worth the *Grecian* sages knew,
They gave our sires the honour due,
They weigh'd the dignity of fowls,
And pry'd into the depth of owls.
Athens, the seat of learned fame,
With gen'ral voice rever'd our name ;
On merit title was conferr'd,　　11
And all ador'd th' *Athenian* bird.
　Brother, you reason well, replies
The solemn mate, with half-shut eyes ;
Right. *Athens* was the seat of learn-
　　ing,
And truly wisdom is discerning.
Besides, on *Pallas*' helm we sit,
The type and ornament of wit :
But now, alas, we're quite neglected,
And a pert sparrow 's more respected.
　A Sparrow, who was lodg'd beside,

O'erhears them sooth each other's
　　pride,　　22
And thus he nimbly vents his heat.
　Who meets a fool must find conceit.
I grant, you were at *Athens* grac'd,
And on *Minerva*'s helm were plac'd,
But ev'ry bird that wings the sky,
Except an owl, can tell you why.
From hence they taught their schools
　　to know
How false we judge by outward show,
That we should never looks esteem, 31
Since fools as wise as you might seem.
Would ye contempt and scorn avoid,
Let your vain-glory be destroy'd ;
Humble your arrogance of thought,
Pursue the ways by nature taught,
So shall ye find delicious fare,
And grateful farmers praise your care,
So shall sleek mice your chase reward,
And no keen cat find more regard. 40

FABLE XXXIII.

The COURTIER *and* PROTEUS.

WHENE'ER a courtier 's out of place,
The country shelters his disgrace ;
Where, doom'd to exercise and health,
His house and gardens own his wealth.
He builds new schemes, in hopes to
　　gain
The plunder of another reign ;
Like *Philip*'s son would fain be
　　doing,
And sighs for other realms to ruin.

　As one of these (without his wand)
Pensive, along the winding strand 10
Employ'd the solitary hour
In projects to regain his power ;
The waves in spreading circles ran,
Proteus arose, and thus began.

Came you from court ?　For in
　　your mien
A self-important air is seen.
　He frankly own'd his friends had
　　trick'd him,
And how he fell his party's victim.
　Know, says the God, by matchless
　　skill
I change to ev'ry shape at will ;　20
But yet, I'm told, at court you see
Those who presume to rival me.
　Thus said.　A snake, with hideous
　　trail,
Proteus extends his scaly mail.
　Know, says the Man, though proud
　　in place,
All courtiers are of reptile race.

Like you, they take that dreadful
  form,
Bask in the sun, and fly the storm ;
With malice hiss, with envy glote,
And for convenience change their
  coat,   30
With new-got lustre rear their head,
Though on a dunghill born and bred.
  Sudden the God a lyon stands,
He shakes his mane, he spurns the
  sands ;
Now a fierce lynx, with fiery glare,
A wolf, an ass, a fox, a bear.
  Had I ne'er lived at court, he cries,
Such transformation might surprise ;
But there, in quest of daily game,
Each able courtier acts the same. 40
Wolves, lyons, lynxes, while in place,

Their friends and fellows are their
  chace ;
They play the bear's and fox's part,
Now rob by force, now steal with art ;
They sometimes in the senate bray ;
Or, chang'd again to beasts of prey,
Down from the lyon to the ape,
Practise the frauds of ev'ry shape.
  So said. Upon the God he flies,
In cords the struggling captive tyes. 50
  Now, *Proteus*, now (to truth com-
  pell'd)
Speak, and confess thy art excell'd.
Use strength, surprise, or what you
  will,
The courtier finds evasion still ;
Not to be bound by any tyes,
And never forc'd to leave his lyes.

48 Practise] *1728 and 1729* Practice *1727.*
49–50 flies . . . tyes] *see Introduction to the Fables, l. 1, n.*

FABLE XXXIV.

The MASTIFF.

THOSE, who in quarrels interpose,
Must often wipe a bloody nose.

  A Mastiff, of true *English* blood,
Lov'd fighting better than his food,
When dogs were snarling for a bone,
He long'd to make the war his own,
And often found (when two contend)
To interpose obtain'd his end ;
He glory'd in his limping pace,
The scars of honour seam'd his face, 10
In ev'ry limb a gash appears,
And frequent fights retrench'd his
  ears.
  As, on a time, he heard from far
Two dogs engag'd in noisy war,
Away he scours and lays about him,
Resolv'd no fray should be without
  him.
  Forth from his yard a tanner flies,
And to the bold intruder cries,

  A cudgel shall correct your
    manners.
Whence sprung this cursed hate to
  tanners ?   20
While on my dog you vent your spite ;
Sirrah, 'tis me you dare not bite.
  To see the battel thus perplext,
With equal rage a butcher vext,
Hoarse-screaming from the circled
  croud,
To the curst Mastiff cries aloud.
  Both *Hockley-hole* and *Mary-bone*
The combats of my dog have known ;
He ne'er, like bullies coward-hearted,
Attacks in publick, to be parted ; 30
Think not, rash fool, to share his fame,
Be his the honour or the shame.
  Thus said, they swore and rav'd
    like thunder,
They dragg'd their fasten'd dogs
    asunder,

Fable XXXIV. MASTIFF] MASTIFFS *early and most late editions (including Dobson),
obviously wrong. Cooke and Underhill have the correction. Compare Fable XV.*

While clubs and kicks from ev'ry side
Rebounded from the Mastiff's hide.

All reeking now with sweat and blood
A while the parted warriors stood,

Then pour'd upon the meddling foe :
Who, worried, howl'd and sprawl'd below :　　40
He rose ; and limping from the fray,
By both sides mangled, sneak'd away.

36–7 *So printed in the Second and Third Editions.　First Edition has no white line here.*

FABLE XXXV.

The BARLEY-MOW *and the* DUNGHILL.

How many saucy airs we meet
From *Temple-bar* to *Aldgate-street* ;
Proud rogues, who shar'd the *South-sea* prey,
And sprung like mushrooms in a day !
They think it mean, to condescend
To know a brother or a friend ;
They blush to hear their mother's name,
And by their pride expose their shame.

As cross his yard, at early day,
A careful farmer took his way,　　10
He stop'd, and leaning on his fork
Observ'd the flail's incessant work ;
In thought he measur'd all his store,
His geese, his hogs he number'd o'er,
In fancy weigh'd the fleeces shorn,
And multiply'd the next year's corn.
A Barley-mow, which stood beside,
Thus to its musing master cry'd.

Say, good sir, is it fit or right　　19
To treat me with neglect and slight ?
Me, who contribute to your cheer,
And raise your mirth with ale and beer !
Why thus insulted, thus disgrac'd,
And that vile dunghill near me plac'd?
Are those poor sweepings of a groom,
That filthy sight, that nauseous fume
Meet objects here ?　Command it hence :
A thing so mean must give offence.
The humble Dunghill thus reply'd.
Thy master hears and mocks thy pride.　　30
Insult not thus the meek and low,
In me thy benefactor know ;
My warm assistance gave thee birth,
Or thou hadst perish'd low in earth ;
But upstarts, to support their station,
Cancell at once all obligation.

Fable XXXV. DUNGHILL] *1728 and 1729*　DUNG-HILL *1727.*
30 pride.] *1728*　pride, *1727 and 1729.*
36 obligation] *1727 and 1729*　Obligation *1728.*

FABLE XXXVI.

PYTHAGORAS *and the* COUNTRYMAN.

PYTHAG'RAS rose at early dawn.
By soaring meditation drawn,
To breathe the fragrance of the day,
Through flow'ry fields he took his way;
In musing contemplation warm,
His steps mis-led him to a farm,

Where, on the ladder's topmost round
A Peasant stood ;　the hammer's sound
Shook the weak barn.　Say, friend, what care
Calls for thy honest labour there ?　10

8 Peasant] pheasant *Underhill.*

The Clown with surly voice replies.
Vengeance aloud for justice cries :
This kite, by daily rapine fed,
My hen's annoy, my turkey's dread,
At length his forfeit life hath paid ;
See, on the wall his wings display'd,
Here nail'd, a terror to his kind,
My fowls shall future safety find,
My yard the thriving poultry feed,
And my barn's refuse fat the breed.
   Friend, says the Sage, the doom is
      wise,   21
For publick good the murd'rer dies ;
But if these tyrants of the air
Demand a sentence so severe,
Think how the glutton man devours ;
What bloody feasts regale his hours !
O impudence of power and might,

Thus to condemn a hawk or kite,
When thou perhaps, carniv-rous
    sinner,   29
Hadst pullets yesterday for dinner !
   Hold, cry'd the Clown, with passion
    heated,
Shall kites and men alike be treated ?
When Heav'n the world with crea-
    tures stor'd,
Man was ordain'd their sov'raign lord.
   Thus tyrants boast, the Sage re-
    ply'd,
Whose murders spring from power
   'and pride.
Own then this manlike kite is slain
Thy greater lux'ry to sustain ;
For * *petty rogues submit to fate*
That great ones may enjoy their state. 40

* *Garth*'s Dispensary.

---

14 hen's . . . turkey's] hens' . . . turkeys' *Bell, Dobson, Underhill.*

FABLE XXXVII.

The FARMER'S WIFE *and the* RAVEN.

WHY are those tears ? Why droops
    your head ?
Is then your other husband dead ?
Or does a worse disgrace betide ?
Hath no one since his death apply'd ?
   Alas ! you know the cause too
    well.
The salt is spilt, to me it fell.
Then to contribute to my loss,
My knife and fork were laid across,
On *friday* too ! the day I dread !
Would I were safe at home in bed ! 10
Last night (I vow to Heav'n 'tis
    true)
Bounce from the fire a coffin flew.

Next post some fatal news shall tell.
God send my *Cornish* friends be well !
   Unhappy widow, cease thy tears,
Nor feel affliction in thy fears ;
Let not thy stomach be suspended,
Eat now, and weep when dinner 's
    ended,
And when the butler clears the table
For thy dissert I'll read my fable. 20

    Betwixt her swagging pannier's
     load
A Farmer's wife to market rode,
And, jogging on, with thoughtful care
Summ'd up the profits of her ware ;

15 *This line does not begin a paragraph in the early editions. Rightly corrected by
Bell.*
   20 dissert] *early editions*   desert *Bell, Cooke, Dobson and most editions*   dessert
Underhill. A pun is perhaps intended between dessert *and* dissertation.
   21 swagging] swaggering *Underhill.*
      pannier's] *early editions, Bell*   panniers' *Cooke, Underhill, and others*   panniers
Dobson. Those who read panniers *here must do so in l. 31 below : the engraving (by
Baron) shows the eggs tumbling out of both baskets. Gay evidently used* pannier *to mean
both baskets together.*

When, starting from her silver dream,
Thus far and wide was heard her
          scream.
     That raven on yon left-hand oak
(Curse on his ill-betiding croak)
Bodes me no good. No more she
          said,
When poor blind *Ball* with stumbling
          tread   30
Fell prone ; o'erturn'd the pannier
          lay,
And her mash'd eggs bestrow'd the
          way.
     She, sprawling in the yellow road,
Rail'd, swore and curst. Thou croak-
          ing toad,

A murrain take thy whoreson throat !
I knew misfortune in the note.
     Dame, quoth the Raven, spare
          your oaths,
Unclench your fist, and wipe your
          cloaths.
But why on me those curses thrown ?
Goody, the fault was all your own ; 40
For had you laid this brittle ware
On *Dun*, the old sure-footed mare,
Though all the ravens of the *Hunderd*
With croaking had your tongue out-
          thunder'd,
Sure-footed *Dun* had kept his legs,
And you, good woman, sav'd your
          eggs.

31 pannier] *Dobson and Underhill* panniers *Cook and a few others.*
43 *Hunderd*] 1727 *Hundred* 1728 and 1729.

FABLE XXXVIII.

The TURKEY *and the* ANT.

IN other men we faults can spy,
And blame the mote that dims their
          eye,
Each little speck and blemish find,
To our own stronger errors blind.

     A Turkey, tir'd of common food,
Forsook the barn, and sought the
          wood,
Behind her ran her infant train,
Collecting here and there a grain.
     Draw near, my birds, the mother
          cries,
This hill delicious fare supplies ;   10
Behold, the busy *Negro* race,
See, millions blacken all the place !
Fear not. Like me, with freedom eat;
An ant is most delightful meat.
How blest, how envy'd were our life,

Could we but 'scape the poult'rer's
          knife !
But man, curst man on turkeys preys,
And *Christmas* shortens all our days ;
Sometimes with oysters we combine,
Sometimes assist the sav'ry chine. 20
From the low peasant to the lord,
The turkey smoaks on ev'ry board.
Sure men for gluttony are curst,
Of the sev'n deadly sins the worst.
     An Ant, who climb'd beyond his
          reach,
Thus answer'd from the neighb'ring
          beech.
Ere you remark another's sin.
Bid thy own conscience look within.
Controul thy more voracious bill,
Nor for a breakfast nations kill.   30

17 turkeys] *1728 and 1729* turkey *1727.*

FABLE XXXIX.

The FATHER *and* JUPITER.

THE Man to *Jove* his suit preferr'd ;
He begg'd a wife ; his prayer was
heard.
Jove wonder'd at his bold addressing.
For how precarious is the blessing !
 A wife he takes. And now for
 heirs
Again he worries heav'n with prayers.
Jove nods assent. Two hopeful boys
And a fine girle reward his joys.
 Now more solicitous he grew,
And set their future lives in view ; 10
He saw that all respect and duty
Were paid to wealth, to power, and
 beauty.
 Once more, he cries, accept my
 prayer,
Make my lov'd progeny thy care :
Let my first hope, my fav'rite boy,
All fortune's richest gifts enjoy.
My next with strong ambition fire,
May favour teach him to aspire,
'Till he the step of power ascend,
And courtiers to their idol bend. 20
With ev'ry grace, with ev'ry charm
My daughter's perfect features arm.
If Heav'n approve, a father 's blest.
Jove smiles, and grants his full re-
 quest.
 The first, a miser at the heart,
Studious of ev'ry griping art,

Heaps hoards on hoards with anxious
 pain,
And all his life devotes to gain. 28
He feels no joy, his cares encrease,
He neither wakes nor sleeps in peace,
In fancy'd want (a wretch compleat)
He starves, and yet he dares not eat.
 The next to sudden honours grew,
The thriving art of courts he knew ;
He reach'd the height of power and
 place,
Then fell, the victim of disgrace.
 Beauty with early bloom supplies
His daughter's cheek, and points her
 eyes :
The vain coquette each suit disdains,
And glories in her lovers pains. 40
With age she fades, each lover flies,
Contemn'd, forlorn, she pines and
 dies.
 When *Jove* the father's grief sur-
 vey'd,
And heard him Heav'n and Fate up-
 braid,
Thus spoke the God. By outward
 show
Men judge of happiness and woe :
Shall ignorance of good and ill
Dare to direct th' eternal will ?
Seek virtue ; and of that possest,
To Providence resign the rest. 50

31 want] *1728 and 1729* want, *1727*.

FABLE XL.

The two MONKEYS.

THE learned, full of inward pride,
The fops of outward show deride ;
The fop, with learning at defiance,
Scoffs at the pedant and the science :
The *Don*, a formal, solemn strutter,
Despises *Monsieur*'s airs and flutter ;

While *Monsieur* mocks the formal
 fool,
Who looks, and speaks, and walks by
 rule.
Britain, a medly of the twain,
As pert as *France*, as grave as *Spain*,

* K 3

In fancy wiser than the rest,   11
Laughs at them both, of both the jest.
Is not the poet's chiming close
Censur'd, by all the sons of prose ?
While bards of quick imagination
Despise the sleepy prose narration.
Men laugh at apes, they men con-
    temn ;
For what are we, but apes to them ?

Two Monkeys went to *Southwark*
    fair,
No criticks had a sourer air.   20
They forc'd their way through drag-
    gled folks,
Who gap'd to catch *Jack-Pudding*'s
    jokes.
Then took their tickets for the show,
And got by chance the foremost row.
To see their grave observing face
Provok'd a laugh thro' all the place.
Brothers, says Pug, and turn'd his
    head,
The rabble 's monstrously ill-bred.
Now through the booth loud hisses
    ran ;
Nor ended 'till the Show began.   30
The tumbler whirles the flip-flap
    round,
With sommersets he shakes the
    ground ;
The cord beneath the dancer springs ;

Aloft in air the vaulter swings,
Distorted now, now prone depends,
Now through his twisted arms
    ascends ;
The croud, in wonder and delight,
With clapping hands applaud the
    sight.
With smiles, quoth Pug; If pranks
    like these
The giant apes of reason please,   40
How would they wonder at our arts !
They must adore us for our parts.
High on the twig I've seen you cling,
Play, twist and turn in airy ring ;
How can those clumsy things, like
    me,
Fly with a bound from tree to tree ?
But yet, by this applause, we find
These emulators of our kind   48
Discern our worth, our parts regard,
Who our mean mimicks thus reward.
Brother, the grinning mate replies,
In this I grant that man is wise,
While good example they pursue,
We must allow some praise is due ;
But when they strain beyond their
    guide,
I laugh to scorn the mimic pride.
For how fantastick is the sight,
To meet men always bolt upright,
Because we sometimes walk on two !
I hate the imitating crew.   60

FABLE XLI.

The OWL *and the* FARMER.

An Owl of grave deport and mien,
Who (like the *Turk*) was seldom seen,
Within a barn had chose his station,
As fit for prey and contemplation :
Upon a beam aloft he sits,
And nods, and seems to think, by fits.
So have I seen a man of news
Or *Post-boy*, or *Gazette* peruse,
Smoak, nod, and talk with voice pro-
    found,

And fix the fate of *Europe* round.   10
Sheaves pil'd on sheaves hid all the
    floor :
At dawn of morn to view his store
The Farmer came. The hooting guest
His self-importance thus exprest.
Reason in man is meer pretence :
How weak, how shallow is his sense !
To treat with scorn the bird of night,
Declares his folly or his spite ;

11 *Dobson and Underhill begin a new paragraph here.*

Then too, how partial is his praise !
The lark's, the linnet's chirping lays 20
To his ill-judging ears are fine ;
And nightingales are all divine.
But the more knowing feather'd race
See wisdom stampt upon my face.
Whene'er to visit light I deign,
What flocks of fowl compose my train !
Like slaves, they croud my flight
    behind,
And own me of superior kind.
    The Farmer laugh'd, and thus
    reply'd.

Thou dull important lump of pride, 30
Dar'st thou with that harsh grating
    tongue
Depreciate birds of warbling song ?
Indulge thy spleen. Know, men and
    fowl
Regard thee, as thou art, an owl.
Besides, proud blockhead, be not vain
Of what thou call'st thy slaves and
    train.
Few follow wisdom or her rules,
Fools in derision follow fools.

FABLE XLII.

The JUGGLERS.

A JUGGLER long through all the town
Had rais'd his fortune and renown ;
You'd think (so far his art transcends)
The devil at his fingers' ends.
    Vice heard his fame, she read his
    bill ;
Convinc'd of his inferior skill,
She sought his booth, and from the
    croud
Defy'd the man of art aloud.
    Is this then he so famed for slight,
Can this slow bungler cheat your
    sight,   10
Dares he with me dispute the prize ?
I leave it to impartial eyes.
    Provok'd, the Juggler cry'd, 'tis
    done.
In science I submit to none.
    Thus said. The cups and balls he
    play'd ;
By turns, this here, that there, con-
    vey'd :
The cards, obedient to his words,
Are by a fillip turn'd to birds ;
His little boxes change the grain,
Trick after trick deludes the train. 20
He shakes his bag, he shows all fair,

His fingers spread, and nothing there,
Then bids it rain with showers of
    gold,
And now his iv'ry eggs are told,
But when from thence the hen he
    draws,
Amaz'd spectators humm applause.
    Vice now stept forth and took the
    place,
With all the forms of his grimace.
    This magick looking-glass, she
    cries,
(There, hand it round) will charm
    your eyes :   30
Each eager eye the sight desir'd,
And ev'ry man himself admir'd.
    Next, to a senator addressing ;
See this *Bank-note* ; observe the
    blessing :
Breathe on the bill. Heigh, pass !
    'Tis gone.
Upon his lips a padlock shone.
A second puff the magick broke,
The padlock vanish'd, and he spoke.
    Twelve bottles rang'd upon the
    board,
All full, with heady liquor stor'd, 40

22 spread] spreads *Dobson and Underhill, mistaking the construction.*
23. *It is tempting to replace the comma at the end of this line with a full stop or semi-colon; but lines 21 to 25 seem to describe two tricks performed with the same bag.*

By clean conveyance disappear,
And now two bloody swords are there.
    A purse she to a thief expos'd ;
At once his ready fingers clos'd ;
He opes his fist, the treasure 's fled,
He sees a halter in its stead.
    She bids Ambition hold a wand,
He grasps a hatchet in his hand.
    A box of charity she shows :
Blow here ; and a church-warden
        blows,   50
'Tis vanish'd with conveyance neat,
And on the table smoaks a treat.
    She shakes the dice, the board she
        knocks,
And from all pockets fills her box.
    She next a meagre rake address ;
This picture see ; her shape, her
        breast !
What youth, and what inviting
        eyes !

Hold her, and have her. With sur-
        prise,
His hand expos'd a box of pills ;
And a loud laugh proclaim'd his ills. 60
    A counter, in a miser's hand,
Grew twenty guineas at command ;
She bids his heir the summ retain,
And 'tis a counter now again.
    A guinea with her touch you see
Take ev'ry shape but Charity ;
And not one thing, you saw, or drew,
But chang'd from what was first in
        view.
    The Juggler now, in grief of heart,
With this submission own'd her art. 70
Can I such matchless slight with-
        stand ?
How practice hath improv'd your
        hand !
But now and then I cheat the throng :
You ev'ry day, and all day long.

          45 fled,] *1727 and 1728* fled. *1729.*   54 all] her *Underhill.*

FABLE XLIII.

The Council of HORSES.

UPON a time a neighing steed,
Who graz'd among a num'rous breed,
With mutiny had fir'd the train,
And spread dissention through the
        plain.
On matters that concern'd the State
The council met in grand debate.
A colt, whose eye-balls flam'd with
        ire,
Elate with strength and youthful fire,
In haste stept forth before the rest,
And thus the list'ning throng addrest.
    Good Gods ! how abject is our
        race,   11
Condemn'd to slav'ry and disgrace !
Shall we our servitude retain,
Because our sires have born the
        chain ?
Consider, friends, your strength and
        might ;
'Tis conquest to assert your right.

How cumb'rous is the gilded coach !
The pride of man is our reproach.
Were we design'd for daily toil,
To drag the plough-share through
        the soil,   20
To sweat in harness through the road,
To groan beneath the carrier's load ?
How feeble are the two-legg'd kind !
What force is in our nerves combin'd !
Shall then our nobler jaws submit
To foam and champ the galling bit ?
Shall haughty man my back be-
        stride ?
Shall the sharp spur provoke my
        side ?
Forbid it Heav'ns ! Reject the rein,
Your shame, your infamy disdain. 30
Let him the lyon first controul,
And still the tyger's famish'd growle ;
Let us, like them, our freedom claim,
And make him tremble at our name.

A general nod approv'd the cause,
And all the circle neigh'd applause.
 When, lo, with grave and solemn pace
A steed advanc'd before the race,
With age and long experience wise,
Around he cast his thoughtful eyes, 40
And, to the murmurs of the train,
Thus spoke the *Nestor* of the plain.
 When I had health and strength, like you,
The toils of servitude I knew ;
Now grateful man rewards my pains,
And gives me all these wide domains ;
At will I crop the year's encrease,
My latter life is rest and peace.
I grant to man we lend our pains,
And aid him to correct the plains ; 50
But doth not he divide the care,
Through all the labours of the year ?
How many thousand structures rise,
To fence us from inclement skies !
For us he bears the sultry day,
And stores up all our winter's hay ;
He sows, he reaps the harvest's gain,
We share the toil and share the grain.
Since ev'ry creature was decreed
To aid each other's mutual need, 60
Appease your discontented mind,
And act the part by Heav'n assign'd.
 The tumult ceas'd. The colt submitted,
And, like his ancestors, was bitted.

FABLE XLIV.

The HOUND *and the* HUNTSMAN.

IMPERTINENCE at first is born
With heedless slight, or smiles of scorn ;
Teaz'd into wrath, what patience bears
The noisy fool who perseveres ?

 The morning wakes, the huntsman sounds,
At once rush forth the joyful hounds ;
They seek the wood with eager pace,
Through bush, through brier explore the chase ;
Now scatter'd wide, they try the plain,
And snuff the dewy turf in vain. 10
What care, what industry, what pains !
What universal silence reigns !
 Ringwood, a dog of little fame,
Young, pert, and ignorant of game,
At once displays his babbling throat ;
The pack, regardless of the note,
Pursue the scent ; with louder strain
He still persists to vex the train. 18
 The Huntsman to the clamour flies,
The smacking lash he smartly plies ;
His ribs all welk'd, with howling tone
The puppy thus exprest his moan.
I know the musick of my tongue
Long since the pack with envy stung ;
What will not spite ? These bitter smarts
I owe to my superior parts.
 When puppies prate, the Huntsman cry'd,
They show both ignorance and pride,
Fools may our scorn, not envy raise,
For envy is a kind of praise. 30
Had not thy forward noisy tongue
Proclaim'd thee always in the wrong,
Thou might'st have mingled with the rest,
And ne'er thy foolish nose confest ;
But fools, to talking ever prone,
Are sure to make their follies known.

FABLE XLV.

The POET *and the* ROSE.

I HATE the man who builds his name
On ruins of another's fame.
Thus prudes by characters o'erthrown
Imagine that they raise their own ;
Thus scriblers, covetous of praise,
Think slander can transplant the
    bays.
Beauties and bards have equal pride,
With both all rivals are decry'd.
Who praises *Lesbia*'s eyes and feature,
Must call her sister, aukward crea-
    ture ;   10
For the kind flatt'ry 's sure to charm,
When we some other nymph disarm.

As in the cool of early day
A Poet sought the sweets of *May*,
The garden's fragrant breath ascends,
And ev'ry stalk with odour bends.
A rose he pluck'd, he gaz'd, admir'd,
Thus singing as the Muse inspir'd.

Go, Rose, my *Chloe*'s bosom grace ;
  How happy should I prove,   20
Might I supply that envy'd place
  With never-fading love !

There, Phenix-like, beneath her eye,
Involv'd in fragrance, burn and
    die !

Know, hapless flower, that thou shalt
    find
  More fragrant roses there ;
I see thy with'ring head reclin'd
  With envy and despair !
One common fate we both must
    prove ;
You die with envy, I with love.   30

Spare your comparisons, reply'd
An angry Rose, who grew beside ;
Of all mankind you should not flout
  us ;
What can a Poet do without us !
In ev'ry love-song roses bloom ;
We lend you colour and perfume.
Does it to *Chloe*'s charms conduce,
To found her praise on our abuse ?
Must we, to flatter her, be made
To wither, envy, pine and fade ?   40

FABLE XLVI.

The CUR, *the* HORSE, *and the* SHEPHERD'S DOG.

THE lad, of all-sufficient merit,
With modesty ne'er damps his spirit,
Presuming on his own deserts,
On all alike his tongue exerts ;
His noisy jokes at random throws,
And pertly spatters friends and foes ;
In wit and war the bully race
Contribute to their own disgrace :
Too late the forward youth shall
  find

That jokes are sometimes paid in
    kind,   10
Or if they canker in the breast,
He makes a foe who makes a jest.

A village-cur, of snappish race,
The pertest puppy of the place,
Imagin'd that his treble throat
Was blest with musick's sweetest
    note ;

In the mid road he basking lay,
The yelping nusance of the way ;
For not a creature past along
But had a sample of his song.   20
  Soon as the trotting steed he hears,
He starts, he cocks his dapper ears,
Away he scowers, assaults his hoof,
Now near him snarles, now barks
    aloof ;
With shrill impertinence attends,
Nor leaves him 'till the village ends.
  It chanc'd, upon his evil day,
A Pad came pacing down the way ;
The Cur, with never-ceasing tongue,

Upon the passing trav'ler sprung, 30
The horse, from scorn provok'd to ire,
Flung backward ; rolling in the mire,
The puppy howl'd, and bleeding lay ;
The Pad in peace pursu'd his way.
  A shepherd's Dog, who saw the
    deed,
Detesting the vexatious breed,
Bespoke him thus. When coxcombs
    prate,
They kindle wrath, contempt, or hate.
Thy teazing tongue had judgment
    ty'd,
Thou hadst not, like a puppy, dy'd. 40

37 coxcombs] *1727 and 1728* Coxcombs *1729.*

FABLE XLVII.

The COURT *of* DEATH.

DEATH, on a solemn night of state,
In all his pomp of terrors sate :
Th' attendants of his gloomy reign,
Diseases dire, a ghastly train,
Croud the vast court. With hollow
    tone
A voice thus thunder'd from the
    throne.
This night our minister we name,
Let ev'ry servant speak his claim ;
Merit shall bear this eban wand.
All, at the word, stretch'd forth their
    hand.   10
Feaver, with burning heat possest,
Advanc'd, and for the wand addrest.
  I to the weekly bills appeal,
Let those express my fervent zeal,
On ev'ry slight occasion near,
With violence I persevere.
  Next Gout appears with limping
    pace,
Pleads how he shifts from place to
    place,
From head to foot how swift he flies,
And ev'ry joint and sinew plys, 20

Still working when he seems supprest,
A most tenacious stubborn guest.
  A haggard spectre from the crew
Crawls forth, and thus asserts his due.
'Tis I who taint the sweetest joy,
And in the shape of love destroy :
My shanks, sunk eyes, and noseless
    face
Prove my pretension to the place.
  Stone urg'd his ever-growing force.
And, next, Consumption's meagre
    corse,   30
With feeble voice, that scarce was
    heard,
Broke with short coughs, his suit
    prefer'd.
  Let none object my lingring way,
I gain, like *Fabius,* by delay,
Fatigue and weaken ev'ry foe
By long attack, secure though slow.
  Plague represents his rapid power,
Who thinn'd a nation in an hour.
  All spoke their claim, and hop'd the
    wand.
Now expectation hush'd the band, 40

2 terrors] *early editions*   terror *all other editions cited.*

When thus the monarch from the throne.
Merit was ever modest known.
What, no physician speak his right !
None here ! But fees their toils require.
Let then Intemp'rance take the wand,
Who fills with gold their zealous hand.

You, Feaver, Gout, and all the rest,
(Whom wary men, as foes, detest,)
Forgo your claim ; no more pretend :
Intemp'rance is esteem'd a friend,   50
He shares their mirth, their social joys,
And, as a courted guest, destroys ;
The charge on him must justly fall,
Who finds employment for you all.

FABLE XLVIII.

The GARDENER *and the* HOG.

A GARD'NER, of peculiar taste,
On a young Hog his favour plac'd,
Who fed not with the common herd,
His tray was to the hall prefer'd,
He wallow'd underneath the board,
Or in his master's chamber snor'd,
Who fondly stroak'd him ev'ry day,
And taught him all the puppy's play ;
Where'er he went, the grunting friend
Ne'er fail'd his pleasure to attend.   10
  As on a time, the loving pair
Walk'd forth to tend the garden's care,
The master thus addrest the swine.
  My house, my garden, all is thine :
On turnips feast whene'er you please,
And riot in my beans and pease,
If the potatoe's taste delights,
Or the red carrot's sweet invites,
Indulge thy morn and evening hours,
But let due care regard my flowers ; 20
My tulips are my garden's pride.
What vast expence those beds supply'd !
  The Hog by chance one morning roam'd
Where with new ale the vessels foam'd ;
He munches now the steaming grains,
Now with full swill the liquor drains ;
Intoxicating fumes arise,
He reels, he rolls his winking eyes,
Then stagg'ring through the garden scowers,

And treads down painted ranks of flowers,   30
With delving snout he turns the soil,
And cools his palate with the spoil.
  The Master came, the ruin spy'd.
Villain, suspend thy rage, he cry'd :
Hast thou, thou most ungrateful sot,
My charge, my only charge forgot ?
What, all my flowers ! No more he said,
But gaz'd, and sigh'd, and hung his head.
  The Hog with stutt'ring speech returns.
Explain, Sir, why your anger burns ,
See there, untouch'd your tulips strown,   41
For I devour'd the roots alone !
  At this, the Gard'ner's passion grows ;
From oaths and threats he fell to blows :
The stubborn brute the blows sustains,
Assaults his leg and tears the veins.
  Ah, foolish swain, too late you find
That sties were for such friends design'd !
  Homeward he limps with painful pace,
Reflecting thus on past disgrace ;   50
Who cherishes a brutal mate
Shall mourn the folly soon or late.

FABLE XLIX.

The MAN *and the* FLEA.

WHETHER on earth, in air, or main,
Sure ev'ry thing alive is vain !
  Does not the hawk all fowls survey,
As destin'd only for his prey ?
And do not tyrants, prouder things,
Think men were born for slaves to kings ?
  When the crab views the pearly strands,
Or *Tagus*, bright with golden sands,
Or crawles beside the coral grove,
And hears the ocean roll above ;   10
Nature is too profuse, says he,
Who gave all these to pleasure me !
  When bord'ring pinks and roses bloom,
And ev'ry garden breathes perfume,
When peaches glow with sunny dyes,
Like *Laura*'s cheek, when blushes rise ;
When with huge figs the branches bend ;
When clusters from the vine depend ;
The snail looks round on flow'r and tree,
And cries, all these were made for me !   20

  What dignity 's in human nature,
Says Man, the most conceited creature,

As from a cliff he cast his eye,
And view'd the sea and arched sky !
The sun was sunk beneath the main,
The moon, and all the starry train
Hung the vast vault of heav'n.   The Man
His contemplation thus began.
  When I behold this glorious show,
And the wide watry world below,   30
The scaly people of the main,
The beasts that range the wood or plain,
The wing'd inhabitants of air,
The day, the night, the various year,
And know all these by heav'n design'd
As gifts to pleasure human kind,
I cannot raise my worth too high ;
Of what vast consequence am I !
  Not of th' importance you suppose,
Replies a Flea upon his nose :   40
Be humble, learn thyself to scan ;
Know, pride was never made for man.
'Tis vanity that swells thy mind.
What, heav'n and earth for thee design'd !
For thee ! made only for our need ;
That more important Fleas might feed.

14 breathes] *1728 and 1729*   breaths *1727*.

FABLE L.

The HARE *and many* FRIENDS.

FRIENDSHIP, like love, is but a name,
Unless to one you stint the flame.
The child, whom many fathers share,
Hath seldom known a father's care ;
'Tis thus in friendships ; who depend
On many, rarely find a friend.

  A Hare, who, in a civil way,
Comply'd with ev'ry thing, like *Gay*,
Was known by all the bestial train,
Who haunt the wood, or graze the plain :   10
Her care was, never to offend,
And ev'ry creature was her friend.

6-7 *Line 7 in the First Edition begins a page.   The Second and Third Editions do not show a white line ; but this is evidently a mistake.*

As forth she went at early dawn
To taste the dew-besprinkled lawn,
Behind she hears the hunter's cries,
And from the deep-mouth'd thunder
    flies ;
She starts, she stops, she pants for
    breath,
She hears the near advance of death,
She doubles, to mis-lead the hound,
And measures back her mazy round ;
Till, fainting in the publick way,   21
Half dead with fear she gasping lay.

What transport in her bosom grew,
When first the horse appear'd in view!

Let me, says she, your back ascend,
And owe my safety to a friend,
You know my feet betray my flight,
To friendship ev'ry burthen 's light.

The horse reply'd, poor honest puss,
It grieves my heart to see thee thus ;
Be comforted, relief is near ;   31
For all your friends are in the rear.

She next the stately bull implor'd ;
And thus reply'd the mighty lord.
Since ev'ry beast alive can tell
That I sincerely wish you well,
I may, without offence, pretend
To take the freedom of a friend ;
Love calls me hence ; a fav'rite cow
Expects me near yon barley mow : 40

And when a lady 's in the case,
You know, all other things give place.
To leave you thus might seem unkind ;
But see, the goat is just behind.

The goat remark'd her pulse was
    high,
Her languid head, her heavy eye ;
My back, says he, may do you harm ;
The sheep 's at hand, and wool is
    warm.

The sheep was feeble, and com-
    plain'd,
His sides a load of wool sustain'd,   50
Said he was slow, confest his fears ;
For hounds eat sheep as well as hares.

She now the trotting calf addrest,
To save from death a friend distrest.
Shall I, says he, of tender age,
In this important care engage ?
Older and abler past you by ;
How strong are those ! how weak
    am I !
Should I presume to bear you hence,
Those friends of mine may take
    offence.   60
Excuse me then. You know my
    heart.
But dearest friends, alas, must part !
How shall we all lament ! Adieu.
For see the hounds are just in view.

48 and] the *Underhill.*   63 lament !] *1727*   lament : *1728 and 1729.*

FABLES.

By the late Mr. GAY.

VOLUME THE SECOND.

LONDON:

Printed for J. and P. KNAPTON, in Ludgate-Street;
and T. COX, under the Royal-Exchange.
M DCC XXXVIII.

ADVERTISEMENT.

These FABLES were finished by Mr. GAY, and intended for the Press, a short time before his Death; when they were left, with his other Papers, to the Care of his noble Friend and Patron, the DUKE of QUEENSBERRY: His Grace has accordingly permitted them to the Press, and they are here printed from the Originals in the Author's own Hand-writing. We hope they will please equally with his former Fables, though mostly on Subjects of a graver and more political Turn: They will certainly shew Him to have been (what he esteemed the best Character) a Man of a truly honest Heart, and a sincere Lover of his Country.

EDITOR'S NOTE

[' Volume the Second ' of the *Fables* was not seen through the press by Gay, nor published until six years after his death. It is, I think, reasonable to re-edit it slightly, so as to make it conform in minor details of style and spelling with the original Fables. I have not carried this process further than I felt obliged. Even in the First Series I have allowed many inconsistencies to remain; and I have not done more than follow the common usages of the poet himself. The following are the chief alterations made; a few others are indicated in the notes. (1) Punctuation within brackets. See Fable XXIII, 1st series, l. 30, n. In the 1738 volume the second bracket almost always ousts the stop. I restore the stop, where necessary, within the bracket. (2) Spelling of *power*, *flower*, &c. In the early editions of the First Series out of some twenty-seven examples of these words there are only four instances of the spelling *pow'r*, *flow'r*. This establishes *power* as Gay's normal spelling. *Flow'ry* occurs twice, each time with the elision; *Prayer* twice, without elision. I adopt these spellings in the Second Series; though the 1738 volume generally uses the elision. The same applies to the word *general*. (3) Spelling of words ending in *-ick*. This is a debatable question. The practice varies in the First Series (see Fable XL, ll. 50, 56, and 57), but on the whole the general practice is to spell such words with a *k*. No distinction can be drawn between nouns and adjectives; nor can it be said that the more modern usage began to prevail with Gay as he wrote his Fables, since the spelling *ick* is more usual in the later than in the earlier Fables. Certain words are never spelt otherwise—*publick* for instance. But in the volume of 1738 the modern spelling, with comparatively few exceptions, is adopted. I restore the antique spelling throughout. (4) Miscellaneous words. I follow the original Fables (as against the volume of 1738) in printing *oft'* not *oft*, *'till* not *till*, *encrease* not *increase*, *lyon* not *lion*. (5) Italics. The volume of 1738 makes no use of italics. I follow the style of the original Fables.]

FABLES.

Second Series.

FABLE I.

The DOG *and the* FOX.

To a *LAWYER.*

I KNOW you Lawyers can, with ease,
Twist words and meanings as you
please ;
That language, by your skill made
pliant,
Will bend to favour ev'ry client ;
That 'tis the fee directs the sense
To make out either side's pretense.
When you peruse the clearest case,
You see it with a double face ;
For scepticism 's your profession ;
You hold there 's doubt in all ex-
pression.   10
  Hence is the bar with fees supply'd,
Hence eloquence takes either side :
Your hand would have but paultry
gleaning,
Could ev'ry man express his meaning.
Who dares presume to pen a deed,
Unless you previously are fee'd ?
'Tis drawn ; and, to augment the
cost,
In dull prolixity engrost :
And now we're well secur'd by law,
'Till the next brother find a flaw. 20
  Read o'er a will.   Was 't ever
known,
But you could make the will your
own ?

For when you read, 'tis with intent
To find out meanings never meant.
Since things are thus, *se defendendo,*
I bar fallacious *innuendo.*
  Sagacious *Porta's* skill could trace
Some beast or bird in ev'ry face ;
The head, the eye, the nose's shape
Prov'd this an owl, and that an ape. 30
When, in the sketches thus design'd,
Resemblance brings some friend to
mind ;
You show the piece, and give the hint,
And find each feature in the print ;
So monstrous like the portrait's found,
All know it and the laugh goes round.
Like him, I draw from gen'ral nature :
Is 't I or you then fix the Satire ?
  So, Sir, I beg you spare your pains
In making comments on my strains :
All private slander I detest,   41
I judge not of my neighbour's breast ;
Party and prejudice I hate,
And write no libels on the state.
  Shall not my fable censure vice,
Because a knave is over-nice ?
And, lest the guilty hear and dread,
Shall not the Decalogue be read ?
If I lash vice in gen'ral fiction,
Is 't I apply or self-conviction ?   50

  25 *se defendendo*] se defendendo *1738. I follow Gay's practice in the Quarto of 1720.*
  26 *innuendo*] innuendo *1738. See note on l. 25. Bell italicizes both phrases.*
  29 shape] shape, *1738. Compare Fable XVIII (1st Series), l. 20, and see Introduction, p. xx.*

Brutes are my theme. Am I to blame,
If men in morals are the same ?
I no man call or ape or ass ;
'Tis his own conscience holds the
  glass.
Thus void of all offence I write :
Who claims the fable, knows his right.

  A shepherd's Dog, unskill'd in
    sports,
Pick'd up acquaintance of all sorts :
Among the rest a Fox he knew ;
By frequent chat their friendship
  grew.   60
  Says *Renard*, 'tis a cruel case,
That man should stigmatize our race.
No doubt, among us rogues you find,
As among dogs and human kind ;
And yet (unknown to me and you)
There may be honest men and true.
Thus slander tries, whate'er it can,
To put us on the foot with man.
Let my own actions recommend ;
No prejudice can blind a friend :   70
You know me free from all disguise ;
My honour as my life I prize.
  By talk like this from all mistrust
The Dog was cur'd, and thought him
  just.
  As on a time the Fox held forth
On conscience, honesty, and worth,
Sudden he stopt ; he cock'd his ear ;
Low dropt his brushy tail with fear.
  Bless us ! the hunters are abroad.
What 's all that clatter on the road ?
  Hold, says the Dog, we 're safe
    from harm :   81
'Twas nothing but a false alarm.
At yonder town 'tis market-day ;
Some farmer's wife is on the way :

'Tis so, (I know her pye-ball'd mare,)
Dame *Dobbins*, with her poultry-
  ware.
  Renard grew huff. Says he, This
    sneer
From you I little thought to hear ;
Your meaning in your looks I see.
Pray, what 's dame *Dobbins*, friend,
  to me ?   90
Did I e'er make her poultry thinner ?
Prove that I owe the dame a dinner.
  Friend, quoth the Cur, I meant no
    harm :
Then why so captious ?   Why so
    warm ?
My words, in common acceptation,
Could never give this provocation.
No lamb (for ought I ever knew)
May be more innocent than you.
  At this, gall'd *Renard* winc'd and
    swore
Such language ne'er was giv'n before.
  What 's lamb to me ?   This saucy
    hint   101
Shows me, base knave, which way
    you squint.
If t'other night your master lost
Three lambs ; am I to pay the cost ?
Your vile Reflections would imply
That I 'm the thief. You dog, you
    lye.
  Thou knave, thou fool, (the Dog re-
    ply'd,)
The name is just, take either side ;
Thy guilt these applications speak :
Sirrah, 'tis conscience makes you
    squeak.   110
  So saying, on the Fox he flies.
The self-convicted felon dies.

<hr>

78 brushy] bushy *Underhill*.

FABLE II.

The VULTUR, *the* SPARROW, *and other Birds.*

To a FRIEND *in the Country.*

E'ER I begin, I must premise
Our ministers are good and wise ;
So, though malicious tongues apply,
Pray, what care they, or what care I ?
  If I am free with courts ; be 't
    known,
I ne'er presume to mean our own.
If general morals seem to joke
On ministers and such like folk,
A captious fool may take offence ;
What then ? He knows his own pre-
    tence.   10
I meddle with no state-affairs,
But spare my jest to save my ears.
Our present schemes are too pro-
    found
For *Machiavel* himself to sound :
To censure 'em I've no pretension ;
I own they're past my comprehension.
  You say your brother wants a
    place,
('Tis many a younger brother's case,)
And that he very soon intends
To ply the court and teaze his friends.
If there his merits chance to find   21
A patriot of an open mind,
Whose constant actions prove him
    just
To both a king's and people's trust,
May he, with gratitude, attend,
And owe his rise to such a friend.
  You praise his parts for bus'ness fit,
His learning, probity, and wit ;
But those alone will never do,
Unless his patron have 'em too.   30
  I've heard of times, (pray God
    defend us,)
We're not so good but he can mend
    us,)

When wicked ministers have trod
On kings and people, law and God ;
With arrogance they girt the throne,
And knew no int'rest but their own.
Then virtue, from preferment barr'd,
Gets nothing but its own reward.
A gang of petty knaves attend 'em,
With proper parts to recommend 'em.
Then, if his patron burn with lust,   41
The first in favour's pimp the first.
His doors are never clos'd to spies,
Who chear his heart with double lyes ;
They flatter him, his foes defame,
So lull the pangs of guilt and shame.
If schemes of lucre haunt his brain,
Projectors swell his greedy train ;
Vile brokers ply his private ear
With jobs of plunder for the year.   50
All consciences must bend and ply,
You must vote on, and not know why ;
Through thick and thin you must go
    on ;
One scruple, and your place is gone.
  Since plagues like these have curst
    a land,
And fav'rites cannot always stand,
Good courtiers should for change be
    ready,
And not have principles too steady ;
For should a knave engross the power,
(God shield the realm from that sad
    hour,)   60
He must have rogues or slavish fools ;
For what 's a knave without his tools?
  Wherever those a people drain,
And strut with infamy and gain,
I envy not their guilt and state,
And scorn to share the publick
    hate.

41 his] their *Underhill.*
58 too] to *The misprint is corrected in later editions.*

Let their own servile creatures rise,
By screening fraud and venting lyes :
Give me, kind heav'n, * a private
    station,
A mind serene for contemplation, 70
Title and profit I resign,
The post of honour shall be mine.
My fable read, their merits view,
Then herd who will with such a crew.

In days of yore (my cautious
    rhimes
Always except the present times)
A greedy Vultur, skill'd in game,
Inur'd to guilt, unaw'd by shame,
Approach'd the throne in evil hour,
And step by step intrudes to power :
When at the royal Eagle's ear   81
He longs to ease the monarch's care :
The monarch grants. With pride
    elate,
Behold him minister of state !
Around him throng the feather'd
    rout ;
Friends must be serv'd, and some
    must out.
Each thinks his own the best pre-
    tension ;
This asks a place, and that a pension.
The Nightingale was set aside :
A forward Daw his room supply'd. 90
    This bird, (says he,) for bus'ness fit,

Hath both sagacity and wit ;
With all his turns and shifts and tricks,
He 's docile, and at nothing sticks :
Then with his neighbours one so free
At all times will connive at me.
    The Hawk had due distinction
        shown,
For parts and talents like his own.
    Thousands of hireling Cocks attend
        him,
As blust'ring bullies, to defend him.
    At once the Ravens were dis-
        carded,   101
And Magpies with their posts re-
    warded.
    Those fowls of omen I detest,
That pry into another's nest :
State lyes must lose all good intent,
For they foresee and croak th' event.
My friends ne'er think, but talk by
    rote,
Speak what they're taught, and so too
    vote.
    When rogues like these (a Sparrow
        cries)
To honours and employments rise, 110
I court no favour, ask no place ;
From such, preferment is disgrace :
Within my thatch'd retreat I find
(What these ne'er feel) true peace of
    mind.

* ————When impious men bear sway,
    The post of honour is a private station.   ADDISON.

81 Eagle] eagle *I follow Bell in restoring capitals where it seems necessary. Otherwise only the* Vultur *and the* Sparrow *would be so dignified !*
    83 pride] proud *Underhill.*
    108 too] to *After the misprint in l. 58* too *seems a certain conjecture.*

FABLE III.

The BABOON and the POULTRY.

To a LEVEE-HUNTER.

WE frequently misplace esteem
By judging men by what they seem.
To birth, wealth, power we should
    allow
Precedence and our lowest bow :
In that is due distinction shown :
Esteem is virtue's right alone.
    With partial eye we 're apt to see
The man of noble pedigree.
We 're prepossess my lord inherits
In some degree his grandsire's merits ;
For those we find upon record,   11
But find him nothing but my lord.
    When we with superficial view
Gaze on the rich, we 're dazled too :
We know that wealth, well under-
    stood,
Hath frequent power of doing good ;
Then fancy that the thing is done,
As if the power and will were one.
Thus oft' the cheated croud adore
The thriving knaves that keep 'em
    poor.   20
    The cringing train of power survey :
What creatures are so low as they !
With what obsequiousness they bend !
To what vile actions condescend !
Their rise is on their meanness built,
And flatt'ry is their smallest guilt.
What homage, rev'rence, adoration,
In ev'ry age, in ev'ry nation,
Have sycophants to power addrest !
No matter who the power possest.   30
Let ministers be what they will,
You find their levees always fill :
Ev'n those who have perplex'd a
    state,
Whose actions claim'd contempt and
    hate,

Had wretches to applaud their
    schemes,
Though more absurd than madmen's
    dreams.
When barb'rous *Moloch* was in-
    vok'd,
The blood of infants only smoak'd ;
But here (unless all hist'ry lyes)
Whole realms have been a sacrifice. 40
    Look through all courts : 'Tis
    power we find
The general idol of mankind ;
There worshipp'd under ev'ry shape :
Alike the lyon, fox and ape
Are follow'd by time-serving slaves,
Rich prostitutes and needy knaves.
    Who then shall glory in his post ?
How frail his pride, how vain his
    boast !
The followers of his prosp'rous hour
Are as unstable as his power.   50
Power, by the breath of flatt'ry nurst,
The more it swells, is nearer burst :
The bubble breaks, the gewgaw
    ends,
And in a dirty tear descends.

    Once on a time, an ancient maid,
By wishes and by time decay'd,
To cure the pangs of restless thought,
In birds and beasts amusement
    sought :
Dogs, parrots, apes her hours em-
    ploy'd ;
With these alone she talk'd and toy'd.
    A huge Baboon her fancy took, 61
(Almost a man in size and look,)
He finger'd ev'ry thing he found,
And mimick'd all the servants round ;

14 dazled] dazzled *1738*.   *But see Fable XI (1st series), l. 14, for Gay's usual spelling.*
34 claim'd] *1738*   claim *Bell and all later. editions.*   44 fox] fox, *1738.*
59 apes] apes, *1738.*

Then too his parts and ready wit
Show'd him for ev'ry bus'ness fit.
With all these talents, 'twas but just
That *Pug* should hold a place of trust ;
So to her fav'rite was assign'd   69
The charge of all her feather'd kind ;
'Twas his to tend 'em eve and morn,
And portion out their daily corn.
  Behold him now, with haughty stride,
Assume a ministerial pride.
The morning rose. In hope of picking,
Swans, turkeys, peacocks, ducks, and chicken,
Fowls of all ranks surround his hut,
To worship his important strut.
The minister appears. The croud
Now here, now there, obsequious bow'd.   80
This praised his parts, and that his face,
T'other his dignity in place :
From bill to bill the flatt'ry ran ;
He hears and bears it like a man :
For, when we flatter self-conceit,
We but his sentiments repeat.
  If we 're too scrupulously just,
What profit 's in a place of trust ?
The common practice of the great
Is, to secure a snug retreat :   90
So *Pug* began to turn his brain
(Like other folks in place) on gain.
  An apple-woman's stall was near,
Well stock'd with fruits through all the year :

Here ev'ry day he cramm'd his guts,
Hence were his hoards of pears and nuts ;
For 'twas agreed (in way of trade)
His payments should in corn be made.
  The stock of grain was quickly spent,
And no account which way it went ;
Then too the poultry's starved condition   101
Caus'd speculations of suspicion.
The facts were prov'd beyond dispute :
Pug must refund his hoards of fruit ;
And, though then minister in chief,
Was branded as a publick thief.
Disgrac'd, despis'd, confin'd to chains,
He nothing but his pride retains.
  A Goose pass'd by ; he knew the face,
Seen ev'ry levee while in place.   110
  What, no respect ! no rev'rence shown !
How saucy are these creatures grown !
Not two days since (says he) you bow'd
The lowest of my fawning croud.
  Proud fool (replies the Goose) 'tis true,
Thy corn a flutt'ring levee drew ;
For that I join'd the hungry train,
And sold thee flatt'ry for thy grain :
But then, as now, conceited Ape,
We saw thee in thy proper shape.   120

109 Goose] goose *1738*.   119 Ape] ape *1738*.

FABLE IV.

The ANT *in Office.*

To a FRIEND.

YOU tell me that you apprehend
My verse may touchy folks offend.
In prudence too you think my rhimes
Should never squint at courtiers crimes ;

For though nor this, nor that is meant,
Can we another's thoughts prevent ?
  You ask me if I ever knew
Court chaplains thus the lawn pursue.
I meddle not with gown or lawn :

Poets, I grant, to rise must fawn. 10
They know great ears are over-nice,
And never shock their patron's vice.
But I this hackney path despise ;
'Tis my ambition not to rise :
If I must prostitute the muse,
The base conditions I refuse.
    I neither flatter nor defame ;
Yet own I would bring guilt to shame.
If I corruption's hand expose,
I make corrupted men my foes. 20
What then ? I hate the paultry tribe.
Be virtue mine : Be theirs the bribe.
I no man's property invade :
Corruption 's yet no lawful trade ;
Nor would it mighty ills produce,
Could I shame brib'ry out of use.
I know 'twould cramp most politi-
    cians,
Were they tied down to these con-
    ditions :
'Twould stint their power, their riches
    bound,
And make their parts seem less pro-
    found. 30
Were they deny'd their proper tools,
How could they lead their knaves and
    fools ?
Were this the case, let 's take a view,
What dreadful mischiefs would ensue.
Though it might aggrandize the state,
Could private lux'ry dine on plate ?
Kings might indeed their friends
    reward,
But ministers find less regard.
Informers, sycophants and spies
Would not augment the year's sup-
    plies : 40
Perhaps too, take away this prop,
An annual job or two might drop.
Besides, if pensions were deny'd,
Could avarice support its pride ?
It might ev'n ministers confound,
And yet the state be safe and sound.
    I care not though 'tis understood ;
I only mean my country's good :
And (let who will my freedom blame)
I wish all courtiers did the same. 50

Nay, though some folks the less might
    get,
I wish the nation out of debt.
I put no private man's ambition
With publick good in competition :
Rather than have our laws defac'd,
I'd vote a minister disgrac'd.
    I strike at vice, be 't where it
    will ;
And what if great folks take it ill ?
I hope, corruption, brib'ry, pension
One may with detestation mention :
Think you the law (let who will take
    it) 61
Can *scandalum magnatum* make it ?
    I vent no slander, owe no grudge,
Nor of another's conscience judge :
At him or him I take no aim,
Yet dare against all vice declaim.
Shall I not censure breach of trust,
Because knaves know themselves
    unjust ?
That steward, whose account is clear,
Demands his honour may appear ; 70
His actions never shun the light ;
He is, and would be prov'd upright.
    But then you think my fable bears
Allusion too to state affairs.
    I grant it does : And who 's so
    great,
That has the privilege to cheat ?
If then in any future reign
(For ministers may thirst for gain)
Corrupted hands defraud the nation,
I bar no reader's application. 80

    An Ant there was, whose forward
    prate
Controul'd all matters in debate ;
Whether he knew the thing or no,
His tongue eternally would go ;
For he had impudence at will,
And boasted universal skill.
Ambition was his point in view.
Thus by degrees to power he grew.
Behold him now his drift attain :
He 's made chief treas'rer of the
    grain. 90

17 nor] or *1738*.
59 pension] pension, *1738*.
39 sycophants] sycophants, *1738*.

But as their ancient laws are just,
And punish breach of publick trust,
'Tis order'd, (lest wrong application
Should starve that wise industrious
 nation,)
That all accounts be stated clear,
Their stock, and what defray'd the
 year ;
That auditors shall these inspect,
And publick rapine thus be check'd.
For this the solemn day was set ;
The auditors in council met.   100
The gran'ry-keeper must explain
And balance his account of grain.
He brought (since he could not refuse
 'em)
Some scraps of paper to amuse 'em.
  An honest Pismire, warm with zeal,
In justice to the publick weal,
Thus spoke. The nation's hoard is
 low.
From whence doth this profusion
 flow ?
I know our annual fund's amount.
Why such expence, and where 's th'
 account ?   110
  With wonted arrogance and pride,
The Ant in office thus reply'd.
  Consider, Sirs, were secrets told,
How could the best-schem'd projects
 hold ?
Should we state mysteries disclose,
'Twould lay us open to our foes.
My duty and my well-known zeal
Bid me our present schemes conceal :
But, on my honour, all th' expence
(Though vast) was for the swarm's
 defence.   120
  They pass'd th' account, as fair and
 just,
And voted him implicit trust.

Next year again the gran'ry drain'd,
He thus his innocence maintain'd.
  Think how our present matters
 stand,
What dangers threat from ev'ry hand :
What hosts of turkeys stroll for food ;
No farmer's wife but hath her brood.
Consider, when invasion 's near,
Intelligence must cost us dear ;   130
And, in this ticklish situation,
A secret told betrays the nation.
But, on my honour, all th' expence
(Though vast) was for the swarm's
 defence.
  Again, without examination,
They thank'd his sage administration.
  The year revolves. Their treasure,
 spent,
Again, in secret service went.
His honour too again was pledg'd
To satisfy the charge alledg'd.   140
  When thus, with panick shame
 possest,
An auditor his friends addrest.
  What are we ? ministerial tools.
We little knaves are greater fools.
At last this secret is explor'd ;
'Tis our corruption thins the hoard.
For ev'ry grain we touch'd, at least
A thousand his own heaps encreas'd.
Then, for his kin and fav'rite spies,
A hundred hardly could suffice.   150
Thus, for a paultry sneaking bribe,
We cheat ourselves and all the tribe ;
For all the magazine contains
Grows from our annual toil and pains.
  They vote th' account shall be in-
 spected ;
The cunning plund'rer is detected :
The fraud is sentenc'd, and his hoard,
As due, to publick use restor'd.

105 Pismire] pismire *1738*.

FABLE V.

The BEAR *in a Boat.*

To a COXCOMB.

THAT man must daily wiser grow,
Whose search is bent himself to know:
Impartially he weighs his scope,
And on firm reason founds his hope ;
He tries his strength before the race,
And never seeks his own disgrace ;
He knows the compass, sail and oar,
Or never launches from the shore ;
Before he builds computes the cost,
And in no proud pursuit is lost :   10
He learns the bounds of human sense,
And safely walks within the fence :
Thus, conscious of his own defect,
Are pride and self-importance check'd.
    If then, self-knowledge to pursue,
Direct our life in ev'ry view,
Of all the fools that pride can boast,
A coxcomb claims distinction most.
    Coxcombs are of all ranks and kind,
They're not to sex or age confin'd,   20
Or rich, or poor, or great, or small ;
And vanity besots 'em all.
By ignorance is pride increas'd ;
Those most assume who know the
    least ;
Their own false balance gives 'em
    weight,
But ev'ry other finds 'em light.
    Not that all coxcombs follies strike,
And draw our ridicule alike ;
To diff'rent merits each pretends :
This in love-vanity transcends ;   30
That, smitten with his face and shape,
By dress distinguishes the ape ;
T'other with learning cramms his
    shelf,
Knows books and all things but him-
    self.
    All these are fools of low condition,
Compared with coxcombs of ambi-
    tion ;

For those, puff'd up with flatt'ry, dare
Assume a nation's various care :
They ne'er the grossest praise mis-
    trust,
Their sycophants seem hardly just; 40
For these, in part alone, attest
The flatt'ry their own thoughts sug-
    gest.
In this wide sphere a coxcomb's
    shown
In other réalms beside his own :
The self-deem'd *Machiavel* at large
By turns controuls in ev'ry charge.
Does commerce suffer in her rights ?
'Tis he directs the naval flights.
What sailor dares dispute his skill ?
He 'll be an adm'ral when he will. 50
Now, meddling in the soldier's trade,
Troops must be hir'd, and levies
    made.
He gives embassadors their cue
His cobbled treaties to renew,
And annual taxes must suffice
The current blunders to disguise.
When his crude schemes in air are
    lost,
And millions scarce defray the cost,
His arrogance (nought undismay'd)
Trusting in self-sufficient aid,   60
On other rocks misguides the realm,
And thinks a pilot at the helm.
He ne'er suspects his want of skill,
But blunders on from ill to ill ;
And, when he fails of all intent,
Blames only unforeseen event.
Lest you mistake the application,
The fable calls me to relation.

    A Bear of shagg and manners
    rough,
    At climbing trees expert enough, 70

18 coxcomb] Coxcomb *all modern editions, wrongly.*

For dextrously, and safe from harm,
Year after year he robb'd the swarm.
Thus, thriving on industrious toil,
He glory'd in his pilfer'd spoil.
   This trick so swell'd him with conceit,
He thought no enterprise too great.
Alike in sciences and arts,
He boasted universal parts ;
Pragmatick, busy, bustling, bold,
His arrogance was uncontroul'd :   80
And thus he made his party good,
And grew dictator of the wood.
   The beasts, with admiration, stare,
And think him a prodigious Bear.
Were any common booty got,
'Twas his each portion to allot ;
For why, he found there might be picking,
Ev'n in the carving of a chicken.
Intruding thus, he by degrees
Claim'd too the butcher's larger fees.
And now his over-weening pride   91
In ev'ry province will preside.
No task too difficult was found.
His blund'ring nose misleads the hound :
In stratagem and subtile arts,
He over-rules the fox's parts.
   It chanc'd, as on a certain day,
Along the bank he took his way,
A boat, with rudder, sail and oar,
At anchor floated near the shore.   100

He stopt, and turning to his train,
Thus pertly vents his vaunting strain.
   What blund'ring puppies are mankind,
In ev'ry science always blind !
I mock the pedantry of schools :
What are their compasses and rules ?
From me that helm shall conduct learn.
And man his ignorance discern.   108
   So saying, with audacious pride
He gains the boat and climbs the side:
The beasts astonish'd line the strand.
The anchor 's weigh'd, he drives from land :
The slack sail shifts from side to side,
The boat untrimm'd admits the tide.
Born down, adrift, at random tost,
His oar breaks short, the rudder 's lost.
The Bear, presuming in his skill,
Is here and there officious still ;
'Till, striking on the dang'rous sands,
Aground the shatter'd vessel stands.
   To see the bungler thus distrest   121
The very fishes sneer and jest ;
Ev'n gudgeons join in ridicule,
To mortify the meddling fool.
The clam'rous watermen appear,
Threats, curses, oaths insult his ear ;
Seiz'd, thresh'd and chain'd, he 's dragg'd to land.
Derision shouts along the strand.

111 line] lin'd *Dobson*   lined *Underhill.*

FABLE VI.

The SQUIRE *and his* CUR.

To a COUNTRY-GENTLEMAN.

THE man of pure and simple heart
Through life disdains a double part ;
He never needs the screen of lyes
His inward bosom to disguise.
In vain malicious tongues assail ;
Let envy snarl, let slander rail,

From virtue's shield (secure from wound)
Their blunted venom'd shafts rebound.
So shines his light before mankind,
His actions prove his honest mind.   10

If in his country's cause he rise,
Debating senates to advise,
Unbrib'd, unaw'd, he dares impart
The honest dictates of his heart ;
No ministerial frown he fears,
But in his virtue perseveres.
 But would you play the politician,
Whose heart 's averse to intuition,
Your lips at all times, nay, your reason
Must be controul'd by place and
  season.   20
What statesman could his power sup-
  port,
Were lying tongues forbid the court ?
Did princely ears to truth attend,
What minister could gain his end ?
How could he raise his tools to place,
And how his honest foes disgrace ?
 That politician tops his part,
Who readily can lye with art ;
The man's proficient in his trade,
His power is strong, his fortune 's
  made.   30
By that the int'rest of the throne
Is made subservient to his own :
By that have kings of old, deluded,
All their own friends for his excluded :
By that, his selfish schemes pursuing,
He thrives upon the publick ruin.
 * Antiochus with hardy pace
Provok'd the dangers of the chace ;
And, lost from all his menial train,
Travers'd the wood and pathless
  plain :   40
A cottage lodg'd the royal guest.
The Parthian clown brought forth
  his best :
The king unknown his feast enjoy'd,
And various chat the hours employ'd.
From wine what sudden friendship
  springs !
Frankly they talk'd of courts and
  kings.
 We country-folk (the clown re-
  plies)

Could ope our gracious monarch's
  eyes :
The king, (as all our neighbours say,)
Might he (God bless him !) have his
  way,   50
Is sound at heart, and means our
  good,
And he would do it, if he cou'd.
If truth in courts were not forbid,
Nor kings nor subjects would be rid.
Were he in power, we need not doubt
  him ;
But that transferr'd to those about
  him,
On them he throws the regal cares :
And what mind they ? their own
  affairs.
If such rapacious hands he trust,
The best of men may seem unjust : 60
From kings to coblers 'tis the same :
Bad servants wound their masters
  fame.
In this our neighbours all agree :
Would the king knew as much as we.
Here he stopt short. Repose they
  sought :
The peasant slept, the monarch
  thought.
 The courtiers learnt, at early dawn,
Where their lost sov'reign was with-
  drawn.
The guard's approach our host
  alarms,
With gaudy coats the cottage
  swarms ;   70
The crown and purple robes they
  bring,
And prostrate fall before the king.
The clown was call'd ; the royal guest
By due reward his thanks exprest.
The king then, turning to the croud,
Who fawningly before him bow'd,
Thus spoke. Since, bent on private
  gain,
Your counsels first misled my reign,

* Plutarch.

47 folk] 1738 folks Bell and all other editions I have cited.
62 masters] 1738 master's all other editions cited.
69 guard's] 1738 guards' all other editions cited.

Taught and inform'd by you alone,
No truth the royal ear hath known 80
'Till here conversing. Hence, ye
    crew,
For now I know myself and you.
    Whene'er the royal ear 's engrost,
State lyes but little genius cost.
The fav'rite then securely robs,
And gleans a nation by his jobs.
Franker and bolder grown in ill,
He daily poisons dares instill ;
And, as his present views suggest,
Inflames or sooths the royal breast. 90
Thus wicked ministers oppress,
When oft' the monarch means redress.
    Would kings their private subjects
        hear,
A minister must talk with fear.
If honesty oppos'd his views,
He dar'd not innocence accuse ;
'Twould keep him in such narrow
        bound,
He could not right and wrong con-
        found.
Happy were kings, could they dis-
        close
Their real friends and real foes !   100
Were both themselves and subjects
        known,
A monarch's will might be his own :
Had he the use of ears and eyes,
Knaves would no more be counted
        wise.
But then a minister might lose
(Hard case !) his own ambitious views.
When such as these have vex'd a
        state,
Pursu'd by universal hate,
Their false support at once hath fail'd,
And persevering truth prevail'd :   110
Expos'd, their train of fraud is seen.
Truth will at last remove the screen.

    A country Squire, by whim di-
        rected,
The true, stanch dogs of chace
        neglected :

Beneath his board no hound was fed ;
His hand ne'er stroak'd the spaniel's
        head :
A snappish cur, alone carest,
By lyes had banish'd all the rest :
Yap had his ear ; and defamation
Gave him full scope of conversation.
His sycophants must be preferr'd ; 121
Room must be made for all his herd :
Wherefore, to bring his schemes about
Old faithful servants all must out.
    The Cur on ev'ry creature flew,
(As other great men's puppies do,)
Unless due court to him were shown,
And both their face and bus'ness
        known.
No honest tongue an audience found,
He worried all the tenants round, 130
For why, he lived in constant fear,
Lest truth by chance should interfere.
If any stranger dar'd intrude,
The noisy Cur his heels pursu'd ;
Now fierce with rage, now struck with
        · dread,
At once he snarled, bit and fled :
Aloof he bays, with bristling hair,
And thus in secret growls his fear.
Who knows but truth, in this dis-
        guise,
May frustrate my best guarded
        · lyes ?   140
Should she (thus mask'd) admittance
        find,
That very hour my ruin 's sign'd.
    Now in his howl's continu'd sound
Their words were lost, the voice was
        drown'd :
Ever in awe of honest tongues,
Thus ev'ry day he strain'd his lungs.
    It happen'd, in ill-omen'd hour,
That *Yap*, unmindful of his power,
Forsook his post, to love inclin'd ;
A fav'rite bitch was in the wind ; 150
By her seduc'd, in am'rous play
They frisk'd the joyous hours away.
Thus by untimely love pursuing,
Like *Antony*, he sought his ruin.

108 Pursu'd] Pursued *1738*.
136 snarled, bit] *1738*   snarl'd, [he] bit, *Dobson and Underhill, wrongly.*
144 the] *1738*   their *Dobson and Underhill.*

For now the Squire, unvex'd with noise,
An honest neighbour's chat enjoys.
Be free, (says he,) your mind impart ;
I love a friendly open heart.
Methinks my tenants shun my gate :
Why such a stranger grown of late ?
Pray tell me what offence they find.
'Tis plain, they're not so well inclin'd.
    Turn off your Cur, (the farmer cries,)   163
Who feeds your ear with daily lyes ;
His snarling insolence offends ;
'Tis he that keeps you from your friends.
Were but that saucy puppy checkt,
You'd find again the same respect.
Hear only him, he'll swear it too,
That all our hatred is to you :   170
But learn from us your true estate ;
'Tis that curst Cur alone we hate.
    The Squire heard truth. Now *Yap* rush'd in ;
The wide hall ecchoes with his din :
Yet truth prevail'd ; and, with disgrace,
The dog was cudgell'd out of place.

164 ear] ears *Underhill*.

FABLE VII.

The COUNTRYMAN *and* JUPITER

To MYSELF.

HAVE you a friend (look round and spy)
So fond, so prepossess'd as I ?
Your faults, so obvious to mankind,
My partial eyes could never find.
When, by the breath of fortune blown,
Your airy castles were o'erthrown,
Have I been over prone to blame,
Or mortified your hours with shame ?
Was I e'er known to damp your spirit,
Or twit you with the want of merit ?
    'Tis not so strange that fortune's frown   11
Still perseveres to keep you down.
Look round, and see what others do.
Would you be rich and honest too ?
Have you (like those she rais'd to place)
Been opportunely mean and base ?
Have you (as times requir'd) resign'd
Truth, honour, virtue, peace of mind?
If these are scruples, give her o'er ;
Write, practice morals, and be poor.
    The gifts of fortune truly rate ;   21
Then tell me what would mend your state.
If happiness on wealth were built,
Rich rogues might comfort find in guilt.
As grows the miser's hoarded store,
His fears, his wants encrease the more.
    Think, *Gay*, (what ne'er may be the case,)
Should fortune take you into grace,
Would that your happiness augment ?
What can she give beyond content ?
    Suppose yourself a wealthy heir,   31
With a vast annual income clear ;
In all the affluence you possess
You might not feel one care the less :
Might you not then (like others) find,
With change of fortune, change of mind ?
Perhaps, profuse beyond all rule,
You might start out a glaring fool ;
Your luxury might break all bounds ;
Plate, table, horses, stewards, hounds,
Might swell your debts : Then lust of play   41
No regal income can defray.
Sunk is all credit, writs assail,
And doom your future life to jail.

     * L

Or were you dignified with power,
Would that avert one pensive hour ?
You might give avarice its swing,
Defraud a nation, blind a king :
Then, from the hirelings in your cause
Though daily fed with false applause,
Could it a real joy impart ?   51
Great guilt knew never joy at heart.
    Is happiness your point in view ?
(I mean th' intrinsick and the true.)
She nor in camps or courts resides,
Nor in the humble cottage hides ;
Yet found alike in ev'ry sphere ;
Who finds content, will find her there.

    O'erspent with toil, beneath the
        shade
A Peasant rested on his spade.   60
    Good Gods, he cries, 'tis hard to
        bear
This load of life from year to year !
Soon as the morning streaks the skies,
Industrious labour bids me rise ;
With sweat I earn my homely fare,
And ev'ry day renews my care.
Jove heard the discontented strain,
And thus rebuk'd the murm'ring
        swain.
    Speak out your wants then, honest
        friend :
Unjust complaints the Gods offend. 70
If you repine at partial fate,
Instruct me what could mend your
        state.
Mankind in ev'ry station see.
What wish you ? tell me what you'd
        be.
So said, upborn upon a cloud,
The clown survey'd the anxious croud.
    Yon face of care, says Jove, be-
        hold ;
His bulky bags are fill'd with gold.
See with what joy he counts it o'er !
That sum to-day hath swell'd his
        store.   80
    Were I that man, (the Peasant
        cry'd),
What blessing could I ask beside ?

Hold, says the god ; first learn to
        know
True happiness from outward show.
This optick glass of intuition—
Here, take it, view his true condition.
    He look'd, and saw the miser's
        breast,
A troubled ocean, ne'er at rest ;
Want ever stares him in the face,
And fear anticipates disgrace :   90
With conscious guilt he saw him
        start ;
Extortion gnaws his throbbing heart,
And never, or in thought or dream,
His breast admits one happy gleam.
    May Jove, he cries, reject my prayer
And guard my life from guilt and
        care ;
My soul abhors that wretch's fate.
O keep me in my humble state !
But see, amidst a gaudy croud,
Yon minister so gay and proud,   100
On him what happiness attends,
Who thus rewards his grateful friends!
First take the glass, the god replies,
Man views the world with partial
        eyes.
    Good gods, exclaims the startled
        wight,
Defend me from this hideous sight !
Corruption, with corrosive smart,
Lies cank'ring on his guilty heart ;
I see him, with polluted hand,
Spread the contagion o'er the land. 110
Now av'rice with insatiate jaws,
Now rapine with her harpy claws,
His bosom tears. His conscious
        breast
Groans with a load of crimes opprest.
I see him, mad and drunk with power,
Stand tott'ring on ambition's tower :
Sometimes, in speeches vain and
        proud,
His boasts insult the nether croud ;
Now, seiz'd with giddiness and fear,
He trembles lest his fall is near.   120
    Was ever wretch like this, he cries ?
Such misery in such disguise !

---

115 I see] See *1738 and all editions. My conjecture is supported by l.* 109.

The change, O *Jove*, I disavow.
Still be my lot the spade and plough.
  He next, confirm'd by speculation,
Rejects the lawyer's occupation ;
For he the statesman seem'd in part,
And bore similitude of heart.
Nor did the soldier's trade inflame
His hopes with thirst of spoil and
    fame :   130
The miseries of war he mourn'd,
Whole nations into desarts turn'd.
  By these have laws and rights been
    brav'd ;
By these was free-born man inslav'd :
When battles and invasion cease,
Why swarm they in the lands of
  peace ?

Such change (says he) may I decline ;
The scythe and civil arms be mine !
  Thus, weighing life in each condi-
    tion,
The clown withdrew his rash peti-
    tion.   140
    When thus the god. How mortals
    err !
If you true happiness prefer,
'Tis to no rank of life confin'd,
But dwells in ev'ry honest mind.
Be justice then your sole pursuit.
Plant virtue, and content 's the fruit.
  So *Jove*, to gratify the clown,
Where first he found him set him
  down.

FABLE VIII.

The MAN, *the* CAT, *the* DOG, *and the* FLY.

To my NATIVE COUNTRY.

HAIL happy land, whose fertile
    grounds
The liquid fence of *Neptune* bounds ;
By bounteous nature set apart,
The seat of industry and art.
O *Britain*, chosen port of trade,
May lux'ry ne'er thy sons invade ;
May never minister (intent
His private treasures to augment)
Corrupt thy state. If jealous foes
Thy rights of commerce dare oppose,
Shall not thy fleets their rapine awe ?
Who is't prescribes the ocean law ? 12
    Whenever neighb'ring states con-
    tend,
'Tis thine to be the general friend.
What is 't, who rules in other lands ?
On trade alone thy glory stands.
That benefit is unconfin'd,
Diffusing good among mankind :
That first gave lustre to thy reigns,
And scatter'd plenty o'er thy plains :
'Tis that alone thy wealth supplies, 21

And draws all *Europe*'s envious eyes
Be commerce then thy sole design ;
Keep that, and all the world is thine.
    When naval traffick ploughs the
    main,
Who shares not in the merchant's
    gain ?
'Tis that supports the regal state,
And makes the farmer's heart elate ;
The num'rous flocks, that cloath the
    land,
Can scarce supply the loom's demand;
Prolifick culture glads the fields, 31
And the bare heath a harvest yields.
    Nature expects mankind should
    share
The duties of the publick care.
Who 's born for sloth ? * To some we
    find
The plough-share's annual toil as-
    sign'd ;
Some at the sounding anvil glow ;
Some the swift-sliding shuttle throw ;

* *Barrow*.

Some, studious of the wind and tide,
From pole to pole our commerce
    guide ;   40
Some (taught by industry) impart
With hands and feet the works of art ;
While some, of genius more refin'd,
With head and tongue assist man-
    kind :
Each, aiming at one common end,
Proves to the whole a needful friend.
Thus, born each other's useful aid,
By turns are obligations paid.
    The monarch, when his table 's
    spread,
Is to the clown oblig'd for bread ;   50
And, when in all his glory drest,
Owes to the loom his royal vest :
Do not the mason's toil and care
Protect him from th' inclement air ?
Does not the cutler's art supply
The ornament that guards his thigh ?
All there, in duty, to the throne
Their common obligations own.
'Tis he (his own and people's cause)
Protects their properties and laws : 60
Thus they their honest toil employ,
And with content the fruits enjoy.
In ev'ry rank, or great or small,
'Tis industry supports us all.

    The animals, by want opprest,
To Man their services addrest :
While each pursu'd their selfish good,
They hunger'd for precarious food ;
Their hours with anxious cares were
    vext ;
One day they fed, and starv'd the
    next.   70
They saw that plenty, sure and rife,
Was found alone in social life ;
That mutual industry profest
The various wants of Man redrest.
    The Cat, half-famish'd, lean and
    weak,
Demands the privilege to speak.
    Well, Puss, (says Man) and what
    can you
To benefit the publick do ?

    The Cat replies ; These teeth, these
    claws,   79
With vigilance shall serve the cause.
The mouse, destroy'd by my pursuit,
No longer shall your feasts pollute ;
Nor rats, from nightly ambuscade,
With wasteful teeth your stores in-
    vade.
    I grant, says Man, to general use
Your parts and talents may conduce ;
For rats and mice purloin our grain,
And threshers whirl the flail in vain :
Thus shall the Cat, a foe to spoil,
Protect the farmer's honest toil.   90
    Then turning to the Dog, he cry'd,
Well, Sir ; be next your merits try'd.
    Sir, says the Dog, by self-applause
We seem to own a friendless cause.
Ask those who know me, if distrust
E'er found me treach'rous or unjust.
Did I e'er faith or friendship break ?
Ask all those creatures ; let them
    speak.
My vigilance and trusty zeal   99
Perhaps might serve the publick weal.
Might not your flocks in safety feed,
Were I to guard the fleecy breed ?
Did I the nightly watches keep,
Could thieves invade you while you
    sleep ?
    The Man replies, 'Tis just and right,
Rewards such service should requite.
So rare, in property, we find
Trust uncorrupt among mankind,
That, taken in a publick view,
The first distinction is your due.   110
Such merits all reward transcend ;
Be then my comrade and my friend.
    Addressing now the Fly. From
    you
What publick service can accrue ?
    From me ! the flutt'ring insect
    said ;
I thought you knew me better bred.
Sir, I'm a gentleman. Is't fit
That I to industry submit ?
Let mean mechanicks, to be fed,
By bus'ness earn ignoble bread :   120

    73 That] That, *1738. But the comma does not help the sense of an awkward couplet :
transferred to the end of the line, as by Dobson and Underhill, it destroys all meaning.*

Lost in excess of daily joys,
No thought, no care my life annoys.
At noon (the lady's matin hour)
I sip the tea's delicious flower :
On cates luxuriously I dine,
And drink the fragrance of the vine.
Studious of elegance and ease,
Myself alone I seek to please.
  The Man his pert conceit derides,
And thus the useless coxcomb chides.
  Hence, from that peach, that
    downy seat ;   131
No idle fool deserves to eat.
Could you have sapp'd the blushing
  rind,
And on that pulp ambrosial din'd,
Had not some hand, with skill and
  toil,

To raise the tree, prepar'd the soil ?
Consider, sot, what would ensue,
Were all such worthless things as you:
You'd soon be forc'd (by hunger
  stung)   139
To make your dirty meals on dung,
On which such despicable need,
Unpitied, is reduc'd to feed.
Besides, vain selfish insect, learn,
(If you can right and wrong discern,)
That he who with industrous zeal
Contributes to the publick weal,
By adding to the common good,
His own hath rightly understood.
  So saying, with a sudden blow
He laid the noxious vagrant low : 150
Crush'd in his luxury and pride,
The spunger on the publick died.

FABLE IX.

The JACKAL, LEOPARD, and other Beasts.

To a MODERN POLITICIAN.

I GRANT corruption sways mankind,
That int'rest too perverts the mind,
That bribes have blinded common
  sense,
Foil'd reason, truth and eloquence ;
I grant you too, our present crimes
Can equal those of former times.
Against plain facts shall I engage,
To vindicate our righteous age ?
I know, that in a modern fist
Bribes in full energy subsist :   10
Since then these arguments prevail,
And itching palms are still so frail,
Hence politicians, you suggest,
Should drive the nail that goes the
  best ;
That it shows parts and penetration,
To ply men with the right temptation.
  To this, I humbly must dissent,
Premising, no reflection 's meant.

  Does justice, or the client's sense,
Teach lawyers either side's defence ?
The fee gives eloquence its spirit ; 21
That only is the client's merit.
Does art, wit, wisdom, or address
Obtain the prostitute's caress ?
The guinea (as in other trades)
From ev'ry hand alike persuades.
Man, scripture says, is prone to evil ;
But does that vindicate the devil ?
Besides, the more mankind are prone,
The less the devil's parts are shown. 30
Corruption 's not of modern date ;
It hath been try'd in ev'ry state :
Great knaves of old their power have
  fenc'd
By places, pensions, bribes, dispens'd;
By these they glory'd in success,
And impudently dar'd oppress ;
By these despotickly they sway'd,

9 fist] fist, *1738.*   23 address] address, *1738.*
37 despotickly] despoticly *1738* despotic'ly *Dobson* despotic'lly *Underhill.*

And slaves extoll'd the hand that
  pay'd ;   38
Nor parts nor genius were employ'd,
By these alone were realms destroy'd.
  Now see these wretches in disgrace,
Stript of their treasures, power and
  place ;
View 'em abandon'd and forlorn,
Expos'd to just reproach and scorn.
What now is all your pride, your
  boast ?   45
Where are your slaves, your flatt'ring
  host ?
What tongues now feed you with ap-
  plause ?
Where are the champions of your
  cause ?
Now ev'n that very fawning train,
Which shar'd the gleanings of your
  gain,   50
Press foremost who shall first accuse
Your selfish jobs, your paultry views,
Your narrow schemes, your breach of
  trust,
And want of talents to be just.
  What fools were these amidst their
    power !
How thoughtless of their adverse
  hour !
What friends were made ? A hireling
  herd,
For temporary votes preferr'd.
Was it, these sycophants to get,
Your bounty swell'd a nation 's debt ?
You're bit.   For these, like Swiss,
  attend ;   61
No longer pay, no longer friend.

  The Lyon is (beyond dispute)
Allow'd the most majestick brute ;
His valour and his gen'rous mind
Prove him superior of his kind.
Yet to Jackalls (as 'tis averr'd)
Some lyons have their power trans-
  ferr'd ;
As if the parts of pimps and spies
To govern forests could suffice.   70

Once, studious of his private good,
A proud Jackall opprest the wood ;
To cramm his own insatiate jaws,
Invaded property and laws :
The forest groans with discontent,
Fresh wrongs the general hate fo-
  ment.
The spreading murmurs reach'd his
  ear ;
His secret hours were vex'd with fear :
Night after night he weighs the case,
And feels the terrors of disgrace.   80
  By friends (says he) I'll guard my
    seat,
By those malicious tongues defeat ;
I'll strengthen power by new allies,
And all my clam'rous foes despise.
  To make the gen'rous beasts his
    friends,
He cringes, fawns and condescends ;
But those repuls'd his abject court,
And scorn'd oppression to support.
Friends must be had.   He can't sub-
  sist.
Bribes shall new proselytes enlist. 90
But these nought weigh'd in honest
  paws ;
For bribes confess a wicked cause :
Yet think not ev'ry paw withstands
What had prevail'd in human hands.
  A tempting turnip's silver skin
Drew a base hog through thick and
  thin :
Bought with a stag's delicious haunch,
The mercenary wolf was stanch ;
The convert fox grew warm and
  hearty,
A pullet gain'd him to the party : 100
The golden pippin in his fist,
A chatt'ring monkey join'd the list.
  But soon, expos'd to publick hate,
The fav'rite's fall redress'd the state.
The Leopard, vindicating right,
Had brought his secret frauds to
  light.
As rats, before the mansion falls,
Desert late hospitable walls,

  61 attend;] attend, *1738*. *All other editions cited have the semicolon, which seems*
to be needed.
  86 fawns] fawns, *1738*.

In shoals the servile creatures run,
To blow before the rising sun.　110
　The hog with warmth exprest his zeal,
And was for hanging those that steal ;
But hop'd, though low, the publick hoard
Might half a turnip still afford.
Since saving measures were profest,
A lamb's head was the wolf's request.
The fox submitted, if to touch
A goslin would be deem'd too much.
The monkey thought his grin and chatter

Might ask a nut or some such matter.
　Ye hirelings, hence, the Leopard cries,　121
Your venal conscience I despise :
He, who the publick good intends,
By bribes needs never purchase friends ;
Who acts this just, this open part,
Is propt by ev'ry honest heart.
Corruption now too late hath show'd,
That bribes are always ill-bestow'd :
By you your bubbled master's taught,
Time-serving tools, not friends, are bought.　130

FABLE X.

The DEGENERATE BEES.

To the Reverend Dr. SWIFT, *Dean of St.* PATRICK'S.

THOUGH courts the practice disallow,
A friend at all times I'll avow.
In politicks I know 'tis wrong ;
A friendship may be kept too long ;
And what they call the prudent part,
Is to wear int'rest next the heart.
As the times take a diff'rent face,
Old friendships should to new give place.
　I know too you have many foes,
That owning you is sharing those ;　10
That ev'ry knave in ev'ry station,
Of high and low denomination,
For what you speak and what you write,
Dread you at once and bear you spite.
Such freedoms in your works are shown,
They can't enjoy what 's not their own.
All dunces too in church and state
In frothy nonsense show their hate,
With all the petty scribbling crew,
(And those pert sots are not a few,)　20
'Gainst you and *Pope* their envy spurt.

The booksellers alone are hurt.
　Good Gods ! by what a powerful race
(For blockheads may have power and place)
Are scandals rais'd, and libels writ,
To prove your honesty and wit !
Think with yourself : Those worthy men
You know have suffer'd by your pen ;
From them you've nothing but your due.
From hence, 'tis plain, your friends are few :　30
Except myself, I know of none,
Besides the wise and good alone.
To set the case in fairer light,
My fable shall the rest recite ;
Which (tho' unlike our present state)
I for the moral's sake relate.

　A Bee, of cunning, not of parts,
Luxurious, negligent of arts,
Rapacious, arrogant and vain,
Greedy of power, but more of gain,　40

30 hence,] hence *1738*.

Corruption sow'd throughout the hive.
By petty rogues the great ones thrive.
  As power and wealth his views supply'd,
'Twas seen in overbearing pride ;
With him loud impudence had merit,
The Bee of conscience wanted spirit ;
And those who follow'd honour's rules
Were laugh'd to scorn for squeamish fools :
Wealth claim'd distinction, favour, grace,
And poverty alone was base ;   50
He treated industry with slight,
Unless he found his profit by 't ;
Rights, laws, and liberties give way,
To bring his selfish schemes in play :
The swarm forgot the common toil,
To share the gleanings of his spoil.
  While vulgar souls, of narrow parts,
Waste life in low mechanick arts,
Let us, (says he,) to genius born,
The drudg'ry of our fathers scorn.   60
The wasp and drone, you must agree,
Live with more elegance than we ;
Like gentlemen they sport and play,
No bus'ness interrupts the day ;
Their hours to luxury they give,
And nobly on their neighbours live.
  A stubborn Bee among the swarm,
With honest indignation warm,

Thus from his cell with zeal replied.
  I slight thy frowns, and hate thy pride.   70
The laws our native rights protect ;
Offending thee, I those respect.
Shall luxury corrupt the hive,
And none against the torrent strive ?
Exert the honour of your race ;
He builds his rise on your disgrace.
'Tis industry our state maintains :
'Twas honest toil and honest gains
That rais'd our sires to power and fame.
Be virtuous ; save yourselves from shame :   80
Know, that in selfish ends pursuing
You scramble for the publick ruin.
  He spoke ; and, from his cell dismiss'd,
Was insolently scoff'd and hiss'd.
With him a friend or two resign'd,
Disdaining the degen'rate kind.
  These drones, (says he,) these insects vile,
(I treat 'em in their proper stile,)
May for a time oppress the state.
They own our virtue by their hate ;
By that our merits they reveal,   91
And recommend our publick zeal ;
Disgrac'd by this corrupted crew,
We're honour'd by the virtuous few.

78 toil] toils *Dobson and Underhill : the misprint occurs in earlier editions, but not in Bell or Cooke.*   81 pursuing] pursuing, *1738.*

FABLE XI.

The PACK-HORSE *and the* CARRIER.

To a YOUNG NOBLEMAN.

BEGIN, my lord, in early youth
To suffer, nay, encourage truth ;
And blame me not for disrespect,
If I the flatt'rer's stile reject ;
With that, by menial tongues supply'd,

You're daily cocker'd up in pride.
  The tree 's distinguish'd by the fruit.
Be virtue then your first pursuit :
Set your great ancestors in view,
Like them deserve the title too ;   10

8 first] sole *Dobson and Underhill.*

Like them ignoble actions scorn :
Let virtue prove you greatly born.
  Though with less plate their side-
    board shone,
Their conscience always was their
    own ;
They ne'er at levees meanly fawn'd,
Nor was their honour yearly pawn'd ;
Their hands, by no corruption stain'd,
The ministerial bribe disdain'd ;
They serv'd the crown with loyal zeal,
Yet jealous of the publick weal   20
They stood the bulwark of our laws,
And wore at heart their country's
    cause ;
By neither place or pension bought,
They spoke and voted as they
    thought.
Thus did your sires adorn their seat ;
And such alone are truly great.
If you the paths of learning slight,
You're but a dunce in stronger light :
In foremost rank, the coward, plac'd,
Is more conspicuously disgrac'd.   30
If you, to serve a paultry end,
To knavish jobs can condescend,
We pay you the contempt that's due ;
In that you have precedence too.
  Whence had you this illustrious
    name ?
From virtue and unblemish'd fame.
By birth the name alone descends ;
Your honour on yourself depends.
Think not your coronet can hide
Assuming ignorance and pride :   40
Learning by study must be won,
'Twas ne'er entail'd from son to son.
Superior worth your rank requires,
For that mankind reveres your sires :
If you degen'rate from your race,
Their merits heighten your disgrace.

A Carrier ev'ry night and morn
Would see his horses eat their corn :
This sunk the hostler's vails, 'tis true ;

But then his horses had their due. 50
Were we so cautious in all cases,
Small gain would rise from greater
    places.
  The manger now had all its mea-
    sure,
He heard the grinding teeth with
    pleasure ;
When all at once confusion rung,
They snorted, jostled, bit and flung.
A Pack-horse turn'd his head aside,
Foaming, his eye-balls swell'd with
    pride.
  Good Gods ! (says he) how hard 's
    my lot !
Is then my high descent forgot ? 60
Reduc'd to drudg'ry and disgrace,
(A life unworthy of my race,)
Must I too bear the vile attacks
Of ragged scrubs and vulgar hacks ?
See scurvy *Roan*, that brute ill-
    bred,
Dares from the manger thrust my
    head !
Shall I, who boast a noble line,
On offals of these creatures dine ?
Kick'd by old *Ball* ! so mean a foe !
My honour suffers by the blow. 70
Newmarket speaks my grandsire's
    fame,
All jockeys still revere his name :
There yearly are his triumphs told,
There all his massy plates enroll'd.
Whene'er led forth upon the plain,
You saw him with a liv'ry train ;
Returning too, with laurels crown'd,
You heard the drums and trumpets
    sound.
Let it then, Sir, be understood,
Respect 's my due ; for I have blood.
  Vain-glorious fool, (the Carrier
    cry'd,)   81
Respect was never paid to pride.
Know 'twas thy giddy, wilful heart
Reduc'd thee to this slavish part.

---

20 weal] weal, *1738.* *I think this makes the sense of the passage clearer.* Dobson
and Underhill *retain the comma after* weal, *but place a semicolon after* zeal *and a comma
after* Yet. *An alternative treatment is to read l. 20 with l. 19, and regard the comma
after* weal *as equivalent to a semicolon.*
23 or] *sic.* My York edition, 1806, *emends to* nor.

Did not thy headstrong youth disdain
To learn the conduct of the rein ?
Thus coxcombs, blind to real merit,
In vicious frolicks fancy spirit.
What is't to me by whom begot ?
Thou restif, pert, conceited sot.   90
Your sires I rev'rence ; 'tis their due :
But, worthless fool, what 's that to you ?
Ask all the carriers on the road,
They'll say thy keeping 's ill-bestow'd.
Then vaunt no more thy noble race,
That neither mends thy strength or pace.
What profits me thy boast of blood ?
An ass hath more intrinsick good.
By outward show let 's not be cheated :   99
An ass should like an ass be treated.

FABLE XII

Pan *and* Fortune.

To a Young Heir.

Soon as your father's death was known,
(As if th' estate had been their own,)
The gamesters outwardly exprest
The decent joy within your breast.
So lavish in your praise they grew,
As spoke their certain hopes in you.
   One counts your income of the year,
How much in ready money clear.
No house, says he, is more compleat,
The garden's elegant and great.   10
How fine the park around it lies !
The timber 's of a noble size.
Then count his jewels and his plate.
Besides, 'tis no entail'd estate.
If cash run low, his lands in fee
Are or for sale or mortgage free.
   Thus they, before you threw the main,
Seem'd to anticipate their gain.
   Would you, when thieves are known abroad,   19
Bring forth your treasures in the road?
Would not the fool abett the stealth,
Who rashly thus expos'd his wealth ?
Yet this you do, whene'er you play
Among the gentlemen of prey.

Could fools to keep their own contrive,
On what, on whom could gamesters thrive ?
Is it in charity you game,
To save your worthy gang from shame ?
Unless you furnish'd daily bread,
Which way could idleness be fed ?   30
Could these professors of deceit
Within the law no longer cheat,
They must run bolder risques for prey,
And strip the trav'ler on the way.
Thus in your annual rents they share,
And 'scape the noose from year to year.
   Consider, e'er you make the bett,
That sum might cross your taylor's debt.
When you the pilf'ring rattle shake,
Is not your honour too at stake ?   40
Must you not by mean lyes evade
To-morrow's duns from ev'ry trade ?
By promises so often paid,
Is yet your taylor's bill defray'd ?

18 Seem'd] *1738.* Seem *all other editions cited.*
19 are] were *Dobson and Underhill : the wrong reading occurs in earlier editions, but not in Bell or Cooke.*
36 'scape] scape *1738.*

Must you not pitifully fawn,
To have your butcher's writ with-
    drawn ?
This must be done. In debts of play
Your honour suffers no delay ;
And not this year's and next year's
    rent
The sons of rapine can content.   50
  Look round. The wrecks of play
    behold,
Estates dismember'd,   mortgag'd,
    sold !
Their owners, now to jails confin'd,
Show equal poverty of mind.
Some, who the spoil of knaves were
    made,
Too late attempt to learn their trade.
Some, for the folly of one hour,
Become the dirty tools of power,
And, with the mercenary list,
Upon court-charity subsist.   60
  You 'll find at last this maxim true,
Fools are the game which knaves
    pursue.

  The forest (a whole cent'ry's shade)
Must be one wasteful ruin made :
No mercy 's shown to age or kind,
The general massacre is sign'd ;
The park too shares the dreadful fate,
For duns grow louder at the gate.
Stern clowns, obedient to the squire,
(What will not barb'rous hands for
    hire ?)   70
With brawny arms repeat the stroke ;
Fall'n are the elm and rev'rend oak ;
Through the long wood loud axes
    sound,
And eccho groans with ev'ry wound.
  To see the desolation spread,
Pan drops a tear, and hangs his head :
His bosom now with fury burns,
Beneath his hoof the dice he spurns ;
Cards too, in peevish passion torn,
The sport of whirling winds are born.
  To snails invet'rate hate I bear,   81
Who spoil the verdure of the year ;
The caterpillar I detest,

The blooming spring's voracious
    pest ;
The locust too, whose rav'nous band
Spreads sudden famine o'er the land.
But what are these ? The dice's
    throw
At once hath laid a forest low :
The cards are dealt, the bett is made,
And the wide park hath lost its shade.
Thus is my kingdom's pride defac'd,
And all its antient glories waste.   92
All this (he cries) is Fortune's doing,
'Tis thus she meditates my ruin :
By Fortune, that false, fickle jade,
More havock in one hour is made,
Than all the hungry insect race,
Combin'd, can in an age deface.
  Fortune, by chance, who near him
    past,
O'erheard the vile aspersion cast.
  Why, *Pan*, (says she,) what 's all
    this rant ?   101
'Tis ev'ry country bubble's cant.
Am I the patroness of vice ?
Is 't I who cog or palm the dice ?
Did I the shuffling art reveal,
To mark the cards, or range the deal ?
In all th' employments men pursue,
I mind the least what gamesters do.
There may (if computation 's just)
One now and then my conduct trust :
I blame the fool ; for what can I,   111
When ninety-nine my power defy ?
These trust alone their fingers ends,
And not one stake on me depends.
Whene'er the gaming board is set,
Two classes of mankind are met ;
But if we count the greedy race,
The knaves fill up the greater space.
'Tis a gross error, held in schools,
That Fortune always favours fools :
In play it never bears dispute ;   121
That doctrine these fell'd oaks con-
    fute.
Then why to me such rancour show ?
'Tis Folly, *Pan*, that is thy foe.
By me his late estate he won,
But he by Folly was undone.

FABLE XIII.

Plutus, Cupid, *and* Time.

Of all the burthens man must bear,
Time seems most galling and severe ;
Beneath this grievous load opprest
We daily meet some friend distrest.
  What can one do ? I rose at nine.
'Tis full six hours before we dine :
Six hours ! no earthly thing to do !
Would I had doz'd in bed 'till two.
  A pamphlet is before him spread,
And almost half a page is read ;   10
Tir'd with the study of the day,
The flutt'ring sheets are tost away.
He opes his snuff-box, hums an air,
Then yawns and stretches in his chair.
  Not twenty, by the minute-hand !
Good Gods, says he, my watch must stand !
How muddling 'tis on books to pore !
I thought I'd read an hour or more.
The morning, of all hours, I hate. 19
One can't contrive to rise too late.
  To make the minutes faster run,
Then too his tiresome self to shun,
To the next coffee-house he speeds,
Takes up the news, some scraps he reads.
Saunt'ring, from chair to chair he trails,
Now drinks his tea, now bites his nails :
He spies a partner of his woe ;
By chat afflictions lighter grow ;
Each other's grievances they share,
And thus their dreadful hours compare. 30
  Says *Tom*, since all men must confess
That time lies heavy more or less ;
Why should it be so hard to get,
'Till two, a party at piquet ?
Play might relieve the lagging morn :
By cards long wintry nights are born.
Does not quadrille amuse the fair,

Night after night, throughout the year ?
Vapours and spleen forgot, at play
They cheat uncounted hours away. 40
  My case, says *Will*, then must be hard,
By want of skill from play debarr'd.
Courtiers kill time by various ways ;
Dependence wears out half their days.
How happy these, whose time ne'er stands !
Attendance takes it off their hands.
Were it not for this cursed shower,
The park had whil'd away an hour.
At court, without or place or view,
I daily lose an hour or two : 50
It fully answers my design,
When I have pick'd up friends to dine.
The tavern makes our burthen light ;
Wine puts our time and care to flight.
At six (hard case !) they call to pay.
Where can one go ? I hate the play.
From six till ten ! Unless in sleep,
One cannot spend the hours so cheap.
The comedy 's no sooner done,
But some assembly is begun. 60
Loit'ring from room to room I stray,
Converse, but nothing hear or say ;
Quite tir'd, from fair to fair I roam.
So soon ! I dread the thoughts of home.
From thence, to quicken slow-pac'd night,
Again my tavern friends invite ;
Here too our early mornings pass,
'Till drowsy sleep retards the glass.
  Thus they their wretched life bemoan, 69
And make each other's case their own.
  Consider, friends, no hour rolls on,
But something of your grief is gone.
Were you to schemes of bus'ness bred,
Did you the paths of learning tread,

Your hours, your days would fly too
    fast ;
You 'd then regret the minute past.
Time 's fugitive and light as wind ;
'Tis indolence that clogs your mind :
That load from off your spirits shake,
You 'll own, and grieve for your mis-
    take.   80
A while your thoughtless spleen sus-
    pend,
Then read ; and (if you can) attend.

As *Plutus*, to divert his care,
Walk'd forth one morn to take the
    air,
Cupid o'ertook his strutting pace.
Each star'd upon the stranger's face,
'Till recollection set 'em right ;
For each knew t' other but by sight.
After some complimental talk,
Time met 'em, bow'd, and join'd their
    walk.   90
Their chat on various subjects ran,
But most, what each had done for
    man.
Plutus assumes a haughty air,
Just like our purse-proud fellows here.
Let kings, (says he,) let coblers tell,
Whose gifts among mankind excell.
Consider courts : What draws their
    train ?
Think you 'tis loyalty or gain ?
That statesman hath the strongest
    hold
Whose tool of politicks is gold :   100
By that, in former reigns, 'tis said,
The knave in power hath senates led :
By that alone he sway'd debates,
Enrich'd himself, and beggar'd states.
Forgo your boast. You must con-
    clude,
That 's most esteem'd that 's most
    pursu'd.
Think too, in what a woful plight
That wretch must live whose pocket 's
    light :
Are not his hours by want deprest ?
Penurious care corrodes his breast :

Without respect, or love, or friends,
His solitary day descends.   112
  You might, says *Cupid*, doubt my
    parts,
My knowledge too in human hearts,
Should I the power of gold dispute,
Which great examples might confute.
I know, when nothing else prevails,
Persuasive money seldom fails ;
That beauty too (like other wares)
Its price, as well as conscience, bears.
Then marriage (as of late profest) 121
Is but a money-job at best :
Consent, compliance may be sold ;
But love 's beyond the price of gold.
Smugglers there are, who, by retale,
Expose what they call love to sale :
Such bargains are an arrant cheat ;
You purchase flatt'ry and deceit.
Those who true love have ever try'd,
(The common cares of life supply'd,)
No wants endure, no wishes make,
But ev'ry réal joy partake ;   132
All comfort on themselves depends,
They want nor power, nor wealth,
    nor friends :
Love then hath ev'ry bliss in store ;
'Tis friendship, and 'tis something
    more :
Each other ev'ry wish they give.
Not to know love, is not to live.
  Or love, or money, (Time reply'd,)
Were men the question to decide, 140
Would bear the prize : on both intent
My boon 's neglected or mispent.
'Tis I who measure vital space,
And deal out years to human race :
Though little priz'd and seldom
    sought,
Without me love and gold are nought.
How does the miser time employ ?
Did I e'er see him life enjoy ?
By me forsook, the hoards he won
Are scatter'd by his lavish son.   150
By me all useful arts are gain'd,
Wealth, learning. wisdom is attain'd.
Who then would think (since such my
    power)

96 excell] excel *1738*.

That e'er I knew an idle hour ?
So subtile and so swift I fly,
Love 's not more fugitive than I.
Who hath not heard coquettes com-
plain
Of days, months, years, mispent in
vain ?
For time misus'd they pine and waste,
And love's sweet pleasures never
taste.   160
Those who direct their time aright,
If love or wealth their hopes excite,

166 known !] known ? *1738*.

In each pursuit fit hours employ'd,
And both by time have been enjoy'd.
How heedless then are mortals grown !
How little is their int'rest known !
In ev'ry view they ought to mind me,
For when once lost they never find me.
He spoke. The gods no more con-
test,
And his superior gift confest ;   170
That Time (when truly understood)
Is the most precious earthly good.

171 Time] time *1738*.

FABLE XIV.

The OWL, *the* SWAN, *the* COCK, *the* SPIDER, *the* ASS, *and the* FARMER.

To a MOTHER.

CONVERSING with your sprightly boys,
Your eyes have spoke the mother's
joys.
With what delight I've heard you
quote
Their sayings in imperfect note !
I grant, in body and in mind,
Nature appears profusely kind.
Trust not to that. Act you your part;
Imprint just morals on their heart ;
Impartially their talents scan :
Just education forms the man.   10
Perhaps (their genius yet unknown)
Each lot of life's already thrown ;
That this shall plead, the next shall
fight,
The last assert the church's right.
I censure not the fond intent ;
But how precarious is th' event !
By talents misapplied and crost,
Consider, all your sons are lost.
One day (the tale 's by *Martial*
penn'd)
A father thus address'd his friend. 20

To train my boy and call forth sense,
You know I've stuck at no expence ;
I've try'd him in the sev'ral arts,
(The lad, no doubt, hath latent parts,)
Yet trying all he nothing knows ;
But crablike rather backward goes.
Teach me what yet remains undone ;
'Tis your advice shall fix my son.
Sir, says the friend, I've weigh'd the
matter ;
Excuse me, for I scorn to flatter ; 30
Make him (nor think his genius
checkt)
A herald or an architect.
Perhaps (as commonly 'tis known,
He heard th' advice and took his own.
The boy wants wit ; he 's sent to
school,
Where learning but improves the
fool :
The college next must give him parts,
And cram him with the lib'ral arts.
Whether he blunders at the bar,
Or owes his infamy to war,   40

Or if by licence or degree
The sexton share the doctor's fee,
Or from the pulpit by the hour
He weekly floods of nonsense pour,
We find (th' intent of nature foil'd)
A taylor or a butcher spoil'd.
   Thus ministers have royal boons
Conferr'd on blockheads and buf-
   foons :
In spite of nature, merit, wit,
Their friends for ev'ry post were fit. 50
   But now let ev'ry muse confess
That merit finds its due success :
Th' examples of our days regard ;
Where's virtue seen without reward ?
Distinguish'd and in place you find
Desert and worth of ev'ry kind.
Survey the rev'rend bench, and see
Religion, learning, piety :
The patron, e'er he recommends,
Sees his own image in his friends. 60
Is honesty disgrac'd and poor ?
What is't to us what was before ?
   We all of times corrupt have heard,
When paultry minions were preferr'd ;
When all great offices, by dozens,
Were fill'd by brothers, sons, and
   cozens.
What matter ignorance and pride ?
The man was happily ally'd.
Provided that his clerk was good,
What though he nothing understood ?
In church and state, the sorry race 71
Grew more conspicuous fools in place.
Such heads, as then a treaty made,
Had bungled in the cobler's trade.
   Consider, patrons, that such elves
Expose your folly with themselves.
'Tis yours, as 'tis the parent's care,
To fix each genius in its sphere.
Your partial hand can wealth dis-
   pense,
But never give a blockhead sense. 80

   An Owl of magisterial air,
Of solemn voice, of brow austere,
Assum'd the pride of human race,
And bore his wisdom in his face.

Not to depreciate learned eyes,
I've seen a pedant look as wise.
   Within a barn, from noise retir'd,
He scorn'd the world, himself admir'd,
And, like an ancient sage, conceal'd
The follies publick life reveal'd. 90
   Philosophers of old, he read,
Their country's youth to science bred,
Their manners form'd for ev'ry sta-
   tion,
And destin'd each his occupation.
When *Xenophon*, by numbers brav'd,
Retreated, and a people sav'd,
That laurel was not all his own ;
The plant by *Socrates* was sown.
To *Aristotle's* greater name
The *Macedonian* ow'd his fame. 100
   Th' *Athenian* bird, with pride re-
   plete,
Their talents equall'd in conceit ;
And, copying the *Socratick* rule,
Set up for master of a school.
Dogmatick jargon learnt by heart,
Trite sentences, hard terms of art,
To vulgar ears seem'd so profound,
They fancy'd learning in the sound.
   The school had fame : the crouded
   place 110
With pupils swarm'd of ev'ry race.
With these the Swan's maternal care
Had sent her scarce-fledg'd cygnet
   heir :
The Hen (though fond and loth to
   part)
Here lodg'd the darling of her heart :
The Spider, of mechanick kind,
Aspir'd to science more refin'd :
The Ass learnt metaphors and tropes,
But most on musick fix'd his hopes.
   The pupils now, advanc'd in age, 120
Were call'd to tread life's busy stage ;
And to the master 'twas submitted,
That each might to his part be fitted.
The Swan, says he, in arms shall
   shine :
The soldier's glorious toil be thine.
   The Cock shall mighty wealth
   attain :

42 share] shares *Dobson and Underhill, and some earlier editions, but not Bell or Cooke.*   60 friends] *1738* friend's *all other editions cited.*

Go, seek it on the stormy main ;
    The court shall be the Spider's
        sphere :
Power, fortune shall reward him there.
    In musick's art the Ass's fame   130
Shall emulate *Corelli's* name.
    Each took the part that he advis'd,
And all were equally despis'd.
A Farmer, at his folly mov'd,
The dull preceptor thus reprov'd.
    Blockhead, says he, by what you 've
        done,
One would have thought 'em each
        your son ;

For parents, to their offspring blind,
Consult nor parts nor turn of mind ;
But ev'n in infancy decree   140
What this, what t'other son shall be.
Had you with judgment weigh'd the
        case,
Their genius thus had fix'd their place :
The Swan had learnt the sailor's art ;
The Cock had play'd the soldier's
        part ;
The Spider in the weaver's trade
With credit had a fortune made ;
But for the fole, in ev'ry class
The blockhead had appear'd an Ass.

148 fole] *1738*   fool *some later editions*   foal *Bell, Cooke, Dobson, Underhill.*

FABLE XV.

The COOK-MAID, *the* TURNSPIT, *and the* OX.

To a POOR MAN.

CONSIDER man in ev'ry sphere ;
Then tell me, is your lot severe ?
'Tis murmur, discontent, distrust,
That makes you wretched.   God is
        just.
I grant that hunger must be fed,
That toil too earns thy daily bread.
What then ! thy wants are seen and
        known ;
But ev'ry mortal feels his own.
We're born a restless needy crew :   9
Show me the happier man than you.
    Adam, though blest above his kind,
For want of social woman pin'd :
Eve's wants the subtile serpent saw,
Her fickle taste transgress'd the law :
Thus fell our sire ; and their disgrace
The curse entail'd on human race.
    When *Philip's* son, by glory led,
Had o'er the globe his empire spread ;

When altars to his name were drest,
That he was man his tears confest.   20
    The hopes of avarice are checkt :
The proud man always wants respect.
What various wants on power attend !
Ambition never gains its end.
Who hath not heard the rich com-
        plain
Of surfeits and corporeal pain ?
He, barr'd from ev'ry use of wealth,
Envies the plowman's strength and
        health ;
Another in a beauteous wife
Finds all the miseries of life ;   30
Domestick jars and jealous fear
Embitter all his days with care.
This wants an heir ; the line is lost :
Why was that vain entail engrost ?
Canst thou discern another's mind ?
What is't you envy ?   Envy's blind.

13 subtile] subtle *1738.*

23 attend !] attend ? *1738.*

Tell envy, when she would annoy,
That thousands want what you enjoy.

The dinner must be dish'd at one.
Where's this vexatious *Turnspit*
        gone ?   40
Unless the skulking cur is caught,
The sir-loin 's spoil'd and I'm in fault.
Thus said ; (for sure you'll think it fit
That I the Cook-maid's oaths omit)
With all the fury of a cook,
Her cooler kitchin *Nan* forsook ;
The broomstick o'er her head she
        waves,
She sweats, she stamps, she puffs, she
        raves ;
The sneaking cur before her flies,
She whistles, calls, fair speech she
        tries,   50
These nought avail ; her choler
        burns,
The fist and cudgel threat by turns.
With hasty stride she presses near,
He slinks aloof, and howls with fear.
    Was ever cur so curs'd, he cry'd,
What star did at my birth preside !
Am I for life by compact bound
To tread the wheel's eternal round ?
Inglorious task ! Of all our race
No slave is half so mean and base. 60
Had fate a kinder lot assign'd,
And form'd me of the lap-dog kind,
I then, in higher life employ'd,
Had indolence and ease enjoy'd,
And, like a gentleman carest,
Had been the lady's fav'rite guest.
Or were I sprung from spaniel line,
Was his sagacious nostril mine,
By me, their never erring guide,
From wood and plain their feasts
        supply'd,   70
Knights, squires, attendant on my
        pace,
Had shar'd the pleasures of the chace.

Endu'd with native strength and fire,
Why call'd I not the lyon sire ?
A lyon ! such mean views I scorn.
Why was I not of woman born ?
Who dares with reason's power con-
        tend ?
On man we brutal slaves depend ;
To him all creatures tribute pay,
And luxury employs his day.   80
    An Ox by chance o'erheard his
        moan,
And thus rebuk'd the lazy drone.
    Dare you at partial fate repine ?
How kind's your lot compared with
        mine !
Decreed to toil, the barb'rous knife
Hath sever'd me from social life ;
Urg'd by the stimulating goad,
I drag the cumbrous waggon's load ;
'Tis mine to tame the stubborn plain,
Break the stiff soil, and house the
        grain ;   90
Yet I without a murmur bear
The various labours of the year.
But then consider that one day
(Perhaps the hour's not far away)
You, by the duties of your post,
Shall turn the spit when I'm the
        roast ;
And for reward shall share the feast,
I mean, shall pick my bones at least.
    'Till now, th' astonish'd Cur replies,
I look'd on all with envious eyes ; 100
How false we judge by what appears !
All creatures feel their sev'ral cares.
If thus yon mighty beast complains,
Perhaps man knows superior pains.
Let envy then no more torment.
Think on the Ox, and learn content.
    Thus said ; close-following at her
        heel,
With chearful heart he mounts the
        wheel.

99 Cur] cur *1738.*

FABLE XVI.

The RAVENS, the SEXTON, and the EARTH-WORM.

To LAURA.

LAURA, methinks you're over nice.
True. Flatt'ry is a shocking vice ;
Yet sure, whene'er the praise is just,
One may commend without disgust.
Am I a privilege deny'd,
Indulg'd by ev'ry tongue beside ?
How singular are all your ways ;
A woman, and averse to praise !
If 'tis offence such truths to tell,
Why do your merits thus excell ?   10
 Since then I dare not speak my mind,
A truth conspicuous to mankind ;
Though in full lustre ev'ry grace
Distinguish your celestial face,
Though beauties of inferior ray
(Like stars before the orb of day)
Turn pale and fade : I check my lays,
Admiring what I dare not praise.
 If you the tribute due disdain,
The muse's mortifying strain   20
Shall, like a woman, in meer spight
Set beauty in a moral light.
 Though such revenge might shock the ear
Of many a celebrated fair ;
I mean that superficial race
Whose thoughts ne'er reach beyond their face,
What's that to you ? I but displease
Such ever-girlish ears as these.
Virtue can brook the thoughts of age,
That lasts the same through ev'ry stage.   30
Though you by time must suffer more
Than ever woman lost before,
To age is such indiff'rence shown,
As if your face were not your own.
 Were you by *Antoninus* taught,
Or is it native strength of thought,

That thus, without concern or fright,
You view yourself by reason's light ?
 Those eyes of so divine a ray,
What are they ? mould'ring, mortal clay.   40
Those features, cast in heav'nly mould,
Shall, like my coarser earth, grow old;
Like common grass, the fairest flower
Must feel the hoary season's power.
 How weak, how vain is human pride !
Dares man upon himself confide ?
The wretch, who glories in his gain,
Amasses heaps on heaps in vain.
Why lose we life in anxious cares
To lay in hoards for future years ?   50
Can those (when tortur'd by disease)
Chear our sick heart, or purchase ease ?
Can those prolong one gasp of breath,
Or calm the troubled hour of death ?
 What's beauty ? Call ye that your own,
A flower that fades as soon as blown ?
What's man in all his boast of sway ?
Perhaps the tyrant of a day.
 Alike the laws of life take place
Through ev'ry branch of human race :   60
The monarch of long regal line
Was rais'd from dust as frail as mine :
Can he pour health into his veins,
Or cool the fever's restless pains ?
Can he (worn down in nature's course)
New-brace his feeble nerves with force ?
Can he (how vain is mortal pow'r !)
Stretch life beyond the destin'd hour ?

Consider, man ; weigh well thy
frame ;
The king, the beggar is the same. 70
Dust form'd us all. Each breathes
his day,
Then sinks into his native clay.

Beneath a venerable yew
That in the lonely church-yard grew,
Two Ravens sate. In solemn croak
Thus one his hungry friend bespoke.
Methinks I scent some rich repast ;
The savour strengthens with the
blast,
Snuff then ; the promis'd feast inhale,
I taste the carcase in the gale. 80
Near yonder trees, the farmer's steed,
From toil and daily drudg'ry freed,
Hath groan'd his last. A dainty
treat !
To birds of taste delicious meat.
A Sexton, busy at his trade,
To hear their chat suspends his spade :
Death struck him with no farther
thought,
Than meerly as the fees he brought.
Was ever two such blund'ring fowls,
In brains and manners less than owls !
Blockheads, says he, learn more re-
spect. 91
Know ye on whom ye thus reflect ?
In this same grave (who does me
right,
Must own the work is strong and
tight)
The squire that yon fair hall possest,
To-night shall lay his bones at rest.
Whence could the gross mistake pro-
ceed ?
The squire was somewhat fat indeed
What then ? The meanest bird of
prey 99
Such want of sense could ne'er betray,
For sure some diff'rence must be found
(Suppose the smelling organ sound)
In carcases, (say what we can,)
Or where's the dignity of man ?

With due respect to human race,
The Ravens undertook the case.
In such similitude of scent,
Man ne'er could think reflection
meant.
As Epicures extol a treat, 109
And seem their sav'ry words to eat,
They prais'd dead horse, luxurious
food,
The ven'son of the prescient brood.
The Sexton's indignation mov'd,
The mean comparison reprov'd ;
Their undiscerning palate blam'd,
Which two-legg'd carrion thus de-
fam'd.
Reproachful speech from either
side
The want of argument supply'd.
They rail, revile : As often ends
The contest of disputing friends. 120
Hold, says the fowl ; since human
pride
With confutation ne'er comply'd,
Let's state the case, and then refer
The knotty point : For taste may
err.
As thus he spoke, from out the
mould
An Earth-worm, huge of size, unroll'd
His monstrous length. They strait
agree
To chuse him as their referee.
So to th' experience of his jaws 129
Each states the merits of the cause.
He paus'd, and with a solemn tone
Thus made his sage opinion known.
On carcases of ev'ry kind
This maw hath elegantly din'd ;
Provok'd by luxury or need,
On beast or fowl or man I feed :
Such small distinction's in the savour,
By turns I chuse the fancy'd flavour ;
Yet I must own (that human beast)
A glutton is the rankest feast. 140
Man, cease this boast ; for human
pride
Hath various tracts to range beside.

82 daily] ev'ry *Bell, Cooke, Underhill. Dobson has the right reading.*
108 reflection] reflections *Bell, Cooke, Dobson, Underhill.*
130 the] his *Dobson and Underhill.*

The prince who kept the world in awe,
The judge whose dictate fix'd the law,
The rich, the poor, the great, the small,
Are levell'd.   Death confounds 'em all.
Then think not that we reptiles share
Such cates, such elegance of fare ;
The only true and real good
Of man was never vermine's food. 150

'Tis seated in th' immortal mind ;
Virtue distinguishes mankind,
And that (as yet ne'er harbour'd here)
Mounts with the soul we know not where.
So good-man Sexton, since the case
Appears with such a dubious face,
To neither I the cause determine,
For diff'rent tastes please diff'rent vermine.

THE
MOHOCKS.

A

Tragi-Comical Farce.

As it was Acted near the

Watch-houſe in *Covent-Garden*.

B Y

Her M A J E S T Y's Servants.

Quo, quo, ſceleſti, ruitis? aut cur dexteris
Aptantur enſes conditi? Hor.

L O N D O N:
Printed for *Bernard Lintott*, at the *Croſs-Keys* between the two *Temple-Gates*, in *Fleet-ſtreet*. 1712.

THE

MOHOCKS.

A

Tragi-Comical Farce.

[*Editions :*
1. THE | MOHOCKS. | A | Tragi-Comical Farce. | As it was Acted near the | Watch-house in *Covent-Garden.* | BY Her MAJESTY's Servants. | *Quo, quo, scelesti, ruitis ? aut cur dexteris | Aptantur enses condili?* Hor. | *LONDON* : | Printed for *Bernard Lintott,* at the *Cross-Keys* be-tween the two *Temple-Gates,* in *Fleet-street.* 1712.
2. *Poetical, Dramatic, and Miscellaneous Works of John Gay.* Vol. 5.   1795.]

There can be little if any doubt that the Farce was written by Gay. The *Biographia Britannica* (1747) says (p. 2184) ' Mr. Gay published another Farce called the Mohocks, but it was never acted '. And the *Biographia Dramatica* (1812) says (iii. 55) ' This piece was never perform'd, but is printed with a dedication to Mr. D**** (Dennis), and has been attributed in general, and truly, to Mr. Gay '.

A Broadside, dated 1712 and entitled *The Town-Rakes : or, The Frolicks of the Mohocks or Hawkubites. With an Account of their Frolicks last Night* &c. [Brit. Mus. 816 m. 19 (74)] relates how ' The Watch in most of the Out-parts of the Town stand in awe of them, because they always come in a Body, and are too strong for them, and when any Watchman, presumes to demand where they are going, they generally misuse them . . . They attack'd the Watch in *Devereux-Court* and *Essex-Street,* made them scower.' Here seems to be the germ of the Play.]

TO

Mr. *D* ✳ ✳ ✳.

S I R,

THERE are several Reasons which induce me to lay this Work at Your
Feet : The Subject of it is *Horrid* and *Tremendous*, and the whole Piece written
according to the exactest Rules of Dramatick Poetry, as I have with great
care collected them from several of your elaborate Dissertations.

The World will easily perceive that the Plot of it is form'd upon that of
Appius and *Virginia*, which Model, indeed, I have in great measure follow'd
throughout the whole Conduct of the Play.

The Action is plain and simple, the Time not above an hour and three
quarters, and the Scene shifted but twice in the whole *Drama* : I am apt
to flatter my self that those two Transitions are extremely natural and easie ;
being only out of the Tavern into the Watch-house, and, *vice versa*, out of
the Watch-house into the Tavern.

I am informed that several of these Scenes have already received your
Approbation in your elegant Retreat in the Country ; where, I have the
Pleasure to learn, that you are laying out your Time in such Rhapsodies and
Speculations as cannot but be beneficial to the Commonwealth of Letters.

As we look upon you to have the Monopoly of *English* Criticism in your
Head, we hope you will very shortly chastise the Insolence of the *Spectator*,
who has lately had the *Audaciousness* to show that there are more Beauties
than Faults in a Modern Writer.

I am not at all concern'd at this *Tragedy's* being rejected by the Players,
when I consider how many of your immortal Compositions have met with
no better Reception.

I am proud to answer the malicious World in this Case, with that memorable
Saying which was formerly apply'd to *Scaliger, I had rather be in the Wrong
with the ingenious Mr.* D ✳ ✳ ✳, *than in the Right with any body else.*

I am, Sir, with great Respect and Gratitude,

> *Your most oblig'd,*
>
> *most obedient,*
>
> *most humble,*

London, April, 1.   *and most devoted Servant,*

W. B.

Dedication. Date omitted ; THE AUTHOR *substituted for* W. B. *in the edition of*
1795.

THE

PROLOGUE.

To be Spoken by the Publisher.

THIS Farce, if the kind Players had thought fit
With Action had supply'd its want of Wit.
Oh Readers! had you seen the Mohocks *rage,*
And frighted Watchmen tremble on the Stage;
Had you but seen our Mighty Emperor *stalk;*
And heard in Cloudy *honest* Dicky *talk,*
Seen Pinkethman *in strutting* Prig *appear,*
And 'midst of Danger wisely lead the Rear,
It might have pleas'd; for now-a-days the Joke
Rises or falls as with Grimace *'tis spoke.*　　　　10
As matters stand; there's but this only way,
T' applaud our disappointed Author's Play:
Let all those Hands that would have clapp'd, combine
To take the whole Impression off from mine.
That's a sure way to raise the Poet's Name:
A New Edition gains immortal Fame.

Dramatis Personæ.

The Emperor of the
   Mohocks.
Abaddon,
Moloch,
Whisker, } *Mohocks.*
Mirmidon,
Cannibal,
Cogmagog,

Constable Prig.
Peter Cloudy,
Starlight,
Frost, } *Watch-*
Windy,   *men.*
Moonshine,
Bleak,
Gentle, *a Beau,*

Joan Cloudy, Cloudy's
  Wife.
Justice Wiseman.
Justice Kindle.
Justice Scruple.
Peg Firebrand, } *Whores.*
Jenny Cracker,

Other Watchmen.

Moloch] Molock *1712, but* Moloch *in text.*

SCENE I. *A Tavern.*

The Emperor of the Mohocks *sitting in State,* Mohocks *attending him.*

A B A D D O N.

T H U S far our Riots with Success are crown'd,
Have found no stop, or what they found o'ercame ;
In vain th' embattell'd Watch in deep array,
Against our Rage oppose their lifted Poles ;
Through Poles we rush triumphant, Watchman rolls
On Watchman ; while their Lanthorns kick'd aloft
Like blazing Stars, illumine all the Air.
   Mol. Such Acts as these have made our Fame immortal,
And wide through all *Britannia's* distant Towns,
The Name of *Mohock* ev'ry Tongue employs ;   10
While each fond Mother at the Sound grows pale
And trembles for her absent Son———
   Whisk. Let's lose no longer time in idle Talk,
Which might be better spent in new Exploits.
Most mighty Emperor, a Noble Youth,
Fir'd with our Deeds to glorious Emulation,
Desires Admittance———
   Emp. Go, Introduce him :
But search with care th' Intentions of his Heart,
See he be not a superficial Sinner,
That talks of Mischiefs which he ne'er perform'd :   20
Those are mean Villains, and unworthy us.
   Mir. I'll answer for him, for I've known him long,
Know him a Subject worthy such a Prince ;

Sashes and Casements felt his early Rage,
H' has twisted Knockers, broken Drawers Heads,
And never flinch'd his Glass, or baulk'd his Wench.
But see he comes——

Enter New Mohock.

New Moh. Great Potentate! who leadst the *Mohock* Squadrons
To nightly Expeditions, whose dread Nod
Gives Law to those, lawless to all besides: 30
To thee I come——to serve beneath thy Banner.
Mischief has long lain dormant in my Bosom
Like smother'd Fire, which now shall blaze abroad
In glorious Enterprize——
    Emp. Bravely resolv'd——henceforth thy Name
Be *Cannibal*——like them, devour Mankind.
But come——Night wears apace——begin the Rites.
                    [*They all take Hands in a Circle and Kneel.*
    Gog. By all the Elements, and all the Powers,
Celestial, nay Terrestrial, and Infernal;
By *Acheron*, and the black Streams of *Styx*,   40
An Oath irrevocable to *Jove* himself,
We swear true Fealty, and firm Allegiance
To our most High and Mighty Emperor.
    All. We swear.
    Gog. That we'll to Virtue bear invet'rate Hate,
Renounce Humanity, defie Religion;
That Villany, and all outragious Crimes
Shall ever be our Glory and our Pleasure.
    All. We swear.
    Gog. Let all Hell's Curses light upon his Head,
That dares to violate this solemn Oath;
May Pains and Aches cramp his rotten Bones;   50
May constant Impotence attend his Lust;
May the dull Slave be bigotted to Virtue;
And tread no more the pleasing Paths of Vice,
And then at last die a mean whining Penitent.
    All. This Curse involve us all.
    Emp. 'Tis well——   [*The* Emperor *stands in the midst of them, and speaks*
                                                      this Speech.
Now bring the generous Bowl—Come—pledge me all—
Rouse up your Souls with this Celestial Nectar.
What gain'd the *Macedonian* Youth the World?
'Twas Wine. What rais'd the Soul of *Catiline*
To such brave, unparallel'd Ambition?   60
Wine, Potent, heav'nly Juice, Immortal Wine.
Slothful awhile inglorious Mortals lay,
But Wine to Noble Action led the Way;
Wine conquers all things——all must Wine obey. [*Drinks.*

A SONG.

[The *Mohocks* stand in a Circle, with the Glasses in their Hands.

> *Come fill up the Glass,*
> *Round, round, let it pass,*
> *'Till our Reason be lost in our Wine :*
> *Leave Conscience's Rules*
> *To Women and Fools,*
> *This only can make us divine.*   70

Chorus. *Then a* Mohock, *a* Mohock *I'll be,*
> *No Laws shall restrain*
> *Our Libertine Reign,*
> *We'll riot, drink on, and be free.*   [All Drink.

> *We will scower the Town,*
> *Knock the Constable down,*
> *Put the Watch and the Beadle to flight :*
> *We'll force all we meet*
> *To kneel down at our Feet,*
> *And own this great Prince of the Night.*   80

Chorus. *Then a* Mohock, *a* Mohock, *&c.*   [All Drink.

> *The Grand Seignior shall own*
> *His Seraglio outdone,*
> *For all Womankind is our booty ;*
> *No Condition we spare*
> *Be they Brown, Black or Fair*
> *We make them fall down, and do Duty.*

Chorus. *Then a* Mohock, *a* Mohock *I'll be,*
> *No Laws shall restrain*
> *Our Libertine Reign*   90
> *We'll riot, drink on, and be free.*   [All Drink.
>   [Exeunt.

SCENE II. *The Street before the Watch-house.*

Moon. Lookye, Brother Watchman, you are a Man of Learning and can read the News.

Windy. Why, Neighbour, for that matter as a Body may say, Mr. Constable is a great Man, a great Man, Neighbour, and fair Words cost nothing ——But as I was saying, *Peter Cloudy* there is ready with his Verses.

Frost. Ay, ay, *Peter's* Verses may be seen pasted up in every Barber's Shop in the Parish ; *Peter* shall be our Spokesman to induce our New Mr. Constable.

Enter Constable.

Come, *Cloudy*, begin.

Cloudy. *O Magistrate, thou art, as I may say,*   10
So Great by Night, as is Queen Anne *by Day,*

> *Stage-direction to Song.* stand] stands *1712.*
> *Scene II. Stage-direction* Enter several watchmen *added 1795.*

And what greater Power can any where be seen?
For you do represent the Person of the Queen.
The greatest Judge in England *cannot do,*
Or execute more greater things than you.
God save you, Master Constable, we pray,
Who are your honest Watch-men Night and Day.

Const. Well said, *Peter*——but heark ye, my Lads, we are like to have hot work on't to Night——the *Mohocks* without doubt will be abroad.

Starl. Oh, Master Constable, bloody-minded Fellows ! that have broke more Windows than the great Storm, and are more mischievous than a Press-gang. 22

Cloudy. You may take my word for it, Mr. Constable——Sufferers may have leave to complain——my Head and Ribs have been thwack'd over and over again like a Flock-bed by them.

Const. Why, they say that they slit Noses, cut and slash all they meet with, poach Folks in the Calves of the Legs, and disturb us and our Officers in our lawful Authority—I charge you all, knock down upon Suspicion——that we may not be forced to cut Capers against our Wills—pox of such Dancing Masters, say I, that will make a Man Dance without a Fiddle.   30

Starl. They make no more of our Poles than so many Straws ; let me tell you, Sir, that I have seen them do such things that would make a Man's Hair stand on end—let me see————ay————to-morrow Night, 'twill be three Nights ago————when I was going my round————I met about five or six and thirty of these *Mohocks*————by the same token 'twas a very windy Morning————they all had Swords as broad as Butchers Cleavers, and hack'd and hew'd down all before them————I saw————as I am a Man of credit, in the Neighbourhood————all the Ground covered with Noses———— as thick as 'tis with Hail-stones after a Storm.   39

Const. So——between Whores and *Mohocks*, we shall not have a Man left with a handle to his Face——Heav'n keep us, say I—and preserve that Member from danger—for a Man of Reputation would never be able to show his Nose after such an Affront.

Frost. Ha, ha, ha————but that is nothing to what I have seen———— I saw them hook a Man as cleverly as a Fisher-man would a great Fish———— and play him up and down from *Charing-Cross* to *Temple-Bar*————they cut off his Ears, and eat them up, and then gave him a swinging Slash in the Arm————told him that bleeding was good for a fright, and so turn'd him loose.

Const. And where was you all the while ?   50

Frost. I blow'd out my Candle, and lay snug in the corner of a Bulk.

Starl. Poh——poh !——that 's nothing at all————I saw them cut off a Fellow's Legs, and if the poor Man had not run hard for it, they had cut off his Head into the bargain.

Cloudy. Poor *John Mopstaff*'s Wife was like to come to damage by them ————for they took her up by the Heels and turn'd her quite inside out ————the poor Woman, they say, will ne'er be good for any thing more— honest *John* can hardly find the Head from the Tail of her.

Windy. Hark ! hark ! what Noise is that ?——oh the *Mohocks*——the *Mohocks*——oh——*Will, Harry, Gregory, Peter, George, Thomas,* to your Poles—quickly—ay———— there——stand to it————stand to it.   61

[*Pushing them forwards.*

15 *than*] *that* 1712.

Const. Where ?——where are they ?——ay, Gentlemen——stand to it.
[Pushing them forwards.

Starl. Oh——there they come——oh——yonder is one with a Face like a Lion——the *Guildhall* Giant is a meer Dwarf to him.

Cloudy. Where, where ?——oh——keep your Ranks, Brothers——hark !

Starl. Nothing but Fancy, Neighbours, all 's well, only a shadow, only a shadow ; but if they had come——

All. Ay, if they had come——
[All with their Poles lifted up and advancing.

Bleak. We would have——hark——keep your Ranks, *Peter,*—stand to them, Boys. *[Pushing 'em.*] Nothing, nothing, Neighbours.   70

Cloudy. I'm afraid these plaguy suspexions are fore-runners of them ; but if they had come——

Const. Ope thy Lanthorn, *Peter.*
[The Constable speaks lighting his Pipe.

The *Mohocks*——are but Men——and——we be Men as well as they be— and—— a Man—is a Man, Neighbours—now——you be the Watch——and I—am the Constable—they may——mayhap——venture upon a single stragling Watchman——but we——are a Garrison——a Garrison, Brothers.

Bleak. Ay, Mr. Constable, and we'll all stand by you with our Lives and Fortunes.   79

Const. A *Mohock*——Brothers——a *Mohock*, I say, will no more come near a Watch-house than a Whore——Here——we are unattackable——but we be——not only to be upon the Defensive——Brothers——I mean, to defend the Watch-house——but upon the Offensive——I mean, to offend—— destroy—knock down——take up——and——commit—and bring *Mohocks* to Justice.—Therefore, Neighbours,——as our Duty requires us——I order the greatest Party of you to go—through all the several——Streets——Lanes and Alleys——to endeavour——to seize——and apprehend the *Mohocks*— if you apprehend them——d'ye hear——bring them hither before me—— But if——they apprehend you——d'ye hear——then——you need not come.—The Justices are now sitting——and have ordered all the *Mohocks* that we shall take, to be immediately brought before them.   91
[They all go out, but the Constable and six Watchmen.

Cloudy. Mr. Constable——d'ye see, Mr. Constable, here is this Pole, Mr. Constable—I'll engage that this Pole—Mr. Constable, if it takes a *Mohock* in the right Place—it shall knock him down as flat as a Flounder, Mr. Con- stable——Pole is the word, Sir——I, one Night, Mr. Constable, clap'd my Back against the Watch-house, and kept nine *Mohocks*, with their Swords drawn, at Pole's length, broke three of their Heads, knock'd down four, and trim'd the Jackets of the other six.

Bleak. I, for my part, remember the ancient *Mohocks* of King *Charles* his Days ; I was a young Man then ; now times are alter'd with me——some of the greatest Men of the Kingdom were *Mohocks*, yet for all that we did not care a Fig for them.   102

Const. There have been *Mohocks* in all Reigns and in all Ages, but, thank Heav'n, there have been Constables too, with heart and hand to suppress them——though a Constable be a Civil Magistrate, yet upon great occasions he is allow'd to take up Arms ; and there is not a Man among you that shall step a Step farther than my self.   *[A noise of the Mohocks.*

97 Pole's] Poles *1712.*

Windy. Mr. Constable stand in the front.

[*Pushing one another forwards.*

Frost. A brave Man ! a gallant Man ! I warrant him.   109

Const. Hold, hold, Gentlemen, let us do all things in order——Do you advance, Gentlemen, d'ye see, and while you advance I'll lead up the Rear.

Enter the Mohocks *singing.*

'*Tis Wine and a Whore,*
That we Mohocks *adore,*
We'll drink 'till our Senses we quench ;
When the Liquor is in
We're heighten'd for Sin ;
Then heigh ! for a brisk jolly Wench.
Fa, la, la, la.

Abad. Hola ! the Watch, down—down with them ; oh, the Devil, down with your Poles you Dogs————upon your Knees—worship the *Mohocks* and be damn'd to you.   121

[*The Watch throw down their Poles and fall on their Knees.*

Starl. Oh for Pity's sake, Gentlemen, I've a Wife and four Children.

Mol. Rot your Wife and Children, make Fricassees of them, Sirrah, and invite the Devil to Supper.

Whisk. And I'll cut off the Noses of all these Rascals to garnish the Dish.

Mirm. Heighday————what, *Peg Firebrand* in Limbo ?

[*Looking towards two Wenches which the Watch have in Custody.*

Gog. Come, you Scoundrel there————unhand the Doxies————upon your Knees, you Dog, and receive Sentence.

Peg. Your humble Servant, Mr. *Mirmidon.*

Jenny. Who thought to have found Mr. *Gogmagog* here !   130

Peg. Pox of these destroyers of Game——and Mr. *Moloch* too ! Mr. *Moloch* I am your humble Servant.

Can. Come, I'll sacrifice this Rascal's Ears to you, *Peg.*

Emp. The Constable is my Prisoner——hark ye, Sirrah, are you married ?

Const. Yes, an please your Honour.

Emp. Then you are a Cuckold, Coxcomb.

Const. Yes——an—an—an—please—you——your Worship.

[*Trembling for fear.*

Abad. This Dog's Face Phiz is scarce worth the spoiling. Come, Sirrah, I'll save your Wife the charge of more Children, and make you cry a dark cloudy Morning like an *Italian.*   140

Cloudy. Oh pray your Honour, good your Honour, my Ears or my Nose is wholly at your Worship's Service ; but pray, good, dear loving Sir, don't let poor *Gillian* lose her only Comfort.

Mol. Come, let's dispatch, cut, slash, and mangle, and pursue more noble Game.

Emp. Hold, hold, for once we'll have a merry frolick. Since we have the Constable and Watch in our Power, we will divest our self of our Imperial Dignity, make them *Mohocks,* and our selves Constable and Watchmen.

All. Agreed, agreed,——come strip, Sirrah, strip, Sirrah.   149

Emp. Ay, ay, come, come, Sirrah, let us put the Lion's Skin upon the Ass.

Const. Yes, Sir, yes ; oh pray, Sir, I'll be an Ass or any thing————but pray your Honour let me be an Ass with Ears.

Starl. Little does my poor Wife at home think what a pitiful taking her Husband is in——Poor Soul——she is sound asleep————and thinks nought of all this.   [*Aside.*

[*The Emperor changes Cloaths with the Constable, and places a Patch like an half Moon in his Forehead ; the other* Mohocks *strip the Watchmen and take their Poles and Lanthorns.*

Mirm. Come, strip this Scoundrel, *Jenny,* and plague the Rogue now thou hast got him in thy power.   158

Jenny. Pox on't, Mr. *Mirmidon*——'tis as dangerous for us to use a Watchman ill, as for a Stage-Coachman to be uncivil to an High-way Man ; for our Trade forces us to travel the Streets all the Year round————Remember, Sirrah, you owe me an Escape without a Fee to the Constable.

Peg. And me.

Whisk. Why, the Dog looks as terrible as a Janizary.

Cloudy. Oh Law, Sir, I'm a poor quiet harmless Fellow, and no Janzary——*Peter Cloudy* by Name——I'm known all the Neighbourhood over, and can bring several good creditable Housekeepers to vouch for my Honesty.

Can. The next Man that speaks a Word forfeits an Ear ; and for the second fault, a Nose————   169

Cloudy. Let me see, oh, ay, I was afraid he had took him off as a Mountebank draws a Tooth—with a Touch.   [*Feeling his Nose. Aside.*

Can. Silence in the Court——while our most mighty Emperor sits in Judgment.

Emp. You *Cannibal,* you *Abaddon,* with *Whisker* and the rest of you, bring all you meet before me.

Enter Gentle.

Mol. Heigh-day, here 's a Fellow got into the Trammels already ; come, you Sir, before the Constable——on, on.   [*They seize* Gentle.

Gent. Pray, Gentlemen, treat a Man of Fashion with more Civility.   179

Can. Damme Sir——you are a *Mohock.*

Gent. I vow and protest Gentlemen, I just now came from my Lady *Pride's* in the City, from playing at Ombre, and had there been a Coach or a Chair to be found, I had not walk'd a-foot.

Abad. Before the Constable——come, come, before the Constable.

Gent. Be civil, I beg you, Gentlemen, disengage your Poles from my full Bottom——and I'll wait upon you.

Emp. Hearkye, Fellow, you seem very suspicious, you have a downcast hanging look.

Gent. A languishing Air, you mean, Sir.   188

Emp. Give an Account of your self, Fellow, whence come you ? whither are you going ? What is your business abroad at this time of Night—take his Sword from him there, lest he should have some evil design against the Queen's Officer.

Gent. I am a Gentleman, Sir.

Emp. A doubtful, a shuffling Answer ! we need no further proof that he is a *Mohock*—commit him.   195

178 *seize*] *size* 1712 and 1795.

Gent. 'Tis a strange thing that the vulgar cannot distinguish the Gentleman—pray Sir, may I ask you one Question—have you ever seen a *Mohock* ? has he that softness in his Look ? that sweetness of delivery in his Discourse ? believe me, Sir, there is a certain *Je ne scay quoi* in my manner that shows my Conversation to have lain altogether among the politer part of the World.

Emp. Look ye, Sir, your Manners in talking *Latin* before her Majesty's Officer, show you to be an ill-designing Person.   202

Gent. Ha, ha, ha, very merry, as I hope to be caress'd. *Latin* and *French* sound alike in the Ears of the vulgar—*Je ne scay quoi* is a *French* Phrase much in vogue at the Court end of the Town, ha, ha, ha.

Emp. Meer Prevarication ! to the Round-house with him——a *Mohock* without dispute——here's Evidence against you, Friend, downright Evidence against you.

Mol. With these very Eyes, Mr. Constable, I saw him in a dark Alley, where one could not see ones Hand, slit a Cinder Wenches Nose, because she would not yield to his Brutality.   211

Gent. Is there any thing in my Appearance that shows a *Goust* for a Cinder Wench ? Improbable ! downright falsity !——this Usage, Sir, will make me complain to some higher Power of your illegal Proceedings.

Emp. What ! dispute my Authority ! bind him, and see you guard him strictly.

Gent. Pray——Gentlemen——indeed——I vow——Gentlemen——you daub my Ruffles ; let not your Lanthorns come nigh my Cloaths——bless me ! my Perriwig !——hold, hold, I vow and protest upon the word of a Gentleman, that I am a civil Person——fogh ! the stench of the Lanthorns confound me——Have a care what you do Mr. Constable, for I shall find redress.   222

Emp. Bind him, bind him, I value not his Threats. *Mohocks* are thus to be treated, where and whenever they shall be taken.   [*They bind Gentle.*

Enter Joan Cloudy.

Gog. Come on, Woman, before the Constable——Here is a Stragler that is just now fallen into my Hands, Mr. Constable.

Joan. Where is *Peter?*—What, is *Peter* going his rounds ? I'm *Peter's* Wife, Mr. Constable——an please your Worship——and am come to take a Pot with him, and take care of him this cold Weather. What, is not *Peter* among you ? What ! is not *Peter* come back from his rounds ?——*Peter,* Mr. Constable, an please your Worship, is a diligent Man in his Office—— I have been in Bed this two hours, and was so strangely a-dream'd of the *Mohocks* that I could not rest, but must come and see him——alas ! alas ! these are strange hazardous Times ! I was a-dream'd methought that the *Mohocks*——   235

Emp. Hold, hold, Woman, are you drunk with Mild, Stale, or Stout ?

Cloudy. Heav'n grant that I may not be made a Cuckold before my own Face——What a plague made her stirring ?   [*Aside.*

Joan. Drunk, Mr. Constable, Drunk ! whether you know it or no, though I am a poor Woman, I am a sober Woman——I work for what I get, and I thank no body for a Maintenance.——Drunk ! tell your Wife of being

Drunk with Mild, Stale, and Stout——would *Peter* was here, he should not hear his Wife affronted after this manner.

Emp. I'll take care and Tongue-tye you, Woman!   244

Joan. To be Tongue-tyed is fit for nothing but Lyars and Swearers. I'll speak the Truth and shame the Devil. Though a Constable be to keep Peace and Quietness, yet the greatest Constable in *England* shall not make me hold my Tongue, when there is occasion for speaking. My Husband is a Watchman, *Peter Cloudy* by Name, a good House-keeper, though he be a poor Man.——— Why these are all strange Faces, methinks. Where is *Peter*, Friend? oh Law! oh Dear! this ugly Dream runs in my Head most strangely.——— [*Spies* Peter.] Oh Gracious! what 's this our *Peter?* why *Peter?*——sure I be'nt out of my Dream yet——why, *Peter*, I say, *Peter*.   [*Bawls.*

                    [Peter *shakes his Head.*

Gog. Ay, why there now, good Woman, while you thought he was upon the Watch, he was about a *Mohocking*———Why he is a *Mohock*, good Woman.   256

Joan. Oh good Lord!

Whisk. Here——we took him in company with these two Wenches.

Joan. What, and Constable *Prig* a *Mohock* too! and honest *Harry Starlight!*

Can. *Mohocks* all, good Woman, every Soul of them.

Joan. Why *Peter*, *Peter*, Mr. *Prig*, *Harry Starlight!* what are you all dumb? [*Cloudy shakes his Head.*] Oh, you ungracious Rogue! you ungodly Wretch! what, must you have your Wenches, Sirrah, while your poor Children at home—ay, and your poor Wife, nay your honest, true and careful Wife, are ready to starve. Why, *Peter*, I say, fye upon't, what, hadst thee no more Wit to be a *Mohock* too?   267

                    [Cloudy *shakes his Head.*

Joan. Why! you notorious Rogue, won't you answer your poor Wife?

                    [Cloudy *shakes his Head.*

Joan. Alack, alack! do I live to see this with my own Eyes? oh, *Peter*, *Peter!* an old Fool of all Fools is the worst——a *Hawkubite!* a Rogue! I hope, I shall see thee at the Gallows for this, Blockhead! What, you there with your hairy Bush upon your Head, I suppose are the Ring-leader of them, I'll *Hawkubite* you, Sirrah.   [*To* Gent.

Gent. I vow and protest, Madam, you do me the greatest Injustice in the World, I am a Gentleman of Honour, but at present labour under the Misfortune of being suspected.   277

Emp. Come, come, Woman, don't be troublesome, we can see through your Designs; you are a Female *Mohock*, I perceive——and under that Denomination I order you to be apprehended.

Joan. I, a Female *Mohock!* a Female Jesuit as soon—

Emp. Bind her, bind her.

Joan. But my Tongue shall still be at Liberty; he must have good Luck, ifackins, that ties a Woman's Tongue. Why, *Peter*, Sirrah, all this comes of your ungracious Tricks, you *Hawkubite* Rogue.   285

Emp. Heigh-day! what 's here— [*Takes a Paper out of the Constable's Pocket.*] a Warrant for the apprehending us *Mohocks!* I find the Justices are sitting in all the several Quarters of the Town this Night to examine

        251 strangely.] strangely? *1712 and 1795.*

                    * M

them ; what think you, my Heroes——shall we improve the Jest ? carry the
Scoundrels before some Justices of a Ward where they are unknown, and so
make them commit their own Officers instead of us.

All. A Merry Frolick ! with all our Hearts.

Emp. We'll immediately carry them before the Justices of the next Ward,
commit the Rascals to the Round-house, and so finish the Night's Adventure.

Whis. Come, come, to the Justices——to the Justices. 295

Emp. Leave this Fellow, and this Female *Mohock* till our Return ; bind
them Back to Back, and there will be no fear of *Peter*'s being Jealous.

[*They bind them.*

Gent. I beg you, Gentlemen ; this Posture is so like Man and Wife, that
a Man of Mode may be perfectly ashamed of it.

Joan. Go you *Hawkubite* Rogue, you ungracious Wretch !

Gent. Figurative Matrimony, as I hope to be caress'd ; one pulls one way,
and the other the other.

[*They bolt* Gentle *and* Joan *into the Watch-house, and Exeunt.*

SCENE III. *A Tavern.*

The Justices sitting.

Scrup. What says the Statute Book, Brother *Wiseman*, in relation to
these kind of Enormities ? I am informed that there were *Mohocks* in Queen
Elizabeth's Days. Have you search'd all the Statutes of her Reign for an Act
in relation to this Affair ?

Kind. What occasion for all these doubts, Mr. Justice *Scruple* ? for where
the Law is silent, there, our Will is the Law——If we have no Precedents of
Mohocks——come, Mr. Justice *Scruple*, my hearty Service to you——if
we have no Precedents, I say, of any *Mohocks*——my hearty Service to you
again, Mr. Justice————yet *Mohocks* inclusively are comprehended in
disorderly Persons, and disturbers of her Majesty's Peace, and as such, I say,
they may and ought to be committed. 11

Scrup. But we must refer to the Statute Books upon all Occasions————
The Statute Books must be our guide in all Cases————and where the
Statutes will not come within our Cases————we must make our Cases
come within the Statute's Cases—That 's the Method of all judicious practising
Lawyers, Brothers.

Wise. Let us act Justice, and be guided by Reason.

Kind. What has Reason to do with Law, Brother *Wiseman* ? if we follow
the Law, we must judge according to the Letter of the Law. 19

Scrup. You are in the Right, Brother *Kindle*————Reason and Law have
been at variance in our Courts these many Years——a mis-spell'd Word,
or a Quibble will baffle the most convincing Argument in the World ; and
therefore if we are guided—Mr. Justice *Wiseman*, my hearty respects to you—
if we are guided, I say, in any measure by the Law, 'tis my Opinion, that we
must keep strictly to the Letter of the Law.

Enter the Mohocks, *Constable and Watchmen.*

Emp. An please your Worship we have brought some *Mohocks* before your
Honours ; This, an please your Honours, is the Emperor, and this his
Grand Vizier, and all the rest are Princes of the Blood.

Abad. I, my own self, an please your Honours, saw this very self-same

Fellow here, tip the Lyon upon five several of her Majesty's true-born Subjects, and afterwards slit all their Noses.   31

Mol. This Fellow here—is a Dancing-Master——an please your Worships, he pricks Passengers in the Calves of the Legs to make them show their Agility.

Whisk. And this Terrible-look'd Fellow, and please your Honours, is their Master Cooper, his Office is to Barrel up old Women——all the rest of them have their proper Employments.

Wise. Where, and how were they taken ?   38

Can. In an Attack upon the Watch-house——after an obstinate fight of about an hour and an half we made them all Prisoners.

Star. The Devil is a most confounded Lyar !   [*Aside.*

Emp. We took this *Mohock*, Mr. Justices, in an actual Assault to ravish these two Women—oh—he 's a Devilish Fellow for a Wench—the Rogue has no Conscience with him—no more Conscience than a Woman—what two Women ! why a Woman with common Modesty in her Demands would not have desired above two Men—what, two Women at once !   46

Peg. He gagg'd me, and please your Worships ; then drew his Sword, and threaten'd to kill me, if I did not—

Jen. And if the Watchman had not come just in the Nick—

Cloudy. If I lose both my Tongues and my Ears——I must and will speak————And please your Worships, I am an honest Watchman—— *Peter Cloudy.*——

Whisk. What are you, Sirrah——what are you——such a Word more———
                                                    [*Aside to him.*
                              [*The* Mohocks *prick* Cloudy *behind.*

Cloudy. I am———oh————yes—— I am——oh——I am a *Mohock* an please your Worships————a Watchman I mean——and this is Mr. Constable *Prig*———oh no——I beg your Worship's Pardon, he is——oh no—— oh no———he is not——   57

Gog. Come, come, confess——   [*Aside to* Cloudy.

Cloudy. Yes, he is——Emperor of the *Mohocks*, an please ye——

Kind. I perceive that you are a prevaricating shuffling Rogue—commit him, commit him——when a Man talks backwards and forwards——I have done with him.

Cloudy. Oh, Dear Mr. Justice——indeed——oh pray sweet, loving, good, kind Mr. Justice——I have been a Watchman, these twenty Years.

Mol. What 's that you say, Rascal ?   [*Aside to* Cloudy.

Cloudy. A *Mohock* these twenty Years, an please your Honours.   66

Kind. Commit them————commit them——we need no further Proof————Impudent————Impudent——Rogue——pretend to be the Queen's Officer !————I'll hear no more——away——away with them.

Scrup. But hold, Brother *Kindle*————though the Case is plain in Relation to this Fellow————yet we must not punish the Guilty with the Innocent——

Kind. The Innocent with the Guilty, you would say, Brother——they are all of a Gang—all Rogues alike————away——away with them.   74

Wise. Do you confess what is alledg'd against you by these honest Watchmen, Friends ? you are accused of being a Riotous sort of Creatures called *Mohocks*—Answer to your Charge——are you Guilty or not Guilty——
                              [*The* Mohocks *prick them behind.*

All. Not Guilty——an please your Worship——Oh yes, yes——Guilty ——Guilty——Guilty.

Kind. What need we examine further ?

Cloudy. But as to the Ravishing——Mr. Justices——oh me !——Yes I will speak [*Aside to the* Mohocks.] as I was saying, Mr. Justices, as to the Ravishing——I know nothing of that matter—oh, oh ! yes, yes——I did Ravish——I did Ravish them———an please your Worships.   84

Kind. A most Impudent Rogue———the Fellow has a confounded Ravishing Look——Heav'n preserve our Wives and Daughters———away, away——they are dangerous Persons——commit them.

[*As they are carrying them out, Enter the other Party of Watch——with* Joan Cloudy *and Beau* Gentle.

1 *Watch.* An please your Worships—we found this Gentleman here, and Woman here, joyn'd together in a very odd Posture.

Kind. As how——Friend, as how ?

1 *Watch.* Why they were tyed together——back to back—an please your Worships.

Wise. A very odd Posture——Brother *Scruple*——a very odd Posture.

Joan. But Mr. Justices—Oh you ungracious Wretch ! Mr. Justices—you are Justices of the Peace, and I hope your Worshipful Honours will do me Justice——Look, how the sneaking Rogue looks upon me now !   96

Scrup. Proceed, Woman, to the Matter in Hand.

Joan. Why, an please your Worshipful Honours, to make short of my Story—this great Boobily Lubber here——it seems, while I thought he was upon the Watch, went about a *Mohocking*——The Laird keep us, say I, from the Great *Turk*, and from Popery ! but to make short of my Story, Mr. Justices,—this Slave here, this *Hawkubite* Rogue, throws away upon two Wenches in one Night, [*Weeping.*] what with good Huswifery would have satisfied his poor Wife for a Fortnight ;——can you deny this, Sirrah, can you deny it ?——but to make short of my Story, an please your worshipful Honours ; when I came to the Watch-house, thinking to find him in his Office, I found him [*Weeping.*] taken up for a *Mohock*.   107

Emp. Faith, 'tis high time for us to sneak off.   [*Aside.*

[*The* Mohocks *are going.*

Wise. Hold——hold !——let us examine further into these Affairs.

2 *Watch.* Why, *Harry*——how comest thee in this Pickle ?

[*Aside to* Starlight.

Gent. These, Gentlemen, Sirs, treat all alike without the least Distinction ———one would rather fall into the Hands of the *Mohocks*, than suffer the Barbarities of these ill-bred sort of Creatures.

Cloudy. Why they are all *Mohocks*———an please your worshipful Honours———they unconstabled the Constable.   115

Star. And unwatch'd the Watch———an please your Honours.

Cloudy. Ay—faith———I don't value your Staring——it shall all out— faith——now I have got all my Friends about me. [*Aside to the* Mohocks.] They stript us——an please your worshipful Honours—made us *Mohocks*, and themselves Constable and Watch.

Kind. Very strange——Brother *Scruple*——very strange.

118 faith] fath *1712*.

Cloudy. This is Mr. Constable *Prig*, an please your Honours.

Starl. And I am *Harry Starlight*, an please ye.   123

Joan. And is not my *Peter* a *Mohock* then !——art not thee a *Hawkubite*, *Peter?*——are not these thy Wenches ?————oh, *Peter* !   [*Hugging him.*

All the Watch. These are all our Brother Watchmen,————we'll vouch for them————an please your Worships.

Wisem. A plain case, Brothers,————Oh, then you are the *Mohocks*, it seems, Gentlemen.

All the Mohocks. We are Gentlemen, Sirs, 'twas only an innocent Frolick.

Wisem. Frolicks for Brutes and not for Men.————Watchmen, seize your Prisoners.   132

Cloudy. Heark ye, Sir——are you a *Mohock*————or are you not a *Mohoc*, ————[*Takes away the Dagger, with which they prick'd him.*] Come, come give up your Poles and your Lanthorns—hold up your Head, Friend— Mr. *Hannibal* I think they call him—oh—I find you have Ears to lose—I was afraid the Pillory had been before-hands with me—come strip.

[*The Watchmen strip the* Mohocks.

Joan. Oh *Peter* ! *Peter* ! and art not thee a *Mohock* then, *Peter ?*

Gent. Have I been a Captive of the *Mohocks*————well——I vow, 'tis mighty happy, that I have preserv'd all my Features entire for the Ladies.

Emp. Pray, Gentlemen, give us our Liberty.   141

All the Mohocks. We'll ask Pardon.

Emp. Treat us like Gentlemen.

Wisem. Let them be brought before us by ten a Clock——You may assure your selves, Gentlemen——these Proceedings of yours shall be punished with the utmost Severity.   [*Exeunt Justices.*

All the Mohocks. We'll submit, ask Pardon, or do any thing.

Const. Come,—let's call up the Musick that is below, and rejoice for our happy Deliverance——Let us show the Emperor here, that we can Dance without his Instructions.   150

All. Agreed.

A Dance of Watchmen.

Const. *This is the Day——the joyful Night indeed*
In which Great Britain's *Sons from the* Mo-hocks *are freed.*
Our Wives and Daughters they may walk the Street,
Nor Mohock *now, nor* Hawkubite *shall meet.*
Mohock *and* Hawkubite, *both one and all,*
Shall from this very Night date their Down——fall.

THE

E P I L O G U E,

Design'd to be spoken by the Person who should have play'd
Joan Cloudy.

W H A T woful things do we poor Folks endure,
To keep our Spouses to our selves secure?
We Wives——(of one and all this may be said,)
Ne'er think our Husbands safe,——but when in Bed.
But now, to quit the Wife——How would it please ye,
Could you dissolve the Marriage Noose as easie.
Marriage would then no more entail for Life,
And Coquets venture on the Name of Wife:
What Woman would not!——if this Scheme would do,
Just for a Frolick——take a Spouse or two.   10
Ye Criticks that are scatter'd o'er the Pit,
And stare and gape to catch descending Wit,
Meer Mohocks, *that on harmless Authors prey,*
And damn for want of Sense a Modern Play,
I vow 'tis hard.——Yet if it must be so,
I still must ask one Favour e'er I go.
If you condemn him, grant him a Reprieve,
Three days of Grace to the young Sinner give,
And then——if his sad Downfal does delight ye,
As witness of his Exit *I invite ye.*   20

F I N I S.

THE WIFE OF *BATH*.

[Editions :
1. THE | WIFE of BATH. | A | COMEDY. As it is Acted at the | THEATRE-ROYAL in *Drury-Lane*, | BY | Her MAJESTY's Servants. | By Mr. *GAY*. |—*Magicis sanos avertere Sacris | Experiar Sensus.* Virg. | *LONDON :* | Printed for BERNARD LINTOTT, at the *Cross-Keys* between | the Two *Temple-Gates* in *Fleetstreet.* MDCCXIII F'cap 4to. Mr. T. J. Wise says (*Catalogue of the Ashley Library*) : ' There are two varieties of the first edition of *The Wife of Bath.* These differ only in the half-title. In the one variety the half-title reads *The | Wife of Bath. | A | Comedy*, and the rest of the page is plain. The other variety has a crude portrait of a stout Falstaff-like character, holding a jug and bowl in either hand, enclosed within a circular frame, imposed upon the lower portion of the page below the letterpress.'
2. The same. 'As it is Acted at the Theatre-Royal in Lincoln's-Inn-Fields. Written by Mr. Gay. Revised and Altered by the Author.' Lintot. 1730. Cr. 4to. Practically a new Play. The characters of Chaucer, Franklyn, and Doublechin omitted ; those of Plowden, Gauntlet, Hubert added.
The Prologue, and the fragments of verse following, are printed in italics in both the early editions.]

PROLOGUE.

IF lavish *Dryden* so profusely writ,
That ev'n his *Prologues* too were cramm'd with Wit ;
'Tis not for us in this our first Essay
To waste in *Prologue* what might starve the *Play* :
Lest we be found, like Marriages in Fashion,
With nothing good besides the Preparation.
So then, like antient Bards, 'tis now our Care,
Only to read his little Bill of Fare.
He draws his Characters from *Chaucer*'s Days,
On which our Grandsires are profuse of Praise ;   10
When all mankind,——(if we'll believe Tradition,)
Jogg'd on in settled Conjugal Fruition :
Then, as Old Wives with serious Nod will tell us,
The wise contented Husband ne'er was jealous ;
The youthful Bride no sep'rate Trading drives,
Ev'n Citizens could——satisfy their Wives.

Prologue. 'Spoken by Mrs. *Mountfort.*' 1713 only.
1–8 *So 1730. The Prologue in 1713 opens thus :*
        If ancient Poets thought the *Prologue* fit,
        To Sport away superfluous Starts of Wit ;
        Why should we Moderns lavish ours away,
        And to supply the *Prologue* starve the *Play* ?
        Thus *Plays* of late, like Marriages in Fashion,
        Have nothing good besides the Preparation.
        How shall we do to help our Author out,
        Who both for *Play* and *Prologue* is in doubt ?

The cautious Virgin, ignorant of Man,
No Glances threw, nor exercis'd the Fan ;
Found Love a Stranger to her easy Breast,
And 'till the Wedding-Night——enjoy'd her Rest.   20
No gilded Chariot drew the Ladies eyes,
Ensnar'd their Hearts, and bore away the Prize ;
Then the strict Father no hard Bargains drove
For Jointures :—All the settlement was Love.
Believe all this who will :——For let me die !
They knew the World as well as You and I.
Lovers would Then, as now-a-days, forswear ;
Seize the soft Moment, and surprize the Fair,
And many a modest, knowing Bride was led
With artful Blushes to the Nuptial Bed.   30
This Picture, tho' in former Ages known,
Points out some Frailties which are still our own :
The *Wife of Bath* in our weak Wives we find ;
And Superstition runs through all the Kind :
We but repeat our Grandsires Actions o'er,
And copy Follies which were theirs before.

18 Fan ;] *1730* Fan, *1713*.
24 For Jointures—all their Settlement was—Love. *1713*.
31–2   Our Author hath from former Ages shown,
        Some ancient Frailties which are still our own ; *1713*.
The Epilogue is printed in the revised edition of 1730 as ' By a Friend ' ; and is therefore not given here.

Fragments.

Alison (sings)

Then who would not be a Bride,
Then who would not be a Bride,
    For the sweetest Kiss,
        Is not half of her Bliss :   40
This all will say,—who have try'd.
                    From Act I. Omitted in 1730.

Alison (speaks)

The best Advice comes sometimes out of season ;
When Reason's on our Side, we side with Reason.
                    End of Act I. 1730 only.

Doggrell (speaks)

To your Relief your ardent Lover flies.
Ah ! those attractive Lips, and dear deluding Eyes !
                    End of Act I. 1713 only.

Alison (speaks)

In love, he 's like the dog, (that foolish glutton)
Who for a shadow lost substantial mutton.
                    End of Act II. 1730 only.

Florinda (*speaks*)
> Since Marriage binds us fast in lasting Bands,
> Love that unites our Hearts, shall join our Hands.
> > End of Act II. 1713 only.

Chaucer (*speaks*)
> Since the kind Stars to mutual Love constrain,   50
> Why should the Tongue conceal our secret Pain ?
> Was it for this, inexorable Fair,
> Your Magick drew me through the distant Air ?
> Tho' some curst Charm your wonted Speech denies,
> At least shed Pity from those radiant Eyes,
> And look me into Hope.— . . .

> We from the Ladies Eyes our Fate may learn,
> And in those Glasses Love or Hate discern.
> > Beginning of Act III. 1713 only.

Alison (*sings*)
> The Maiden and the Batchelor,
> > Pardie . . . are simple Elves,   60
> And 'till they grow to Man and Wife,
> > Know nothing of themselves.

> Then since we're each others by Nature design'd
> > Let's unite, and our Knowledge improve ;
> Here 's a Health to the Lass that is passively kind,
> > And the Youth that is active in Love.   [*Drinks.*
> > Act III. 1713 only.

Alison (*speaks*)
> Women's Love is like Wild-fire
> The more it burneth the more it doth desire.
> > Act III. 1713 only.

Alison (*speaks*)
> There 's double danger in an assignation ;
> Though we resist the man's solicitation,   70
> We're often lost by woman's inclination.
> > End of Act III. 1730 only.

Alison (*speaks*)
> Beauty, like Colour, owes it self to Light ;
> For Youth and Age boast equal Charms by Night ;
> And we can still please ev'ry Sense—but Sight.
> > End of Act III. 1713 only.

Chaucer (*disguised as a Conjurer*)
> Thrice I wave my Wand around,
> And Consecrate this Spot of Ground.
> *Zutphin*, and *Zephin*,—ye that Reign
> Far beyond the Northern Main.
> Quickly, quickly take your Flight,
> And leave the dark Abyss of Night ;

He puts off the Conjurer's Cap and Beard, and puts on his Hat, &c. and peeps over Myrtilla's Shoulder, as she looks in the Glass.

* M 3

Hither, hither, gently fly,   81
Ye milder Spirits of the Sky,
Let now my Science be your Care,
And bring her Lover to the Fair.

   .   .   .   .   .

Swiftly, swiftly haste away,   He puts on his Dis-
And my inverted Wand obey: guise again.
Let no hurly-burly rise;
Nor Storms the Face of Heav'n disguise;
Let the Winds in silence lye,
Nor dreadful Lightnings streak the Sky;   90
Let Thunder sleep, and Calmness reign,
In Fire, in Air, in Earth, and Main,
Lightly skim the tops of Mountains,
Nor blast the Corn, nor taint the Fountains,
Swiftly, swiftly haste away,
And my inverted Wand obey.
                       Act IV.   1713 only.

Sir Harry Gauntlet (reads Doggrel's verses aloud)

    Ye Gods! did *Jove* e'er taste such charms,
    When prest in fair *Alcmena*'s arms?
      I'm sure it could not be!
    A triple night would not have done,   100
    He would have blotted out the Sun,
      Had he been pleas'd like me.

    .   .   .   .   .

    Beneath the sable veil's disguise,
    Had you not hid your killing eyes,
      It had been worse for me.
    My *Nun* had then appear'd like *Jove*,
    I had been light'ning-struck for love
      And dy'd like *Semele*.
                    Act IV.   1730.

Chaucer (reads Doggrel's verses aloud)

    S T A N Z A S, upon a Fair Lady making me **Happy.**

    Ye Gods! did *Jove* e'er taste such Charms,
    When prest in fair *Alcmena*'s Arms,   110
      O ye Immortal Pow'rs!
    For He in all his triple Night,
    Did ne'er enjoy such soft Delight,
      As I in half a one of yours.

    .   .   .   .   .

    Oh Ecstasie! what Wit can tell,
    Those Charms that lie beneath your Veil
      Those Lightnings of your Eye?

No longer then your Beauty shroud,
Nor place the Sun behind a Cloud,
   For ah! fair Nun, I faint, I die.   120
                    Act IV. 1713.

Busy (speaks)

I'll act with zeal that never yet was shown;
First do my lady's job, and next my own.
                    End of Act IV. 1730.

Chaucer (speaks)

Now Blithe and Debonnaire, I'll relish Life,
Nor sour it with that lasting Evil—Wife:
My Love at random through the Sex shall fly,
And Treach'rous Vows allure them to comply:
I'll artfully each tender Fair subdue,
And, like themselves, for half an hour be true.
                    End of Act IV. 1713.

Chaucer (extemporizes some verses)

I.

Daphne, a coy and foolish Dame,
   Flew from *Apollo*'s Charms,   130
Had he confess'd in Verse his Flame,
   She had flown into his Arms.

II.

Whenever *Orpheus* touch'd the Lyre,
   Or sung melodious Airs,
He made the very Stones admire,
   And tam'd the fiercest Bears.

III.

Are Ladies Hearts more hard than Stone,
   Are Wolves and Bears less fierce?
Then, prithee, Nymph, no longer frown,
   But own the Pow'r of Verse.   140
                    Act V. 1713 only.

Chaucer (speaks)

Marriage, the chiefest Good that Mortals know,
Doubles our Joy, while it divides our Woe:
What anxious Cares can then our Bliss controul,
When Heav'n assents, and Love unites our Soul?
                    Act V. 1713 only.

Florinda (speaks)

Love like an Apparition's unconfin'd,
And scorns a Leading-String though young and blind;
Woman by Nature all Restraint disdains;
And she that wears will chuse the Nuptial Chains.
                    Act V. 1713 only.

Alison (sings)

I.

There was a Swain full fair,
 Was tripping it over the Grass,   150
And there he spy'd with her Nut-brown Hair,
 A Pretty tight Country Lass.
  Fair Damsel, says he,
  With an Air brisk and free,
Come let us each other know ;
  She blush'd in his Face,
  And reply'd with a Grace,
Pray forbear, Sir,——no, no, no, no.

II.

The Lad being bolder grown,
 Endeavour'd to steal a Kiss,   160
She cry'd, Pish !—let me alone,
 But held up her Nose for the Bliss.
  And when he begun,
  She would never have done,
But unto his Lips she did grow,
  Near smother'd to Death,
  As soon as she'ad Breath,
She stammer'd out, no, no, no, no.

III.

Come, come, says he, pretty Maid,
 Let's walk to yon' private Grove,   170
Cupid always delights in the cooling Shade,
 There, I'll read thee a Lesson of Love.
  She mends her Pace,
  And hastes to the Place,
But if her Love Lecture you'd know ;
  Let a bashful young Muse,
  Plead the Maiden's Excuse,
And answer you,—no, no, no, no.
       Act V. 1713 only.

Doggrel (' *hums a Tune* ')

  Fair *Amaryllis* in a pleasant Grove,
  For her dear Boy a flow'ry Garland wove.   180
  For *Damon* stay'd ;—*Damon*, the Loveliest Swain;
  And she the fairest Nymph of all the Plain.
  Thus she complains, while all the Feather'd Throng,
  And Silence, list'ned to the mournful Song.
       Act V. 1713 only.

Sir Harry Gauntlet (speaks)

  When superstition hath the mind engross'd,
  Judgment is laid asleep, and reason lost ;

154 free,] free *1713*.   171 Shade,] Shade *1713*.

By fancy'd omens we have joy and sorrow,
Sit moap'd at home, or gad abroad to-morrow ;
By that we sink our joys, our fears enhance,
And all we do, is right or wrong by chance.   190
But shall I censure visionary schemes ?
Myrtilla, no.—I thank your stars and dreams.

Alison (*speaks*)

For through the sex this pious humour runs ;
Were there no men, all women would be nuns.
End of Act V.   1730.

Chaucer (*speaks*)

She who by Rules of Superstition goes,
Upon her self does rig'rous Laws impose ;
While Fancy gives or takes away Repose.
Yet why should I this female whim deride,
Since to her Stars I owe my beauteous Bride ?
Through the whole Sex this Pious Humour runs,   200
Were there no Men, all Women would be Nuns.
End of Act V.   1713.

[*Editions :*
1. THE | *WHAT D'YE CALL IT :* | A | Tragi-Comi-Pastoral | FARCE. | By Mr. *GAY.* | —*Spirat Tragicum satis, & feliciter audet.* | Hor. |—*Locus est & pluribus Umbris.* | Hor. | *LONDON :* | Printed for BERNARD LINTOTT between the | two *Temple* Gates in *Fleet-street.*

    8vo. No date. Published 19 March, 1715. Engraved frontispiece, unsigned.
2. The Second Edition. No date.
    8vo.
3. The Third Edition. 1716.
    8vo.
4. An edition published in Dublin for George Grierson. No date.
    8vo.
5. *Poems on Several Occasions.* 1720.
6. The Fourth Edition. 1725.
    8vo.
7. *Poems on Several Occasions.* 1731.

Not included in the editions of Bell (1777), Cooke (1804), and Underhill.]

THE

WHAT D'YE CALL IT :

A

Tragi - Comi - Paſtoral

F A R C E.

----*Spirat Tragicum ſatis, & feliciter audet.* Hor.

----*Locus eſt & pluribus Umbris.* Hor.

THE

PREFACE.

A S I am the first who have introduced this kind of Dramatick entertainment upon the stage, I think it absolutely necessary to say something by way of Preface, not only to shew the nature of it, but to answer some objections that have been already rais'd against it by the graver sort of Wits, and other interested people.

We have often had Tragi-Comedies upon the English *Theatre with success: but in that sort of composition the Tragedy and Comedy are in distinct Scenes, and may be easily separated from each other. But the whole Art of the* Tragi-Comi-Pastoral Farce *lies in interweaving the several kinds of the Drama with each other, so that they cannot be distinguish'd or separated.*

The objections that are rais'd against it as a Tragedy, *are as follow.*   10

First, As to the Plot, they deny it to be Tragical, because its Catastrophe is a wedding, which hath ever been accounted Comical.

Secondly, As to the Characters; that those of a Justice of Peace, a Parish-Clark, *and an* Embryo's Ghost, *are very improper to the dignity of Tragedy, and were never introduc'd by the Antients.*

Thirdly, They say the Sentiments are not Tragical, because they are those of the lowest country people.

Lastly, They will not allow the Moral to be proper for Tragedy, because the end of Tragedy being to shew human life in its distresses, imperfections and infirmities, thereby to soften the mind of man from its natural obduracy and haughtiness, the Moral ought to have the same tendency; but this Moral, they say, seems entirely calculated to flatter the Audience in their vanity and self-conceitedness.   23

You all have sense enough to find it out.

To the first objection I answer, that it is still a disputable point, even among the best Criticks, whether a Tragedy may not have a happy Catastrophe; *that the* French *Authors are of this opinion, appears from most of their Modern Tragedies.*

In answer to the second objection, I cannot affirm, that any of the Antients have either a Justice of Peace, a Parish Clark, *or an* Embryo Ghost *in their Tragedies; yet whoever will look into* Sophocles, Euripides, *or* Seneca, *will find that they greatly affected to introduce* Nurses *in all their pieces, which every one must grant to be an inferior Character to a Justice of Peace; in imitation of which also, I have introduced a Grandmother and an Aunt.*   33

To the third objection, which is the meanness of the sentiments, I answer that the sentiments of Princes and clowns have not in reality that difference which they seem to have: their thoughts are almost the same, and they only differ as the same thought is attended with a meanness or pomp of diction, or receive

1 who] 1720, 1731   that 8vos.

a different light from the circumstances each Character is conversant with. But these Criticks have forgot the precept of their Master Horace, *who tells them,*

—Tragicus plerumque dolet sermone pedestri.

In answer to the objection against the Moral, I have only this to alledge, That the Moral of this piece is conceal'd ; and Morals that are couch'd so as to exercise the judgments of the audience, have not been disapprov'd by the best Criticks.* And I would have those that object against it as a piece of Flattery, consider, that there is such a Figure as the Irony.   45

The Objections against it as a Comedy *are,*

First, They object to the Plot, that it throws the Characters into the deepest circumstances of distress : Inferiors trampled upon by the Tyranny of Power, a soldier to be shot for desertion, and an innocent maid in the utmost despair.

Secondly, That Ghosts are introduced, which move terror, a Passion not proper to be moved in Comedy.

Thirdly, They will not allow the Sentiments to be comical, because they are such as naturally flow from the deep distresses above-mentioned. The Speech of a dying man, and his last advice to his child, are what one could not reasonably expect should raise the mirth of an audience.   55

First, that the Plot is comical, I argue from the Peripaetia *and the* Catastrophe. Peascod's *change of fortune upon the reprieve's being produced,* Kitty's *distress ending in the discharge of her sweetheart, and the wedding, are all incidents that are truly comical.*

To the second objection I answer, That Ghosts have not been omitted in the antient Comedy ; Aristophanes *having laid the Scene of his* Βάτραχοι *among the shades ; and* Plautus *has introduced a* Lar familiaris *in his Prologue to the* Aulularia, *which tho' not actually a Ghost, is very little better.*

As to the third objection, That the Sentiments are not Comical, I answer, That the Ghosts are the only characters which are objected to as improper for Comedy, which I have already proved to be justly introduced, as following the manner of the old Comedy ; but as they allow that the Sentiments naturally flow from the characters, those of the Justice, Clowns, &c. *which are indisputably Comical characters, must be Comical. For the Sentiments being conveyed in number and rhime, I have the authority of the best Modern* French *Comedies.*   71

The only objection against it as a Pastoral *falls upon the characters, which they say are partly* Pastoral, *and partly not so. They insist particularly, that a Sergeant of Granadiers is not a pastoral character, and that the others are so far from being in the state of innocence, that the clowns are whoremasters, and the damsels with child.*

To this I reply, that Virgil *talks of Soldiers among his Shepherds.*

Impius haec tam culta Novalia miles habebit.

And the character of the Sergeant is drawn according to the Epithet of Virgil, Impius Miles, *which may be seen in that speech of his,*   80

You Dog, die like a Soldier——and be damn'd.

---

* *See* Bossu's *Chapter* of concealed Sentences.

38 *with*] 1720, 1731 *in* 8vos

For, in short, a Soldier *to a* Swain *is but just the same thing that a* Wolf *is to his* Flocks, *and is as naturally talk'd of or introduc'd. As for the rest of the characters, I can only say I have copied nature, making the youths amorous before wedlock, and the damsels complying and fruitful. Those that are the most conversant in the country are the best judges of this sort of nature.*

Lastly, They object against it as a Farce.

First, Because the irregularity of the Plot should answer to the Extravagance of the characters, which they say this piece wants, and therefore is no Farce.

Secondly, They deny the characters to be Farcical, because they are actually in nature.   91

Thirdly, If it was a true Farce, *the Sentiments ought to be strain'd, to bear a proportional irregularity with the plot and characters.*

To the First I answer, That the Farcical Scene of the Ghosts is introduced without any coherence with the rest of the piece, might be entirely left out, and would not be allowed in a regular Comedy. There are indeed a great number of Dramatick entertainments, where are Scenes of this kind ; but those pieces in reality are not Comedies, *but* five Act Farces.

Secondly, Let the Criticks consider only the nature of Farce, that it is made up of absurdities and incongruities, and that those pieces which have these Qualities in the greatest degree are the most Farces ; and they will allow this to be so from the characters, and particularly from that of the speaking Ghost of an Embryo, *in the conclusion of the first Act. I have, 'tis true,* Aristophanes's *Authority for things of this sort in Comedy, who hath introduced a* Chorus of Frogs, *and made them talk in the following manner :*   105

> Βρεκεκεκὲξ, κοὰξ, κοὰξ,
> Βρεκεκεκὲξ, κοὰξ, κοὰξ,
> Λιμναῖα κρηνῶν τέκνα, &c.

Mr. D'Urfey *of our own nation has given all the fowls of the air the faculty of speech equal with the parrot. Swans and elbow-chairs in the Opera of* Dioclesian *have danc'd upon the English Stage with good success.* Shakespear *hath some characters of this sort, as a* speaking wall, *and* Moonshine.* The former he designed to introduce (as he tells us himself) with something rough cast about him, and the latter comes in with a lanthorn and candle ; which in my opinion are characters that make a good figure in the modern Farce.*   115

Thirdly, The sentiments are truly of the Farce kind, as they are the sentiments of the meanest Clowns convey'd in the pomp of numbers and rhyme ; which is certainly forc'd and out of nature, and therefore Farcical.

After all I have said, I would have these Criticks only consider, when they object against it as a Tragedy, that I design'd it something of a Comedy ; when

---

* *See his* Midsummer Night's Dream.

---

83 *and is*] 1720, 1731 *and* 8vos.
96 *a great number*] 1720, 1731 *great numbers* 8vos.
103 Aristophanes's] Aristophanes' *first, second, and third editions (8vo).*
117 *rhyme*] 1720, 1731 *rhime* 8vos.

they cavil at it as a Comedy, that I had partly a view to Pastoral ; when they attack it as a Pastoral, that my endeavours were in some degree to write a Farce ; and when they would destroy its character as a Farce, that my design was a Tragi-Comi-Pastoral : I believe when they consider this, they will all agree, that I have happily enough executed what I purpos'd, which is all I contend for. Yet that I might avoid the cavils and misinterpretations of severe Criticks, I have not call'd it a Tragedy, Comedy, Pastoral, or Farce, but left the name entirely undetermin'd in the doubtful appellation of the What d'ye call it, *which name I thought unexceptionable ; but I added to it a* Tragi-Comi-Pastoral Farce, *as it comprized all those several kinds of the* Drama. 130

The Judicious Reader will easily perceive, that the unities are kept as in the most perfect pieces, that the Scenes are unbroken, and Poetical Justice strictly observ'd ; the Ghost of the Embryo *and the* Parish-Girle *are entire new characters. I might enlarge further upon the conduct of the particular Scenes, and of the piece in general, but shall only say, that the Success this piece has met with upon the Stage, gives encouragement to our Dramatick Writers to follow its Model ; and evidently demonstrates that this sort of* Drama *is no less fit for the Theatre than those they have succeeded in.* 138

Dramatis Personae.

M E N.

Sir *Roger*	Mr. *Miller.*
Sir *Humphry*	Mr. *Cross.*
Justice *Statute*	Mr. *Shepherd.*
Squire *Thomas,* Sir *Roger's* Son, alias, *Thomas Filbert*	} Mr. *Johnson.*
Jonas Dock, alias *Timothy Peascod*	Mr. *Penkethman.*
Peter Nettle, the Sergeant	Mr. *Norris.*
Steward to Sir *Roger*	Mr. *Quin.*
Constable	Mr. *Penroy.*
Corporal	Mr. *Weller.*
Stave, a Parish-Clark.	
The Ghost of a Child unborn	Mr. *Norris* Junior.
Countrymen, Ghosts, and Soldiers.	

W O M E N.

Kitty, the Steward's Daughter, alias *Kitty Carrot*	} Mrs. *Bicknell.*
Dorcas, Peascod's Sister	Mrs. *Willis* Senior.
Joyce, Peascod's Daughter left upon the Parish	} Miss *Younger.*
Aunt	Mrs. *Baker.*
Grandmother.	

THE
WHAT D'YE CALL IT:
A
Tragi-Comi-Pastoral
F A R C E.

SCENE, *A Country Justice's Hall, adorn'd with Scutcheons and Stags Horns.*

Enter Steward, Squire, Kitty, Dock, *and others in Country Habits.*

Steward. So, you are ready in your parts, and in your dress too, I see ; your own best cloaths do the business. Sure never was Play and actors so suited. Come, range your selves before me, women on the right, and men on the left. Squire *Thomas*, you make a good figure.

[*The Actors range themselves.*

Squire. Ay, thanks to *Barnaby*'s Sunday cloaths ; but call me *Thomas Filbert*, as I am in the Play.

Steward. Chear up, daughter, and make *Kitty Carrot* the shining part : Squire *Thomas* is to be in love with you to night, girle.   8

Kitty. Ay, I have felt Squire *Thomas*'s love to my cost. I have little stomach to play, in the condition he hath put me into.   [*Aside.*

Steward. *Jonas Dock*, dost thou remember thy name ?

Dock. My name ? *Jo—Jo—Jonas.* No—that was the name my God-fathers gave me. My play name is *Timothy Pea—Pea—Peascod* ; ay, *Peascod* —and am to be shot for a deserter.—

Steward. And you, *Dolly?*   15

Dolly. An't please ye, I am *Dorcas*, *Peascod*'s sister, and am to be with child, as it were.

1 *Countryman.* And I am to take her up, as it were—I am the Constable.

2 *Countryman.* And I am to see *Tim* shot, as it were—I am the Corporal.

Steward. But what is become of our sergeant ?

PRELIMINARY SCENE. *I print this after the style of the 8vos. The editions of 1720 and 1731 print the names of the speakers as in the body of the Play, between the speeches.*

Dorcas. Why *Peter Nettle, Peter, Peter.* [*Enter* Nettle.

Nettle. These stockings of *Susan's* cost a woundy deal of pains the pulling on : But what 's a sergeant without red stockings ? 23

Dock. I'll dress thee, *Peter,* I'll dress thee. Here, stand still, I must twist thy neckcloth ; I would make thee hold up thy head, and have a ruddy complexion ; but pr'ythee don't look black in the face, man. [*Rolling his Neckcloth.*] Thou must look fierce and dreadful. [*Making whiskers with a burnt cork.*] But what shall we do for a grenadier's cap ? 28

Steward. Fetch the leathern bucket that hangs in the belfry ; that is curiously painted before, and will make a figure.

Nettle. No, no, I have what 's worth twenty on't : the Pope's mitre, that my master Sir *Roger* seiz'd, when they would have burnt him at our market town.

Steward. So, now let ev'ry body withdraw, and prepare to begin the play. [*Exeunt Actors.*] My daughter debauched ! and by that booby Squire ! well, perhaps the conduct of this play may retrieve her folly, and preserve her reputation. Poor girle ! I cannot forget thy tears. [*Enter Sir* Roger. 37

Sir Roger. Look ye, Steward, don't tell me you can't bring them in. I will have a ghost ; nay, I will have a competence of ghosts. What, shall our neighbours think we are not able to make a ghost ? A play without a ghost is like, is like,—i'gad it is like nothing.

Steward. Sir, be satisfied ; you shall have ghosts.

Sir Roger. And is the play as I order'd it, both a Tragedy and a Comedy ? I would have it a Pastoral too : and if you could make it a Farce, so much the better—and what if you crown'd all with a spice of your Opera ? You know my neighbours never saw a Play before ; and d'ye see, I would shew them all sorts of Plays under one. 47

Steward. Sir *Roger,* it is contrived for that very purpose.

[*Enter two* Justices.

Sir Roger. Neighbours, you are welcome. Is not this Steward of mine a pure ingenious fellow now, to make such a Play for us these *Christmas* holidays. [*Exit Steward bowing.*]—A rare headpiece ! he has it here, i'faith. [*Pointing to his own head.*] But indeed, I gave him the hint—To see now what contrivance some folks have ! We have so fitted the parts to my tenants, that ev'ry man talks in his own way !—and then we have made just three justices in the play, to be play'd by us three justices of the *Quorum.* 55

1 *Justice.* Zooks !—so it is ;—main ingenious.—And can we sit and smoke at the same time we act ?

Sir Roger. Ay, ay,—we have but three or four words to say—and may drink and be good company in peace and silence all the while after.

2 *Justice.* But how shall we know when we are to say these same words ?

Sir Roger. This shall be the signal—when I set down the tankard, then speak you, Sir *Humphry,*—and when Sir *Humphry* sets down the tankard, speak you, Squire *Statute.*

1 *Justice.* Ah, Sir *Roger,* you are an old dog at these things.

2 *Justice.* To be sure. 65

Sir Roger. Why neighbours, you know, experience, experience—I remember your *Harts* and your *Bettertons*—But to see your *Othello,* neighbours,—how

26 *Rolling*] 1720, 1731 *Twisting* 8vos.   41 i'gad] 1720, 1731   igad *8vos.*
64 an old] *1731*   old *1720 and 8vos.*

he would rave and roar, about a foolish flower'd handkerchief!—and then he would groul so manfully,—and he would put out the light, and put the light out so cleverly ! but hush—the Prologue, the Prologue.

[*They seat themselves with much ceremony at the table, on which are pipes and tobacco, and a large silver tankard.*

THE

PROLOGUE,

Spoken by Mr. *Pinkethman.*

THE entertainment of this night—or day,
This something, or this nothing of a Play,
Which strives to please all palates at a time,
With ghosts and men, songs, dances, prose and rhime,
This comic story, or this tragic jest,   5
May make you laugh, or cry, as you like best ;
May exercise your good, or your ill-nature,
Move with distress, or tickle you with satyr.
All must be pleas'd too with their Parts, we think :
Our maids have sweethearts, and their Worships drink.
Criticks, we know, by ancient rules may maul it ;
But sure Gallants must like—the What d'ye call it.

ACT I. SCENE I.

Sir ROGER, *Sir* HUMPHRY, *Justice* STATUTE, CONSTABLE, FILBERT, SERGEANT, KITTY, DORCAS, GRANDMOTHER, AUNT.

Sir ROGER.

HERE, Thomas Filbert, answer to your name,
Dorcas hath sworn to you she owes her shame :
Or wed her strait, or else you're sent afar,
To serve his gracious Majesty in war.

FILBERT.

'Tis false, 'tis false—I scorn thy odious touch,
                              [*Pushing* Dorcas *from him.*

DORCAS.

When their turn 's serv'd, all men will do as much.

KITTY.

Ah, good your Worships, ease a wretched maid,
To the right father let the child be laid.

Art thou not perjur'd ?—mark his harmless look.
How canst thou, *Dorcas*, kiss the Bible book ?   10
Hast thou no conscience, dost not fear *Old Nick?*
Sure sure the ground will ope, and take thee quick.

S E R G E A N T.

Zooks ! never wed, 'tis safer much to roam ;
For what is war abroad to war at home ?
Who wou'd not sooner bravely risque his life ;
For what 's a cannon to a scolding wife ?

F I L B E R T.

Well, if I must, I must—I hate the wench,
I'll bear a musquet then against the *French.*
From door to door I'd sooner whine and beg,
Both arms shot off, and on a wooden leg,   20
Than marry such a trapes—No, no, I'll not :
—Thou wilt too late repent when I am shot.
But, *Kitty*, why dost cry ?—

G R A N D M O T H E R.

————Stay, Justice, stay :
Ah, little did I think to see this day !
Must Grandson *Filbert* to the wars be prest ?
Alack ! I knew him when he suck'd the breast,
Taught him his catechism, the fescue held,
And join'd his letters, when the bantling spell'd.
His loving mother left him to my care.   30
Fine child, as like his Dad as he could stare !
Come *Candlemas*, nine years ago she dy'd,
And now lies buried by the yew-tree's side.

A U N T.

O tyrant Justices ! have you forgot
How my poor brother was in *Flanders* shot ?
You press'd my brother—he shall walk in white,
He shall—and shake your curtains ev'ry night.
What though a paultry hare he rashly kill'd,
That cross'd the furrows while he plough'd the Field ?   39
You sent him o'er the hills and far away ;
Left his old mother to the parish pay,
With whom he shar'd his ten pence ev'ry day.
Wat kill'd a bird, was from his farm turn'd out ;
You took the law of *Thomas* for a trout :
You ruin'd my poor uncle at the sizes,
And made him pay nine pound for *Nisiprises.*
Now will you press my harmless nephew too ?
Ah, what has conscience with the rich to do !

46 pound] *1731*   pounds *1720 and 8vos.*

[Sir Roger *takes up the Tankard.*

Though in my hand no silver tankard shine,

Nor my dry lip be dy'd with claret wine,   50

Yet I can sleep in peace—

Sir R O G E R.   *[After having drunk.*

————————————Woman, forbear.

Sir H U M P H R Y.   *[Drinking.*

The man 's within the act————

Justice S T A T U T E.   *[Drinking also.*

——————————The law is clear.

S E R G E A N T.

Haste, let their Worships orders be obey'd.

K I T T Y.   *[Kneeling.*

Behold how low you have reduc'd a maid.

Thus to your Worships on my knees I sue,

(A posture never known but in the pew)

If we can money for our taxes find,

Take that—but ah! our sweethearts leave behind.   60

To trade so barb'rous he was never bred,

The blood of vermine all the blood he shed :

How should he, harmless youth, how should he then

Who kill'd but poulcats, learn to murder men ?

D O R C A S.

O *Thomas, Thomas!* hazard not thy life ;

By all that 's good, I'll make a loving wife :

I'll prove a true pains-taker day and night,

I'll spin and card, and keep our children tight.

I can knit stockings, you can thatch a barn ;

If you earn ten-pence, I my groat can earn.   70

How shall I weep to hear this infant cry ?

[Her hand on her belly.

He'll have no father——and no husband I.

K I T T Y.

Hold, *Thomas*, hold, nor hear that shameless witch :

I can sow plain-work, I can darn and stitch ;

I can bear sultry days and frosty weather ;

Yes, yes, my *Thomas*, we will go together ;

Beyond the seas together will we go,

In camps together, as at harvest, glow.

This arm shall be a bolster for thy head,

I'll fetch clean straw to make my soldier's bed ;   80

There, while thou sleep'st, my apron o'er thee hold,

Or with it patch thy tent against the cold.

Pigs in hard rains I've watch'd, and shall I do

That for the pigs, I would not bear for you ?

50 be] *1720, 1731* is *8vos.*

FILBERT.

Oh, *Kitty, Kitty,* canst thou quit the rake,
And leave these meadows for thy sweetheart's sake?
Canst thou so many gallant soldiers see,
And captains and lieutenants slight for me?
Say, canst thou hear the guns, and never shake,
Nor start at oaths that make a christian quake?   90
Canst thou bear hunger, canst thou march and toil
A long long way, a thousand thousand mile?
And when thy *Tom*'s blown up, or shot away,
Then canst thou starve?—they'll cheat thee of my pay.

Sir ROGER.   [*Drinking.*

Take out that wench——

Sir HUMPHRY.   [*Drinking.*

——————————But give her pennance meet.

Justice STATUTE.   [*Drinking also.*

I'll see her stand—next Sunday—in a sheet.

DORCAS.

Ah! why does nature give us so much cause
To make kind-hearted lasses break the laws?
Why should hard laws kind-hearted lasses bind,   100
When too soft nature draws us after kind?

SCENE II.

Sir ROGER, *Sir* HUMPHRY, *Justice* STATUTE, FILBERT,
SERGEANT, KITTY, GRANDMOTHER, AUNT, SOLDIER.

SOLDIER.

Sergeant, the captain to your quarters sent;
To ev'ry ale-house in the town I went.
Our Corp'ral now has the deserter found;
The men are all drawn out, the pris'ner bound.

SERGEANT.   [*To* Filbert.

Come, soldier, come——

KITTY.

——————————Ah! take me, take me too.

GRANDMOTHER.

Stay, forward wench;——

AUNT.

——————————What would the creature do?
This week thy mother means to wash and brew.

97 Sunday] sunday *1720 and 1731.*

KITTY.

Brew then she may herself, or wash or bake;   10
I'd leave ten mothers for one sweetheart's sake.
O justice most unjust!——

FILBERT.

——————————O tyranny!

KITTY.

How can I part?——

FILBERT.

——————Alas! and how can I?

KITTY.

O rueful day!——

FILBERT.

——————Rueful indeed, I trow.

KITTY.

O woeful day!

FILBERT.

——————A day indeed of woe!

KITTY.

When gentlefolks their sweethearts leave behind,   20
They can write letters, and say something kind;
But how shall *Filbert* unto me endite,
When neither I can read, nor he can write?
   Yet Justices, permit us e'er we part
To break this ninepence, as you've broke our heart.

   FILBERT.   [*Breaking the Ninepence.*
As this divides, thus are we torn in twain.

   KITTY.   [*Joining the Pieces.*
And as this meets, thus may we meet again.
      [*She is drawn away on one side of the Stage by
       Aunt and Grandmother.*
Yet one look more——

FILBERT.

      [*Haul'd off on the other side by the Sergeant.*
——————One more e'er yet we go.

KITTY.

To part is death.——   30

FILBERT.

——————'Tis death to part.

KITTY.

——————————Ah!

FILBERT.

——————————————Oh!

SCENE III.

Sir ROGER, *Sir* HUMPHRY, *Justice* STATUTE, *and* CONSTABLE.

Sir ROGER.   [*Drinking.*
See constable, that ev'ry one withdraw.

Sir HUMPHRY.   [*Drinking.*
We've business————

Justice STATUTE.   [*Drinking also.*
————————————To discuss a point of Law.

SCENE IV.

Sir ROGER, *Sir* HUMPHRY, *Justice* STATUTE.

They seem in earnest discourse.

Sir ROGER.

I say the Press-act plainly makes it out.

Sir HUMPHRY.

Doubtless, Sir *Roger.*————

Justice STATUTE.

————————————Brother, without doubt.

A Ghost rises.

1 GHOST.

I'm *Jeffry Cackle.*————You my death shall rue ;
For I was press'd by you, by you, by you.
[*Pointing to the Justices.*

Another Ghost rises.

2 GHOST.

I'm *Smut* the farrier.—You my death shall rue ;
For I was press'd by you, by you, by you.

A Woman's Ghost rises.

3 GHOST.

I'm *Bess* that hang'd my self for *Smut* so true ;
So owe my death to you, to you, to you.

A Ghost of an Embryo rises.

4 GHOST.

I was begot before my mother married,   10
Who whipt by you, of me poor child miscarried.

Another Woman's Ghost rises.

5 *G H O S T.*

Its mother I, whom you whipt black and blue;
Both owe our deaths to you, to you, to you.
[*All Ghosts shake their heads.*

Sir R O G E R.

Why do you shake your mealy heads at me?
You cannot say I did it————

B O T H   J U S T I C E S.

————————————No—nor we,

1 *G H O S T.*

All three————

2 *G H O S T.*

————All three————

3 *G H O S T.*

————————All three————   20

4 *G H O S T.*

————————————All three———

5 *G H O S T.*

——————————————————All three.

A SONG sung dismally by a GHOST.

Y E goblins, and fairys,
With frisks and vagarys,
Ye fairys and goblins,
With hoppings and hobblings,
  Come all, come all
To Sir Roger's great hall.

All fairys and goblins,
All goblins and fairys,
With hoppings and hobblings,
With frisks and vagarys.   30

C H O R U S.

Sing, goblins and fairys,
Sing, fairys and goblins,
With frisks and vagarys,
And hoppings and hobblings.

[*The ghosts dance round the Justices, who go off in a fright, and
the ghosts vanish.*

ACT II. SCENE I.

A Field.

TIMOTHY PEASCOD *bound* ; CORPORAL, SOLDIERS *and*
COUNTRYMEN.

C O R P O R A L.

Stand off there, countrymen ; and you, the guard,
Keep close your pris'ner——see that all's prepar'd.
Prime all your firelocks——fasten well the stake.

P E A S C O D.

'Tis too much, too much trouble for my sake.
O fellow-soldiers, countrymen and friends,
Be warn'd by me to shun untimely ends :
For evil courses am I brought to shame,
And from my soul I do repent the same.
Oft my kind *Grannam* told me——*Tim*, take warning,
Be good—and say thy pray'rs—and mind thy learning.   10
But I, sad wretch, went on from crime to crime ;
I play'd at nine-pins first in sermon time :
I rob'd the parson's orchard next ; and then
(For which I pray forgiveness) stole—a hen.
When I was press'd, I told them the first day
I wanted heart to fight, so ran away ;
                         [*Attempts to run off, but is prevented.*
For which behold I die.   'Tis a plain case,
'Twas all a judgment for my want of grace.
                         [*The soldiers prime, with their muskets towards him.*
Hold, hold, my friends ; nay hold, hold, hold, I pray ;
They may go off——and I have more to say.   20

1 *C O U N T R Y M A N.*

Come, 'tis no time to talk——

2 *C O U N T R Y M A N.*

——————————Repent thine ill,
And pray in this good book.——   [*Gives him a Book.*

P E A S C O D.

——————————————I will, I will.
Lend me thy handkercher—*The Pilgrim's pro*————
                         [*Reads and weeps.*
(I cannot see for tears) *Pro—Progress*—Oh !
The Pilgrim's Progress—eighth—edi—ti—on
Lon-don-prin-ted—for—Ni-cho-las Bod-ding-ton
With new ad-di-tions never made before.   29
Oh ! 'tis so moving, I can read no more.   [*Drops the book.*

SCENE II.

PEASCOD, CORPORAL, SOLDIERS, COUNTRYMEN, SERGEANT, FILBERT.

SERGEANT.

What whining 's this ?—boys, see your guns well ramm'd.
You dog, die like a soldier—and be damn'd.

FILBERT.

My friend in ropes !————————

PEASCOD.

——————————————I should not thus be bound,
If I had Means, and could but raise five pound.
The cruel Corp'ral whisper'd in my ear,
Five pounds, if rightly tipt, would set me clear.

FILBERT.

Here——*Peascod*, take my pouch—'tis all I own.
(For what is Means and like when *Kitty*'s gone !)
'Tis my press-money——can this silver fail ?
'Tis all, except one sixpence spent in ale.
This had a ring for *Kitty*'s finger bought,
Kitty on me had by that token thought.
But for thy life, poor *Tim*, if this can do't ;
Take it, with all my soul——thou'rt welcome to't.

[*Offers him his purse.*

1 COUNTRYMAN.

And take my fourteen pence————

2 COUNTRYMAN.

——————————————And my cramp-ring.
Would, for thy sake, it were a better thing.

3 COUNTRYMAN.

And master Sergeant, take my box of copper.

4 COUNTRYMAN.

And my wife's thimble————

5 COUNTRYMAN.

——————————————And this 'bacco-stopper.

SERGEANT.

No bribes. Take back your things—I'll have them not.

PEASCOD.

Oh ! must I die ?————

10 press-money] *1720, 1731*   press money *8vos.*
11 all,] *1720, 1731*   all *8vos.*

CHORUS of COUNTRYMEN.

————————Oh ! must poor *Tim* be shot !

PEASCOD.

But let me kiss thee first——　　　　　[*Embracing* Filbert.

SCENE III.

PEASCOD, CORPORAL, SOLDIERS, COUNTRYMEN, SERGEANT, FILBERT, DORCAS.

DORCAS.

————————————Ah, brother *Tim.*
Why these close hugs ? I owe my shame to him.
He scorns me now, he leaves me in the lurch ;
In a white sheet poor I must stand at church.
O marry me—[*To* Filbert.] Thy sister is with child.　　[*To* Tim.
And he, 'twas he my tender heart beguil'd.

PEASCOD.

Could'st thou do this ? could'st thou—　　[*In anger to* Filbert.

SERGEANT.

————————————————Draw out the men :
Quick to the stake ; he must be dead by ten.

DORCAS.

Be dead ! must *Tim* be dead !——　　　　　　　　10

PEASCOD.

————————————————He must—he must.

DORCAS.

Ah ! I shall sink downright ; my heart will burst.
—Hold, Sergeant, hold—yet ere you sing the Psalms,
Ah ! let me ease my conscience of its qualms.
O brother, brother ! *Filbert* still is true.
I fouly wrong'd him——do forgive me, do.　　　[*To* Filb.
The Squire betray'd me ; nay,—and what is worse,
Brib'd me with two gold guineas in this purse,
To swear the child to *Filbert*.————

PEASCOD.

————————————————What a *Jew*　　20
My sister is !——Do, *Tom*, forgive her, do.　　[*To* Filb.

FILBERT.　　　　[*Kisses* Dorcas.

But see thy base-born child, thy babe of shame,
Who left by thee, upon our parish came,
Comes for thy blessing.————

9 he] *1731*　you *1720 and 8vos.*　　　16 do forgive] do, forgive *all editions.*
24 blessing.—] *8vos.*　blessing— *1720, 1731.*

SCENE IV.

PEASCOD, CORPORAL, SOLDIERS, COUNTRYMEN, SERGEANT,
FILBERT, DORCAS, JOYCE.

PEASCOD.

————————————————Oh ! my sins of youth !
Why on the haycock didst thou tempt me, *Ruth* ?
O save me, Sergeant :——how shall I comply ?
I love my daughter so——I cannot die.

JOYCE.

Must father die ! and I be left forlorn ?
A lack a day ! that ever *Joyce* was born !
No grandsire in his arms e'er dandled me,
And no fond mother danc'd me on her knee.
They said, if ever father got his pay,
I should have two-pence ev'ry market-day.   10

PEASCOD.

Poor child ; hang sorrow, and cast care behind thee,
The parish by this badge is bound to find thee.
                    [*Pointing to the badge on her arm.*

JOYCE.

The parish finds indeed——but our church-wardens
Feast on the silver, and give us the farthings.
Then my school-mistress, like a vixen *Turk*,
Maintains her lazy husband by our work :
Many long tedious days I've worsted spun ;
She grudg'd me victuals when my task was done.
Heav'n send me a good service ! for I now
Am big enough to wash, or milk a cow.   20

PEASCOD.

O that I had by charity been bred !
I then had been much better——taught than fed.
Instead of keeping nets against the law,
I might have learnt accounts, and sung *Sol-fa*.
Farewell, my child ; spin on, and mind thy book,
And send thee store of grace therein to look.
Take warning by thy shameless Aunt ; lest thou
Should'st o'er thy bastard weep——as I do now.
Mark my last words——an honest living get ;
Beware of Papishes, and learn to knit.   30
                    [Dorcas *leads out* Joyce *sobbing and crying.*

10 market-day] *8vos.* market day *1720, 1731.*
22 better—taught] *1720, 1731* better taught— *8vos.*

*   N

SCENE V.

PEASCOD, CORPORAL, SOLDIERS, COUNTRYMEN, SERGEANT,
FILBERT.

FILBERT.

Let's drink before we part——for sorrow's dry.
To *Tim*'s safe passage———
                    [*Takes out a brandy-bottle, and drinks.*

1 *COUNTRYMAN.*

———————————————I'll drink too.

2 *COUNTRYMAN.*

————————————————And I.

PEASCOD.

Stay, let me pledge—'tis my last earthly liquor.   [*Drinks.*
——When I am dead you'll bind my grave with wicker.
                    [*They lead him to the stake.*

1 *COUNTRYMAN.*

He was a special ploughman————   [*Sighing.*

2 *COUNTRYMAN.*

————————————————Harrow'd well!

3 *COUNTRYMAN.*

And at our may-pole ever bore the bell!

PEASCOD.

Say, is it fitting in this very field,   10
Where I so oft have reap'd, so oft have till'd ;
This field, where from my youth I've been a carter,
I, in this field, should die for a deserter ?

FILBERT.

'Tis hard, 'tis wondrous hard !——

SERGEANT.

————————————Zooks, here 's a pother.
Strip him ; I'd stay no longer for my brother.

PEASCOD.

                    [*Distributing his things among his friends.*
Take you my 'bacco-box——my neckcloth, you.
To our kind Vicar send this bottle-skrew.
But wear these breeches, *Tom* ; they're quite bran-new.

FILBERT.

Farewell———   20

6 dead you'll] *1720, 1731*   dead—you'll *8vos.*

1 *COUNTRYMAN.*

————B'ye, *Tim.*————

2 *COUNTRYMAN.*

————————B'ye, *Tim.*

3 *COUNTRYMAN.*

————————————Adieu.

4 *COUNTRYMAN.*

————————————————Adieu.

[*They all take leave of* Peascod *by shaking hands with him.*

SCENE VI.

PEASCOD, CORPORAL, SOLDIERS, COUNTRYMEN, SERGEANT,
FILBERT, *to them a* SOLDIER *in great haste.*

SOLDIER.

Hold——why so furious, Sergeant ? by your leave,
Untye the pris'ner—see, here 's a reprieve.   [*Shows a paper.*

CHORUS of *COUNTRYMEN.*   [*Huzzaing.*

A reprieve, a reprieve, a reprieve !
                    [Peascod *is unty'd, and embraces his friends.*

SCENE VII.

PEASCOD, CORPORAL, SOLDIERS, COUNTRYMEN, SERGEANT,
FILBERT, CONSTABLE.

CONSTABLE.

Friends, reprehend him, reprehend him there.

SERGEANT.

For what ?——

CONSTABLE.

————————For stealing gaffer *Gap*'s gray mare.
                            [*They seize the* Sergeant.

PEASCOD.

Why, heark ye, heark, ye, friend ; you'll go to pot.
Would you be rather hang'd—hah !——hang'd or shot ?

SERGEANT.

Nay, hold, hold, hold——

PEASCOD.

————————————————Not if you were my brother.   10
Why, friend, should you not hang as well's another ?

CONSTABLE.

Thus said Sir *John*—the law must take its course ;
'Tis law that he may 'scape who steals a horse.
But (said Sir *John*) the statutes all declare,
The man shall sure be hang'd—that steals a mare.

P E A S C O D.   [*To the* Sergeant.

Ay—right—he shall be hang'd that steals a mare.
He shall be hang'd—that 's certain ; and good cause.
A rare good sentence this—how is't ?—the laws
No—not the laws—the statutes all declare,
The man that steals a mare shall sure—be—hang'd,   20
No, no—he shall be hang'd that steals a mare.

[*Exit* Sergeant *guarded,* Countrymen, &c. *huzzaing after him.*

S C E N E   V I I I.

KITTY, *with her hair loose,* GRANDMOTHER, AUNT, HAYMAKERS,
CHORUS *of* SIGHS *and* GROANS.

K I T T Y.

Dear happy fields, farewell ; ye flocks, and you
Sweet meadows, glitt'ring with the pearly dew :
And thou, my rake, companion of my cares,
Giv'n by my mother in my younger years :
With thee the toils of full eight springs I've known,
'Tis to thy help I owe this hat and gown ;
On thee I lean'd, forgetful of my work,
While *Tom* gaz'd on me, propt upon his fork :
Farewell, farewell ; for all thy task is o'er,
Kitty shall want thy service now no more.   10
[*Flings away the rake.*

C H O R U S of S I G H S *and* G R O A N S.

Ah———O !———Sure never was the like before!

K I T T Y.

Happy the maid, whose sweetheart never hears
The soldier's drum, nor writ of Justice fears.
Our ban thrice bid ! and for our wedding day
My kerchief bought ! then press'd, then forc'd away !

C H O R U S of S I G H S *and* G R O A N S.

Ah ! O ! poor soul ! alack ! and well a day !

5 I've] have *first and second editions.*
7 I lean'd] *1731* I've lean'd *8vos.*
15 press'd,] press'd *first and second editions.*

KITTY.

You, *Bess*, still reap with *Harry* by your side;
You, *Jenny*, shall next *Sunday* be a bride:
But I forlorn!——This ballad shews my care;
                             [*Gives Susan a ballad.*
Take this sad ballad, which I bought at fair: 20
Susan can sing——do you the burthen bear.

A BALLAD.

I.

'TW*AS when the seas were roaring*
   With hollow blasts of wind;
A damsel lay deploring,
   All on a rock reclin'd.
Wide o'er the rolling billows
   She cast a wistful look;
Her head was crown'd with willows
   That tremble o'er the brook.

II.

Twelve months are gone and over,   30
   And nine long tedious days.
Why didst thou, vent'rous lover,
   Why didst thou trust the seas?
Cease, cease, thou cruel ocean,
   And let my lover rest:
Ah! what's thy troubled motion
   To that within my breast?

III.

The merchant, rob'd of pleasure,
   Sees tempests in despair;
But what's the loss of treasure   40
   To losing of my dear?
Should you some coast be laid on
   Where gold and di'monds grow,
You'd find a richer maiden,
   But none that loves you so.

A BALLAD. Probably not published separately by Gay before the publication
of the *What d'ye Call it* in 1715. At any rate I have not traced any such publication.
    Besides the editions enumerated above, it appears separately in Pope's *Eloisa to
Abelard*, the second edition, Lintot, 1720. This volume included a few pieces by
other hands than Pope's.
    Also in Pope's *Miscellany Poems* (' Fifth Edition '), vol. i, 1726. See p. 88.
    The setting used in the performance and attributed to Handel will be found in the
British Museum—H 1601 (427).
    27 wistful] wishful *MP 1726.*   28 willows] willows, *El. to Ab. 1720, MP 1726.*
    34 Cease, cease thou cruel Ocean, *MP 1726.*
    45 Not one that loves you so. *MP 1726.*

IV.

How can they say that nature
  Has nothing made in vain ;
Why then beneath the water
  Should hideous rocks remain ?
No eyes the rocks discover,   50
  That lurk beneath the deep,
To wreck the wand'ring lover,
  And leave the maid to weep.

V.

All melancholy lying,
  Thus wail'd she for her dear ;
Repay'd each blast with sighing,
  Each billow with a tear ;
When, o'er the white wave stooping,
  His floating corpse she spy'd ;
Then like a lily drooping,   60
  She bow'd her head, and dy'd.

K I T T Y.

Why in this world should wretched *Kitty* stay ?
What if these hands should make my self away ?
I could not sure do otherways than well.
A maid so true's too innocent for hell.
But hearkye, *Cis*———   [*Whispers and gives her a penknife.*

A U N T.

————————I'll do't——'tis but to try
If the poor soul can have the heart to die.
                    [*Aside to the* Haymakers.
Thus then I strike——but turn thy head aside.

K I T T Y.

'Tis shameless sure to fall as pigs have dy'd.   70
No—take this cord—   [*Gives her a cord.*

A U N T.

————————————With this thou shalt be sped.
                [*Putting the noose round her neck.*

K I T T Y.

But curs are hang'd.———

A U N T.

————————————Christians should die in bed.

K I T T Y.

Then lead me thither ; there I'll moan and weep,
And close these weary eyes in death.

58 When o'er the white wave stooping *MP 1726.*

A U N T.

——————————————————————or sleep.   [*Aside.*

K I T T Y.

When I am cold, and stretch'd upon my bier,
My restless sprite shall walk at midnight here :
Here shall I walk——for 'twas beneath yon tree   80
Filbert first said he lov'd——lov'd only me.   [Kitty *faints.*

G R A N D M O T H E R.

She swoons, poor Soul—help, *Dolly.*

A U N T.

——————————————————————She 's in fits.
Bring water, water, water.———   [*Screaming.*

G R A N D M O T H E R.

——————————————————Fetch her wits.
        [*They throw water upon her.*

K I T T Y.

Hah.!—I am turn'd a stream—look all below ;
It flows, and flows, and will for ever flow.
The meads are all afloat—the haycocks swim.
Hah ! who comes here !—my *Filbert !* drown not him.
Bagpipes in butter, flocks in fleecy fountains,   90
Churns, sheep-hooks, seas of milk, and honey mountains.

S C E N E   I X.

Kitty, Grandmother, Aunt, Haymakers, Filbert.

K I T T Y.

It is his ghost——or is it he indeed ?
Wert thou not sent to war ? hah, dost thou bleed ?
No——'tis my *Filbert.*

F I L B E R T.   [*Embracing her.*

——————————————————Yes, 'tis he, 'tis he,
Dorcas confess'd ; the Justice set me free.
I'm thine again.———

K I T T Y.

——————————————I thine————

F I L B E R T.

——————————————————————Our fears are fled.
Come, let's to Church, to Church.———

SCENE IX. *The 8vos wrongly print* Chorus *of* Sighs *and* Groans *after* Haymakers.

KITTY.
————————————————————To wed.   10

FILBERT.
————————————————————To bed.

CHORUS of HAYMAKERS.
A wedding, a bedding ; a wedding, a bedding.
[*Exeunt all the Actors.*

Sir Roger. Ay now for the Wedding. Where 's he that plays the Parson ?
Now, neighbours, you shall see what was never shewn upon the *London* stage.
——Why, heigh day ! what 's our Play at a stand ?   [*Enter a Countryman.*
Countryman. So please your worship, I should have play'd the Parson,
but our Curate would not lend his gown, for he says it is a profanation.   17
Sir Roger. What a scrupulous whim is this ? an innocent thing ! believe
me, an innocent thing.   [*The Justices assent by nods and signs.*
[*Enter* Stave *the Parish-clerk.*
Stave. Master Doctor saith he hath two and twenty good reasons against
it from the Fathers, and he is come himself to utter them to your Worship.
Sir Roger. What, shall our Play be spoil'd ? I'll have none of his reasons—
call in Mr. *Inference.*   [*Stave goes out and re-enters.*
Stave. Sir, he saith he never greatly affected stage Plays.
[*Within.*]   *Stave, Stave, Stave.*   25
Sir Roger. Tell him that I say——
[*Within.*]   *Stave, Stave.*
Sir Roger. What, shall the Curate controul me ? have not I the presenta-
tion ? tell him that I will not have my Play spoil'd ; nay, that he shall marry
the couple himself—I say, he shall.   [*Stave goes out and re-enters.*
Stave. The steward hath persuaded him to join his hands in the
parlour within—but he saith he will not, and cannot in conscience consent
to expose his character before neighbouring gentlemen ; neither will he enter
into your worship's hall ; for he calleth it a stage *pro tempore.*
Sir Humphry. Very likely : The good man may have reason.   35
Justice Statute. In troth, we must in some sort comply with the scrupulous
tender conscienc'd doctor.
Sir Roger. Why, what 's a Play without a marriage ? and what is a marriage
if one sees nothing of it ? Let him have his humour—but set the doors wide
open, that we may see how all goes on.   [*Exit* Stave.
[*Sir* Roger *at the door pointing.*
So natural ! d'ye see now, neighbours ? the ring i'faith. To have and to hold !
right again—well play'd, doctor ; well play'd, Son *Thomas.* Cóme, come,
I'm satisfy'd—now for the fiddles and dances.
[*Enter* Steward, *Squire* Thomas, Kitty, Stave, *&c.*
Steward. Sir *Roger*, you are very merry.

So comes a reck'ning when the banquet's o'er,   45
The dreadful reck'ning, and men smile no more.

41 i' faith. To] *1720, 1731* i'faith—to *8vos.*

I wish you joy of your Play, and of your daughter. I had no way but this
to repair the injury your son had done my child—she shall study to deserve
your favour.   [*Presenting* Kitty *to Sir* Roger.
  Sir Roger. Married! how married! can the marriage of *Filbert* and *Carrot*
have any thing to do with my son ?
  Steward. But the marriage of *Thomas* and *Katherine* may, Sir *Roger.*
  Sir Roger. What a plague, am I trick'd then ? I must have a stage Play,
with a pox !   54
  Sir Humphry. If this speech be in the play, remember the tankard,
Sir *Roger.*
  Squire Thomas. Zooks, these stage plays are plaguy dangerous things—
but I am no such fool neither, but I know this was all your contrivance.
  Justice Statute. Ay, Sir *Roger*, you told us it was you that gave him the hint.
  Sir Roger. Why blockhead ! puppy ! had you no more wit than to say
the ceremony ? he should only have married you in rhime, fool.   61
  Squire Thomas. Why, what did I know, ha ? but so it is—and since murder
will out, as the saying is ; look ye father, I was under some sort of a promise
too, d'ye see—so much for that—If I be a husband, I be a husband, there's
an end on't.—sure I must have been married some time or other.
          [*Sir* Roger *walks up and down fretting, and goes out in a passion.*
  Sir Humphry. In troth, it was in some sort my opinion before ; it is
good in law.
  Justice Statute. Good in law, good in law—but hold, we must not lose the
dance.   70

A D A N C E.

E P I L O G U E.

S T A V E.

Our stage Play has a moral——and no doubt
You all have sense enough to find it out.

THREE HOURS AFTER MARRIAGE

PROLOGUE.

[*Editions :*
1. *Three Hours after Marriage.* | A | COMEDY, | As it is Acted at the | *Theatre* Royal. | *Rumpatur, quisquis rumpitur invidia.* MART. | *LONDON* : | Printed for BERNARD LINTOT between the | *Temple Gates, Fleetstreet.* 1717. Post 8vo.
The *Advertisement*, signed by *John Gay*, acknowledges ' the Assistance I have receiv'd in this Piece from two of my friends '—viz. Pope and Arbuthnot.
2. Miscellanies in Verse, 1727. (Prologue only ; text as given here.)
3. Miscellanies. The Fourth Volume, 1747.]

AUTHORS are judg'd by strange capricious Rules ;
The great ones are thought mad, the small ones Fools :
Yet sure the Best are most severely fated,
For Fools are only laugh'd at, Wits are hated.
Blockheads with Reason Men of Sense abhor ;
But Fool 'gainst Fool, is barb'rous civil War.
Why on all Authors then should Cricks fall ?
Since some have writ, and shewn no wit at all.
Condemn a Play of theirs, and they evade it,
Cry, "Damn not us, but damn the *French* that made it."　　10
By running Goods, these graceless Owlers gain ;
Theirs are the *Rules* of *France*, the *Plots* of *Spain* :
But Wit like Wine, from happier Climates brought,
Dash'd by these Rogues, turns *English* common Draught.
They pall *Moliere's* and *Lopez'* sprightly Strain,
And teach dull *Harlequins* to grin in vain.
　How shall our Author hope a gentle Fate,
Who dares most impudently—not translate.
It had been civil, in these ticklish Times,
To fetch his Fools and Knaves from foreign Climes ;　　20
Spaniard and *French* abuse to the World's End,
But spare old *England*, lest you hurt a Friend.
If any Fool is by our Satire bit,
Let him hiss loud, to show you all, he 's hit.
Poets make Characters, as *Salesmen* Cloaths,
We take no Measure of your Fops and Beaus,
But here all Sizes and all Shapes ye meet,
And fit your selves, like Chaps in *Monmouth-Street.*

10 *No inverted commas. 1717.*　　17 *No new paragraph. 1717.*
23 Satire] *Satyr* 1717.　　24 *to show you all—he 's hit.* 1717.

    Gallants look here, This * *Fool's Cap* has an Air—
Goodly and Smart, with Ears of *Issachar*.   30
Let no one Fool engross it, or confine :
A common Blessing ! now 'tis yours, now mine.
But Poets in all ages had the Care
To keep this Cap, for such as will, to wear.
Our Author has it now, (for ev'ry Wit
Of Course resign'd it to the next that writ :)
And thus upon the Stage 'tis fairly † thrown ;
Let him that takes it, wear it as his own.

   * *Shews a Cap with Ears.*   † *Flings down the Cap, and* Exit.

FRAGMENTS.

Maid (reads with an affected Tone Mrs. Phoebe Clinket's Lines writ upon
    the *Deluge*).
        Swell'd with a Dropsy, sickly Nature lies,
        And melting in a Diabetes, dies.   40

Clinket (composing further on the same theme)
        ' The roaring Seas o'er the tall Woods have broke,
        And Whales now perch upon the sturdy Oak.'
Roaring ? Stay. Rumbling, roaring, rustling. No ; raging seas.
        ' The raging Seas o'er the tall Woods have broke,
        Now perch, thou Whale, upon the sturdy Oak.'
Sturdy Oak ? No ; steady, strong, strapping, stiff. Stiff ? No, stiff is too
short.
        ' What Feast for Fish ! Oh too luxurious Treat !
        When hungry Dolphins feed on Butchers Meat.'

Further fragments from Mrs. Clinket's Play *The Universal Deluge*, or *The
    Tragedy of Deucalion and Pyrrha.*
        Tho' Heav'n wrings all the Sponges of the Sky,
        And pours down Clouds, at once each Cloud a Sea.
        Not the Spring-Tides——

      .   .   .   .   .   .
                          Why do the Stays   50
        Taper my Waste, but for thy circling Arms ?

Fossile (reads a letter to his wife)
    Verses on Mrs. *Susanna Townley*, in the front Box dress'd in Green.
        In You the Beautys of the Spring are seen,
        Your Cheeks are Roses, and your Dress is Green.

Mrs. Townley (concealing Plotwell under her petticoat from Fossile)
        Thus *Venus*, when approaching Foes assail,
        Shields her *Aeneas* with a Silken Veil.

   30 *Goodly and Smart,—with* etc. *1717.*   35-6 *No brackets.* 1717.

Plotwell (dress'd like a Mummy)

> Thus trav'ling far from his *Egyptian* Tomb
> Thy *Antony* salutes his *Cleopatra*.

Mrs. Townley. Thus *Cleopatra*, in desiring Arms,
Receives her *Antony*—

Underplot (*concealed in an alligator, crawling forward and embracing Mrs. Townley*)

> Thus *Jove* within the *Serpent's* scaly Folds,
> Twin'd round the *Macedonian* Queen.

EPILOGUE.

Spoken by MRS. OLDFIELD.

THE ancient *Epilogue*, as Criticks write,
Was, clap your Hands, excuse us, and good-night.
The modern always was a kind Essay
To reconcile the Audience to the Play:
More polish'd we, of late have learnt to fly
At Parties, Treaties, Nations, Ministry.
Our Author more genteelly leaves these Brawls
To *Coffee-houses*, and to Coblers Stalls.
His very Monsters are of sweet Condition,
None but the *Crocodile's* a Politician;   10
He reaps the Blessings of his double Nature,
And, *Trimmer* like, can live on Land or Water:
Yet this same Monster should be kindly treated,
He lik'd a Lady's Flesh—but not to eat it.
  As for my other Spark, my fav'rite Mummy,
His Feats were such, smart Youths! as might become ye,
Dead as he seem'd, he had sure Signs of Life;
His Hieroglyphicks pleas'd the Doctor's Wife.
  Whom can our well-bred Poetess displease?
She writ like Quality—with wondrous Ease: 20
All her Offence was harmless want of Wit;
Is that a Crime?—Ye Powers, preserve the Pit!
  My Doctor, too, to give the Devil his due,
When ev'ry Creature did his Spouse pursue,
(Men sound and living, bury'd Flesh, dry'd Fish),
Was e'en as civil as a Wife could wish.
Yet he was somewhat saucy with his Vial;
What, put young Maids to that unnat'ral Trial!
So hard a Test! why, if you needs will make it,
Faith, let us marry first—and then we'll take it.   30
  Who could be angry, though like *Fossile* teaz'd?
Consider, in three Hours, the Man was eas'd.

How many of you are for Life beguil'd,
And keep as well the Mother, as the Child !
None but a *Tar* could be so tender-hearted,
To claim a Wife that had been three Years parted ;
Would you do this, my Friends ?—Believe me, never ;
When modishly you part—you part for ever.
  Join then your Voices, be the Play excus'd
For once, though no one living is abus'd ;   40
To that bright Circle which commands our Duties,
To you superior Eighteen-penny Beauties,
To the lac'd Hat and Cockard of the Pit,
To All, in one Word, we our Cause submit,
Who think Good-breeding is a-kin to Wit.

D I O N E.

A

Pastoral Tragedy

—————————*Sunt numina amanti,*
Sævit et injustâ lege relicta Venus.
Tibull. Eleg. 5. Lib. 1.

[*Editions :*
1. *Poems on Several Occasions.* 1720.
2. Ditto, 1731 (with a frontispiece by Fourdrinier, showing the funeral pyre and tomb of Dione, the latter inscribed with her name and visited by five Cupids).
3. Cooke's Edition of Gay's Poems ; 1804. The Prologue only was included in the editions of Bell and Underhill.
The edition of 1731 is occasionally altered from that of 1720, and is followed by Cooke. The text follows the later version, and the readings of 1720 are recorded in the notes without reference to the editions, unless such reference is necessary for clearness.
Dione was translated into German about the middle of the eighteenth century.]

PROLOGUE.

Design'd for the Pastoral Tragedy of D I O N E.

THERE was a time (Oh were those days renew'd !)
Ere tyrant laws had woman's will subdu'd ;
Then nature rul'd, and love, devoid of art,
Spoke the consenting language of the heart.
Love uncontroul'd ! insipid, poor delight !
'Tis the restraint that whets our appetite.
Behold the beasts who range the forests free,
Behold the birds who fly from tree to tree ;
In their amours see nature's power appear !
And do they love ?   Yes——One month in the year.   10
Were these the pleasures of the golden reign ?
And did free nature thus instruct the swain ?
I envy not, ye nymphs, your am'rous bowers :
Such harmless swains !——I'm ev'n content with ours.
But yet there's something in these sylvan scenes
That tells our fancy what the lover means ;
Name but the mossy bank, and moon-light grove,
Is there a heart that does not beat with love ?
    To-night we treat you with such country fare,
Then for your lover's sake our author spare.   20
He draws no *Hemskirk* boors, or home-bred clowns,
But the soft shepherds of *Arcadia*'s downs.
    When *Paris* on the three his judgment past ;
I hope, you'll own the shepherd show'd his taste :
And *Jove*, all know, was a good judge of beauty,
Who made the nymph *Calisto* break her duty ;
Then was the country nymph no awkward thing.
See what strange revolutions time can bring !
    Yet still methinks our author's fate I dread.
Were it not safer beaten paths to tread   30
Of Tragedy ; than o'er wide heaths to stray,
And seeking strange adventures lose his way ?
No trumpet's clangor makes his Heroine start,
And tears the soldier from her bleeding heart ;
He, foolish bard ! nor pomp nor show regards.
Without the witness of a hundred guards
His Lovers sigh their vows.——If sleep should take ye,
He has no battel, no loud drum to wake ye.
What, no such shifts ? there's danger in't, 'tis true ;
Yet spare him, as he gives you something new.   40

PROLOGUE. *Design'd etc.*] In the *Poems on Several Occasions* the Prologue was
printed separately from the Play, several short pieces intervening.
    29 our] an *Cooke.*   37 If] if *1720 and 1731.*

Dramatis Personæ.

M E N.

Evander under the name of *Lycidas*.
Cleanthes.
Shepherds.

W O M E N.

Dione under the name of *Alexis*.
Parthenia.
Laura.

Scene *A R C A D I A.*

ACT I. SCENE I.

A Plain, at the foot of a steep craggy mountain.

D I O N E. L A U R A.

L A U R A.

WHY dost thou fly me ? stay, unhappy fair,
Seek not these horrid caverns of despair ;
To trace thy steps the midnight air I bore,
Trod the brown desart, and unshelter'd moor :
Three times the lark has sung his matin lay,
And rose on dewy wing to meet the day,
Since first I found thee, stretch'd in pensive mood,
Where laurels border *Ladon*'s silver flood.

D I O N E.

O let my soul with grateful thanks o'erflow !
'Tis to thy hand my daily life I owe.   10
Like the weak lamb you rais'd me from the plain,
Too faint to bear bleak winds and beating rain ;
Each day I share thy bowl and clean repast,
Each night thy roof defends the chilly blast.
But vain is all thy friendship, vain thy care :
Forget a wretch abandon'd to despair.

L A U R A.

Despair will fly thee, when thou shalt impart
The fatal secret that torments thy heart;
Disclose thy sorrows to my faithful ear,
Instruct these eyes to give thee tear for tear.   20
Love, love's the cause; our forests speak thy flame,
The rocks have learnt to sigh *Evander*'s name.
If faultring shame thy bashful tongue restrain,
If thou hast look'd, and blush'd, and sigh'd in vain;
Say, in what grove thy lovely shepherd strays,
Tell me what mountains warble with his lays;
Thither I'll speed me, and with moving art
Draw soft confessions from his melting heart.

D I O N E.

Thy gen'rous care has touch'd my secret woe.
Love bids these scalding tears incessant flow,   30
Ill-fated love! O, say, ye sylvan maids,
Who range wide forests and sequester'd shades,
Say where *Evander* bled, point out the ground
That yet is purple with the savage wound.
Yonder he lies; I hear the bird of prey;
High o'er those cliffs the raven wings his way;
Hark how he croaks! he scents the murder near.
O may no greedy beak his visage tear!
Shield him, ye *Cupids*; strip the *Paphian* grove,
And strow unfading myrtle o'er my love!   40
Down, heaving heart.

L A U R A.

——————————The mournful tale disclose.

D I O N E.

Let not my tears intrude on thy repose.
Yet if thy friendship still the cause request;
I'll speak; though sorrow rend my lab'ring breast.
Know then, fair shepherdess; no honest swain
Taught me the duties of the peaceful plain;
Unus'd to sweet content, no flocks I keep,
Nor browzing goats that overhang the steep.
Born where *Orchomenos*' proud turrets shine,   50
I trace my birth from long illustrious line.
Why was I train'd amidst *Arcadia*'s Court?
Love ever revells in that gay resort.
Whene'er *Evander* past, my smitten heart
Heav'd frequent sighs, and felt unusual smart.
Ah! hadst thou seen with what sweet grace he mov'd!
Yet why that wish? for *Laura* then had lov'd.

22 The] And

L A U R A.

Distrust me not ; thy secret wrongs impart.

D I O N E.

Forgive the sallies of a breaking heart.
Evander's sighs his mutual flame confest,   60
The growing passion labour'd in his breast ;
To me he came ; my heart with rapture sprung,
To see the blushes, when his faultring tongue
First said, I love. My eyes consent reveal,
And plighted vows our faithful passion seal.
Where 's now the lovely youth ? he 's lost, he 's slain,
And the pale corse lies breathless on the plain !

L A U R A.

Are thus the hopes of constant lovers paid ?
If thus—ye Powers, from love defend the maid !

D I O N E.

Now have twelve mornings warm'd the purple east,   70
Since my dear hunter rous'd the tusky beast ;
Swift flew the foaming monster through the wood,
Swift as the wind, his eager steps pursu'd :
'Twas then the savage turn'd ; then fell the youth,
And his dear blood distain'd the barb'rous tooth.

L A U R A.

Was there none near ? no ready succour found ?
Nor healing herb to stanch the spouting wound ?

D I O N E.

In vain through pathless woods the hunters crost,
And sought with anxious eye their master lost ;
In vain their frequent hollows eccho'd shrill,   80
And his lov'd name was sent from hill to hill ;
Evander hears you not. He 's lost, he 's slain,
And the pale corse lies breathless on the plain.

L A U R A.

Has yet no clown (who, wandring from the way,
Beats ev'ry bush to raise the lamb astray)
Observ'd the fatal spot ?

D I O N E.

———————————————O, if ye pass
Where purple murder dies the wither'd grass,
With pious finger gently close his eyes,
And let his grave with decent verdure rise.   [*Weeps.*

L A U R A.

Behold the turtle who has lost her mate ;   91
Awhile with drooping wing she mourns his fate,

Sullen, awhile she seeks the darkest grove,
And cooing meditates the murder'd dove ;
But time the rueful image wears away,
Again she 's chear'd, again she seeks the day.
Spare then thy beauty, and no longer pine.

DIONE.

Yet sure some turtle's love has equall'd mine,
Who, when the hawk has snatch'd her mate away,
Hath never known the glad return of day.   100
  When my fond father saw my faded eye,
And on my livid cheek the roses dye ;
When catching sighs my wasted bosom mov'd,
My looks, my sighs confirm'd him that I lov'd.
He knew not that *Evander* was my flame,
Evander dead ! my passion still the same !
He came, he threaten'd ; with paternal sway
Cleanthes nam'd, and fix'd the nuptial day :
O cruel kindness ! too severely prest !
I scorn his honours, and his wealth detest.   110

LAURA.

How vain is force ! Love ne'er can be compell'd.

DIONE.

Though bound by duty, yet my heart rebell'd.
One night, when sleep had hush'd all busy spys,
And the pale moon had journey'd half the skies ;
Softly I rose and drest ; with silent tread,
Unbarr'd the gates ; and to these mountains fled.
Here let me sooth the melancholy hours !
Close me, ye woods, within your twilight bowr's !
Where my calm soul may settled sorrow know,
And no *Cleanthes* interrupt my woe   120
      [*Melancholy musick is heard at a distance.*
With importuning love.—On yonder plain
Advances slow a melancholy train ;
Black Cypress boughs their drooping heads adorn.

LAURA.

Alas ! *Menalcas* to his grave is born.
Behold the victim of *Parthenia's* pride !
He saw, he sigh'd, he lov'd, was scorn'd and dy'd.

DIONE.

Where dwells this beauteous tyrant of the plains ?
Where may I see her ?

104 The certain signs confirm'd &c.
107-10   Now he with threats asserts paternal sway,
      With rich *Cleanthes* names my nuptial day ;
      Cleanthes long his ardent vows had prest ;
      But I his honours and his wealth detest.

L A U R A.

————————————Ask the sighing swains.
They best can speak the conquests of her eyes,   130
Whoever sees her, loves ; who loves her, dies.

D I O N E.

Perhaps untimely fate her flame hath crost,
And she, like me, hath her *Evander* lost.
How my soul pitys her !

L A U R A.

————————————If pity move
Your generous bosom, pity those who love.
There late arriv'd among our sylvan race
A stranger shepherd, who with lonely pace
Visits those mountain pines at dawn of day,
Where oft' *Parthenia* takes her early way   140
To rouse the chace ; mad with his am'rous pain,
He stops and raves ; then sullen walks again.
Parthenia's name is born by passing gales,
And talking hills repeat it to the dales.
Come, let us from this vale of sorrow go,
Nor let the mournful scene prolong thy woe.   *[Exeunt.*

    132 hath] has   133 hath] has

---

* S C E N E   I I.

*Shepherds and Shepherdesses, (crown'd with garlands of Cypress and Yew)
bearing the body of* Menalcas.

1 *S H E P H E R D.*

Here gently rest the corse.—With faultring breath
Thus spake *Menalcas* on the verge of death.
' Belov'd *Palemon*, hear a dying friend ;
' See, where yon hills with craggy brows ascend,
' Low in the valley where the mountain grows,
' There first I saw her, there began my woes.
' When I am cold, may there this clay be laid ;
' There often strays the dear the cruel maid,
' There as she walks, perhaps you'll hear her say,
' (While a kind gushing tear shall force its way)   10
' How could my stubborn heart relentless prove ?
' Ah poor *Menalcas*—all thy fault was love !

2 *S H E P H E R D.*

When pitying lions o'er a carcase groan,
And hungry tygers bleeding kids bemoan ;

* *This and the following Scene are form'd upon the novel of* Marcella *in* Don Quixote.

When the lean wolf laments the mangled sheep;
Then shall *Parthenia* o'er *Menalcas* weep.

1 *S H E P H E R D.*

When famish'd panthers seek their morning food,
And monsters roar along the desart wood;
When hissing vipers rustle through the brake,
Or in the path-way rears the speckled snake;   20
The wary swain th'approaching peril spys,
And through some distant road securely flys.
Fly then, ye swains, from beauty's surer wound.
Such was the fate our poor *Menalcas* found!

2 *S H E P H E R D.*

What shepherd does not mourn *Menalcas* slain?
Kill'd by a barbarous woman's proud disdain!
Whoe'er attempts to bend her scornful mind,
Crys to the desarts, and pursues the wind.

1 *S H E P H E R D.*

With ev'ry grace *Menalcas* was endow'd,
His merits dazled all the sylvan croud.   30
If you would know his pipe's melodious sound,
Ask all the ecchoes of these hills around,
For they have learnt his strains; who shall rehearse
The strength, the cadence of his tuneful verse?
Go, read those lofty poplars; there you'll find
Some tender sonnet grow on ev'ry rind.

2 *S H E P H E R D.*

Yet what avails his skill? *Parthenia* flies.
Can merit hope success in woman's eyes?

1 *S H E P H E R D.*

Why was *Parthenia* form'd of softest mould?
Why does her heart such savage nature hold?   40
O ye kind gods! or all her charms efface,
Or tame her heart.—So spare the shepherd race.

2 *S H E P H E R D.*

As fade the flowers which on the grave I cast;
So may *Parthenia's* transient beauty waste!

1 *S H E P H E R D.*

What woman ever counts the fleeting years,
Or sees the wrinkle which her forehead wears?
Thinking her feature never shall decay,
This swain she scorns, from that she turns away.
But know, as when the rose her bud unfolds,
Awhile each breast the short-liv'd fragrance holds;   50

42 So] so *1720 and 1731.*

When the dry stalk lets drop her shrivell'd pride,
The lovely ruin's ever thrown aside.
So shall *Parthenia* be.

2 S H E P H E R D.

———————————————See, she appears,
To boast her spoils, and triumph in our tears.

S C E N E I I I.

Parthenia appears from the mountain.

P A R T H E N I A. S H E P H E R D S.

1 S H E P H E R D.

Why this way dost thou turn thy baneful eyes,
Pernicious Basilisk ? Lo ! there he lies,
There lies the youth thy cursed beauty slew ;
See, at thy presence, how he bleeds anew !
Look down, enjoy thy murder.

P A R T H E N I A.

—————————————————Spare my fame ;
I come to clear a virgin's injur'd name.
If I'm a Basilisk, the danger fly,
Shun the swift glances of my venom'd eye :
If I'm a murd'rer, why approach ye near,   10
And to the dagger lay your bosom bare ?

1 S H E P H E R D.

What heart is proof against that face divine ?
Love is not in our power.

P A R T H E N I A.

—————————————Is love in mine ?
If e'er I trifled with a shepherd's pain,
Or with false hope his passion strove to gain ;
Then might you justly curse my savage mind,
Then might you rank me with the serpent kind :
But I ne'er trifled with a shepherd's pain,
Nor with false hope his passion strove to gain :   20
'Tis to his rash pursuit he owes his fate,
I was not cruel ; he was obstinate.

1 S H E P H E R D.

Hear this, ye sighing shepherds, and despair.
Unhappy *Lycidas*, thy hour is near !
Since the same barb'rous hand hath sign'd thy doom,
We'll lay thee in our lov'd *Menalcas'* tomb.

P A R T H E N I A.

Why will intruding man my peace destroy ?
Let me content, and solitude enjoy ;
Free was I born, my freedom to maintain,
Early I sought the unambitious plain.   30
Most women's weak resolves, like reeds, will ply,
Shake with each breath, and bend with ev'ry sigh ;
Mine, like an oak, whose firm roots deep descend,
No breath of love can shake, no sigh can bend.
If ye unhappy *Lycidas* would save ;
Go seek him, lead him to *Menalcas'* grave ;
Forbid his eyes with flowing grief to rain,
Like him *Menalcas* wept, but wept in vain ;
Bid him his heart-consuming groans give o'er :
Tell him, I heard such piercing groans before,   40
And heard unmov'd. O *Lycidas*, be wise,
Prevent thy fate.—Lo ! there *Menalcas* lies.

1 *S H E P H E R D.*

Now all the melancholy rites are paid,
And o'er his grave the weeping marble laid ;
Let's seek our charge ; the flocks dispersing wide,
Whiten with moving fleece the mountain's side.
Trust not, ye swains, the lightning of her eye,
Lest ye like him, should love, despair, and dye.

[*Exeunt* Shepherds, *&c.* Parthenia *remains in a melancholy posture looking on the grave of* Menalcas. *Enter* Lycidas.

31 resolves,] *Cooke* resolves *1720 and 1731.*

S C E N E I V.

L Y C I D A S. P A R T H E N I A.

L Y C I D A S.

When shall my steps have rest ? through all the wood,
And by the winding banks of *Ladon's* flood
I sought my love. O say, ye skipping fawns,
(Who range entangled shades and daisy'd lawns)
If ye have seen her ! say, ye warbling race,
(Who measure on swift wing th' aerial space,
And view below hills, dales, and distant shores)
Where shall I find her whom my soul adores !

SCENE V.

LYCIDAS. PARTHENIA. DIONE. LAURA.
[Dione *and* Laura *at a distance.*

LYCIDAS.

What do I see ? no. Fancy mocks my eyes,
And bids the dear deluding vision rise.
'Tis she. My springing heart her presence feels.
See, prostrate *Lycidas* before thee kneels.
[*Kneeling to* Parthenia.
Why will *Parthenia* turn her face away ?

PARTHENIA.

Who calls *Parthenia* ? hah !
[*She starts from her melancholy ; and seeing* Lycidas, *flys into
the wood.*

LYCIDAS.

————————————————Stay, virgin, stay.
O wing my feet, kind Love. See, see, she bounds,
Fleet as the mountain roe, when prest by hounds.
[*He pursues her.* Dione *faints in the arms of* Laura.

LAURA.

What means this trembling ? all her colour flies,   10
And life is quite unstrung. Ah ! lift thy eyes,
And answer me ; speak, speak, 'tis *Laura* calls.
Speech has forsook her lips.——She faints, she falls.
Fan her, ye Zephyrs, with your balmy breath,
And bring her quickly from the shades of death :
Blow, ye cool gales. See, see, the forest shakes
With coming winds ! she breaths, she moves, she wakes.

DIONE.

Ah false *Evander!*

LAURA.

————————————Calm thy sobbing breast.
Say, what new sorrow has thy heart opprest.   20

DIONE.

Didst thou not hear his sighs and suppliant tone ?
Didst thou not hear the pityirg mountain groan ?
Didst thou not see him bend his suppliant knee ?
Thus in my happy days he knelt to me,
And pour'd forth all his soul ! see how he strains,
And lessens to the sight o'er yonder plains
To keep the fair in view ! run, virgin, run,
Hear not his vows ; I heard, and was undone !

L A U R A.

Let not imaginary terrors fright.
Some dark delusion swims before thy sight.   30
I saw *Parthenia* from the mountain's brow,
And *Lycidas* with prostrate duty bow ;
Swift, as on faulcon's wing, I saw her fly,
And heard the cavern to his groans reply.
Why stream thy tears for sorrows not thy own ?

D I O N E.

Oh ! Where are honour, faith, and justice flown ?
Perjur'd *Evander !*

L A U R A.

————————————Death has laid him low.
Touch not the mournful string that wakes thy woe.

D I O N E.

That am'rous swain, whom *Lycidas* you name,   40
(Whose faithless bosom feels another flame)
Is my once kind *Evander*—yes—'twas he.
He lives—but lives, alas ! no more for me.

L A U R A.

Let not thy frantick words confess despair.

D I O N E.

What, know I not his voice, his mien, his air ?
Yes, I that treach'rous voice with joy believ'd,
That voice, that mien, that air my soul deceiv'd.
If my dear shepherd love the lawns and glades,
With him I'll range the lawns and seek the shades,
With him through solitary desarts rove.   50
But could he leave me for another love ?
O base ingratitude !

L A U R A.

————————————Suspend thy grief,
And let my friendly counsel bring relief
To thy desponding soul. *Parthenia*'s ear
Is barr'd for ever to the lover's prayer ;
Evander courts disdain, he follows scorn,
And in the passing winds his vows are born.
Soon will he find that all in vain he strove
To tame her bosom ; then his former love   60
Shall wake his soul, then, will he sighing blame
His heart inconstant and his perjur'd flame :
Then shall he at *Dione*'s feet implore,
Lament his broken faith, and change no more.

D I O N E.

Perhaps this cruel nymph well knows to feign
Forbidding speech, coy looks, and cold disdain,

36 are] is   51 But could] And can

To raise his passion. Such are female arts,
To hold in safer snares inconstant hearts !

L A U R A.

Parthenia's breast is steel'd with real scorn.

D I O N E.

And dost thou think *Evander* will return ?   70

L A U R A.

Forgo thy sex, lay all thy robes aside,
Strip off these ornaments of female pride ;
The shepherd's vest must hide thy graceful air,
With the bold manly step a swain appear ;
Then with *Evander* may'st thou rove unknown,
Then let thy tender eloquence be shown ;
Then the new fury of his heart controul,
And with *Dione*'s sufferings touch his soul.

D I O N E.

Sweet as refreshing dews, or summer showers
To the long parching thirst of drooping flowers ;   80
Grateful as fanning gales to fainting swains,
And soft as trickling balm to bleeding pains,
Such are thy words. The sex shall be resign'd,
No more shall breaded gold these tresses bind ;
The shepherd's garb the woman shall disguise.
If he has lost all love, may friendship's tyes
Unite me to his heart !

L A U R A.

———————————————Go, prosp'rous maid,
May smiling love thy faithful wishes aid.
Be now *Alexis* call'd. With thee I'll rove,   90
And watch thy wand'rer through the mazy grove ;
Let me be honour'd with a sister's name ;
For thee, I feel a more than sister's flame.

D I O N E.

Perhaps my shepherd has outstript her haste.
Think'st thou, when out of sight, she flew so fast ?

70 And dost thou think] Canst thou believe
71 *In the edition of 1720 Laura's speech begins*
          If thou the secrets of his heart wouldst find,
          And try to cure the fever of his mind ;
          If thy soft speech his passions knows to move,
          If thou canst plead *Dione*'s injur'd love,
          Forgo thy sex, *etc.*
94 *In the edition of 1720 Dione's speech begins*
          Come then my guardian, sister, friend and guide ;
          Strait let these female robes be laid aside.
          Perhaps my shepherd *etc.*

One sudden glance might turn her savage mind ;
May she like *Daphne* fly, nor look behind,
Maintain her scorn, his eager flame despise,
Nor view *Evander* with *Dione*'s eyes !

ACT II. SCENE I.

Lycidas *lying on the grave of* Menalcas.

LYCIDAS.

WHEN shall these scalding fountains cease to flow ?
How long will life sustain this load of woe ?
Why glows the morn ? roll back, thou source of light,
And feed my sorrows with eternal night.
Come, sable Death ! give, give the welcome stroke ;
The raven calls thee from yon' blasted oak.
What pious care my ghastful lid shall close ?
What decent hand my frozen limbs compose ?
O happy shepherd, free from anxious pains,
Who now art wandring in the sighing plains   10
Of blest *Elysium* ; where in myrtle groves
Enamour'd ghosts bemoan their former loves.
Open, thou silent grave ; for lo ! I come
To meet *Menalcas* in the fragrant gloom ;
There shall my bosom burn with friendship's flame,
The same our passion, and our fate the same ;
There, like two nightingales on neighb'ring boughs,
Alternate strains shall mourn our frustrate vows.
But if cold Death should close *Parthenia*'s eye,
And should her beauteous form come gliding by ;   20
Friendship would soon in jealous fear be lost,
And kindling hate pursue thy rival ghost.

SCENE II.

LYCIDAS. DIONE *in a shepherd's habit.*

LYCIDAS.

Hah ! who comes here ? turn hence, be timely wise ;
Trust not thy safety to *Parthenia*'s eyes.
As from the bearing faulcon flies the dove,
So, wing'd with fear, *Parthenia* flies from love.

DIONE.

If in these vales the fatal beauty stray,
From the cold marble rise ; let's haste away.
Why lye you panting, like the smitten deer ?
Trust not the dangers which you bid me fear.

4 So,] So   7 lye you] liest thou   8 you bid] thou bid'st

L Y C I D A S.

Bid the lur'd lark, whom tangling nets surprise,
On soaring pinion rove the spacious skies;   10
Bid the cag'd linnet range the leafy grove;
Then bid my captive heart get loose from love.
The snares of death are o'er me. Hence; beware;
Lest you should see her, and like me despair.

D I O N E.

No. Let her come; and seek this vale's recess,
In all the beauteous negligence of dress;
Though *Cupid* send a shaft in ev'ry glance,
Though all the Graces in her step advance,
My heart can stand it all. Be firm, my breast;
Th' ensnaring oath, the broken vow detest: 20
That flame, which other charms have power to move,
O give it not the sacred name of love!
'Tis perj'ry, fraud, and meditated lies.
Love's seated in the soul, and never dies.
What then avail her charms? my constant heart
Shall gaze secure, and mock a second dart.

L Y C I D A S.

But you perhaps a happier fate have found,
And the same hand that gave, now heals the wound;
Or art thou left abandon'd and forlorn,
A wretch, like me, the sport of pride and scorn?   30

D I O N E.

O tell me, shepherd, hath thy faithless maid
False to her vow thy flatter'd hope betray'd?
Did her smooth speech engage thee to believe?
Did she protest and swear, and then deceive?
Such are the pangs I feel!

L Y C I D A S.

————————————————The haughty fair
Contemns my suff'rings, and disdains to hear.
Let meaner Beauties learn'd in female snares
Entice the swain with half-consenting airs;
Such vulgar arts ne'er aid her conqu'ring eyes,   40
And yet, where-e'er she turns, a lover sighs.
Vain is the steady constancy you boast;
All other love at sight of her is lost.

D I O N E.

True constancy no time no power can move.
He that hath known to change, ne'er knew to love.
Though the dear author of my hapless flame
Pursue another; still my heart's the same.

14 you should] thou shoud'st   27 you ... have] thou ... hast
31 hath] has   41 yet, ... turns,] yet ... turns   47 Pursue] Pursues

Am I for ever left ? (excuse these tears)
May your kind friendship soften all my cares!

LYCIDAS.

What comfort can a wretch, like me, bestow ?   50

DIONE.

He best can pity who hath felt the woe.

LYCIDAS.

Since diff'rent objects have our souls possest,
No rival fears our friendship shall molest.

DIONE.

Come, let us leave the shade of these brown hills,
And drive our flocks beside the steaming rills.
Should the fair tyrant to these vales return,
How would thy breast with double fury burn !
Go hence, and seek thy peace.

51 hath] has   52 objects] passions
55 steaming] *The emendation* streaming *is too obvious.* Brown *and* steaming *are
meant to suggest intense heat.*   56 the] thy

SCENE III.

LYCIDAS. DIONE. LAURA.

LAURA.

————————————————Fly, fly this place ;
Beware of love ; the proudest of her race
This way approaches : from among the pines,
Where from the steep the winding path declines,
I saw the nymph descend.

LYCIDAS.

————————————————She comes, she comes ;
From her the passing Zephyrs steal perfumes,
As from the vi'let's bank ; with odours sweet
Breaths ev'ry gale ; spring blooms beneath her feet.
Yes, 'tis my fairest ; here she 's wont to rove.   10

LAURA.

Say, by what signs I might have known thy Love ?

LYCIDAS.

My Love is fairer than the snowy breast
Of the tall swan, whose proudly-swelling chest
Divides the wave ; her tresses loose behind,
Play on her neck, and wanton in the wind ;
The rising blushes, which her cheek o'erspread,
Are op'ning roses in the lilly's bed.
Know'st thou *Parthenia ?*

LAURA.

———————————————Wretched is the slave
Who serves such pride ! behold *Menalcas'* grave !
Yet if *Alexis* and this sighing swain   20
Wish to behold the Tyrant of the plain,
Let us behind these myrtle's twining arms
Retire unseen ; from thence survey her charms.
Wild as the chaunting thrush upon the spray,
At man's approach she swiftly flies away.
Like the young hare, I've seen the panting maid
Stop, listen, run ; of ev'ry wind afraid.

LYCIDAS.

And wilt thou never from thy vows depart ?
Shepherd, beware——now fortifie thy heart.   [*To* Dione.
        [Lycidas, Dione, *and* Laura *retire behind the boughs.*

SCENE IV.

PARTHENIA. LYCIDAS. DIONE. LAURA.

PARTHENIA.

This melancholy scene demands a groan.
Hah ! what inscription marks the weeping stone ?
O *pow'r of beauty ! here* Menalcas *lies.*
Gaze not, ye shepherds, on Parthenia's *eyes.*
Why did heav'n form me with such polish'd care ?
Why cast my features in a mold so fair ?
If blooming beauty was a blessing meant,
Why are my sighing hours deny'd content ?
The downy peach, that glows with sunny dyes,
Feeds the black snail, and lures voracious flies ;   10
The juicy pear invites the feather'd kind,
And pecking finches scoop the golden rind ;
But beauty suffers more pernicious wrongs,
Blasted by envy, and censorious tongues.
How happy lives the nymph, whose comely face
And pleasing glances boast sufficient grace
To wound the swain she loves ! no jealous fears
Shall vex her nuptial state with nightly tears,
Nor am'rous youths, to push their foul pretence,
Infest her days with dull impertinence.   20
But why talk I of love ? my guarded heart
Disowns his power, and turns aside the dart.
Hark ! from his hollow tomb *Menalcas* crys,
Gaze not, ye shepherds, on Parthenia's *eyes.*
Come, *Lycidas,* the mournful lay peruse,
Lest thou, like him, *Parthenia's* eyes accuse.
      [*She stands in a melancholy posture, looking on the tomb.*

LYCIDAS.

Call'd she not *Lycidas?*——I come, my fair;
See, gen'rous pity melts into a tear,
And her heart softens. Now's the tender hour,
Assist me, Love, exert thy sov'raign power   30
To tame the scornful maid.

DIONE.

——————————————————Rash swain, be wise:
'Tis not from thee or him, from love she flies.
Leave her, forget her.   [*They hold* Lycidas.

LAURA.

——————————————Why this furious haste?

LYCIDAS.

Unhand me; loose me.

DIONE.

——————————————Sister, hold him fast.
To follow her, is, to prolong despair.
Shepherd, you must not go.

LYCIDAS.

——————————————————Bold youth, forbear.   40
Hear me, *Parthenia.*

PARTHENIA.

——————————————From behind the shade
Methought a voice some list'ning spy betray'd.
Yes, I'm observ'd.   [*She runs out.*

LYCIDAS.

——————————————Stay, nymph; thy flight suspend.
She hears me not—when will my sorrows end!
As over-spent with toil, my heaving breast
Beats quick. 'Tis death alone can give me rest.
          [*He remains in a fixt melancholy.*

31 the scornful] th'obdurate

SCENE V.

LYCIDAS. DIONE. LAURA.

LAURA.

Recall thy scatter'd sense, bid reason wake,
Subdue thy passion.

LYCIDAS.

——————————————Shall I never speak?
She's gone, she's gone.—Kind shepherd, let me rest
My troubled head upon thy friendly breast.

The forest seems to move.——O cursed state !
I doom'd to love, and she condemn'd to hate !
Tell me, *Alexis*, art thou still the same ?
Did not her brighter eyes put out the flame
Of thy first love ? did not thy flutt'ring heart,   10
Whenc'er she rais'd her look, confess the dart ?

D I O N E.

I own the nymph is fairest of her race,
Yet I unmov'd can on this beauty gaze,
Mindful of former promise ; all that 's dear,
My thoughts, my dreams ; my ev'ry wish is there.
Since then our hopes are lost ; let friendship's tye
Calm our distress, and slighted love supply ;
Let us together drive our fleecy store,
And of ungrateful woman think no more.

L Y C I D A S.

'Tis death alone can rase her from my breast.   20

L A U R A.

Why shines thy Love so far above the rest ?
Nature, 'tis true, in ev'ry outward grace,
Her nicest hand employ'd ; her lovely face
With beauteous feature stampt ; with rosy dyes
Warm'd her fair cheek ; with lightning arm'd her eyes ;
But if thou search the secrets of her mind,
Where shall thy cheated soul a virtue find ?
Sure hell with cruelty her breast supply'd.
How did she glory when *Menalcas* dy'd !
Pride in her bosom reigns ; she 's false, she 's vain ;   30
She first entices, then insults the swain ;
Shall female cunning lead thy heart astray ?
Shepherd, be free ; and scorn for scorn repay.

L Y C I D A S.

How woman talks of woman !

D I O N E.

————————————————Hence depart ;
Let a long absence cure thy love-sick heart.
To some far grove retire, her sight disclaim,
Nor with her charms awake the dying flame.
Let not an hour thy happy flight suspend ;
But go not, *Lycidas*, without thy friend.   40

14–16 *In the edition of 1720 the passage runs :*

> Mindful of former promise ; though my love,
> Inconstant like the bee, the meadows rove,
> And skim each beauteous flower ; nor time nor place
> Shall the dear image from my breast efface.
> Since all thy hopes are lost ; let friendship's tye *etc.*

21 Love] *1720* love *1731 Cooke.*

* O

Together let us seek the chearful plains,
And lead the dance among the sportive swains,
Devoid of care.

L A U R A.

——————————————Or else the groves disdain
Nor with the sylvan walk indulge thy pain.
Haste to the town ; there (I have oft' been told)
The courtly nymph her tresses binds with gold,
To captivate the youths ; the youths appear
In fine array ; in ringlets waves their hair
Rich with ambrosial scents, the fair to move,   50
And all the business of the day is love.
There from the gawdy train select a dame,
Her willing glance shall catch an equal flame.

L Y C I D A S.

Name not the Court.—The thought my soul confounds,
And with *Dione*'s wrongs my bosom wounds.
Heav'n justly vindicates the faithful maid ;
And now are all my broken vows repaid.
Perhaps she now laments my fancy'd death
With tears unfeign'd ; and thinks my gasping breath
Sigh'd forth her name. O guilt, no more upbraid !   60
Yes. I fond innocence and truth betray'd.   [*Aside.*
                               [Dione *and* Laura *apart.*

D I O N E.

Hark ! how reflection wakes his conscious heart.
From my pale lids the trickling sorrows start ;
How shall my breast the swelling sighs confine !

L A U R A. .

O smooth thy brow, conceal our just design :
Be yet awhile unknown. If grief arise,
And force a passage through thy gushing eyes,
Quickly retire, thy sorrows to compose ;
Or with a look serene disguise thy woes.
               [Dione *is going out.* Laura *walks at a distance.*

L Y C I D A S.

Canst thou, *Alexis*, leave me thus distrest ?   70
Where 's now the boasted friendship of thy breast ?
Hast thou not oft' survey'd the dappled deer
In social herds o'er-spread the pastures fair,
When op'ning hounds the warmer scent pursue,
And force the destin'd victim from the crew,
Oft' he returns, and fain would join the band,
While all their horns the panting wretch withstand ?
Such is thy friendship ; thus might I confide.

59 and thinks] thinks, how

D I O N E.

Why wilt thou censure what thou ne'er hast try'd ?
Sooner shall swallows leave their callow brood,   80
Who with their plaintive chirpings cry for food ;
Sooner shall hens expose their infant care,
When the spread kite sails wheeling in the air,
Than I forsake thee when by danger prest ;
Wrong not by jealous fears a faithful breast.

L Y C I D A S.

If thy fair-spoken tongue thy bosom shows,
There let the secrets of my soul repose.

D I O N E.

Far be suspicion ; in my truth confide.
O let my heart thy load of cares divide !

L Y C I D A S.

Know then, *Alexis*, that in vain I strove   90
To break her chain, and free my soul from love ;
On the lim'd twig thus finches beat their wings,
Still more entangled in the clammy strings.
The slow-pac'd days have witness'd my despair,
Upon my weary couch sits wakeful care ;
Down my flush'd cheek the flowing sorrows run,
As dews descend to weep the absent sun.
O lost *Parthenia* !

D I O N E.

—————————These wild thoughts suspend ;
And in thy kind commands instruct thy friend.   100

L Y C I D A S.

Whene'er my faultring tongue would urge my cause,
Deaf is her ear, and sullen she withdraws.
Go then, *Alexis* ; seek the scornful maid,
In tender eloquence my suff'rings plead ;
Of slighted passion you the pangs have known ;
O judge my secret anguish by your own !

D I O N E.

Had I the skill inconstant hearts to move,
My longing soul had never lost my Love.

79 *In the edition of 1720 Dione's speech runs :*
         Why wilt thou censure what thou ne'er hast try'd ?
         Should some lean wolf to seise thee swift descend,
         And gnawing famine wide his jaws distend ;
         I'd rush between, the monster to engage,
         And my life's blood should glut his thirsty rage.
         Sooner shall swallows *etc.*
105 you . . . have] thou . . . hast   106 your] thy

My feeble tongue, in these soft arts untry'd,
Can ill support the thunder of her pride;   110
When she shall bid me to thy bower repair,
How shall my trembling lips her threats declare !
How shall I tell thee, that she could behold,
With brow serene, thy corse all pale and cold
Beat on the dashing billow ? shouldst thou go
Where the tall hill o'er-hangs the rocks below,
Near thee thy tyrant could unpitying stand,
Nor call thee back, not stretch a saving hand.
Wilt thou then still persist to tempt thy fate,
To feed her pride and gratifie her hate ?   120

L Y C I D A S.

Know, unexperienc'd youth, that woman's mind
Oft' shifts her passions, like th' inconstant wind;
Sudden she rages, like the troubled main,
Now sinks the storm, and all is calm again.
Watch the kind moment, then my wrongs impart,
And the soft tale shall glide into her heart.

D I O N E.

No. Let her wander in the lonely grove,
And never hear the tender voice of love.
Let her awhile, neglected by the swain,
Pass by, nor sighs molest the cheerful plain ;   130
Thus shall the fury of her pride be laid ;
Thus humble into love the haughty maid.

L Y C I D A S.

Vain are attempts my passion to controul.
Is this the balm to cure my fainting soul ?

D I O N E.

Deep then among the green-wood shades I'll rove,
And seek with weary'd pace thy wander'd Love ;   136
Prostrate I'll fall, and with incessant prayers
Hang on her knees, and bath her feet with tears ;
If sighs of pity can her ear incline,
(O *Lycidas*, my life is wrapt in thine !)   [*Aside.*
I'll charge her from thy voice to hear the tale,
Thy voice more sweet than notes along the vale
Breath'd from the warbling pipe : the moving strain
Shall stay her flight, and conquer her disdain.   144
Yet if she hear ; should love the message speed,
Then dies all hope ;—then must *Dione* bleed.   [*Aside.*

L Y C I D A S.

Haste then, dear faithful swain. Beneath those yews
Whose sable arms the brownest shade diffuse,

136 weary'd] weary   144 conquer her disdain] o'er her passions gain

Where all around, to shun the fervent skie,
The panting flocks in ferny thickets lye ;   150
There with impatience shall I wait my friend,
O'er the wide prospect frequent glances send
To spy thy wish'd return.   As thou shalt find
A tender welcome, may thy Love be kind !

[*Ex.* Lycidas.

SCENE VI.

DIONE. LAURA.

DIONE.

Methinks I'm now surrounded by despair,
And all my with'ring hopes are lost in air.
Thus the young linnet on the rocking bough
Hears through long woods autumnal tempests blow,
With hollow blasts the clashing branches bend,
And yellow show'rs of rustling leaves descend ;
She sees the friendly shelter from her fly,
Nor dare her little pinions trust the sky ;
But on the naked spray in wintry air,
All shiv'ring, hopeless, mourns the dying year.   10
What have I promis'd ? rash, unthinking maid !
By thy own tongue thy wishes are betray'd !

[Laura *advances.*

LAURA.

Why walk'st thou thus disturb'd with frantick air ?
Why roll thy eyes with madness and despair ?

DIONE.   [*Musing.*

How wilt thou bear to see her pride give way ?
When thus the yielding nymph shall bid thee say,
' Let not the shepherd seek the silent grave,
' Say, that I bid him live.—if hope can save.

LAURA.

Hath he discern'd thee through the swain's disguise,
And now alike thy love and friendship flys ?   20

DIONE.

Yes.   Firm and faithful to the promise made,
I'll range each sunny hill, each lawn and glade.

LAURA.

'Tis *Laura* speaks.   O calm your troubled mind.

19 Hath] Has   23 Wilt thou not answer ?   Calm thy troubled mind.

D I O N E.

Where shall my search this envy'd Beauty find ?
I'll go, my faithless shepherd's cause to plead,
And with my tears accuse the rival maid.
Yet, should her soften'd heart to love incline !

L A U R A.

If those are all thy fears ; Evander's thine.

D I O N E.

Why should we both in sorrow waste our days ?
If love unfeign'd my constant bosom sways,   30
His happiness alone is all I prize,
And that is center'd in Parthenia's eyes.
Haste then, with earnest zeal her love implore,
To bless his hours ;—when thou shalt breathe no more.

24 envy'd Beauty] happy rival   26 the rival] th' ungrateful

ACT III. SCENE I.

Dione lying on the ground by the side of a Fountain.

D I O N E.

HERE let me rest : and in the liquid glass
View with impartial look my fading face.
Why are Parthenia's striking beauties priz'd ?
And why Dione's weaker glance despis'd ?
Nature in various molds has beauty cast,
And form'd the feature for each different taste :
This sighs for golden locks and azure eyes ;
That, for the gloss of sable tresses, dyes.
Let all mankind these locks, these eyes detest,
So I were lovely in Evander's breast !   10
When o'er the garden's knot we cast our view,
While summer paints the ground with various hue ;
Some praise the gaudy tulip's streaky red,
And some the silver lilly's bending head ;
Some the junquil in shining yellow drest,
And some the fring'd carnation's varied vest ;
Some love the sober vi'let's purple dyes.
Thus beauty fares in diff'rent lovers eyes.
But bright Parthenia like the rose appears,
She in all eyes superior lustre bears.   20

SCENE II.

DIONE. LAURA.

LAURA.

Why thus beneath the silver willow laid,
Weeps fair *Dione* in the pensive shade ?
Hast thou yet found the over-arching bower,
Which guards *Parthenia* from the sultry hour ?

DIONE.

With weary step in paths unknown I stray'd,
And sought in vain the solitary maid.

LAURA.

Seest thou the waving tops of yonder woods,
Whose aged arms imbrown the cooling floods ?
The cooling floods o'er breaking pebbles flow,
And wash the soil from the big roots below ;   10
From the tall rock the dashing waters bound.
Hark, o'er the fields the rushing billows sound !
There, lost in thought, and leaning on her crook,
Stood the sad nymph, nor rais'd her pensive look ;
With settled eye the bubbling waves survey'd,
And watch'd the whirling eddys, as they play'd.

DIONE.

Thither to know my certain doom I speed,
For by this sentence life or death's decreed.   [*Exit.*

4 *In the edition of 1720 Laura's speech continues :*
    Has not her pride confirm'd the youth's despair ?
    Or does thy passion still a rival fear ?

SCENE III.

LAURA. CLEANTHES.

LAURA.

But see ! some hasty stranger bends his way ;
His broider'd vest reflects the sunny ray :
Now through the thinner boughs I mark his mien,
Now veil'd, in thicker shades he moves unseen
Hither he turns ; I hear a mutt'ring sound ;
Behind this rev'rend oak with ivie bound
Quick I'll retire ; with busy thought possest,
His tongue betrays the secrets of his breast.

[*She hides her self.*

C L E A N T H E S.

The skillful hunter with experienc'd care
Traces the doubles of the circling hare ;   10
The subtle fox (who breaths the weary hound
O'er hills and plains) in distant brakes is found ;
With ease we track swift hinds and skipping roes.
But who th' inconstant ways of woman knows ?
They say, she wanders with the sylvan train,
And courts the native freedoms of the plain ;
Shepherds explain their wish without offence,
Nor blush the nymphs ;—for Love is innocence.
O lead me where the rural youth retreat,
Where the slope hills the warbling voice repeat.   20
Perhaps on daisy'd turf reclines the maid,
And near her side some rival clown is laid.
Yet, yet I love her.—O lost nymph return,
Let not thy fire with tears incessant mourn ;
Return, lost nymph ; bid sorrow cease to flow
And let *Dione* glad the house of woe.

L A U R A.

Call'd he not lost *Dione?* hence I'll start,
Cross his slow steps, and sift his op'ning heart.   [*Aside.*

C L E A N T H E S.

Tell me, fair nymph, direct my wandring way ;
Where, in close bowers, to shun the sultry ray,   30
Repose the swains ; whose flocks with bleating fill
The bord'ring forest and the thymy hill.
But if thou frequent join those sylvan bands,
Thy self can answer what my soul demands.

L A U R A.

Seven years I trod these fields, these bowers, and glades,
And by the less'ning and the length'ning shades
Have mark'd the hours ; what time my flock to lead
To sunny mountains, or the watry mead :
Train'd in the labours of the sylvan crew :
Their sports, retreats, their cares and loves I knew.   40

C L E A N T H E S.

Instruct me then, if late among your race,
A stranger nymph is found, of noble grace,
In rural arts unskill'd, no charge she tends ;
Nor when the morn and ev'ning dew descends
Milks the big-udder'd ewe. Her mien and dress
The polish'd manners of the Court confess.

L A U R A.

Each day arrive the neighb'ring nymphs and swains
To share the pastime of our jovial plains ;

33 those] these

How can I there thy roving beauty trace,
Where not one nymph is bred of vulgar race ?　　50

CLEANTHES.

If yet she breath, what tortures must she find !
The curse of disobedience tears her mind.
If e'er your breast with filial duty burn'd,
If e'er you sorrow'd when a parent mourn'd ;
Tell her, I charge you, with incessant groans
Her drooping sire his absent child bemoans.

LAURA.

Unhappy man !

CLEANTHES.

———— ————With storms of passion tost,
When first he learnt his vagrant child was lost,
On the cold floor his trembling limbs he flung,　　60
And with thick blows his hollow bosom rung ;
Then up he started, and with fixt surprise,
Upon her picture threw his frantick eyes,
While thus he cry'd. ' In her my life was bound,
' Warm in each feature is her mother found !
' Perhaps despair has been her fatal guide,
' And now she floats upon the weeping tide ;
' Or on the willow hung, with head reclin'd,
' All pale and cold she wavers in the wind.
' Did I not force her hence by harsh commands ?　　70
' Did not her soul abhor the nuptial bands ?

LAURA.

Teach not, ye fires, your daughters to rebell,
By counsel rein their wills, but ne'er compel.

CLEANTHES.

Ye duteous daughters, trust these tender guides ;
Nor think a parent's breast the tyrant hides.

LAURA.

From either lid the scalding sorrows roll ;
The moving tale runs thrilling to my soul.

CLEANTHES.

Perhaps she wanders in the lonely woods,
Or on the sedgy borders of the floods ;
Thou know'st each cottage, forest, hill and vale,　　80
And pebbled brook that winds along the dale.
Search each sequester'd dell to find the fair ;
And just reward shall gratifie thy care,

LAURA.

O ye kind boughs protect the virgin's flight,
And guard *Dione* from his prying sight !　　[*Aside.*

* O 3

C L E A N T H E S.

Mean while I'll seek the shepherd's cool abodes,
Point me, fair nymph, along these doubtful roads.

L A U R A.

Seest thou yon' mountain rear his shaggy brow ?
In the green valley graze the flocks below :
There ev'ry gale with warbling musick floats,   90
Shade answers shade, and breaths alternate notes.

[*Ex.* Cleanthes.

He's gone ; and to the distant vales is sent,
Nor shall his force *Dione*'s love prevent.
But see, she comes again with hasty pace,
And conscious pleasure dimples on her face.

S C E N E   I V.

L A U R A.   D I O N E.

D I O N E.

I found her laid beside the crystal brook,
Nor rais'd she from the stream her settled look,
Till near her side I stood ; her head she rears,
Starts sudden, and her shrieks confess her fears.

L A U R A.

Did not thy words her thoughtful soul surprise,
And kindle sparkling anger in her eyes ?

D I O N E.

Thus she reply'd, with rage and scorn possest.
' Will importuning love ne'er give me rest ?
' Why am I thus in desarts wild pursu'd,
' Like guilty consciences when stain'd with blood ?   10
' Sure boding ravens, from the blasted oak,
' Shall learn the name of *Lycidas* to croak,
' To sound it in my ears ! As swains pass by,
' With look askance, they shake their heads and cry,
' Lo ! this is she for whom the shepherd dy'd !
' Soon *Lycidas*, a victim to her pride,
' Shall seek the grave ; and in the glimm'ring glade,
' With look all pale, shall glide the restless shade
' Of the poor swain ; while we with haggard eye
' And bristled hair the fleeting phantom fly.   20
' Still let their curses innocence upbraid :
' Heav'n never will forsake the virtuous maid.

21-22 *Given in all editions without inverted commas, as Dione's own addition to her*
report of Parthenia's outburst. But clearly these two lines belong to Parthenia. The
' swains ' *were the cause of the confusion.*

L A U R A.

Didst thou persist to touch her haughty breast ?

D I O N E.

She still the more disdain'd, the more I prest.

L A U R A.

When you were gone, these walks a stranger crost,
He turn'd through ev'ry path, and wander'd lost ;
To me he came ; with courteous speech demands
Beneath what bowers repos'd the shepherd bands ;
Then further asks me, if among that race
A shepherdess was found of courtly grace ;   30
With proffer'd bribes my faithful tongue essays ;
But for no bribe the faithful tongue betrays.
In me *Dione*'s safe. Far hence he speeds,
Where other hills resound with other reeds.

D I O N E.

Should he come back ; Suspicion's jealous eyes
Might trace my feature through the swain's disguise.
Now ev'ry noise and whistling wind I dread,
And in each sound approaches human tread.

L A U R A.

He said, he left your house involv'd in cares,
Sighs swell'd each breast, each eye o'erflow'd with tears ;   40
For his lost child thy pensive father mourns,
And sunk in sorrow to the dust returns.
Go back, obedient daughter ; hence depart,
And still the sighs that tear his anxious heart.
Soon shall *Evander*, wearied with disdain,
Forgo these fields, and seek the town again.

D I O N E.

Think, *Laura*, what thy hasty thoughts persuade.
If I return, to Love a victim made,
My wrathful Sire will force his harsh command,
And with *Cleanthes* join my trembling hand.   50

L A U R A.

Trust a fond father ; raise him from despair.

D I O N E.

I fly not him ; I fly a life of care.
On the high nuptials of the Court look round ;
Where shall, alas, one happy pair be found !
There, marriage is for servile int'rest sought :
Is love for wealth or power or title bought ?

51–53 *In the edition of 1720 the passage runs :*
        LAURA.   Yet the kind parent soft persuasion trys,
                       And what his power compells not, may advise.
        DIONE.   On the high nuptials *etc.*

'Tis hence domestick jars their peace destroy,
And loose adult'ry steals the shameful joy.
But search we wide o'er all the blissful plains,
Where love alone, devoid of int'rest, reigns.   60
What concord in each happy pair appears !
How fondness strengthens with the rolling years !
Superior power ne'er thwarts their soft delights,
Nor jealous accusations wake their nights.

L A U R A.

May all those blessings on *Dione* fall.

D I O N E.

Grant me *Evander*, and I share them all.
Shall a fond parent give perpetual strife,
And doom his child to be a wretch for life ?
Though he bequeath'd me all these woods and plains,
And all the flocks the russet down contains ;   70
With all the golden harvests of the year,
Far as where yonder purple mountains rear :
Can these the broils of nuptial life prevent ?
Can these, without *Evander*, give content ?
But see, he comes.

L A U R A.

——————————————I'll to the vales repair,
Where wanders by the stream my fleecy care.
Mayst thou the rage of this new flame controul,
And wake *Dione* in his tender soul !   [*Ex.* Laura.

67 parent] father

S C E N E V.

D I O N E. L Y C I D A S.

L Y C I D A S.

Say, my *Alexis*, can thy words impart
Kind rays of hope to cheer a doubtful heart ?
How didst thou first my pangs of love disclose ?
Did her disdainful brow confirm my woes ?
Or did soft pity in her bosom rise,
Heave on her breast, and languish in her eyes ?

D I O N E.

How shall my tongue the fault'ring tale explain !
My heart drops blood to give the shepherd pain.

L Y C I D A S.

Pronounce her utmost scorn ; I come prepar'd
To meet my doom. Say, is my death declar'd ?   10

D I O N E.

Why should thy fate depend on woman's will?
Forget this tyrant, and be happy still.

L Y C I D A S.

Didst thou beseech her not to speed her flight,
Nor shun with wrathful glance my hated sight?
Will she consent my sighing plaint to hear,
Nor let my piercing crys be lost in air?

D I O N E.

Can mariners appease the tossing storm,
When foaming waves the yawning deep deform?
When o'er the sable cloud the thunder flies,
Say, who shall calm the terror of the skies?   20
Who shall the lion's famish'd roar asswage?
And can we still proud woman's stronger rage?
Soon as my faithful tongue pronounc'd thy name,
Sudden her glances shot resentful flame:
Be dumb, she crys, this whining love give o'er,
And vex me with the teazing theme no more.

L Y C I D A S.

'Tis pride alone that keeps alive her scorn.
Can the mean swain in humble cottage born,
Can Poverty that haughty heart obtain,
Where avarice and strong ambition reign?   30
If Poverty pass by in tatter'd coat,
Curs vex his heels and stretch their barking throat;
If chance he mingle in the female croud,
Pride tosses high her head, Scorn laughs aloud;
Each nymph turns from him to her gay gallant,
And wonders at the impudence of Want.
'Tis vanity that rules all woman-kind,
Love is the weakest passion of their mind.

D I O N E.

Though one is by those servile views possest,
O *Lycidas*, condemn not all the rest.   40

L Y C I D A S.

Though I were bent beneath a load of years,
And seventy winters thin'd my hoary hairs;
Yet if my olive branches dropt with oil,
And crooked shares were brighten'd in my soil
If lowing herds my fat'ning meads possest,
And my white fleece the tawny mountain drest;
Then would she lure me with love-darting glance,
Then with fond mercenary smiles advance.
Though hell with ev'ry vice my soul had stain'd,
And froward anger in my bosom reign'd,   50

Though avarice my coffers cloath'd in rust,
And my joints trembled with enfeebled lust ;
Yet were my ancient name with titles great,
How would she languish for the gawdy bait !
If to her love all-tempting wealth pretend,
What virtuous woman can her heart defend !

D I O N E.

Conquests, thus meanly bought, men soon despise,
And justly slight the mercenary prize.

L Y C I D A S.

I know these frailties in her breast reside,
Direct her glance and ev'ry action guide.   60
Still let *Alexis'* faithful friendship aid,
Once more attempt to bend the stubborn maid.
Tell her, no base-born swain provokes her scorn,
No clown, beneath the sedgy cottage born ;
Tell her, for her this sylvan dress I took,
For her my name and pomp of Courts forsook ;
My lofty roofs with golden sculpture shine,
And my high birth descends from ancient line.

D I O N E.

Love is a sacred voluntary fire,
Gold never bought that pure, that chast desire,   70
Who thinks true love for lucre to possess,
Shall grasp false flatt'ry and the feign'd caress ;
Can we believe that mean, that servile wife,
Who vilely sells her dear-bought love for life,
Would not her virtue for an hour resign,
If in her sight the proffer'd treasure shine.

L Y C I D A S.

Can reason (when by winds swift fires are born
O'er waving harvests of autumnal corn)
The driving fury of the flame reprove ?
Who then shall reason with a heart in love !   80

D I O N E.

Yet let me speak ; O may my words persuade
The noble youth to quit this sylvan maid !
Resign thy crook, no more to plains resort,
Look round on all the beauties of the Court ;
There shall thy merit find a worthy flame,
Some nymph of equal wealth and equal name.
Think, if these offers should thy wish obtain,
And should the rustick beauty stoop to gain :
Thy heart could ne'er prolong th' unequal fire,
The sudden blaze would in one year expire ;   90

Then thy rash folly thou too late shalt chide,
To Poverty and base-born blood ally'd ;
Her vulgar tongue shall animate the strife,
And hourly discord vex thy future life.

L Y C I D A S.

Such is the force thy faithful words impart,
That like the galling goad they pierce my heart!
You think fair virtue in my breast resides,
That honest truth my lips and actions guides ;
Deluded shepherd, could you view my soul,
You'd see it with deceit and treach'ry foul ;   100
I'm base, perfidious. E'er from Court I came,
Love singled from the train a beauteous dame ;
The tender maid my fervent vows believ'd,
My fervent vows the tender maid deceiv'd.
Why dost thou tremble ?——why thus heave thy sighs ?
Why steal the silent sorrows from thy eyes ?

D I O N E.

Sure the soft lamb hides rage within his breast,
And cooing turtles are with hate possest ;
When from so sweet a tongue flow fraud and lies,
And those meek looks a perjur'd heart disguise.   110
Ah ! who shall now on faithless man depend ?
The treach'rous lover proves as false a friend.

L Y C I D A S.

When with *Dione*'s love my bosom glow'd,
Firm constancy and truth sincere I vow'd ;
But since *Parthenia*'s brighter charms were known,
My love, my constancy and truth are flown.

D I O N E.

Are not thy hours with conscious anguish stung ?
Swift vengeance must o'ertake the perjur'd tongue.
The Gods the cause of injur'd love assert,
And arm with stubborn pride *Parthenia*'s heart.   120

L Y C I D A S.

Go, try her ; tempt her with my birth and state,
Stronger ambition will subdue her hate.

D I O N E.

O rather turn thy thoughts on that lost maid,
Whose hourly sighs thy faithless oaths upbraid !
Think you behold her at the dead of night,
Plac'd by the glimm'ring taper's paly light,

97 You think] Thou think'st   99 could you] couldst thou
100 You'd] Thou'dst   125 you behold] thou beheld'st

With all your letters spread before her view,
While trickling tears the tender lines bedew;
Sobbing she reads the perj'rys o'er and o'er,
And her long nights know peaceful sleep no more.   130

L Y C I D A S.
Let me forget her.

D I O N E.
——————————O false youth, relent;
Think should *Parthenia* to thy hopes consent;
When *Hymen* joins your hands, and musick's voice
Makes the glad ecchoes of thy domes rejoyce,
Then shall *Dione* force the crouded hall,
Kneel at thy feet and loud for justice call:
Could you behold her weltring on the ground,
The purple dagger reeking from the wound?
Could you unmov'd this dreadful sight survey?   140
Such fatal scenes shall stain thy bridal day.

L Y C I D A S.
The horrid thought sinks deep into my soul,
And down my cheek unwilling sorrows roll.

D I O N E.
From this new flame you may as yet recede.
Or have you doom'd that guiltless maid shall bleed?

L Y C I D A S.
Name her no more.——Haste, seek the sylvan Fair.

D I O N E.
Should the rich proffer tempt her list'ning ear,
Bid all your peace adieu. O barb'rous youth,
Can you forgo your honour, love and truth?
Yet should *Parthenia* wealth and title slight,   150
Would justice then restore *Dione*'s right?
Would you then dry her ever-falling tears;
And bless with honest love your future years?

L Y C I D A S.
I'll in yon' shade thy wish'd return attend;
Come, quickly come, and cheer thy sighing friend.

                                                    [*Exit* Lycidas.

D I O N E.
Should her proud soul resist the tempting bait,
Should she contemn his proffer'd wealth and state,
Then I once more his perjur'd heart may move,
And in his bosom wake the dying love.

127 your] thy   138, 140 Could you] Could'st thou
144 you may] thou may'st   145 have you] hast thou   148 your] thy
149 Can you ... your] Canst thou ... thy   152 Would you] Would'st thou
153 And bless with love and joy thy future years?
155 Come, quickly] *1720* Come quickly *1731*.

As the pale wretch involv'd in doubts and fears,   160
All trembling in the judgment-hall appears ;
So shall I stand before *Parthenia's* eyes,
For as she dooms, *Dione* lives or dies.

ACT IV. SCENE I.

L Y C I D A S. P A R T H E N I A asleep in a bower.

L Y C I D A S.

MAY no rude wind the rustling branches move ;
Breathe soft, ye silent gales, nor wake my Love.
Ye shepherds, piping homeward on the way,
Let not the distant ecchoes learn your lay ;
Strain not, ye nightingales, your warbling throat,
May no loud shake prolong the shriller note,
Lest she awake ; O sleep, secure her eyes,
That I may gaze ; for if she wake, she flies.
While easy dreams compose her peaceful soul,
What anxious cares within my bosom roll !   10
If tir'd with sighs beneath the beech I lye,
And languid slumber close my weeping eye,
Her lovely vision rises to my view,
Swift flys the nymph, and swift would I pursue ;
I strive to call, my tongue has lost its sound ;
Like rooted oaks, my feet benumm'd are bound ;
Struggling I wake. Again my sorrows flow,
And not one flatt'ring dream deludes my woe.
What innocence ! how meek is ev'ry grace !
How sweet the smile that dimples on her face,   20
Calm as the sleeping seas ! but should my sighs
Too rudely breathe, what angry storms would rise !
Though the fair rose with beauteous blush is crown'd,
Beneath her fragrant leaves the thorn is found ;
The peach, that with inviting crimson blooms,
Deep at the heart the cank'ring worm consumes ;
'Tis thus, alas ! those lovely features hide
Disdain and anger and resentful pride.

S C E N E I I.

L Y C I D A S. D I O N E. P A R T H E N I A.

L Y C I D A S.

Hath proffer'd greatness yet o'ercome her hate ?
And does she languish for the glitt'ring bait ?
Against the swain she might her pride support.
Can she subdue her sex, and scorn a Court ?

Perhaps in dreams the shining vision charms,
And the rich bracelet sparkles on her arms ;
In fancy'd heaps the golden treasure glows :
Parthenia wake ; all this thy swain bestows.

D I O N E.

Sleeps she in these close bowers ?

L Y C I D A S.

————————————————Lo ! there she lies.   10

D I O N E.

O may no startling sound unseal her eyes,
And drive her hence away. 'Till now, in vain
I trod the winding wood and weary plain.
Hence, *Lycidas* ; beyond those shades repose,
While I thy fortune and thy birth disclose.

L Y C I D A S.

May I *Parthenia* to thy friendship owe !

D I O N E.

O rather think on lost *Dione*'s woe !
Must she thy broken faith for ever mourn,
And will that juster passion ne'er return ?

L Y C I D A S.

Upbraid me not ; but go. Her slumbers chase ;   20
And in her view the bright temptation place.   [*Ex.* Lycidas.

12 *In the edition of 1720 the passage runs :*
                        'Till now, in vain
          I trod the winding wood and weary plain ;
          Ign'rant as yet what grandeur courts her scorn,
          She thinks thee train'd in fields, and vulgar-born.
          Hence, Lycidas ; *etc.*
16 May kind success upon the message wait.
17 woe !] fate !
20 I'll hear no more : go then, her slumbers chase,

S C E N E   I I I.

D I O N E.   P A R T H E N I A.

D I O N E.

Now flames the western skie with golden beams,
And the ray kindles on the quiv'ring streams ;
Long flights of crows, high-croaking from their food,
Now seek the nightly covert of the wood ;
The tender grass with dewy crystal bends,
And gath'ring vapour from the heath ascends.

Shake off this downy rest ; wake, gentle maid,
Trust not thy charms beneath the noxious shade.
Parthenia, rise.

P A R T H E N I A.

——————————What voice alarms my ear ?   10
Away. Approach not. Hah ! *Alexis* there !
Let us together to the vales descend,
And to the folds our bleating charge attend ;
But let me hear no more that shepherd's name,
Vex not my quiet with his hateful flame.

D I O N E.

Can I behold him gasping on the ground,
And seek no healing herb to stanch the wound ?
For thee continual sighs consume his heart,
'Tis you alone can cure the bleeding smart.
Once more I come the moving cause to plead,   20
If still his suff'rings cannot intercede,
Yet let my friendship do his passion right,
And show thy lover in his native light.

P A R T H E N I A.

Why in dark myst'ry are thy words involv'd ?
If *Lycidas* you mean ; know, I'm resolv'd.

D I O N E.

Let not thy kindling rage my words restrain.
Know then ; *Parthenia* slights no vulgar swain.
For thee he bears the scrip and sylvan crook,
For thee the glories of a Court forsook.
May not thy heart the wealthy flame decline !   30
His honours, his possessions, all are thine.

P A R T H E N I A.

If he 's a Courtier, O ye Nymphs, beware ;
Those who most promise are the least sincere.
The quick-ey'd hawk shoots headlong from above,
And in his pounces bears the trembling dove ;
The pilf'ring wolf o'er-leaps the fold's defence.
But the false Courtier preys on innocence.
If he 's a Courtier ; O ye Nymphs, beware :
Those who most promise are the least sincere.

D I O N E.

Alas ! thou ne'er hast prov'd the sweets of State,   40
Nor known that female pleasure, to be great.
'Tis for the town ripe clusters load the poles,
And all our Autumn crowns the Courtier's bowles ;
For him our woods the red-ey'd pheasant breed,
And annual coveys in our harvest feed ;

  19 you . . . can] thou . . . canst   30 decline !] decline,

For him with fruit the bending branch is stor'd,
Plenty pours all her blessings on his board.
If (when the market to the city calls)
We chance to pass beside his palace walls,
Does not his hall with musick's voice resound,   50
And the floor tremble with the dancer's bound ?
Such are the pleasures *Lycidas* shall give,
When thy relenting bosom bids him live.

PARTHENIA.

See yon gay goldfinch hop from spray to spray,
Who sings a farewell to the parting day ;
At large he flies o'er hill and dale and down ;
Is not each bush, each spreading tree his own ?
And canst thou think he'll quit his native brier,
For the bright cage o'er-arch'd with golden wire ?
What then are honours, pomp and gold to me ?   60
Are those a price to purchase liberty !

DIONE.

Think, when the *Hymeneal* torch shall blaze,
And on the solemn rites the virgins gaze ;
When thy fair locks with glitt'ring gems are grac'd,
And the bright zone shall sparkle round thy waste,
How will their hearts with envious sorrow pine,
When *Lycidas* shall join his hand to thine !

PARTHENIA.

And yet, *Alexis*, all that pomp and show
Are oft' the varnish of internal woe.
When the chast lamb is from her sisters led,   70
And interwoven garlands paint her head ;
The gazing flock, all envious of her pride,
Behold her skipping by the Priestess' side ;
Each hopes the flow'ry wreath with longing eyes ;
While she, alas ! is led to sacrifice !
Thus walks the bride in all her state array'd,
The gaze and envy of each thoughtless maid.

DIONE.

As yet her tongue resists the tempting snare,
And guards my panting bosom from despair.   [*Aside.*
Can thy strong soul this noble flame forgo ?   80
Must such a lover waste his life in woe ?

PARTHENIA.

Tell him, his gifts I scorn ; not all his art,
Not all his flattery shall seduce my heart.
Courtiers, I know, are disciplin'd to cheat,
Their infant lips are taught to lisp deceit ;

To prey on easy nymphs they range the shade,
And vainly boast of innocence betray'd ;
Chast hearts, unlearn'd in falsehood, they assail,
And think our ear will drink the grateful tale :
No. *Lycidas* shall ne'er my peace destroy,   90
I'll guard my virtue, and content enjoy.

D I O N E.

So strong a passion in my bosom burns,
Whene'er his soul is griev'd, *Alexis* mourns !
Canst thou this importuning ardor blame ?
Would not thy tongue for friendship urge the same ?

P A R T H E N I A:

Yes, blooming swain. You show an honest mind ;
I see it, with the purest flame refin'd.
Who shall compare love's mean and gross desire
To the chast zeal of friendship's sacred fire ?
By whining love our weakness is confest ;   100
But stronger friendship shows a virtuous breast.
In Folly's heart the short-liv'd blaze may glow,
Wisdom alone can purer friendship know.
Love is a sudden blaze which soon decays,
Friendship is like the sun's eternal rays ;
Not daily benefits exhaust the flame,
It still is giving, and still burns the same ;
And could *Alexis* from his soul remove
All the low images of grosser love ;
Such mild, such gentle looks thy heart declare,   110
Fain would my breast thy faithful friendship share.

D I O N E.

How dare you in the diff'rent sex confide ?
And seek a friendship which you ne'er have try'd ?

P A R T H E N I A.

Yes, I to thee could give up all my heart.
From thy chast eye no wanton glances dart ;
Thy modest lips convey no thought impure,
With thee may strictest virtue walk secure.

D I O N E.

Yet can I safely on the nymph depend,
Whose unrelenting scorn can kill my friend !

P A R T H E N I A.

Accuse me not, who act a generous part ;   120
Had I, like city maids, a fraudful heart,
Then had his proffers taught my soul to feign
Then had I vilely stoopt to sordid gain,

96 You show] Thou show'st   112 dare you] dar'st thou
113 you . . . have] thou . . . hast

Then had I sigh'd for honours, pomp and gold,
And for unhappy chains my freedom sold.
If you would save him, bid him leave the plain,
And to his native city turn again ;
There, shall his passion find a ready cure,
There, not one dame resists the glitt'ring lure.

DIONE.

All this I frequent urg'd, but urg'd in vain.   130
Alas ! thou only canst asswage his pain !

126 you would] thou would'st

SCENE IV.

DIONE. PARTHENIA. LYCIDAS, [listening.

LYCIDAS.

Why stays *Alexis* ? can my bosom bear
Thus long alternate storms of hope and fear ?
Yonder they walk ; no frowns her brow disguise,
But love consenting sparkles in her eyes ;
Here will I listen, here, impatient wait.
Spare me, *Parthenia*, and resign thy hate.   [*Aside.*

PARTHENIA.

When *Lycidas* shall to the Court repair,
Still let *Alexis* love his fleecy care ;
Still let him chuse cool grots and sylvan bowers,
And let *Parthenia* share his peaceful hours.   10

LYCIDAS.

What do I hear ? my friendship is betray'd ;
The treach'rous rival has seduc'd the maid.   [*Aside.*

PARTHENIA.

With thee, where bearded goats descend the steep,
Or where, like winter's snow, the nibbling sheep
Cloath the slope hills ; I'll pass the cheerful day,
And from thy reed my voice shall catch the lay.
But see, still Ev'ning spreads her dusky wings,
The flocks, slow-moving from the misty springs,
Now seek their fold. Come, shepherd, let's away,
To close the latest labours of the day.   [*Exeunt hand in hand.*

2 alternate storms] th' alternate storm

S C E N E V.

L Y C I D A S.

My troubled heart what dire disasters rend !
A scornful mistress, and a treach'rous friend !
Would ye be cozen'd, more than woman can ;
Unlock your bosom to perfidious man.
One faithful woman have these eyes beheld,
And against her this perjur'd heart rebell'd :
But search as far as earth's wide bounds extend,
Where shall the wretched find one faithful friend ?

S C E N E V I.

L Y C I D A S. D I O N E.

L Y C I D A S.

Why starts the swain ? why turn his eyes away,
As if amidst his path the viper lay ?
Did I not to thy charge my heart confide ?
Did I not trust thee near *Parthenia*'s side,
As here she slept ?

D I O N E.

————————————She strait my call obey'd,
And downy slumber left the lovely maid ;
As in the morn awakes the folded rose,
And all around her breathing odour throws ;
So wak'd *Parthenia*.   10

L Y C I D A S.

————————————Could thy guarded heart,
When her full beauty glow'd, put by the dart ?
Yet on *Alexis* let my soul depend.
'Tis most ungen'rous to suspect a friend.
And thou, I hope, hast well that name profest.

D I O N E.

O could thy piercing eye discern my breast !
Could'st thou the secrets of my bosom see,
There ev'ry thought is fill'd with cares for thee.

L Y C I D A S.

Is there, against hypocrisie, defence,
Who cloaths her words and looks with innocence !   [*Aside.*
Say, shepherd, when you proffer'd wealth and state,   21
Did not her scorn and suppled pride abate ?

D I O N E.

As sparkling di'monds to the feather'd train,
Who scrape the winnow'd chaff in search of grain ;
Such to the shepherdess the Court appears :
Content she seeks, and spurns those glitt'ring cares.

L Y C I D A S.

'Tis not in woman grandeur to despise,
'Tis not from Courts, from me alone she flies.
Did not my passion suffer like disgrace,
While she believ'd me born of sylvan race ?   30
Dost thou not think, this proudest of her kind
Has to some rival swain her heart resign'd ?

D I O N E.

No rival shepherd her disdain can move ;
Her frozen bosom is averse to love.

L Y C I D A S.

Say, art thou sure, that this ungrateful fair
Scorns all alike, bids all alike despair ?

D I O N E.

How can I know the secrets of her heart !

L Y C I D A S.

Answer sincere, nor from the question start.
Say, in her glance was never love confest,
And is no swain distinguish'd from the rest ?   40

D I O N E.

O *Lycidas*, bid all thy troubles cease ;
Let not a thought on her disturb thy peace.
May justice bid thy former passion wake ;
Think how *Dione* suffers for thy sake :
Let not a broken oath thy honour stain,
Recall thy vows, and seek the town again.

L Y C I D A S.

What means *Alexis* ? where 's thy friendship flown ?
Why am I banish'd to the hateful town ?
Hath some new shepherd warm'd *Parthenia*'s breast ?
And does my love his am'rous hours molest ?   50
Is it for this thou bid'st me quit the plain ?
Yes, yes, thou fondly lov'st this rival swain.
When first my cheated soul thy friendship woo'd,
To my warm heart I took the vip'rous brood.
O false *Alexis* !

50 his] her

D I O N E.

———————————————Why am I accus'd ?
Thy jealous mind is by weak fears abus'd.

L Y C I D A S.

Was not thy bosom fraught with false design ?
Didst thou not plead his cause, and give up mine ?
Let not thy tongue evasive answer seek ;   60
The conscious crimson rises on thy cheek :
Thy coward conscience, by thy guilt dismaid,
Shakes in each joint, and owns that I'm betray'd.

D I O N E.

How my poor heart is wrong'd! O spare thy friend !

L Y C I D A S.

Seek not detected falsehood to defend.

D I O N E.

Beware ; lest blind suspicion rashly blame.

L Y C I D A S.

Own thy self then the rival of my flame.
If this be she for whom *Alexis* pin'd,
She now no more is to thy vows unkind.
Behind the thicket's twisted verdure laid,   70
I witness'd ev'ry tender thing she said ;
I saw bright pleasure kindle in her eyes,
Love warm'd each feature at thy soft replys.

D I O N E.

Yet hear me speak.

L Y C I D A S.

———————————————In vain is all defence.
Did not thy treach'rous hand conduct her hence ?
Haste, from my sight. Rage burns in ev'ry vein ;
Never approach my just revenge again.

D I O N E.

O search my heart ; there injur'd truth thou'lt find.

L Y C I D A S.

Talk not of Truth ; long since she left mankind.   80
So smooth a tongue ! and yet so false a heart !
Sure Courts first taught thee fawning friendship's art !
No. Thou art false by nature.

D I O N E.

———————————————Let me clear
This heavy charge, and prove my trust sincere.

L Y C I D A S.

Boast then her favours; say, what happy hour
Next calls to meet her in th' appointed bower;
Say, when and where you met.

D I O N E.

——————————Be rage supprest.
In stabbing mine, you wound *Parthenia*'s breast.   90
She said, she still defy'd Love's keenest dart;
Yet purer friendship might divide her heart,
Friendship's sincerer bands she wish'd to prove.

L Y C I D A S.

A woman's friendship ever ends in love.
Think not these foolish tales my faith command;
Did not I see thee press her snowy hand?
O may her passion like thy friendship last!
May she betray thee e'er a day be past!
Hence then. Away. Thou'rt hateful to my sight,
And thus I spurn the fawning hypocrite.   [*Ex.* Lycidas.

S C E N E   V I I.

D I O N E.

Was ever grief like mine! O wretched maid!
My friendship wrong'd! my constant love betray'd!
Misfortune haunts my steps where-e'er I go,
And all my days are over-cast with woe.
Long have I strove th' encreasing load to bear,
Now faints my soul, and sinks into despair.
O lead me to the hanging mountain's cell,
In whose brown cliffs the fowls of darkness dwell;
Where waters, trickling down the rifted wall,
Shall lull my sorrows with the tinkling fall.   10
There, seek thy grave. How canst thou bear the light,
When banish'd ever from *Evander*'s sight!

S C E N E   V I I I.

D I O N E.   L A U R A.

L A U R A.

Why hangs a cloud of grief upon thy brows?
Does the proud nymph accept *Evander*'s vows?

D I O N E.

Can I bear life with these new pangs opprest!
Again he tears me from his faithless breast:

A perjur'd Lover first he sought these plains,
And now my friendship like my love disdains.
As I new offers to *Parthenia* made,
Conceal'd he stood behind the woodbine shade.
He says, my treach'rous tongue his heart betray'd,
That my false speeches have mis-led the maid ;   10
With groundless fear he thus his soul deceives ;
What frenzy dictates, jealousy believes.

L A U R A.

Resign thy crook, put off this manly vest,
And let the wrong'd *Dione* stand confest ;
When he shall learn what sorrows thou hast born,
And find that nought relents *Parthenia*'s scorn,
Sure he will pity thee.

D I O N E.

——————————No, *Laura*, no.
Should I, alas ! the sylvan dress forgo,
Then might he think that I her pride foment,   20
That injur'd love instructs me to resent ;
Our secret enterprize might fatal prove :
Man flys the plague of persecuting love.

L A U R A.

Avoid *Parthenia* ; lest his rage grow warm,
And jealousie resolve some fatal harm.

D I O N E.

O *Laura*, if thou chance the youth to find,
Tell him what torments vex my anxious mind ;
Should I once more his awful presence seek,
The silent tears would bathe my glowing cheek;
By rising sighs my fault'ring voice be stay'd,   30
And trembling fear too soon confess the maid.
Haste, *Laura*, then ; his vengeful soul asswage,
Tell him, I'm guiltless ; cool his blinded rage ;
Tell him that truth sincere my friendship brought,
Let him not cherish one suspicious thought.
Then to convince him, his distrust was vain,
I'll never, never see that nymph again.
This way he went.

L A U R A.

——————————See, at the call of night,
The star of ev'ning sheds his silver light   40
High o'er yon western hill : the cooling gales
Fresh odours breathe along the winding dales ;
Far from their home as yet our shepherds stray,
To close with cheerful walk the sultry day.

Methinks from far I hear the piping swain :
Hark, in the breeze now swells, now sinks the strain !
Thither I'll seek him.

D I O N E.

———————————————While this length of glade
Shall lead me pensive through the sable shade ;
Where on the branches murmur rushing winds,   50
Grateful as falling floods to love-sick minds.
O may this path to Death's dark vale descend !
There only, can the wretched hope a friend.   [*Ex. severally.*

ACT V. SCENE I.

A Wood.

D I O N E. C L E A N T H E S, (*who lies wounded
in a distant part of the stage.*)

D I O N E.

THE Moon serene now climbs th' aerial way ;
See, at her sight ten thousand stars decay :
With trembling gleam she tips the silent grove,
While all beneath the checquer'd shadows move.
Turn back thy silver axles, downward roll,
Darkness best fits the horrors of my soul.
Rise, rise, ye clouds ; the face of heav'n deform,
Veil the bright Goddess in a sable storm :
O look not down upon a wretched maid !
Let thy bright torch the happy lover aid,   10
And light his wandring footsteps to the bower,
Where the kind nymph attends th' appointed hour.
Yet thou hast seen unhappy love, like mine ;
Did not thy lamp in Heav'n's blue forehead shine,
When *Thisbe* sought her Love along the glade ?
Didst thou not then behold the gleaming blade,
And gild the fatal point that stabb'd her breast ?
Soon I, like her, shall seek the realms of rest.
Let groves of mournful yew a wretch surround !
O sooth my ear with melancholy sound !   20
The village curs now stretch their yelling throat,
And dogs from distant cotts return the note ;
The rav'nous wolf along the valley prowls,
And with his famish'd crys the mountain howls.
But hark ! what sudden noise advances near ?
Repeated groans alarm my frighted ear !

C L E A N T H E S.

Shepherd, approach ; ah ! fly not through the glade.
A wretch all dy'd with wounds invokes thy aid.

D I O N E.

Say then, unhappy stranger, how you bled ;
Collect thy spirits, raise thy drooping head.   30
                    [Cleanthes *raises himself on his arm.*
O horrid sight ! *Cleanthes* gasping lies ;
And Death's black shadows float before his eyes.
Unknown in this disguise, I'll check my woe,
And learn what bloody hand has struck the blow.   [*Aside.*
Say, youth, ere Fate thy feeble voice confounds,
What led thee hither ? whence these purple wounds ?

C L E A N T H E S.

Stay, fleeting life ; may strength a-while prevail,
Lest my clos'd lips confine th' imperfect tale.
Ere the streak'd East grew warm with amber ray,
I from the city took my doubtful way,   40
Far o'er the plains I sought a beauteous maid,
Who from the Court, in these wide forests stray'd,
Wanders unknown ; as I, with weary pain,
Try'd ev'ry path, and op'ning glade in vain ;
A band of thieves, forth-rushing from the wood,
Unsheath'd their daggers warm with daily blood ;
Deep in my breast the barb'rous steel is dy'd,
And purple hands the golden prey divide.
Hence are these mangling wounds. Say, gentle swain,
If thou hast known among the sylvan train   50
The vagrant nymph I seek ?

D I O N E.

——————————————What mov'd thy care,
Thus, in these pathless wilds to search the fair ?

C L E A N T H E S.

I charge you, O ye daughters of the grove,
Ye *Naiads*, who the mossy fountains love,
Ye happy swains, who range the pastures wide,
Ye tender nymphs, who feed your flocks beside ;
If my last gasping breath can pity move,
If e'er ye knew the pangs of slighted love,
Show her, I charge you, where *Cleanthes* dy'd ;   60
The grass yet reeking with the sanguine tide.
A father's power to me the virgin gave,
But she disdain'd to live a nuptial slave ;
So fled her native home.

DIONE.

—————————————'Tis then from thee
Springs the foul source of all her misery.
Could'st thou, thy selfish appetite to please,
Condemn to endless woes another's peace ?

CLEANTHES.

O spare me ; nor my hapless love upbraid,
While on my heart Death's frozen hand is laid !   70
Go, seek her, guide her where *Cleanthes* bled ;
When she surveys her lover pale and dead,
Tell her, that since she fled my hateful sight,
Without remorse I sought the realms of night.
Methinks I see her view these poor remains,
And on her cheek indecent gladness reigns !
Full in her presence cold *Cleanthes* lies,
And not one tear stands trembling in her eyes !
O let a sigh my hapless fate deplore !
Cleanthes now controuls thy love no more.   80

DIONE.

How shall my lids confine these rising woes ?   [*Aside.*

CLEANTHES.

O might I see her, ere Death's finger close
These eyes for ever ! might her soften'd breast
Forgive my love with too much ardor prest !
Then I with peace could yield my latest breath.

DIONE.

Shall I not calm the sable hour of death,
And show my self before him !——Hah ! he dies.
See, from his trembling lip the spirit flies !   [*Aside.*
Stay yet awhile. *Dione* stands confest.
He knows me not. He faints, he sinks to rest.   90

CLEANTHES.

Tell her, since all my hopes in her were lost,
That death was welcome——   [*Dies.*

DIONE.

What sudden gusts of grief my bosom rend !
A parent's curses o'er my head impend
For disobedient vows ; O wretched maid,
Those very vows *Evander* hath betray'd.
See, at thy feet *Cleanthes* bath'd in blood !
For love of thee he trod this lonely wood ;
Thou art the cruel authress of his fate ;
He falls by thine, thou, by *Evander*'s hate.   100

When shall my soul know rest ? *Cleanthes* slain
No longer sighs and weeps for thy disdain.
Thou still art curst with love. Bleed, virgin, bleed.
How shall a wretch from anxious life be freed!
My troubled brain with sudden frenzy burns,
And shatter'd thought now this now that way turns.
What do I see thus glitt'ring on the plains ?
Hah ! the dread sword yet warm with crimson stains !

[*Takes up the dagger.*

102 disdain.] disdain,

SCENE II.

DIONE. PARTHENIA.

PARTHENIA.

Sweet is the walk when night has cool'd the hour.
This path directs me to my sylvan bower. [*Aside.*

DIONE.

Why is my soul with sudden fear dismay'd !
Why drops my trembling hand the pointed blade ?
O string my arm with force ! [*Aside.*

PARTHENIA.

————————————Methought a noise
Broke through the silent air, like human voice. [*Aside.*

DIONE.

One well-aim'd blow shall all my pangs remove,
Grasp firm the fatal steel, and cease to love. [*Aside.*

PARTHENIA.

Sure 'twas *Alexis*. Hah ! a sword display'd ! 10
The streaming lustre darts a-cross the shade. [*Aside.*

DIONE.

May Heav'n new vigour to my soul impart,
And guide the desp'rate weapon to my heart ! [*Aside.*

PARTHENIA.

May I the meditated death arrest ! [*Holds* Dione's *hand.*
Strike not, rash shepherd ; spare thy guiltless breast.
O give me strength to stay the threaten'd harm,
And wrench the dagger from his lifted arm !

DIONE.

What cruel hand with-holds the welcome blow ?
In giving life, you but prolong my woe.

O may not thus th' expected stroke impend !   20
Unloose thy grasp, and let swift death descend.
But if yon' murder thy red hands hath dy'd ;
Here.   Pierce me deep ; let forth the vital tide.

[Dione *quits the dagger*.

P A R T H E N I A.

Wait not thy fate ; but this way turn thy eyes :
My virgin hand no purple murder dyes.
Turn then, *Alexis* ; and *Parthenia* know,
'Tis she protects thee from the fatal blow.

D I O N E.

Must the night-watches by my sighs be told ?
And must these eyes another morn behold
Through dazling floods of tears ? ungen'rous maid,   30
The friendly stroke is by thy hand delay'd ;
Call it not mercy to prolong my breath ;
'Tis but to torture me with lingring death.

P A R T H E N I A.

What moves thy hand to act this bloody part ?
Whence are these gnawing pangs that tear thy heart ?
Is that thy friend who lies before thee slain ?
Is it his wound that reeks upon the plain ?
Is't *Lycidas* ?

D I O N E.

——————————————No.   I the stranger found,
E'er chilly death his frozen tongue had bound.   40
He said ; as at the rosy dawn of day,
He from the city took his vagrant way,
A murd'ring band pour'd on him from the wood,
First seiz'd his gold, then bath'd their swords in blood.

P A R T H E N I A.

You, whose ambition labours to be great,
Think on the perils which on riches wait.
Safe are the shepherd's paths ; when sober Even
Streaks with pale light the bending arch of heaven,
From danger free, through desarts wild he hies,
The rising smoak far o'er the mountain spies,   50
Which marks his distant cottage ; on he fares,
For him no murd'rers lay their nightly snares ;
They pass him by, they turn their steps away :
Safe Poverty was ne'er the villain's prey.
At home he lies secure in easy sleep,
No bars his ivie-mantled cottage keep ;
No thieves in dreams the fancy'd dagger hold,
And drag him to detect the buried gold ;

22 hath] has

Nor starts he from his couch aghast and pale
When the door murmurs with the hollow gale,   60
While he, whose iron coffers rust with wealth,
Harbours beneath his roof Deceit and Stealth;
Treach'ry with lurking pace frequents his walks,
And close behind him horrid Murder stalks.
'Tis tempting lucre makes the villain bold.
There lies a bleeding sacrifice to gold.

DIONE.

To live, is but to wake to daily cares,
And journey through a tedious vale of tears.
Had you not rush'd between, my life had flown;
And I, like him, no more had sorrow known.   70

PARTHENIA.

When anguish in the gloomy bosom dwells,
The counsel of a friend the cloud dispells.
Give thy breast vent, the secret grief impart,
And say what woe lies heavy at thy heart.
To save thy life kind Heav'n has succour sent,
The Gods by me thy threaten'd fate prevent.

DIONE.

No.   To prevent it, is beyond thy power;
Thou only canst defer the welcome hour.
When you the lifted dagger turn'd aside,
Only one road to death thy force deny'd;   80
Still fate is in my reach.   From mountains high,
Deep in whose shadow craggy ruines lie,
Can I not headlong fling this weight of woe,
And dash out life against the flints below?
Are there not streams, and lakes, and rivers wide,
Where my last breath may bubble on the tide?
No.   Life shall never flatter me again,
Nor shall to-morrow bring new sighs and pain.

PARTHENIA.

Can I this burthen of thy soul relieve,
And calm thy grief?   90

DIONE.

———————————If thou wilt comfort give;
Plight me thy word, and to that word be just;
When poor *Alexis* shall be laid in dust,
That pride no longer shall command thy mind,
That thou wilt spare the friend I leave behind.
I know his virtue worthy of thy breast.
Long in thy love may *Lycidas* be blest!

PARTHENIA.

That swain (who would my liberty controul,
To please some short-liv'd transport of his soul)

* P

Shows, while his importuning flame he moves,   100
That 'tis not me, himself alone he loves.
O live, nor leave him by misfortune prest ;
'Tis shameful to desert a friend distrest.

D I O N E.

Alas ! a wretch like me no loss would prove,
Would kind *Parthenia* listen to his love.

P A R T H E N I A.

Why hides thy bosom this mysterious grief ?
Ease thy o'erburthen'd heart, and hope relief.

D I O N E.

What profits it to touch thy tender breast,
With wrongs, like mine, which ne'er can be redrest ?
Let in my heart the fatal secret dye,   110
Nor call up sorrow in another's eye !

S C E N E   I I I.

D I O N E.   P A R T H E N I A.   L Y C I D A S.

L Y C I D A S.

If *Laura* right direct the darksome ways,
Along these paths the pensive shepherd strays.   [*Aside.*

D I O N E.

Let not a tear for me roll down thy cheek.
O would my throbbing sighs my heart-strings break !
Why was my breast the lifted stroke deny'd ?
Must then again the deathful deed be try'd ?
Yes.   'Tis resolv'd.   [*Snatches the dagger from* Parthenia.

P A R T H E N I A.

——————————————Ah, hold ; forbear, forbear !

L Y C I D A S.

Methought Distress with shrieks alarm'd my ear !

P A R T H E N I A.

Strike not.   Ye Gods, defend him from the wound !   10

L Y C I D A S.

Yes.   'Tis *Parthenia*'s voice, I know the sound.
Some sylvan ravisher would force the maid,
And *Laura* sent me to her virtue's aid.
Die, villain, die ; and seek the shades below.
            [Lycidas *snatches the dagger from* Dione, *and stabs her.*

D I O N E.

Whoe'er thou art, I bless thee for the blow.

L Y C I D A S.

Since Heav'n ordain'd this arm thy life should guard,
O hear my vows ! be love the just reward.

P A R T H E N I A.

Rather let vengeance, with her swiftest speed
O'ertake thy flight, and recompence the deed !
Why stays the thunder in the upper skie ?   20
Gather, ye clouds ; ye forky lightnings, fly :
On thee may all the wrath of heav'n descend,
Whose barb'rous hand hath slain a faithful friend.
Behold *Alexis* !

L Y C I D A S.

——————————Would that treach'rous boy
Have forc'd thy virtue to his brutal joy ?
What rous'd his passion to this bold advance ?
Did e'er thy eyes confess one willing glance ?
I know, the faithless youth his trust betray'd ;
And well the dagger hath my wrongs repay'd.   30

D I O N E,   [*raising herself on her arm.*

Breaks not *Evander's* voice along the glade ?
Hah ! is it he who holds the reeking blade !
There needed not or poyson, sword, or dart ;
Thy faithless vows, alas ! had broke my heart.   [*Aside.*

P A R T H E N I A.

O tremble, shepherd, for thy rash offence,
The sword is dy'd with murder'd innocence !
His gentle soul no brutal passion seiz'd,
Nor at my bosom was the dagger rais'd ;
Self-murder was his aim ; the youth I found
Whelm'd in despair, and stay'd the falling wound.   40

D I O N E.

Into what mischiefs is the lover led,
Who calls down vengeance on his perjur'd head !
O may he ne'er bewail this desperate deed,
And may, unknown, unwept, *Dione* bleed !   [*Aside.*

L Y C I D A S.

What horrors on the guilty mind attend !
His conscience had reveng'd an injur'd friend,
Hadst thou not held the stroke. In death he sought
To lose the heart-consuming pain of thought.
Did not the smooth-tongu'd boy perfidious prove,
Plead his own passion, and betray my love ?   50

23 hath] has

D I O N E.

O let him ne'er this bleeding victim know ;
Lest his rash transport, to revenge the blow,
Should in his dearer heart the dagger stain !
That wound would pierce my soul with double pain.   [*Aside.*

P A R T H E N I A.

How did his faithful lips (now pale and cold)
With moving eloquence thy griefs unfold !

L Y C I D A S.

Was he thus faithful ? thus, to friendship true ?
Then I'm a wretch.   All peace of mind, adieu !
If ebbing life yet beat within thy vein,
Alexis, speak ; unclose those lids again.   60
                [*Flings himself on the ground near* Dione.
See at thy feet the barb'rous villain kneel !
'Tis *Lycidas* who grasps the bloody steel,
Thy once lov'd friend.—Yet e'er I cease to live,
Canst thou a wretched penitent forgive ?

D I O N E.

When low beneath the sable mould I rest,
May a sincerer friendship share thy breast !
Why are those heaving groans ? (ah ! cease to weep !)
May my lost name in dark oblivion sleep ;
Let this sad tale no speaking stone declare,
From future eyes to draw a pitying tear.   70
Let o'er my grave the lev'ling plough-share pass,
Mark not the spot ; forget that e'er I was.
Then may'st thou with *Parthenia*'s love be blest,
And not one thought on me thy joys molest !
My swimming eyes are over-power'd with light,
And darkning shadows fleet before my sight.
May'st thou be happy ! ah ! my soul is free.   [*Dies.*

L Y C I D A S.

O cruel shepherdess, for love of thee   [*To* Parthenia.
This fatal deed was done.

S C E N E *the last.*

L Y C I D A S. P A R T H E N I A. L A U R A.

L A U R A.
————————————*Alexis* slain !

L Y C I D A S.

Yes.   'Twas I did it.   See this crimson stain !
My hands with blood of innocence are dy'd.
O may the Moon her silver beauty hide
In rolling clouds ! my soul abhors the light ;
Shade, shade the murd'rer in eternal night !

LAURA.

No rival shepherd is before thee laid;
There bled the chastest, the sincerest maid
That ever sigh'd for love. On her pale face,
Cannot thy weeping eyes the feature trace   10
Of thy once dear *Dione*? with wan care
Sunk are those eyes, and livid with despair!

LYCIDAS.

Dione!

LAURA.

———————There pure Constancy lies dead!

LYCIDAS.

May Heav'n shower vengeance on this perjur'd head!
As the dry branch that withers on the ground,
So, blasted be the hand that gave the wound!
Off; hold me not. This heart deserves the stroke;
'Tis black with treach'ry. Yes: the vows are broke
                                            [*Stabs himself.*
Which I so often swore. Vain world, adieu!   20
Though I was false in life, in death I'm true.   [*Dies.*

LAURA.

To morrow shall the funeral rites be paid,
And these Love victims in one grave be laid.

PARTHENIA.

There shall the yew her sable branches spread,
And mournful cypress rear her fringed head.

LAURA.

From thence shall thyme and myrtle send perfume,
And laurel ever-green o'ershade the tomb.

PARTHENIA.

Come, *Laura*; let us leave this horrid wood,
Where streams the purple grass with lovers blood;
Come to my bower. And as we sorrowing go,   30
Let poor *Dione*'s story feed my woe
With heart-relieving tears.——

LAURA,   [*pointing to* Dione.

——————————————Unhappy maid,
Hadst thou a Parent's just command obey'd,
Thou yet had'st liv'd.——But who shall Love advise?
Love scorns command, and breaks all other tyes.
Henceforth, ye swains, be true to vows profest;
For certain vengeance strikes the perjur'd breast.

ACIS and *GALATEA:*

AN ENGLISH

PASTORAL OPERA.

[*Editions* :
   ACIS and *GALATEA* : | AN ENGLISH | PASTORAL OPERA. | In THREE
ACTS. | As it is Perform'd at the | NEW THEATRE *in the* HAY-MARKET, | Set to
MUSICK | By Mr. *HANDEL.* | *LONDON* : | Printed for J. WATTS at the Printing-
Office in | *Wild-Court* near Lincoln's-Inn-Fields. | MDCCXXXII. | [Price Six Pence.]
Post 8vo.
   Numerous editions were published in the eighteenth and early nineteenth
centuries.
   The version given by Bell (1777) is entitled ' A Serenata. In Two Parts '. Part II
covering Acts II and III. The stage-directions of 1732 are all omitted. So is the
Argument. The following description of the scene is given.
   A rural prospect, diversified with rocks, groves, and a river. Acis and Galatea
seated by a fountain. Chorus of nymphs and shepherds, distributed about the landscape,
and Polyphemus discovered sitting upon a mountain.

   Of the numerous later editions I have also used that of 1764. *Acis and Galatea,*
a Serenata : As it is Perform'd at the Theatre-Royal in Covent-Garden. The Musick
composed by Mr. Handel. London : Printed for the Administrator of J. Watts. . . .
1764. [*Price One Shilling.*] This is in 4to. It agrees with Bell's version, except
that it is in three parts (not acts), and except also for a few textual differences
recorded in the notes.
   Another edition (? Oxford, no date, 4to) which I have looked at is *The Masque of*
Acis and Galatea, As it is Perform'd At the Theatre in Oxford. It is a mangled version ;
I mention it for the sake of one delightful emendation, to wit : ' Thou trusty Pine,
Prop of my *portly* steps.' The original epithet would have fallen offensively upon the
ears of so many Doctors of Divinity.

   Acis and Galatea has always been attributed to Gay, though the earlier editions
bear no name on the title-page. Austin Dobson, in the article upon Gay in the *D.N.B.*,
says definitely that ' both the words and the music had been written some ten years
before ' the first performance in 1732. The strong and definite tradition (supported
by *The Thespian Dictionary* (1802) and the more authoritative *Biographia Dramatica*
(1812), as well as the collected editions) is in agreement with the character of the
' Opera ' itself.]

THE

ARGUMENT

Acis *was the Son of* Faunus, *and the Nymph* Symethis. *He loved and was beloved of the Nymph* Galatea, *Daughter to* Nereus, *the Son of* Oceanus *and* Tethys. *Acis was allowed to be the handsomest Youth of all* Sicily ; *he was happy in his Amours with* Galatea, *till* Polyphemus *the Cyclop, Son of* Neptune, *fell in love with her, who surprising 'em together, with a Piece of a Rock overwhelmed* Acis. *Galatea, by her Persuasion, gained her Father* Nereus's *Consent to change him into a River. The Story at large is mentioned in* Ovid's *Metamorphoses, Lib.* xiii.

Dramatis Personæ

MEN.

Acis.   Mr. *Mountier.*
Polyphemus.   Mr. *Waltz.*
Damon.   Mrs. *Mason.*

WOMEN.

Galatea.   Miss *Arne.*

Chorus of Shepherds and Shepherdesses.

ACT I.

CHORUS.

O the Pleasure of the Plains,
Happy Nymphs and happy Swains,
Harmless, Merry, Free, and Gay,
Dance and sport the Hours away.
For us the Zephyr blows,
    For us distils the Dew,
For us unfolds the Rose,
    And Flowers display their Hue,
For us the Winters rain,
    For us the Summers shine,   10
Spring swells for us the Grain,
    And Autumn bleeds the Vine.
    O the, &c.   [Exeunt.

Enter GALATEA.

RECITATIVO

Gal. Ye verdant Plains and woody Mountains,
Purling Streams, and bubbling Fountains,
Ye painted Glories of the Field ;
Vain are the Pleasures which ye yield,
Too thin the Shadow of the Grove,
Too faint the Gales, to cool my Love,

AIR.

Hush, ye pretty warbling Quire,   20
    Your thrilling Strains,
        Awake my Pains,
    And kindle soft Desire.
Cease your Song, and take your Flight ;
Bring back my Acis *to my Sight.*   [Exit.
    Hush ye, &c.

Enter ACIS.

AIR.

Where shall I seek the charming Fair,
    Direct the way, king Genius of the Mountains,
O tell me if you saw my Dear,
    Seeks she the Groves, or Bathes in Crystal Fountains? 30
        Where, &c.

3 Later editions enclose this line in brackets.
9, 10 *Winters rain . . . Summers shine*] *Winter's rain . . . Summer's shine* Bell.
26 *ye*] *you* Bell.

Enter D A M O N.

R E C I T A T I V O.

Dam. Stay, Shepherd, stay, see how thy Flocks
In yonder Valley stray;
What means this melancholy Air,
No more thy tuneful Pipe we hear.

A I R.

Shepherd, what art thou pursuing?
Heedless running to thy ruining;
Share our Joy, our Pleasure share,
Leave thy Passion till to-morrow,
   Let this Day be free from sorrow,   40
Free from Love and free from Care.
  Shepherd, &c.

A C I S.

R E C I T A T I V O.

Acis. Lo! here my Love, turn *Galatea,* hither turn thine Eyes.
See at thy Feet the loving *Acis* lies.

A I R.

Love in her Eyes sits playing,
  And sheds delicious Death;
Love in her Lips sits straying,
  And warbling in her Breath.
Love on her Breast sits panting,
  And swells with soft Desire,   50
No Grace, no Charm is wanting,
  To set the Heart on Fire.
  Love in, &c.

Enter G A L A T E A.

R E C I T A T I V O.

Gal. O didst thou know the Pains of absent Love.
Acis would ne'er from *Galatea* rove.

A I R.

  As when the Dove,
  Laments her Love,
All on the naked Spray,
  When he returns,
  No more she mourns,   60
But loves the live-long Day.

32 Stay, Shepherd ! stay ; | See how etc. *1764, Bell.*
37 *ruining*] *ruin* 1764, Bell.
  43 And see my Love ! | Turn, *Galatea* etc. *1764* Lo here, my Love ! | Turn,
Galatea ! etc. *Bell.*
44 loving] longing *1764,* Bell.
45 This song was included in John Hughes's *Poems on Several Occasions,* 1735.
47 *sits straying*] *is straying* 1764, Bell.
51 *no Charm*] *nor Charm* 1764, Bell.   57 *her*] *his* Bell.

> *Billing, cooing,*
> *Panting, wooing,*
> *Melting Murmurs fill the Grove,*
> *Melting Murmurs, lasting love.*
> *As when, &c.*   [Exeunt.

Enter ACIS, *and* GALATEA.

DUETTO.

Both.	*Happy, happy Pair,*
	Happy, happy we,
Gal.	*What Joys I feel.*
Acis.	*What Charms I see.*
Gal.	*Of all Youths, thou dearest Boy,* 70
Acis.	*Of all Nymphs, thou brightest Fair.*
Both.	*Thou art all my Bliss,*
	Thou all my Joy.
	Happy, &c. [Exeunt.

65 *Murmurs*,] 1764, Bell   *Murmurs* 1732.
66–74 *In* 1764 *and Bell* :

ACIS *and* GALATEA.
Happy we.
What Joys I feel!—what Charms I see!
Of all Youths, thou dearest Boy!
Of all Nymphs, thou brightest Fair!
Thou all my Bliss, thou all my Joy!   Da capo.
CHORUS.
Happy we, etc.

71 *Nymphs*,] *Nymphs* 1732.

ACT II.

Enter SHEPHERDS.

CHORUS.

Wretched Lovers, Fate has past
This sad Decree, no Joy shall last,
Wretched Lovers, quit your Dream,
Behold the Monster, Polypheme.
See what ample Strides he takes,
The Mountain nods, the Forest shakes,
The Waves run frighted to the Shores.
Hark! how the thund'ring Giant roars.

ACT II.] PART II. *A Concerto on the organ.* 1764, Bell.
7 *frighted*] *frighten'd* 1764, Bell.

P O L Y P H E M U S.

R E C I T A T I V O.

Polyph. I rage, I melt, I burn,
The feeble God has stab'd me to the Heart.   10
Thou trusty Pine, Prop of my Godlike Steps,
I lay thee by.

Bring me an hundred Reeds of decent growth,
To make a Pipe for my capacious Mouth.
In soft enchanting Accents let me breathe,
Sweet *Galatea*'s Beauty, and my Love.

A I R.

O ruddier than the Cherry,
O sweeter than the Berry,
   O Nymph more bright
   Than Moonshine Night,   20
Like Kidlings blith and merry.
Ripe as the melting Cluster,
No Lilly has such Lustre,
   Yet hard to tame,
   As raging Flame,
And fierce as Storms that bluster.
   O Ruddier, &c.

P O L Y P H E M U S.

R E C I T A T I V O.

Polyph. Whither, Fairest, art thou running?
Still my warm Embraces shunning.

G A L A T E A.

Gal. The lion calls not to his Prey,   30
Nor bids the Wolf the Lambkin stay.

P O L Y P H E M U S.

Polyph. Thee, *Polyphemus,* great as *Jove,*
Calls to Empire and to Love,
To his Palace in the Rock,
To his Dairy, to his Flock,
To the Grape of purple Hue,
To the Plumb of Glossy Blue,
Wildings which expecting stand,
Proud to be gathered by thy Hand.
   Gal. Of Infant limbs to make my Food,   40
And swill full Draughts of Humane Blood!
Go, Monster, bid some other Guest;
I loath the Host, and loath the Feast.   [*Exit.*

    11 Thou trusty Pine, | Prop etc. *1764, Bell.*
    43 and loath] I loath *1764, Bell.*

POLYPHEMUS.

AIR.

Polyph.　*Cease to Beauty to be suing,*
　　　Ever whining, Love disdaining,
　　　Let the Brave, their Aims pursuing,
　　　Still be conqu'ring, not complaining.
　　　　　　　Cease to, &c.

DAMON.

AIR.

Dam.　*Wou'd you gain the tender creature?*
　　　Softly, gently, kindly treat her;　　　　50
　　　Suff'ring is the Lover's Part:
　　　Beauty by constraint, possessing,
　　　You enjoy but half the Blessing,
　　　Lifeless Charms, without the Heart.
　　　　　　　Wou'd you, &c.
　　　　　　　[Exeunt *Polyph.* and *Dam.*

Enter ACIS.

RECITATIVO.

Acis.　His hideous Love provokes my Rage,
Weak as I am, I must engage ;
Inspir'd by thy victorious Charms,
The God of Love will lend his Arms.

AIR.

Love sounds the Alarm, and Fear is a flying ;　　60
When Beauty's the Prize, what Mortal fears dying?
In Defence of my Treasure I'll bleed at each Vein ;
Without her, no Pleasure, for Life is a Pain.
　　　　　　　Love sounds, &c.

45 *Ever whining,*] *Ever-whining* Bell.

A C T   I I I.

Enter A c i s *in a melancholy Posture,* D a m o n *following him.*

A I R.

> *Consider, fond Shepherd,*
> > *How fleeting's the Pleasure,*
> *That flatters our Hopes,*
> > *In pursuit of the Fair ;*
> *The Joys that attend it,*
> > *By Moments we measure,*
> *But life is too little*
> > *To measure our Care.*

Enter G a l·a t e a.

R e c i t a t i v o.

Gal. Cease, O cease ! thou gentle Youth,
Trust my Constancy and Truth ;   10
Trust my Truth and Pow'rs above,
The Pow'rs propitious still to love.

A I R.

Both.   *The Flocks shall leave the Mountains,*
> *The Woods the Turtle-Dove,*
> *The Nymphs forsake the Fountains,*
> *Ere I forsake my love.*

Enter P o l y p h e m u s.

Polyph.   *Torture, Fury, Rage, Despair,*
> *I cannot, no, I cannot bear.*
Both.   *Not Show'rs to Larks so pleasing,*
> *Nor Sunshine to the Bee ;*   20
> *No Sleep to Toil so easing,*
> > *As these dear Smiles to me.*   [Exit.
Polyph.   *Fly swift, thou massy Ruin, fly,*
> *Presumptuous Acis, die.*
> [*Polyphemus* kills *Acis* with a great Stone, which he gathers
> from a Rock.

ACT III.] *In Bell Part II continues without a break.*
13 *Flocks*] *flock 1764,* Bell.
14 *Woods*] *1764,* Bell   *Floods 1732,* evidently a misprint.
18 *I cannot, cannot, cannot bear. 1764,* Bell.
24 *Die, presumptuous Acis ! die. 1764,* Bell.

Enter A C I S, *supported by* S H E P H E R D S.

R E C I T A T I V O.

Acis. Help, *Galatea*, help ye Parent Gods,
And take me dying to your deep Abodes.

C H O R U S *of Shepherds and Shepherdesses.*

Mourn all the Muses, weep all the Swains,
  Tune your Reeds to doleful Strains ;
Groans, Cries, and Howlings, fill the neighb'ring Shore ;   30
Ah! the gentle Acis *is no more.*

G A L A T E A.

Gal. Must I my *Acis* still bemoan,
Inglorious, crush'd beneath that Stone ?

C H O R U S.

Cease, Galatea, *cease to grieve,*
Bewail not whom you can't relieve.

G A L A T E A.

Gal. Must the lovely charming Youth,
Die for his Constancy and Truth ?

C H O R U S.

Cease, Galatea, *cease to grieve,*
Bewail not whom you can't relieve.
Call forth thy Pow'r, employ thy Art,   40
The Goddess soon can heal the Smart,

G A L A T E A.

Gal. Say, what Comfort can I find,
For dark Despair o'er-clouds my Mind ?   [*Exit.*

C H O R U S.

To kindred Gods the Youth return,
Through verdant Plains to roll his Urn.

Enter G A L A T E A.

R E C I T A T I V O.

Gal. 'Tis done, thus I exert my Pow'r Divine,
Be thou immortal, tho' thou art not mine.

25 ye Parent Gods] *1764, Bell*   the Parent Gods *1732.*
28-9 *Mourn, all ye Muses ! weep, ye Swains !*
    Tune, tune etc. 1764, Bell.
34-5 *Chorus omitted in 1764 and Bell.*
38-41 *Chorus omitted in 1764 and Bell.*   42 can I] can you *1764, Bell.*
44-5 *The Choruses omitted above are introduced here in 1764 and Bell.*
44 *return*] 1764, Bell *returns* 1732.

A I R.

Heart, the Seat of soft Delight,
Be thou now a Fountain bright;
Purple be no more thy Blood,
Glide thou like a Crystal Flood;
Through the Plains he joys to rove,
Murm'ring still his gentle Love.

50

C H O R U S.

Galatea, *dry thy Tears,*
Acis *now a God appears;*
See how he rears him from his Bed!
See the Wreath that binds his Head!
Hail, thou gentle murm'ring Stream,
Shepherds Pleasure, Muses Theme,
Through the Plain still joy to rove,
Murm'ring still thy gentle Love.

60

48 *the Seat*] *thou seat* 1764, Bell.
51 Here follow in 1764 two new lines:
         Rock, thy hollow Womb disclose
     The bubbling Fountain, lo! it flows.
         Thro' the Plains etc.
So too Bell, with a semi-colon after *disclose*

THE

CAPTIVES.

A

TRAGEDY.

Splendidè mendax, & in omne Virgo
Nobilis ævum.   HOR.

[*Editions :*
1. THE | CAPTIVES. | A | TRAGEDY.   As it is Acted at the | THEATRE-ROYAL
in *Drury-lane,* | BY | His MAJESTY'S SERVANTS. | *Splendidè mendax, & in omne Virgo* |
Nobilis ævum. Hor. | *LONDON* : | Printed for J. TONSON at *Shakespear's-Head* | in
the *Strand.* MDCCXXIV.
2. *The Plays,* 1760.]

P R O L O G U E.

Spoken by Mr. *WILKS*.

I Wish some author, careless of renown,
Would without formal prologue risque the town.
For what is told you by this useless ditty ?
Only that tragedy should move your pity :
That when you see theatric heroes shown,
Their virtues you should strive to make your own.
What gain we by this solemn way of teaching ?
Our precepts mend your lives no more than preaching.
  Since then our Bard declines this beaten path ;
What if we lash'd the criticks into wrath ?
Poets should ne'er be drones ; mean, harmless things ;
But guard, like bees, their labours by their stings.
That mortal sure must all ambition smother,
Who dares not hurt one man to please another.
What, sink a joke ! That's but a meer pretence :
He shows most wit who gives the most offence.
But still our squeamish author satyr loaths,
As children, physick ; or as women, oaths.
He knows he's at the bar, and must submit ;
For ev'ry man is born a judge of wit.
How can you err ? Plays are like paintings try'd,
You first enquire the hand, and then decide :
Yet judge him not before the curtain draws,
Lest a fair hearing should reverse the cause.

Dramatis Personæ.

MEN.

Phraortes,	Mr. *Wilks.*
Sophernes,	Mr. *Booth.*
Hydarnes,	Mr. *Mills.*
Araxes,	Mr. *Williams.*
Orbasius,	Mr. *Bridgewater.*
Magi.	
Conspirators.	

WOMEN.

Astarbe,	Mrs. *Porter.*
Captive,	Mrs. *Oldfield.*
Doraspe,	Mrs. *Campbell.*

ACT I. Scene I.

The PALACE.

Hydarnes. Conspirators.

1*st Consp.* Is night near spent?
2*d Consp.* 'Tis yet the dead of night;
And not a glimm'ring ray behind yon hills
Fore-runs the morning's dawn.
1*st Consp.* Thus far w'are safe.
2*d Consp.* Silence and Sleep throughout the Palace reign.
1*st Consp.* Success is now secure.
2*d Consp.* Are all assembled?
1*st Consp.* Our number's not compleat.
2*d Consp.* What, not yet come!   10
Those two were over-zealous. It looks ill.
1*st Consp.* Why fear ye? I'm their pledge. I know them brave.
They'll soon be with us and partake our glory.
Hyd. What mean these murmurs?
1*st Consp.* If mistrust divide us,
Our enterprize is foil'd, and we are lost.
Hyd. My vengeful heart pants for the glorious deed,
And my thirst quickens for *Phraortes'* blood.

Why stops the lazy night ?—O morning, rise ;
Call up the drowsy Priests to the day's task ;
The King to day the holy hill ascends,
And prostrate falls before the rising sun.

   1st Consp. The sun shall rise, but rise to him no more.
For as he passes from the royal chamber
This strikes him home.

   2d Consp. Let each man give him death.
We cannot be too sure.

   Hyd. Revenge is mine.
By him my father fell, by him my brothers ;
They fail'd, they perish'd in the great design :
Success and vengeance are reserv'd for me.
My father led the *Median* hosts to battle,
And all the hosts of *Media* sung his triumphs.

   1st Consp. The people's hearts were his.

   Hyd. The people saw
His royal virtues. He, to please his country,
Grasp'd at the sceptre which *Phraortes* holds.
For this he suffer'd ignominious death :
His house was raz'd ; my brave, unhappy brothers
Fell in his ruin ; I alone escap'd ;
In banishment I've sigh'd whole years away,
Unknown, forgot.—But now, even in his glory,
Now, while he leads the *Persian* Princes captive,
And overflows whole nations with his armies,
I'll stab him to the heart.

   2d Consp. What sound was that ?

   1st Consp. Lights pass a-cross the rooms, and hasty steps
Move to the King's apartment. Sleep is fled,
And all the palace lives ; *Phraortes* wakes.

   2d Consp. Hush ! hark again !

   1st Consp. The ecchoes of the night
Catch ev'ry whisper.

   2d Consp. Some have overheard us.

   1st Consp. It must be so. The guards have took th' alarm.
Our Lives, (what's worse) our enterprize is lost !

   2d Consp. Retreat, my friends ; let us reserve ourselves
For some more prosp'ious hour.

   Hyd. You raise up phantoms,
Then start at them your selves. Some sickly qualm
Has wak'd the King too soon. Hence spring your fears,
Hence grows this mean surprize. Are these your boasts ?
Danger but whets the edge of resolution,
And at each noise I grasp my dagger faster.
Is every thing dispos'd to give th' alarm
Among the *Persian* captives ? Hope of freedom
Will arm them on our side.

   1st Consp. Were the blow struck,
The rest would follow.

Hyd. See a gleam of light
Darts from the King's apartment. Man your hearts,   70
Be firm, be ready. Let not trembling fear
Misguide your aim ; let ev'ry wound be mortal.
   1st Consp. This way and that way danger presses near us.
Where shall we fly ? The tread of nimble feet
Hurries from room to room, and all the palace
Swarms as at noon.
   2d Consp. Let us consult our safety.
   1st Consp. To stay and to be taken is despair ;
And what 's despair ? but poor, mean cowardice.
By timely caution heroes are preserv'd   80
For glorious enterprize, and mighty kingdoms
Are levell'd with the dust.
   Hyd. Withdraw yourselves.
Be still, and listen. These will best inform us
If still it may be done ; or if the blow
Must be deferr'd. But hush, they come upon us.

SCENE II.

*Orbasius, Araxes at one door, two Magi at the other, servants with lights.
Hydarnes and Conspirators listning.*

   Ara. Whence come ye, rev'rend Fathers ; why these looks
Of terror and amaze ? why gaze ye back
As if the strides of Death stalk'd close behind you ?
   1st Mag. The King ev'n at this solemn hour of Night
Sent privately to call us to his presence.
Ye Gods preserve him !
   Ara. Why this wild confusion ?
In ev'ry passing face I read suspicion,   *[People crossing the Stage.*
And haggard fear. Has sickness seiz'd the King,
And groans he with the latest pang of death ?   10
Speak forth your terrors.
   2d Mag. May *Phraortes* live !
   Orba. Tell us the cause. If violence or treachery,
Our duty bids us interpose our lives
Between the King and death. O Heaven, defend him !
   1st Mag. The King, disturb'd by visionary dreams,
Bad the most learn'd Magicians stand before him.
We stood before the King ; and the King trembled
While he declar'd his dream ; and thus I spoke
' O may the great *Phraortes* live for ever !   20
' Avert the dire presages of the dream !
' This night the Gods have warn'd thee to beware
' Of deep-laid treasons, ripe for execution ;
' Assassination lurks within the palace,

' And murder grasps the dagger for the blow.
' If the King trusts his steps beyond his chamber,
' I see him bleed ! I hear his dying groan !
' Obey the voice of Heav'n.
   2d Mag. The King is wise ;
And therefore to the will of Heav'n assented ;   30
Nor will he trust his life, a nation's safety,
From out the royal chamber. See the dawn
Breaks in the East, and calls us to devotion.
It is not Man ; but 'tis the Gods he fears.   [*Exeunt* Magi.

SCENE III.

Orbasius. Araxes. [Conspirators *apart.*]

   Hyd. Let 's quit the palace while retreat is safe.
The deed must be deferr'd. Revenge, be calm.
This day is his, to-morrow shall be ours.
      [*Ex. Conspirators on one side. Enter guards on the other.*
   Orba. See that each centinel is on strict watch.
Let all the Guards be doubled ; bar the gates,
That not a man pass forth without observance.   [*Exit a party of Soldiers.*
Go you ; and with the utmost vigilance
Search ev'ry room ; for treason lyes in wait.   [*Exit a party of Soldiers.*
   Ara. Divide yourselves this instant o'er the palace.
Think *Media* is in danger ; and remember   10
That he who takes a traytor, saves the King.   [*Exeunt Soldiers.*
   Orba. Whence can these dangers threaten ?
   Ara. From the *Persians.*
Captivity 's a yoke that galls the shoulders
Of new-made slaves, and makes them bold and resty.
He that is born in chains may tamely bear them ;
But he that once has breath'd the air of freedom,
Knows life is nothing when depriv'd of that.
Our lord the King has made a people slaves,
And ev'ry slave is virtuously rebellious.   20
I fear the *Persian* Prince.
   Orba. You injure him.
I know him, have convers'd with him whole days,
And ev'ry day I stronger grew in virtue.
Load not th' unhappy with unjust suspicion ;
Adversity ne'er shakes the heart of honour :
He who is found a villain, in distress,
Was never virtuous.
   Ara. Who suspects his virtue ?
'Tis not dishonest to demand our right ;   30
And freedom is the property of man.

   18 Stage-direction in Plays 1760 reads *Exit* Araxes.   27 villain], villian *1724*
and *1760.*

Orba. That glorious day when *Persia* was subdu'd,
Sophernes fought amidst a host of foes,
Disdaining to survive his country's fate.
When the whole torrent of the war rush'd on,
Phraortes interpos'd his shield, and sav'd him.
And canst thou think this brave, this gen'rous Prince
Would stab the man to whom he owes his life ?
    Ara. Whoever is, must feel himself, a slave.
And 'tis worth struggling to shake off his chains.   40
    Orba. But gratitude has cool'd his soul to patience.
Ingratitude 's a crime the *Persians* hate ;
Their laws are wise, and punish it with death.

SCENE IV.

Guards with Sophernes. Orbasius. Araxes.

    Ara. Behold, *Orbasius* ; have I wrong'd your friend ?
Behold a slave oblig'd by gratitude
To wear his chains with patience ! This is he
Phraortes honours with his royal favours !
This is the man that I accus'd unjustly !
Soldiers, advance, and bring the prisoner near us.
    Soph. Why am I thus insulted ? why this force ?
If 'tis a crime to be unfortunate,
I well deserve this usage.
    Ara. 'Tis our duty.   10
If you are innocent, let justice clear you.
Orbasius, to your charge I leave the Prince ;
Mean while I'll search the palace. On this instant
Perhaps the safety of the King depends.
Come, soldiers, there are others to be taken,
Mine be that care. I'll bring them face to face,
When each man conscious of the other's crime
Shall in his guilty look confess his own.
Guard him with strictness, as you prize your life.

                    [*Exeunt* Araxes *and some Guards.*

SCENE V.

Orbasius. Sophernes.

    Orba. Keep off a while, and leave us to ourselves.
                    [*Guards retire to the back part of the stage.*
I own, I think this rash suspicion wrongs you ;
For murder is the mean revenge of cowards,
And you are brave.
    Soph. By whom am I accus'd ?
Let him stand forth. Of murder, murder say you ?

Bear I the marks of an abandon'd wretch ?
How little man can search the heart of man !
   Orba.   Our Priests are train'd up spies by education ;
They pry into the secrets of the state,   10
And then by way of prophecy reveal them ;
'Tis by such artifice they govern Kings.
The last night's rumour of conspiracy
Form'd the King's dream, and from that very rumour
They venture to speak out, what we but whisper'd.
'Twas they that call'd us to this early watch.
'Twas they inform'd us that assassination
Lies hid, ev'n now, within the palace walls.
And we but execute the King's command
In seizing all we find.   20
   Soph.   It is your duty,
And I submit. You cannot be too watchful
To guard the life of such a worthy prince.
I saw his prowess in the rage of battel,
I found his mercy in the flush of conquest.
Do not I share his palace, though a captive ?
What can set limits to his gen'rous soul,
Or close his lib'ral hand ? Am I a viper
To sting the man that warms me in his bosom ?
   Orba.   Why is power given into the hands of Kings,   30
But to distinguish virtue and protect it ?
If then *Phraortes* loves and honours you,
Why seek you thus to nourish your misfortunes
With midnight walks and pensive solitude ?
   Soph.   To lose the pomp and glories of a crown,
Is not a circumstance so soon forgot !
But I have humbled me to this affliction.
To lead the flower of *Persia* forth to battel,
And meet with overthrow and foul defeat,
Is no such trifle in a soldier's breast !   40
But I submit ; for 'tis the will of Heaven.
To see a father bleed amidst the carnage,
Must touch the heart of filial piety.
Why was his lot not mine ? His fall was glorious.
To see my brave, but now unhappy people
Bow down their necks in shameful servitude,
Is not a spectacle of slight compassion.
All these calamities I have subdu'd.
But——my dear wife ! *Cylene* !
   Orba.   Still there 's hope.   50
Can you support the load of real ills,
And sink beneath imaginary sorrows ?
Perhaps she still may live,
   Soph.   Had I that hope,
'Twou'd banish from my heart all other cares.
Perhaps she still may live ! no : 'tis impossible.

When storms of arrows clatter'd on our shields,
Love arm'd her breast, and where I led she follow'd ;
Then Victory broke our ranks, and like a torrent
Bore my *Cylene* from my sight for ever.   60
But say, she did survive that fatal day ;
Was she not then the spoil of some rude soldier,
Whose blood was riotous and hot with conquest ?
—Who can gaze on her beauty and resist it !
Methinks I see her now, ev'n now before me,
The hand of Lust is tangled in her hair
And drags her to his arms :——
I see her snatch the dagger from his grasp
And resolutely plunge it in her bosom.
    Orba. Yet think she may have found a milder fate.   70
All soldiers are not of that savage temper ;
May she not chance to be some brave man's captive ?
And Valour ever lov'd to shield Distress.
    Soph. Can I think thus ? I cannot be so happy.
    Orba. Is still the King a stranger to this sorrow
That day and night lies rankling in your breast ?
    Soph. A grateful heart is all I've left to pay him.
Phraortes is as liberal as Heaven,
And daily pours new benefits upon me.
Last night he led me to the royal garden,   80
(His talk all bent to soften my misfortunes)
Like a fond friend he grew inquisitive,
And drew the story from me.
    Orba. All his heart
Is turn'd to your relief. What further happen'd ?
    Soph. The King was mov'd, and strait sent forth commands
That all the female captives of his triumph
Should stand before his presence. Thus (says he)
Unhappy Prince, I may retrieve your peace,
And give *Cylene* to your arms again.   90
O source of light ! O Sun, whose piercing eye
Views all below on earth, in sea or air ;
Who at one glance can comprehend the globe,
Who ev'ry where art present, point me out
Where my *Cylene* mourns her bitter bondage.——
If she yet live !
    Orba. Why will you fear the worst ?
Why seek you to anticipate misfortune ?
The King commands. Obedience on swift wing
Flies through his whole dominions to redress you ;   100
From hence you soon will learn what chance befell her.
'Tis soon enough to feel our adverse fortune
When there 's no room for hope. This last distress
I know must move the King to tend'rest pity.
    Soph. He dwelt on ev'ry little circumstance,
And as I talk'd, he sigh'd.

Orba. It reach'd his heart.
A tale of love is fuel to a lover.
Phraortes dotes with such excess of fondness,
All his pursuits are lost in that of love. 110
Astarbe suffers him to hold the sceptre,
But she directs his hand which way to point.
The King's decrees weie firm and absolute,
Not the whole earth's confederate powers could shake 'em ;
But now a frown, a smile from fair *Astarbe*
Renders them light as air.
Soph. If you have lov'd,
You cannot think this strange.
Orba. Yet this same woman,
To whom the King has given up all himself, 120
Can scarce prevail upon her haughty temper
To show dissembled love. She loves his power,
She loves his treasures ; but she loaths his person :
Thus ev'ry day he buys dissimulation.
Whene'er a woman knows you in her power,
She never fails to use it.
Soph. That 's a sure proof
Of cold indifference and fixt dislike.
In love both parties have the power to govern,
But neither claims it. Love is all compliance. 130
Astarbe seem'd to me of gentlest manners,
A tender softness languish'd in her eyes,
Her voice, her words, bespoke an easy temper.
I thought I scarce had ever seen till then
Such beauty and humility together.
Orba. How beauty can mis-lead and cheat our reason !
The Queen knows all the ways to use her charms
In their full force, and *Media* feels their power.
Whoever dares dispute her hourly will,
Wakens a busy fury in her bosom. 140
Sure, never love exerted greater sway ;
For her he breaks through all the regal customs,
For she is not confin'd like former Queens,
But with controuling power enjoys full freedom.
I am to blame, to talk upon this subject.
Soph. My innocence had made me quite forget
That I'm your prisoner. Load me with distresses,
They better suit my state. I've lost my kingdom,
A palace ill befits me. I'm a captive,
And captives should wear chains. My fellow soldiers 150
Now pine in dungeons, and are gall'd with irons,
And I the cause of all ! Why live I thus
Amidst the pomp and honours of a court ?
Why breathe I morn and ev'n in fragrant bowers ?
Why am I suffer'd to behold the day ?
For I am lost to ev'ry sense of pleasure.

Give me a dungeon, give me chains and darkness ;
Nor courts, nor fragrant bowers, nor air, nor day-light
Give me one glimpse of joy——O lost *Cylene!*
  Orba. Misfortunes are the common lot of man,   160
And each man has his share of diff'rent kinds :
He who has learnt to bear them best is happiest.
But see *Araxes* comes with guards and prisoners.

SCENE VI.

Orbasius. Sophernes. Araxes. Hydarnes. Conspirators, *with guards.*

  Arax. Behold your leader. Where are now your hopes
                                                [To the Conspirators.
Of murd'ring Kings and over-turning nations ?
See with what stedfast eyes they gaze upon him,
As thinking him the man that has betray'd them.
Angry Suspicion frowns on ev'ry brow,
They know their guilt, and each mistrusts the other.
We seiz'd them in th'attempt to make escape,
All arm'd, all desperate, all of them unknown,
And ev'ry one is obstinately dumb.   *[To* Orbasius.
I charge you, speak. Know you that prisoner there ?   10
Ay, view him well. Confess, and merit grace.
What, not a word ! Will you accept of life ?   *[To* Hydarnes.
Speak, and 'tis granted. Tortures shall compel you.
Will you, or you, or you, or any of you ?
What, all resolv'd on death ! Bring forth the chains.   *[Exit Soldier.*
  Orba. Be not too rash, nor treat the Prince too roughly.
He may be innocent.
  Arax. You are too partial.
I know my duty. Justice treats alike
Those who alike offend, without regard   20
To dignity or office. Bring the chains.   *[Enter Soldiers with chains.*
  Orba. This over-zeal perhaps may give offence,
The Prince is treated like no common slave.
Phraortes strives to lessen his affliction,
Nor would he add a sigh to his distresses :
Astarbe too will talk to him whole hours
With all the tender manners of her sex,
To shorten the long tedious days of bondage.
I'll be his guard. My life shall answer for him.
  Ara. My life must answer for him. He's my charge,   30
And this is not a time for courtesy.
Are you still resolute and bent on death ?   *[To the Conspirators.*
Once more I offer mercy. When the torture
Cracks all your sinews and disjoints your bones,
And death grins on you arm'd with all his terrors,
'Twill loose your stubborn tongue. Know ye this man ?

Hyd. We know him not ; nor why we wear these chains.
We ask no mercy, but appeal to justice.
Now you know all we know : lead to our dungeons.
                              [*Exeunt* Hydarnes *and* Conspirators *guarded.*
   Orba. How have you wrong'd the Prince ! these shameful irons 40
Should not disgrace the hands of innocence.
Let 's set him free.
   Ara. This is all artifice,
To let their leader scape. Guards, take him hence,
And let him be confin'd till further orders.
   Soph. Who shall plead for me in a foreign land !
My words will find no faith ; for I'm a stranger :
And who holds friendship with adversity ?
So Fate may do its worst. I'm tir'd of life.   [*Exit guarded.*

SCENE VII.

Araxes. Orbasius.

   Ara. I've done my duty, and I've done no more.
Why wear you that concern upon your brow ?
It misbecomes you in this time of joy.
Strait let us to the King, and learn his pleasure.
Justice is ours, but mercy 's lodg'd in him.
   Orba. I never can believe the Prince so vile
To mix with common murderers and assassins.
I think him virtuous, and I share his suff'rings.
All generous souls must strong reluctance find,
In heaping sorrows on th'afflicted mind.   [*Exeunt.* 10

ACT II. Scene I.

The Queen's Apartment.

Astarbe.

How expectation can prolong an hour,
And make it seem a day ! a tedious day !
What not yet come ! the wonted hour is past.
In vain I turn my eye from walk to walk,
Sophernes is not there.—Here, every morn
I watch his pensive steps along the garden,
And gaze and wish till I am lost in love !
What not yet come ! But hark ! methinks I hear
The sound of feet ! How my heart pants and flutters !
No. 'Twas the wind that shook yon cypress boughs.   10

Where are my views of wealth, of power, of State ?   *[Rises.*
They're blotted from my mind. I've lost ambition.
O love, thou hast me all. My dreams, my thoughts,
My every wish is center'd in *Sophernes.*
Hence, Shame, thou rigid tyrant of our sex,
I throw thee off——and I'll avow my passion.
Doraspe. I can bear to think no longer.   *[Sits again.*

SCENE II.

Doraspe. Astarbe.

Dor. Why sits the queen thus overcast with thought ?
Is Majesty all plac'd in outward pomp ?
Is it a Queen, to have superior cares ?
And to excell in sorrows and distresses ?
'Tis in your power to have superior pleasures,
And feel your self a Queen.
    Ast. This mighty empire
I know I do command, and him that rules it.
That was a pleasure once, but now 'tis past !
To you alone I have disclos'd my heart.   10
I know you faithful.
    Dor. What avails my service ?
Can I redress you ? can I calm your mind ?
    Ast. Thou know'st, *Doraspe,* amidst all this power,
That I'm a slave, the very worst of slaves.
The yoke of bondage, and the dungeon's horrors
Are easy suff'rings, if compar'd with mine.
I am confin'd to dwell with one I hate,
Confin'd for life to suffer nauseous love,
Like a poor mercenary prostitute.   20
His fondness is my torture.
    Dor. Love is a pleasure for inferior minds ;
Your lot is rais'd above that vulgar passion.
Ambition is the pleasure of the great,
That fills the heart, and leaves no room for love.
Think you're a Queen, enjoy your pomp, your power ;
Love is the paradise of simple shepherds.
You hold a sceptre.
    Ast. O insipid greatness !
She who has never lov'd, has never liv'd.   30
All other views are artificial pleasures
For sluggish minds incapable of love.
My soul is form'd for this sublimer passion :
My heart is temper'd for the real joy ;
I sigh, I pant, I burn, I'm sick of love !

26 power ;] *Plays 1760*   power, *1724.*

Yes, *Media,* I renounce thy purple honours.   [*Rises.*
Farewell the pomp, the pageantry of state,
Farewell ambition, and the lust of empire;
I've now no passion, no desire but love.
O may my eyes have power!—I ask no more.   40
Where stays *Sophernes?* Were he now before me,
My tongue should own what oft my eyes have spoke,
For love has humbled pride.—Why this intrusion?
Who call'd you here a witness to my frailties?
Away and leave me.
    Dor. I obey my Queen.
    Ast. Doraspe, stay. Excuse this start of passion;
My mind is torn with wishes, doubts, and fears;
I had forgot myself.—Should fortune frown,
And tear the diadem from off my brow,   50
Couldst thou be follower of my adverse fortune?
I think thou couldst.
    Dor. If I might give that proof,
Without your sufferings, I could wish the tryal;
So firm I know my heart.
    Ast. Life, like the seasons,
Is intermix'd with sun-shine days and tempests.
Prosperity has many thousand friends;
They swarm around us in our summer hours,
But vanish in the storm.   60
    Dor. What means my Queen,
To wound her faithful servant with suspicion?
    Ast. Whene'er my mind is vex'd and torn with troubles,
In thee I always find the balm of counsell:
And can I then mistrust thee? No, *Doraspe,*
Suspicion ne'er with-held a thought from thee,
Thou know'st the close recesses of my heart:
And now, ev'n now I fly to thee for comfort.
    Dor. How my soul longs to learn the Queen's commands!
    Ast. When conquest over-power'd my father's legions,   70
We were made captives of the war together;
Phraortes saw me, rais'd me to his throne,
Heav'n knows with what reluctance I consented!
For my heart loath'd him. But O curs'd ambition!
I gave my self a victim to his love,
To be a Queen, the outside of a Queen.
I then was, what I'm now, a wretch at heart!
Whene'er I was condemn'd to hours of dalliance,
All *Media's* gems lay glitt'ring at my feet,
To buy a smile, and bribe me to compliance.   80
But what's ambition, glory, riches, empire?
The wish of misers, and old doating courtiers;
My heart is fill'd with love——Go, my *Doraspe,*
Enquire the cause that has detain'd *Sophernes*

74 But] 1724 But, Plays 1760.

From his accustom'd walk.——I'm fix'd, determin'd,
To give up all for love.——A life of love.
With what impatience shall I wait thy coming!
    Dor.   Happy *Sophernes!*
    Ast.   If you chance to meet him,
Talk of me to him, watch his words, his eyes;   90
Let all you say be turn'd to wake desire;
Prepare him for the happy interview,
For my heart bursts, and I must tell it all.
To what an abject state am I reduc'd?
To proffer love! Was beauty given for this?
Yes. 'Tis more gen'rous; and I'll freely give
What kneeling monarchs had implor'd in vain.
    Dor.   This well rewards him for an empire lost.   [*Exit.*

SCENE III.

Astarbe.

    Ast.   Have I not caught the eyes of wondring nations,
While warm desire has glow'd on ev'ry cheek,
Ev'n when I wore the pride of majesty?
When opportunity awakes desire,
Can he then gaze, insensible of beauty?
When ardent wishes speak in ev'ry glance,
When love and shame by turns in their full force,
Now pale, now red, possess my guilty cheek,
When heaving breasts, and sighs, and kindling blushes
Give the most strong assurance of consent   10
In the convincing eloquence of love;
Will he then want a proof that's less sincere?
And must I speak?—O love, direct my lips,
And give me courage in that hour of shame!

SCENE IV.

Astarbe. Doraspe.

    Dor.   May the Queen never know a moment's sorrow,
Nor let my words offend!—the Prince *Sophernes,*
Leagu'd with a crew of daring desperate men,
Had meditated to destroy *Phraortes,*
And let loose war and rapine o'er the land.
But Heav'n has made their machinations vain;
And they now groan in dungeons.
    Ast.   Then I'm wretched,
And ev'ry pleasing view of life is lost.
Was it confirm'd? or was it only rumour?   10

Dor. *Araxes* said *Sophernes* was his prisoner.
My haste would not allow me further question :
And this is all I learnt.
    Ast. Have I not power ?
I have. Why then, I'll give *Sophernes* freedom,
I'll give him life.—I think you nam'd *Araxes* ;
That man to me owes all his growth of fortune ;
And if I judge him right, he 's very grateful.
Tell him the Queen admits him to her presence.   [*Exit* Doraspe.
O Heaven ! I thank thee for this blest occasion.   20
Did ever proof of fondness equal mine ?
And sure so strong a proof must find return.
With what excess of transport shall I go
To lead him forth from heavy chains and darkness
To liberty and love !—But see, *Araxes.*

SCENE V.

Astarbe. Doraspe. Araxes.

    Ara. All health attend the mighty Queen of *Media.*
    Ast. I'm told, *Araxes*, that the *Persian* Prince
Hath join'd in horrid league, and hath conspir'd
The murther of my lord and king *Phraortes.*
Speak forth ; say what thou know'st.
    Ara. The hand of heaven
Protects the King ; and all the black design
Is shown in open daylight. The foul traitor
Is taken in the snares of death he laid.
Sophernes is my charge. O base ingratitude,   10
That he, whom the King honour'd next himself,
That he, whom the King's mercy spar'd in battle,
Should mix with vile assassins ! Justice longs
To punish the vast crime.
    Ast. Owns he the guilt ?
    Ara. No. With the calmest face of innocence,
With looks known only to hypocrisy,
He solemnly deny'd it.
    Ast. Is he confin'd ?
    Ara. Yes, with the strictest guard and heaviest irons.   20
The prison joining to the Queen's apartment
Lodges the horrid crew in sep'rate dungeons.
To-day the King will mount the judgment-seat,
And death shall be their portion.
    Ast. Is *Sophernes*
Stubborn and sullen ? made he no confession ?
I often have convers'd with that vile man,
That hypocrite, whose talk was always honest.
How have I been deceiv'd !—Yet, ere his sentence,
With secresy I fain once more would see him.   30

* Q

Ara. I'm happy to obey my Queen's commands.
His prison lies so close to these apartments,
That unobserv'd I can conduct him hither.
    Ast. I know thee faithfull, and such ready zeal
Shall always find reward.
    Ara. The Queen is gracious.   [*Exit.*

36 Exit.] 1760 only.

S C E N E   V I.

Astarbe. Doraspe.

    Ast. Now my design is ripe for execution.
Then let *Doraspe* well consult her heart,
If she will share with me all change of fortune.
    Dor. Doubt not your faithfull servant. I'm prepar'd.
I know, however heinous is his crime,
Your intercession always must prevail.
His gratitude will kindle into love,
And in possession every wish be lost.
    Ast. How little thou hast div'd into my thoughts !
My purposes are otherways determin'd.   10
I'll shake off bondage, and abandon empire ;
For him disrobe my self of majesty ;
Then to my native *Parthia* will I fly
With all my soul holds dear—my guide *Sophernes.*
    Dor. Let me not find my gracious Queen's displeasure
If I dissent, and offer other counsel.
Why will you quit your crown ? why fly from *Media?*
Does jealousy restrain your liberty ?
Your love, your empire, both are in your power.
    Ast. Mine 's not the common passion of our sex,   20
Which ev'ry day we. can command at pleasure,
And shift and vary as occasion offers.
My love is real and unchangeable,
Controuls my heart, and governs absolute.
My eyes, words, actions, are no more my own :
My ev'ry thought 's *Sophernes.*—Other women,
Who have the power to practise little arts
To cheat a husband, and delude his fondness,
Ne'er knew the burning passion that I feel.
Those are the trifling wanton airs of women,   30
All vanity, and only love in name.
No. She who loves, must give up all her self ;
She ne'er can be content with a stol'n minute,
Then pass whole days and nights with him she hates.
Advise no further—for I am determin'd.
    Dor. *Araxes*, with the *Persian* prince !
    Ast. Retire.   [*Exit* Doraspe.

37 Exit Doraspe.] 1760 only.

SCENE VII.

Astarbe. Araxes. Sophernes.

It is not meet, while in the royal presence,
That he should wear these irons. Take them off.   [Ara. *takes off the chains.*
Now leave me ; and without attend my pleasure.   [*Exit* Araxes.

3 *Exit* Araxes.] *1760 only.*

SCENE VIII.

Astarbe. Sophernes.

Be not surpriz'd that I have call'd you hither,
Most noble Prince, in this your hour of trouble ;
For I ev'n bear a part in your misfortunes.
Who 's your accuser ?—whence those shameful chains ?
    Soph. I'm charg'd with crimes of the most heinous nature.
If 'tis Heav'n's will to try me with afflictions,
I will not, like a dastard, sink beneath them,
But resolutely strive to stem the torrent.
Not the dark dungeon, nor the sharpest torture
Can ruffle the sweet calm of innocence.   10
My chains are grievous, but my conscience free.
    Ast. I long have mark'd your virtues, and admir'd them.
Against a resolute and steady mind
The tempest of affliction beats in vain.
When we behold the hero's manly patience,
We feel his suff'rings, and my tears have own'd
That what you bore with courage touch'd my heart.
And when compassion once has reach'd the mind,
It spurs us on to charity and kindness.
Instruct me then which way to cure your sorrows.   20
    Soph. The Queen is gracious and delights in mercy.
    Ast. I speak with the sincerity of friendship.
Friendship is free and open, and requires not
Such distant homage and respectful duty.
Forget that I'm a Queen : I have forgot it ;
And all my thoughts are fixt on thy relief.
Draw near me then, and as from friend to friend,
Let us discharge our hearts of all their cares.
    Soph. How beautiful a virtue is compassion !
It gives new grace to every charm of woman !   30
When lovely features hide a tender soul,
She looks, she speaks, all harmony divine.
    Ast. Tell me, *Sophernes*, does not slav'ry's yoke
Gall more and more through ev'ry pace of life ?
I am a slave, like you. And though a Queen

Possest of all the richest gems of *Media*,
I know no pleasure ; this distasteful thought
Imbitters all my hours ; the royal bed
Is loathsome, and a stranger to delight.
I'm made the drudge to serve another's pleasure.   40
O when shall I be free ! take, take your empire,
And give me peace and liberty again.
    Soph.   The strokes of fortune must be born with patience.
    Ast.   But I have lost all patience.—Give me counsel,
Give me thy friendship, and assist a wretch
Who thirsts and pants for freedom.
    Soph.   Who seeks succour
From one whose hands are bound in double irons ?
I am a slave, and captive of the war,
Accus'd of treason and ingratitude,   50
And must from hence go back to chains and darkness.
But had I power, such beauty might command it.
    Ast.   But I have power, and all my power is thine.
If I had arm'd my self with resolution
To quit the pompous load of majesty,
To fly far off from this detested empire,
To seek repose within my native land,
Wouldst thou then be companion of my flight,
And share in my distresses and my fortune ?
    Soph.   The Queen intends to try a wretched man,   60
Whether he'd break all hospitable laws,
The strictest oaths and tyes of gratitude,
To sacrifice his honour to such beauty
That can command all hearts.
    Ast.   Tell me directly,
Wouldst thou accept of freedom on these terms ?
    Soph.   How shall I answer ?
    Ast.   Is thy heart of ice ?
Or are my features so contemptible
That thou disdain'st to fix thy eyes upon me ?   70
Can you receive this offer with such coldness ?
I make it from my heart ; my warm heart speaks :
Distrust me not. What, not a word ! no answer !
    Soph.   O may the Queen excuse her prostrate servant,
And urge no more a tryal too severe.
    Ast.   What means *Sophernes?* Why this abject posture ?
'Tis I should kneel ; 'tis I that want compassion.   [*Gives him her hand.*
Thou art unpractis'd in the ways of women,
To judge that I could trifle on this subject.
Think how severe a conflict I have conquer'd,   80
To over-rule ev'n nature and my sex,
Think what confusion rises in my face
To ask what (to be ask'd) would kindle blushes
In ev'ry modest cheek !—where 's shame ? where 's pride ?
Sophernes has subdu'd them. Women, I own,

Are vers'd in little frauds, and sly dissemblings :
But can we rule the motions of the blood ?
These eyes,—this pulse—these tremblings—this confusion
Make truth conspicuous, and disclose the soul.
Think not I fly with man for his protection ;   90
For only you I could renounce a kingdom,
For you, ev'n in the wild and barren desart
Forget I was a Queen ; ev'n then more happy
Than seated on a throne. Say, wilt thou chuse
Or liberty, and life, and poor *Astarbe*,
Or dungeons, chains, and ignominious death !
   Soph. O how I struggle in the snares of beauty !
Those eyes could warm pale elders to desire,
I feel them at my heart ; the feaver rages,
And if I gaze again——how shall I answer !   100
   Ast. How is my pride brought low ! how vilely treated!
The worst of scorn is cold deliberation.
   Soph. *Cylene* may be found. What, take me from her !
How can I go and leave my hopes for ever ?
Can I renounce my love, my faith, my all ?
Who can resist those eyes ?—I go—I'm lost !
Cylene holds me back, and curbs desire.   [*Aside.*
   Ast. Resolve and answer me. For soon as night
Favours our flight I'll gather up my treasures.
Prepare thee then, lest death should intercept thee,   110
And murder all my quiet.
   Soph. If in her sight
I've favour found, the Queen will hear me speak.
How can my heart refuse her ? how obey her ?
Can I deny such generous clemency ?
Join'd with all beauties ever found in woman ?
Yet think on my unhappy circumstance.
I've giv'n my word, the strictest tye of honour,
Never to pass beyond my bounds prescrib'd ;
And shall I break my faith ? Who holds society   120
With one who 's branded with that infamy ?
Did not *Phraortes* in the heat of battle
Stay the keen sword that o'er me menac'd death ?
Do not I share his palace, and his friendship ?
Does he not strive by daily curtesies
To banish all the bitter cares of bondage ?
And shall I seise and tear his tend'rest heart-string ?
Shall I conspire to rob him of all peace ?
For on the Queen hangs ev'ry earthly joy,
His ev'ry pleasure is compriz'd in you !   130
What virtue can resist such strong temptation ?
O raise not thus a tempest in my bosom !
What shall I do ?—my soul abhors ingratitude.
Should I consent, you must detest and loath me,
And I should well deserve those chains and death.

Ast. Is this thy best return for proffer'd love ?
Such coldness, such indifference, such contempt !
Rise, all ye Furies, from th' infernal regions,
And prompt me to some great, some glorious vengeance
Vengeance is in my power, and I'll enjoy it.   140
But majesty perhaps might awe his passion,
And fear forbid him to reveal his wishes.
That could not be. I heard, I saw him scorn me ;
All his disdainful words his eyes confirm'd.
Ungrateful man ! Hence, traytor, from my sight.
Revenge be ready. Slighted love invokes thee.
Of all the injuries that rack the soul,
Mine is most exquisite ! Hence, to thy dungeon.
Araxes !

S C E N E   I X.

Astarbe. Sophernes. Araxes.

Take the villain from my presence,
His crimes are black as hell. I'll turn away,
Lest my heart melt and cool into compassion.
His sight offends me. Bind his irons fast.   [*Ara. puts on his Irons.*
So : lead him hence ; and let *Doraspe* know
The Queen permits her entrance.   [*Exeunt* Araxes *and* Sophernes.

SCENE IX.] *Wrongly numbered* VIII *in 1724 ; and so to end of Act.*
6 *Exeunt* etc.] *1760 only.*

S C E N E   X.

Astarbe. Doraspe.

Dor. What 's the Queen's pleasure ? See your servant ready.
Why are your eyes thus fixt upon the ground ?
Why that deep sigh ? and why these trembling lips ?
This sudden paleness, and these starts of frenzy ?
You're sick at heart.
    Ast. Yes ; I will be reveng'd.
    Dor. Lift up your eyes, and know me. 'Tis *Doraspe.*
    Ast. Look on me, tell me, is my beauty blighted ?
And shrunk at once into deformity ?
Slighted ! despis'd ! my charms all set at nought !   10
Yes. I will be reveng'd.——O my *Doraspe,*
I've met with foul contempt, and cold disdain :
And shall the wretch who gave me guilt and shame,
The wretch who 's conscious of my infamy
Out-live that crime ? he must not, nay, he shall not.

Dor. Let reason mitigate and quell this feaver ;
The safest, surest, is the cool revenge.
Rash anger, like the hasty scorpion's fury,
Torments and wounds it self.
    Ast. It is in vain   20
The torrent rushes on ; it swells, ferments,
And strongly bears away all opposition.
What means that hurry in the antichamber ?
What are those crowds ?
    Dor. The King intends to mount the judgment-seat,
And the conspirators now wait their sentence.
    Ast. Go, tell *Araxes* (if with privacy
He could conduct him) I would see their chief ;
The desp'rate instrument of this bold scheme ;
This instant ; ere he stands before the Presence.   [*Exit* Doraspe. 30

30 *Exit* Doraspe.] *1760 only.*

SCENE XI.

Astarbe.

Revenge, I thank thee for this ready thought.
Death now shall reach *Sophernes*, shamefull death
Thus will I satiate love. His death alone
Can raze him from my heart, and give me peace.

SCENE XII.

Araxes *conducts in* Hydarnes, *and retires.*

Astarbe. Hydarnes.

The King is gracious, and delights in mercy ;
And know that free confession merits life :
I'll intercede. Know you the Prince *Sophernes?*
You are unhappy men betray'd to ruin :
And will ye suffer for another's crime ?
Speak of him, as ye ought ; 'twas he betray'd you.
    Hyd. If racks and tortures cannot tear confession
From innocence, shall woman's flattery do it ?
No ; my heart's firm, and I can smile on death.
    Ast. Think not to hide what is already known.   10
'Tis to *Sophernes* that you owe those chains,
We've fathom'd his designs, they're all laid open ;
We know him turbulent and enterprizing.
By the foul murder of my lord the King,
He meant to set his captive nation free.
Unfold this truth, and I'll insure thy pardon.

Hyd. What ! lead a hateful life of ignominy !
And live the bane of all society !
Shun'd like a pestilence, a curst informer !
Yet since the fate of kingdoms may depend   20
On what I speak ; truth shall direct my lips.
The Queen has offer'd grace. I know the terms.
    Ast. By the King's life, I swear.

S C E N E X I I I.

Astarbe. Hydarnes. Araxes.

Ara. Excuse this entrance,
The pris'ner must attend.   ′
    Ast. I'm satisfy'd.
This man seems open, and may be of service.

> [*Exeunt* Araxes *and* Hydarnes.

4 *Exeunt* etc.] *1760 only.*

S C E N E X I V.

Astarbe.

How my heart bleeds, thus to pursue revenge
Against the man I love ! But me he scorns ;
And from my beauty turns his head away
With saucy arrogance and proud contempt.
I could forgive him ev'ry other crime,
Ev'n the base murder of my dearest friend ;
But slighted love no woman can forgive.
For thro' our life we feel the bitter smart,
And guilt and shame lye festring at the heart.

A C T I I I. Scene I.

A Room of State with a Throne.

Hydarnes. Conspirators. Orbasius. Guards.

1st Conspirator. THE information of those two vile cowards,
Who mingled with us brave and active spirits,
Hath giv'n us death. Let those mean creatures live,
They're fitter for the world.
    2d Consp. Lead us to death.

Hyd. Death is pronounc'd on you, on me, on all.
Would I could take your guilt upon my self,
So to preserve some virtue in the world.
But those informers have deny'd me that ;
We all must perish, and fall unreveng'd.   10
But since I cannot take your crimes upon me ;
I'll live, and execute our great design,
And thus revenge your deaths.
   1st Consp. Could this be done !
   Hyd. It can.
   1st Consp. You flatter us.
   Hyd. I say, I'll do it.
Soon as the King returns to sign our sentence,
Only confirm the words which I shall speak,
And I'll revenge you soon, and soon be with you.   [*Talks to them apart* 20
   Orba. The guilty perish ; innocence is freed.
Suspicion has not cast the smallest stain
Upon the virtuous *Persian.* Those accusers,
Who have condemn'd their fellows, know him not.
Of all the pleasures that a monarch tastes,
Sure mercy is most sweet ! 'Tis heavenly pleasure,
To take the galling chains from off the hands
Of injur'd innocence ! That privilege
O'er-ballances the cares that load a crown.

SCENE II.

Phraortes *seats himself on the Throne.* Magi. Orbasius.   Araxes.
Sophernes. Hydarnes. *Guards and Attendants.*

   Ara. Make room ; The *Persian* Prince attends his sentence.
   Phra. Most noble Prince, I grieve that you were injur'd.
When foul conspiracy molests a state
The ear of Kings is open to suspicion,
And we grow jealous of our bosom friends.
When calumny would blast a virtuous man,
And justice has made clear his innocence ;
It only throws a brighter lustre on him,
And serves to make his virtues more conspicuous.
Approach the throne ; and let the King's embrace   10
Make some attonement for your shameful bonds.
I feel your suff'rings, and my heart grows fonder.
Now bring the pris'ners to receive their sentence.
Justice cries loud for vengeance on your crimes.
Say, have ye ought to plead to ward the blow,
Ere I enroll your names among the dead ?
   Hyd. That I design'd to bath these hands in blood,
Even in thy blood, O King, I dare confess,
And glory in th' attempt. I know thy power ;
I know that death with all his dreadful tortures   20

* Q 3

Stands ready at thy nod. Give then the signal,
For I unmov'd can face the ghastly terror.
How is thy wisdom foil'd ! Prepare to follow.
Think not with us our enterprize is lost.
A King shall bleed to pacifie our ghosts.
Come, lead to death. Spend all thy wrath on us.
The raging tyger bites the shaft that wounds him,
And spares the man who threw it. I have done.
 Phra. These are the starts and ravings of despair.
Think'st thou by threats to force me into mercy ?   30
 Hyd. I grow impatient ; lead me to my fate.
 Phra. Know you that I have life within my power ?
 Hyd. I know the utmost of thy power is death.
 Mag. Ye Gods avert his words, and save the King !
 Phra. What said he ? Speak again.
 Hyd. Death is my choice.
 Phra. I will be satisfy'd.
 Hyd. I've said too much.
 Phra. Say more, or torture shall extort it from you.
 Hyd. Let torture do its worst. You dare not try it.   40
 Mag. If memory can recal the solemn speech.
These were his very words,
A King shall bleed to pacifie our ghosts.
The raging tyger bites the shaft that wounds him,
But spares the man who threw it. Was it thus ?
 Hyd. Now let your wisdom fathom this deep secret.
I answer no more questions.
 Phra. Reverend fathers,
What may these words portend ? Expound the mystery.
 Mag. Thy sacred life, O King, is still in danger.   50
While justice pours down vengeance on these wretches,
These mean subservient instruments of mischief,
Their leader scapes, and lives for future crimes.
 Hyd. Go on.
 Mag. The words imply no more.
 Hyd. 'Tis well.
All 's safe.—I'm ready.—Why is death delay'd ?
 Phra. Thus speaks the voice of Mercy from my lips.
Th' irrevocable sentence is not sign'd,
And still there 's room for hope. Attend, and live :   60
By this bright sceptre, by the throne of *Media*,
By yon great light that rules the rolling year,
If you lay ope the depth of this foul treason,
And point me out that undetected villain,
I swear, to grant you life and liberty.
Speak now, or death shall seal your lips for ever.
 Hyd. The royal word is giv'n, and I accept it.
The King shall live, and all his foes shall perish.
Danger stands near the throne. How blind is Justice !
The *Persian* Prince !   70

Phra.   Sophernes!
Hyd. He 's a traytor.
'Twas he that put the dagger in my hand.
So. Now I have betray'd. O love of life!
Where was my resolution ? I'm a coward ;
And cowards can endure a life of shame.
    Phra. Sophernes!—Let strong proof confirm your charge,
I must have proof.
    Hyd. Call in my fellow-prisoners.
    Soph. What can set bounds to man's impiety,   80
And where is virtue safe ? Accus'd thus falsely,
With all the strongest circumstance of guilt,
By one I know not ! Heav'n has then determin'd
That I must fall. Shall man contest with *Jove?*
'Tis all in vain. The will of Fate be done.
    Hyd. Those who accus'd us, brib'd with *Persian* gold,
Conceal'd the author of our enterprize.

SCENE III.

The Aforesaid and Conspirators.

Know ye that man ?
    1*st Consp.* Would he had been unknown.
    Hyd. The King has trac'd our mischief to the source.
Who was it prompted you to this attempt ?
Had ye not views to set a nation free ?
And to restore him to his crown and kingdom ?
    1*st Consp.* By him we fell, 'tis just that he fall with us.
    2*d Consp.* So, now one ruin has involv'd us all.
    Phra. Death is the lot of those that thirst for blood.
Conduct them hence. This hour prepare to suffer.   10
                                        [*Exeunt* Conspirators.
            10 *Exeunt* Conspirators.] *1760 only.*

SCENE IV.

Phraortes. Magi. Orbasius. Araxes. Sophernes.
Hydarnes. Guards *and* Attendants.

Ungrateful Prince !
    Soph. Since 'tis the will of Heaven
To load me with calamities and shame,
Since the most searching eye cannot discern
The heart of man ; O where shall I find justice !
I am a stranger, in adversity,
Bereft of wealth and power, without a friend.
    Phra. Hence, base dissembler. Take him from my presence
When hypocrites are stript of Virtue's plumes,

Vice then appears most hideous and deform'd.   10
Back to thy dungeon, to remorse and death.
  Soph. Vain are excuse and solemn protestation ;
How shall my words prevail, and truth appear,
When there 's a crowd of witnesses against me !
The Guilty perish with remorse and horror,
But innocence ne'er feels the sting of death.
Death is a blessing to adversity ;
Anxiety, calamity and sorrow,
And all the daily fretting cares of life
Are shook from off our shoulders ; and we rest. [*Exit* Sophernes *guarded.*

20 *Exit* etc.] *1760 only.*

S C E N E V.

Phraortes. Magi. Orbasius. Araxes. Hydarnes.
Guards *and* Attendants.

  Hyd. Safety now guards the throne, and *Media*'s happy.
  Phra. I ratifie my word, and give you life,
I give you liberty ; but on conditions.
Those I shall send you soon, and then you're free.
O Sun, I thank thee ; thy all-seeing eye
Has trac'd the villain through his secret ways,
And now the hand of Justice is upon him.
  Ara. *Media* rejoice.
  All. May the King live for ever !
  Phra. Proclaim a festival for seven days space ;   10
Let the Court shine in all its pomp and lustre :
Let all our streets resound with shouts of joy ;
Let Musick's care-dispelling voice be heard ;
The sumptuous banquet and the flowing goblet
Shall warm the cheek, and fill the heart with gladness.
For *Media*'s foes are put to shame and death.
Astarbe shall sit soveraign of the feast,
That Queen of beauty shall direct our pleasures.
I'll to her bower.—I would have no attendance.   [*Exeunt* Phraortes, *&c.*

19 *Exeunt* etc.] *1760 only.*

S C E N E VI.

Araxes. Doraspe.

  Dor. Inform me, what has past ?
  Ara. The Queen's conjectures
The King has now confirm'd. The *Persian* Prince,
That hypocrite is known, and prov'd a traytor,
And leader of that crew of vile assassins.   5
But see the Queen.—The King is gone to seek her.
Excuse my haste ; for Duty calls me hence.   [*Exit.*

7 *Exit.*] *1760 only.*

S C E N E   V I I.

Doraspe. Astarbe.

Ast. 'Twas downright arrogance. I saw his scorn.
A Lover reads the thought of every look,
And needs no comment or interpreter.
What woman can forgive that worst of insults ?
Not ev'n the most deform'd of all our sex
Can bear contempt. And shall I pardon it ?
To pardon it, is to insult myself,
And own that I deserve it. [*Aside*]. Know you ought
Of what the King in judgment has determin'd ?
   Dor. *Sophernes* was accus'd.   10
   Ast. Was he found guilty ?
   Dor. Yes, prov'd a traytor.
   Ast. Then I'm satisfy'd.
   Dor. How one affliction crouds upon another,
To punish this ungrateful man !
   Ast. What mean y.ou ?
   Dor. It is confirm'd among the captive women
(Who now attend to pass before the presence)
His wife was slain in battle.
   Ast. Would he were dead !   20
Yet were he dead, would he dye in my thoughts ?
Talk to me, speak ; leave me not to reflection.   [*To* Doraspe.
Yet what will talk avail ?—I've lost attention.
Were her words soft and soothing as the lyre,
Or strong and sprightly as th' enlivening trumpet,
I could hear nought but conscience. Would he were dead !
You shall not leave me.
   Dor. See the king returns.   [*Exit.*

28 *Exit.*] *1760 only.*

S C E N E   V I I I.

Phraortes. Astarbe.

Phra. Welcome, my Queen ; how my heart springs to meet thee
Each day, each hour, thy beauty grows upon me,
Ev'n while I gaze some undiscover'd charm
Opens it self, and wounds my heart anew.
Rejoyce, *Astarbe* ; *Media* is deliver'd :
The gathering storm that threaten'd desolation
Is over-blown, and all is now serene.
Then let us give our future days to pleasure ;
My ev'ry pleasure is compris'd in thee.
   Ast. Be firm in justice, nor give way to mercy,   10
'Tis the mind's frailty, and the nurse of crimes.
Punish. And root out treason from the land.

Phra. *Sophernes* was their chief.

Ast. Ungrateful villain !

Phra. How he deceiv'd me !

Ast. Your too easy nature
Must always harbour mischiefs in your empire.
Does he still live ?

Phra. His death is fix'd and sign'd.

Ast. Each hour he lives, your people doubt your justice.   20
Would you deter the populace from crimes,
Let punishment be sudden. That's true mercy.

Phra. He never shall behold another Sun.
But why should cares of state intrude upon us ?

Ast. Why this reproof ?   In what have I deserv'd it ?
All my concern was for the peace of *Media*,
And for your safety.   I have said too much.

Phra. What has *Astarbe* ask'd, that I refus'd ?
Thy beauty has all power.   Who waits without ?
Go ;   let the Captives be dismiss'd the palace,   [*Speaks at the door.*   30
The King resigns his privilege of choice.
Should the selected beauties of the world   [*To* Astarbe.
In full temptation stand before my presence,
Still would my heart and eye be fixt on thee.
Thy charms would (like the Sun's all-powerful rays)
Make all those little stars of beauty fade.
Why that dejected look ?   that thoughtful sigh ?
In what have I offended ?   If to love,
Be to offend ; *Phraortes* is most wretched.

SCENE IX.

Phraortes. Astarbe. Araxes.

Ara. I spoke the King's commands ;   when from the crowd
One of the Captives rose, and humbly pray'd
Admission to the throne.

Phra. I hear no suits.

Ara. She wish'd to speak a matter of importance.

Phra. Dismiss them all.   Let us retire, my Queen.

Ast. *Araxes*, stay.   [Araxes *going out.*

Phra. What is *Astarbe's* pleasure ?

Ast. This matter should be search'd.   The fate of Empires
Turns often on the slightest information ;   10
And were my counsell worthy to be heard,
I would admit her.

Phra. Let her be admitted.   [*Exit* Araxes.

[Phraortes *seats* Astarbe *on the throne, then places himself by her. The
Guards enter, and range themselves on each side.*

SCENE X.

Phraortes. Captive. Doraspe. Araxes. Attendants.

Phra. Arise, fair maid ; and let thy suit be heard.
Cap. The King has done his prostrate servant justice.   [*Kneeling.*
Thus low I pay my thanks to Heaven and you.
Phra. Rise from that humble posture, and speak forth.
Cap. The *Persian* Prince, to whom we owe our bondage,   [*Rises.*
'Tis said, is doom'd to death for horrid treachery.
Phra. He well deserves it. If you fall before me,
To melt me into mercy with your tears,
Woman, your tears are frustrate. Take her hence.
Cap. I speak for mercy ! No. I sue for tortures.   10
With rapture I could gaze upon his sufferings,
Enjoy his agonies and dying groans,
And then this hand could stab him to the heart.
Phra. Whence rose this furious spirit of revenge ?
Cap. By brutal violence he slew my husband.
Excuse my tears. Love calls them from my eyes ;
With him I lost all joy, all peace and comfort.
Phra. What mov'd *Sophernes* to the barbarous deed ?
Cap. My husband was distinguish'd in his armies ;
With him I always shar'd the toils of war,   20
The tedious marches, and the scorching suns,
For Love makes all fatigue seem light and easy.
Sophernes saw me, sigh'd, and spoke his passion.
I spurn'd his offers, and despis'd his suit.
He still persisted, and my virtue strengthen'd :
'Till on a day, inflam'd with loose desire,
He sent my Lord upon some feign'd command ;
I in his tent sate waiting his return,
Then suddenly the ravisher rush'd in.   [*Weeps.*
Phra. Go on.   30
Cap. He seiz'd me, tore me, dragg'd me to his Arms ;
In vain I struggled ; by resistance weaken'd,
I lost all strength, and so—he spoil'd my Honour.
O shame ! O brutal force !   [*Weeps.*
Phra. Unhappy woman !
Proceed.
Cap. Just in the moment of my shame
My husband enter'd. Strait the villain left me,
And, desperate by the stings of guilt and terror,
He stabb'd him to the heart.   [*Weeps.* 40
Phra. Most monstrous villain !
His life 's a series of the blackest crimes.
Cap. I in the hurry of the murder fled,
And 'scap'd the tyrant's power. Alone, disguis'd,
I've past away my restless hours in sorrow.
Revenge was all my wish, and all my comfort,

†   *

For that I watch'd him thro' long weary marches,
And Revenge gave me strength and resolution.
Why fell he not by me ?   His crime requir'd it.
Vengeance o'ertakes him for another guilt,   50
And I have lost revenge.   O may he feel
The pain and horror due to both his crimes.
   Phra.   His death is sign'd.
   Cap.   That is his due for treachery.
   Phra.   What would Revenge have more ?   Th' offender's blood
Allays its strongest thirst.
   Cap.   Most gracious King,   [*Kneels.*
Hear an unhappy woman's just petition,
And may my prayer find favour and acceptance !
Grant me to see him in his latest gasp ;   60
Let my appearance strike him with confusion,
Let me awake fresh terrors in his conscience,
And bring my murther'd husband to his view.
Entrust the sword of justice in my hand ;
The stroke shall then be sure.
   Phra.   What fortitude
Lies hid beneath that face of softest feature !
The death of his confederates is sign'd,
And he with privacy this very evening
Shall be dispatch'd in prison.   Now you're satisfy'd.   70
   Cap.   O, were that office mine !
   Ast.   For such offence
He cannot feel too much ;   her suit is just.
Then let me intercede in her behalf ;
Grant her request.   Give her the fatal signet.
Give her the dagger.—Such revenge is virtue.
   Phra.   Take this ;   your boon is granted.   Soon my orders
                      [*Gives her his dagger.*
Shall send you to revenge a husband's murther.
Let her attend without.   Draw near, *Araxes*.   [*Exit* Captive.

      47 I] *1724* I've Plays *1760*.   79 *Exit* Captive.] *1760 only.*

SCENE XI.

Phraortes.   Astarbe.   Doraspe.   Araxes.   Attendants.

                [Phraortes *talks aside to* Araxes.
   Ast.   What, sue to her !   and when I sued disdain me !
How my disgrace grows on me !   Let him perish,
And perish by that woman.   My resentment
Kindles and burns, to take her charge upon me.
Yet still would he relent, I could forgive him.
   Dor.   His wife is dead, on whom his heart was fix'd :
That obstacle's remov'd
   Ast.   And Death hangs o'er him.
That sight perhaps may shake his resolution.

If I could hope, I would delay his sentence.   10
I dread his death. What is there to be done ?
I'll see him ere he dies. O abject thought !
Yes, I will see him, and renew my offers
In his last moments ; For whene'er he dies
My mind will ne'er know peace. I will defer it.
I'll sooth the king in his soft hours of love,
When all his strongest purposes are nothing.
When 'tis deferr'd—Would I could cease from thought !
    Phra. Tell her as soon as justice is perform'd,
The King requires her thanks—She 's wondrous fair !   20
You know my will ; these are my last commands,
Let punctual care and diligence obey me.   [*Exit* Araxes.

SCENE XII.

Phraortes. Astarbe. Doraspe. Attendants.

Go, bid the priests prepare the sacrifice ;
This ev'ning shall the fragrance of devotion
Smoak in our temples, and perfume the skies.
Phraortes shall attend the solemn rites,
To pay his grateful thanks in songs of joy.
                                    [*Exeunt* Doraspe *and Attendants.*
Astarbe, come.—One glance of those bright eyes
Dispells all care, and empires are forgot.
In what is man superior to the brute ?
Brutes eat, drink, sleep ; like us, have all the senses.
The male and female meet, then coldly part,   10
Part with indifference, and desire is cloy'd,
In love alone we feel th' immortal part,
And that celestial fire refines the heart.

        12 th' immortal] *1724*   the immortal *Plays 1760.*

A C T I V. Scene I.

A Prison.

Hydarnes. Conspirators.

    Hyd. I shall survive but for a little space ;
Doubt not my plighted faith, and dye in peace.
What is an hour of life ! an hour of torment.
Think then what I shall suffer for your sake,
How I shall long and pant to be among you !
To him who fears not death Revenge is sure,
To him who fears not death Revenge is speedy.

Soon as the chains are struck from off these hands,
I'll dye them purple in the royal blood ;
I'll watch all time. The throne shall not secure him,   10
The solemn temple, ev'n that sacred ground
Shall not protect him from my resolution.
Would it were done ; that we might fall together !
   1st Consp. May all success attend thy glorious purpose !
Thinking upon thy brave undaunted spirit,
I shall forget my pains, and smile in torture,
Ev'n when the sharpest pang of death is on me.
   Hyd. Ere you are cold my Ghost shall overtake you,
And bring the welcome news.—Impatience racks me.
   2d Consp. We thank our bold revenger, and will dye   20
Like men that well deserv'd so great a chief.
   3d Consp. Farewell. And when you lift the dagger for the blow
Think on my friendship.
   4th Consp. And on mine,
   5th Consp. And mine.
   1st Consp. Think of us all, and give him death for each.
   Hyd. Farewell, unhappy friends ; you're brave and true,
And you entrust one who deserves such friendships.
Your prayers and wishes shall direct the dagger
Deep in his heart. And when this deed is done   30
I've done my task of life ; and I'll resign it.

29 wishes] *Plays 1760* wishes, *1724.*

SCENE II.

Hydarnes. Conspirators. Araxes. Officers.

   Ara. Time presses on us, and your hour is come.
We must obey our orders. Lead them hence.
Torture and Death expect you.
   1st Consp. Well. Lead on.
   Ara. 'Tis your last moment.   5
   1st Consp. We're impatient for it.
   Ara. Stay here till my return. To you, my message   *[To* Hyd.
Is of a sweeter sound. 'Tis life, 'tis freedom.
I'll see them to the scaffold ; then discharge you.

[Exeunt Araxes, Conspirators, and Officers.

9 *Exeunt* etc.] *1760 only.*

SCENE III.

Hydarnes.

   Hyd. What's death to that I feel within ! 'Tis nothing.
Tortures but tear the flesh, and crush the bones,
But guilt and horror tear my restless soul,
And ev'ry thought's an arrow in my heart.

Sophernes is condemn'd, and I accused him.
For what ?—For means to satiate my revenge,
And that 's sufficient.—O Revenge, support me !
What, am I grown a coward ? Does repentance,
Does vile contrition sink my boasted **courage** ?
Does resolution stagger ! Hence, away,   10
I will not hear thee, dastard, medling conscience !
No. I'll go on, I feel my spirits rise :
My heart grows harder, and I scorn remorse,
That 's the poor whining refuge of a Coward.
My friends are now expiring. Hark, their groans
Start me from thought, and summon me to vengeance !
I come, my friends ; in that great deed I'll fall.

S C E N E I V.

Hydarnes. Araxes.

Ara. *Phraortes* sends you life and liberty.
Twelve days are granted you to pass the confines
Of his Domains : to stay beyond that time
Annuls his pardon, and your life is forfeit.
You're now discharg'd. Be grateful for this mercy,   5
Pray for the peace of *Media*, and repent.
    Hyd. *Media*, farewell. With all the wings of speed
I fly thy bounds. Let me forget thy name ;
'Twill bring to my remembrance my lost friends.   *[Exit.*

9 *Exit.*] *1760 only.*

S C E N E V.

Araxes. Sophernes.

Ara. Come forth, unhappy Prince ; excuse my words :
                                        [*Unlocks the dungeon.*
'Tis with reluctance that I bring the message.
Your death 's at hand,
    Soph. Death is the only friend
That I have left ; thy message is most welcome.
My friend 's at hand ; O how long I to meet him !
In him is all my hope, in him my refuge,
He shall disburthen me of all misfortune,
He shall wipe off calamity and sorrow,
And give me peace and everlasting rest.   10
I thank thee for the news.
    Ara. Such unconcern,
Such steady fortitude amidst afflictions
Was never seen till now.

468 THE CAPTIVES. ACT IV.

Soph. My wife is dead !
And I have no attachment to the world.
What is 't to live ? And who counts life a blessing ?
It is to see Injustice hold the scale,
And weigh with partial hand the deeds of men ;
It is to see a race of servile flatterers   20
Worship the author of all mischief, Gold ;
To see Oppression rich, and Virtue starving.
Death only closes this distasteful scene.
    Ara. This scorn of death appears like innocence.
    Soph. All mortal justice errs. Heav'n knows the heart.
'Tis easy in my circumstance to dye,
For I have no possessions to forgo,
My kingdom is another's. Round my couch
No faithful servants stand with weeping eyes ;
No darling children cling around my neck,   30
And with fond kisses warm my hollow cheek ;
No wife, who, (worn, and wearied out with grief)
Faints in my arms. These give the pangs of death ;
These make us covet life. But I leave nothing.
    Ara. What manly resolution ! I grieve for you.
    Soph. At death's approach the guilty conscience trembles,
But I have not those horrors.——Hark, he knocks.   [*Knocking heard.*
With what impatient joy I come to meet thee !
    Ara. Farewell, thou most unfortunate of men ;
A mind so great, unshaken by distress,   40
Deserved a nobler end. Forgive my duty,
It seems severe, but 'tis the King's command.
The dungeon must confine you.
    Soph. I submit.   [Araxes *locks him in the dungeon.*

SCENE VI.

Araxes. Captive.

    Cap. This letter will instruct you in your duty.
    Ara. The prisoner shall be given into your hands.
    Cap. And he shall perish by an injur'd woman.
Thus has the King decreed ; so shall he suffer
Both for his treason, and my murder'd lord.
To see me arm'd with such just resolution,
My husband's ghost is pleas'd, and smiles upon me.
Phraortes gave this dagger. This shall end him.
    Ara. Within that iron gate he mourns in darkness.   [*Gives the Keys.*
This will conduct you.—'Tis the King's command,   10
Soon as the bloody office is perform'd,
That you present your self once more before him.
    Cap. His will shall be obey'd.
    Ara. He 's now your charge.

Cap. And soon my charge shall end.—Leave me to justice.
How will my sight dismay his guilty soul!
Ev'n while that terror preys upon his heart,
I'll hurle him to the deepest shades below.
But I delay; and justice grows impatient.
I'd be alone. You now have done your duty.   [*Exit* Araxes.   20

20 *Exit* Araxes.] *1760 only.*

SCENE VII.

Captive. Sophernes.

Cap. Come forth, *Sophernes.*   [*Unlocks the Dungeon.*
Soph. I will meet thee, Death.
Cap. Draw near.
Soph. Hark! was it not a woman's voice?
That voice no more is sweet;—*Cylene's* dead.
Yes. 'Tis the Queen. Here satiate thy revenge,
My bosom heaves, and longs to meet the dagger.
Why is thy hand so slow?
    Cap. Look on this face,   [*Lifts up her veil.*
I's not thy heart acquainted with these eyes?   10
And is thy ear a stranger to this voice?
What, not a word!
    Soph. O dear delusion!   [*Faints.*
    Cyl. Wake.
'Tis thy *Cylene* calls, thy lost *Cylene.*
Cannot this bosom warm thee into life?
Cannot this voice recall thy sinking spirits?
Cannot these lips restore thee? O look up;
Thy voice, thy lips, could call me from the dead.
Look up, and give me comfort.   20
    Soph. 'Tis *Cylene.*
'Tis no delusion. Do I live to see thee?
And must I be torn from thee? cruel thought!
O tyrant Death, now thou hast made me fear thee!
    Cyl. When will misfortunes leave us?
    Soph. Death must end them.
'Twas said you fell in battle; from that time
I lost all pleasure, and desire of life.
    Cyl. In that sad day of our adversity,
When *Persia* was made captive, every eye   30
Wept for the fall of my dear Lord *Sophernes,*
For you they sorrow'd, and forgot their bondage.
I lost my self in heart-consuming grief,
And lest a conqueror's arrogance and pride
Should tempt him to condemn a captive Queen
To his loose hours, industriously I spread

The rumour of my death ; and by those means
Have sigh'd away my days obscure, unknown.
    Soph. How gain'd you this access ? and why that dagger ?
    Cyl. This is no time for talk ; consult thy safety.   40
Catch at the present moment, for the next
May throw us back again into despair.
    Soph. What means, my love ? No innocence can stand
Against the voice of perjur'd calumny.
    Cyl. This dagger was design'd to murder thee ;
And I am sent upon that bloody errand.
This hand that now is thrown about thy neck
Was to have done the deed. O horrid thought !
Unknown, among a train of captive women,
They brought me to the palace : there I learnt   50
The tale of thy unhappy sufferings,
And how the King had sign'd the fatal sentence.
I fell before the throne, extoll'd his justice ;
Then, with feign'd tears, and well dissembled speech
Charg'd thee with violation of my honour,
And murder of a husband. He was mov'd ;
Pleas'd with my bold request, he heard my prayer,
And for revenge and justice gave me this.   [*Shews the dagger.*
But the time flies. I come. my Lord, to save thee.
'Tis by that hope, I live.   60
    Soph. That hope is past :
It is impossible. Resentment, power,
And perjury, all work against my life.
O how I fear to dye ! for thee, I fear,
To leave thee thus expos'd, a helpless Captive,
In a strange land, and not one friend to chear thee !
    Cyl. I think thou lov'st me.
    Soph. Sure thou long hast known it.
    Cyl. Is there ought that I could deny *Sophernes?*
No. I have try'd my heart !   70
    Soph. What mean these doubts ?
I never gave you cause.
    Cyl. Then promise, swear,
That you will not refuse me what I ask ;
Thus on her knees *Cylene* begs it of you.
    Soph. Does this appear like love ? speak, and 'tis granted.
    Cyl. I thank thee. Thou hast given me all my wishes,
For now thy life is safe ; and sav'd by me.
Here, take this veil ; this shall secure thy flight,
With this thou shalt deceive the watchful guard.   80
O blest occasion ! fly, my Lord, with speed ;
I never wish'd to part till now.
    Soph. What, go and leave thee thus ! my heart forbids it.
No. Death is all that I am doom'd to suffer ;
But thy distress is more.
    Cyl. Dispute it not.
Hast thou not sworn ?

Soph. What never can be done.
Why wilt thou force severer torture on me ?
No. Give me death ; I chuse the slighter pain.   90
When I am dead, may the just Gods relieve thee.
  Cyl. Was ever love thus obstinately cruel !
Only thy life can save me ; think on that.
                    [Sophernes *fixes his eyes on the ground.*
Like the deaf rock he stands immoveable.
How my fears grow, and chill my shiv'ring heart !
Has then thy stubbornness resolv'd to kill me ?
  Soph. Shall I that was her shield in every danger
Abandon her to the rude hand of power ?
  Cyl. Hear me, my Lord ; embrace the happy moment ;
This is, perhaps, the last that is allow'd us.   100
  Soph. What ! give her my distress !
  Cyl. Look up, and answer.   ·
Have my words lost all int'rest in thy heart ?
Hear then my purpose ; and I will perform it.
I'll never feel the pang of that sad hour
When thou shalt suffer. No. I'll dye before thee.
How gracious was this Present of the King.
'Tis kind, 'tis merciful, 'twill give me peace,
And show me more compassion than *Sophernes.*
  Soph. O give me strength, ye Powers, to break my chains,   110
That I may force the lifted weapon from her !
Spare, spare thy dearer life ! I grant thee all.
I will abandon thee to my distresses ;
I'll fly this instant ; by our loves, I will.
The Gods are kind. O may their mercy save her !
  Cyl. From thy dear hands I take the galling chains.
Lest danger intercept thee, haste, be gone ;
And as thou valuest mine, secure thy life.
Thou hadst no hope. Who knows but my offence
May find forgiveness ! 'tis a crime of love ;   120
And love 's a powerful advocate to mercy.
  Soph. O how I struggle to unloose my heart-strings,
That are so closely knit and twin'd with thine !
Is't possible that we may meet again ?
That thought has filled my soul with resolution.
Farewell : may Heaven support thee, and redress us !   [*Exit.*

            126 *Exit.*] *1760 only.*

SCENE VIII.

Cylene.

  Cyl. O blessed opportunity, I thank thee.
If for this pious act of love I perish,
Let not *Sophernes* rashly follow me.
Live to revenge me, and the world shall praise thee.
Though all my hours be doom'd to chains and darkness,

The pleasing thought that I have giv'n thee safety,
Will chear me more than liberty and day-light.
Though I'm condemned to suffer shameful death,
Ev'n in that hour I shall forget his terrors,
And knowing that preserv'd thee, dye with pleasure.   10
But hark ! what noise was that ?   New fears alarm me.
Is he detected ?—Heaven has more compassion.
Be still, my heart.   I go to take his place,
And wait th' event with steady resignation.   [*Enters the dungeon.*

S C E N E   I X.

Araxes.   Astarbe

[*Cylene in the Dungeon.*
Ast.   I bring the royal mandate, read your order.
The sentence of *Sophernes* is suspended ;
I'd question him in private.   Guide me to him.
Ara.   He 's dead.
Ast.   *Sophernes* dead !   when ?   how ?   by whom ?
Ara.   The captive woman by whose hand he fell,
Is gone before the King ;   just now she parted.
Ast.   My guilt, my hate, my love, all war within,
And conscience and distraction will betray me.   [*Aside.*
Ara.   Within that dungeon lyes the breathless body.   10
Ast.   Name him no more.   Begone ;   I'd be alone.
You know my pleasure.
Ara.   I am all Obedience.   [*Exit.*

    1 Cylene *in the Dungeon.*] *Omitted 1760.*
    13 *Exit.*] *1760 only.*

S C E N E   X.

Astarbe.   Cylene *in the Dungeon.*

Ast.   Who shall appease this tempest of my soul ?
'Tis done.   He 's dead :   now it will rage for ever !
Yet why ?   Hence, conscience.   All I did was justice.
Am I the cause ?   I proffer'd life and love.
The murder was not mine.   Why then this horror ?
Could a Queen bear such insolence and scorn ?
Was I not injured ?   shall I not resent ?
He well deserv'd his fate.   Ungrateful man !
The bloody spectacle shall please revenge,
And fix eternal hatred in my heart.   [*Cylene comes forth.*   10
Hah !   speak :   what art ?——
It moves !   it comes !   where shall I hide me from it ?
Nature shrinks back, and shivers at the sight.   [*Hides her face.*

Cyl.   See at your feet a poor unhappy captive.   [*Kneeling.*
O may the Queen be gracious to her servant!
   Ast.   *Araxes* said that he had let you forth,
And by command you went before the King.
Why has he thus deceiv'd me?
   Cyl.   Turn not away;
Bestow one look of pity on a wretch,   20
Who lifts her eyes to you for grace and pardon.
   Ast.   Pardon! for what? you did it by command.
Is it a crime t'obey the voice of justice?
And did not thy own wrongs demand his blood?
What has detain'd thee in that horrid place?
Was it to hear him in the pangs of death,
And taste the pleasure of his dying groan?
Stretch forth thy hands.   Where are the crimson stains?
Where lies the reeking sword?   Is he yet cold?
'Twas bravely done.—Go, haste, before the Throne;   30
Phraortes shall reward thee for this service.
   Cyl.   When I shall stand before that awful presence,
How shall I stem the torrent of his wrath!
Then let the Queen instill soft mercy in him,
And intercede to spare a wretched wife.
   Ast.   Make known thy crime.
   Cyl.   All my offence is love.
Sophernes is my husband.
   Ast.   Hast thou kill'd him?
   Cyl.   No.   I dar'd disobey.   My love has sav'd him.   40
With lying speeches I deceiv'd the King,
Accus'd *Sophernes* of imagin'd crimes,
And thus have giv'n him life.   My veil conceal'd him,
And brought him forth from death.   This is my guilt.
If e'er your heart has felt the tender passion,
You will forgive this just, this pious fraud.
Who would not do the same for him she loves?
Consult thy heart; and Pity will plead for me.
   Ast.   How dar'd you contradict the King's command?
   Cyl.   No power on earth commands the heart but Love,   [*Rises.*   50
And I obey'd my heart.
   Ast.   Thy life is forfeit.
Dar'st thou avow thy crime?
   Cyl.   I glory in it.
If 'tis a crime, when innocence is wrong'd
To snatch it from the rage of credulous Power;
If 'tis a crime to succour the distrest;
If 'tis a crime to relieve injur'd virtue;
If 'tis a crime to be a faithful wife;
Those crimes are mine.   For I have sav'd my husband.   60
   Ast.   Is this an answer turn'd to move compassion!
Such insolence is only match'd in him.
Thine is the most consummate pitch of treason.

Who gave thee power ?   Are traytors at thy mercy ?
Let not hope flatter thee.   Nor prayers nor tears
Shall turn away the sword of justice from thee.
Rash woman, know, thy life shall pay his ransom.
   Cyl.   Alas ! my life is of too little price ;
Such as it is, I freely give it for him.
May safety guard his days, and watch his nights !   [*Kneeling.*   70
May ev'ry sun rise happier than the last,
'Till he shall reascend his native throne !
Then think upon *Cylene.*   Heaven shall aid thee
To punish *Media* for thy murder'd wife.
   Ast. Araxes!   Seize this bold presumptuous woman.
Your charge, beneath her veil is fled from justice,
And she dares own the crime.   I fear your duty
Will be suspected.   Lead her to the dungeon.
There wait thy fate.
   Cyl.   Ye Gods, preserve *Sophernes.*   [*She is lock'd into the Dungeon,*   80

SCENE XI.

Astarbe. Araxes.

   Ast.   If I had power, this instant she should die.
   Ara.   I fear the King will soften into mercy.
   Ast.   Why that suspicion ?
   Ara.   While she spoke before him,
I saw the King with the most fond attention
Hang on her words, and as she spoke he languish'd,
And ev'ry look he gave was love or pity.
   Ast.   She shall not live an hour.   Lest with each moment
His passion strengthen, and my power diminish.
Did beauty strike all hearts as well as eyes,   10
For me the rival world would be in arms ;
Beauty 's admir'd and prais'd, not always lov'd.
Some eyes are dazled with too strong a lustre,
That gaze with pleasure on a fainter object ;
This homely captive then may steal his heart,
And bring disgrace upon me.   I'll prevent her.
This hour I'll see her bleed, and thus remove
At once the rival of my throne and love.

A C T V. Scene I.

A Temple.

Astarbe.

Doraspe knows,—and I am in her power.
Araxes was employ'd ; he may suspect me.
One crime supports another—I must on.
I fear them both. How shall I lose my fear ?
Their deaths must end it. But they may be honest.
I'll sift them—for my Soul has lost all rest.
But see *Doraspe.*

S C E N E I I.

Astarbe. Doraspe.

Thou sometimes wert known
To miss Devotion's hours. How comes it then
Thou'rt now so soon ? hast thou ought that concerns me ?
Think'st thou *Araxes* honest ? I have doubts.
I fear the prisoner 'scap'd by his connivance.
Are my commands obey'd ?
　Dor. 'Tis not yet done.
He could not gain admission to the King.
　Ast. Does he not know a frown of mine can crush him ?
　Dor. I know his heart and hand are wholly yours.　　　10
He waits the King's commands.
　Ast. Are mine then nothing ?
And want I power to justify the deed ?
Why was she not dispatch'd ? He knew my pleasure.
My pleasure is his duty, 'Twas I rais'd him ;
And dares he now dispute what I ordain ?
Tell him, I'll have it done ; that I command it.
Thou too art false. Then on her self alone
Astarbe shall depend. Away, thou flatterer.
Go hence, and tremble at the Queen's displeasure.　　　20
She shall this instant die. For see *Phraortes.*
Astarbe now has all things at her nod.
Of this day's worship I'll appoint the victim.

SCENE III.

Phraortes.　Astarbe.　*A solemn Procession of Priests.*

[The Queen talks apart to Phraortes.
Phra.　Bid them suspend a while the sacrifice,
The Queen requires a private conference
On matters that concern the state.　Withdraw.　　*[Exeunt Priests.*
Now speak, my Queen ;　I'm ready to obey.
Ast.　All is not safe.　Your state still harbours treason.
Ev'n now I tremble for my Lord the King ;
For through the dark the traytor's arrow flies ;
And which way will you turn your shield against it ?
Phra.　What means my Queen ?
Ast.　Cast off all clemency ;　　　　　　　　　　　　10
So shall your throne stand firm to latest time.
Phra.　And has my danger giv'n *Astarbe* fear ?
Where shall I find reward for so much goodness ?
I swear by *Jove*, and yon wide sapphire Heaven,
Astarbe's will shall fix the King's decree.
Ast.　What shall be done to him, whose lying lips
Mis-lead the King from the strait paths of justice ?
Phra.　*Media* decrees that death shall be his portion.
Ast.　What is ordain'd for him, who (when the King
Entrusts the royal signet in his hands)　　　　　　　20
Dares contradict the sacred mandate ?
Phra.　Death.
Ast.　What shall our laws inflict on that bold miscreant,
Who saves th' offender whom the King condemns ?
Phra.　The fatal sentence falls upon his head.
Ast.　Let justice then support the throne of *Media*,
Let justice then preserve thy sacred life !
All these offences are that captive woman's,
Who with feign'd tears beg'd pity and revenge.
With lying lips she fell before the throne,　　　　　30
She turn'd the King from the strait paths of justice,
The royal seal was trusted in her hands ;
Presumptuously she broke the sacred mandate,
She spar'd whom you condemn'd, and with vile treachery
Hath set *Sophernes* free.　So this assassin
Shall kindle new rebellions in your Empire.
Phra.　These flagrant crimes demand immediate death.
Ast.　Let it be so.　The King is wise and just.
Phra.　She shall this instant bleed.　Audacious woman !
Ast.　Let her endure the shameful pomp of death,　　40
Expose her through the city's publick street ;
So shall your people's shouts extol your justice ;
So shall you strike your enemies with fear,

And awe them to subjection. Bring her forth ;
Here let her bleed, ev'n on this holy ground,
Before the presence ; *Jove* delights in justice,
The righteous sacrifice shall please the Gods.

S C E N E   I V.

Phraortes. Astarbe. Orbasius. Magi. Attendants.

Phra. Come from the croud, *Orbasius* ; hear and obey.
Haste to the Prison, and bring forth that woman
(Who freed *Sophernes* from the hand of power)
To publick justice. She shall bleed before me.
Let her be led a publick spectacle.   5
Dispatch. Remember that the King expects you.   [*Exit* Orbasius.

6 *Exit* Orbasius.] *1760 only.*

S C E N E   V.

Phraortes. Astarbe. Magi. Attendants.

The shield of heaven has turn'd Destruction from us ;
And Gratitude requires our thanks and praise.
Call up the Priests. Begin the sacred rites.
  1st Mag. Turn all your eyes to yon bright arch of Heaven.
  2d Mag. When *Jove* in thunder threatens impious men,
May the red lightnings scatter *Media*'s foes,
And lay their cities desolate and waste !
  1st Mag. May the vast globe of inexhausted light,
That rolls its living fires from east to west,
Strow all his paths with fragrant herbs and flowers,   10
And bless his people with perpetual spring !
  2d Mag. May the bright lamp of night, the silver moon,
And all the starry myriad that attend her,
Guard and defend his midnight couch from dangers !
  1st Mag. May everliving springs supply our fountains,
And wind in fertile rivers through the land !
  2d Mag. Bless him, ye winds, with ever-prosp'rous gales !
  1st Mag. Pour not your wrath in tempests on his people.
Let your sweet breath chase dearth and pestilence,
And cool our summers with eternal health !   20

SCENE VI.

Phraortes. Astarbe. Magi. Orbasius. Attendants.
Cylene *as led to execution.*

[*Orbasius talks apart to the King.*

Phra. Again we must defer the solemn worship.
Bid the procession move towards the Temple :
And let th' offender stand before the presence.   [*To* Orbasius.
    Ast. *Sophernes* has expos'd me to this woman ;
And while she lives, I live in fear and shame.
Shall she then triumph in a Queen's disgrace ?   [*Aside.*
    Cyl. Most gracious King, consider my transgression.   [*Kneels.*
My life is forfeit ; justice has condemn'd me.
I broke th' inviolable laws of *Media.*
Yet let *Phraortes* with impartial scale   10
Weigh my offence ; he'll find my crime was virtue.
Sure Heaven that trys the heart will pardon me.
And Kings, who imitate the Gods in justice,
Should not forsake them in the paths of mercy.
    Phra. Have not thy lying lips deceiv'd the King ?
How shall thy words find faith ! They're air, they're nothing !
    Cyl. O be not rash in judgment ! Hear me speak,
What mov'd my tongue to practice this deceit ?
Was it ambition and the lust of power ?
Was it to vex your empire with rebellion ?   20
Was it the meaner views of sordid gain ?
Was it to hurt the lowest of your people ?
All my offence is faithful love and duty :
Sophernes is my husband, and I sav'd him.
    Phra. Thy husband !
    Ast. Hear her not : woman, away.
Remember you have sworn.
    Phra. Thy husband, say'st thou ?
    Ast. Think on your oath, and spurn dissimulation.
    Phra. Am I debarr'd the chief delight of Kings ?   30
Have I the power to punish ; not to pardon ?
But I have sworn.
    Cyl. If there 's no room for mercy   [*Rises.*
My life is well bestow'd. My death is glorious ;
I chose it ; and repine not at my fate.
    Ast. Turn from her. Listen not to fraud and guile.
    Cyl. Think not I shudder at th' approach of death,
That the keen sword which glitters in my eyes
Makes my heart fail, and sinks me to despair.
I fear not for my self ; for him I fear.   40
How will he bear my death ?—As I could his.
    Phra. Why have I bound the tender hands of mercy ?   [*Musing.*
    Ast. You but delay. The royal oath is sacred.

Cyl. Well then. Lead on. His punishment is mine.
Live, live, *Sophernes*, and forget *Cylene* ;
Lest grief destroy thy peace, and make thee wretched.
I'm ready.
    Phra. How shall I pronounce the sentence !
    Ast. For your oath's sake.
    Phra. 'Tis granted. Let her dye.   50
But let me first perform my due devotions,
To beg that mercy which I must refuse.
As soon as I have paid my solemn vows,
I'll make the sign. Then let the blow be given.
See all be ready. Now renew the rites.

SCENE VII.

The Aforesaid. Hydarnes *disguis'd.*

    Hyd. Thus far I'm undiscover'd.—Now 's my time.
The King of *Media*'s given into my hands.
And when he leaves his guards to trust the Gods,
Ev'n while he prostrate falls, and lifts his eyes
To the bright God of day, th' all-seeing sun ;
This shall dispatch him first, and then *Hydarnes*.
    1st Mag. Now let the King advance.
    Phra. O glorious Sun !   [*Kneeling.*
    [Hydarnes *attempting to stab* Phraortes, *is stab'd by* Sophernes *dis-*
        guis'd, who is seiz'd by the Magi.
What means this consternation in all eyes ?
Whence this alarm, and all this wild disorder ?   10
Hah ! who lies here thus weltring in his blood,
Gasping for life ? what means this horrid murder ?
Strike not till I command, [*To the Executioner*]. Who did this deed ?
    1st Mag. Behold the man. What bounty can reward him ?
What shall be done for him who sav'd the King ?
    Phra. Say who, and whence thou art ?
    Soph. A wretched man
Who comes to take his sentence on him, death.
Sophernes was condemn'd ; 'tis he must suffer.
Spare then that pattern of heroic virtue.   20
The sentence is not hers ; I claim my right.
Sophernes stands before you, and demands it.   [*Throws off his disguise.*
    Cyl. O stay not for the signal. Give the blow.
Save him, ye Gods ! Why is the stroke delay'd ?
The King has sworn. O may my death preserve him !
    Phra. Suspend her sentence till my further orders.
Who slew this man ? what mov'd thee to the murder ?
Why hast thou stain'd this holy place with blood ?
    Soph. That villain who lies groveling there before thee,
Had rais'd his arm to take thy life, O King ;   30
And as the point descended, in the moment

I laid him low ; and Heaven has done me justice.
If favour shall reward me for this deed,
Spare my *Cylene*, grant her your protection.
I ask not life, for without her 'tis nothing.
    Ast. Where will this end ? How are my schemes destroy'd !
Fear chills my heart, and guilt lies heavy on me.
Leave me not, Hell ; desert not now thy cause.
I've gone too far. O blind the eyes of justice !
And sink me not in ruin and perdition.   [*Aside.* 40
    Phra. Know you this bold Assassin ? View him well.
    Hyd. Ay, gaze upon me.
    Orba. Sure I've seen this man.
    Soph. Among the crowd I mark'd this perjur'd wretch,
Who charg'd me with ingratitude and treason.
With fury in his looks, and hasty strides
He stept before me ; strait he rais'd his dagger :
In justice to my self and thee, I smote him.
    Ast. Where shall I hide me ? how my fears distract me !
Who knows the torment of the guilty wretch,   50
When accusation stares him in the face ?
Then all our spirits sink into despair,
And when we want most strength, then most it fails us.
He speaks, and I'm betray'd. Why err'd the dagger !
To bring confusion, shame and death upon me.
Where shall I fly ?—for conscience will detect me,
'Twill faulter on my tongue, and stain my cheek.
O horror ! O disgrace !—I fly from shame.   [*Exit.*

SCENE VIII.

Phraortes. Cylene. Sophernes. Magi. Orbasius. Araxes.
Executioner. Attendants.

    Soph. 'Twas I that gave thee death.
    Hyd. Thou hast done justice.
    Phra. What sayest thou ? speak again.
    Hyd. He has done justice.
I barb'rously accus'd him of my crimes ;
That guilt upbraids me ; and I ask forgiveness.   [*To* Sophernes.
    Phra. Whence art thou ?—why this zealous rage against me ?
    Hyd. I grieve not that I perish'd by his hand ;
But that he disappointed my Revenge
I can't forgive him. Had he stay'd 'till then,   10
Hydarnes had faln greatly. But that 's past.
Still I shall wound thee in the tenderest part,   [*To* Phraortes.
I faint. O grant me strength to give it utterance !
Draw near, *Araxes*. Speak, inform the King ;
Did not you guide me to the Queen's apartment ?
You know why I was call'd. Disclose the secret.
    Ara. What past I know not.
    Hyd. What you fear to own,

I dare reveal : hear then a dying man.
The Queen, on promise of my life and pardon,   20
Prevail'd upon me to accuse this Prince ;
I knew him not.   Yet to pursue thy life,
And gratify revenge, I undertook it.
    Phra.   It is impossible.   Advance, my Queen,
And let thy presence strike him with confusion.
Come forth, *Astarbe*.   Hah ! she 's fled ; she 's guilty !
Haste, bring her back.   I will extort confession.
What mov'd her to this perjur'd information ?   [*Exeunt* Officers.
Whence sprung this hate and malice to *Sophernes?*   [*To* Hydarnes.
    Hyd.   Ask her.   I speak the truth, and know no further.
Look on me, Tyrant, and observe my features ;
Seest thou not here the lines of brave *Lysamnes?*
He by thy power was led to shameful death,
His son now dyes, and never has reveng'd him.   [*Dyes.*

SCENE IX.

Phraortes.   Astarbe *brought in by* Officers.   Cylene.   Sophernes.
Magi.   Attendants.

    Ast.   Bring me before the King.
    Phra.   Perfidious woman !
Look on that wretch, who there lyes pale and cold
Was he not brought in private to your chamber ?
Who gave instructions to accuse *Sophernes?*
Who promis'd life and pardon to *Hydarnes?*
    Ast.   All then is lost.   *Astarbe* is betray'd.
But shall I stoop to lead a life of shame ?
No.   This shall close a scene of long remorse.   [*Stabs her self.*
    Phra.   *Astarbe!* hold !   10
    Ast.   Forgive me !   [*Dyes.*
    Phra.   Her foul treachery
My soul detests.   But love will force a tear.
What mov'd her hatred thus against your life ?
    Soph.   She was unhappy.   Let her be forgot.
    Phra.   Draw near, *Cylene*.   May heav'n bless your loves !
                        [*Gives her to* Sophernes.
    Cyl.   Shall he then live ?   My heart o'erflows with joy.
Now life is worth accepting, worth desiring,
Worth. ev'ry wish, and ev'ry daily prayer.
    Phra.   By you the royal vestment shall be worn,   20
And next the King, all honour shall be paid
To you who sav'd him.   [*To* Sophernes.
    Soph.   What I did was due.
I've only paid a debt of gratitude ;
What would your bounty more ?—you've giv'n me all.
For in these arms I ev'ry wish possess.

Phra. Life is a voyage, and we with pain and labour
Must weather many a storm, to reach the port.
  Soph. Since 'tis not giv'n to mortals to discern
Their real good and ill ; let men learn patience :   30
Let us the toils of adverse fate sustain,
For through that rugged road our hopes we gain.

E P I L O G U E.

Spoken by Mrs. *O L D F I E L D.*

SHALL authors teaze the town with tragic passion,
When we've more modern moral things in fashion ?
Let poets quite exhaust the Muse's treasure ;
Sure Masquerades must give more feeling pleasure,
Where we meet finer sense and better measure ;
The marry'd Dame, whose business must be done,
Puts on the holy vestments of a Nun ;
And brings her unprolifick spouse a son.
Coquettes, with whom no lover could succeed,
Here pay off all arrears, and love in—deed ;   10
Ev'n conscious Prudes are so sincere and free,
They ask each man they meet—do you know me ?
  Do not our Operas unbend the mind,
Where ev'ry soul' s to ecstasy refin'd ?
Entranc'd with sound sits each seraphic Toast.
All Ladies love the play that moves the most.
Ev'n in this house I've known some tender fair,
Touch'd with meer sense alone, confess a tear.
But the soft voice of an Italian wether,
Makes them all languish three whole hours together.   20
And where 's the wonder ? Plays, like Mass, are sung,
(Religious Drama) !—in an unknown tongue.
  Will Poets ne'er consider what they cost us ?
What tragedy can take, like Doctor Faustus ?
Two stages in this moral show excell,
To frighten vicious youth with scenes of hell ;
Yet both these Faustuses can warn but few.
For what 's a Conj'rer's fate to me or—you ?
  Yet there are wives who think heav'n worth their care,
But first they kindly send their spouses there.   30
When you my lover's last distress behold,
Does not each husband's thrilling blood run cold ?
Some heroes only dye.—Ours finds a wife.
What 's harder than captivity for life ?
Yet Man, ne'er warn'd, still court their own undoing :
Who, for that circle, would but venture ruin ?

Epilogue. *Printed here in 1760 ; immediately after Prologue in edition of 1724.*
19 *wether,*] Weather 1724 Wether 1760

THE

BEGGAR'S

OPERA.

——Nos haec novimus esse nihil.   MART.

[*Editions :*

1. THE | *BEGGAR's* | OPERA. | As it is Acted at the | THEATRE-ROYAL ; IN | *LINCOLNS-INN-FIELDS.* | Written by Mr. *GAY.* | —*Nos haec novimus esse nihil.* Mart. | To which is Added, | *The* MUSICK *Engrav'd on* COPPER- | PLATES. | *LONDON :* | Printed for JOHN WATTS, at the Printing-Office | in *Wild-Court*, near *Lincoln's-Inn-Fields.* | MDCCXXVIII. | [Price 1s. 6d.]

Post 8vo. Two issues, the first with, and the second without, the Air, *A cobbler there was, &c.* [AIR LVI]—both music and words. See the *Catalogue of the Ashley Library*, 1923, vol. ii, pp. 140, 141. In the first issue the music of the Air is printed in the text ; it follows that the Air was added after the rest of the music had been engraved. Since it reappears in all subsequent editions, one would naturally have supposed that the ' second issue ' (without the Air) was the first, and the ' first issue ' the second. But Mr. Wise shows that the readjustment necessitated by the omission of the Air produced a blank page at the end of the text of the ' second issue ', immediately before the advertisements, and that the advertisements were continued *back* into this extra page. It seems, then, that the Air was added at the last moment, was then discarded (perhaps because the music was thought to spoil the appearance of the text), to be restored in later editions.

Of this second issue Mr. Wise has two copies, one of them a large-paper copy, with a presentation four-line inscription on the blank fly-leaf, given in this edition under the Minor Miscellaneous Pieces. This large-paper copy is the only known specimen. ' The fact that the details of its collation agree with those of the " second issue " furnish additional evidence that the copies without " Air LVI " are the second issue, for any large-paper copies would as a matter of course not be produced until the regular published edition of the book had been completed. In the ordinary copies of the second issue the music was re-engraved upon a smaller scale. In the large-paper copy still further modifications were introduced into the sixteen pages of engraved music : they therefore appear in three distinct states.' (*Cat. Ash. Lib., loc. cit.*)

The airs are numbered separately for each Act. [Ref. *1728*¹.]

2. ' The Second Edition : To which is Added The Ouverture in Score ; *And the* Musick *prefix'd to each* Song.' John Watts. 1728.

Post 8vo. In this and subsequent editions the airs are numbered continuously through the Play. [Ref. *1728*².]

3. A ' Third Edition ' [*sic*] printed in Dublin by S. Powell, for George Risk, George Ewing, and William Smith, in 1728.

Fcap 8vo. [Ref. *1728*³.]

4. ' The Third Edition : With the Ouverture in Score, *The* Songs, *and the* Basses, (The Ouverture and Basses Compos'd by Dr. Pepusch) *Curiously Engrav'd on* Copper Plates.' John Watts. 1729.

Crown 4to. Title-page in red and black. The motto from Martial contains the misprint *novissimus*, repeated in the *Plays* 1760.

I follow the style of this edition, which is more carefully considered (in spite of a few misprints) than the 8vo editions. The points of difference are few. The 8vos use capital letters much more freely. They always print ' &c. ' after the name of each Air ; the 4to only when the sentence is incomplete. The 4to gives the music at the end, as does the first edition (1728), whereas the 2nd edition of 1728 and all subsequent editions give it in the text ; but the musical notation used is much finer and clearer, and moreover this is the only edition in which a Bass is given, and the words are fitted to the music. The spelling of the 8vos is on the whole more antique than that of the 4to. [Ref. *1729*.]

5. ' The Third Edition : To which is Added The Ouverture in Score ; *And the* Musick *prefix'd to each* Song.' John Watts. 1733.

Post 8vo.

6. ' The Fourth Edition.' John Watts. 1735. etc.

Modern Editions Consulted.

7. *Plays written by Mr. John Gay.* London. Tonson. 1760. [Ref. *Plays 1760.*]

8. Bell's edition in the '*British Theatre*'. ['Distinguishing also the Variations of the Theatre, as performed at the Theatre-Royal in Drury-Lane, Regulated from the Prompt-Book, *By Permission of the Managers,* By Mr. Hopkins, Prompter.'] London : John Bell. 1777. [Ref. *Bell.*]

9. *Dicks' Standard Plays.* Number 45. ['New and complete edition.—Price One Penny.']

These were published weekly. ? date. [Ref. *Dicks.*]

10. Number III of '*The King's Library,* Edited by Professor Gollancz, De La More Press Quartos'. 'At the De La More Press 32 George Street Hanover Square London W MDCCCCV.' Edited, with a Preface, Notes, and Bibliography, by G. Hamilton MacLeod.

Fcap 4to. Limited to 20 copies on Vellum and 250 on hand-made Paper. [Ref. *MacLeod.*]

11. *Representative English Dramas from Dryden to Sheridan.* Edited by Frederick Tupper and James W. Tupper. New York, Oxford University Press, 1914.

12. *The Beggar's Opera.* London. Martin Secker. 1920. 'The present text follows that of the edition of 1765, which has been collated with the first.'

Crown 8vo.

13. *The Beggar's Opera.* Heinemann, 1921.

Post 4to.

Limited edition of 430 numbered copies on hand-made paper, 350 for sale in the United Kingdom, 50 for sale in the United States, and 30 for presentation.

With the music prefixed to each song, a memoir of Lovat Fraser, a note on the scene and costumes at the Lyric Theatre, Hammersmith, and head- and tail-pieces in black and white, and eight plates in colour from Fraser's paintings.

14. The same in Royal 8vo for ordinary sale.

Both 13 and 14 follow the edition of 1765, and renumber the scenes in the modern method denoting actual changes of place or time.

In 12, 13, and 14 Air XXIV and a part of the Dialogue are omitted.

The differences between the texts are exceedingly small. The edition of 1729, which I follow, is also followed as a rule by the *Plays* 1760, by Bell, and Dicks. These editions (nos. 4, 7, 8, 9 in the above list) are occasionally referred to in the notes by the letter B, A denoting all the other editions enumerated.]

Dramatis Personae.

M E N.

Peachum.		Mr. *Hippesley.*
Lockit.		Mr. *Hall.*
Macheath.		Mr. *Walker.*
Filch.		Mr. *Clark.*
Jemmy Twitcher.		Mr. *H. Bullock.*
Crook-finger'd Jack.		Mr. *Houghton.*
Wat Dreary.		Mr. *Smith.*
Robin *of* Bagshot.	} *Macheath's* Gang. {	Mr. *Lacy.*
Nimming Ned.		Mr. *Pit.*
Harry Padington.		Mr. *Eaton.*
Mat *of the* Mint.		Mr. *Spiller.*
Ben Budge.		Mr. *Morgan.*
Beggar.		Mr. *Chapman.*
Player.		Mr. *Milward.*

Constables, Drawer, Turnkey, &c.

W O M E N.

Mrs. Peachum.		Mrs. *Martin.*
Polly Peachum.		Miss *Fenton.*
Lucy Lockit.		Mrs. *Egleton.*
Diana Trapes.		Mrs. *Martin.*
Mrs. Coaxer.		Mrs. *Holiday.*
Dolly Trull.		Mrs. *Lacy.*
Mrs. Vixen.		Mrs. *Rice.*
Betty Doxy.	} *Women of the Town.* {	Mrs. *Rogers.*
Jenny Diver.		Mrs. *Clarke.*
Mrs. Slammekin.		Mrs. *Morgan.*
Suky Tawdry.		Mrs. *Palin.*
Molly Brazen.		Mrs. *Sallee.*

In the edition of 1733 a second cast is printed, giving the names of the players at Drury Lane as well as Lincoln's-Inn-Fields. The whole cast is entirely different.

INTRODUCTION.

B E G G A R. P L A Y E R.

BEGGAR.

IF Poverty be a title to Poetry, I am sure no-body can dispute mine. I own myself of the company of Beggars ; and I make one at their weekly festivals at St. *Giles*'s. I have a small yearly Salary for my Catches, and am welcome to a dinner there whenever I please, which is more than most Poets can say.

Player. As we live by the Muses, it is but gratitude in us to encourage poetical merit where-ever we find it. The Muses, contrary to all other ladies, pay no distinction to dress, and never partially mistake the pertness of embroidery for wit, nor the modesty of want for dulness. Be the author who he will, we push his Play as far as it will go. So (though you are in want) I wish you success heartily.

Beggar. This piece I own was originally writ for the celebrating the marriage of *James Chanter* and *Moll Lay*, two most excellent ballad-singers. I have introduc'd the Similes that are in all your celebrated *Operas* : The *Swallow*, the *Moth*, the *Bee*, the *Ship*, the *Flower*, &c. Besides, I have a Prison Scene, which the ladies always reckon charmingly pathetick. As to the parts, I have observ'd such a nice impartiality to our two ladies, that it is impossible for either of them to take offence. I hope I may be forgiven, that I have not made my Opera throughout unnatural, like those in vogue ; for I have no Recitative : excepting this, as I have consented to have neither Prologue nor Epilogue, it must be allow'd an Opera in all its forms. The piece indeed hath been heretofore frequently represented by ourselves in our great room at St. *Giles*'s, so that I cannot too often acknowlege your charity in bringing it now on the stage.

Player. But I see 'tis time for us to withdraw ; the Actors are preparing to begin. Play away the Ouverture. [*Exeunt.*

THE

BEGGAR's OPERA.

A C T I. Scene I.

S C E N E Peachum's *House.*

Peachum *sitting at a Table with a large Book of Accounts before him.*

A I R I. An old woman cloathed in gray.

THROUGH all the employments of life
Each neighbour abuses his brother ;
Whore and Rogue they call Husband and Wife :
All professions be-rogue one another.
The Priest calls the Lawyer a cheat,   5
The Lawyer be-knaves the Divine ;
And the Statesman, because he 's so great,
Thinks his trade as honest as mine.

A Lawyer is an honest employment, so is mine. Like me too he acts in a double capacity, both against Rogues and for 'em ; for 'tis but fitting that we should protect and encourage Cheats, since we live by 'em.

8 as] is as *Underhill.*   10 'em ;] them *1728* [1 and 3].

S C E N E I I.

P E A C H U M, F I L C H.

Filch. Sir, black *Moll* hath sent word her tryal comes on in the afternoon, and she hopes you will order matters so as to bring her off.

Peach. Why, she may plead her belly at worst ; to my knowledge she hath taken care of that security. But as the wench is very active and industrious, you may satisfy her that I'll soften the evidence.

Filch. Tom *Gagg,* Sir, is found guilty.

Peach. A lazy dog ! When I took him the time before, I told him what he would come to if he did not mend his hand. This is death without reprieve. I may venture to book him. [*Writes.*] For *Tom Gag,* forty pounds. Let *Betty Sly* know that I'll save her from Transportation, for I can get more by her staying in *England.*   11

Filch. Betty hath brought more goods into our Lock to-year than any five of the gang ; and in truth, 'tis a pity to lose so good a customer.

Peach. If none of the gang take her off, she may, in the common course of business, live a twelve-month longer. I love to let women scape. A good sportsman always lets the Hen-Partridges fly, because the breed of the game depends upon them. Besides, here the Law allows us no reward ; there is nothing to be got by the death of women——except our wives.   **18**

Filch. Without dispute, she is a fine woman ! 'Twas to her I was oblig'd for my education, and (to say a bold word) she hath train'd up more young fellows to the business than the Gaming-table.

Peach. Truly, *Filch*, thy observation is right. We and the Surgeons are more beholden to women than all the professions besides.

A I R I I. The bonny gray-ey'd morn, &c.

Filch.   *'Tis woman that seduces all mankind,*
     By her we first were taught the wheedling arts: **25**
Her very eyes can cheat; when most she's kind,
She tricks us of our money with our hearts.
For her, like Wolves by night we roam for prey,
And practise ev'ry fraud to bribe her charms;
For suits of love, like law, are won by pay,
And Beauty must be fee'd into our arms.

Peach. But make haste to *Newgate*, boy, and let my friends know what I intend ; for I love to make them easy one way or other.

Filch. When a gentleman is long kept in suspence, penitence may break his spirit ever after. Besides, certainty gives a man a good air upon his tryal, and makes him risque another without fear or scruple. But I'll away, for 'tis a pleasure to be the messenger of comfort to friends in affliction.

14 take] takes *Plays 1760, Bell, Dicks.*   20 hath] had *McLeod.*

S C E N E I I I.

P E A C H U M.

But 'tis now high time to look about me for a decent Execution against next Sessions. I hate a lazy rogue, by whom one can get nothing 'till he is hang'd. A Register of the Gang. [*Reading.*] Crook-finger'd *Jack*. A year and a half in the service : Let me see how much the stock owes to his industry ; one, two, three, four, five gold Watches, and seven silver ones. A mighty clean-handed fellow ! sixteen Snuff-boxes, five of them of true gold. Six dozen of Handkerchiefs, four silver-hilted Swords, half a dozen of Shirts, three Tye-perriwigs, and a piece of Broad Cloth. Considering these are only the fruits of his leisure hours, I don't know a prettier fellow, for no man alive hath a more engaging presence of mind upon the road. *Wat Dreary*, alias *Brown Will*, an irregular dog, who hath an underhand way of disposing his goods. I'll try him only for a Sessions or two longer upon his good behaviour. *Harry Paddingdon*, a poor petty-larceny rascal, without the least genius ; that fellow, though he were to live these six months, will never come to the gallows with any credit. Slippery *Sam* ; he goes off the next Sessions, for the villain hath the impudence to have views of following his trade as a Taylor, which he calls an honest employment. *Mat* of the *Mint* ; listed not above a month ago, a promising sturdy fellow, and diligent in his way ; somewhat too bold and hasty, and may raise good contributions on the publick, if he does not cut himself short by murder. *Tom Tipple*, a guzzling soaking sot, who is always too drunk to stand himself, or to make others stand. A cart is absolutely necessary for him. *Robin* of *Bagshot*, alias *Gorgon*, alias *Bluff Bob*, alias *Carbuncle*, alias *Bob Booty*.

SCENE IV.

P E A C H U M, Mrs. *P E A C H U M*.

Mrs. Peach. What of *Bob Booty*, husband ? I hope nothing bad hath betided him. You know, my dear, he 's a favourite customer of mine. 'Twas he made me a present of this ring.

Peach. I have set his name down in the black-list, that 's all my dear ; he spends his life among women, and as soon as his money is gone, one or other of the ladies will hang him for the reward, and there 's forty pound lost to us for-ever.

Mrs. Peach. You know, my dear, I never meddle in matters of Death ; I always leave those affairs to you. Women indeed are bitter bad judges in these cases, for they are so partial to the brave that they think every man handsome who is going to the Camp or the Gallows.   11

A I R I I I.   Cold and raw, *&c.*

If any wench Venus's *girdle wear,*
   Though she be never so ugly,
Lillies and roses will quickly appear,
   And her face look wond'rous smuggly.
Beneath the left ear, so fit but a cord,
   (A rope so charming a Zone is !)
The youth in his cart hath the air of a lord,
   And we cry, There dies an Adonis !

But really, husband, you should not be too hard-hearted, for you never had a finer, braver set of men than at present. We have not had a murder among them all, these seven months. And truly, my dear, that is a great blessing.

Peach. What a dickens is the woman always a whimpring about murder for ? No gentleman is ever look'd upon the worse for killing a man in his own defence ; and if business cannot be carried on without it, what would you have a gentleman do ?   26

Mrs. Peach. If I am in the wrong, my dear, you must excuse me, for no-body can help the frailty of an over-scrupulous Conscience.

Peach. Murder is as fashionable a crime as a man can be guilty of. How many fine gentlemen have we in *Newgate* every year, purely upon that article ? If they have wherewithal to perswade the jury to bring it in manslaughter, what are they the worse for it ? So, my dear, have done upon this subject.

31 perswade] *1729* persuade *remainder.*

Was captain *Macheath* here this morning, for the bank-notes he left with you last week ?   34

Mrs. *Peach.*   Yes, my dear ; and though the Bank hath stopt payment, he was so cheerful and so agreeable !   Sure there is not a finer gentleman upon the road than the Captain !   If he comes from *Bagshot* at any reasonable hour he hath promis'd to make one this evening with *Polly*, and me, and *Bob Booty*, at a party of Quadrille.   Pray, my dear, is the Captain rich ?

Peach.   The Captain keeps too good company ever to grow rich.   *Marybone* and the Chocolate-houses are his undoing.   The man that proposes to get money by play should have the education of a fine gentleman, and be train'd up to it from his youth.   43

Mrs. *Peach.*   Really, I am sorry upon *Polly's* account the Captain hath not more discretion.   What business hath he to keep company with lords and gentlemen ?   he should leave them to prey upon one another.

Peach.   Upon *Polly's* account !   What, a plague, does the woman mean ?— Upon *Polly's* account !

Mrs. *Peach.*   Captain *Macheath* is very fond of the girl.

Peach.   And what then ?

Mrs. *Peach.*   If I have any skill in the ways of women, I am sure *Polly* thinks him a very pretty man.   52

Peach.   And what then ?   you would not be so mad to have the wench marry him ?   Gamesters and highwaymen are generally very good to their whores, but they are very devils to their wives.

Mrs. *Peach.*   But if *Polly* should be in love, how should we help her, or how can she help herself ?   Poor girl, I am in the utmost concern about her.

A I R   I V.   Why is your faithful slave disdain'd ?

> *If love the virgin's heart invade,*
> *How, like a Moth, the simple maid*
> *Still plays about the flame!*   60
> *If soon she be not made a wife,*
> *Her honour's sing'd, and then for life,*
> *She's—what I dare not name.*

Peach.   Look ye, wife.   A handsome wench in our way of business, is as profitable as at the bar of a *Temple* coffee-house, who looks upon it as her livelihood to grant every liberty but one.   You see I would indulge the girl as far as prudently we can.   In any thing, but marriage ! after that, my dear, how shall we be safe ?   are we not then in her husband's power ?   for a husband hath the absolute power over all a wife's secrets but her own.   If the girl had the discretion of a court lady, who can have a dozen young fellows at her ear without complying with one, I should not matter it ; but *Polly* is tinder, and a spark will at once set her on a flame.   Married ! If the wench does not know her own profit, sure she knows her own pleasure better than to make herself a property !   My daughter to me should be, like a court lady to a minister of state, a key to the whole gang.   Married !   If the affair is not already done, I'll terrify her from it, by the example of our neighbours.   76

Mrs. *Peach.*   May-hap, my dear, you may injure the girl.   She loves to imitate the fine ladies, and she may only allow the Captain liberties in the view of interest.

Peach. But 'tis your duty, my dear, to warn the girl against her ruin, and to instruct her how to make the most of her beauty. I'll go to her this moment, and sift her. In the mean time, wife, rip out the coronets and marks of these dozen of cambric handkerchiefs, for I can dispose of them this afternoon to a chap in the city.

SCENE V.

Mrs. *PEACHUM.*

Never was a man more out of the way in an argument, than my husband ! Why must our *Polly*, forsooth, differ from her sex, and love only her husband ? And why must our *Polly*'s marriage, contrary to all observation, make her the less followed by other men ? All men are thieves in love, and like a woman the better for being another's property.

AIR V. Of all the simple things we do, *&c.*

> *A Maid is like the golden oar,*
> *Which hath guineas intrinsical in't,*
> *Whose worth is never known, before*
> *It is try'd and imprest in the mint.*
> *A Wife 's like a guinea in gold,*   10
> *Stampt with the name of her spouse ;*
>   *Now here, now there ; is bought, or is sold ;*
> *And is current in every house.*

SCENE VI.

Mrs. *PEACHUM, FILCH.*

Mrs. *Peach.* Come hither, *Filch.* I am as fond of this child, as though my mind misgave me he were my own. He hath as fine a hand at picking a pocket as a woman, and is as nimble-finger'd as a juggler. If an unlucky session does not cut the rope of thy life, I pronounce, boy, thou wilt be a great man in history. Where was your post last night, my boy ?

Filch. I ply'd at the Opera, madam ; and considering 'twas neither dark nor rainy, so that there was no great hurry in getting chairs and coaches, made a tolerable hand on't. These seven handkerchiefs, madam.

Mrs. *Peach.* Colour'd ones, I see. They are of sure sale from our ware-house at *Redriff* among the sea-men.   10

Filch. And this snuff-box.

Mrs. *Peach.* Set in gold ! A pretty encouragement this to a young beginner.

Filch. I had a fair tug at a charming gold watch. Pox take the Taylors for making the fobs so deep and narrow ! It stuck by the way, and I was forc'd to make my escape under a coach. Really, madam, I fear I shall be cut off in the flower of my youth, so that every now and then (since I was pumpt) I have thoughts of taking up and going to Sea.   17

Mrs. *Peach.* You should go to *Hockley in the hole*, and to *Marybone*, child,

to learn valour. These are the schools that have bred so many brave men.
I thought, boy, by this time, thou hadst lost fear as well as shame. Poor lad !
how little does he know yet of the *Old-Baily !* For the first fact I'll ensure
thee from being hang'd ; and going to Sea, *Filch,* will come time enough upon
a sentence of transportation. But now, since you have nothing better to do,
ev'n go to your book, and learn your catechism ; for really a man makes but
an ill figure in the Ordinary's paper, who cannot give a satisfactory answer
to his questions. But, hark you, my lad, Don't tell me a lye ; for you know
I hate a lyar. Do you know of any thing that hath past between captain
Macheath and our *Polly?*   28

Filch. I beg you, Madam, don't ask me : for I must either tell a lye to
you or to Miss *Polly ;* for I promis'd her I would not tell.

Mrs. *Peach.* But when the honour of our family is concern'd—

Filch. I shall lead a sad life with Miss *Polly,* if ever she come to know that
I told you. Besides, I would not willingly forfeit my own honour by betraying
any body.

Mrs. *Peach.* Yonder comes my husband and *Polly.* Come *Filch,* you shall
go with me into my own room, and tell me the whole story. I'll give thee
a glass of a most delicious cordial that I keep for my own drinking.

S C E N E   V I I.

P E A C H U M,   P O L L Y.

Polly. I know as well as any of the fine ladies how to make the most of
my self and of my man too. A woman knows how to be mercenary, though
she hath never been in a court or at an assembly. We have it in our natures,
papa. If I allow captain *Macheath* some trifling liberties, I have this watch
and other visible marks of his favour to show for it. A girl who cannot grant
some things, and refuse what is most material, will make a poor hand of her
beauty, and soon be thrown upon the common.

A I R   V I.   What shall I do to show how much I love her ?

> *Virgins are like the fair flower in its lustre,*
> *Which in the garden enamels the ground ;*
> *Near it the Bees in play flutter and cluster,*   10
> *And gaudy Butterflies frolick around.*
> *But, when once pluck'd, 'tis no longer alluring,*
> *To* Covent-garden *'tis sent, (as yet sweet,)*
> *There fades, and shrinks, and grows past all enduring,*
> *Rots, stinks, and dies, and is trod under feet.*

Peach. You know, *Polly,* I am not against your toying and trifling with
a customer in the way of business, or to get out a secret, or so. But if I find
out that you have play'd the fool and are married, you jade you, I'll cut
your throat, hussy. Now you know my mind.

SCENE VIII.

PEACHUM, POLLY, Mrs. PEACHUM.

AIR VII. Oh *London* is a fine Town.

Mrs. Peachum, [*in a very great passion.*]

Our Polly *is a sad slut! nor heeds what we have taught her.*
I wonder any man alive will ever rear a daughter!
For she must have both hoods and gowns, and hoops to swell her pride,
With scarfs and stays, and gloves and lace; and she will have men beside;
And when she's drest with care and cost, all-tempting, fine and gay,
As men should serve a Cowcumber, she flings herself away.

You baggage! you hussy! you inconsiderate jade! had you been hang'd,
it would not have vex'd me, for that might have been your misfortune; but
to do such a mad thing by choice! The wench is married, husband.   9

Peach. Married? the Captain is a bold man, and will risque any thing for
money; to be sure he believes her a fortune. Do you think your mother and
I should have liv'd comfortably so long together, if ever we had been married?
Baggage!

Mrs. Peach. I knew she was always a proud slut; and now the wench
hath play'd the fool and married, because forsooth she would do like the
Gentry. Can you support the expence of a husband, hussy, in gaming,
drinking and whoring? have you money enough to carry on the daily
quarrels of man and wife about who shall squander most? There are not
many husbands and wives, who can bear the charges of plaguing one another
in a handsome way. If you must be married, could you introduce no-body
into our family, but a highwayman! Why, thou foolish jade, thou wilt be
as ill us'd, and as much neglected, as if thou hadst married a Lord!   22

Peach. Let not your anger, my dear, break through the rules of decency,
for the Captain looks upon himself in the military capacity, as a gentleman
by his profession. Besides what he hath already, I know he is in a fair way
of getting, or of dying; and both these ways, let me tell you, are most
excellent chances for a wife. Tell me hussy, are you ruin'd, or no?

Mrs. Peach. With *Polly*'s fortune, she might very well have gone off to
a person of distinction. Yes, that you might, you pouting slut!   29

Peach. What, is the wench dumb! Speak, or I'll make you plead by
squeezing out an answer from you. Are you really bound wife to him, or
are you only upon liking?   [*Pinches her.*

Polly. Oh!   [*Screaming.*

Mrs. Peach. How the mother is to be pitied who hath handsome daughters!
Locks, bolts, bars, and lectures of morality are nothing to them: they break
through them all. They have as much pleasure in cheating a father and
mother, as in cheating at cards.

Peach. Why, *Polly*, I shall soon know if you are married, by *Macheath*'s
keeping from our house.   39

6 So B. A add: *Our* Polly *is a sad Slut*, &c.

AIR VIII. Grim King of the Ghosts, &c.

Polly.

Can Love be controul'd by advice?
Will Cupid our mothers obey?
Though my heart were as frozen as Ice,
  At his flame 'twould have melted away.
When he kist me so closely he prest,
  'Twas so sweet, that I must have comply'd:
So I thought it both safest and best
  To marry, for fear you should chide.

Mrs. Peach. Then all the hopes of our family are gone for ever and ever !
Peach. And *Macheath* may hang his father and mother-in-law, in hope to
get into their daughter's fortune.   50
Polly. I did not marry him (as 'tis the fashion) cooly and deliberately for
honour or money. But, I love him.
Mrs. Peach. Love him ! worse and worse ! I thought the girl had been
better bred. Oh husband, husband ! her folly makes me mad ! my head
swims ! I'm distracted ! I can't support myself—Oh !   [*Faints.*
Peach. See, wench, to what a condition you have reduced your poor
mother ! a glass of cordial, this instant. How the poor woman takes it to
heart !   [Polly *goes out, and returns with it.*
Ah, hussy, now this is the only comfort your mother has left !
Polly. Give her another glass, Sir ; my Mamma drinks double the quantity
whenever she is out of order. This, you see, fetches her.   61
Mrs. Peach. The girl shows such a readiness, and so much concern, that
I could almost find in my heart to forgive her.

AIR IX. O *Jenny*, O *Jenny*, where hast thou been.

O Polly, you might have toy'd and kist.
By keeping men off, you keep them on.

Polly.
          But he so teaz'd me,
          And he so pleas'd me,
What I did, you must have done.

Mrs. Peach. Not with a highway-man.——You sorry slut !   69
Peach. A word with you, wife. 'Tis no new thing for a wench to take
man without consent of Parents. You know 'tis the frailty of woman, my dear.
Mrs. Peach. Yes, indeed, the sex is frail. But the first time a woman is
frail, she should be somewhat nice methinks, for then or never is the time to
make her fortune. After that, she hath nothing to do but to guard herself
from being found out, and she may do what she pleases.
Peach. Make your self a little easy ; I have a thought shall soon set all
matters again to rights. Why so melancholy, *Polly?* since what is done
cannot be undone, we must all endeavour to make the best of it.
Mrs. Peach. Well, *Polly* ; as far as one woman can forgive another, I
forgive thee.—Your father is too fond of you, hussy.   80
Polly. Then all my sorrows are at an end.

40–47 *So B.   A divide into two quatrains.*
49 hope] hopes *Bell, Plays 1760, Dick.*

Mrs. *Peach.* A mighty likely speech, in troth, for a wench who is just married !

AIR X. *Thomas, I cannot, &c.*

Polly.
I, like a ship in storms, was tost :
Yet afraid to put into Land ;
For seiz'd in the port the vessel's lost,
Whose treasure is contreband.
The waves are laid,
My duty's paid.
O joy beyond expression !   90
Thus, safe a-shore,
I ask no more,
My all is in my possession.

Peach. I hear customers in t'other room ; go, talk with 'em, *Polly* ; but come to us again, as soon as they are gone.—But, heark ye, child, if 'tis the gentleman who was here yesterday about the repeating watch, say, you believe we can't get intelligence of it, till to-morrow. For I lent it to *Suky Straddle*, to make a figure with to-night at a tavern in *Drury-Lane*. If t'other gentleman calls for the silver-hilted sword ; you know beetle-brow'd *Jemmy* hath it on, and he doth not come from *Tunbridge* till *Tuesday* night ; so that it cannot be had till then.

SCENE IX.

PEACHUM, Mrs. PEACHUM.

Peach. Dear wife, be a little pacified. Don't let your passion run away with your senses. *Polly*, I grant you, hath done a rash thing.

Mrs. *Peach.* If she had had only an intrigue with the fellow, why the very best families have excus'd and huddled up a frailty of that sort. 'Tis marriage, husband, that makes it a blemish.

Peach. But money, wife, is the true fuller's earth for reputations, there is not a spot or a stain but what it can take out. A rich rogue now-a-days is fit company for any gentleman ; and the world, my dear, hath not such a contempt for roguery as you imagine. I tell you, wife, I can make this match turn to our advantage.   10

Mrs. *Peach.* I am very sensible husband, that captain *Macheath* is worth money, but I am in doubt whether he hath not two or three wives already, and then if he should die in a Session or two, *Polly*'s dower would come into dispute.

Peach. That, indeed, is a point which ought to be consider'd.

AIR XI. A Soldier and a Sailor.

A Fox may steal your hens, sir,
A whore your health and pence, sir,
Your daughter rob your chest, sir,
Your wife may steal your rest, sir,
A thief your goods and plate.   20

> *But this is all but picking,*
> *With rest, pence, chest and chicken ;*
> *It ever was decreed, sir,*
> *If Lawyer's hand is fee'd, sir,*
> *He steals your whole estate.*

The Lawyers are bitter enemies to those in our way. They don't care that any body should get a clandestine livelihood but themselves.

SCENE X.

Mrs. *P E A C H U M, P E A C H U M, P O L L Y.*

Polly. 'Twas only Nimming *Ned*. He brought in a damask window-curtain, a hoop-petticoat, a pair of silver candlesticks, a perriwig, and one silk stocking, from the fire that happen'd last night.

Peach. There is not a fellow that is cleverer in his way, and saves more goods out of the fire than *Ned*. But now, *Polly*, to your affair ; for matters must not be left as they are. You are married then, it seems ?

Polly. Yes, Sir.

Peach. And how do you propose to live, child ?

Polly. Like other women, Sir, upon the industry of my husband.   9

Mrs. Peach. What, is the wench turn'd fool ? A highway-man's wife, like a soldier's, hath as little of his pay, as of his company.

Peach. And had not you the common views of a gentlewoman in your marriage, *Polly ?*

Polly. I don't know what you mean, Sir.

Peach. Of a jointure, and of being a widow.

Polly. But I love him, Sir : how then could I have thoughts of parting with him ?   16

Peach. Parting with him ! Why, that is the whole scheme and intention of all Marriage-articles. The comfortable estate of widowhood, is the only hope that keeps up a wife's spirits. Where is the woman who would scruple to be a wife, if she had it in her power to be a widow whenever she pleas'd ? If you have any views of this sort, *Polly*, I shall think the match not so very unreasonable.

Polly. How I dread to hear your advice ! Yet I must beg you to explain yourself.   24

Peach. Secure what he hath got, have him peach'd the next Sessions, and then at once you are made a rich widow.

Polly. What, murder the man I love ! The blood runs cold at my heart with the very thought of it.

Peach. Fye, *Polly !* what hath murder to do in the affair ? Since the thing sooner or later must happen, I dare say, the Captain himself would like that we should get the reward for his death sooner than a stranger. Why, *Polly*, the Captain knows, that as 'tis his employment to rob, so 'tis ours to take Robbers ; every man in his business. So that there is no malice in the case.   34

Mrs. Peach. Ay, husband, now you have nick'd the matter. To have him peach'd is the only thing could ever make me forgive her.

　　　　A I R　X I I.　Now ponder well, ye parents dear.

Polly.　　　　　*Oh, ponder well! be not severe;*
　　　　　　　　So save a wretched wife!
　　　　　　　　For on the rope that hangs my dear
　　　　　　　　Depends poor Polly's life.　　　　40

Mrs. Peach. But your duty to your parents, hussy, obliges you to hang him. What would many a wife give for such an opportunity!

Polly. What is a jointure, what is widow-hood to me? I know my heart. I cannot survive him.

　　　　A I R　X I I I.　Le printemps rappelle aux armes.

　　　　The Turtle thus with plaintive crying,
　　　　Her lover dying,
　　　　The turtle thus with plaintive crying
　　　　Laments her Dove.
　　　　Down she drops quite spent with sighing,
　　　　Pair'd in death, as pair'd in love.　　　　50

Thus, Sir, it will happen to your poor *Polly.*

Mrs. Peach. What, is the fool in love in earnest then? I hate thee for being particular: Why, wench, thou art a shame to thy very Sex.

Polly. But hear me, mother.—If you ever lov'd—

Mrs. Peach. Those cursed Play-books she reads have been her ruin. One word more, hussy, and I shall knock your brains out, if you have any.

Peach. Keep out of the way, *Polly*, for fear of mischief, and consider of what is propos'd to you.

Mrs. Peach. Away, hussy. Hang your husband, and be dutiful.

　　　49 *sighing,*] *sighing* 1729.

S C E N E　X I.

Mrs. *P E A C H U M, P E A C H U M.*

　　　　　　　　　　　　　　[Polly *listning.*

Mrs. Peach. The thing, husband, must and shall be done. For the sake of intelligence we must take other measures, and have him peach'd the next Session without her consent. If she will not know her duty, we know ours.

Peach. But really, my dear, it grieves one's heart to take off a great man. When I consider his personal bravery, his fine stratagem, how much we have already got by him, and how much more we may get, methinks I can't find in my heart to have a hand in his death. I wish you could have made *Polly* undertake it.

Mrs. Peach. But in a case of necessity—our own lives are in danger.　　9

Peach. Then, indeed, we must comply with the customs of the world, and make gratitude give way to interest.—He shall be taken off.

Mrs. Peach. I'll undertake to manage *Polly.*

Peach. And I'll prepare matters for the *Old-Baily.*

SCENE XII.

POLLY.

Now I'm a wretch, indeed.—Methinks I see him already in the cart, sweeter and more lovely than the nosegay in his hand !—I hear the crowd extolling his resolution and intrepidity !—What vollies of sighs are sent from the windows of *Holborn*, that so comely a youth should be brought to disgrace !— I see him at the tree ! the whole Circle are in tears !—even Butchers weep !—— *Jack Ketch* himself hesitates to perform his duty, and would be glad to lose his fee, by a reprieve. What then will become of *Polly* !—As yet I may inform him of their design, and aid him in his escape.—It shall be so.—But then he flies, absents himself, and I bar my self from his dear, dear conversation ! that too will distract me.—If he keeps out of the way, my Papa and Mama may in time relent, and we may be happy.—If he stays, he is hang'd, and then he is lost for ever !—He intended to lye conceal'd in my room, 'till the dusk of the evening : If they are abroad I'll this instant let him out, lest some accident should prevent him.   [*Exit, and returns.*

SCENE XIII.

POLLY, MACHEATH.

AIR XIV. Pretty Parrot, say, *&c.*

Mach.   *Pretty* Polly, *say,*
                         When I was away,
                         Did your fancy never stray
                         To some newer lover ?
Polly.   *Without disguise,*
                         Heaving sighs,
                         Doating eyes,
                         My constant heart discover.
                         Fondly let me loll !
Mach.   *O pretty, pretty* Poll.   10

Polly. And are *you* as fond as ever, my dear ?
Mach. Suspect my honour, my courage, suspect any thing but my love.— May my pistols miss fire, and my mare slip her shoulder while I am pursu'd, if I ever forsake thee !
Polly. Nay, my dear, I have no reason to doubt you, for I find in the Romance you lent me, none of the great Heroes were ever false in love.

9 *Fondly let me loll !*] given to Macheath by *Plays 1760, and Underhill.*
11 And are *you* etc.] And are you as fond of me as ever, my dear ? *Bell, Dick. Plays 1760 has* you *but not of* me.

AIR XV. Pray, fair one, be kind.

Mach.

> *My heart was so free,*
> *It rov'd like the Bee,*
> *'Till Polly my passion requited;*
> *I sipt each flower,*   20
> *I chang'd ev'ry hour,*
> *But here ev'ry flower is united.*

Polly. Were you sentenc'd to Transportation, sure, my dear, you could not leave me behind you——could you?

Mach. Is there any power, any force that could tear me from thee? You might sooner tear a pension out of the hands of a Courtier, a fee from a Lawyer, a pretty woman from a looking-glass, or any woman from *Quadrille.*—But to tear me from thee is impossible!

AIR XVI. Over the hills and far away.

> *Were I laid on Greenland's coast,*
> *And in my arms embrac'd my lass;*   30
> *Warm amidst eternal frost,*
> *Too soon the half year's night would pass.*

Polly.

> *Were I sold on Indian soil.*
> *Soon as the burning day was clos'd,*
> *I could mock the sultry toil,*
> *When on my charmer's breast repos'd.*

Mach.   *And I would love you all the day,*
Polly.   *Every night would kiss and play,*
Mach.   *If with me you'd fondly stray*
Polly.   *Over the hills and far away.*   40

Polly. Yes, I would go with thee. But oh!——how shall I speak it? I must be torn from thee. We must part.

Mach. How! Part!

Polly. We must, we must.—My Papa and Mama are set against thy life. They now, even now are in search after thee. They are preparing evidence against thee. Thy life depends upon a moment.

AIR XVII. Gin thou wert mine awn thing.

> *O what pain it is to part!*
> *Can I leave thee, can I leave thee?*
> *O what pain it is to part!*
> *Can thy Polly ever leave thee?*   50
> *But lest death my love should thwart,*
> *And bring thee to the fatal cart,*
> *Thus I tear thee from my bleeding heart!*
> *Fly hence, and let me leave thee.*

One kiss and then—one kiss—begone—farewell.

Mach. My hand, my heart, my dear, is so riveted to thine, that I cannot unloose my hold.

Polly. But my Papa may intercept thee, and then I should lose the very glimmering of hope. A few weeks, perhaps, may reconcile us all. Shall thy *Polly* hear from thee ?   60
Mach. Must I then go ?
Polly. And will not absence change your love ?
Mach. If you doubt it, let me stay——and be hang'd.
Polly. O how I fear ! how I tremble !—Go—but when safety will give you leave, you will be sure to see me again ; for 'till then *Polly* is wretched.

AIR XVIII. O the broom, &c.

Mach.
> *The Miser thus a shilling sees,*
> *Which he's oblig'd to pay,*
> *With sighs resigns it by degrees.*
> *And fears 'tis gone for aye.*

[Parting, and looking back at each other with fondness ; he at one door, she at the other.

Polly.
> *The Boy thus, when his Sparrow's flown,*
> *The bird in silence eyes ;*
> *But soon as out of sight 'tis gone,*
> *Whines, whimpers, sobs and cries.*   70

ACT II. Scene I.

A Tavern near Newgate.

Jemmy Twitcher, *Crook-finger'd* Jack, Wat Dreary, Robin *of* Bagshot, Nimming Ned, Henry Padington, Matt *of the* Mint, Ben Budge, *and the rest of the Gang, at the Table, with Wine, Brandy and Tobacco.*

Ben.

But pr'ythee, *Matt*, what is become of thy brother *Tom ?* I have not seen him since my return from transportation.
Matt. Poor brother *Tom* had an accident this time twelvemonth, and so clever a made fellow he was, that I could not save him from those fleaing rascals the Surgeons ; and now, poor man, he is among the Otamys at *Surgeon's Hall.*
Ben. So it seems, his time was come.
Jem. But the present time is ours, and no body alive hath more. Why are the laws levell'd at us ? are we more dishonest than the rest of mankind ? what we win, gentlemen, is our own by the law of arms, and the right of conquest.
Crook. Where shall we find such another set of practical philosophers, who to a man are above the fear of Death ?   13
Wat. Sound men, and true !
Robin. Of try'd courage, and indefatigable industry !
Ned. Who is there here that would not dye for his friend ?
Harry. Who is there here that would betray him for his interest ?
Matt. Show me a gang of Courtiers that can say as much.

Ben. We are for a just partition of the world, for every man hath a right to enjoy life.   20

Matt. We retrench the superfluities of mankind. The world is avaritious, and I hate avarice. A covetous fellow, like a Jack-daw, steals what he was never made to enjoy, for the sake of hiding it. These are the robbers of mankind, for money was made for the free-hearted and generous, and where is the injury of taking from another, what he hath not the heart to make use of ?

Jem. Our several stations for the day are fixt. Good luck attend us all. Fill the glasses.

AIR XIX. Fill ev'ry glass, *&c.*

Matt.

> *Fill ev'ry glass, for wine inspires us,*
> > *And fires us*   30
> *With courage, love and joy.*
> *Women and wine should life employ.*
> *Is there ought else on earth desirous ?*

Chorus.

> *Fill ev'ry glass, &c.*

SCENE II.

To them enter MACHEATH.

Mach. Gentlemen, well met. My heart hath been with you this hour ; but an unexpected affair hath detain'd me. No ceremony, I beg you.

Matt. We were just breaking up to go upon duty. Am I to have the honour of taking the air with you, Sir, this evening upon the Heath ? I drink a dram now and then with the Stage-coachmen in the way of friendship and intelligence ; and I know that about this time there will be passengers upon the western road, who are worth speaking with.

Mach. I was to have been of that party—but——

Matt. But what, Sir ?

Mach. Is there any man who suspects my courage ?   10

Matt. We have all been witnesses of it.

Mach. My honour and truth to the gang ?

Matt. I'll be answerable for it.

Mach. In the division of our booty, have I ever shown the least marks of avarice or injustice ?

Matt. By these questions something seems to have ruffled you. Are any of us suspected ?

Mach. I have a fixt confidence, gentlemen, in you all, as men of honour, and as such I value and respect you. *Peachum* is a man that is useful to us.

Matt. Is he about to play us any foul play ? I'll shoot him through the head.   21

Mach. I beg you, gentlemen, act with conduct and discretion. A pistol is your last resort.

Matt. He knows nothing of this meeting.

15 injustice ?] injustice ! *1729.*

Mach. Business cannot go on without him. He is a man who knows the world, and is a necessary agent to us. We have had a slight difference, and till it is accommodated I shall be oblig'd to keep out of his way. Any private dispute of mine shall be of no ill consequence to my friends. You must continue to act under his direction, for the moment we break loose from him, our gang is ruin'd.   30

Matt. As a bawd to a whore, I grant you he is to us of great convenience.

Mach. Make him believe I have quitted the gang, which I can never do but with life. At our private quarters I will continue to meet you. A week or so will probably reconcile us.

Matt. Your instructions shall be observ'd. 'Tis now high time for us to repair to our several duties ; so till the evening, at our quarters in *Moor-fields*, we bid you farewell.

Mach. I shall wish my self with you. Success attend you.
                                                   [*Sits down melancholy at the Table.*

A I R X X.   March in *Rinaldo*, with Drums and Trumpets.

Matt.   *Let us take the road.*
                         Hark ! I hear the sound of coaches !   40
                         The hour of attack approaches,
                         To your arms, brave boys, and load.
                         See the ball I hold !
                         Let the Chymists toil like asses,
                         Our fire their fire surpasses,
                         And turns all our lead to gold.

[The Gang rang'd in the front of the Stage, load their pistols, and stick them under their girdles ; then go off singing the first part in Chorus.

SCENE III.

M A C H E A T H, D R A W E R.

Mach. What a fool is a fond wench ! *Polly* is most confoundedly bit.——
I love the sex. And a man who loves money, might as well be contented with one guinea, as I with one woman. The town perhaps hath been as much oblig'd to me, for recruiting it with free-hearted ladies, as to any recruiting Officer in the army. If it were not for us and the other gentlemen of the sword, *Drury-lane* would be uninhabited.

A I R X X I.   Would you have a young Virgin, *&c.*

                   If the heart of a man is deprest with cares,
                   The mist is dispell'd when a woman appears ;
                   Like the notes of a fiddle, she sweetly, sweetly
                   Raises the spirits, and charms our ears.   10
                       Roses and lillies her cheeks disclose,
                       But her ripe lips are more sweet than those.

> *Press her,*
> *Caress her,*
> *With blisses,*
> *Her kisses*
> *Dissolve us in pleasure, and soft repose.*

I must have women. There is nothing unbends the mind like them. Money is not so strong a cordial for the time.——Drawer.——[*Enter Drawer.*] Is the Porter gone for all the ladies, according to my directions ?   20

Draw. I expect him back every minute. But you know, Sir, you sent him as far as *Hockley in the Hole*, for three of the ladies, for one in *Vinegar Yard*, and for the rest of them somewhere about *Lewkner's Lane.* Sure some of them are below, for I hear the barr bell. As they come I will show them up.——Coming, coming.

SCENE IV.

Macheath, *Mrs.* Coaxer, Dolly Trull, *Mrs.* Vixen, Betty Doxy, Jenny Diver, *Mrs.* Slammekin, Suky Tawdry, *and* Molly Brazen.

Mach. Dear Mrs. *Coaxer*, you are welcome. You look charmingly to-day. I hope you don't want the repairs of quality, and lay on paint.——*Dolly Troll !* kiss me, you slut ; are you as amorous as ever, hussy ? You are always so taken up with stealing hearts, that you don't allow your self time to steal any thing else.—Ah *Dolly*, thou wilt ever be a Coquette !——Mrs. *Vixen*, I'm yours, I always lov'd a woman of wit and spirit ; they make charming mistresses, but plaguy wives.——*Betty Doxy !* come hither, hussy. Do you drink as hard as ever ? You had better stick to good wholesome beer ; for in troth, *Betty*, strong-waters will in time ruin your constitution. You should leave those to your betters.——What ! and my pretty *Jenny Diver* too ! As prim and demure as ever ! There is not any Prude, though ever so high bred, hath a more sanctify'd look, with a more mischievous heart. Ah ! thou art a dear artful hypocrite.——Mrs. *Slammekin !* as careless and genteel as ever ! all you fine ladies, who know your own beauty, affect an undress.—— But see, here's *Suky Tawdry* come to contradict what I was saying. Every thing she gets one way she lays out upon her back. Why, *Suky*, you must keep at least a dozen Tally-men. *Molly Brazen !* [*She kisses him.*] That's well done. I love a free-hearted wench. Thou hast a most agreeable assurance, girl, and art as willing as a Turtle.——But hark ! I hear musick. The Harper is at the door: *If musick be the food of Love, play on.* E'er you seat your selves, ladies, what think you of a dance ? Come in. [*Enter Harper.*] Play the *French* Tune, that Mrs. *Slammekin* was so fond of.   22

[*A Dance* à la ronde *in the* French *manner ; near the end of it this Song and Chorus.*

A I R X X I I. Cotillon.

> *Youth's the season made for joys,*
> *Love is then our duty ;*
> *She alone who that employs,*
> *Well deserves her beauty.*

Let's be gay,
While we may,
Beauty's a flower despis'd in decay.

Chorus.   *Youth's the season, &c.*   30

Let us drink and sport to-day,
Ours is not to-morrow.
Love with youth flies swift away,
Age is nought but sorrow.
Dance and sing,
Time's on the wing,
Life never knows the return of spring.

Chorus.   *Let us drink, &c.*

Mach. Now pray ladies, take your places. Here Fellow, [*Pays the Harper.*]
Bid the Drawer bring us more wine. [*Ex. Harper.*] If any of the ladies
chuse gin, I hope they will be so free to call for it.   41

Jenny. You look as if you meant me. Wine is strong enough for me.
Indeed, Sir, I never drink strong-waters, but when I have the Cholic.

Mach. Just the excuse of the fine ladies ! Why, a lady of quality is never
without the Cholic. I hope, Mrs. *Coaxer*, you have had good success of late in
your visits among the Mercers.

Coax. We have so many interlopers——Yet with industry, one may still
have a little picking. I carried a silver-flower'd lutestring and a piece of black
padesoy to Mr. *Peachum*'s Lock but last week.

Vix. There's *Molly Brazen* hath the ogle of a Rattlesnake. She rivitted
a Linnen-draper's eye so fast upon her, that he was nick'd of three pieces of
cambric before he could look off.   52

Braz. O dear madam !——But sure nothing can come up to your handling
of laces ! And then you have such a sweet deluding tongue ! To cheat a man
is nothing ; but the woman must have fine parts indeed who cheats a woman !

Vix. Lace, madam, lyes in a small compass, and is of easy conveyance.
But you are apt, madam, to think too well of your friends.

Coax. If any woman hath more art than another, to be sure, 'tis *Jenny
Diver.* Though her fellow be never so agreeable, she can pick his pocket as
cooly, as if money were her only pleasure. Now that is a command of the
passions uncommon in a woman !   61

Jenny. I never go to the tavern with a man, but in the view of business.
I have other hours, and other sort of men for my pleasure. But had I your
address, madam———

Mach. Have done with your compliments, ladies ; and drink about :
You are not so fond of me, *Jenny*, as you use to be.

Jenny. 'Tis not convenient, Sir, to show my fondness among so many
rivals. 'Tis your own choice, and not the warmth of my inclination, that will
determine you.

A I R X X I I I. All in a misty morning.

Before the barn-door crowing,   70
The Cock by Hens attended,
His eyes around him throwing,
Stands for a while suspended:

Then one he singles from the crew,
And cheers the happy Hen;
With how do you do, and how do you do,
And how do you do again.

Mach. Ah *Jenny!* thou art a dear slut.

Trull. Pray, madam, were you ever in keeping?

Tawd. I hope, madam, I ha'nt been so long upon the town, but I have met with some good fortune as well as my neighbours.   81

Trull. Pardon me, madam, I meant no harm by the question; 'twas only in the way of conversation.

Tawd. Indeed, madam, if I had not been a fool, I might have liv'd very handsomely with my last friend. But upon his missing five guineas, he turn'd me off. Now I never suspected he had counted them.

Slam. Who do you look upon, madam, as your best sort of keepers?

Trull. That, madam, is thereafter as they be.

Slam. I, madam, was once kept by a *Jew*; and, bating their religion, to women they are a good sort of people.   90

Tawd. Now for my part, I own I like an old fellow: for we always make them pay for what they can't do.

Vix. A spruce Prentice, let me tell you, ladies, is no ill thing, they bleed freely. I have sent at least two or three dozen of them, in my time, to the Plantations.

Jenny. But to be sure, Sir, with so much good fortune as you have had upon the road, you must be grown immensely rich.

Mach. The road, indeed, hath done me justice, but the gaming-table hath been my ruin.

A I R   X X I V.   When once I lay with another man's wife.

Jen.   *The Gamesters and Lawyers are jugglers alike,*   100
If they meddle your all is in danger:
Like Gypsies, if once they can finger a souse,
Your pockets they pick, and they pilfer your house,
And give your estate to a stranger.

A man of courage should never put any thing to the risque, but his life. These are the tools of a man of honour. Cards and Dice are only fit for cowardly cheats, who prey upon their friends.   107

[*She takes up his Pistol.* Tawdry *takes up the other.*

Tawd. This, Sir, is fitter for your hand. Besides your loss of money, 'tis a loss to the ladies. Gaming takes you off from women. How fond could I be of you! but before company, 'tis ill bred.

Mach. Wanton hussies!

Jen. I must and will have a kiss to give my wine a zest.

[*They take him about the neck, and make signs to* Peachum *and Constables*; *who rush in upon him.*

105 A man of courage . . . life. *This sentence occurs in the 2nd and subsequent editions: it is not given in 1728* [1] *and* [2].

SCENE V.

To them P E A C H U M and Constables.

Peach. I seize you, Sir, as my prisoner.——

Mach. Was this well done, *Jenny?*——Women are decoy Ducks ; who can trust them ! Beasts, Jades, Jilts, Harpies, Furies, Whores !

Peach. Your case, Mr. *Machecth*, is not particular. The greatest Heroes have been ruin'd by women. But, to do them justice, I must own they are a pretty sort of creatures, if we could trust them. You must now, Sir, take your leave of the ladies, and if they have a mind to make you a visit, they will be sure to find you at home. The gentleman, ladies, lodges in *Newgate.* Constables, wait upon the Captain to his lodgings.

AIR XXV.   When first I laid siege to my *Chloris.*

Mach.   *At the Tree I shall suffer with pleasure,*   10
          At the Tree I shall suffer with pleasure,
             Let me go where I will,
             In all kinds of ill,
          I shall find no such Furies as these are.

Peach. Ladies, I'll take care the reckoning shall be discharg'd.

          [*Exit* Macheath, *guarded with* Peachum *and Constables.*

SCENE VI.

The Women remain.

Vix. Look ye, Mrs. *Jenny*, though Mr. *Peachum* may have made a private bargain with you and *Suky Tawdry* for betraying the Captain, as we were all assisting, we ought all to share alike.

Coax. I think, Mr. *Peachum*, after so long an acquaintance, might have trusted me as well as *Jenny Diver.*

Slam. I am sure at least three men of his hanging, and in a year's time too, (if he did me justice) should be set down to my account.

Trull. Mrs. *Slammekin*, that is not fair. For you know one of them was taken in bed with me.   9

Jenny. As far as a bowl of punch or a treat, I believe Mrs. *Suky* will join with me.——As for any thing else, ladies, you cannot in conscience expect it.

Slam. Dear madam——

Trull. I would not for the world——

Slam. 'Tis impossible for me——

Trull. As I hope to be sav'd, madam——

Slam. Nay, then I must stay here all night——

Trull. Since you command me.   [*Exeunt with great Ceremony.*

S C E N E   V I I.   *Newgate.*

L O C K I T, Turnkeys, M A C H E A T H, Constables.

Lock. Noble Captain, you are welcome.   You have not been a lodger of mine this year and half.   You know the custom, Sir.   Garnish, Captain, garnish.   Hand me down those fetters there.

Mach. Those, Mr. *Lockit*, seem to be the heaviest of the whole set.   With your leave, I should like the further pair better.

Lock. Look ye, Captain, we know what is fittest for our prisoners.   When a gentleman uses me with civility, I always do the best I can to please him— Hand them down I say—We have them of all prices, from one guinea to ten, and 'tis fitting every gentleman should please himself.   9

Mach. I understand you, Sir.   [*Gives money.*]   The fees here are so many, and so exorbitant, that few fortunes can bear the expence of getting off handsomly, or of dying like a gentleman.

Lock. Those, I see, will fit the Captain better.——Take down the further pair.   Do but examine them, Sir—Never was better work.——How genteely they are made!——They will fit as easy as a glove, and the nicest man in *England* might not be asham'd to wear them.   [*He puts on the chains.*]   If I had the best gentleman in the land in my custody I could not equip him more handsomly.   And so, Sir—I now leave you to your private meditations.

S C E N E   V I I I.

M A C H E A T H.

A I R   X X V I.   Courtiers, courtiers think it no harm.

> *Man may escape from rope and gun ;*
> *Nay, some have out-liv'd the Doctor's pill :*
> *Who takes a woman must be undone,*
> *That Basilisk is sure to kill.*
> *The Fly that sips treacle is lost in the sweets,*
> *So he that tastes woman, woman, woman,*
> *He that tastes woman, ruin meets.*

To what a woful plight have I brought my self!   Here must I (all day long, 'till I am hang'd) be confin'd to hear the reproaches of a wench who lays her ruin at my door.——I am in the custody of her father, and to be sure if he knows of the matter, I shall have a fine time on't betwixt this and my execution.——But I promis'd the wench marriage.——What signifies a promise to a woman ?   does not man in marriage itself promise a hundred things that he never means to perform ?   Do all we can, women will believe us ; for they look upon a promise as an excuse for following their own inclinations.—— But here comes *Lucy*, and I cannot get from her——wou'd I were deaf!

SCENE IX.

MACHEATH, LUCY.

Lucy. You base man, you,——how can you look me in the face after what hath past between us ?——See here, perfidious wretch, how I am forc'd to bear about the load of Infamy you have laid upon me——O *Macheath !* thou hast robb'd me of my quiet——to see thee tortur'd would give me pleasure.

AIR XXVII. A lovely Lass to a Friar came.

> *Thus when a good huswife sees a Rat*
> *In her trap in the morning taken,*
> *With pleasure her heart goes pit a pat,*
> *In revenge for her loss of bacon.*
>   *Then she throws him*   10
>   *To the Dog or Cat,*
> *To be worried, crush'd and shaken.*

Mach. Have you no bowels, no tenderness, my dear *Lucy,* to see a husband in these circumstances ?

Lucy. A husband !

Mach. In ev'ry respect but the form, and that, my dear, may be said over us at any time.——Friends should not insist upon ceremonies. From a man of honour, his word is as good as his bond.

Lucy. 'Tis the pleasure of all you fine men to insult the women you have ruin'd.   20

AIR XXVIII. 'Twas when the Sea was roaring.

> *How cruel are the traytors,*
> *Who lye and swear in jest,*
> *To cheat unguarded creatures*
> *Of virtue, fame, and rest !*
> *Whoever steals a shilling,*
> *Thro' shame the guilt conceals :*
> *In love the perjur'd villain*
> *With boasts the theft reveals.*

Mach. The very first opportunity, my dear, (have but patience) you shall be my wife in whatever manner you please.   30

Lucy. Insinuating monster ! And so you think I know nothing of the affair of Miss *Polly Peachum.*——I could tear thy eyes out !

Mach. Sure, *Lucy,* you can't be such a fool as to be jealous of *Polly !*

Lucy. Are you not married to her, you brute, you ?

Mach. Married ! Very good. The wench gives it out only to vex thee, and to ruin me in thy good opinion. 'Tis true, I go to the house ; I chat with the girl, I kiss her, I say a thousand things to her (as all gentlemen do) that mean nothing, to divert myself ; and now the silly jade hath set it about that I am married to her, to let me know what she would be at. Indeed, my dear *Lucy,* these violent passions may be of ill consequence to a woman in your condition.   41

Lucy. Come, come, Captain, for all your assurance, you know that Miss *Polly* hath put it out of your power to do me the justice you promis'd me.

Mach. A jealous woman believes ev'ry thing her passion suggests. To convince you of my sincerity, if we can find the Ordinary, I shall have no scruples of making you my wife ; and I know the consequence of having two at a time.

Lucy. That you are only to be hang'd, and so get rid of them both.

Mach. I am ready, my dear *Lucy,* to give you satisfaction——if you think there is any in marriage.——What can a man of honour say more ? 50

Lucy. So then it seems you are not married to *Miss Polly.*

Mach. You know, *Lucy,* the girl is prodigiously conceited. No man can say a civil thing to her, but (like other fine ladies) her vanity makes her think he 's her own for ever and ever.

A I R X X I X. The Sun had loos'd his weary teams.

The first time at the looking-glass
The mother sets her daughter,
The Image strikes the smiling lass
With self-love ever after.
Each time she looks, she, fonder grown,
Thinks ev'ry charm grows stronger :   60
But alas, vain maid, all eyes but your own
Can see you are not younger.

When women consider their own beauties, they are all alike unreasonable in their demands ; for they expect their lovers should like them as long as they like themselves.

Lucy. Yonder is my father——perhaps this way we may light upon the Ordinary, who shall try if you will be as good as your word.——For I long to be made an honest woman.

S C E N E X.

P E A C H U M, L O C K I T with an Account-Book.

Lock. In this last affair, brother *Peachum,* we are agreed. You have consented to go halves in *Macheath.*

Peach. We shall never fall out about an execution.—But as to that article, pray how stands our last year's account ?

Lock. If you will run your eye over it, you'll find 'tis fair and clearly stated.

Peach. This long arrear of the government is very hard upon us ! Can it be expected that we should hang our acquaintance for nothing, when our betters will hardly save theirs without being paid for it. Unless the people in employment pay better, I promise them for the future, I shall let other rogues live besides their own.   10

Lock. Perhaps, brother, they are afraid these matters may be carried too far. We are treated too by them with contempt, as if our profession were not reputable.

Peach. In one respect indeed, our employment may be reckoned dishonest, because, like great Statesmen, we encourage those who betray their friends.

Lock. Such language, brother, any where else, might turn to your prejudice. Learn to be more guarded, I beg you.

AIR XXX. How happy are we, &c.

> *When you censure the age,*
> *Be cautious and sage,*
> *Lest the Courtiers offended should be :*　　　20
> *If you mention vice or bribe,*
> *'Tis so pat to all the tribe ;*
> *Each cries—That was levell'd at me.*

Peach. Here's poor *Ned Clincher*'s name, I see. Sure, brother *Lockit*, there was a little unfair proceeding in *Ned*'s case : for he told me in the condemn'd hold, that for value receiv'd, you had promis'd him a Session or two longer without molestation.

Lock. Mr. *Peachum*,—this is the first time my honour was ever call'd in question.

Peach. Business is at an end—if once we act dishonourably.　　30

Lock. Who accuses me ?

Peach. You are warm, brother.

Lock. He that attacks my honour, attacks my livelyhood.—And this usage—Sir—is not to be born.

Peach. Since you provoke me to speak—I must tell you too, that Mrs. *Coaxer* charges you with defrauding her of her information-money, for the apprehending of curl-pated *Hugh*. Indeed, indeed, brother, we must punctually pay our Spies, or we shall have no Information.　　38

Lock. Is this language to me, Sirrah——who have sav'd you from the gallows, Sirrah !　　　　　　　　　　　　　　[*Collaring each other.*

Peach. If I am hang'd, it shall be for ridding the world of an arrant rascal.

Lock. This hand shall do the office of the halter you deserve, and throttle you—you dog !—

Peach. Brother, brother,—we are both in the wrong—we shall be both losers in the dispute—for you know we have it in our power to hang each other. You should not be so passionate.

Lock. Nor you so provoking.　　47

Peach. 'Tis our mutual interest ; 'tis for the interest of the world we should agree. If I said any thing, brother, to the prejudice of your character, I ask pardon.

Lock. Brother *Peachum*—I can forgive as well as resent.—Give me your hand. Suspicion does not become a friend.

Peach. I only meant to give you occasion to justifie yourself : But I must now step home, for I expect the gentleman about this Snuff-box, that *Filch* nimm'd two nights ago in the Park. I appointed him at this hour.

14-15 dishonest, because, like] dishonest; like *Plays 1760*　dishonest; because like *Bell, Dicks.*

SCENE XI.

LOCKIT, LUCY.

Lock. Whence come you, hussy ?

Lucy. My tears might answer that question.

Lock. You have then been whimpering and fondling, like a Spaniel, over the fellow that hath abus'd you.

Lucy. One can't help love ; one can't cure it. 'Tis not in my power to obey you, and hate him.   6

Lock. Learn to bear your husband's death like a reasonable woman. 'Tis not the fashion, now-a-days, so much as to affect sorrow upon these occasions. No woman would ever marry, if she had not the chance of mortality for a release. Act like a woman of spirit, hussy, and thank your father for what he is doing.

AIR XXXI. Of a noble Race was *Shenkin*.

Lucy.   *Is then his fate decreed, Sir,*   12
            Such a man can I think of quitting ?
            When first we met, so moves me yet,
            O see how my heart is splitting !

Lock. Look ye, *Lucy*—there is no saving him.——So, I think, you must ev'n do like other widows—buy your self weeds, and be cheerful.

AIR XXXII.

You'll think, e'er many days ensue,
This sentence not severe ;
I hang your husband, child, 'tis true,   20
But with him hang your care.
Twang dang dillo dee.

Like a good wife, go moan over your dying husband. That, child, is your duty—consider, girl, you can't have the man and the money too—so make yourself as easy as you can by getting all you can from him.

12 The 3rd edition (1729) gives this Air to Polly.

SCENE XII.

LUCY, MACHEATH.

Lucy. Though the Ordinary was out of the way to day, I hope, my dear, you will, upon the first opportunity, quiet my scruples—Oh Sir !—my father's hard heart is not to be soften'd, and I am in the utmost despair.

Mach. But if I could raise a small sum—would not twenty Guineas, think you, move him ?—Of all the arguments in the way of business, the perquisite is the most prevailing.——Your father's perquisites for the escape of prisoners must amount to a considerable sum in the year. Money well tim'd, and properly apply'd, will do any thing.

A I R   X X X I I I.   *London* Ladies.

If you at an Office solicit your due,
  And would not have matters neglected ;
You must quicken the Clerk with the perquisite too,
  To do what his duty directed.
Or would you the frowns of a lady prevent,
  She too has this palpable failing,
The perquisite softens her into consent ;
  That reason with all is prevailing.

10

Lucy. What love or money can do shall be done : for all my comfort depends upon your safety.

S C E N E   X I I I.

L U C Y, M A C H E A T H, P O L L Y.

Polly. Where is my dear husband ?—Was a rope ever intended for this neck !—O let me throw my arms about it, and throttle thee with love !—Why dost thou turn away from me ?—'Tis thy *Polly*—'tis thy wife.
Mach. Was ever such an unfortunate rascal as I am !
Lucy. Was there ever such another villain !
Polly. O *Macheath* ! was it for this we parted ?   Taken ! Imprison'd ! Try'd ! Hang'd !—cruel reflection ! I'll stay with thee 'till death—no force shall tear thy dear wife from thee now.—What means my love ?—Not one kind word ! not one kind look ! think what thy *Polly* suffers to see thee in this condition.   10

A I R   X X X I V.   All in the Downs, *&c.*

Thus when the Swallow, seeking prey,
  Within the sash is closely pent,
His consort with bemoaning lay,
  Without sits pining for th' event.
Her chatt'ring lovers all around her skim ;
She heeds them not (poor bird) her soul 's with him.

Mach. I must disown her. [*Aside.*] The wench is distracted.
Lucy. Am I then bilk'd of my virtue ?   Can I have no reparation ?   Sure men were born to lye, and women to believe them ! O Villain ! Villain !
Polly. Am I not thy wife ?—Thy neglect of me, thy aversion to me too severely proves it.—Look on me.—Tell me, am I not thy wife ?   21
Lucy. Perfidious wretch !
Polly. Barbarous husband !
Lucy. Hadst thou been hang'd five months ago, I had been happy.
Polly. And I too—If you had been kind to me 'till death, it would not have vex'd me—And that 's no very unreasonable request, (though from a wife) to a man who hath not above seven or eight days to live.
Lucy. Art thou then married to another ?   Hast thou two wives, monster ?

16 bird)] B   bird !) A

Mach. If women's tongues can cease for an answer—hear me.
Lucy. I won't.—Flesh and blood can't bear my usage.   30
Polly. Shall I not claim my own ?   Justice bids me speak.

A I R   X X X V.   Have you heard of a frolicksome ditty.

Mach.
>How happy could I be with either,
>   Were t'other dear charmer away !
>But while you thus teaze me together,
>   To neither a word will I say ;
>   But tol de rol, &c.

Polly. Sure, my dear, there ought to be some preference shown to a wife !
At least she may claim the appearance of it.   He must be distracted with
his misfortunes, or he cou'd not use me thus !   39
Lucy. O Villain, Villain ! thou hast deceiv'd me—I could even inform
against thee with pleasure.   Not a Prude wishes more heartily to have facts
against her intimate acquaintance, than I now wish to have facts against
thee.   I would have her satisfaction, and they should all out.

A I R   X X X V I.   Irish Trot.

Polly. I'm bubbled.
Lucy. ——————I'm bubbled.
Polly. Oh how I am troubled !
Lucy. Bambouzled, and bit !
Polly. ——————————My distresses are doubled.
Lucy. When you come to the Tree, should the Hangman refuse,
These fingers, with pleasure, could fasten the noose.   50
Polly. I'm bubbled, &c.

Mach. Be pacified, my dear *Lucy*—This is all a fetch of *Polly*'s to make me
desperate with you in case I get off.   If I am hang'd, she would fain have the
credit of being thought my widow—Really, *Polly*, this is no time for a dispute
of this sort ;   for whenever you are talking of marriage, I am thinking of
hanging.
Polly. And hast thou the heart to persist in disowning me ?
Mach. And hast thou the heart to persist in persuading me that I am
married ?   Why, *Polly*, dost thou seek to aggravate my misfortunes ?
Lucy. Really, Miss *Peachum*, you but expose yourself.   Besides, 'tis
barbarous in you to worry a gentleman in his circumstances.   61

A I R   X X X V I I.

Polly.
>Cease your funning ;
>Force or cunning
>Never shall my heart trapan.
>   All these sallies
>   Are but malice
>To seduce my constant man.
>   'Tis most certain,
>   By their flirting
>Women oft have envy shown :   70

39 his misfortunes,] misfortunes *Plays 1760.*

> *Pleas'd, to ruin*
> *Others wooing ;*
> *Never happy in their own !*

Polly. Decency, madam, methinks might teach you to behave yourself with some reserve with the husband, while his wife is present.

Mach. But seriously, *Polly*, this is carrying the joke a little too far.

Lucy. If you are determin'd, madam, to raise a disturbance in the prison, I shall be oblig'd to send for the Turnkey to shew you the door. I am sorry, madam, you force me to be so ill-bred.

Polly. Give me leave to tell you, madam ; these forward Airs don't become you in the least, madam. And my duty, madam, obliges me to stay with my husband, madam.   82

     A I R   X X X V I I I.   Good-morrow, Gossip *Joan.*

Lucy.   *Why how now, madam* Flirt ?
             If you thus must chatter,
             And are for flinging dirt,
                Let 's try who best can spatter ;
                         Madam Flirt !

Polly.   *Why how now, saucy Jade ;*
             Sure the wench is tipsy !
             How can you see me made   [To him.
             The scoff of such a Gipsy ?
                      Saucy Jade !   [To her.

S C E N E   X I V.

L U C Y,   M A C H E A T H,   P O L L Y,   P E A C H U M.

Peach. Where 's my wench ? Ah hussy ! hussy !—Come you home, you slut ; and when your fellow is hang'd, hang yourself, to make your family some amends.

Polly. Dear, dear father, do not tear me from him—I must speak ; I have more to say to him—Oh ! twist thy fetters about me, that he may not haul me from thee !

Peach. Sure all women are alike ! If ever they commit the folly, they are sure to commit another by exposing themselves—Away—Not a word more— You are my prisoner now, hussy.

     A I R   X X X I X.   Irish Howl.

Polly.   *No power on earth can e'er divide*   10
             The knot that sacred Love hath ty'd.
             When parents draw against our mind,
             The true-love's knot they faster bind.
                Oh, oh ray, oh Amborah—oh, oh, &c.
                 [*Holding* Macheath, Peachum *pulling her.*

11 *sacred*] *secret* Underhill.   15 *Stage-direction omitted in Plays 1760.*

SCENE XV.

LUCY, MACHEATH.

Mach. I am naturally compassionate, wife; so that I could not use the wench as she deserv'd; which made you at first suspect there was something in what she said.

Lucy. Indeed, my dear, I was strangely puzzled.

Mach. If that had been the case, her father would never have brought me into this circumstance—No, *Lucy*,—I had rather dye than be false to thee.

Lucy. How happy am I, if you say this from your heart! For I love thee so, that I could sooner bear to see thee hang'd than in the arms of another.

Mach. But couldst thou bear to see me hang'd?

Lucy. O *Macheath*, I can never live to see that day.   10

Mach. You see, *Lucy*, in the account of Love you are in my debt; and you must now be convinc'd, that I rather chuse to die than be another's.— Make me, if possible, love thee more, and let me owe my life to thee—If you refuse to assist me, *Peachum* and your father will immediately put me beyond all means of escape.

Lucy. My father, I know, hath been drinking hard with the Prisoners: and I fancy he is now taking his nap in his own room—If I can procure the keys, shall I go off with thee, my dear?

Mach. If we are together, 'twill be impossible to lye conceal'd. As soon as the search begins to be a little cool, I will send to thee—'Till then my heart is thy prisoner.   21

Lucy. Come then, my dear husband—owe thy life to me—and though you love me not—be grateful—But that *Polly* runs in my head strangely.

Mach. A moment of time may make us unhappy for-ever.

AIR XL. The Lass of *Patie's* Mill.

Lucy.
> *I like the Fox shall grieve,*
> *Whose mate hath left her side,*
> *Whom Hounds, from morn to eve,*
> *Chase o'er the country wide.*
> *Where can my lover hide?*
> *Where cheat the wary pack?*   30
> *If Love be not his guide,*
> *He never will come back!*

30 *wary*] *weary* Underhill.

ACT III. Scene I.

SCENE *Newgate.*

LOCKIT, LUCY.

LOCKIT.

To be sure, wench, you must have been aiding and abetting to help him to this escape.

Lucy. Sir, here hath been *Peachum* and his daughter *Polly*, and to be sure they know the ways of *Newgate* as well as if they had been born and bred in the place all their lives. Why must all your suspicion light upon me ?

Lock. Lucy, Lucy, I will have none of these shuffling answers.

Lucy. Well then——If I know any thing of him I wish I may be burnt !

Lock. Keep your temper, *Lucy*, or I shall pronounce you guilty.

Lucy. Keep yours, Sir,——I do wish I may be burnt. I do——And what can I say more to convince you ?   10

Lock. Did he tip handsomely ?——How much did he come down with ? Come hussy, don't cheat your father ; and I shall not be angry with you—— Perhaps, you have made a better bargain with him than I could have done—— How much, my good girl ?

Lucy. You know, Sir, I am fond of him, and would have given money to have kept him with me.

Lock. Ah, *Lucy* ! thy education might have put thee more upon thy guard ; for a girl in the bar of an Alehouse is always besieg'd.

Lucy. Dear Sir, mention not my education——for 'twas to that I owe my ruin.   20

AIR XLI. If Love's a sweet passion, *&c.*

> *When young at the bar you first taught me to score,*
> *And bid me be free with my lips, and no more ;*
> *I was kiss'd by the Parson, the Squire, and the Sot :*
> *When the guest was departed, the kiss was forgot.*
> *But his kiss was so sweet, and so closely he prest,*
> *That I languish'd and pin'd 'till I granted the rest.*

If you can forgive me, Sir, I will make a fair confession, for to be sure he hath been a most barbarous villain to me.

Lock. And so you have let him escape, hussy——have you ?

Lucy. When a woman loves ; a kind look, a tender word can persuade her to any thing——and I could ask no other bribe.   31

Lock. Thou wilt always be a vulgar slut, *Lucy*——If you would not be look'd upon as a fool, you should never do any thing but upon the foot of interest. Those that act otherwise are their own bubbles.

Lucy. But Love, Sir, is a misfortune that may happen to the most discreet woman, and in love we are all fools alike.——Notwithstanding all he swore, I am now fully convinc'd that *Polly Peachum* is actually his wife.——Did

I let him escape, (fool that I was!) to go to her?——*Polly* will wheedle her self into his money, and then *Peachum* will hang him, and cheat us·both.

Lock. So I am to be ruin'd, because, forsooth, you must be in love!—— a very pretty excuse! 41

Lucy. I could murder that impudent happy strumpet:——I gave him his life, and that creature enjoys the sweets of it.——Ungrateful *Macheath*!

A I R X L I I. *South-Sea* Ballad.

> *My love is all madness and folly,*
>   *Alone I lye,*
>   *Toss, tumble, and cry,*
> *What a happy creature is* Polly !
> *Was e'er such a wretch as I !*
> *With rage I redden like scarlet,*
> *That my dear inconstant Varlet,* 50
>   *Stark blind to my charms,*
>   *Is lost in the arms*
> *Of that Jilt, that inveigling Harlot !*
>   *Stark blind to my charms,*
>   *Is lost in the arms*
> *Of that Jilt, that inveigling Harlot !*
> *This, this my resentment alarms.*

Lock. And so, after all this mischief, I must stay here to be entertain'd with your catterwauling, mistress Puss!——Out of my sight, wanton Strumpet! you shall fast and mortify yourself into reason, with now and then a little handsome discipline to bring you to your senses.——Go.

SCENE II.

L O C K I T.

Peachum then intends to outwit me in this affair; but I'll be even with him.——The dog is leaky in his liquor, so I'll ply him that way, get the secret from him, and turn this affair to my own advantage.——Lions, Wolves, and Vulturs don't live together in herds, droves or flocks.——Of all animals of prey, man is the only sociable one. Every one of us preys upon his neighbour, and yet we herd together.——*Peachum* is my companion, my friend—— According to the custom of the world, indeed, he may quote thousands of Precedents for cheating me——And shall not I make use of the privilege of friendship to make him a return?

A I R X L I I I. *Packington's* Pound.

> *Thus Gamesters united in friendship are found,* 10
> *Though they know that their industry all is a cheat;*
> *They flock to their prey at the Dice-box's sound,*
> *And join to promote one another's deceit.*

> *But if by mishap*
> *They fail of a chap,*
> *To keep in their hands, they each other entrap.*
> *Like Pikes, lank with hunger, who miss of their ends,*
> *They bite their companions, and prey on their friends.*

Now, *Peachum*, you and I, like honest Tradesmen, are to have a fair tryal which of us two can over-reach the other.——*Lucy*.——[*Enter* Lucy.] Are there any of *Peachum*'s people now in the house ?   21

Lucy. *Filch*, Sir, is drinking a quartern of Strong-waters in the next room with black *Moll*.

Lock. Bid him come to me.

S C E N E III.

L O C K I T , F I L C H .

Lock. Why, boy, thou lookest as if thou wert half starv'd ; like a shotten Herring.

Filch. One had need have the constitution of a horse to go thorough the business.——Since the favourite Child-getter was disabled by a mis-hap, I have pick'd up a little money by helping the ladies to a pregnancy against their being call'd down to sentence.——But if a man cannot get an honest livelihood any easier way, I am sure, 'tis what I can't undertake for another Session.   8

Lock. Truly, if that great man should tip off, 'twould be an irreparable loss. The vigor and prowess of a Knight-errant never sav'd half the ladies in distress that he hath done.——But, boy, can'st thou tell me where thy master is to be found ?

Filch. At his * Lock, Sir, at the *Crooked Billet*.   13

Lock. Very well.——I have nothing more with you. [*Ex.* Filch.] I'll go to him there, for I have many important affairs to settle with him ; and in the way of those transactions, I'll artfully get into his secret.——So that *Macheath* shall not remain a day longer out of my clutches.

* A Cant word, signifying, a Warehouse where stolen goods are deposited.

7 livelihood] Livelyhood *1728* [1 and 2].

S C E N E IV. *A Gaming-House.*

M A C H E A T H , *in a fine tarnish'd Coat,* B E N   B U D G E , M A T T *of the* M I N T .

Mach. I am sorry, gentlemen, the road was so barren of money. When my friends are in difficulties, I am always glad that my fortune can be serviceable to them. [*Gives them money.*] You see, gentlemen, I am not a meer Court friend, who professes every thing and will do nothing.

A I R   X L I V.   Lillibulero.

The modes of the Court so common are grown,
That a true friend can hardly be met ;
Friendship for interest is but a loan,
Which they let out for what they can get.
'Tis true, you find
Some friends so kind,   10
Who will give you good counsel themselves to defend.
In sorrowful ditty,
They promise, they pity,
But shift you for money, from friend to friend.

But we, gentlemen, have still honour enough to break through the corruptions of the world.—And while I can serve you, you may command me.

Ben. It grieves my heart that so generous a man should be involv'd in such difficulties, as oblige him to live with such ill company, and herd with gamesters.   19

Matt. See the partiality of mankind !—One man may steal a horse, better than another look over a hedge.—Of all mechanics, of all servile handycraftsmen, a gamester is the vilest. But yet, as many of the Quality are of the profession, he is admitted amongst the politest company. I wonder we are not more respected.

Mach. There will be deep play to-night at *Marybone*, and consequently money may be pick'd up upon the road. Meet me there, and I'll give you the hint who is worth setting.

Matt. The fellow with a brown coat with a narrow gold binding, I am told, is never without money.

Mach. What do you mean, *Matt ?*—Sure you will not think of meddling with him !—He's a good honest kind of a fellow, and one of us.   31

Ben. To be sure, Sir, we will put our selves under your direction.

Mach. Have an eye upon the money-lenders.—A *Rouleau*, or two, would prove a pretty sort of an expedition. I hate extortion.

Matt. Those *Rouleaus* are very pretty things.—I hate your Bank bills—there is such a hazard in putting them off.

Mach. There is a certain man of distinction, who in his time hath nick'd me out of a great deal of the ready. He is in my cash, *Ben* ;—I'll point him out to you this evening, and you shall draw upon him for the debt.—The company are met ; I hear the Dice-box in the other room. So, gentlemen, your servant. You'll meet me at *Marybone*.

15 corruptions] corruption *Plays 1760.*

S C E N E V. Peachum's *Lock*.

A Table with Wine, Brandy, Pipes and Tobacco.

P E A C H U M , L O C K I T .

Lock. The Coronation account, brother *Peachum*, is of so intricate a nature, that I believe it will never be settled.

Peach. It consists indeed of a great variety of articles.—It was worth to our people, in fees of different kinds, above ten instalments.—This is part of the account, brother, that lies open before us.

Lock. A lady's tail of rich Brocade—that, I see, is dispos'd of.

Peach. To Mrs. *Diana Trapes*, the Tally-woman, and she will make a good hand on't in shoes and slippers, to trick out young ladies, upon their going into keeping.—

Lock. But I don't see any article of the Jewels.   10

Peach. Those are so well known, that they must be sent abroad—you'll find them enter'd under the article of Exportation.—As for the Snuff-boxes, Watches, Swords, &c.—I thought it best to enter them under their several heads.

Lock. Seven and twenty women's pockets compleat ; with the several things therein contain'd ; all seal'd, number'd, and enter'd.

Peach. But, brother, it is impossible for us now to enter upon this affair.— We should have the whole day before us.—Besides, the account of the last half year's Plate is in a book by it self, which lies at the other Office.   19

Lock. Bring us then more liquor.—To-day shall be for pleasure—to-morrow for business.—Ah brother, those daughters of ours are two slippery hussies— keep a watchful eye upon *Polly*, and *Macheath* in a day or two shall be our own again.

A I R X L V. Down in the North Country.

Lock.   *What Gudgeons are we men !*
                Ev'ry woman 's easy prey.
                Though we have felt the hook, agen
                We bite, and they betray.

                The bird that hath been trapt,
                When he hears his calling mate,
                To her he flies, again he 's clapt   30
                Within the wiry grate.

Peach. But what signifies catching the Bird, if your daughter *Lucy* will set open the door of the Cage ?

Lock. If men were answerable for the follies and frailties of their wives and daughters, no friends could keep a good correspondence together for two days.—This is unkind of you, brother ; for among good friends, what they say or do goes for nothing.

Enter a Servant.

Serv. Sir, here 's Mrs. *Diana Trapes* wants to speak with you.

Peach. Shall we admit her, brother *Lockit* ?   39

Lock. By all means—she 's a good customer, and a fine-spoken woman— and a woman who drinks and talks so freely will enliven the conversation.

Peach. Desire her to walk in.   [*Exit Servant.*

SCENE VI.

PEACHUM, LOCKIT, Mrs. *TRAPES.*

Peach. Dear Mrs. *Dye*, your servant—one may know by your kiss, that your Ginn is excellent.

Trap. I was always very curious in my liquors.

Lock. There is no perfum'd breath like it—I have been long acquainted with the flavour of those lips—han't I, Mrs. *Dye*?

Trap. Fill it up.—I take as large draughts of liquor, as I did of love.— I hate a Flincher in either.

AIR XLVI. A Shepherd kept sheep, *&c.*

In the days of my youth I could bill like a Dove, fa, la, la, &c.
Like a Sparrow at all times was ready for love, fa, la, la, &c.
The life of all mortals in kissing should pass,   10
Lip to lip while we're young—then the lip to the glass, fa, la, &c.

But now, Mr. *Peachum*, to our business.—If you have blacks of any kind, brought in of late; Mantoes—Velvet Scarfs—Petticoats—let it be what it will—I am your chap—for all my ladies are very fond of mourning.

Peach. Why, look ye, Mrs. *Dye*—you deal so hard with us, that we can afford to give the gentlemen, who venture their lives for the goods, little or nothing.   17

Trap. The hard times oblige me to go very near in my dealing.—To be sure, of late years I have been a great sufferer by the Parliament.—Three thousand pounds would hardly make me amends.—The Act for destroying the Mint was a severe cut upon our business—'till then, if a customer stept out of the way—we knew where to have her—no doubt you know Mrs. *Coaxer* —there's a wench now ('till to-day) with a good suit of cloaths of mine upon her back, and I could never set eyes upon her for three months together.— Since the Act too against imprisonment for small sums, my loss there too hath been very considerable, and it must be so, when a lady can borrow a handsome petticoat, or a clean gown, and I not have the least hank upon her! And, o' my conscience, now-a-days most ladies take a delight in cheating, when they can do it with safety.   29

Peach. Madam, you had a handsome gold watch of us t'other day for seven Guineas.—Considering we must have our profit—to a gentleman upon the road, a gold watch will be scarce worth the taking.

Trap. Consider, Mr. *Peachum*, that watch was remarkable, and not of very safe sale.—If you have any black Velvet Scarfs—they are a handsome winter wear; and take with most gentlemen who deal with my customers.— 'Tis I that put the ladies upon a good foot. 'Tis not youth or beauty that fixes their price. The gentlemen always pay according to their dress, from half a crown to two guineas; and yet those hussies make nothing of bilking of me.—Then too, allowing for accidents.—I have eleven fine customers now down under the Surgeon's hands,—what with fees and other expences, there are great goings-out, and no comings-in, and not a farthing to pay for at least a month's cloathing.—We run great risques—great risques indeed.   42

40 hands,] hand *Plays 1760, Bell.*

Peach. As I remember, you said something just now of Mrs. *Coaxer.*

Trap. Yes, Sir.—To be sure I stript her of a suit of my own cloaths about two hours ago ; and have left her as she should be, in her shift, with a lover of hers at my house. She call'd him up stairs, as he was going to *Marybone* in a hackney-coach.—And I hope, for her own sake and mine, she will perswade the Captain to redeem her, for the Captain is very generous to the ladies.

Lock. What Captain ?

Trap. He thought I did not know him.—An intimate acquaintance of yours, Mr. *Peachum*—only Captain *Macheath*—as fine as a Lord.　　51

Peach. To-morrow, dear Mrs. *Dye,* you shall set your own price upon any of the goods you like—we have at least half a dozen Velvet Scarfs, and all at your service. Will you give me leave to make you a present of this suit of night-cloaths for your own wearing ?—But are you sure it is Captain *Macheath* ?

Trap. Though he thinks I have forgot him ; no body knows him better. I have taken a great deal of the Captain's money in my time at second-hand, for he always lov'd to have his ladies well drest.

Peach. Mr. *Lockit* and I have a little business with the Captain ;—you understand me—and we will satisfie you for Mrs. *Coaxer's* debt.　　61

Lock. Depend upon it—we will deal like men of honour.

Trap. I don't enquire after your affairs—so whatever happens, I wash my hands on't.—It hath always been my Maxim, that one friend should assist another.—But if you please—I'll take one of the Scarfs home with me, 'tis always good to have something in hand.

47 perswade] *1728* [1] and [2], *1729.*

S C E N E V I I. *Newgate.*

L U C Y.

Jealousy, rage, love and fear are at once tearing me to pieces. How I am weather-beaten and shatter'd with distresses !

A I R X L V I I.　One evening having lost my way.

I'm like a skiff on the Ocean tost,
　　Now high, now low, with each billow born,
With her rudder broke, and her anchor lost,
　　Deserted and all forlorn.
While thus I lie rolling and tossing all night,
That Polly *lyes sporting on seas of delight !*
　　Revenge, revenge, revenge.
Shall appease my restless sprite.　　10

I have the Rats-bane ready.—I run no risque ; for I can lay her death upon the Ginn, and so many dye of that naturally that I shall never be call'd in question.—But say I were to be hang'd—I never could be hang'd for any thing that would give me greater comfort, than the poysoning that slut.

Enter Filch.

Filch. Madam, here 's our Miss *Polly* come to wait upon you.

Lucy. Show her in.

SCENE VIII.

L U C Y , P O L L Y .

Lucy. Dear madam, your servant.—I hope you will pardon my passion, when I was so happy to see you last.—I was so over-run with the spleen, that I was perfectly out of my self. And really when one hath the spleen, every thing is to be excus'd by a friend.

A I R X L V I I I. Now *Roger,* I'll tell thee, because thou'rt my son.

> *When a wife's in her pout,*
> *(As she's sometimes, no doubt)*
> *The good husband as meek as a lamb,*
> *Her vapours to still,*
> *First grants her her will,*
> *And the quieting draught is a dram.*   10
> *Poor man! And the quieting draught is a dram.*

—I wish all our quarrels might have so comfortable a reconciliation.

Polly. I have no excuse for my own behaviour, madam, but my misfortunes.—And really, madam, I suffer too upon your account.

Lucy. But, Miss *Polly*—in the way of friendship, will you give me leave to propose a glass of Cordial to you?

Polly. Strong-waters are apt to give me the head-ache—I hope, Madam, you will excuse me.

Lucy. Not the greatest lady in the land could have better in her closet, for her own private drinking.—You seem mighty low in Spirits, my dear. 20

Polly. I am sorry, madam, my health will not allow me to accept of your offer.—I should not have left you in the rude manner I did when we met last, madam, had not my Papa haul'd me away so unexpectedly.—I was indeed somewhat provok'd, and perhaps might use some expressions that were disrespectful.—But really, madam, the Captain treated me with so much contempt and cruelty, that I deserv'd your pity, rather than your resentment.

Lucy. But since his escape, no doubt all matters are made up again.—Ah *Polly! Polly!* 'tis I am the unhappy wife; and he loves you as if you were only his mistress. 29

Polly. Sure, madam, you cannot think me so happy as to be the object of your jealousy.—A man is always afraid of a woman who loves him too well—so that I must expect to be neglected and avoided.

Lucy. Then our cases, my dear *Polly,* are exactly alike. Both of us indeed have been too fond.

A I R X L I X. *O Bessy Bell, &c.*

Polly.	*A curse attends that woman's love,*
	Who always would be pleasing.
Lucy.	*The pertness of the billing Dove,*
	Like tickling, is but teazing.

Polly.	*What then in love can woman do?*	
Lucy.	*If we grow fond they shun us.*	40
Polly.	*And when we fly them, they pursue:*	
Lucy.	*But leave us when they've won us.*	

Lucy. Love is so very whimsical in both sexes, that it is impossible to be lasting.—But my heart is particular, and contradicts my own observation.

Polly. But really, mistress *Lucy* by his last behaviour, I think I ought to envy you.—When I was forc'd from him, he did not shew the least tenderness.—But perhaps, he hath a heart not capable of it.

A I R L. Wou'd Fate to me *Belinda* give.

> *Among the men, Coquets we find,*
> *Who court by turns all woman-kind;*
> *And we grant all their hearts desir'd,*   50
> *When they are flatter'd and admir'd.*

The Coquets of both sexes are self-lovers, and that is a love no other whatever can dispossess. I fear, my dear *Lucy*, our husband is one of those.

Lucy. Away with these melancholy reflections,——indeed, my dear *Polly*, we are both of us a cup too low.—Let me prevail upon you, to accept of my offer.

A I R L I. Come, sweet lass.

> *Come, sweet lass,*
> *Let's banish sorrow*
> *'Till to-morrow;*
> *Come sweet lass,*
> *Let's take a chirping glass.*   60
> *Wine can clear*
> *The vapours of despair;*
> *And make us light as air;*
> *Then drink, and banish care.*

I can't bear, child, to see you in such low spirits.—And I must persuade you to what I know will do you good.—I shall now soon be even with the hypocritical Strumpet.   [*Aside.*

S C E N E I X.

P O L L Y.

Polly. All this wheedling of *Lucy* cannot be for nothing.—At this time too! when I know she hates me!—The dissembling of a woman is always the fore-runner of mischief.—By pouring Strong-waters down my throat, she thinks to pump some secrets out of me—I'll be upon my guard, and won't taste a drop of her liquor, I'm resolv'd.   5

SCENE X.

L U C Y, with Strong-waters. P O L L Y.

Lucy. Come, Miss *Polly.*

Polly. Indeed, child, you have given yourself trouble to no purpose.—You must, my dear, excuse me.

Lucy. Really, Miss *Polly*, you are so squeamishly affected about taking a cup of Strong-waters, as a lady before company. I vow, *Polly*, I shall take it monstrously ill if you refuse me.—Brandy and Men (though women love them never so well) are always taken by us with some reluctance—unless 'tis in private.

Polly. I protest, madam, it goes against me.—What do I see ! *Macheath* again in custody !—Now every glimmering of happiness is lost.   10

> [*Drops the glass of liquor on the ground.*

Lucy. Since things are thus, I'm glad the wench hath escap'd : for by this event, 'tis plain, she was not happy enough to deserve to be poison'd.

SCENE XI.

L O C K I T, M A C H E A T H, P E A C H U M, L U C Y, P O L L Y.

Lock. Set your heart to rest, Captain.—You have neither the chance of Love or Money for another escape—for you are order'd to be call'd down upon your Tryal immediately.

Peach. Away, hussies !—This is not a time for a man to be hamper'd with his wives.—You see, the gentleman is in chains already.

Lucy. O husband, husband, my heart long'd to see thee ; but to see thee thus distracts me !

Polly. Will not my dear husband look upon his *Polly* ? Why hadst thou not flown to me for protection ? with me thou hadst been safe.

A I R L I I. The last time I went o'er the Moor.

Polly.	*Hither, dear husband, turn your eyes.* 10
Lucy.	*Bestow one glance to cheer me.*
Polly.	*Think with that look, thy* Polly *dyes.*
Lucy.	*O shun me not,—but hear me.*
Polly.	*'Tis* Polly *sues.*
Lucy.	————————*'Tis* Lucy *speaks.*
Polly.	*Is thus true love requited ?*
Lucy.	*My heart is bursting.*
Polly.	————————*Mine too breaks.*
Lucy.	*Must I,*
Polly.	————————*Must I be slighted ?* 20

Mach. What would you have me say, ladies ?——You see, this affair will soon be at an end, without my disobliging either of you.

Peach. But the settling this point, Captain, might prevent a Law-suit between your two widows.

AIR LIII. *Tom Tinker's* my true love, *&c.*

Mach.   *Which way shall I turn me—how can I decide?*
Wives, the day of our death, are as fond as a bride.
One wife is too much for most husbands to hear,
But two at a time there's no mortal can bear.
This way, and that way, and which way I will,
What would comfort the one, t'other wife would take ill.   30

Polly. But if his own misfortunes have made him insensible to mine—
a Father sure will be more compassionate.—Dear, dear Sir, sink the material
evidence, and bring him off at his Tryal—*Polly upon her knees begs it of you.*

AIR LIV. I am a poor Shepherd undone.

When my Hero in court appears,
   And stands arraign'd for his life,
Then think of poor Polly's *tears;*
   For ah! poor Polly's *his wife.*
Like the Sailor he holds up his hand,
   Distrest on the dashing wave.
To die a dry death at land,   40
   Is as bad as a watry grave.
And alas, poor Polly!
   Alack, and well-a-day!
Before I was in love,
   Oh! every month was May.

Lucy. If *Peachum's* heart is harden'd; sure you, Sir, will have more
compassion on a daughter.——I know the evidence is in your power.——How
then can you be a tyrant to me?   [*Kneeling.*

AIR LV. *Ianthe* the lovely, *&c.*

When he holds up his hand arraign'd for his life,
O think of your daughter, and think I'm his wife!   50
What are cannons, or bombs, or clashing of swords?
For death is more certain by witnesses words.
Then nail up their lips; that dread thunder allay;
And each month of my life will hereafter be May.

Lock. *Macheath's* time is come, *Lucy.*—We know our own affairs, therefore
let us have no more whimpering or whining.

AIR LVI. A Cobler there was, *&c.*

Our selves, like the Great, to secure a retreat,
When matters require it, must give up our gang:
   And good reason why,
   Or, instead of the fry,   60
   Ev'n Peachum *and I,*
Like poor petty rascals, might hang, hang;
Like poor petty rascals, might hang.

Air LVI. *Omitted in the second issue of the first edition.*

Peach. Set your heart at rest, *Polly.*——Your husband is to dye to day.——
Therefore, if you are not already provided, 'tis high time to look about for
another. There's comfort for you, you slut.

Lock. We are ready, Sir, to conduct you to the *Old Baily.*

AIR LVII. Bonny *Dundee.*

Mach.

> *The charge is prepar'd ; the Lawyers are met ;*
> *The Judges all rang'd (a terrible show !)*
> *I go, undismay'd.—For death is a debt,*
> *A debt on demand.—So, take what I owe.*
> *Then, farewell, my love—dear charmers, adieu.*
> *Contented I die—'tis the better for you.*
> *Here ends all dispute the rest of our lives,*
> *For this way at once I please all my wives.*

70

Now, Gentlemen, I am ready to attend you.

SCENE XII.

LUCY, POLLY, FILCH.

Polly. Follow them, *Filch,* to the Court. And when the Tryal is over,
bring me a particular account of his behaviour, and of every thing that
happen'd.—You'll find me here with Miss *Lucy.* [*Ex.* Filch.] But why is
all this Musick ?   6

Lucy. The Prisoners, whose tryals are put off till next Session, are diverting
themselves.

Polly. Sure there is nothing so charming as Musick ! I'm fond of it to
distraction—But alas !—now, all mirth seems an insult upon my affliction.——
Let us retire, my dear *Lucy,* and indulge our sorrows.—The noisy crew, you
see, are coming upon us.   [*Exeunt.*

A Dance of Prisoners in chains, &c.

SCENE XIII. *The Condemn'd Hold.*

M A C H E A T H, in a melancholy posture.

AIR LVIII. Happy Groves.

> *O cruel, cruel, cruel case !*
> *Must I suffer this disgrace ?*

AIR LIX. Of all the girls that are so smart.

> *Of all the friends in time of grief,*
> *When threat'ning Death looks grimmer,*
> *Not one so sure can bring relief,*
> *As this best friend a brimmer.*

[Drinks.

A I R L X. *Britons* strike home.

Since I must swing,—I scorn, I scorn to wince or whine.   [Rises.

A I R L X I. Chevy Chase.

But now again my spirits sink ;
I'll raise them high with wine. [Drinks a glass of wine.

A I R L X I I. To old Sir *Simon* the King.

But valour the stronger grows,   10
The stronger liquor we're drinking.
And how can we feel our woes,
When we've lost the trouble of thinking ?   [Drinks.

A I R L X I I I. Joy to great *Caesar.*

If thus—A man can die
Much bolder with brandy.   [Pours out a bumper of brandy.

A I R L X I V. There was an old woman, *&c.*

So I drink off this bumper—And now I can stand the test,
And my Comrades shall see, that I die as brave as the best. [Drinks.

A I R L X V. Did you ever hear of a gallant sailor.

But can I leave my pretty hussies,
Without one tear, or tender sigh ?

A I R L X V I. Why are mine eyes still flowing.

Their eyes, their lips, their busses   20
Recall my love—Ah must I die !

A I R L X V I I. Green sleeves.

Since laws were made for ev'ry degree,
To curb vice in others, as well as me,
I wonder we han't better company
Upon Tyburn *tree !*
But gold from law can take out the sting ;
And if rich men like us were to swing,
'Twould thin the land, such numbers to string
Upon Tyburn *tree !*

Jailor. Some friends of yours, Captain, desire to be admitted—I leave you together.

16 *off*] *of* Underhill.
Air LXVI. Why are mine eyes etc.] *Printed by Underhill as part of Airs LXV and LXVI, which he combines into one.*

S C E N E   X I V.

M A C H E A T H, B E N B U D G E, M A T of the Mint.

Mach. For my having broke Prison, you see, gentlemen, I am ordered immediate execution.——The Sheriffs officers, I believe, are now at the door.——That *That Jemmy Twitcher* should peach me, I own supriz'd me !— 'Tis a plain proof that the world is all alike, and that even our Gang can no more trust one another than other people. Therefore, I beg you, gentlemen, look well to your selves, for in all probability you may live some months longer.

Mat. We are heartily sorry, Captain, for your misfortune.—But 'tis what we must all come to.   9

Mach. *Peachum* and *Lockit*, you know, are infamous Scoundrels. Their lives are as much in your power, as yours are in theirs——Remember your dying friend !——'Tis my last request.——Bring those villains to the Gallows before you, and I am satisfied.

Mat. We'll do't.

Jailor. Miss *Polly* and Miss *Lucy* intreat a word with you.

Mach. Gentlemen, adieu.

S C·E N E   X V.

L U C Y, M A C H E A T H, P O L L Y.

Mach. My dear *Lucy*——my dear *Polly*——Whatsoever hath past between us, is now at an end.—If you are fond of marrying again, the best advice I can give you, is to ship yourselves off for the *West-Indies*, where you'll have a fair chance of getting a husband a-piece ; or by good luck, two or three, as you like best.

Polly. How can I support this sight !

Lucy. There is nothing moves one so much as a great man in distress.

A I R L X V I I I. All you that must take a leap, &c.

Lucy.	*Wou'd I might be hang'd !*
Polly.	————————————*And I would so too !*
Lucy.	*To be hang'd with you,* 10
Polly.	——————————*My dear, with you.*
Mach.	*O leave me to thought ! I fear ! I doubt !*
	I tremble ! I droop !——See my courage is out.
	[Turns up the empty bottle.
Polly.	*No token of love ?*
Mach.	——————————*See my courage is out.*
	[Turns up the empty pot.
Lucy.	*No token of love ?*
Polly.	——————————*Adieu.*
Lucy.	——————————*Farewell.*
Mach.	*But hark ! I hear the toll of the bell.*

Chorus.   *Tol de rol lol*, &c.   20

Jailor. Four women more, Captain, with a child a-piece! See, here they come.   [*Enter women and children.*

Mach. What—four wives more!—This is too much.—Here—tell the Sheriff's Officers I am ready.   [*Exit* Macheath *guarded.*

24 *Stage direction omitted by Plays 1760 and Bell.*

SCENE XVI.

To them, Enter P L A Y E R and B E G G A R.

Play. But honest friend, I hope you don't intend that *Macheath* shall be really executed.

Beg. Most certainly, Sir.—To make the piece perfect, I was for doing strict poetical Justice.—*Macheath* is to be hang'd; and for the other personages of the Drama, the Audience must have suppos'd they were all either hang'd or transported.

Play. Why then, friend, this is a down-right deep Tragedy. The catastrophe is manifestly wrong, for an Opera must end happily.   8

Beg. Your objection, Sir, is very just; and is easily remov'd. For you must allow, that in this kind of Drama, 'tis no matter how absurdly things are brought about—So—you rabble there—run and cry a Reprieve—let the prisoner be brought back to his wives in triumph.

Play. All this we must do, to comply with the taste of the town.

Beg. Through the whole piece you may observe such a similitude of manners in high and low life, that it is difficult to determine whether (in the fashionable vices) the fine gentlemen imitate the gentlemen of the road, or the gentlemen of the road the fine gentlemen.——Had the Play remain'd, as I at first intended, it would have carried a most excellent moral. 'Twould have shown that the lower sort of people have their vices in a degree as well as the rich: And that they are punish'd for them.   20

SCENE XVII.

To them M A C H E A T H with Rabble, &c.

Mach. So, it seems, I am not left to my choice, but must have a wife at last.——Look ye, my dears, we will have no controversie now. Let us give this day to mirth, and I am sure she who thinks her self my wife will testifie her joy by a dance.

All. Come, a Dance——a Dance.

Mach. Ladies, I hope you will give me leave to present a Partner to each of you. And (if I may without offence) for this time, I take *Polly* for mine.— And for life, you Slut,—for we were really marry'd.——As for the rest.——But at present keep your own secret.   [*To Polly.*

A   D A N C E.

AIR LXIX. Lumps of Pudding, &c.

Thus I stand like a Turk, *with his doxies around ;*   10
From all sides their glances his passion confound ;
For black, brown, and fair, his inconstancy burns,
And the different beauties subdue him by . ras :
Each calls forth her charms, to provoke his desires :
Though willing to all ; with but one he retires.
But think of this maxim, and put off your sorrow,
The wretch of to-day, may be happy to morrow.

Chorus.   *But think of this maxim,* &c.

16 *off your*] *of all*   Plays 1760.

P O L L Y :

A N

O P E R A.

[*Editions :*
1. POLLY : | AN | OPERA. | BEING THE | SECOND PART | OF THE |
BEGGAR's OPERA. | Written by Mr. GAY. | *Raro antecedentem scelestum | Deseruit
pede pœna claudo.* Hor. | *LONDON :* | Printed for the AUTHOR. MDCCXXIX.
   Crown 4to. Title-page in red and black. Uniform with the 3rd (4to) edition of
The Beggar's Opera ; the Airs (no Overture is included) given at the end, with a
Bass, and with the words fitted to the music.
   No other authorized edition seems to have been published in Gay's lifetime ; but
numerous pirated editions appeared—such as Jeffery Walker's and T. Read's, both
8vo, without the music, and J. Thomson's, 8vo, with the music.
2. The *Plays*, 1760.
3. Bell's *British Theatre*, 1777.
4. *Polly : an Opera* etc. *The Foreword by Oswald Doughty, M.A. Lecturer in
English, University College, London. . . . London* : Daniel O'Connor. . . . MCMXXII.]

PREFACE.

AFTER *Mr.* Rich *and I were agreed upon terms and conditions for bringing this Piece on the stage, and that every thing was ready for a Rehearsal ; The Lord Chamberlain sent an order from the country to prohibit Mr.* Rich *to suffer any Play to be rehears'd upon his stage till it had been first of all supervis'd by his Grace. As soon as Mr.* Rich *came from his Grace's secretary (who had sent for him to receive the before-mentioned order) he came to my lodgings and acquainted me with the orders he had received.*

Upon the Lord Chamberlain's coming to town, I was confined by sickness, but in four or five days I went abroad on purpose to wait upon his Grace with a faithful and genuine copy of this Piece, excepting the erratas of the transcriber.

It was transcribed in great haste by Mr. Stede *the Prompter of the Playhouse, that it might be ready against his Grace's return from the country : As my illness at that time would not allow me to read it over, I since find in it many small faults, and here and there a line or two omitted. But lest it should be said I had made any one alteration from the copy I deliver'd to the Lord Chamberlain : I have caused every error in the said copy to be printed (litteral faults excepted) and have taken notice of every omission. I have also pointed out every amendment I have made upon the revisal of my own copy for the Press, that the reader may at one view see what alterations and amendments have been made.*

E R R O R S *as they stood in the copy delivered to the* Lord Chamberlain *(occasion'd by the haste of the transcriber) corrected in this edition ; by which will appear the most minute difference between that and my own copy.*

P for page. l for line. sc. for scene. what was added mark'd thus *. What was left out, thus †.

The names of all the tunes †. The scenes not divided and number'd. The marginal directions for the Actors were often omitted.

Act I. p. 2. l. 16. *ever* †. l. 18. after more, *too* *. p. 4. l. 1. before part *not* *. l. 11. *take* †. sc. 2. l. 12. *to* †. Air 5. l. 10. *thus* instead of *they.* p. 9. l. 20. *wherewith* for *wherewithal.* l. 19. *my* †. l. 26. *will* †. p. 10. l. 1. *you* for *it.* p. 11. l. 20. *no* †. Air 10. l. 5. *with a twinkum twankum* †. p. 14. l. 18. *complaisance* for

E M E N D A T I O N S *of my own copy on revising it for the Press.*

* Is the mark for anything added.
† The mark for what is left out.
‡ The mark of what stood in the original Copy.

Act I. p. 2. l. 36. *pictures* *. sc. 4. l. 2. *thousand* *. p. 18. l. 28. *But unhappy love, the more virtuous that is* ‡. Air 21. l. 13. *my steps direct, my truth protect a faithful,* &c. ‡. Act. 2. Air 23. l. 3. *sick imagination* ‡. l. 4. then *alone I forget* to weep ‡. l. 7. for *whole* years ‡. l. 11. *'Tis* a dream ‡. l. 12. *'Tis* our utmost ‡. Air 27. l. 9. you ne'er were drawn to cringe and fawn among the spawn who &c. ‡. Air 28. l. 2. *for* *. l. 4. *alike* for *both.* p. 40. l. 12. all women expect ‡. Air 39. l. 3. thus colts let loose, by want of use grow ‡. Air 40. *unextinguish'd* ray ‡. Recitative. *Away* for *Hence* ‡. p. 46. l. 1. *pardons* for

The third paragraph, and the lists of Errors and Emendations are omitted from the preface in Plays 1760, and Bell 1777.

compliance. sc. 9. l. 1. *part from.* p. 18. l. 9. *surely* for *sure.* l. 13. *And* †. sc. 14, l. 20. insult me *thus.* p. 24. l. 18. *her* †. l. 21. young and handsome. Act 2. Air 25. l. 8. *charms* for *arms.* p. 29. the speech between Air 25 and Air 26.†. Air 27. l. 2. *why* for *who.* Air 29. with a mirleton, *&c.* †. sc. 7. l. 2. a bawdy-house bully, p. 42. l. 26 *is* †. Air 42. l. 6. *is* for *are.* p. 44. l. 7. *none* for *no more.* Act 3. p. 52. l. 18. are *all* at stake. p. 53. l. 9. *ever* †. p. 54. l. 9. *found* †. Air 51. Thus to battle we will go †. Air 52. with a fa, la, la, †. sc. 8. l. 4. *prey* for *pay.* p. 63, l. 26. *no* notions. p. 65. l. 28. or redress 'em †. Air 71. the repetition of the Chorus †.

persons ‡. Air 45. . 1. when as ambition's ‡. l. 2. *mighty* *. l. 4. *fraud and* *. Air 48. l. 2. *Thus* *. l. 3. what expence and what care ‡. l. 7. *sage* politicians ‡. Act. 3. sc. 1, 2, 3, 4, 5, 6. are transpos'd with no alteration of the words, but instead of *On then; hope and conquer,* is put p. 55. l. 2. *let us then to our posts.* p. 57. l. 12. *after* enterprize, *let us now to our posts* ‡. Air 58. l. 4. *cheers* my breast. ‡. Air 62. l. 7. by turns we *take* ‡. Air 63. l. 7. Tis jealous rage ‡. Air 64. l. 3. is of *the* noxious ‡. folded arms hide its charms, all the night free from blight, *&c.* ‡. *Polly's* speech before Air 64 was plac'd after it, but without any alteration ‡. Air 69. l. 7. *sure* to virtue ‡.

Excepting these errors and emendations, this Edition is a true and faithful Copy as I my-self in my own hand writing delivered it to Mr. Rich, *and afterwards to the Lord Chamberlain, for the truth of which I appeal to his Grace.*

As I have heard several suggestions and false insinuations concerning the copy : I take this occasion in the most solemn manner to affirm, that the very copy I delivered to Mr. Rich *was written in my own hand some months before at the* Bath *from my own first foul blotted papers ; from this, that for the Playhouse was transcribed, from whence the above-mention'd Mr.* Stede *copied that which I delivered to the Lord Chamberlain, and excepting my own foul blotted papers ; I do protest I know of no other copy whatsoever, than those I have mention'd.*

The Copy I gave into the hands of Mr. Rich *had been seen before by several Persons of the greatest distinction and veracity, who will be ready to do me the honour and justice to attest it ; so that not only by them, but by Mr.* Rich *and Mr.* Stede, *I can (against all insinuation or positive affirmation) prove in the most clear and undeniable manner, if occasion required, what I have here upon my own honour and credit asserted. The Introduction indeed was not shown to the Lord Chamberlain, which, as I had not then quite settled, was never transcribed in the Playhouse copy.*

'Twas on Saturday *morning* December 7th, 1728, *that I waited upon the Lord Chamberlain ; I desir'd to have the honour of reading the Opera to his Grace, but he order'd me to leave it with him, which I did upon expectation of having it return'd on the* Monday *following, but I had it not 'till* Thursday December 12, *when I receiv'd it from his Grace with this answer ; that it was not allow'd to be acted, but commanded to be supprest. This was told me in general without any reasons assign'd, or any charge against me of my having given any particular offence.*

Since this prohibition I have been told that I am accused, in general terms, of having written many disaffected libels and seditious pamphlets. As it hath ever been my utmost ambition (if that word may be us'd upon this occasion) to lead a quiet and inoffensive life, I thought my innocence in this particular would never have requir'd a justification ; and as this kind of writing is, what I have ever detested and never practic'd, I am persuaded so groundless a calumny can never be believ'd but by those who do not know me. But when general aspersions of this sort have been cast upon me, I think my-self call'd upon to declare my principles ;

and I do with the strictest truth affirm, that I am as loyal a subject and as firmly attach'd to the present happy establishment as any of those who have the greatest places or pensions. I have been inform'd too, that in the following Play, I have been charg'd with writing immoralities ; that it is fill'd with slander and calumny against particular great persons, and that Majesty it-self is endeavour'd to be brought into ridicule and contempt.

As I knew that every one of these charges was in every point absolutely false and without the least grounds, at first I was not at all affected by them ; but when I found they were still insisted upon, and that particular passages which were not in the Play were quoted and propagated to support what had been suggested, I could no longer bear to lye under these false accusations ; so by printing it, I have submitted and given up all present views of profit which might accrue from the stage, which undoubtedly will be some satisfaction to the worthy gentlemen who have treated me with so much candour and humanity, and represented me in such favourable colours.

But as I am conscious to my-self that my only intention was to lash in general the reigning and fashionable vices, and to recommend and set virtue in as amiable a light as I could ; to justify and vindicate my own character, I thought my-self obliged to print the Opera without delay in the manner I have done.

As the Play was principally design'd for representation, I hope when it is read it will be considered in that light : And when all that hath been said against it shall appear to be intirely misunderstood or misrepresented ; if, some time hence, it should be permitted to appear on the stage, I think it necessary to acquaint the publick, that as far as a contract of this kind can be binding ; I am engag'd to Mr. Rich to have it represented upon his Theatre.

March 25. 1729.

INTRODUCTION.

POET, PLAYER.

Poet. A SEQUEL to a Play is like more last words. 'Tis a kind of absurdity; and really, Sir, you have prevail'd upon me to pursue this subject against my judgment.

1st Player. Be the success as it will, you are sure of what you have contracted for; and upon the inducement of gain no body can blame you for undertaking it.

Poet. I know, I must have been look'd upon as whimsical, and particular if I had scrupled to have risqu'd my reputation for my profit; for why should I be more squeamish than my betters? and so, Sir, contrary to my opinion I bring *Polly* once again upon the Stage.

1st Player. Consider, Sir, you have prepossession on your side.

Poet. But then the pleasure of novelty is lost; and in a thing of this kind I am afraid I shall hardly be pardon'd for imitating my-self, for sure pieces of this sort are not to be followed as precedents. My dependance, like a tricking bookseller's, is, that the kind reception the first part met with will carry off the second be it what it will.

1st Player. You should not disparage your own works; you will have criticks enough who will be glad to do that for you: and let me tell you, Sir, after the success you have had, you must expect envy.

Poet. Since I have had more applause than I can deserve, I must, with other authors, be content, if criticks allow me less. I should be an arrant courtier or an arrant beggar indeed, if as soon as I have receiv'd one undeserved favour I should lay claim to another; I don't flatter my-self with the like success.

1st Player. I hope, Sir, in the catastrophe you have not run into the absurdity of your last Piece.

Poet. I know that I have been unjustly accus'd of having given up my moral for a joke, like a fine gentleman in conversation; but whatever be the event now, I will not so much as seem to give up my moral.

1st Player. Really, Sir, an author should comply with the customs and taste of the town.——I am indeed afraid too that your Satyr here and there is too free. A man should be cautious how he mentions any vice whatsoever before good company, lest somebody present should apply it to himself.

Poet. The Stage, Sir, hath the privilege of the pulpit to attack vice however dignified or distinguish'd, and preachers and poets should not be too well bred upon these occasions: Nobody can overdo it when he attacks the vice and not the person.

1st Player. But how can you hinder malicious applications?

Poet. Let those answer for 'em who make 'em. I aim at no particular persons; my strokes are at vice in general: but if any men particularly vicious are hurt, I make no apology, but leave them to the cure of their flatterers. If an author write in character, the lower people reflect on the follies and vices of the rich and great, and an *Indian* judges and talks of *Europeans* by those he hath seen and convers'd with, *&c.* And I will venture to own that I wish every man of power or riches were really and apparently virtuous, which would soon amend and reform the common people who act by imitation.

1st Player. But a little indulgence and partiality to the vices of your own country without doubt would be look'd upon as more discreet. Though your Satyr, Sir, is on vices in general, it must and will give offence ; every vicious man thinks you particular, for conscience will make self-application. And why will you make your-self so many enemies ? I say no more upon this head, As to us I hope you are satisfy'd we have done all we could for you ; for you will now have the advantage of all our best singers.

Enter 2d Player.

2d Player. 'Tis impossible to perform the Opera to night, all the fine singers within are out of humour with their parts. The Tenor, says he was never offer'd such an indignity, and in a rage flung his clean lambskin gloves into the fire ; he swears that in his whole life he never did sing, would sing, or could sing but in true kid.

1st Player. Musick might tame and civilize wild beasts, but 'tis evident it never yet could tame and civilize musicians.

Enter 3d Player.

3d Player. Sir, *Signora Crotchetta* says she finds her character so low that she had rather dye than sing it.

1st Player. Tell her by her contract I can make her sing it.

Enter Signora Crotchetta.

Crotchetta. Barbarous Tramontane ! Where are all the lovers of *Virtù* ? Will they not all rise in arms in my defence ? make me sing it ! good Gods ! should I tamely submit to such usage I should debase my-self through all *Europe.*

1st Player. In the Opera nine or ten years ago, I remember, Madam, your appearance in a character little better than a fish.

Crotchetta. A fish ! monstrous ! Let me inform you, Sir, that a Mermaid or Syren is not many removes from a sea-Goddess ; or I had never submitted to be that fish which you are pleas'd to call me by way of reproach. I have a cold, Sir ; I am sick. I don't see, why I may not be allowed the privilege of sickness now and then as well as others. If a singer may not be indulg'd in her humours, I am sure she will soon become of no consequence with the town. And so, Sir, I have a cold ; I am hoarse. I hope now you are satisfied.

[*Exit* Crotchetta *in a fury.*

Enter 4th Player.

4th Player. Sir, the base voice insists upon pearl-colour'd stockings and red-heel'd shoes.

1st Player. There is no governing caprice. But how shall we make our excuses to the house ?

4th Player. Since the town was last year so good as to encourage an Opera without singers ; the favour I was then shown obliges me to offer my-self once more, rather than the audience should be dismiss'd. All the other Comedians upon this emergency are willing to do their best, and hope for your favour and indulgence.

1st Player. Ladies and Gentlemen, as we wish to do every thing for your diversion, and that singers only will come when they will come, we beg you to excuse this unforeseen accident, and to accept the proposal of the Comedians, who relye wholly on your courtesie and protection.   [*Exeunt.*

The OUVERTURE.

Dramatis Personæ.

Ducat.
Morano.
Vanderbluff.
Capstern.
Hacker.

Culverin.
Laguerre.
Cutlace.
Pohetohee.
Cawwawkee.

Servants. Indians. Pyrates. Guards, &c.

Polly.
Mrs. Ducat.
Trapes.

Jenny Diver.
Flimzy.
Damaris.

SCENE. *In the* WEST-INDIES.

ACT I. Scene I.

SCENE Ducat's *House.*

DUCAT. TRAPES.

Trapes. THOUGH you were born and bred and live in the *Indies,* as you are a subject of *Britain* you shou'd live up to our customs. Prodigality there, is a fashion that is among all ranks of people. Why, our very younger brothers push themselves into the polite world by squandering more than they are worth. You are wealthy, very wealthy, Mr. *Ducat*; and I grant you the more you have, the taste of getting more should grow stronger upon you. 'Tis just so with us. But then the richest of our Lords and Gentlemen, who live elegantly, always run out. 'Tis genteel to be in debt. Your luxury should distinguish you from the vulgar. You cannot be too expensive in your pleasures.   10

AIR I. The disappointed Widow.

The manners of the Great affect;
Stint not your pleasure :
If conscience had their genius checkt,
How got they treasure ?

The more in debt, run in debt the more,
Careless who is undone ;
Morals and honesty leave to the poor,
As they do at London.

Ducat. I never thought to have heard thrift laid to my charge. There is not a man, though I say it, in all the *Indies* who lives more plentifully than my self ; nor, who enjoys the necessaries of life in so handsome a manner. 21

Trapes. There it is now. Who ever heard a man of fortune in *England* talk of the necessaries of life ? If the necessaries of life would have satisfied such a poor body as me, to be sure I had never come to mend my fortune to the Plantations. Whether we can afford it or no, we must have superfluities. We never stint our expence to our own fortunes, but are miserable if we do not live up to the profuseness of our neighbours. If we could content our selves with the necessaries of Life, no man alive ever need be dishonest. As to woman now ; why, look ye, Mr. *Ducat*, a man hath what we may call every thing that is necessary in a wife. 30

Ducat. Ay, and more !

Trapes. But for all that, d'ye see, your married men are my best customers. It keeps wives upon their good behaviours.

Ducat. But there are jealousies and family lectures, Mrs. *Trapes.*

Trapes. Bless us all ! how little are our customs known on this side the herring-pond ! Why, jealousy is out of fashion even among our common country-gentlemen. I hope you are better bred than to be jealous. A husband and wife should have a mutual complaisance for each other. Sure, your wife is not so unreasonable to expect to have you always to her self. 39

Ducat. As I have a good estate, Mrs. *Trapes*, I would willingly run into every thing that is suitable to my dignity and fortune. No body throws himself into the extravagancies of life with a freer spirit. As to conscience and musty morals, I have as few drawbacks upon my profits or pleasures as any man of quality in *England* ; in those I am not in the least vulgar. Besides, Madam, in most of my expences I run into the polite taste. I have a fine library of books that I never read ; I have a fine stable of horses that I never ride ; I build, I buy plate, jewels, pictures, or any thing that is valuable and curious, as your great men do, merely out of ostentation. But indeed I must own, I do still cohabit with my wife ; and she is very uneasy and vexatious upon account of my visits to you. 50

Trapes. Indeed, indeed, Mr. *Ducat*, you shou'd break through all this usurpation at once, and keep ——. Now too is your time ; for I have a fresh cargo of ladies just arriv'd : no body alive shall set eyes upon 'em till you have provided your self. You should keep your lady in awe by her maid ; place a handsome, sprightly wench near your wife, and she will be a spy upon her into the bargain. I would have you show your self a fine gentleman in every thing.

Ducat. But I am somewhat advanc'd in life, Mrs. *Trapes*, and my duty to my wife lies very hard upon me ; I must leave keeping to younger husbands and old batchelors. 60

Trapes. There it is again now ! Our very vulgar pursue pleasures in the flush of youth and inclination, but our great men are modishly profligate when their appetite hath left 'em.

33 behaviours.] behaviour *Plays 1760, Bell 1777.*

AIR II. *The* Irish *ground.*

BASS.

Ducat.

What can wealth
When we're old ?
Youth and health
Are not sold.

TREBLE.

Trapes.

When love in the pulse beats low,
(As haply it may with you)
A girl can fresh youth bestow,   70
And kindle desire anew,
Thus, numm'd in the brake,
Without motion, the snake
Sleeps cold winter away :
But in every vein
Life quickens again
On the bosom of May.   77

We are not here, I must tell you, as we are at *London,* where we can have fresh goods every week by the waggon. My maid is again gone aboard the vessel ; she is perfectly charm'd with one of the ladies ; 'twill be a credit to you to keep her. I have obligations to you, Mr. *Ducat,* and I would part with her to no man alive but your self. If I had her at *London,* such a lady would be sufficient to make my fortune ; but, in truth, she is not impudent enough to make herself agreeable to the sailors in a publick-house in this country. By all accounts, she hath a behaviour only fit for a private family.

Ducat. But how shall I manage matters with my wife ?   86

Trapes. Just as the fine gentlemen do with us. We could bring you many great precedents for treating a wife with indifference, contempt, and neglect ; but that, indeed, would be running into too high life. I would have you keep some decency, and use her with civility. You should be so obliging as to leave her to her liberties and take them too yourself. Why, all our fine ladies, in what they call pin-money, have no other views ; 'tis what they all expect.

Ducat. But I am afraid it will be hard to make my wife think like a gentlewoman upon this subject ; so that if I take her, I must act discreetly and keep the affair a dead secret.   95

Trapes. As to that, Sir, you may do as you please. Should it ever come to her knowledge, custom and education perhaps may make her at first think it somewhat odd. But this I can affirm with a safe conscience, that many a lady of quality have servants of this sort in their families, and you can afford an expence as well as the best of 'em.   100

Ducat. I have a fortune, Mrs. *Trapes,* and would fain make a fashionable figure in life ; if we can agree upon the price I'll take her into the family.

Trapes. I am glad to see you fling your self into the polite taste with a spirit. Few, indeed, have the turn or talents to get money ; but fewer know how to spend it handsomely after they have got it. The elegance of luxury consists in variety, and love requires it as much as any of our appetites and passions, and there is a time of life when a man's appetite ought to be whetted by a delicacy.   108

Ducat. Nay, Mrs. *Trapes*, now you are too hard upon me. Sure you cannot think me such a clown as to be really in love with my Wife ! We are not so ignorant here as you imagine ; why, I married her in a reasonable way, only for her money.

A I R   I I I.   Noel *Hills.*

He that weds a beauty
*   Soon will find her cloy ;*
When pleasure grows a duty,
*   Farewell love and joy :*
He that weds for treasure
*   (Though he hath a wife)*
Hath chose one lasting pleasure
*   In a married life.*   120

S C E N E   I I.

D U C A T,   T R A P E S,   D A M A R I S.

Ducat. Damaris, [*Calling at the door.*] *Damaris*, I charge you not to stir from the door, and the instant you see your lady at a distance returning from her walk, be sure to give me notice.

Trapes. She is in most charming rigging ; she won't cost you a penny, Sir, in cloaths at first setting out. But, alack-a-day ! no bargain could ever thrive with dry lips : a glass of liquor makes every thing go so glibly.

Ducat. Here, *Damaris* ; a glass of Rum for Mrs. *Dye.* [*Damaris goes out and returns with a bottle and glass.*]   8

Trapes. But as I was saying, Sir, I would not part with her to any body alive but your self ; for, to be sure, I could turn her to ten times the profit by jobbs and chance customers. Come, Sir, here 's to the young lady's health.

S C E N E   I I I.

D U C A T,   T R A P E S,   F L I M Z Y.

Trapes. Well, *Flimzy* ; are all the ladies safely landed, and have you done as I order'd you ?

Flimzy. Yes, Madam. The three ladies for the run of the house are safely lodg'd at home ; the other is without in the hall to wait your commands. She is a most delicious creature, that 's certain. Such lips, such eyes, and such flesh and blood ! If you had her in *London* you could not fail of the custom of all the foreign Ministers. As I hope to be sav'd, Madam, I was forc'd to tell her ten thousand lyes before I could prevail upon her to come with me. Oh Sir, you are the most lucky, happy man in the world ! Shall I go call her in ?   10

Trapes. 'Tis necessary for me first to instruct her in her duty and the ways of the family. The girl is bashful and modest, so I must beg leave to prepare her by a little conversation, and afterwards, Sir, I shall leave you to your private conversations.

Flimzy. But I hope, Sir, you won't forget poor *Flimzy* ; for the richest man alive could not be more scrupulous than I am upon these occasions, and the bribe only can make me excuse it to my conscience. I hope, Sir, you will pardon my freedom. [*He gives her money.*]

A I R I V. Sweetheart, think upon me.

> *My conscience is of courtly mold,*
> *Fit for highest station.*   20
> *Where 's the hand, when touch'd with gold,*
> *Proof against temptation ?*   [*Exit* Flimzy.

Ducat. We can never sufficiently encourage such useful qualifications. You will let me know when you are ready for me.   [*Exit.*

24 *Exit.*] not in 1729.

S C E N E I V.

T R A P E S.

Trapes. I wonder I am not more wealthy ; for, o' my conscience, I have as few scruples as those that are ten thousand times as rich. But, alack-a-day ! I am forc'd to play at small game. I now and then betray and ruine an innocent girl. And what of that ? Can I in conscience expect to be equally rich with those who betray and ruine provinces and countries ? Introth, all their great fortunes are owing to situation ; as for genius and capacity I can match them to a hair : were they in my circumstance they would act like me ; were I in theirs, I should be rewarded as a most profound penetrating politician.

A I R V. 'Twas within a furlong.

> *In pimps and politicians*   10
> *The genius is the same ;*
> *Both raise their own conditions*
> *On others guilt and shame :*
> *With a tongue well-tipt with lyes*
> *Each the want of parts supplies,*
> *And with a heart that 's all disguise*
> *Keeps his schemes unknown.*
> *Seducing as the devil,*
> *They play the tempter's part,*
> *And have, when most they're civil,*   20
> *Most mischief in their heart.*
> *Each a secret commerce drives,*
> *First corrupts and then connives,*
> *And by his neighbours vices thrives,*
> *For they are all his own.*

24 neighbours] neighbour's 1729, corrected in Errata

SCENE V.

TRAPES, FLIMZY, POLLY.

Trapes. Bless my eye-sight! what do I see? I am in a dream, or it is Miss *Polly Peachum!* mercy upon me! Child, what brought you on this side of the water?

Polly. Love, Madam, and the misfortunes of our family. But I am equally surpris'd to find an acquaintance here; you cannot be ignorant of my unhappy story, and perhaps from you, Mrs. *Dye*, I may receive some information that may be useful to me.

Trapes. You need not be much concern'd, Miss *Polly*, at a sentence of transportation, for a young lady of your beauty hath wherewithal to make her fortune in any country.					10

Polly. Pardon me, Madam; you mistake me. Though I was educated among the most profligate in low life, I never engag'd in my father's affairs as a thief or a thief-catcher, for indeed I abhorr'd his profession. Would my Papa had never taken it up, he then still had been alive and I had never known *Macheath!*

AIR VI. Sortez des vos retraites.

She who hath felt a real pain
  By Cupid's dart,
Finds that all absence is in vain
  To cure her heart.
Though from my lover cast					20
  Far as from Pole to Pole,
Still the pure flame must last,
  For love is in the Soul.

You must have heard, Madam, that I was unhappy in my marriage. When *Macheath* was transported all my peace was banished with him; and my Papa's death hath now given me liberty to pursue my inclinations.

Trapes. Good lack-a-day! poor Mr. *Peachum!* Death was so much oblig'd to him that I wonder he did not allow him a reprieve for his own sake. Truly, I think he was oblig'd to no-body more except the physicians: but they dye it seems too. Death is very impartial; he takes all alike, friends and foes.					31

Polly. Every monthly Sessions-paper like the apothecary's files (if I may make the comparison) was a record of his services. But my Papa kept company with gentlemen, and ambition is catching. He was in too much haste to be rich. I wish all great men would take warning. 'Tis now seven months since my Papa was hang'd.

Trapes. This will be a great check indeed to your men of enterprizing genius; and it will be unsafe to push at making a great fortune, if such accidents grow common. But sure, Child, you are not so mad as to think of following *Macheath*.					40

Polly. In following him I am in pursuit of my quiet. I love him, and like a troubled ghost shall never be at rest till I appear to him. If I can receive any information of him from you, it will be a cordial to a wretch in despair.

Trapes. My dear Miss *Polly*, you must not think of it. 'Tis now above a year and a half since he robb'd his master, ran away from the plantation and turn'd pyrate. Then too what puts you beyond all possibility of redress, is, that since he came over he married a transported slave, one *Jenny Diver*, and she is gone off with him. You must give over all thoughts of him for he is a very devil to our sex ; not a woman of the greatest vivacity shifts her inclinations half so fast as he can. Besides, he would disown you, for like an upstart he hates an old acquaintance. I am sorry to see those tears, Child, but I love you too well to flatter you.   52

Polly. Why have I a heart so constant ? cruel love !

A i r   V I I. O Waly, Waly, up the bank.

> *Farewell, farewell, all hope of bliss !*
> *For* Polly *always must be thine.*
> *Shall then my heart be never his,*
> *Which never can again be mine ?*
> *O Love, you play a cruel part,*
> *Thy shaft still festers in the wound ;*
> *You should reward a constant heart,*   60
> *Since 'tis, alas, so seldom found !*

Trapes. I tell you once again, Miss *Polly*, you must think no more of him. You are like a child who is crying after a butterfly that is hopping and fluttering upon every flower in the field ; there is not a woman that comes in his way but he must have a taste of ; besides there is no catching him. But, my dear girl, I hope you took care, at your leaving *England*, to bring off wherewithal to support you.

Polly. Since he is lost, I am insensible of every other misfortune. I brought indeed a summ of money with me, but my chest was broke open at sea, and I am now a wretched vagabond expos'd to hunger and want, unless charity relieve me.   71

Trapes. Poor child ! your father and I have had great dealings together, and I shall be grateful to his memory. I will look upon you as my daughter ; you shall be with me.

Polly. As soon as I can have remittances from *England*, I shall be able to acknowledge your goodness : I have still five hundred pounds there which will be return'd to me upon demand ; but I had rather undertake any honest service that might afford me a maintenance than be burthensome to my friends.   79

Trapes. Sure never any thing happen'd so luckily ! Madam *Ducat* just now wants a servant, and I know she will take my recommendation ; and one so tight and handy as you must please her : then too, her husband is the civilest, best-bred man alive. You are now in her house and I won't leave it 'till I have settled you. Be cheerful, my dear Child, for who knows but all these misfortunes may turn to your advantage ? You are in a rich creditable family, and I dare say your person and behaviour will soon make you a favourite. As to captain *Macheath*, you may now safely look upon your self as a widow, and who knows, if Madam *Ducat* should tip off, what may happen ? I shall recommend you, Miss *Polly*, as a gentlewoman.   89

AIR VIII. O Jenny come tye me.

Despair is all folly ;   90
Hence, melancholy,
Fortune attends you while youth is in flower.
By beauty's possession
Us'd with discretion,
Woman at all times hath joy in her power.

Polly. The service, Madam, you offer me, makes me as happy as I can be in my circumstances, and I accept of it with ten thousand obligations.

Trapes. Take a turn in the hall with my maid for a minute or two, and I'll take care to settle all matters and conditions for your reception. Be assur'd, Miss *Polly*, I'll do my best for you.   100

SCENE VI.

TRAPES, DUCAT.

Trapes. Mr. *Ducat*. Sir. You may come in. I have had this very girl in my eye for you ever since you and I were first acquainted ; and to be plain with you, Sir, I have run great risques for her : I had many a stratagem, to be sure, to inviegle her away from her relations ! she too herself was exceeding difficult. And I can assure you, to ruine a girl of severe education is no small addition to the pleasure of our fine gentlemen. I can be answerable for it too, that you will have the first of her. I am sure I could have dispos'd of her upon the same account for at least a hundred guineas to an alderman of *London* ; and then too I might have had the disposal of her again as soon as she was out of keeping ; but you are my friend, and I shall not deal hard with you.   11

Ducat. But if I like her I would agree upon terms beforehand ; for should I grow fond of her, I know you have the conscience of other trades-people and would grow more imposing ; and I love to be upon a certainty.

Trapes. Sure you cannot think a hundred pistoles too much ; I mean for me. I leave her wholly to your generosity. Why your fine men, who never pay any body else, pay their pimps and bawds well ; always ready money. I ever dealt conscientiously, and set the lowest price upon my ladies ; when you see her, I am sure you will allow her to be as choice a piece of beauty as ever you laid eyes on.   20

Ducat. But, dear Mrs. *Dye*, a hundred pistoles say you ? why, I could have half a dozen negro princesses for the price.

Trapes. But sure you cannot expect to buy a fine handsome christian at that rate. You are not us'd to see such goods on this side of the water. For the women, like the cloaths, are all tarnish'd and half worn out before they are sent hither. Do but cast your eye upon her, Sir ; the door stands half open ; see, yonder she trips in conversation with my maid *Flimzy* in the hall.

Ducat. Why truly I must own she is handsome.

Trapes. Bless me, you are no more mov'd by her than if she were your wife. Handsom ! what a cold husband-like expression is that ! nay, there   30 is no harm done. If I take her home, I don't question the making more money of her. She was never in any body's house but your own since she was landed. She is pure, as she was imported, without the least adulteration.

Ducat. I'll have her. I'll pay you down upon the nail. You shall leave her with me. Come, count your money, Mrs. *Dye.*

Trapes. What a shape is there ! she 's of the finest growth.

Ducat. You make me mis-reckon. She even takes off my eyes from gold.

Trapes. What a curious pair of sparkling eyes !

Ducat. As vivifying as the sun. I have paid you ten.

Trapes. What a racy flavour must breath from those lips !   40

Ducat. I want no provoking commendations. I'm in youth ; I'm on fire ! twenty more makes it thirty ; and this here makes it just fifty.

Trapes. What a most inviting complexion ! how charming a colour ! In short, a fine woman has all the perfections of fine wine, and is a cordial that is ten times as restorative.

Ducat. This fifty then makes it just the sum. So now, Madam, you may deliver her up.

─────────────────────────────

SCENE VII.

DUCAT, TRAPES, DAMARIS.

Damaris. Sir, Sir, my Mistress is just at the door.   [*Exit.*

Ducat. Get you out of the way this moment, dear Mrs. *Dye* ; for I would not have my wife see you. But don't stir out of the house till I am put in possession. I'll get rid of her immediately.   [*Exit* Trapes.

─────────────────────────────

SCENE VIII.

DUCAT, Mrs. *DUCAT.*

Mrs. *Ducat.* I can never be out of the way, for an hour or so, but you are with that filthy creature. If you were young, and I took liberties, you could not use me worse ; you could not, you beastly fellow. Such usage might force the most vertuous woman to resentment. I don't see why the wives in this country should not put themselves upon as easy a foot as in *England.* In short, Mr. *Ducat,* if you behave your self like an *English* husband, I will behave my self like an *English* wife.

A i r I X. Red House.

I will have my humours, I'll please all my senses,
I will not be stinted——in love or expences.
I'll dress with profusion, I'll game without measure ;   10
You shall have the business, I will have the pleasure :
*   Thus every day I'll pass my life,*
*   My home shall be my least resort ;*
*   For sure 'tis fitting that your wife*
*   Shou'd copy ladies of the court.*

      8 *all my senses,*] *all senses* 1729, corrected in Errata.

Ducat. All these things I know are natural to the sex, my dear. But husbands like colts, are restif, and they require a long time to break 'em. Besides, 'tis not the fashion as yet, for husbands to be govern'd in this country. That tongue of yours, my dear, hath not eloquence enough to persuade me out of my reason. A woman's tongue, like a trumpet, only serves to raise my courage. 21

A I R X. Old *Orpheus* tickl'd, *&c.*

When billows come breaking on the strand,
The rocks are deaf and unshaken stand :
Old oaks can defy the thunder's roar,
And I can stand woman's tongue—that's more,
    With a twinkum, twankum, &c.

With that weapon, women, like pyrates, are at war with the whole world. But I thought, my dear, your pride would have kept you from being jealous. 'Tis the whole business of my life to please you ; but wives are like children, the more they are flatter'd and humour'd the more perverse they are. Here now have I been laying out my money, purely to make you a present, and I have nothing but freaks and reproaches in return. You wanted a maid, and I have bought you the handiest creature ; she will indeed make a very creditable servant. 34

Mrs. *Ducat.* I will have none of your hussies about me. And so, Sir, you would make me your convenience, your bawd. Out upon it !

Ducat. But I bought her on purpose for you, Madam.

Mrs. *Ducat.* For your own filthy inclinatiohs, you mean. I won't bear it. What keep an impudent strumpet under my nose ! Here's fine doings indeed ! 40

Ducat. I will have the directions of my family. 'Tis my pleasure it shall be so. So, Madam, be satisfy'd.

A I R X I. Christ-Church Bells.

	When a woman jealous grows,
	Farewell all peace of life !
Mrs. Ducat.	*But e'er man roves, he should pay what he owes.*
	And with her due content his wife.
Ducat.	*'Tis man's the weaker sex to sway.*
Mrs. Ducat.	*We too, whene'er we list, obey.*
Ducat.	*'Tis just and fit*
	You should submit. 50
Mrs. Ducat.	*But sweet kind husband—not to day.*
Ducat.	*Let your clack be still.*
Mrs. Ducat.	*Not till I have my will.*
	If thus you reason slight,
	There's never an hour
	While breath has power,
	But I will assert my right. 57

45 *what he owes.*] *Printed by Underhill as a separate line.*
56 *power,*] Plays 1760, Bell 1777, Underhill *power.* 1729.

Would I had you in *England*; I should have all the women there rise in arms in my defence. For the honour and prerogative of the sex, they would not suffer such a precedent of submission. And so Mr. *Ducat*, I tell you once again, that you shall keep your trollops out of the house, or I will not stay in it.

Ducat. Look'ee, Wife; you will be able to bring about nothing by pouting and vapours. I have resolution enough to withstand either obstinacy or stratagem. And I will break this jealous spirit of yours before it gets a head. And so, my dear, I order that upon my account you behave your self to the girl as you ought.

Mrs. Ducat. I wish you would behave your self to your Wife as you ought; that is to say, with good manners, and compliance. And so, Sir, I leave you and your minx together. I tell you once again, that I would sooner dye upon the spot, than not be mistress in my own house. [*Exit in a passion.*

SCENE IX.

DUCAT, DAMARIS.

Ducat. If by these perverse humours, I should be forc'd to part with her, and allow her a separate maintenance; the thing is so common among people of condition, that it could not prove to my discredit. Family divisions, and matrimonial controversies are a kind of proof of a man's riches; for the poor people are happy in marriage out of necessity, because they cannot afford to disagree. *Damaris*, saw you my Wife?   [*Enter* Damaris. Is she in her own room? What said she? Which way went she?

Damaris. Bless me, I was perfectly frighten'd, she look'd so like a fury! Thank my stars, I never saw her look so before in all my life; tho' mayhap you may have seen her look so before a thousand times. Woe be to the servants that fall in her way! I'm sure I'm glad to be out of it.   11

AIR XII. Cheshire-rounds.

> *When kings by their huffing*
> *Have blown up a squabble,*
> *All the charge and cuffing*
> *Light upon the rabble.*
> *Thus when Man and Wife*
> *By their mutual snubbing,*
> *Kindle civil strife,*
> *Servants get the drubbing.*   19

Ducat. I would have you, *Damaris*, have an eye upon your mistress. You should have her good at heart, and inform me when she has any schemes afoot; it may be the means to reconcile us.

Damaris. She's wild, Sir. There's no speaking to her. She's flown into the garden! Mercy upon us all, say I! How can you be so unreasonable to contradict a woman, when you know we can't bear it?   25

Ducat. I depend upon you, *Damaris*, for intelligence. You may observe her at a distance ; and as soon as she comes into her own room, bring me word. There is the sweetest pleasure in the revenge that I have now in my head ! I'll this instant go and take my charge from Mrs. *Trapes*. [*Aside*.] *Damaris*, you know your instructions.   [*Exit*.

SCENE X.

D A M A R I S.

Damaris. Sure all masters and mistresses, like politicians, judge of the conscience of mankind by their own, and require treachery of their servants as a duty ! I am employ'd by my master to watch my mistress, and by my mistress to watch my master. Which party shall I espouse ? To be sure my mistress's. For in hers, jurisdiction and power, the common cause of the whole sex, are at stake. But my master I see is coming this way. I'll avoid him, and make my observations.   [*Exit*.

SCENE XI.

D U C A T, P O L L Y.

Ducat. Be cheerful, *Polly*, for your good fortune hath thrown you into a family, where, if you rightly consult your own interest, as every body now-a-days does, you may make your self perfectly easy. Those eyes of yours, *Polly*, are a sufficient fortune for any woman, if she have but conduct and know how to make the most of 'em.

Polly. As I am your servant, Sir, my duty obliges me not to contradict you ; and I must hear your flattery tho' I know my self undeserving. But sure, Sir, in handsome women, you must have observ'd that their hearts often oppose their interest ; and beauty certainly has ruin'd more women than it has made happy.   10

> A I R X I I I.   The bush a boon traquair.
>
> *The crow or daw thro' all the year*
> *No fowler seeks to ruin ;*
> *But birds of voice or feather rare*
> *He's all day long persuing.*
> *Beware, fair maids ; so scape the net*
> *That other beauties fell in ;*
> *For sure at heart was never yet*
> *So great a wretch as* Helen !

If my Lady, Sir, will let me know my duty, gratitude will make me study to please her.   20

Ducat. I have a mind to have a little conversation with you, and I would not be interrupted.   [*Bars the door.*

5 know] knew *all editions.*
15 *Beware, fair maids, to scape the net* Underhill.

Polly. I wish, Sir, you would let me receive my Lady's commands.

Ducat. And so, *Polly*, by these downcast looks of yours you would have me believe you don't know you are handsome, and that you have no faith in your looking-glass. Why, every pretty woman studies her face, and a looking-glass to her is what a book is to a Pedant ; she is poring upon it all day long. In troth, a man can never know how much love is in him by conversations with his Wife. A kiss on those lips would make me young again. [*Kisses her.*]

A i r X I V. Bury Fair.

Polly.	*How can you be so teazing ?*	30
Ducat.	*Love will excuse my fault.*	
	How can you be so pleasing !	[Going to kiss her.
Polly.	*I vow I'll not be naught.*	
Ducat.	*All maids I know at first resist.*	[Struggling.
	A master may command.	
Polly.	*You're monstrous rude ; I'll not be kiss'd :*	
	Nay, fye, let go my hand.	
Ducat.	*'Tis foolish pride—*	
Polly.	*'Tis vile, 'tis base*	
	Poor innocence to wrong ;	40
Ducat.	*I'll force you,*	
Polly.	*Guard me from disgrace.*	
	You find that vertue 's strong.	[Pushing him away.

'Tis barbarous in you, Sir, to take the occasion of my necessities to insult me.

Ducat. Nay, hussy, I'll give you money.

Polly. I despise it. No, Sir, tho' I was born and bred in *England*, I can dare to be poor, which is the only thing now-a-days men are asham'd of.

Ducat. I shall humble these saucy airs of yours, Mrs. *Minx.* Is this language from a servant ! from a slave !

Polly. Am I then betray'd and sold !   50

Ducat. Yes, hussy, that you are ; and as legally my property, as any woman is her husband's, who sells her self in marriage.

Polly. Climates that change constitutions have no effect upon manners. What a profligate is that *Trapes !*

Ducat. Your fortune, your happiness depends upon your compliance. What, proof against a bribe ! Sure, hussy, you belye your country, or you must have had a very vulgar education. 'Tis unnatural.

A i r X V. Bobbing Joan.

Maids like courtiers must be woo'd,
Most by flattery are subdu'd ;
Some capricious, coy or nice   60
Out of pride protract the vice ;
    But they fall,
    One and all,
When we bid up to their price.

Besides, hussy, your consent may make me your slave ; there 's power to tempt you into the bargain. You must be more than woman if you can stand that too.

Polly. Sure you only mean to try me ! but 'tis barbarous to trifle with my distresses. 69

Ducat. I'll have none of these airs. 'Tis impertinent in a servant, to have scruples of any kind. I hire honour, conscience and all, for I will not be serv'd by halves. And so, to be plain with you, you obstinate slut, you shall either contribute to my pleasure or my profit ; and if you refuse play in the bed-chamber, you shall go work in the fields among the planters. I hope now I have explain'd my self.

Polly. My freedom may be lost, but you cannot rob me of my vertue and integrity : and whatever is my lot, having that, I shall have the comfort of hope, and find pleasure in reflection.

A i r X V I. A Swain long tortur'd with Disdain.

> *Can I or toil or hunger fear ?*
> *For love's a pain that's more severe.* 80
> *The slave, with vertue in his breast,*
> *Can wake in peace, and sweetly rest.*

But love, when unhappy, the more vertuous it is, the more it suffers. [*Aside.*

Ducat. What noise is that ?

Damaris. [*Without.*] Sir, Sir.

Ducat. Step into the closet ; I'll call you out immediately to present you to my wife. Don't let bashfulness ruin your fortune. The next opportunity I hope you will be better dispos'd. [*Exit* Polly.

Damaris. Open the door, Sir. This moment, this moment.

SCENE XII.

D U C A T, D A M A R I S, Servants, Mrs. *D U C A T,* &c.

Ducat. What's the matter ? Was any body about to ravish you ? Is the house o' fire ? Or my Wife in a passion ?

Damaris. O Sir, the whole country is in an uproar ! The pyrates are all coming down upon us ; and if they should raise the militia, you are an officer you know. I hope you have time enough to fling up your commission.

[*Enter* 1st *Footman.*

1st *Footman.* The neighbours, Sir, are all frighted out of their wits ; they leave their houses, and fly to yours for protection. Where's my Lady, your Wife ? Heaven grant, they have not taken her !

Ducat. If they only took what one could spare.

1st *Footm.* That's true, there were no great harm done. 10

Ducat. How are the musquets ?

1st *Footm.* Rusty Sir, all rusty and peaceable ! For we never clean 'em but against training-day.

Damaris. Then, Sir, your honour is safe, for now you have a just excuse against fighting. [*Enter* 2d *Footman.*

2d *Footman.* The *Indians,* Sir, with whom we are in alliance are all in arms ; there will be bloody work to be sure. I hope they will decide the matter before we can get ready. [*Enter* Mrs. Ducat.

Mrs. *Ducat*. O dear Husband, I'm frighten'd to death ! What will become
of us all ! I thought a punishment for your wicked lewdness would light
upon you at last.   21

Ducat. Presence of mind, my dear, is as necessary in dangers as courage.

Damaris. But you are too rich to have courage. You should fight by
deputy. 'Tis only for poor people to be brave and desperate, who cannot
afford to live.   [*Enter Maids*, &c. *one after another*.

1st *Maid*. The pyrates, Sir, the pyrates ! Mercy upon us, what will become
of us poor helpless women !

2d *Maid*. We shall all be ravish'd.

1st *Old Woman*. All be ravish'd !

2d *Old Woman*. Ay to be sure, we shall be ravish'd ; all be ravish'd !   30

1st *Old Wom*. But if fortune will have it so, patience is a vertue, and we
must undergo it.

2d *Old Wom*. Ay, for certain we must all bear it, Mrs. *Damaris*.

3d *Footm*. A soldier, Sir, from the *Indian* Camp, desires admittance.
He 's here, Sir.   [*Enter* Indian.

Indian. I come, Sir, to the *English* colony, with whom we are in alliance,
from the mighty King *Pohetohee*, my lord and master, and address my self
to you, as you are of the council, for succours. The pyrates are ravaging and
plund'ring the country, and we are now in arms, ready for battle, to oppose 'em.

Ducat. Does *Macheath* command the enemy ?   40

Indian. Report says he is dead. Above twelve moons are pass'd since we
heard of him. *Morano*, a Negro villain, is their chief, who in rapine and
barbarities is even equal to him.

Ducat. I shall inform the council, and we shall soon be ready to joyn you.
So acquaint the King your master.   [*Exit* Indian.

A i r XVII.   March in *Scipio*.

	Brave boys prepare.	[To the men.
	Ah ! Cease, fond Wife to cry.	[To her.
Servant.	*For when the danger 's near,*	
	We've time enough to fly.	
Mrs. Ducat.	*How can you be disgrac'd !*	50
	For wealth secures your fame.	
Servant.	*The rich are always plac'd*	
	Above the sense of shame.	
Mrs. Ducat.	*Let honour spur the slave,*	
	To fight for fighting's sake :	
Ducat.	*But even the rich are brave*	
	When money is at stake.	

Be satisfy'd, my dear, I shall be discreet. My servants here will take care
that I be not over-rash, for their wages depend upon me. But before I go to
council—come hither *Polly* ; I intreat you, Wife, to take her into your service.
[*Enter Polly*.] And use her civilly. Indeed, my dear, your suspicions are
very frivolous and unreasonable.   62

Mrs. *Ducat*. I hate to have a handsome wench about me. They are always
so saucy !

Ducat. Women, by their jealousies, put one in mind of doing that which otherwise we should never think of. Why you are a proof, my dear, that a handsome woman may be honest.

Mrs. Ducat. I find you can say a civil thing to me still.

Ducat. Affairs, you see, call me hence. And so I leave her under your protection.   70

S C E N E X I I I.

Mrs. *D U C A T, D A M A R I S.*

Mrs. Ducat. Away, into the other room again. When I want you, I'll call you. [*Exit Polly.*] Well, *Damaris*, to be sure you have observ'd all that has pass'd. I will know all. I'm sure she's a hussy.

Damaris. Nay, Madam, I can't say so much. But——

Mrs. Ducat. But what?

Damaris. I hate to make mischief.

A i r X V I I I. Jig-it-o'Foot.

> *Better to doubt*
> *All that's doing,*
> *Than to find out*
> *Proofs of ruin.*   10
> *What servants hear and see*
> *Should they tattle,*
> *Marriage all day would be*
> *Feuds and battle.*

A servant's legs and hands should be under your command, but, for the sake of quiet, you should leave their tongues to their own discretion.

Mrs. Ducat. I vow, *Damaris*, I will know it.

Damaris. To be sure, Madam, the door was bolted, and I could only listen. There was a sort of a bustle between 'em, that's certain. What past I know not. But the noise they made, to my thinking, did not sound very honest.

Mrs. Ducat. Noises that did not sound very honest, said you?   21

Damaris. Nay, Madam, I am a maid, and have no experience. If you had heard them, you would have been a better judge of the matter.

Mrs. Ducat. An impudent slut! I'll have her before me. If she be not a thorough profligate, I shall make a discovery by her behaviour. Go call her to me.   [*Exit* Damaris *and returns.*

S C E N E X I V.

Mrs. *D U C A T, D A M A R I S, P O L L Y.*

Mrs. Ducat. In my own house! Before my face! I'll have you sent to the house of correction, strumpet. By that over-honest look, I guess her to be a horrid jade. A mere hypocrite, that is perfectly whitewash'd with innocence. My blood rises at the sight of all strumpets, for they are smuglers in love, that ruin us fair traders in matrimony. Look upon me, Mrs. brazen.

She has no feeling of shame. She is so us'd to impudence, that she has not
a blush within her. Do you know, madam, that I am Mr. *Ducat's* wife ?

Polly. As your servant, Madam, I think my self happy.

Mrs. *Ducat.* You know Mr. *Ducat*, I suppose. She has beauty enough to
make any woman alive hate her.   10

A i r   X I X.   Trumpet Minuet.

Abroad after misses most husbands will roam,
Tho' sure they find woman sufficient at home.
To be nos'd by a strumpet ! Hence, hussy you'd best.
Would he give me my due, I wou'd give her the rest.

I vow I had rather have a thief in my house. For to be sure she is that
besides.

Polly. If you were acquainted with my misfortunes, Madam, you could
not insult me.

Mrs. *Ducat.* What does the wench mean ?   19

Damaris. There 's not one of these common creatures, but, like common
beggars, hath a moving story at her finger's ends, which they tell over, when
they are maudlin, to their lovers. I had a sweetheart, Madam, who was
a rake, and I know their ways very well, by hearsay.

Polly. What villains are hypocrites ! For they rob those of relief, who are
in real distress. I know what it is to be unhappy in marriage.

Mrs. *Ducat.* Married !

Polly. Unhappily.

Mrs. *Ducat.* When, where, to whom ?

Polly. If woman can have faith in woman, may my words find belief.
Protestations are to be suspected, so I shall use none. If truth can prevail,
I know you will pity me.   31

Mrs. *Ducat.* Her manner and behaviour are so particular, that is to say,
so sincere, that I must hear her story. Unhappily married ! That is a misfortune not to be remedied.

Polly. A constant woman hath but one chance to be happy ; an inconstant
woman, tho' she hath no chance to be very happy, can never be very unhappy.

Damaris. Believe me, Mrs. *Polly*, as to pleasures of all sorts, 'tis a much
more agreeable way to be inconstant.

A i r   X X.   *Polwart* on the Green.

Love now is nought but art,
'Tis who can juggle best ;   40
To all men seem to give your heart,
But keep it in your breast.
What gain and pleasure do we find,
Who change whene'er we list !
The mill that turns with every wind
Must bring the owner grist.

Polly. My case, Madam, may in these times be look'd upon as singular ;
for I married a man only because I lov'd him. For this I was look'd upon as
a fool by all my acquaintance ; I was us'd inhumanly by my father and

mother ; and to compleat my misfortunes, my husband, by his wild behaviour, incurr'd the sentence of the law, and was separated from me by banishment. Being inform'd he was in this country, upon the death of my father and mother, with most of my small fortune, I came here to seek him.　　　53

Mrs. Ducat. But how then fell you into the hands of that consummate bawd, *Trapes ?*

Polly. In my voyage, Madam, I was robb'd of all I had. Upon my landing in a strange country, and in want, I was found out by this inhuman woman, who had been an acquaintance of my father's : She offer'd me at first the civilities of her own house. When she was inform'd of my necessities, she propos'd to me the service of a Lady ; of which I readily accepted. 'Twas under that pretence that she treacherously sold me to your husband as a mistress. This, Madam, is in short the whole truth. I fling my self at your feet for protection. By relieving me, you make your self easy.　　　63

Mrs. Ducat. What is't you propose ?

Polly. In conniving at my escape, you save me from your husband's worrying me with threats and violence, and at the same time quiet your own fears and jealousies. If it is ever in my power, Madam, with gratitude I will repay you my ransom.

Damaris. Besides, Madam, you will effectually revenge your self upon your husband ; for the loss of the money he paid for her will touch him to the quick.　　　71

Mrs. Ducat. But have you consider'd what you request ? We are invaded by the pyrates : The *Indians* are in arms ; the whole country is in commotion, and you will every where be expos'd to danger.

Damaris. Get rid of her at any rate. For such is the vanity of man, that when once he has begun with a woman, out of pride he will insist upon his point.

Polly. In staying with you, Madam, I make two people unhappy. And I chuse to bear my own misfortunes, without being the cause of another's.

Mrs. Ducat. If I let her escape before my husband's return, he will imagine she got off by the favour of this bustle and confusion.　　　81

Polly. May heaven reward your charity.

Mrs. Ducat. A woman so young and so handsome must be expos'd to continual dangers. I have a suit of cloaths by me of my nephew's, who is dead. In a man's habit you will run fewer risques. I'll assist you too for the present with some money ; and, as a traveller, you may with greater safety make enquiries after your husband.

Polly. How shall I ever make a return for so much goodness ?

Mrs. Ducat. May love reward your constancy. As for that perfidious monster *Trapes*, I will deliver her into the hands of the magistrate. Come, *Damaris*, let us this instant equip her for her adventures.　　　91

Damaris. When she is out of the house, without doubt, Madam, you will be more easy. And I wish she may be so too.

Polly. May vertue be my protection ; for I feel within me hope, cheerfulness, and resolution.

50 compleat] compleat, *1729.*

A i r X X I. St. *Martin*'s Lane.

As pilgrims thro' devotion
To some shrine pursue their way,
They tempt the raging ocean,
   And thro' desarts stray.
With zeal their hope desiring,   100
The saint their breast inspiring
   With cheerful air,
   Devoid of fear,
   They every danger bear.
Thus equal zeal possessing,
I seek my only blessing.
   O love, my honest vow regard !
   My truth protect,
   My steps direct,
   His flight detect,   110
A faithful wife reward.   [Exit.

ACT II. Scene I.

The View of an I n d i a n *Country.*

P O L L Y *in Boy's Cloaths.*

A i r X X I I. La Villanella.

Why did you spare him,
O'er seas to bear him,
Far from his home, and constant bride ?
   When Papa 'peach'd him,
   If death had reach'd him,
I then had only sigh'd, wept, and dy'd !

If my directions are right, I cannot be far from the village. With the habit, I must put on the courage and resolution of a man ; for I am every where surrounded with dangers. By all I can learn of these pyrates, my dear *Macheath* is not of the crew. Perhaps I may hear of him among the slaves of the next plantation. How sultry is the day ! the cool of this shade will refresh me. I am jaded too with reflection. How restless is love ! [*Musick. Two or three bars of the dead March.*] My imagination follows him every where, would my feet were as swift. The world then could not hide him from me. [*Two or three bars more.*] Yet even thought is now bewilder'd in pursuing him. [*Two or three bars more.*] I'm tir'd, I'm faint. [*The Symphony.*]

AIR XXIII. Dead March in *Coriolanus.*

> *Sleep, O sleep,*
> *With thy rod of incantation,*
> *Charm my imagination.*
> *Then, only then, I cease to weep.* 20
> *By thy power,*
> *The virgin, by time o'ertaken,*
> *For years forlorn, forsaken,*
> *Enjoys the happy hour.*
> *What's to sleep?*
> *'Tis a visionary blessing;*
> *A dream that's past expressing;*
> *Our utmost wish possessing;*
> *So may I always keep.*   [Falls asleep.

SCENE II.

CAPSTERN, HACKER, CULVERIN, LAGUERRE, CUTLACE. Polly *asleep in a distant part of the stage.*

Hacker. We shall find but a cool reception from *Morano,* if we return without either booty or intelligence.

Culverin. A man of invention hath always intelligence ready. I hope we are not exempted from the privilege of travellers.

Capstern. If we had got booty, you know we had resolv'd to agree in a lye. And, gentlemen, we will not have our diligence and duty call'd in question for that which every common servant has at his finger's end for his justification.

Laguerre. Alack, gentlemen, we are not such bunglers in love or politicks, but we must know that either to get favour or keep it, no man ever speaks what he thinks, but what is convenient. 10

AIR XXIV. Three Sheep-skins.

Cutlace.   *Of all the sins that are money-supplying;*
> *Consider the world, 'tis past all denying,*
> *With all sorts,*
> *In towns or courts*
> *The richest sin is lying.*

Culverin. Fatigue, gentlemen, should have refreshment. No man is requir'd to do more than his duty. Let us repose our selves a-while. A sup or two of our cag would quicken invention.   [*They sit and drink.*
All. Agreed. 19

Hacker. I had always a genius for ambition. Birth and education cannot keep it under. Our profession is great, brothers. What can be more heroic than to have declar'd war with the whole world?

Culverin. 'Tis a pleasure to me to recollect times past, and to observe by what steps a genius will push his fortune.

Hacker. Now as to me, brothers, mark you me. After I had rubb'd through my youth with variety of adventures, I was prefer'd to be footman to an eminent gamester, where, after having improv'd my self by his manners and conversation, I left him, betook my self to his politer profession, and cheated like a gentleman. For some time I kept a *Pharaon*-Bank with success, but unluckily in a drunken bout was stript by a more expert brother of the trade. I was now, as 'tis common with us upon these occasions, forc'd to have recourse to the highway for a recruit to set me up ; but making the experiment once too often, I was try'd, and receiv'd sentence ; but got off for transportation. Which hath made me the man I am.　　　　　　　　　　34

Laguerre. From a footman I grew to be a pimp to a man of quality. Considering I was for sometime in that employment, I look upon my self as particularly unlucky, that I then miss'd making my fortune. But, to give him his due, only his death could have prevented it. Upon this, I betook my self to another service, where my wages not being sufficient for my pleasures, I robb'd my master, and retir'd to visit foreign parts.　　　40

Capstern. Now, you must know, I was a drawer of one of the fashionable taverns, and of consequence was daily in the politest conversations. Tho' I say it, no body was better bred. I often cheated my master, and as a dutiful servant, now and then cheated for him. I had always my gallantries with the ladies that the lords and gentlemen brought to our house. I was ambitious too of a gentleman's profession, and turn'd gamester. Tho' I had great skill and no scruples, my play would not support my extravagancies : So that now and then I was forc'd to rob with pistols too. So I also owe my rank in the world to transportation.　　　　　　　　　　49

Culverin. Our chief, *Morano*, brothers, had never been the man he is, had he not been train'd up in *England*. He has told me, that from his infancy he was the favourite page of a lady. He had a genius too above service, and, like us, ran into higher life. And, indeed, in manners and conversation, tho' he is black, no body has more the air of a great man.

Hacker. He is too much attach'd to his pleasures. That mistress of his is a clog to his ambition. She 's an arrant *Cleopatra*.

Laguerre. If it were not for her, the *Indies* would be our own.

A I R X X V.　Rigadoon.

> *By women won*
> *We're all undone,*
> *Each wench hath a* Syren's *charms.*　　　60
> *The lover's deeds*
> *Are good or ill,*
> *As whim succeeds*
> *In woman's will :*
> *Resolution is lull'd in her arms.*

Hacker. A man in love is no more to be depended on than a man in liquor, for he is out of himself.

A I R X X V I.　Ton humeur est Catharine.

> *Woman 's like the flatt'ring ocean,*
> *Who her pathless ways can find ?*
> *Every blast directs her motion*　　　70
> *Now she 's angry, now she 's kind.*

> *What a fool's the vent'rous lover,*
> *Whirl'd and toss'd by every wind!*
> *Can the bark the port recover*
> *When the silly Pilot's blind?*

Hacker. A good horse is never turn'd loose among mares, till all his good deeds are over. And really your heroes should be serv'd the same way ; for after they take to women, they have no good deeds to come. That inviegling gipsey, brothers, must be hawl'd from him by force. And then—the kingdom of *Mexico* shall be mine. My lot shall be the kingdom of *Mexico*.   80

Capstern. Who talks of *Mexico?* [*All rise.*] I'll never give it up. If you outlive me, brother, and I dye without heirs, I'll leave it to you for a legacy. I hope now you are satisfy'd. I have set my heart upon it, and no body shall dispute it with me.

Laguerre. The island of *Cuba*, methinks, brother, might satisfy any reasonable man.

Culverin. That I had allotted for you. *Mexico* shall not be parted with without my consent, captain *Morano* to be sure will choose *Peru* ; that's the country of gold, and all your great men love gold. *Mexico* hath only silver, nothing but silver. Governor of *Cartagena*, brother, is a pretty snug employment. That I shall not dispute with you.   91

Capstern. Death, Sir,—I shall not part with *Mexico* so easily.

Hacker. Nor I.

Culverin. Nor I.

Laguerre. Nor I.

Culverin. Nor I.

Hacker. Draw then, and let the survivor take it.   [*They fight.*

Polly. Bless me, what noise was that ! Clashing of swords and fighting ! Which way shall I fly, how shall I escape ?   99

Capstern. Hold, hold, gentlemen, let us decide our pretensions some other time. I see booty. A prisoner. Let us seize him.

Culverin. From him we will extort both ransom and intelligence.

Polly. Spare my life gentlemen. If you are the men I take you for, I sought you to share your fortunes.

Hacker. Why, who do you take us for, friend ?

Polly. For those brave spirits, those *Alexanders*, that shall soon by conquest be in possession of the *Indies*.

Laguerre. A mettl'd young fellow.

Capstern. He speaks with respect too, and gives us our titles.

Culverin. Have you heard of captain *Morano ?*   110

Polly. I came hither in meer ambition to serve under him.

AIR XXVII. Ye nymphes and sylvan gods.

> *I hate those coward tribes,*
> *Who by mean sneaking bribes,*
> *By tricks and disguise,*
> *By flattery and lies,*
> *To power and grandeur rise.*
> *Like heroes of old*
> *You are greatly bold,*

> *The sword your cause supports.*
> *Untaught to fawn,*   120
> *You ne'er were drawn*
> *Your truth to pawn,*
> *Among the spawn,*
> *Who practise the frauds of courts.*

I would willingly choose the more honourable way of making a fortune.

Hacker. The youth speaks well. Can you inform us, my lad, of the disposition of the enemy ? Have the *Indians* joyn'd the factory ? We should advance towards 'em immediately. Who knows but they may side with us ? May-hap they may like our tyranny better.   129

Polly. I am a stranger, gentlemen, and entirely ignorant of the affairs of this country : But in the most desperate undertaking, I am ready to risque your fortunes.

Hacker. Who, and what are you, friend !

Polly. A young fellow, who has genteely run out his fortune with a spirit, and would now with more spirit retrieve it.

Culverin. The lad may be of service. Let us bring him before *Morano*, and leave him to his disposal.

Polly. Gentlemen, I thank you.

A I R   X X V I I I.   Minuet.

Culverin.   *Cheer up my lads, let us push on the fray.*
            For battles, like women, are lost by delay.   140
            Let us seize victory while in our power ;
            Alike war and love have their critical hour.
              Our hearts bold and steady
              Should always be ready,
            So, think war a widow, a kingdom the dower.   [Exeunt.

                    145 *dower.*] *dower,* 1729.

S C E N E   I I I.

Another Country Prospect.

M O R A N O ,   J E N N Y.

Morano. Sure, hussy, you have more ambition and more vanity than to be serious in persuading me to quit my conquests. Where is the woman who is not fond of title ? And one bold step more, may make you a queen, you gipsy. Think of that.

A I R   X X I X.   Mirleton.

When I'm great, and flush of treasure,
Check'd by neither fear or shame,
You shall tread a round of pleasure,
Morning, noon, and night the same.
    With a Mirleton, &c.

Like a city wife or beauty 10
You shall flutter life away ;
And shall know no other duty,
But to dress, eat, drink, and play.
With a Mirleton, *&c.*

When you are a queen, *Jenny*, you shall keep your coach and six, and shall game as deep as you please. So, there's the two chief ends of woman's ambition satisfy'd.

A i r X X X.   Sawny was tall, and of noble race.

	Shall I not be bold when honour calls ?
	You've a heart that would upbraid me then.
Jenny.	*But, ah, I fear, if my hero falls,* 20
	Thy Jenny *shall ne'er know pleasure again.*
Morano.	*To deck their wives fond tradesmen cheat ;*
	I conquer but to make thee great.
Jenny.	*But if my hero falls, — ah then*
	Thy Jenny *shall ne'er know pleasure again !*

Morano. Insinuating creature ! but you must own *Jenny*, you have had convincing proofs of my fondness ; and if you were reasonable in your love, you should have some regard to my honour, as well as my person.

Jenny. Have I ever betray'd you, since you took me to your self ? That's what few women can say, who ever were trusted. 30

Morano. In love, *Jenny*, you cannot out-do me. Was it not entirely for you that I disguis'd my self as a black, to skreen my self from women who laid claim to me where-ever I went ? Is not the rumour of my death, which I purposely spread, credited thro' the whole country ? *Macheath* is dead to all the world but you. Not one of the crew have the least suspicion of me.

Jenny. But, dear captain, you would not sure persuade me that I have all of you. For tho' women cannot claim you, you now and then lay claim to other women. But my jealousy was never teazing or vexatious. You will pardon me, my dear. 39

Morano. Now you are silly, *Jenny*. Pr'ythee—poh ! Nature, girl, is not to be corrected at once. What do you propose ? What would you have me do ? Speak out, let me know your mind.

Jenny. Know when you are well.

Morano. Explain your self ; speak your sentiments freely.

Jenny. You have a competence in your power. Rob the crew, and steal off to *England*. Believe me, Captain, you will be rich enough to be respected by your neighbours.

Morano. Your opinion of me startles me. For I never in my life was treacherous but to women ; and you know men of the nicest punctilio make nothing of that. 50

Jenny. Look round among all the snug fortunes that are made, and you will find most of 'em were secur'd by a judicious retreat. Why will you bar your self from the customs of the times ?

13 *play.*] *play 1729.*   40 Nature, girl,] Nature girl *1729.*

A i r X X X I. Northern *Nancy.*

How many men have found the skill
Of power and wealth acquiring ?
But sure there 's a time to stint the will
And the judgment is in retiring.
    For to be displac'd,
    For to be disgrac'd,
Is the end of too high aspiring.   6ɔ

Enter Sailor.

Sailor. Sir, Lieutenant *Vanderbluff* wants to speak with you. And he hopes your honour will give him the hearing.   [*Exit.*

Morano. Leave me, *Jenny*, for a few minutes. Perhaps he would speak with me in private.

Jenny. Think of my advice before it is too late. By this kiss I beg it of you.   [*Exit.*

S C E N E I V.

M O R A N O, V A N D E R B L U F F.

Vanderbluff. For shame, Captain ; what, hamper'd in the arms of a woman, when your honour and glory are all at stake ! while a man is grappling with these gil-flirts, pardon the expression, Captain, he runs his reason a-ground ; and there must be a woundy deal of labour to set it a-float again.

A i r X X X I I. Amante fuggite cadente belta.

Fine women are devils, compleat in their way,
They always are roving and cruising for prey.
When we flounce on their hook, their views they obtain,
Like those too their pleasure is giving us pain.   8

Excuse my plain speaking, Captain ; a boatswain must swear in a storm, and a man must speak plain, when he sees foul weather a-head of us.

Morano. D'you think me like the wheat-ear, only fit for sunshine, who cannot bear the least cloud over him ? No *Vanderbluff*, I have a heart that can face a tempest of dangers. Your blust'ring will but make me obstinate. You seem frighten'd, Lieutenant.

Vanderbluff. From any body but you, that speech should have had another-guess answer than words. Death, Captain, are not the *Indies* in dispute ? an hour's delay may make their hands too many for us. Give the word, Captain, this hand shall take the *Indian* King pris'ner, and keel-hawl him afterwards, 'till I make him discover his gold. I have known you eager to venture your life for a less prize.   20

Morano. Are *Hacker, Culverin, Capstern, Laguerre* and the rest, whom we sent out for intelligence, return'd, that you are under this immediate alarm ?

Vanderbluff. No, Sir ; but from the top of yon' hill, I my self saw the enemy putting themselves in order of battle.

7 *we*] *omitted by Underhill.*

Morano. But we have nothing at all to apprehend ; for we have still a safe retreat to our ships.

Vanderbluff. To our woman, you mean. Furies ! you talk like one. If our Captain is bewitch'd, shall we be be-devil'd, and lose the footing we have got ? [*Draws.*

Morano. Take care, Lieutenant. This language may provoke me. I fear no man. I fear nothing, and that you know. Put up your cutlace, Lieutenant, for I shall not ruin our cause by a private quarrel. 32

Vanderbluff. Noble Captain, I ask pardon.

Morano. A brave man should be cool till action, Lieutenant ; when danger presses us, I am always ready. Be satisfy'd, I'll take my leave of my wife, and then take the command.

Vanderbluff. That 's what you can never do till you have her leave. She is but just gone from you, Sir. See her not ; hear her not ; the breath of a woman has ever prov'd a contrary wind to great actions. 39

Morano. I tell you I will see her. I have got rid of many a woman in my time, and you may trust me——

Vanderbluff. With any woman but her. The husband that is govern'd is the only man that never finds out that he is so.

Morano. This then, Lieutenant, shall try my resolution. In the mean time, send out parties and scouts to observe the motions of the *Indians.*

A i r   X X X I I I.   Since all the world's turn'd upside down.

> *Tho' different passions rage by turns,*
> *Within my breast fermenting ;*
> *Now blazes love, now honour burns,*
> *I'm here, I'm there consenting.*
> *I'll each obey, so keep my oath,* 50
> *That oath by which I won her :*
> *With truth and steddiness in both,*
> *I'll act like a man of honour.*

Doubt me not, Lieutenant. But I'll now go with you, to give the necessary commands, and after that return to take my leave before the battle.

SCENE V.

M O R A N O,   V A N D E R B L U F F,   J E N N Y,   C A P S T E R N, C U L V E R I N,   H A C K E R,   L A G U E R R E,   P O L L Y.

Jenny. *Hacker*, Sir, and the rest of the party are return'd with a prisoner. Perhaps from him you may learn some intelligence that may be useful. See, here they are. —— A clever sprightly young fellow ! I like him. [*Aside.*

Vanderbluff. What cheer, my lads ? has fortune sent you a good prize ?

Jenny. He seems some rich planter's son.

Vanderbluff. In the common practice of commerce you should never slip an opportunity, and for his ransome, no doubt, there will be room for comfortable extortion.

Morano. Hath he inform'd you of any thing that may be of service ? where pick'd you him up ? whence is he ? 10

Hacker. We found him upon the road. He is a stranger it seems in these parts. And as our heroes generally set out, extravagance, gaming and debauchery have qualify'd him for a brave man.

Morano. What are you, friend ?

Polly. A young fellow, who hath been robb'd by the world ; and I came on purpose to join you, to rob the world by way of retaliation. An open war with the whole world is brave and honourable. I hate the clandestine pilfering war that is practis'd among friends and neighbours in civil societies. I would serve, Sir.

AIR XXXIV. Hunt the Squirrel.

The world is always jarring ;   20
   This is pursuing
   T'other man's ruin,
Friends with friends are warring,
   In a false cowardly way.
Spurr'd on by emulations,
   Tongues are engaging,
   Calumny, raging
Murthers reputations,
   Envy keeps up the fray.
Thus, with burning hate,   30
Each, returning hate,
Wounds and robs his friends.
   In civil life,
   Even man and wife
Squabble for selfish ends.

Jenny. He really is a mighty pretty man.   [*Aside.*

Vanderbluff. The lad promises well, and has just notions of the world.

Morano. Whatever other great men do, I love to encourage merit. The youth pleases me ; and if he answers in action——d'you hear me, my lad ?—— your fortune is made. Now Lieutenant *Vanderbluff*, I am for you.   40

Vanderbluff. Discipline must not be neglected.

Morano. When every thing is settled, my dear *Jenny*, I will return to take my leave. After that, young gentleman, I shall try your mettle. In the mean time, *Jenny*, I leave you to sift him with farther questions. He has liv'd in the world, you find, and may have learnt to be treacherous.

SCENE VI.

JENNY, POLLY.

Jenny. How many women have you ever ruin'd, young gentleman !

Polly. I have been ruin'd by women, madam. But I think indeed a man's fortune cannot be more honourably dispos'd of ; for those have always a kind of claim to their protection, who have been ruin'd in their service.

Jenny. Were you ever in love ?

Polly. With the sex.

Jenny. Had you never a woman in love with you ?

Polly.   All the women that ever I knew were mercenary.

Jenny.   But sure you cannot think all women so.   9

Polly.   Why not as well as all men ?   The manners of courts are catching.

Jenny.   If you have found only such usage, a generous woman can the more oblige you.   Why so bashful, young spark ?   You don't look as if you would revenge your self on the sex.

Polly.   I lost my impudence with my fortune.   Poverty keeps down assurance.

Jenny.   I am a plain-spoken woman, as you may find, and I own I like you. And, let me tell you, to be my favourite may be your best step to preferment.

A I R   X X X V.   Young *Damon* once the loveliest swain.

> *In love and life the present use.*
> *One hour we grant, the next refuse ;*
> *Who then would risque a nay ?*   20
> *Were lovers wise they would be kind,*
> *And in our eyes the moment find ;*
> *For only then they may.*

Like other women I shall run to extremes.   If you won't make me love you, I shall hate you.   There never was a man of true courage, who was a coward in love.   Sure you are not afraid of me, stripling ?   [*Taking* Polly *by the hand.*

Polly.   I know you only railly me.   Respect, madam, keeps me in awe.

Jenny.   By your expression and behaviour, one would think I were your wife.   If so, I may make use of her freedoms, and do what I please without shame or restraint.   [*Kisses her.*]   Such raillery as this, my dear, requires replication.   31

Polly.   You'll pardon me then, Madam.   [*Kisses her.*

Jenny.   What, my cheek !   let me dye, if by your kiss, I should not take you for my brother or my father.

Polly.   I must put on more assurance, or I shall be discover'd.   [*Aside.*] Nay then, Madam, if a woman will allow me liberties, they are never flung away upon me.   If I am too rude—   [*Kisses her.*

Jenny.   A woman never pardons the contrary fault.

A I R   X X X V I.   Catharine Ogye.

	We never blame the forward swain,	
	Who puts us to the tryal.	40
Polly.	*I know you first would give me pain,*	
	Then baulk me with denial.	
Jenny.	*What mean we then by being try'd ?*	
Polly.	*With scorn and slight to use us.*	
	Most beauties, to indulge their pride,	
	Seem kind but to refuse us.	

Jenny.   Come then, my dear, let us take a turn in yonder grove.   A woman never shews her pride but before witnesses.

Polly.   How shall I get rid of this affair ?   [*Aside.*]   *Morano* may surprize us.

Jenny.   That is more a wife's concern.   Consider, young man, if I have put my self in your power, you are in mine.   51

Polly. We may have more easy and safe opportunities. Besides, I know, Madam, you are not serious.

Jenny. To a man who loses one opportunity, we never grant a second. Excuses! consideration! he hath not a spark of love in him. I must be his aversion! go, monster, I hate you, and you shall find I can be reveng'd.

A i r X X X V I I. Roger a Coverly.

My heart is by love forsaken,
I feel the tempest growing.
A fury the place hath taken,   60
I rage, I burn, I'm glowing.
Tho' Cupid's arrows are erring,
Or indifference may secure ye,
When woman's revenge is stirring,
You cannot escape that fury.

I could bear your excuses, but those looks of indifference kill me.

S C E N E V I I.

J E N N Y, P O L L Y, M O R A N O.

Jenny. Sure never was such insolence! how could you leave me with this bawdy-house bully? for if he had been bred a page, he must have made his fortune. If I had given him the least encouragement, it would not have provok'd me. Odious creature!

Morano. What-a-vengeance is the matter?

Jenny. Only an attempt upon your wife. So ripe an assurance! he must have suck'd in impudence from his mother.

Morano. An act of friendship only. He meant to push his fortune with the husband. 'Tis the way of the town, my dear.

A i r X X X V I I I. Bacchus m'a dit.

By halves no friend   10
Now seeks to do you pleasure.
Their help they lend
In every part of life ;
If husbands part,
The friend hath always leisure ;
Then all his heart
Is bent to please the wife.

Jenny. I hate you for being so little jealous.   13

Morano. Sure, *Jenny*, you know the way of the world better, than to be surpriz'd at a thing of this kind. 'Tis a civility that all you fine ladies expect; and, upon the like occasion, I could not have answer'd for my self. I own, I have a sort of partiality to impudence. Perhaps too, his views might be

54. Excuses] excuses *1729.*

honourable. If I had been kill'd in battle, 'tis good to be beforehand. You know 'tis a way often practis'd to make sure of a widow.

Jenny. If I find you so easy in these affairs, you may make my vertue less obstinate.

A I R X X X I X. Health to *Betty.*

If husbands sit unsteady,
Most wives for freaks are ready.
Neglect the rein
The steed again   30
Grows skittish, wild and heady.

Your behaviour forces me to say, what my love for you will never let me put in practice. You are too safe, too secure, to think of pleasing me.

Morano. Tho' I like impudence, yet 'tis not so agreeable when put in practice upon my own wife : and jesting apart, young fellow, if I ever catch you thinking this way again, a cat-o'-nine-tails shall cool your courage.

SCENE VIII.

M O R A N O, J E N N Y, P O L L Y, V A N D E R B L U F F,
C A P S T E R N, L A G U E R R E, &c. *with*
C A W W A W K E E Prisoner.

Van. The party, captain, is return'd with success. After a short skirmish, the *Indian* prince *Cawwawkee* here was made prisoner, and we want your orders for his disposal.

Mor. Are all our troops ready and under arms ?

Van. They wait but for your command. Our numbers are strong. All the ships crews are drawn out, and the slaves that have deserted to us from the plantations are all brave determin'd fellows, who must behave themselves well.

Mor. Look'e lieutenant, the trussing up this prince, in my opinion, would strike a terror among the enemy. Besides, dead men can do no mischief. Let a gibbet be set up, and swing him off between the armies before the onset.

Van. By your leave, captain, my advice blows directly contrary. Whatever may be done hereafter, I am for putting him first of all upon examination. The *Indians* to be sure have hid their treasures, and we shall want a guide to show us the best plunder.   14

Mor. The counsel is good. I will extort intelligence from him. Bring me word when the enemy are in motion, and that instant I'll put myself at your head. [*Exit Sailor.*] Do you know me, prince ?

Caw. As a man of injustice I know you, who covets and invades the properties of another.

Mor. Do you know my power ?   20

Caw. I fear it not.

Mor. Do you know your danger ?

Caw. I am prepar'd to meet it.

A i r X L. Cappe de bonne Esperance.

The body of the brave may be taken,
If chance bring on our adverse hour ;
But the noble soul is unshaken,
For that still is in our power :
'Tis a rock whose firm foundation
Mocks the waves of perturbation ;
'Tis a never-dying ray,
Brighter in our evil Day.   30

Mor. Meer downright Barbarians, you see lieutenant. They have our notional honour still in practice among 'em.

Van. We must beat civilizing into 'em, to make 'em capable of common society, and common conversation.

Mor. Stubborn prince, mark me well. Know you, I say, that your life is in my power ?

Caw. I know too, that my virtue is in my own.

Mor. Not a mule, or an old out-of-fashion'd philosopher could be more obstinate. Can you feel pain ?

Caw. I can bear it.   40

Mor. I shall try you.

Caw. I speak truth, I never affirm but what I know.

Mor. In what condition are your troops ? What numbers have you ? How are they dispos'd ? Act reasonably and openly, and you shall find protection.

Caw. What, betray my friends ! I am no coward, *European.*

Mor. Torture shall make you squeak.

Caw. I have resolution ; and pain shall neither make me lie or betray. I tell thee once more *European*, I am no coward.   49

Van. What, neither cheat nor be cheated ! There is no having either commerce or correspondence with these creatures.

Jen. We have reason to be thankful for our good education. How ignorant is mankind without it !

Cap. I wonder to hear the brute speak.

Lag. They would make a shew of him in *England.*

Jen. Poh, they would only take him for a fool.

Cap. But how can you expect any thing else from a creature, who hath never seen a civiliz'd country ? Which way should he know mankind ?

Jen. Since they are made like us, to be sure, were they in *England* they might be taught.   60

Lag. Why we see country gentlemen grow into courtiers, and country gentlewomen, with a little polishing of the town, in a few months become fine ladies.

Jen. Without doubt, education and example can do much.

Pol. How happy are these savages ! Who would not wish to be in such ignorance.   [*Aside.*

Mor. Have done, I beg you, with your musty reflections : You but interrupt the examination. You have treasures, you have gold and silver among you, I suppose.   69

Caw. Better it had been for us if that shining earth had never been brought to light.

Mor. That you have treasures then you own, it seems. I am glad to hear you confess something.

Caw. But out of benevolence we ought to hide it from you. For, as we have heard, 'tis so rank a poison to you *Europeans*, that the very touch of it makes you mad.

A I R X L I.   When bright Aurelia tripp'd the plain.

> *For gold you sacrifice your fame,*
> *Your honour, life and friend :*
> *You war, you fawn, you lie, you game,*
> *And plunder without fear or shame ;*   80
> *Can madness this transcend ?*

Mor. Bold savage, we are not to be insulted with your ignorance. If you would save your lives, you must, like the beaver, leave behind you what we hunt you for, or we shall not quit the chase. Discover your treasures, your hoards, for I will have the ransacking of 'em.

Jen. By his seeming to set some value upon gold, one would think that he had some glimmering of sense.

A I R X L I I.   Peggy's Mill.

> *When gold is in hand,*
> *It gives us command ;*
> *It makes us lov'd and respected.*   90
> *'Tis now, as of yore,*
> *Wit and sense, when poor,*
> *Are scorn'd, o'erlook'd and neglected.*
> *Tho' peevish and old,*
> *If women have gold.*
> *They have youth, good-humour and beauty ;*
> *Among all mankind*
> *Without it we find*
> *Nor love, nor favour nor duty.*   99

Mor. I will have no more of these interruptions. Since women will be always talking, one would think they had a chance now and then to talk in season. Once more I ask you, obstinate, audacious savage, if I grant you your life, will you be useful to us ? For you shall find mercy upon no other terms. I will have immediate compliance, or you shall undergo the torture.

Caw. With dishonour life is nothing worth.

Mor. Furies ! I'll trifle no longer.

R E C I T A T I V E.   Sia suggetta la plebe *in* Coriolan.

> *Hence let him feel his sentence.*
> *Pain brings repentance.*

Lag. You would not have us put him to death, captain ?   109

93. *o'erlook'd*] *o'rlook'd* 1729.

Mor. Torture him leisurely, but severely. I shall stagger your resolution, *Indian.*

RECITATIVE.

Hence let him feel his sentence.
Pain brings repentance.

But hold, I'll see him tortur'd. I will have the pleasure of extorting answers from him myself. So keep him safe till you have my directions.

Lag. It shall be done.

Mor. As for you, young gentleman, I think it not proper to trust you till I know you farther. Let him be your prisoner too till I give order how to dispose of him.   [*Exeunt* Caw. *and* Polly *guarded.*

SCENE IX.

MORANO, JENNY, VANDERBLUFF.

Van. Come, noble captain, take one hearty smack upon her lips, and then steer off ; for one kiss requires another, and you will never have done with her. If once a man and woman come to grappling, there 's no hawling of 'em asunder. Our friends expect us.

Jen. Nay, lieutenant *Vanderbluff*, he shall not go yet.

Van. I'm out of all patience. There is a time for all things, Madam. But a woman thinks all times must be subservient to her whim and humour. We should be now upon the spot.

Jen. Is the captain under your command, lieutenant ?   9

Van. I know women better than so. I shall never dispute the command with any gentleman's wife. Come captain, a woman will never take the last kiss ; she will always want another. Break from her clutches.

Mor. I must go—— But I cannot.

AIR XLIII. Excuse me.

Honour calls me from thy arms,	[To him.
With glory my bosom is beating.	
Victory summons to arms : then to arms	
Let us haste, for we're sure of defeating.	
One look more—and then——	[To her.
Oh, I am lost again !	
What a Power has beauty !	20
But honour calls, and I must away.	[To him.
But love forbids, and I must obey.	[To her.
You grow too bold ;	[Vanderbluff *pulling him away.*
Hence, loose your hold,	[To him.
For love claims all my duty.	[To her.

They will bring us word when the enemy is in motion. I know my own time, lieutenant.

Van. Lose the *Indies* then, with all my heart. Lose the money, and you lose the woman, that I can tell you, captain. Furies, what would the woman be at !   30

Jen. Not so hasty and choleric, I beg you, lieutenant. Give me the hearing, and perhaps, whatever you may think of us, you may once in your life hear a woman speak reason.

Van. Dispatch then. And if a few words can satisfy you, be brief.

Jen. Men only slight women's advice thro' an overconceit of their own opinions. I am against hazarding a battle. Why should we put what we have already got to the risque ? We have money enough on board our ships to secure our persons, and can reserve a comfortable subsistance besides. Let us leave the *Indies* to our comrades. 39

Van. Sure you are the first of the sex that ever stinted herself in love or money. If it were consistent with our honour, her counsel were worth listening to.

Jen. Consistent with our honour ! For shame, lieutenant ; you talk downright *Indian.* One would take you for the savage's brother or cousin-german at least. You may talk of honour, as other great men do : But when interest comes in your way, you should do as other great men do.

A I R X L I V. Ruben.

Honour plays a bubble's part,
  Ever bilk'd and cheated ;
Never in ambition's heart,
  Int'rest there is seated. 50
Honour was in use of yore,
  Tho' by want attended :
Since 'twas talk'd of, and no more ;
  Lord, how times are mended !

Van. What think you of her proposal, noble captain ? We may push matters too far.

Jen. Consider, my dear, the *Indies* are only treasures in expectation. All your sensible men, now a days, love the ready. Let us seize the ships then, and away for *England,* while we have the opportunity. 59

Van. Sure you can have no scruple against treachery, captain. 'Tis as common a money-getting vice as any in fashion ; for who now-a-days ever boggles at giving up his crew ?

Mor. But the baulking of a great design——

Van. 'Tis better baulking our own designs, than have 'em baulk'd by others ; for then our designs and our lives will be cut short together.

A I R X L V. Troy Town.

When ambition's ten years toils
Have heap'd up mighty hoards of gold ;
Amid the harvest of the spoils,
Acquir'd by fraud and rapin bold,
Comes justice. The great scheme is crost, 70
At once wealth, life, and fame, are lost.

This is a melancholy reflection for ambition, if it ever could think reasonably.

Mor. If you are satisfy'd, and for your security, *Jenny.* For any man may allow that he has money enough, when he hath enough to satisfy his wife.

Van. We may make our retreat without suspicion, for they will readily impute our being mist to the accidents of war.

SCENE X.

M O R A N O, J E N N Y, V A N D E R B L U F F, S A I L O R.

Sail. There is just now news arriv'd, that the troops of the plantation have intercepted the passage to our ships ; so that victory is our only hope. The *Indian* forces too are ready to march, and ours grow impatient for your presence, noble captain.

Mor. I'll be with 'em. Come then, lieutenant, for death or the world.

Jen. Nay then, if affairs are desperate, nothing shall part me from you. I'll share your dangers.

Mor. Since I must have an empire, prepare yourself, *Jenny*, for the cares of royalty. Let us on to battle, to victory. Hark the trumpet.

[*Trumpet sounds.*

A i r X L V I. We've cheated the Parson.

	Despair leads to battle, no courage so great.	10
	They must conquer or die who've no retreat.	
Van.	*No retreat.*	
Jen.	*No retreat.*	
Mor.	*They must conquer or die who've no retreat.*	[Exeunt.

S C E N E X I. *A room of a poor cottage.*

C A W W A W K E E in chains, P O L L Y.

Pol. Unfortunate prince ! I cannot blame your disbelief, when I tell you that I admire your virtues, and share in your misfortunes.

Caw. To be oppress'd by an *European* implies merit. Yet you are an *European*. Are you fools ? Do you believe one another ? Sure speech can be of no use among you.

Pol. There are constitutions that can resist a pestilence.

Caw. But sure vice must be inherent in such constitutions. You are asham'd of your hearts, you can lie. How can you bear to look into yourselves ?

Pol. My sincerity could even bear your examination.

Caw. You have cancell'd faith. How can I believe you ? You are cowards too, for you are cruel. 11

Pol. Would it were in my power to give you proofs of my compassion.

Caw. You can be avaritious. That is a complication of all vices. It comprehends them all. Heaven guard our country from the infection.

Pol. Yet the worst men allow virtue to be amiable, or there would be no hypocrites.

Caw. Have you then hypocrisy still among you ? For all that I have experienc'd of your manners is open violence, and barefac'd injustice. Who that had ever felt the satisfaction of virtue would ever part with it ?

A i r X L V I I. T'amo tanto.

> *Virtue's treasure* 20
> *Is a pleasure,*
> *Cheerful even amid distress ;*
> *Nor pain nor crosses,*
> *Nor grief nor losses,*
> *Nor death itself can make it less :*
> *Here relying,*
> *Suff'ring, dying,*
> *Honest souls find all redress.*

Pol. My heart feels your sentiments, and my tongue longs to join in 'em.

Caw. *Virtue 's treasure* 30
Is a pleasure,
Pol. *Cheerful even amid distress ;*
Caw. *Nor pain nor crosses,*
Pol. *Nor grief nor losses,*
Caw. *Nor death itself can make it less.*
Pol. *Here relying,*
Caw. *Suff'ring, dying,*
Pol. *Honest souls find all redress.*

Caw. Having this, I want no other consolation. I am prepar'd for all misfortune. 40

Pol. Had you means of escape, you could not refuse it. To preserve your life is your duty.

Caw. By dishonest means, I scorn it.

Pol. But stratagem is allow'd in war ; and 'tis lawful to use all the weapons employ'd against you. You may save your friends from affliction, and be the instrument of rescuing your country.

Caw. Those are powerful inducements. I seek not voluntarily to resign my life. While it lasts, I would do my duty.

Pol I'll talk with our guard. What induces them to rapin and murther, will induce 'em to betray. You may offer them what they want, and from no hands, upon no terms, corruption can resist the temptation. 51

Caw. I have no skill. Those who are corrupt themselves know how to corrupt others. You may do as you please. But whatever you promise for me, contrary to the *European* custom, I will perform. For tho' a knave may break his word with a knave, an honest tongue knows no such distinctions.

Pol. Gentlemen, I desire some conference with you, that may be for your advantage.

SCENE XII.

POLLY, CAWWAWKEE, LAGUERRE, CAPSTERN.

Pol. Know you that you have the *Indian* prince in your custody ?   10
Lag. Full well.
Pol. Know you the treasures that are in his power ?
Lag. I know too that they shall soon be ours.
Pol. In having him in your possession they are yours.
Lag. As how, friend ?
Pol. He might well reward you.
Lag. For what ?
Pol. For his liberty.
Caw. Yes, *European*, I can and will reward you.
Cap. He 's a great man, and I trust no such promises.
Caw. I have said it, *European : * And an *Indian*'s heart is always answerable for his words.
Pol. Think of the chance of war, gentlemen. Conquest is not so sure when you fight against those who fight for their liberties.
Lag. What think you of the proposal ?
Cap. The prince can give us places ; he can make us all great men. Such a prospect I can tell you, *Laguerre*, would tempt our betters.
Lag. Besides, if we are beaten, we have no retreat to our ships.
Cap. If we gain our ends what matter how we come by it ?   20
Lag. Every man for himself, say I. There is no being even with mankind, without that universal maxim. Consider, brother, we run no risque.
Cap. Nay, I have no objections.
Lag. If we conquer'd, and the booty were to be divided among the crews, what would it amount to ? Perhaps this way we might get more than would come to our shares.
Cap. Then too, I always lik'd a place at court. I have a genius to get, keep it, and make the most of an employment.
Lag. You will consider, prince, our own politicians would have rewarded such meritorious services : We'll go off with you.   30
Cap. We want only to be known to be employ'd.
Lag. Let us unbind him then.
Pol. 'Tis thus one able politician outwits another ; and we admire their wisdom. You may rely upon the prince's word as much as if he was a poor man.
Cap. Our fortunes then are made.

AIR XLVIII. Down in a meadow.

Pol. *The sportsmen keep hawks, and their quarry they gain ;*
Thus the woodcock, the partridge, the pheasant is slain.
What care and expence for their hounds are employ'd !
Thus the fox, and the hare, and the stag are destroy'd.
The spaniel they cherish, whose flattering way
Can as well as their masters cringe, fawn and betray.
Thus stanch politicians, look all the world round,
Love the men who can serve as hawk, spaniel or hound.   [Exeunt.

ACT III. Scene I.

The I N D I A N *Camp.*

P O H E T O H E E, Attendants, D U C A T.

Ind. Sir, a party from the *British* factory have join'd us. Their chief attends your majesty's orders for their disposition.

Pohe. Let them be posted next my command ; for I would be witness of their bravery. But first let their officer know I would see him. [*Exit* Indian.

Enter Ducat.

Duc. I would do all in my power to serve your majesty. I have brought up my men, and now, Sir,——I would fain give up. I speak purely upon your majesty's account. For as to courage and all that—I have been a colonel of the militia these ten years.

Poh. Sure, you have not fear. Are you a man ? 9

Duc. A married man, Sir, who carries his wife's heart about him, and that indeed is a little timorous. Upon promise to her, I am engag'd to quit in case of a battle ; and her heart hath ever govern'd me more than my own. Besides, Sir, fighting is not our business ; we pay others for fighting ; and yet 'tis well known we had rather part with our lives than our money.

Poh. And have you no spirit then to defend it ? Your families, your liberties, your properties are at stake. If these cannot move you, you must be born without a heart.

Duc. Alas, Sir, we cannot be answerable for human infirmities.

A I R X L I X. There was an old man, and he liv'd.

> *What man can on virtue or courage repose,*
> *Or guess if the touch 'twill abide ?* 20
> *Like gold, if intrinsick sure no body knows,*
> *Till weigh'd in the ballance and try'd.*

Poh. How different are your notions from ours ! We think virtue, honour, and courage as essential to man as his limbs, or senses ; and in every man we suppose the qualities of a man, till we have found the contrary. But then we regard him only as a brute in disguise. How custom can degrade nature !

Duc. Why should I have any more scruples about myself, than about my money ? If I can make my courage pass currant, what matter is it to me whether it be true or false ? 'Tis time enough to own a man's failings when they are found out. If your majesty then will not dispense with my duty to my wife, with permission, I'll to my post. 'Tis wonderful to me that kings ever go to war, who have so much to lose, and nothing essential to get. [*Exit.*

SCENE II.

POHETOHEE, Attendants.

Poh. My Son a Prisoner ! Tortur'd perhaps and inhumanly butcher'd !
Human nature cannot bear up against such afflictions. The war must suffer
by his absence. More then is requir'd from me. Grief raises my resolution,
and calls me to relieve him, or to a just revenge. What mean those shouts ?

[*Enter* Indian.

Ind. The prince, Sir, is return'd. The troops are animated by his presence.
With some of the pyrates in his retinue, he waits your majesty's commands.

SCENE III.

*POHETOHEE, CAWWAWKEE, POLLY,
LAGUERRE, CAPSTERN,* &c.

Poh. Victory then is ours. Let me embrace him. Welcome, my son.
Without thee my heart could not have felt a triumph.

Caw. Let this youth then receive your thanks. To him are owing my life
and liberty. And the love of virtue alone gain'd me his friendship.

Poh. This hath convinc'd me that an *European* can be generous and
honest.

Caw. These others, indeed, have the passion of their country. I owe their
services to gold, and my promise is engag'd to reward them. How it gauls
honour to have obligations to a dishonourable man !

Lag. I hope your majesty will not forget our services.   10

Poh. I am bound for my son's engagements.

Caw. For this youth, I will be answerable. Like a gem found in rubbish,
he appears the brighter among these his country men.

AIR L. Iris la plus charmante.

> *Love with beauty is flying,*
> *At once 'tis blooming and dying,*
> *But all seasons defying,*
> *Friendship lasts on the year.*
> *Love is by long enjoying,*
>   *Cloying ;*
> *Friendship, enjoy'd the longer,*   20
>   *Stronger.*
> *O may the flame divine*
> *Burn in your breast like mine !*

Pol. Most noble prince, my behaviour shall justify the good opinion you
have of me ; and my friendship is beyond professions.

Poh. Let these men remain under guard, till after the battle. All promises
shall then be made good to you.   [*Exeunt* Pyrates *guarded.*

SCENE IV.

POHETOHEE, CAWWAWKEE, POLLY.

Caw. May this young man be my companion in the war. As a boon I request it of you. He knows our cause is just, and that is sufficient to engage him in it.

Poh. I leave you to appoint him his command. Dispose of him as you judge convenient.

Pol. To fall into their hands is certain torture and death. As far as my youth and strength will permit me, you may rely upon my duty.

Enter Indian.

Ind. Sir, the enemy are advancing towards us.   8

Poh. Victory then is at hand. Justice protects us, and courage shall support us. Let us then to our posts.   [*Exeunt.*

SCENE V. *The field of battle.*

CULVERIN, HACKER, PYRATES.

A i r L I. There was a Jovial Beggar.

1 Pyr.
When horns, with cheerful sound,
Proclaim the active day ;
Impatience warms the hound,
He burns to chase the prey.

Chorus.
Thus to battle we will go, &c.

2 Pyr.
How charms the trumpet's breath !
The brave, with hope possess'd,
Forgetting wounds and death,
Feel conquest in their breast.

Chorus.
Thus to battle, &c.   10

Cul. But yet I don't see, Brother *Hacker*, why we should be commanded by a Neger. 'Tis all along of him that we are led into these difficulties. I hate this land fighting. I love to have sea-room.

Hac. We are the council, brother. If ever we get on board again, my vote shall be for calling of him to account for these pranks. Why should we be such fools to be ambitious of satisfying another's ambition ?

Cul. Let us mutiny. I love mutiny as well as my wife.

1 *Pyr.* Let us mutiny.

2 *Pyr.* Ay, let us mutiny.   19

Hac. Our captain takes too much upon him. I am for no engrosser of power. By our articles he hath no command but in a fight or in a storm. Look'ee, brothers, I am for mutiny as much as any of you, when occasion offers.

Cul. Right, brother, all in good season. The pass to our ships is cut off by the troops of the Plantation. We must fight the *Indians* first, and we have a mutiny good afterwards.

Hac. Is *Morano* still with his doxy ?

Cul. He 's yonder on the right, putting his troops in order for the onset.

Hac. I wish this fight of ours were well over. For, to be sure, let soldiers say what they will, they feel more pleasure after a battle than in it.　　30

Cul. Does not the drum-head here, quarter-master, tempt you to fling a merry main or two ?　　　　　　　　　*[Takes dice out of his pocket.*

Hac. If I lose my money, I shall reimburse myself from the *Indians.* I have set.

Cul. Have at you. A nick.　　　　　　　　　　　　*[Flings.*

Hac. Throw the dice fairly out. Are you at me again !

Cul. I'm at it. Seven or eleven. *[Flings.]* Eleven.

Hac. Furies ! A manifest cog ! I won't be bubbled, Sir. This would not pass upon a drunken country gentleman. Death, Sir, I won't be cheated.

Cul. The money is mine. D'you take me for a sharper, Sir ?　　40

Hac. Yes, Sir.

Cul. I'll have satisfaction.

Hac. With all my heart.　　　　　　　　　　　　*[Fighting.*

SCENE VI.

HACKER, CULVERIN, PYRATES, MORANO, VANDERBLUFF, &c.

Mor. For shame, gentlemen ! *[Parting them.]* Is this a time for private quarrel ? What do I see ! Dice upon the drum-head ! If you have not left off those cowardly tools, you are unworthy your profession. The articles you have sworn to, prohibit gaming for money. Friendship and society cannot subsist where it is practis'd. As this is the day of battle, I remit your penalties. But let me hear no more of it.

Cul. To be call'd sharper, captain ! is a reproach that no man of honour can put up.

Hac. But to be one, is what no man of honour can practice.　　9

Mor. If you will not obey orders, quarter-master, this pistol shall put an end to the dispute. *[Claps it to his head.]* The common cause now requires your agreement. If gaming is so rife, I don't wonder that treachery still subsists among you.

Hac. Who is treacherous ?

Mor. *Capstern* and *Laguerre* have let the prince and the stripling you took prisoner escape, and are gone off with them to the *Indians.* Upon your duty, gentlemen, this day depends our all.

Cul. Rather than have ill blood among us, I return the money. I value your friendship more. Let all animosities be forgot.　　19

Mor. We should be *Indians* among ourselves, and shew our breeding and parts to every body else. If we cannot be true to one another, and false to all the world beside, there is an end of every great enterprize.

Hac. We have nothing to trust to but death or victory.

Mor. Then hey for victory and plunder, my lads !

AIR LII. To you fair ladies.

By bolder steps we win the race.

1 Pyr.   *Let's haste where danger calls.*
Mor.   *Unless ambition mend its pace,*
               It totters, nods and falls.
1 Pyr.   *We must advance or be undone.*
Mor.   *Think thus, and then the battle's won.*   30
Chor.   *With a fa la la, &c.*

Mor. You see your booty, your plunder, gentlemen. The *Indians* are
just upon us. The great must venture death some way or other, and the less
ceremony about it, in my opinion, the better. But why talk I of death !
Those only talk of it, who fear it. Let us all live, and enjoy our conquests.
Sound the charge.

AIR LIII. Prince Eugene's march.

When the tyger roams
And the timorous flock is in his view,
Fury foams,
He thirsts for the blood of the crew.   40
His greedy eyes he throws,
Thirst with their number grows,
On he pours, with a wide waste pursuing,
Spreading the plain with a general ruin,
Thus let us charge, and our foes o'erturn :
Van.   *Let us on one and all !*
1 Pyr.   *How they fly, how they fall !*
Mor.   *For the war, for the prize I burn.*

Van. Were they dragons, my lads, as they sit brooding upon treasure, we
would fright them from their nests.   50
Mor. But see, the enemy are advancing to close engagement. Before the
onset, we'll demand a parley, and if we can, obtain honourable terms——We
are overpower'd by numbers, and our retreat is cut off.

SCENE VII.

Enter POHETOHEE, CAWWAWKEE, POLLY, &c.,
    with the Indian *Army drawn up against the Pyrates.*

Poh. Our hearts are all ready. The enemy halts. Let the trumpets give
the signal.

AIR LIV. The marlborough.

Caw.   *We the sword of justice drawing,*
               Terror cast in guilty eyes ;
               In its beam false courage dies ;
           'Tis like lightning keen and awing.
               Charge the foe,
               Lay them low,
           On then and strike the blow.

> *Hark, victory calls us. See, guilt is dismay'd :*   10
> *The villain is of his own conscience afraid.*
> *In your hands are your lives and your liberties held,*
> *The courage of virtue was never repell'd.*

Pyr. Our chief demands a parley.
Poh. Let him advance.

> *Art thou,* Morano, *that fell man of prey ?*
> *That foe to justice ?*
Mor.   *Tremble and obey.*
> *Art thou great* Pohetohee *styl'd ?*
Poh.   *the same.*   20
> *I dare avow my actions and my name.*

Mor. Thou know'st then, king, thy son there was my prisoner. Pay us the ransom we demand, allow us safe passage to our ships, and we will give you your lives and liberties.

Poh. Shall robbers and plunderers prescribe rules to right and equity ? Insolent madman ! Composition with knaves is base and ignominious. Tremble at the sword of justice, rapacious brute.

A I R   L V.   Les rats.

Mor.
> *Know then, war 's my pleasure.*
> *Am I thus controll'd ?*
> *Both thy heart and treasure*   30
> *I'll at once unfold.*
> *You, like a miser, scraping, hiding,*
> *Rob all the world ; you're but mines of gold.*
> *Rage my breast alarms :*
> *War is by kings held right-deciding ;*
> *Then to arms, to arms ;*
> *With this sword I'll force your hold.*

By thy obstinacy, king, thou hast provok'd thy fate ; and so expect me.
Poh. Rapacious fool ; by thy avarice thou shalt perish.
Mor. Fall on.   40
Poh. For your lives and liberties.   [*Fight.* Pyrates *beat off.*

S C E N E   V I I I.
D U C A T.

Duc. A slight wound now would have been a good certificate ; but who dares contradict a soldier ? 'Tis your common soldiers who must content themselves with mere fighting ; but 'tis we officers that run away with the most fame as well as pay. Of all fools, the fool-hardy are the greatest, for they are not even to be trusted with themselves. Why should we provoke men to turn again upon us, after they are run away ? For my own part, I think it wiser to talk of fighting, than only to be talk'd of. The fame of a talking hero will satisfy me ; the sound of whose valour amazes and astonishes all peaceable men, women, and children. Sure a man may be allow'd a little lying in his own praise, when there's so much going about to his discredit. Since every other body gives a man less praise than he deserves, a man, in justice to himself, ought to make up deficiencies. Without this privilege, we should have fewer good characters in the world than we have.   13

A i r L V I.   Mad Robin.

How faultless does the nymph appear,
  When her own hand the picture draws !
But all others only smear
  Her wrinckles, cracks and flaws.
Self-flattery is our claim and right,
  Let men say what they will ;
Sure we may set our good in sight,   20
  When neighbours set our ill.

So, for my own part, I'll no more trust my reputation in my neighbours hands than my money.   But will turn them both myself to the best advantage.

S C E N E   I X.

P O H E T O H E E ,   C A W W A W K E E ,   D U C A T ,
I N D I A N S .

Poh.   Had *Morano* been taken or slain, our victory had been compleat.
Duc.   A hare may escape from a mastiff.   I could not be a greyhound too.
Poh.   How have you dispos'd of the prisoners ?
Caw.   They are all under safe guard, till the king's justice, by their exemplary punishment, deters others from the like barbarities.
Poh.   But all our troops are not as yet return'd from the pursuit : I am too for speedy justice, for in that there is a sort of clemency.   Besides, I would not have my private thoughts worried by mercy to pardon such wretches. I cannot be answerable for the frailties of my nature.   9
Caw.   The youth who rescu'd me from these cruel men is missing ; and amidst all our successes I cannot feel happiness.   I fear he is among the slain. My gratitude interested itself so warmly in his safety that you must pardon my concern.   What hath victory done for me ?   I have lost a friend.

A i r L V I I.   Thro' the wood laddy.

As sits the sad turtle alone on the spray ;
  His heart sorely beating,
  Sad murmur repeating,
Indulging his grief for his consort astray ;
For force or death only could keep her away.
Now he thinks of the fowler, and every snare ;
  If guns have not slain her,   20
  The net must detain her,
Thus he'll rise in my thoughts, every hour with a tear,
If safe from the battle he do not appear.

Poh. Dead or alive, bring me intelligence of him ; for I share in my son's affliction. [*Exit* Indian.

Duc. I had better too be upon the spot, or my men may embezzle some plunder which by right should be mine. [*Exit.*

Enter Indian.

Ind. The youth, Sir, with a party is just return'd from the pursuit. He 's here to attend your majesty's commands. 29

S C E N E X.

P O H E T O H E E, C A W W A W K E E,
P O L L Y, I N D I A N S.

Caw. Pardon, Sir, the warmth of my friendship, if I fly to meet him, and for a moment intercept his duty. [*Embracing.*

A i r L V I I I. Clasp'd in my dear Melinda's arms.

Pol.	*Victory is ours.*
Caw.	————————*My fond heart is at rest.*
Pol.	*Friendship thus receives its guest.*
Caw.	*O what transport fills my breast !*
Pol.	*Conquest is compleat,*
Caw.	*Now the triumph's great.*
Pol.	*In your life is a nation blest.*
Caw.	*In your life I'm of all possess'd.* 10

Poh. The obligations my son hath receiv'd from you, makes me take a part in his friendship. In your safety victory has been doubly kind to me. If *Morano* hath escap'd, justice only reserves him to be punish'd by another hand.

Pol. In the rout, Sir, I overtook him, flying with all the cowardice of guilt upon him. Thousands have false courage enough to be vicious ; true fortitude is founded upon honour and virtue ; that only can abide all tests. I made him my prisoner, and left him without under strict guard, till I receiv'd your majesty's commands for his disposal.

Poh. Sure this youth was sent me as a guardian. Let your prisoner be brought before us. 21

S C E N E X I.

P O H E T O H E E, C A W W A W K E E, P O L L Y,
M O R A N O *guarded.*

Mor. Here 's a young treacherous dog now, who hangs the husband to come at the wife. There are wives in the world, who would have undertaken that affair to have come at him. Your son's liberty, to be sure, you think better worth than mine ; so that I allow you a good bargain if I take my own for his ransom, without a gratuity. You know, king, he is my debtor.

Poh. He hath the obligations to thee of a sheep who hath escap'd out of the jaws of the wolf, beast of prey !

Mor. Your great men will never own their debts, that's certain.

Poh. Trifle not with justice, impious man. Your barbarities, your rapin, your murthers are now at an end.   10

Mor. Ambition must take its chance. If I die, I die in my vocation.

A I R   L I X.   Parson upon Dorothy.

> *The soldiers, who by trade must dare*
>   *The deadly cannon's sounds ;*
> *You may be sure, betimes prepare*
>   *For fatal blood and wounds.*
> *The men, who with adventrous dance,*
>   *Bound from the cord on high,*
> *Must own they have the frequent chance*
>   *By broken bones to die.*
>   *Since rarely then*   20
>   *Ambitious men*
> *Like others lose their breath ;*
>   *Like these, I hope,*
>   *They know a rope*
> *Is but their natural death.*

We must all take the common lot of our professions.

Poh. Would your *European* laws have suffer'd crimes like these to have gone unpunish'd !

Mor. Were all I am worth safely landed, I have wherewithal to make almost any crime sit easy upon me.   30

Poh. Have ye notions of property ?

Mor. Of my own.

Poh. Would not your honest industry have been sufficient to have supported you ?

Mor. Honest industry ! I have heard talk of it indeed among the common people, but all great genius's are above it.

Poh. Have you no respect for virtue ?

Mor. As a good phrase, Sir. But the practicers of it are so insignificant and poor, that they are seldom found in the best company.

Poh. Is not wisdom esteem'd among you ?   40

Mor. Yes, Sir : But only as a step to riches and power ; a step that raises ourselves, and trips up our neighbours.

Poh. Honour, and honesty, are not those distinguish'd ?

Mor. As incapacities and follies. How ignorant are these *Indians !* But indeed I think honour is of some use ; ·it serves to swear upon.

Poh. Have you no consciousness ? Have you no shame ?

Mor. Of being poor.

Poh. How can society subsist with avarice ! Ye are but the forms of men. Beasts would thrust you out of their herd upon that account, and man should cast you out for your brutal dispositions.   50

Mor. *Alexander* the great was more successful. That's all.

Air L X. The collier has a daughter.

When right or wrong's decided
In war or civil causes,
We by success are guided
To blame or give applauses.
Thus men exalt ambition,
In power by all commended,
But when it falls from high condition,
Tyburn *is well attended.*   59

Poh. Let justice then take her course, I shall not interfere with her decrees. Mercy too obliges me to protect my country from such violences. Immediate death shall put a stop to your further mischiefs.

Mor. This sentence indeed is hard. Without the common forms of trial! Not so much as the counsel of a newgate attorney! Not to be able to lay out my money in partiality and evidence! Not a friend perjur'd for me! This is hard, very hard.

Poh. Let the sentence be put in execution. Lead him to death. Let his accomplices be witnesses of it, and afterwards let them be securely guarded till farther orders.

Air L X I. Mad Moll.

Mor.

All crimes are judg'd like fornication;   70
While rich we are honest no doubt.
Fine ladies can keep reputation,
Poor lasses alone are found out.
If justice had piercing eyes,
Like ourselves to look within,
She'd find power and wealth a disguise
That shelter the worst of our kin.   [Exit guarded.

SCENE XII.

POHETOHEE, CAWWAWKEE, POLLY.

Poh. How shall I return the obligations I owe you? Every thing in my power you may command. In making a request, you confer on me another benefit. For gratitude is oblig'd by occasions of making a return: And every occasion must be agreeable, for a grateful mind hath more pleasure in paying than receiving.

Caw. My friendship too is impatient to give you proofs of it. How happy would you make me in allowing me to discharge that duty!

Air L X I I. Prince George.

Pol.

All friendship is a mutual debt,
The contract's inclination:

Caw.

We never can that bond forget   10
Of sweet retaliation.

Pol.	*All day, and every day the same*
	We are paying and still owing ;
Caw.	*By turns we grant by turns we claim*
	The pleasure of bestowing.
Both.	*By turns we grant, &c.*

Pol. The pleasure of having serv'd an honourable man is a sufficient return. My misfortunes, I fear, are beyond relief.

Caw. That sigh makes me suffer. If you have a want let me know it.

Poh. If it is in a king's power, my power will make me happy.   20

Caw. If you believe me a friend, you are unjust in concealing your distresses from me. You deny me the privilege of friendship ; for I have a right to share them, or redress them.

Poh. Can my treasures make you happy ?

Pol. Those who have them not think they can ; those who have them know they cannot.

Poh. How unlike his countrymen !

Caw. While you conceal one want from me, I feel every want for you. Such obstinacy to a friend is barbarity.   29

Pol. Let not my reflection interrupt the joys of your triumph. Could I have commanded my thoughts, I would have reserv'd them for solitude.

Caw. Those sighs and that reservedness are symptoms of a heart in love. A pain that I am yet a stranger to.

Pol. Then you have never been compleatly wretched.

A i r L X I I I.   Blithe Jockey young and gay.

> *Can words the pain express*
> *Which absent lovers know ?*
> *He only mine can guess*
> *Whose heart hath felt the woe.*
> *'Tis doubt, suspicion, fear,*
> *Seldom hope, oft' despair ;*   40
> *'Tis jealousy, 'tis rage, in brief*
> *'Tis every pang and grief.*

Caw. But does not love often deny itself aid and comfort, by being too obstinately secret ?

Pol. One cannot be too open to generosity ; that is a sun, of universal benignity. In concealing ourselves from it we but deny ourselves the blessings of its influence.

A i r L X I V.   In the fields in frost and snow.

> *The modest lilly, like the maid,*
> *Its pure bloom defending,*
> *Is of noxious dews afraid,*   50
> *Soon as even's descending.*

1 3 *we are*] *Were are* Underhill.
5 1 *even's*] *eve's* Underhill.

> *Clos'd all night,*
> *Free from blight,*
> *It preserves the native white*
> *But at morn unfolds its leaves,*
> *And the vital sun receives.*

Yet why should I trouble your majesty with the misfortunes of so inconsiderable a wretch as I am ?

Poh. A king's beneficence should be like the sun. The most humble weed
should feel its influence as well as the most gaudy flower. But I have the
nearest concern in any thing that touches you.   61

Pol. You see then at your feet the most unhappy of women.

[Kneels. He raises her-

Caw. A woman ! Oh my heart !

Poh. A woman !

Pol. Yes, Sir, the most wretched of her sex. In love ! married ! abandon'd,
and in despair !

Poh. What brought you into these countries ?

Pol. To find my husband. Why had not the love of virtue directed my
heart ? But, alas, 'tis outward appearance alone that generally engages a
woman's affections ! And my heart is in the possession of the most profligate
of mankind.   71

Poh. Why this disguise ?

Pol. To protect me from the violences and insults to which my sex might
have expos'd me.

Caw. Had she not been married, I might have been happy.   *[Aside.*

Pol. He ran into the madness of every vice. I detest his principles, tho'
I am fond of his person to distraction. Could your commands for search and
enquiry restore him to me, you reward me at once with all my wishes. For
sure my love still might reclaim him.

Caw. Had you conceal'd your sex, I had been happy in your friendship ;
but now, how uneasy, how restless is my heart !   81

A i r L X V. Whilst I gaze on Chloe.

> *Whilst I gaze in fond desiring,*
>   *Every former thought is lost.*
> *Sighing, wishing and admiring,*
>   *How my troubled soul is tost !*
> *Hot and cold my blood is flowing,*
> *How it thrills in every vein !*
> *Liberty and life are going,*
>   *Hope can ne'er relieve my pain.*

Enter Indian.

Ind. The rest of the troops, Sir, are return'd from the pursuit with more
prisoners. They attend your majesty's commands.   91

Poh. Let them be brought before us. *[Ex.* Ind.] Give not yourself up to
despair ; for every thing in my power you may command.   *[To* Pol.

Caw. And every thing in mine. But, alas, I have none ; for I am not in
my own !

S C E N E   X I I I.

P O H E T O H E E,   C A W W A W K E E,   P O L L Y,
D U C A T,   J E N N Y   guarded,   &c.

Jen. Spare my husband, *Morano* is my husband.

Poh. Then I have reliev'd you from the society of a monster.

Jen. Alas, Sir, there are many husbands who are furious monsters to the rest of mankind, that are the tamest creatures alive to their wives. I can be answerable for his duty and submission to your majesty, for I know I have so much power over him, that I can even make him good.

Poh. Why then had you not made him so before ?

Jen. I was, indeed, like other wives, too indulgent to him, and as it was agreeable to my own humour, I was loth to baulk his ambition. I must, indeed, own too that I had the frailty of pride. But where is the woman who hath not an inclination to be as great and rich as she can be ?   11

Poh. With how much ease and unconcern these *Europeans* talk of vices, as if they were necessary qualifications.

A I R   LXVI.   The Jamaica.

Jen.

> *The sex, we find,*
> *Like men inclin'd*
> *To guard against reproaches ;*
> *And none neglect*
> *To pay respect*
> *To rogues who keep their coaches.*   19

Indeed, Sir, I had determin'd to be honest myself, and to have made him so too, as soon as I had put myself upon a reasonable foot in the world ; and that is more self-denial than is commonly practis'd.

Poh. Woman, your profligate sentiments offend me ; and you deserve to be cut off from society, with your husband. Mercy would be scarce excusable in pardoning you. Have done then. *Morano* is now under the stroke of justice.

Jen. Let me implore your majesty to respite his sentence. Send me back again with him into slavery, from whence we escap'd. Give us an occasion of being honest, for we owe our lives and liberties to another.   29

Duc. Yes, Sir, I find some of my run-away slaves among the crew ; and I hope my services at least will allow me to claim my own again.

Jen. *Morano*, Sir, I must confess hath been a free liver, and a man of so many gallantries, that no woman could escape him. If *Macheath's* misfortunes were known, the whole sex would be in tears.

Pol. Macheath !

Jen. He is so black, Sir, but under that disguise, for my sake, skreen'd himself from the claims and importunities of other women. May love intercede for him ?

Pol. Macheath ! Is it possible ? Spare him, save him, I ask no other reward.   40

Poh. Haste, let the sentence be suspended.   [*Exit* Ind.

Pol. Fly; a moment may make me miserable. Why could not I know him? All his distresses brought upon him by my hand! Cruel love, how could'st thou blind me so?

AIR LXVII. Tweed Side.

> *The stag, when chas'd all the long day*
> *O'er the lawn, thro' the forest and brake;*
> *Now panting for breath and at bay,*
> *Now stemming the river or lake;*
> *When the treacherous scent is all cold,*
> *And at eve he returns to his hind,*   50
> *Can her joy, can her pleasure be told?*
> *Such joy and such pleasure I find.*

But, alas, now again reflection turns fear upon my heart. His pardon may come too late, and I may never see him more.

Poh. Take hence that profligate woman. Let her be kept under strict guard till my commands.

Jen. Slavery, Sir, slavery, is all I ask. Whatever becomes of him, spare my life; spare an unfortunate woman. What can be the meaning of this sudden turn! Consider, Sir, if a husband be never so bad, a wife is bound to duty.   60

Poh. Take her hence, I say; let my orders be obey'd. [*Ex.* Jenny *guarded*.

SCENE XIV.

POHETOHEE, CAWWAWKEE, POLLY, DUCAT, &c.

Pol. What, no news, yet? Not yet return'd!

Caw. If justice hath overtaken him, he was unworthy of you.

Pol. Not yet! Oh how I fear.

AIR LXVIII. One Evening as I lay.

> *My Heart forebodes he's dead,*
> *That thought how can I bear?*
> *He's gone, for ever fled,*
> *My soul is all despair!*
> *I see him pale and cold,*
> *The noose hath stop'd his breath,*
> *Just as my dream foretold,*   10
> *Oh had that sleep been death!*

SCENE XV.

POHETOHEE, CAWWAWKEE, POLLY, DUCAT, INDIANS.

Enter Indians.

Pol. He's dead, he's dead! Their looks confess it. Your tongues have no need to give it utterance to confirm my misfortunes! I know, I see, I feel it! Support me! O *Macheath!*

Duc. Mercy upon me! Now I look upon her nearer, bless me, it must be *Polly.* This woman, Sir, is my slave, and I claim her as my own. I hope, if your majesty thinks of keeping her, you will reimburse me, and not let me be a loser. She was an honest girl to be sure, and had too much virtue to thrive, for, to my knowledge, money could not tempt her.

Poh. And if she is virtuous, *European*, dost thou think I'll act the infamous part of a ruffian, and force her? 'Tis my duty as a king to cherish and protect virtue. 11

Caw. Justice hath reliev'd you from the society of a wicked man. If an honest heart can recompence your loss, you would make me happy in accepting mine. I hope my father will consent to my happiness.

Poh. Since your love of her is founded upon the love of virtue and gratitude, I leave you to your own disposal.

Caw. What, no reply?

Pol. Abandon me to my sorrows. For in indulging them is my only relief.

Poh. Let the chiefs have immediate execution. For the rest, let 'em be restor'd to their owners, and return to their slavery. 20

AIR LXIX. Buff-coat.

Caw.	*Why that languish!*
Pol.	*Oh he's dead! O he's lost for ever!*
Caw.	*Cease your anguish, and forget your grief.*
Pol.	*Ah, never!*
	What air, grace and stature!
Caw.	*How false in his nature!*
Pol.	*To virtue my love might have won him.*
Caw.	*How base and deceiving!*
Pol.	*But love is believing.*
Caw.	*Vice, at length, as 'tis meet, hath undone him.* 30

By your consent you might at the same time give me happiness, and procure your own. My titles, my treasures, are all at your command.

AIR LXX. An *Italian* Ballad.

Pol.　　*Frail is ambition, how weak the foundation!*
　　　　Riches have wings as inconstant as wind;
　　　　My heart is proof against either temptation,
　　　　Virtue, without them, contentment can find.

I am charm'd, Prince, with your generosity and virtues. 'Tis only by the pursuit of those we secure real happiness. Those that know and feel virtue in themselves, must love it in others. Allow me to give a decent time to my sorrows. But my misfortunes at present interrupt the joys of victory. 40

Caw. Fair princess, for so I hope shortly to make you, permit me to attend you, either to divide your griefs, or, by conversation, to soften your sorrows.

Poh. 'Tis a pleasure to me by this alliance to recompence your merits. [*Ex.* Caw. *and* Pol.] Let the sports and dances then celebrate our victory.

[*Exit.*

D A N C E.

A I R L X X I. The temple.

1 Ind.	*Justice long forbearing,*
	Power or riches never fearing,
	Slow, yet persevering,
	Hunts the villain's pace.
Chor.	Justice long, *&c.*
2 Ind.	*What tongues then defend him?* 50
	Or what hand will succour lend him?
	Even his friends attend him,
	To foment the chace.
Chor.	Justice long, *&c.*
3 Ind.	*Virtue, subduing,*
	Humbles in ruin
	All the proud wicked race.
	Truth, never-failing,
	Must be prevailing,
	Falsehood shall find disgrace. 60
Chor.	Justice long forbearing, *&c.*

ACHILLES.

AN

OPERA.

—————————————————deceperat omnes
(In quibus Ajacem) sumptae fallacia vestis.
                                    Ovid. Metam. lib. xiii.

Naturam expellas furcâ licet, usque recurret.   Hor.

[Gay's opera 'Achilles' was produced at the Theatre-Royal in Covent-Garden on February 10, 1733, the year after his death. (Burnet, in his 'Key' dated Monday, February 12, refers to 'the Representation of the Opera...last *Saturday*'.) Although, to quote Burnet, 'There runs a Rumour . . . that the Publick are not to have the Pleasure of *reading* this Piece; for as POLLY was debarred the Stage, ACHILLES will be debarred the *Press* '—the Piece was published later in the year, with the title-page:

ACHILLES. | AN | OPERA. | As it is Perform'd at the | Theatre-Royal in *Covent-Garden.* | *—deceperat omnes* | (*In quibus Ajacem*) *sumptæ fallacia vestis.* | Ovid. Metam. Lib. 13. | *Naturam expellas furcâ licet, usque recurret.* Hor. | Written by the late Mr. *GAY.* | With the MUSICK prefix'd to each SONG. | *LONDON:* | Printed for J. WATTS at the Printing-Office in | *Wild-Court,* near *Lincoln's-Inn-Fields.* | MDCCXXXIII. | Price One Shilling and Six Pence.
    Post 8vo.
    No further edition appeared till the volume of *Plays*, 1760, reprinted in 1772.
    An edition of some importance is that in *Bell's British Theatre*, vol. ix, 1777. The following description is taken from the title-page:
    Achilles. An Opera. As written by John Gay. Distinguishing also the Variations of the Theatre, as perform'd, in Two Acts, at the Theatre-Royal, in Covent-Garden. Regulated from the Prompt-Book, by Permission of the Managers, by Mr. Wild, Prompter.
    These ' Variations ' (both omissions, additions, and transpositions) were introduced at a revival of the piece (the date is unknown to me) when the three Acts were compressed into two, and the part of *Thetis* omitted. As Gay had nothing to do with these ' variations ' I have thought it better not to disfigure the text by indicating them. On its first performance the opera seems to have been played in its entirety.
    Burnet's key *Achilles Dissected* was published in 1733, before the publication of *Achilles*. I take the following passage from it.
    ' Your Ladyship is not to look upon this as a finished Piece, but only as a posthumous Fragment; for I am inclined to believe, Mr. *Gay* intended to lengthen it to five Acts. Some Songs were likewise wanting, and his Friends Mr. *Pope*, Dr. *Arbuthnot*, etc. who have undertaken to supply that Defect, have really overloaded it; for by their Frequency, in my Opinion, the Narrative is too much interrupted: But as *Ballads* seem to be the *high Taste* of the present Age, the Number of them are by the Audience looked upon as the greatest Beauties in the Entertainment: Some of them are very *low*, and others very *luscious*.'
    The editions collated are those of 1733, 1760, and 1777. References to the Key are **by the** name *Burnet*.]

PROLOGUE.

Written by Mr. *GAY.*

Spoken by Mr. *Q U I N.*

I Wonder not our Author doubts Success ;
One in his Circumstance can do no less.
The Dancer on the Rope that tries at all,
In each unpractis'd Caper risques a Fall :
I own I dread his ticklish Situation,
Criticks detest Poetic Innovation.
Had Ic'rus been content with solid Ground,
The giddy vent'rous ·Youth had ne'er been drown'd.
The Pegasus *of old had Fire and Force,*
But your true Modern is a Carrier's Horse,   10
Drawn by the foremost Bell, afraid to stray,
Bard following Bard jogs on the beaten Way.
Why is this Man so obstinate an Elf ?
Will he, alone, not imitate himself ?
     His Scene now shews the Heroes of old Greece ;
But how ? 'tis monstrous ! In a Comic Piece.
To Buskins, Plumes and Helmets what Pretence,
If mighty Chiefs must speak but common Sense ?
Shall no bold Diction, no Poetic Rage,
Fome at our Mouths and thunder on the Stage ?   20
No—'tis Achilles, *as he came from* Chiron,
Just taught to sing as well as wield cold Iron ;
And whatsoever Criticks may suppose,
Our Author holds, that what He spoke was Prose.

Written by etc.] *These words are omitted from the 1777 edition. Burnet says that*
the Prologue was 'written by Mr. Pope.'
   6 *Criticks*] *Critics* 1733 ; but in l. 23 *Criticks.*

Dramatis Personae.

MEN.

Lycomedes,	Mr. *Quin.*
Diphilus,	Mr. *Aston.*
Achilles,	Mr. *Salway.*
Ulysses,	Mr. *Chapman.*
Diomedes,	Mr. *Laguerre.*
Ajax,	Mr. *Hall.*
Periphas,	Mr. *Walker.*
Agyrtes,	Mr. *Leveridge.*

WOMEN.

Thetis,	Mrs. *Buchanan.*
Theaspe,	Mrs. *Cantrel.*
Deïdamia,	Miss *Norsa.*
Lesbia,	Miss *Binks.*
Philoe,	Miss *Oates.*
Artemona,	Mrs. *Egleton.*

Courtiers, Guards, &c.

SCENE, *SCYROS.*

ACT I.

SCENE, *The Palace.*

SCENE I.

THETIS, ACHILLES.

THETIS.

Before I leave you, Child, I must insist upon your Promise, that you will never discover yourself without my Leave. Don't look upon it as capricious Fondness, nor think (because 'tis a Mother's Advice) that in Duty to yourself you are oblig'd not to follow it.

Ach. But my Character! my Honour!—Wou'd you have your Son live with Infamy?—On the first Step of a young Fellow depends his Character for Life.—I beg you, Goddess, to dispense with your Commands.

Thet. Have you then no Regard to my Presentiment? I can't bear the Thoughts of your going, for I know that odious Siege of *Troy* wou'd be the Death of thee.   10

Ach. Because you have the natural Fears of a Mother, wou'd you have me insensible that I have the Heart of a Man? The World, Madam, must look upon my absconding in this Manner, and at this particular Juncture, as infamous Cowardice.

> A I R I.   A Clown in *Flanders* once there was.
>
> *What's Life? No Curse is more severe,*
> *Than bearing Life with Shame.*
> *Is this your Fondness? this your Care?*
> *O give me Death with Fame.*

Thet. Keep your Temper, *Achilles* :—'Tis both impious and undutiful to call my Prescience in question.   20

Ach. Pardon me, Goddess, for had you, like other Mothers, been a meer Woman only, I shou'd have taken the Liberty of other Sons, and shou'd (as 'tis my Duty) have heard your Advice, and follow'd my own.

Thet. I positively shall not be easy, Child, unless you give me your Word and Honour.—You know my Commands.

Ach. My word, Madam, I can give you; but my Honour is already sacrific'd to my Duty. That I gave you when I submitted to put on this Woman's Habit.

The division into scenes exists only in the edition of 1733. The later editions employ the modern *Enter* and *Exit.*

14 Cowardice] Cowardise *1733*.   28 Woman's] Womans *1733*.

Thet. Believe me, *Achilles*, I have a tender Regard for your Honour, as well as Life.—By preventing your running head-long to your Destiny, I preserve you for future Glory. Therefore, Child, I once more insist upon your solemn Promise.   32

Ach. Was I a Woman (as I appear to be) I cou'd without Difficulty give you a Promise to have the Pleasure of breaking it; but when I promise, my Life is pledg'd for the Performance.—Your Commands, Madam, are sacred.— Yet I intreat you, Goddess, to consider the ignominious Part you make me act.—In obeying you, I prove my self unworthy of you.

Thet. My will, *Achilles*, is not to be controverted. Your Life depends upon your Duty; and positively, Child, you shall not go to this Siege.

A I R I I. *Gudgeon's* Song.

Why thus am I held at Defiance ?   40
A Mother, a Goddess obey !
Will Men never practice Compliance,
Till Marriage hath taught 'em the Way ?

Ach. But why must I lead the Life of a Woman ? why was I stolen away from my Preceptor ? Was I not as safe under the Care of *Chiron* ?—I know the Love he had for me; I feel his Concern; and I dare swear that good Creature is now so distress'd for the Loss of me, that he will quite founder himself with galloping from Place to Place to look after me.

Thet. I'll hear no more. Obey, and seek to know no further.—Can you imagine that I wou'd have taken all this Trouble to have lodg'd you under the Protection of *Lycomedes*, if I had not seen the absolute Necessity of it ?   51

Ach. Were I allow'd to follow my Inclinations, what wou'd you have to fear ?—I shou'd do my Duty, and die with Honour.—Was I to live an Age, I cou'd do no more.

Thet. You are so very obstinate, that really, Child, there's no enduring you.—Your Impatience seems to forget that I am a Goddess: Have I not degraded my self into the Character of a distress'd *Grecian* Princess ? 'Tis owing to my Artifice and Insinuation that we have the Protection of the King of *Scyros*. Have I not won *Lycomedes* his Friendship and Hospitality to that degree as to place you, without the least Suspicion, among his Daughters ?— And for what, dear *Achilles* ?—Your Safety and future Fame requir'd it.   61

Ach. 'Tis impossible, Madam, to bear it much longer.—My Words, my Actions, my aukward Behaviour, must one Day inevitably discover me.— I had been safer under the Tuition of *Chiron*.

Thet. Hath not the Prophet *Calchas* persuaded the Confederates that the Success of their Expedition against *Troy* depends upon your being among 'em ? Have they not Emissaries and Spies almost every where in search of you ? 'Tis here only, and in this Disguise, that I can believe you out of the Reach of Suspicion.—You have so much Youth, and such a Bloom, that there is no Man alive but must take you for a Woman. What I am most afraid of is, that when you are among the Ladies you shou'd be so little Master of your Passions as to find your self a Man.   72

40 at] at a *Underhill.*
59 *Lycomedes* his] *Lycomedes's* 1760 and 1777.

A I R I I I. Did you ever hear of a galant Sailor.

Ach.
> *The Woman always in Temptation,*
> *Must do what Nature bids her do ;*
> *Our Hearts feel equal Palpitation,*
> *For we've unguarded Minutes too.*
> *By Nature greedy,*
> *When lank and needy,*
> *Within your Fold the Wolf confine ;*
> *Then bid the Glutton*   80
> *Not think of Mutton ;*
> *Can you persuade him not to dine ?*

Thet. Now, dear Child, let me beg you to be discreet.—I have some Sea-Affairs that require my Attendance, which (much against my Will) oblige me for a time to leave you to your own Conduct.

80 'The Songs, in which was expected so much Pointedness of Wit, are so far from equalling those in the *Beggar's Opera*, that had they not been made publick by Mr. *Gay's* Friends, and under his Name, they might have passed for the Productions of some of those dull Pack-Horses of Imitators ridiculed in the Prologue.—In the first Scene, where *Achilles* tells his Mamma, that the Course of Nature is difficult to be averted ; with a surprizing Poignancy he assures her he thirsts for Fame and Glory,—as
> —*the* Glutton
> *Does after* Mutton.—
How peculiar a *Taste* soever the Author of *this* Turn of *Wit* might have for *that Dish*, as to think the Simile smart, I am afraid few in the Pit or Boxes thought it either *Wit* or Humour.'
Anonymous letter to The Daily Courant, *quoted by Burnet.*

Scene II.

Thetis, Achilles, Artemona.

Art. The Princesses, Lady *Pyrrha*, have been sitting at their Embroidery above a Quarter of an Hour, and are perfectly miserable for want of you.

Thet. *Pyrrha* is so very unhandy, and so monstrously aukward at her Needle, that I know she must be diverting. Her passion for Romances (as you must have observ'd in other Girls) took her off from every Part of useful Education.   6

Ach. For the many Obligations I have to the Princesses, I should (no doubt) upon all Occasions shew my self ready to be the But of their Ridicule.—'Tis a Duty that all great People expect from (what they call) their Dependants.

Art. How can you, Lady *Pyrrha*, misinterpret a Civility ? I know they have a Friendship, an Esteem for you ; and have a Pleasure in instructing you.

Thet. For Heaven's sake, *Pyrrha*, let not your captious Temper run away with your Good-manners. You cannot but be sensible of the King's and their Civilities, both to you and me.—How can you be so horridly out of Humour ?   15

Ach. All I mean, Madam, is ; that when People are sensible of their own Defects, they are not the proper Objects of Ridicule.

Thet. You are so very touchy, *Pyrrha*, that there is no enduring you.—— How can you be so unsociable a Creature as to deny a Friend the Liberty of laughing at your little Follies and Indiscretions ? For what do you think Women keep Company with one another ?

Ach. Because they hate one another, despise one another, and seek to have the Pleasure of seeing and exposing one another's Faults and Follies. 23

Thet. Now, dear *Pyrrha*, tell me, is Work a thing you pique yourself upon ? Suppose too they shou'd smile at an Absurdity in your Dress, it could not be such a Mortification as if (like most Women) you had made it the chief Business of your Life ?

Art. Don't they treat one another with equal Familiarity ?

Ach. But a Reply from me (whatever was the Provocation) might be look'd upon as impertinent. I hate to be under the Restraint of Civility when I am ill-us'd.   31

Art. Will you allow me, Madam, to make your Excuses to the Princesses ? —The Occasion of your Highness's leaving her, I see, troubles her.—Perhaps I may interrupt Conversation.

Thet. 'Tis astonishing, Child, how you can have so little Complaisance. This sullen Behaviour of your's must be disagreeable. I hope, Madam, she is not always in this way ?

Art. Never was any Creature more entertaining ! Such Spirits, and so much Vivacity ! The Princesses are really fond of her to Distraction.— The most chearful Tempers are liable to the Spleen, and 'tis an Indulgence that one Woman owes to another.   41

Ach. The Spleen, Madam, is a Female Frailty that I have no Pretensions to, nor any of its Affections.

A I R I V. Si vous vous moquez de nous.

When a Woman sullen sits,
And wants Breath to conquer Reason,
Always these affected Fits
Are in Season :
Since 'tis in her Disposition,
Make her be her own Physician.

Nay, dear Madam, you shall not go without me.——Though I have my particular Reasons to be out of Humour, I cannot be deficient in Good-manners.

Art. I know they would take it mortally ill if they thought your Complaisance had put yourself under the least Restraint.   53

Ach. I can't forgive myself for my Behaviour.——You must excuse me, Madam ; for Absence in Conversation is an Incivility that I am but too liable to.

Art. You know we all rally you upon your being in Love, as that is one of its most infallible Symptoms.

Thet. I charge you, upon my Blessing ;—as you expect Fame, Glory, Immortality, obey me.   [*To* Achilles.

[Thetis *kisses him.   Exeunt* Achilles *and* Artemona.

Scene III.

Thetis.

As for his Face, his Air, his Figure, I am not under the least Apprehension ; all my Concern is from the Impetuosity of his Temper.—Yet, after all, why *shou'd* I fear a Discovery ? for Women have the same Passions, though they employ 'em upon different Objects.

AIR V. A Minuet.

Man's so touchy, a Word that's injurious
   Wakes his Honour ; he's sudden as Fire.
Woman kindles, and is no less furious
   For her Trifles, or any Desire.
     Man is testy,
     Or sour, or resty,   10
If balk'd of Honours, or Pow'r, or Pelf.
   Woman's Passions can no less molest ye,
   And all for Reasons she keeps to her self.

He is sudden, he is impatient. What then ? Are Women less so ? Ask almost all Servants what they know of their Mistresses.—He is wilful, testy, and untractable. Can't Thousands of Husbands say as much of their Wives ? Then as for his Obstinacy—that can never show him less a Woman. But he hath not that Command of his Tongue I cou'd wish him : He is too vehement, too severe in his Expressions. In this Particular, indeed, few Women take equal Liberties to one another's Faces, but they make ample Amends for it behind each other's Backs ; so that, with all these Infirmities of Man, he may with the least Conduct very well pass for a fine-spirited Woman.—This Reflexion hath cur'd my Anxiety, and will make me believe him secure.

Scene IV.

Thetis, Lycomedes.

Thet. 'Tis with the utmost Gratitude that I return your Majesty Thanks for the Honours and hospitable Favours shewn to me and my Daughter.

Lycom. You wou'd oblige me more, Madam, if your Affairs wou'd allow you to accept 'em longer.

Thet. I have presum'd, Sir, to trespass further on your Generosity, in leaving my Daughter under your Protection.—I hope *Pyrrha*'s Behaviour will deserve it.

AIR VI. To you, my Dear, and to no other.

   Must then, alas, the fondest Mother
     Desert her child ?
Lycom.   ———————*Ah, why this Tear ?*   10
   She'll in Theaspe *find another ;*
   In me paternal Love and Care.

Had you taken her with you, my Daughters wou'd have been miserable beyond Expression. Theirs and her Education shall be the same.

Thet. I beg you, Sir, not to regard my Gratitude like the common Obligations of Princes ; for neither Time nor Interest can ever cancel it.

Lycom. Affairs of Consequence may require your Presence. Importunity upon these Occasions is troublesome and unhospitable.—I ask no Questions, Madam, because I choose not to pry into Secrets.   19

Thet. I can only thank, and rely upon your Majesty's Goodness.—My Duty to the Queen, Sir, calls me hence to own my Obligations, and receive her Commands.

Scene V.

Lycomedes, Diphilus.

Lycom. The Princess *Calista* hath taken her Leave ; she is but just gone out of the Room.

Diph. That *Pyrrha*, Sir, was a most delicious Piece.

Lycom. With all her little vixen Humours, to my Taste she is infinitely agreeable.

Diph. Your parting with her, Sir, in this easy manner, is astonishing. One too so excessively fond of you !

Lycom. Parting with her, *Diphilus !*

Diph. But no Prince alive hath so great a Command of his Passions.

Lycom. Dear *Diphilus*, let me understand you.   10

Diph. To my Knowledge you might have had her.

Lycom. Can I believe thee ?

Diph. I really thought the Queen began to be a little uneasy, and, for the Quiet of the Family (since she is gone) I must own I am heartily glad of it.

AIR VII. *John* went suiting unto *Joan.*

> *How your Patience had been try'd,*
> *Had this haughty Dame comply'd !*
> *What's a Mistress and a Wife ?*
> *Joy for Moments ; Plague for Life.*

Lycom. I am not so unhappy, *Diphilus.*—Her Mother hath left her to my Care.   20

Diph. Just as I wish'd.

Lycom. Wou'd she had taken her with her !

Diph. It might have been better. For beyond dispute, Sir, both you and the Queen wou'd have been easier.

Lycom. Why did she trust her to me ?

Diph. There cou'd be but one Reason.

Lycom. I cannot answer for myself.

Diph. 'Twas upon that very Presumption you was trusted.

Lycom. Wou'd I could believe thee !

SCENE V.] ' In the representation, the first Act begins here.' *Foot-note, 1777.*

Diph. 'Tis an apparent manifest Scheme, Sir, and you wou'd disappoint both Mother and Daughter if your Majesty did not betray your Trust.—You love her, Sir, you say. 　　　　　　　　　　　　　　　　32

Lycom. To Distraction, *Diphilus.*

Diph. And was the betraying a Trust ever as yet an Obstacle to that Passion ? What wou'd you have a Mother do more upon such an Occasion ? Ladies of her Rank cannot transact an Affair of this kind, but with some *Decorum.*

Lycom. But you can never suppose *Pyrrha* knows any thing of the Matter.

Diph. Why not, Sir ?

Lycom. From me she cannot ; for I have never as yet made any downright Professions. 　　　　　　　　　　　　　　　　41

Diph. There lies the true Cause of her Thoughtfulness ; 'tis nothing but Anxiety, for fear her Scheme shou'd not take place ; for, no doubt, her Mother hath instructed her not to be too forward, to make you more so — Believe me, Sir, you will have no Difficulties in this Affair, but those little ones that every Woman knows how to practice to quicken a Lover.

Lycom. Be it as it will, *Diphilus,* I must have her.

Diph. Had I been acquainted with your Pleasure sooner, your Majesty by this time had been tir'd of her.—How happy shall I make her, if I may have the Honour of your Majesty's commands to hint your Passion to her !

Lycom. Never did Eyes receive a Passion with such Coldness, such Indifference ! 　　　　　　　　　　　　　　　　52

A I R　V I I I.　Groom's Complaint.

Whene'er my Looks have spoke Desire,
　I sigh'd, I gaz'd in vain ;
No Glance confess'd her secret Fire ;
　And Eyes the Heart explain.

Diph. Though 'tis what she wishes, what she longs for, what she sighs for, Respect and Awe are a Restraint upon her Eyes as well as Tongue. I have often told you, Sir, she dares not understand you ; she dares not believe herself so happy. 　　　　　　　　　　　　　　　　60

Lycom. This Ring, *Diphilus.*—I must leave the rest to your Discretion.

Diph. There may be a manner in giving it her, a little Hint or so—but the Present will speak for itself ; 'tis the most successful Advocate of Love, and never wants an Interpreter.

Lycom. Say every thing for me, *Diphilus ;* for I feel I cannot speak for myself.

Diph. Cou'd I be as successful in all my other Negotiations ! Yet there may be Difficulties, for, if I mistake not, the Lady hath something of the Coquette about her ; and what Self-Denial will not those Creatures suffer to give a Lover Anxiety ! 　　　　　　　　　　　　　　　　70

A I R　I X.　O'er Bogie.

Observe the **wanton** *Kitten's Play,*
　Whene'er a Mouse appears ;
You there the true Coquette survey
　In all her flirting Airs :

Now pawing,
Now clawing,
Now in fond Embrace
Till 'midst her Freaks,
He from her breaks,
Steals off, and bilks the Chase.   80

Lycom. Dear *Diphilus,* what do you mean ? I never saw a Woman so little of that Character.

Diph. Pardon me, Sir ; your Situation is such, that you can never see what Mankind really are. In your Presence every one is acting a Part ; no one is himself, and was it not for the Eyes and Tongues of your faithful Servants, how little wou'd your Subjects be known to you ! Though she is so prim and reserv'd before you, she is never at a Loss for Airs to draw all the young flirting Lords of the Court about her.

Lycom. Beauty must always have its Followers.   89

Diph. If I mistake not, General *Ajax* too (who is sent to solicit your Quota for the *Trojan* War) hath another Solicitation more at heart.——But suppose she had ten thousand Lovers ; a Woman's prevalent Passion is Ambition, which must answer your Ends.——The Queen is coming this way, and her Commands may detain me.—I go, Sir, to make *Pyrrha* the happiest Creature upon Earth.

75 'The Description of the Coquet is not a less happy comparison ; where the *Coquet-Cat* having got a Mouse

> Now pawing,
> Now toying ;
> —Mouse gets loose
> And bilks her Chace—

The Ladies in the Boxes must think this a *strong Satire* on the sprightly and gay Part of their Sex ; and the *Delicacy* of the Thought will excuse any Reflection on the *whole* in general.'—*Letter to* The Daily Courant *ap.* Burnet.

SCENE VI.

Lycomedes, Theaspe.

Theas. I think the Princess *Calista* might as well have taken her Daughter with her.—That Girl is so intolerably forward, that I cannot imagine such Conversation can possibly be of any great Advantage to your Daughters Education.

Lycom. You seem of late to have taken an Aversion to the Girl. She hath Spirit and Vivacity, but not more than is becoming the Sex ; and I never saw any thing in her Behaviour but what was extremely modest.   7

Theas. For Heaven's sake, Sir, allow me to believe my own Eyes. Her Forwardness must give the Fellows some Encouragement, or there wou'd not be that intolerable Flutter about her.—But perhaps she hath some Reasons to be more upon her Guard before you.

3 Daughters] *1777* Daughter's *1733 and 1760.*
6 and I never] and *yet* I never *1777.*

Lycom. How can you be so unreasonably censorious ?

Theas. I can see her Faults, Sir. I see her as a Woman sees a Woman. The Men, it seems, think the aukward Creature handsome.

A I R X. *Dutch* Skipper. First Part.

Lycom.

> *When a Woman's censorious,*
> *And attacks the meritorious ;*
> *In the Scandal she shews her own malicious Thought.*
> *If real Guilt she blames,*
> *Then Pride her Heart inflames ;*
> *And she fansies she's better for another's Fault.*   20
> *Thus seeking to disclose*
> *The Slips of Friends and Foes,*
> *By her Envy she does herself alone. expose.*

Nay, dear Child, your attacking her in this peevish way can be nothing but downright Antipathy.

Theas. Nay, dear Sir, your defending her in this feeling manner can be nothing but downright Partiality.

Lycom. I own myself partial to Distress, and I see her in that Circumstance.

Theas. But there are other Reasons that may make a man Partial.

A I R X I. *Dutch* Skipper. Second. Part.

> *As you, Sir, are my Husband, no doubt you're prone*   30
> *To turn each new Face*
> *To a Wife's Disgrace ;*
> *And for no other Cause, but that she's your own ;*
> *Nay, Sir, 'tis an evident Case.*
> *'Tis strange that all Husbands should prove so blind,*
> *That a Wife's real Merits they ne'er can find,*
> *Tho' they strike all the rest of Mankind.*

Lycom. How can you be so ridiculous ? By these Airs, Madam, you would have me believe you are jealous.   39

Theas. Whence had you this contemptible Opinion of me ? Jealous ! If I was so I have a Spirit above owning it. I wou'd never heighten your Pleasure by letting you have the Satisfaction of knowing I was uneasy.

Lycom. Let me beg you, my Dear, to keep your Temper.

Theas. Since I have been so unguarded as to own it ; give me leave to tell you, Sir, that was I of a lower Rank it wou'd keep you in some Awe, because you wou'd then know I cou'd take my Revenge.

Lycom. You forget your Duty, Child.

Theas. There is a Duty too due from a Husband.

Lycom. How can you give way to these Passions ?

Theas. Because you give way to yours.   50

Lycom. But to be so unreasonably jealous !

Theas. Unreasonably ! Wou'd it were so !

A I R X I I. Black Joke.

Lycom.	*Then must I bear eternal Strife,*
	Both Night and Day put in mind of a Wife,
	By her Pouts, Spleen, and passionate Airs!
Theas.	*D'ye think I'll bear eternal Slight,*
	And not complain when I'm robb'd of my Right?
	Call you this, Sir, but whimsical Fears?
Lycom.	*Can nought then still this raging Storm?*
Theas.	*Yes. What you promis'd if you wou'd perform.*
Lycom.	*Pr'ythee teaze me no more.*
Theas.	*I can never give o'er,*
	Till I find you as fond and as kind as before.
Lycom.	*Will you ne'er ask*
	A possible Task?

61

Wou'd you have me so unhospitable as to deny her my Protection ?
  Theas. 'Tis not, Sir, that I presume to controul you in your Pleasures.——
Yet you might, methinks, have shew'd that Tenderness for me to have acted
with a little more Reserve. Women are not so blind as Husbands imagine.——
Were there no other Circumstances,—your Coolness to me, your Indifference.
—How I despise my self for this Confession !—Pardon me, Sir, Love made me
thus indiscreet.

72

A I R X I I I. Ye Shepherds and Nymphs.

Theaspe *weeping.*

O Love, *plead my Pardon, nor plead it in vain ;*
'Twas you that was jealous, 'twas you was in Pain ;
Yet why should you speak? To what Purpose or End
I must be unhappy if Love can offend.

Yet was ever a Design of this kind so manifest, so bare-fac'd !

A I R X I V. The Goddesses.

Theaspe *angry.*

To what a Pitch is Man profuse,
And all for ostentatious Pride !
Ev'n Misses are not kept for Use,
But for mere Show, and nought beside.
For might a Wife speak out,
She cou'd prove beyond all doubt,
With more than enough he was supply'd.

80

The Princess *Calista* hath shewn an uncommon Confidence in your Majesty.
The Woman, no doubt, depends upon it, that her Daughter's Charms are not
to be resisted.
  Lycom. Nay, dear Child, don't be scandalous.

A I R X V.   *Joan's* Placket.

Reputations hack'd and hew'd,   90
  Can never be mended again ;
Yet nothing stints the tattling Prude,
  Who joys in another's Pain.
    Thus while she rends
    Both Foes and Friends,
  By both she's torn in twain.
Reputations hack'd and hew'd,
  Can never be mended again.

Theas. You are in so particular a manner oblig'd to her, that I am not surpris'd at your taking her Part.   100

Lycom. But, dear Madam, why at present is all this violent Fluster ?

Theas. Ask your own Heart, ask your own Conduct. Those can best inform you.—'Twou'd have been more obliging if *Pyrrha* and you had kept me out of this impudent Secret.—You know, Sir, I have Reason.

· *Lycom.* If one Woman's Virtue depended upon another's Suspicions, where shou'd we find a Woman of Common Modesty ! Indeed, Child, I think you injure her ; I believe her virtuous.

Theas. When a Man hath ruin'd a Woman, he thinks himself oblig'd in Honour to stand up for her Reputation.   109

Lycom. If you will believe only your own unaccountable Suspicions, and are determin'd not to hear Reason, I must leave you to your perverse Humours. What wou'd you have me say ? What wou'd you have me do ?

Theas. Shew your Hospitality (as you call it) to me, and put that Creature out of the Palace.

Lycom. I have a greater Regard to yours and my own Quiet, than ever to comply with the extravagant Passions of a jealous Woman.

Theas. You have taken then your Resolutions, I find ; and I am sentenc'd to Neglect.——Did ever a Woman marry but with the Probability of having at least one Man in her Power ?—What a wretched Wife am I !   [*Weeps.*

Lycom. Jealousy from a Wife, even to a Man of Quality, is now look'd upon as Ill-manners, though the Affair be never so publick.—But without a Cause !—I beg you, Madam, to say no more upon this Subject.   122

90. ' The Quaintness of the Turn in
         Reputations hack'd and cut,
         Can never be mended again :
by *epigrammatical* concluding,
         Reputation hack'd and cut,
         Can never be mended ;
cannot but raise some *Admiration* in the Audience ; and for the *Sharpness* of the *Sting,* is admirably equalled in another Catch on a jealous Woman ; who
         —herself deceives
         Raising Fears, which she believes.
Though there are but few Songs, through the whole, which are not wrote in the same style, and with the same happy Poignancy. Quotations are not so easy, as it has not yet appeared in Print, (and will be *wisely* concealed from public Examination.) '

Letter to The Daily Courant, *ap.* Burnet.

106 Indeed, Child,] Indeed, *1760.*

Theas. Though you, Sir, may think her fit Company for you ; methinks the very same Reasons might tell you that she is not so very reputable a Companion for your Daughters.

Lycom. Since a passionate Woman will only believe herself, I must leave you, Madam, to enjoy your Obstinacy. I know but that way of putting an end to the Dispute.

A I R X V I. We've cheated the Parson, *&c.*

Though Woman's glib Tongue, when her Passions are fir'd,
Eternally go, a Man's Ear can be tir'd.
Since Woman will have both her Word and her Way,   130
I yield to your Tongue ; but my Reason obey.
    I obey,
      Nothing say,
Since Woman will have both her Word and her Way.

S c e n e V I I.

Theaspe.

Theas. Wou'd I had been more upon the Reserve ! But Husbands are horridly provoking ; they know the Frailty of the Sex, and never fail to take the Advantage of our Passions to make us expose ourselves by Contradiction. —*Artemona.*

S c e n e V I I I.

Theaspe, Artemona.

Art. Madam.

Theas. Is that Creature, that (what do you call her) that Princess gone ?

Art. Yes, Madam.

Theas. Why did not she take that awkward Thing, her Daughter, with her ?

Art. The Advantages she might receive in her Education, might be an Inducement to leave her.

Theas. Might *that* be an Inducement ?

Art. Besides, in her present Circumstance, it might be inconvenient to take her Daughter with her.   10

Theas. Can't you find out any *other* Reason for leaving her ?

Art. Your Courtesy, Madam ; your Hospitality.

Theas. No *other* Reason !

Art. No other Reason ?——

Theas. Wou'd I cou'd believe there was no other !

Art. 'Tis not for me to pry into your Majesty's Secrets.

Theas. I hate a Girl that is so intolerably forward.

Art. I never observ'd any thing but those little Liberties that Girls of her Age will take, when they are among themselves.—Perhaps those particular Distinctions the Princesses shew her, may have made her too familiar.— I am not, Madam, an Advocate for her Behaviour.   21

Theas. A Look so very audacious ! Now the filthy Men, who love every thing that is impudent, call that Spirit.—But there are, *Artemona*, some particular distinctions from a certain Person, who of late hath been very particular to me, that might *indeed* make her too familiar.

Art. Heaven forbid !

Theas. How precarious is the Happiness of a Wife, when it is in the Power of every new Face to destroy it !—Now, dear *Artemona*, tell me sincerely, don't you, from what you yourself have observed, think I have Reason to be uneasy ?   30

Art. That I have observ'd !

Theas. Dear *Artemona*, don't frighten thyself.—I am not accusing you but talking to you as a Friend.

A I R   X V I I.   Fairy Elves.

Art.

> *O guard your Hours from Care,*
> *Of Jealousy beware ;*
> *For she with fancy'd Sprites,*
> *Herself torments and frights.*
> *Thus she frets, and pines, and grieves,*
> *Raising Fears that she believes.*   39

Theas. I hate myself too for having so much Condescension and Humility as to be jealous. 'Tis flattering the Man that uses one ill ; and 'tis wanting the natural Pride that belongs to the Sex. What a wretched, mean, contemptible Figure is a jealous Woman ! How have I expos'd myself !

Art. Your Majesty is safe in the Confidence repos'd in me.

Theas. That is not the Case, *Artemona*. *Lycomedes* knows I am unhappy. I have own'd it, and was so unguarded as to accuse him.

Art. Upon mere Suspicion only ?

Theas. Beyond Dispute he loves her. I know it, *Artemona* ; and can one imagine that Girl hath Virtue enough to withstand such a Proposal.

A I R   X V I I I.   *Moll Peatly.*

> *All Hearts are a little frail*   50
> *When Temptation is rightly apply'd.*
> *What can Shame or Fear avail*
> *When we sooth both Ambition and Pride ?*
> *All Women have Power in view ;*
> *Then there's Pleasure to tempt her too.*
> *Such a sure Attack there's no defying,*
> *No denying ;*
> *Since complying*
> *Gives her another's Due.*

32 accusing you]. accusing, *1760*.

* X

——I can't indeed (if you mean that) positively affirm that he hath yet had her.

Art. Then it may be still only Suspicion.   61

Theas. I have trusted too my Daughter *Deidamia* with my Weakness; that she, by her Intimacies and Friendship with *Pyrrha*, may get into her Secrets. In short, I have plac'd her as my Spy about her. That Girl (out of Good-nature, and to prevent Family-disputes) may deceive me. She insists upon it, that I have nothing to fear from *Pyrrha*; and is so positive in this Opinion, that she offers to be answerable for her Conduct.

Art. Why then, Madam, will you still believe your own Jealousies?   68

Theas. All I say is, that *Deidamia* may deceive me; for whatever is in the Affair, 'tis impossible but she must know it; I have order'd it so that she is scarce ever from her; they have one and the same Bed-Chamber; yet such is my Distemper, that I suspect every Body, and can only believe my own Imaginations.—There must be some Reason that *Deidamia* hath not been with me this Morning.——I am impatient to see her.

AIR XIX. *John Anderson* my *Jo.*

Art.

> Let Jealousy no longer
>   A fruitless Search pursue;   76
> You make his Flame the Stronger,
>   And wake Resentment too.
> This self-tormenting Care give o'er;
>   For all you can obtain
> Is, what was only Doubt before,
>   To change for real Pain.

A C T   I I.

S C E N E   I.

Diphilus, Achilles.

Ach. I am very sensible, my Lord, of the particular Honours that are shewn me.

Diph. Honours, Madam! *Lycomedes* is still more particular. How happy must that Woman be whom he respects!

Ach. What do you mean, my Lord?

Diph. Let this speak both for him and me: The Present is worthy him to give, and you to receive.

Ach. I have too many Obligations already.

Diph. 'Tis in your Power, Madam, to return 'em all.

Ach. Thus I return 'em. And, if you dare be honest, tell him this Ring had been a more *honourable* Present to *Theaspe*.   11

A I R X X.   Abroad as I was walking.

Diph.   [Offering the Ring a second time.]

> *Such Homage to her Beauty,*
> *What Coyness can reject ?*
> *Accept, as 'tis your Duty,*
> *The Tribute with Respect.*
> *What more can Beauty gain thee ?*
> *With Love I offer Power.*
> *What Shame can ever stain thee,*
> *Restrain thee,*
> *Or pain thee,*   20
> *When blest with such a Dower ?*

Diph.   'Tis but an earnest, Madam, of future Favours.—When *Lycomedes* his Power is yours, I intreat your Highness not to forget your Servant.

Ach.   I shall remember thee with Contempt and Abhorrence.

Diph.   I beg you, Madam, to consider your present Situation.——This uncommon Distinction requires a softer Answer.   26

Ach.   I shall give no other, my Lord.—I dare say, *Diphilus*, you think yourself highly honour'd by your present Negotiation.—Is there no Office too mean for Ambition ?—Was you not a Man of Quality, was you not a Favourite, the World, my Lord, wou'd call you a Pimp, a Pandar, a Bawd, for this very honourable Proposal of yours.   31

Diph.   What an unmerciful Weapon is a Woman's Tongue !—I beg your Highness to confine yourself within the Bounds of common Civility, and to consider who I am.

Ach.   I do consider it, *Diphilus*, and that makes thee a thousand times the more contemptible.

A I R X X I.   Butter'd Pease.

> *Shou'd the Beast of the noblest Race*
> *Act the Brute of the lowest Class ;*
> *Tell me, which do you think more base,*
> *Or the Lion or the Ass ?*   40
> *Boast not then of thy Rank or State ;*
> *That but shews thee the meaner Slave.*
> *Take thy due then of Scorn and Hate.*
> *As thou'rt but the greater Knave.*

Diph.   Though the Sex have the Privilege of unlimited Expression, and that a Woman's Words are not to be resented ; yet a Lady, Madam, may be ill-bred. Ladies too are generally passionate enough without a Provocation, so that a Reply at present would be unnecessary.   48

Ach.   Are such the Friends of Power ?—How unhappy are Princes to have their Passions so very readily put in Execution, that they seldom know the Benefit of Reflexion ! Go, and for once make your Report faithfully and without Flattery.

16 *What more can Beauty gain thee ?*] Omitted by Plays 1760, and by Underhill.

S c e n e   II.

Diphilus.

Diph. This Girl is so excessively ill-bred, and such an arrant Termagant, that I cou'd as soon fall in love with a Tigress. She hath a handsome Face, 'tis true, but in her Temper she is a very Fury.—But *Lycomedes* likes her ; and 'tis not for me to dispute either his Taste or Pleasure.—Notwithstanding she is such a Spitfire, 'tis my Opinion the thing may still do : Things of this Nature shou'd be always transacted in Person, for there are Women so ridiculously half-modest, that they are asham'd in Words to consent to what (when a Man comes to the Point) they will make no Difficulties to comply with.   9

1 This Girl] The girl *1777*.

S c e n e   III.

Lycomedes, Diphilus.

Lycom. Well, *Diphilus*, in what manner did she receive my Present ?
Diph. 'Tis my Opinion, Sir, that she will accept it only from your Hands. From me she absolutely refuses it.

A I R   X X I I. Come open the Door sweet *Betty*.

Lycom.   *What, must I remain in Anguish ?*
                      And did not her Eyes consent ?
                   No Sigh, not a Blush, nor Languish
                      That promis'd a kind Event !
                   It must be all Affectation,
                      The Tongue hath her Heart bely'd ;
                   That oft hath withstood Temptation,   10
                      When ev'ry thing else comply'd.

Lycom. How did she receive you ? Did you watch her Eyes ? What was her Behaviour when you first told her I lov'd her ?
Diph. She seem'd to be desperately disappointed, that you had not told her so your self.
Lycom. But when you press'd it to her—
Diph. She had all the Resentment and Fury of the most complying Prude.
Lycom. But did not she soften upon Consideration ?
Diph. She seem'd to take it mortally ill of me, that my meddling in the Affair had delay'd your Majesty's Application.   20
Lycom. What no favourable Circumstance !
Diph. Nay, I was not in the least surpris'd at her Behaviour. Love at second-hand to a Lady of her warm Constitution ! It was a Disappointment, Sir ; and she cou'd not but treat it accordingly.—Whatever was my Opinion, 'twas my Duty, Sir, to obey you, but I found just the Reception I expected. Apply to her your self, Sir ; answer her Wishes, and (if I know any thing of Woman) she will then answer yours, and behave herself as she ought.

Lycom. But, dear *Diphilus*, I grow more and more impatient.   28

Diph. That too by this time is her Case.—To save the Appearances of Virtue, the most easy Woman expects a little gentle Compulsion, and to be allow'd the Decency of a little feeble Resistance. For the Quiet of her own Conscience a Woman may insist upon acting the Part of Modesty, and you must comply with her Scruples.—You will have no more trouble but what will heighten the Pleasure.

Lycom. *Pyrrha !*—This is beyond my Hopes.—*Diphilus*, lay your Hand upon my Breast. Feel how my Heart flutters.   36

Diph. Did *Pyrrha* feel these Assurances of Love she wou'd not appear so thoughtful.

Lycom. *Deidamia* too not with her !

Diph. She is with the Queen, Sir.

Lycom. My other Daughters, who seem less fond of her, are in the Garden ; so all 's safe.—Leave me, *Diphilus*, and let none, upon Pain of my Displeasure, presume to intrude.

29 case.] case *1733*.

S C E N E IV.

Lycomedes, Achilles.

Lycom. Lady *Pyrrha*, my dear Child, why so thoughtful ?

Ach. Thoughts may not be so respectful ; they may be too familiar, too friendly, too true : And who about you presumes to communicate 'em ? Words and Forms only are for your Ear, Sir.

Lycom. You know, *Pyrrha*, you was never receiv'd upon the Foot of Ceremony, but Friendship ; so that it wou'd be more respectful, if you was less shy and less reserv'd.—'Tis your Behaviour, *Pyrrha*, that keeps me at a Distance.   8

Ach. If I was wanting, Sir, either in Duty to you or my self, my own Heart wou'd be the first to reproach me. Your Majesty's Generosity is too solicitous upon my Account ; and your Courtesy and Affability may even now detain you from Affairs of Importance.—If you have no Commands, Sir, the Princesses expect me in the Garden.

Lycom. Nay, positively, my dear *Pyrrha*, you shall not go.

Ach. But why, Sir ?—For Heaven's Sake, what hath set you a trembling ? ——I fear, Sir, you are out of Order.——Who waits there ?   16

Lycom. I did not call, *Pyrrha*.

Ach. Let me then, Sir, know your Commands.—

A I R X X I I I.   Altro Giorno in compagnia.

Lycom.   *If my Passion want explaining,*
            This way turn and read my Eyes ;   20
          These will tell thee, without feigning,
          What in Words I must disguise.

Ach. Why do you fix your Eyes so intensely upon me ?—Speak your Pleasure, speak to me then.—Why am I seiz'd ?—Spare me, Sir, for I have a Temper that can't bear Provocation.

Lycom. I know there are a thousand necessary Affectations of Modesty, which Women, in Decency to themselves, practice with common Lovers before Compliance.—But my Passion, *Pyrrha*, deserves some Distinction.

Ach. I beg you then, Sir, don't lay violent Hands upon me.

Lycom. The Present you refus'd from *Diphilus* accept from me.   30

Ach. Why will you persist ?—Nay, dear Sir, I can't answer for my Passions.

Lycom. 'Tis not *Diphilus*, but I give it you.

Ach. That *Diphilus*, Sir, is your Enemy.

Lycom. 'Tis I that offer it.

Ach. Your very worst Enemy, your Flatterer.

Lycom. You shou'd strive, Child, to conquer these extravagant Passions.

Ach. How I despise that Fellow ! that Pimp, that Pandar !

A I R X X I V. Trip to the Laundry.

How unhappy are the Great,
   Thus begirt with servile Slaves !
Such with Praise your Reason cheat.   40
   Flatt'rers are the meanest Knaves.
They, in Friendship's Guise accost you ;
   False in all they say or do.
When these Wretches have ingross'd you,
   Who 's the Slave, Sir, they or you ?

Lycom. Is this reproachful Language, *Pyrrha*, befitting my Presence ?

Ach. Nay, dear Sir, don't worry me. By *Jove*, you'll provoke me.

Lycom. Your Affectation, *Pyrrha*, is intolerable. There 's enough of it.— Those Looks of Aversion are insupportable.—I will have no struggling.

Ach. Then, Sir, I must have no Violence.   50

A I R X X V. As I walk'd along *Fleetstreet*.

Lycom.   *When the Fort on no Condition*
   Will admit the gen'rous Foe,
   Parley but delays Submission ;
   We by Storm shou'd lay it low.

Lycom. I am in earnest, Lady.—I will have no trifling, no coquetting ; you may spare those little Arts of Women, for my Passion is warm and vehement enough without 'em.—Do you know, *Pyrrha*, that Obedience is your Duty ?

Ach. I know my Duty, Sir ; and, had it not been for that Sycophant *Diphilus*, perhaps you had known yours.   59

Lycom. I am not, Lady, to be aw'd and frighten'd by stern Looks and Frowns.—Since your obstinate Behaviour then makes Violence necessary——

Ach. You make Self-preservation, Sir, as necessary.

Lycom. I won't be refus'd.

A I R X X V I. The Lady's New-Year's Gift.

Lycom.   *Why such Affectation ?*
Ach.   *Why this Provocation ?*
Lycom.   *Must I bear Resistance still !*
Ach.   *Check your Inclination.*

Lycom.	*Dare you then deny me ?*	
Ach.	*You too far may try me.*	
Lycom.	*Must I then against your Will !*	70
Ach.	*Force shall never ply me.*	

Lycom. Never was such a Termagant !
Ach. By *Jove*, never was such an Insult !
Lycom. Will you ?—Dare you ?—Never was such Strength !—
  [Achilles *pushes him from him with great Violence, and throws him down.*
Ach. Desist then.
Lycom. Audacious Fury, know you what you have done ?—

A I R   X X V I I.   Puppet-Show Trumpet Tune.

[*Achilles* holding *Lycomedes* down.]

Ach.	*What Heart hath not Courage, by Force assail'd,*	
	To brave the most desperate Fight ?	80
	'Tis Justice and Virtue that hath prevail'd ;	
	Power must yield to Right.	

Lycom. Am I so ignominiously to be got the better of !
Ach. You are.
Lycom. By a Woman !
Ach. You now, Sir, find you had acted a greater Part, if (in Spite of your Flatterers) you had got the better of your own Passions.

S C E N E V.

Lycomedes, Achilles, Diphilus, Courtiers.

1 *Court.* An Attempt upon the King's Life !—The Guards ! where are the Guards ?
2 *Court.* Such an open, bare-fac'd Assassination !
  [*They seize* Achilles, *and raise* Lycomedes.
3 *Court.* And by a Woman too !
1 *Court.* Where are your Wounds, Sir.
2 *Court.* Take the Dagger from her, that she do no farther Mischief.
3 *Court.* The Dagger ! Where ? What Dagger ?
1 *Court.* You will find it some where or other conceal'd ; examine her, search her.
Ach. Save your Zeal, Sirs, for times of real Danger. Let *Lycomedes* accuse me.—He knows my Offence.   11
Lycom. How have I expos'd my self !——*Diphilus*, bid these over-officious Friends leave me, and, as they value my Favour, that they say nothing of what they have seen.—[Diphilus *talks apart with the Courtiers, who go out.*] Though the Insult from any other Person had been unpardonable ; there are ways that you, Madam, might still take to reconcile me.
Ach. Self-defence, Sir, is the Privilege of Mankind. I know your Power, but as I have offended no Law I rely upon your Justice.

Lycom. 'Twou'd be safer, Madam, to rely on your own future Behaviour.
Ach. Who was the Aggressor, Sir ?   20
Lycom. Beauty, Inclination, Love. If you will merit Favour you know
the Conditions.

AIR XXVIII. Old King Cole.

No more be coy ;
Give a Loose to Joy,
And let Love for thy Pardon sue.
A Glance cou'd all my Rage destroy,
And light up my Flame anew.
For though a Man can stand at Bay
Against a Woman's Will ;
And keep, amid the loudest Fray,   30
His Resolution still :
Yet when consenting Smiles accost,
The Man in her Arms is lost.

Scene VI.

Lycomedes, Achilles, Diphilus.

Ach. If your Resentment wants only the Show of Justice, let this *honourable*
Man here be my Accuser ; it may be necessary for him to trump up a horrid
Conspiracy to skreen his own infamous Practices.
Diph. Your Majesty hath had too much Confidence in this Woman.
The Lives of Kings are sacred, and the Matter (trivial as it seems) deserves
further Inquiry.—There must be some secret villainous Design in this Affair.
Ach. And are not you, *Diphilus*, conscious of that secret villainous Design ?
Diph. 'Tis an Offence, Sir, that is not to be pardon'd. Your Dignity, Sir,
calls upon you (notwithstanding your Partiality to her) to make her an
Example. There must be Things of Consequence that we are still ignorant
of ; and she ought to undergo the severest Examination.—My zeal for your
Service, Sir, was never as yet at a loss for Witnesses upon these Occasions.
                                                              [*To* Lycomedes.
Lycom. Don't you see the Queen coming this Way ? Have done with this
Discourse, dear *Diphilus*, and leave me.—Wou'd I cou'd forget this ridiculous
Affair ! For the present, *Pyrrha*, I trust you to return to the Ladies ; though
(considering your passionate Temper) I have little Reason to rely on your
Discretion.

Scene VII.

Lycomedes, Theaspe, Deidamia.

Theas. I thought I had heard *Pyrrha*'s Voice.
Lycom. A jealous Woman's Thoughts are her own and her Husband's
eternal Plague ; so I beg you, my Dear, say no more of her.
Theas. And have I no reason but my own Thoughts, my Liege ?

AIR XXIX. Dicky's Walk in Dr. *Faustus.*

Theas.	*What give o'er !*
	I must and will complain.
Lycom.	*You plague us both in vain.*
Theas.	*You won't then hear a Wife !*
Lycom.	*I must, it seems, for Life.*
	Teaze no more. 10
Theas.	*Nay, Sir, you know 'tis true,*
	That 'tis to her I owe my Due.
	No Thanks to you !

It behoves Kings, Sir, to have the severest Guard upon their Actions ; for as their great ones are trumpeted by Fame, their little ones are as certainly and as widely convey'd from Ear to Ear by a whisper.

Lycom. These chimerical Jealousies, Madam, may provoke my Patience.

Theas. Chimerical Jealousies !—And do you really, Sir, think your ignominious Affair is still a Secret ?—Am I to be ignorant of a Thing that is already whisper'd every where ?   20

AIR XXX. Puddings and Pyes.

Lycom.	*The Slips of a Husband you Wives*
	Will never forget :
	Your Tongue for the Course of our Lives
	Is never in debt.
	'Tis now funning, 25
	And then dunning ;
	Intent on our Follies alone,
	'Tis so fully employ'd that you never can think of your own.

Theas. My Suspicions have, *indeed*, wrong'd *Pyrrha.*—How I respect and honour that Girl !—*Deidamia*, that honourable, that virtuous Creature *Pyrrha*, well deserves both your Friendship and mine.—As soon as you have found her bring her to me, that I may acknowledge the Merits she hath to me.

===

SCENE VIII.

Lycomedes, Theaspe.

Theas. After the Repulse and Disgrace you have very justly met with, you might with Reason censure me for want of Duty and Respect shou'd I upbraid you.—'Tis past ; and if you will never again put me in mind, I choose to forget it.—Yet, wou'd you reward Virtue, and had you any Regard for my Quiet.—

AIR XXXI. My Dilding, my Dalding.

Ah ! shou'd you ever find her
Complying and kinder ;
Though now you have resign'd her ;
What then must ensue !

1 After the Repulse] *But* after the repulse *1777.*

Your Flame, though now 'tis over,   10
Again will recover ;
You'll prove as fond a Lover,
As I'm now of you.

Lycom. **What** wou'd you have me do ?

Theas. I wou'd have you distrust your self and remove the Temptation.—
I have long had it at Heart to find a Match for my Nephew *Periphas,* and
I really think we can never meet with a more deserving Woman.

Lycom. Whatever Scheme you have for her, *I* shall not interfere with you.
—I have had enough of her termagant Humours ; she hath not the common
Softness of the Sex.—'Tis my Opinion, that *Periphas* will not find himself
much oblig'd to you ; for the Man that marries her must either conquer his
own Passions, or hers, and one of 'em (according to my Observation) is not
to be conquer'd.   23

Theas. Marriage, Sir, hath broke many a Woman's Spirit ; and that will
be only his Affair.—When he takes her with him, your own Family at least will
be easy.

Lycom. Her Presence just now wou'd be shocking.—I cou'd not stand the
Shame and Confusion.—I see her, and *Deidamia* with her.—Do with her as
you please ; you have my Consent.

Scene IX.

Theaspe, Deidamia, Achilles.

Theas. The Character *Deidamia* hath given of you, and your own Behaviour,
Child, have so charm'd me, that I think I never can sufficiently reward your
Merits.

Ach. *Deidamia's* Friendship may make her partial.—My only Merit,
Madam, is Gratitude.

Theas. To convince you of the Opinion I have of you—But I must first
ask you a Question—Don't you think, Lady *Pyrrha,* that my Nephew *Periphas*
is very agreeable ?

Ach. That Impatience of his, to serve as a Volunteer with the Troops of
Lycomedes at the Siege of *Troy,* is becoming his Birth.—So much Fire, and so
much Spirit !—I don't wonder your Majesty is fond of him.   11

Theas. But I am sure, *Pyrrha,* you must think his Person agreeable.

Ach. No Woman alive can dispute it.

Theas. I don't know, every way, so deserving a young Man ; and I have
that Influence upon him, and at the same time that Regard for him, that
I wou'd have him happy.—Don't think, child, that I wou'd make him
happy at your Expence ; for knowing him, I know you will be so.—Was
the Princess *Calistra* here, 'tis a Match she cou'd not disapprove of ; therefore let that be no Obstacle, for every thing, in regard to her, I take upon
my self.   20

Ach. Wou'd you make me the Obstacle to his Glory ? Pardon me, Madam,
I know my self undeserving.

A I R X X X I I. How happy are you and I.

First let him for Honour roam,
And martial Fame obtain :
Then (if he shou'd come Home)
Perhaps I may explain.
Since then alone the Hero's Deeds
Can make my Heart give way ;
'Till Ilion *falls and* Hector *bleeds,*
I must my Choice delay.   30

Theas. Nay, *Pyrrha,* I won't take these romantick Notions of yours for an Answer.—*Deidamia* is so much your Friend, that, I am sure, she must be happy with this Alliance ; so, while I make the Proposal to my Nephew, I leave you two to talk over the Affair together.

Scene X.

Deidamia, Achilles.

Ach. Was there ever a Man in so whimsical a Circumstance !
Deid. Was there ever a Woman in so happy and so unhappy a one as mine !
Ach. Why did I submit ? why did I plight my Faith thus infamously to conceal my self ?—What is become of my Honour ?
Deid. Ah *Pyrrha, Pyrrha,* what is become of mine !
Ach. When shall I behave my self as a Man !
Deid. Wou'd you had never behav'd yourself as one !

A I R X X X I I I. Fy gar rub her o'er with Straw.

Deid.   *Think what Anguish tears my Quiet,*
            Since I suffer'd Shame for thee :
            Man at large may rove and riot,   10
            We are bound but you are free.
            Are thy Vows and Oaths mistaken ?
            See the Birds that wing the Sky ;
            These their Mates have ne'er forsaken,
            'Till their Young at least can fly.

Ach. Pester'd and worried thus from every Quarter 'tis impossible much longer to prevent discovery !
Deid. Dear, dear *Pyrrha,* confide in me. Any other Discovery but to me only wou'd be inevitable Perdition to us both.—Am I treated like a common Prostitute ? Can your Gratitude (wou'd I might say Love !) refuse to let me know the Man to whom I owe my Ruin ?   21
Ach. You must rely, my dear Princess, upon my Honour ; for I am not, like a fond weak Husband, to be teaz'd into the breaking my Resolution.

A I R X X X I V. *Beggar's* Opera. Hornpipe.

Ach.	*Know that Importunity's in vain.*
Deid.	*Can then nothing move thee ?*
Ach.	*Ask not, since Denial gives me Pain.*
Deid.	*Think how much I love thee.*
Ach.	*What 's a Secret in a Woman's Breast ?*
Deid.	*Canst thou thus upbraid me !*
Ach.	*Let me leave thy Heart and Tongue at rest.* 30
Deid.	*Love then hath betray'd me.*

Ach. For Heaven's sake, *Deidamia*, if you regard my Love, give me Quiet.
—Intreaties, Fondness, Tears, Rage and the whole matrimonial Rhetorick
of Woman to gain her Ends are all thrown away upon me ; for, by the Gods,
my dear *Deidamia*, I am inexorable.

Deid. But, my dear *Pyrrha*, (for you oblige me still to call you by that
Name) only imagine what must be the Consequence of a Month or two.—
Think of my unhappy Condition.—To save my Shame (if you are a Man of
Honour) you must then come to some Resolution. 39

Ach. 'Till I deserve these Suspicions, *Deidamia*, methinks it wou'd be more
becoming your Professions of Love to spare 'em.—I have taken my Resolutions;
and when the time comes, you shall know 'em : till then be easy, and press
me no farther.

A I R X X X V. My time, O ye Muses.

Deid.	*How happy my Days and how sweet was my Rest,*
	Ere Love with his Passions my Bosom distrest !
	Now I languish with Sorrow, I doubt and I fear :
	But Love hath me all when my Pyrrha is near.
	Yet why have I griev'd ?—Ye vain Passions adieu !
	I know my own Heart and I'll think thee as true ;
	And as you know my Heart, 'twou'd be folly to range ; 50
	For who'd be inconstant to lose by the Change ?

Deid. My Life, my Honour, then I implicitly intrust with you.

Ach. Who wou'd have the trouble of putting on a Character that does
not naturally belong to him ! the Life of a Hypocrite must be one continual
Scene of Anxiety. When shall I appear as I am, and extricate my self out
of this Chain of Perplexities !—I have no sooner escap'd being ravish'd but
I am immediately to be made a Wife.

Deid. But, dear *Pyrrha*, for my sake, for your own, have a particular
Regard to your Behaviour till your Resolution is ripe for Execution.—You
now and then take such intolerable Strides, that I vow you have set me
a blushing. 61

Ach. Considering my continual Restraint, and how much the Part I act
differs from my Inclinations, I am surpriz'd at my own Behaviour.

A I R X X X V I. I am come to your House.

Ach.	*Your Dress, your Conversations,*
	Your Airs of Joy and Pain,
	All these are Affectations
	We never can attain.

> *The Sex so often varies,*
> *'Tis Nature more than Art :*
> *To play their whole Vagaries*   70
> *We must have Woman's Heart.*

Deid. Your Swearing too, upon certain Occasions, sounds so very mascu-line—an Oath startles me.——Wou'd I cou'd cure my self of these violent Apprehensions !

Ach. As for that matter, there are Ladies who, in their Passions, can take all the Liberties of Speech.   76

Deid. Then too, you very often look so agreeably impudent upon me, that, let me die, if I have not been mortally afraid my Sisters wou'd find you out.

Ach. Impudent ! are Women so censorious that Looks cannot escape 'em ?—May not one Woman look kindly upon another without Scandal ?

Deid. But such Looks !—Nay, perhaps I may be particular, and it may be only my own Fears ; for (notwithstanding your Dress) whenever I look upon you, I have always the Image of a Man before my eyes.

Ach. Do what we will, Love at some Moments will be unguarded.—But what shall I do about this *Periphas ?*   85

Deid. His Heart is so set upon the Siege, that I know you can have but very little Persecution upon his Account.

Ach. Wou'd I cou'd go with him !

Deid. And cou'd you leave me thus ?

Ach. Have you only a womanish Fondness ? I thought, *Deidamia,* you lov'd me. And you cannot truly love and esteem, if in every Circumstance of Life you have not a just Regard for my Honour.   92

Deid. Dear *Pyrrha,* don't mention it ; the very Thought of it kills me. You have set my Heart in a most violent Palpitation.—Let us talk no more upon this disagreeable Subject.—My Sisters will grow very impatient.—Shou'd we stay longer together I might again be importunate and ask to know you, and I had rather bear the eternal Plague of unsatisfied Curiosity, than give you a Moment's Disquiet.—They are now expecting us in the Garden, and, considering my present Circumstances, I wou'd not give 'em occasion to be impertinent, for of late they have been horridly prying and inquisitive.—Let us go to 'em.   101

Ach. I envy that *Periphas.* His Honour, his Fame, his Glory is **not** shackled by a Woman.

A I R X X X V I I. The Clarinette.

Ach.	*Ah, why is my Heart so tender !*
	My Honour incites me to Arms :
	To Love shall I Fame surrender ?
	By Laurels I'll merit thy Charms.
Deid.	*How can I bear the Reflection ?*
Ach.	*I balance ; and Honour gives way.* 109
Deid.	*Reward my Love by Affection ;*
	I ask thee no more than I pay.

108 *Reflection ?*] *Reflection* 1733.

A C T   I I I.

S c e n e   I.

Theaspe, Periphas, Artemona.

Theas. *Periphas,* I have a Favour to ask of you, and positively I will not be refus'd.

Per. Your Majesty may command.

Theas. Nay, Nephew, 'tis for your own good.

Per. To obey your Commands, Madam, must be so.

Theas. I am not, *Periphas,* talking to you as a Queen, but as a Relation, a Friend.—I must have no Difficulties; therefore I insist upon your absolute Promise.

Per. I am not in my own Power, Madam.—*Lycomedes,* you know hath acceded to the Treaty of Alliance ; that to furnish his Quota, his Troops are already embark'd, and that I have engag'd my self in his Service.   10

Theas. Why will you raise Obstacles before you know the Conditions ? 'Tis a thing I have set my heart upon, and I tell you 'tis what in Honour you can comply with.

Per. My Duty, my Obligations, put me entirely in your Disposal.

Theas. You promise then solemnly, faithfully—

Per. I do.

Theas. I have remark'd, *Periphas,* that you are prodigiously fond of the princess *Calista's* Daughter.

Per. I fond of her, Madam !

Theas. Nay, *Periphas,* are not you eternally at her Ear ?   20

Art. How I have seen that formidable Hero General *Ajax* suffer upon your Account !—Of all his Rivals you are his eternal Torment.—He reddens, sighs, and (as much as is consistent with such a blustering Soldier's Valour) languishes whenever you are near her.

Theas. You may safely own your Passion, *Periphas,* for I know you think her agreeable.

Art. Besides her being the fashionable Beauty of the Court (which is sufficient Vanity to make all the young Fellows follow her) you, of all Mankind, in Gratitude ought to like her.—I know all of 'em envy the particular Distinctions she shews you.   30

Theas. I am convinc'd of her Merits ; and your marrying her I know wou'd make you both happy.

Per. Let me perish, Madam, if I ever once thought of it !

Theas. Your Happiness you see hath been in my Thoughts.—I take the settling of this Affair upon my self.

Per. How cou'd you, Madam, imagine I had any Views of this kind !— What, be a Woman's Follower with Intention to marry her ! Why, the very Women themselves wou'd laugh at a Man who had so vulgar a Notion of

Act III]   ' In the representation, the second Act begins here.' *Foot-note, 1777.*

Galantry, and knew so little of their Inclinations.—The Man never means it, and the Woman never expects it ; and for the most part they have every other View but Marriage.   41

Theas. But I am serious, Nephew, and insist upon your Promise.

AIR X X X V I I I. No sooner had *Jonathan* leap'd from the Boat.

> *What are the Jests that on Marriage you quote ?*
> *All ignorant Batchelors censure by Rote ;*
> *Like Criticks you view it with Envy or Spleen.*
> *You pry out its Faults, but the Good is o'erseen.*

Per. 'Tis not in my Power, Madam ; 'tis not in my Inclinations.—A Soldier can have but one Inducement to marry, (and the Woman may have the same Reason too) which is, the Opportunities of Absence.

Theas. You know, Nephew, you have promis'd.   50

Per. But suppose I am already engag'd.

Theas. That will be another Merit to her.

Per. 'Tis impossible, Madam.—In a Day or two you know I am to set out for the Campaign.

Theas. A Lady of her romantic Spirit can have no Objections to following the Camp.

A I R X X X I X. Love 's a Dream of mighty Pleasure.

> *Soldier, think before you marry ;*
> *If your Wife the Camp attends,*
> *You but a Convenience carry,*
>   *For (perhaps) a hundred Friends.*   60
> *If at home she 's left in Sorrow,*
>   *Absence is convenient too ;*
> *Neighbours now and then may borrow*
>   *What is of no Use to you.*

Theas. I indeed fear'd *Pyrrha* might have started some Difficulties, but if you rightly consider the Proposal you can have none.

Per. What is the Cause of the War we are now engaged in ? Does not the Fate of *Menelaus* stare me in the Face ?   63

Theas. I will have no more of your trifling Objections, *Periphas* ; and as to your Part, from this time I will look upon the Affair as happily concluded. —All that now remains to be done is with *Pyrrha.* I have left her to *Deidamia*'s Management ; and without doubt her good Offices must prevail, for you can never have a better Advocate.—But shou'd the girl be perverse and obstinate ! —'Tis impossible. For however her Heart is already engag'd, no Woman alive can resist the Ambition of such an Alliance.

S c e n e I I.

Periphas.

Per. Had I so little Taste of Liberty as to be inclin'd to marry; that Girl is of so termagant a Spirit!—The bravest Man must have the dread of an eternal Domestic War.—In a Tongue-combat Woman is invincible, and the Husband must come off with Shame and Infamy; for though he lives in perpetual Noise and Tumult, the poor Man is only ridiculous to his Neighbours.—How can we ever get rid of her?—*Hercules* conquered the seven-headed *Hydra*, but his Wife was a venom'd Shirt that stuck to him to the last.

7. It is worth noting, as a curious circumstance, that the anonymous critic, already quoted, writes (in continuation of the passages cited):
'But the humorous Description of

> Hercules's *Shirt-a*
> *Which burnt him to—Dirt-a,*
> *And set him all on a Fire-a,*
> *Contriv'd by his* Deianira.

has so peculiar a Quaintness of Expression, it could not pass unheeded
No such lyric occurs in the opera as printed.

S c e n e I I I.

Periphas, Ajax.

Ajax. This Rencounter, *Periphas*, is as I wish'd.——The Liberties you have taken——you know what I mean—when my Honour is concern'd—an Indignity and all that!—'Tis not to be put up; and I must insist upon an Explanation.—There is a particular Affair, my Lord.——

Per. Your accosting me in this particular manner, Lord *Ajax*, requires Explanation.—For let me die, if I comprehend you!

Ajax. Death, my Lord, I explain! I am not come here to be ask'd Questions.—'Tis sufficient that I know the Affront, and that you know I will have Satisfaction.——So, now you are answer'd——

Per. I can't say much to *my* Satisfaction, my Lord; for I can't so much as guess at your meaning.

Ajax. A Man of Honour, *Periphas*, is not to be trifled withal.

Per. But a Man of Honour, *Ajax*, is not oblig'd in Courage to be unintelligible.

Ajax. I hate talking.——The Tongue is a Woman's Weapon. Whenever I am affronted; by the Gods, this Sword is my only Answer.

Per. 'Tis not, *Ajax*, that I decline the Dispute, or wou'd upon any Account deny you the Pleasure of fighting; yet (if it is not too much Condescension in a Man of Honour) before I fight I wou'd willingly know the Provocation.

A I R X L. *Maggy Lawther.*

Ajax.　　　*What is all this idle Chat ?*　　　20
Words are out of Season.
Whether 'tis or this or that,
　　The Sword shall do me reason.
Honour call'd me to the Task ;
　　No matter for explaining :
'Tis a fresh Affront to ask
　　A Man of Honour's meaning.

Ajax. Be it as it will, *Periphas* ; we have gone too far already to retract.
—You know, I suppose, of my Pretensions to a certain Lady.—Now are you
satisfied ?

Per. If you had her, my Lord, it had been much more to my Satisfaction.—
I admire your Courage.

A I R X L I. Lord *Frog* and Lady *Mouse.*

Oh, then it seems you want a Wife !
　　Shou'd I consent,
　　You may repent,
And all her daily Jars and Strife
　　You may on me resent.
Thus ev'ry Day and ev'ry Night,
If things at home shou'd not go right,
We three must live in constant Fight.
　　Take her at all Event.

Ajax. Hell, and Furies ! I am not to be rally'd out of my Resentment.

Per. Now in my Opinion 'tis flinging away your Courage to fight without
a Cause ; though indeed the Men of uncommon Prowess, by their loving to
make the most of every Quarrel, seem to think the contrary.

Ajax. You are not so sure of the Lady, *Periphas*, as you flatter yourself ;
for whenever I am a Rival, by *Jove*, 'tis not her Consent, but my Sword, that
must decide the Question.

Per. Sure never a Rival (as you will call me) had a better Reason for fighting
than I have at present ; for if I am kill'd, I shall be out of danger of having
the Woman.

Ajax. You might spare your Jokes, *Periphas*, for my Courage wants no
Provocation.—If I fall, *Pyrrha* may be yours : You will then deserve her.—
'Till then—

Per. So he that conquers, as a Reward, I find is to be married.—Now dear
Ajax, is that worth fighting for ?

Ajax. Your Passion for that Lady, *Periphas*, is too publick to bear Dispute.
—Have not I seen you whisper her, laugh with her ?　And by some particular
Looks at the same time 'twas too evident that I was the Subject of your
Mirth.

Per. Looks, *Ajax !*

Ajax. Yes Looks, my Lord ; and I never did or will take an impertinent
one from any Man.

Per. Impertinent one !

Ajax. Furies! This calm Mockery is not to be born.—I won't have my Words repeated.

Per. Such Language, *Ajax*, may provoke me.

AIR XLII. *Richmond* Ball.

Per.	*What means all this Ranting ?*
Ajax.	*Cease your joking ;*
	'Tis provoking.
Per.	*I to my Honour will n'er be wanting.*
Ajax.	*Will you do me right ?*
Per.	*What means all this Ranting ?*
Ajax.	*Cease your joking ;*
	'Tis provoking.
Per.	*I to my Honour will ne'er be wanting.*
Ajax.	*Talk not then, but fight.*
	Give then by Action
	Satisfaction.
Per.	*I'm not in awe, Sir.*
Ajax.	*Death ! will you draw, Sir ?*
	Tittle-tattle
	Is a Battle
	You may safer try.
Per.	*Yet, first, I'd fain know why.*

Ajax. By *Jupiter, Periphas,* 'till now I never thought you a Coward.

Per. Nay then—since my own Honour calls upon me.—Take notice, *Ajax*, that I *don't* fight for the Woman.   [*They fight.*

Scene IV.

Periphas, Ajax, Theaspe, Artemona, Guards.

1 *Guard.* Part 'em.—Beat down their swords.   [*They are parted.*

2 *Guard.* How dar'd you presume to fight in the Royal Gardens ?

1 *Guard.* Nay, in the very Presence !—For see, the Queen.

Ajax. 'Tis very hard, Sirs, that a Man shou'd be deny'd the Satisfaction of a Gentleman.

Theas. Lord *Ajax*, for this unparallel'd Presumption we forbid you the Palace.

Ajax. I shall take some other Opportunity, my Lord.

Scene V.

Theaspe, Artemona, Periphas.

Theas. And as for you, *Periphas*—

Per. Your Majesty's Rigor can do no less than forbid me the Woman.

Theas. The Woman, *Periphas*, is the only thing that can reconcile me to your Behaviour.

Per. That blundering Hero *Ajax* will have it that I am his Rival. The Man will be almost as miserable without her, as 'tis probable he might be with her. — Oblige us both then, Madam, and let the General be miserable in his own way.

Theas. I cou'd not have imagin'd that obstinate Girl cou'd have had any Scruples to the Match ; but *Deidamia* tells me she finds her as difficult as you.

Per. Since you know, Madam, that *Pyrrha* will have her own way ; for both our sakes, and to save yourself unnecessary Trouble, your Majesty had better give up this Impossibility. 32

Scene VI.

Theaspe, Artemona, Periphas, Diphilus, Guards.

Diph. To prevent future Mischief my Lord, his Majesty puts you under Arrest, and commands you to attend him. General *Ajax* is already in Custody. —'Tis his Pleasure too, that (after you have paid your Duty to him) you embark with the Troops immediately ; and you are not to come ashore again upon pain of his Majesty's Displeasure.

AIR XLIII.

Per.
In War we've nought but Death to fear,
How gracious is the Sentence !
For that is easier far to bear,
Than Marriage with Repentance.
Begirt with Foes, by Numbers brav'd, 13
I'd bless the happy Crisis ;
The Man from greater Danger sav'd
The lesser ones despises.

Per. Your Majesty then, you find, must dispense with my Promise 'till after the Expedition.—If the General shou'd be so happy, to bring *Pyrrha* with him to the Camp, perhaps we may like one another better.

Diph. The King, Madam, wants to talk to your Majesty upon Affairs of Consequence.—You will find him in the Royal Apartment.

Theas. My Daughter with *Pyrrha* have just turn'd the Walk, and are coming this way.—You may stay with 'em, *Artemona*, till I send for you.

Air XLIII. *The editions do not indicate by whom this Air is sung. As it suits the part of Periphas rather than that of Diphilus, I have printed it accordingly.*

Scene VII.

Artemona, Philoe, Lesbia.

Phil. 'Tis horridly mortifying that these Trades-People will never get any thing New against a Birth-day. They are all so abominably stupid, that a Woman of Fancy cannot possibly have the Opportunity of shewing her Genius.

Lesb. The Fatigue one hath of talking to those Creatures for at least a Month before a Birth-day is insupportable ; for you know, Sister, when the time draws so very near, a Woman can think of nothing else.

Phil. After all, Sister, though their things are detestable, one must make choice of something or other. I have sent to the Fellows to be with me this Morning.   10

Lesb. You are so eternally sending for 'em, one wou'd imagine you was delighted with their Conversation. For those hideous Stuffs they will shew us from Year to Year are frightful, are shocking. How can a Woman have so ill a Taste as to expose herself in a last Year's Pattern !

Phil. Dear Madam, I beg your Pardon. Let me die, if I saw you !

Lesb. Our meeting her was lucky beyond Expression, for I never felt so uneasy a thing as a Secret.

Phil. You know, Sister, we had agreed to trust her with our Suspicions.

Lesb. Yet after all when a Sister's Reputation is concern'd.

Phil. But is not the Honour of a Family of greater Consequence ?   20

Lesb. Tho she is a Woman and a Favourite, I dare say, if *Artemona* promises, whatever she suffers she will inviolably keep it to herself.

Art. If I had not this Quality I had little deserv'd *Theaspe*'s Friendship. —By all that 's Sacred, Ladies, you may safely trust me.

Phil. 'Tis impossible, Sister, but she herself must have observ'd it.

Lesb. Whatever People have observ'd, 'tis a thing you know, that no Creature alive can presume to talk upon.

Phil. Deal fairly and openly with us, *Artemona*.—Have you remark'd nothing particular of *Deidamia* yonder of late ?

Art. Of *Deidamia* !   30

Lesb. Only look upon her, Madam.

Phil. Well—what do you think of her ?

Lesb. Are you blind, *Artemona*, or dare not you believe your Eyes.

Art. Her particular Intimacy with *Pyrrha* do you mean ?

Phil. Dear Madam !—Then I find we must speak first.

Lesb. Now, dear *Artemona*, can any Woman alive imagine that Shape of hers within the compass of common Modesty ?

Art. But how can one possibly have those Suspicions ?

Phil. She is a Woman, Madam ; she hath Inclinations and may have had her Opportunities that we know nothing of.   40

A I R X L I V. Minuet of *Corelli* in the Ninth *Concerto.*

Phil.

> *We may resolve to resist Temptation ;*
> *And that 's all we can do :*
> *For in the Hour of Inclination*
> *What cou'd—I or you ?*

Lesb. Though the thing is improbable, 'tis so monstrously evident that it cannot bear a Dispute.

Phil. Then her Bosom too is so preposterously impudent !—One wou'd think a Woman in her Condition was not conscious of her own Shame.

Lesb. Or imagin'd other People cou'd overlook it as well as herself.

Phil. Then she is so squeamish and so frequently out of order.—   50

Lesb. That she hath all the outward Marks of Female Frailty must be visible to all Womankind.

Phil. But how she came by 'em, there, *Artemona*, is still the Secret.

Lesb. I must own that, by her particular Intimacies with that forward Creature *Pyrrha*, I suspect her to be her Confident in this Accident.

Art. I beg you, Ladies, to turn this Discourse ; for *Deidamia* and *Pyrrha* are just coming upon us to join the Conversation.

Scene VIII.

Philoe, Lesbia, Artemona, Deidamia, Achilles.

Lesb. Now I dare swear that careless Creature *Pyrrha* hath not once thought of her Clothes.

Art. Nay, dear Lady *Pyrrha*, the thing is not such a trifle, for 'tis the only Mark of Respect that most People are capable of shewing. And though that is not your Case, I know your Gratitude can never omit this publick Occasion.

AIR XLV. *Tom* and *Will* were Shepherds twain.

Art.
Think of Dress in ev'ry Light ;
'Tis Woman's chiefest Duty ;
Neglecting that, our selves we slight
And undervalue Beauty.
That allures the Lover's Eye,　　　　10
And graces ev'ry Action ;
Besides, when not a Creature's by,
'Tis inward Satisfaction.

Ach. As I am yet a Stranger, Ladies, to the Fashions of the Country, 'tis your Fancy that must determine me.

Phil. How can a Woman of common Sense be so unsolicitous about her Dress !

Lesb. And trust a Woman to choose for her ! 'Tis a Temptation to be spiteful that very few of us can resist ; for we have not many Pleasures that can equal that of seeing another Woman ridiculous.　　　20

Phil. But you have not, *Pyrrha*, misplac'd your Confidence.

Scene IX.

Philoe, Lesbia, Deidamia, Achilles, Artemona, Servant.

Serv. Your Embroiderer, Madam.

Phil. That Woman is everlastingly pestering me for Employment. Now can she imagine that to promote her tawdry Trade I can be talk'd into making myself ridiculous by appearing eternally in her odious Embroidery ?—I can't see her now.—But perhaps I may want her for some trivial thing or other.—Let her call again to morrow.

Serv. The Anti-chamber, Madam is crowded with Trades-People.

Phil. Did not I tell you that I wou'd not be troubled with those impertinent Creatures ?—But hold—I had forgot I sent for 'em.—Let 'em wait.

Lesb. But if those foreign Merchants who lately came into Port are among 'em—   11

Phil. There, Sister, is all my Hope. I shall be horridly disappointed if they don't shew us something charming.

Lesb. Shou'd any Woman alive get Sight of their things before us—

Phil. I cou'd not bear it.—To appear in what another Woman had refus'd wou'd make the Creature so intolerably vain !

Lesb. Are those Merchants I ask you among 'em ?

Serv. They have been waiting, Madam, above this half Hour.

Lesb. And did not you know our Impatience ?—How cou'd you be so stupid !—Let us see them this Instant.

S C E N E X.

Artemona, Philoe, Lesbia, Deidamia, Achilles.
Ulysses, Diomedes, Agyrtes. [*Disguis'd as Merchants.*]

Art. Unless you have any thing that is absolutely new and very uncommon, you will give us and your selves, Gentlemen, but unnecessary Trouble.

Ulys. Our Experience, Madam, must have profited very little by the Honour of dealing with Ladies, if we cou'd imagine they cou'd possibly be pleas'd twice with the same thing.

Diom. You might as well offer 'em the same Lover.

Ulys. We have learnt the good Manners, Madam, to distinguish our Customers.—To produce any thing that had ever been seen before wou'd be a downright Insult upon the Genius of a Lady of Quality.

Diom. Novelty is the very Spirit of Dress.   10

Lesb. Let me die, if the Fellows don't talk charmingly !

Phil. Sensibly, Sister.

Lesb. 'Tis evident they must have had Dealings with Ladies of Condition.

Diom. We only wait your Commands.

Ulys. We have things of all kinds, Ladies.

Phil. Of all kinds !—Now that is just what I wanted to see.

Lesb. Are not these, Sister, most delightful Creatures ?

Ulys. We know a Lady can never fix unless we first cloy her Curiosity.

Diom. And if Variety can please, we have every thing that Fancy can wish.

A I R X L V I. The Bob-tail Lass.

In Dress and Love by like Desires   20
  Is Woman's Heart perplext ;
The Man and the Gown she one Day admires,
  She wishes to change the next.
The more you are fickle, we're more employ'd,
  And Love hath more Customers too ;
For Men are as fickle, and soon are cloy'd,
  Unless they have something New.

Lesb. But, dear Man, consider our Impatience.

Ulys. Wou'd you command the things, Ladies, to be brought here, or wou'd you see 'em in your own Apartment ?   30

Phil. How intolerably these Fellows love talking !

Lesb. How canst thou, Man, ask such a Question !

Phil. Here——immediately.

Ulys. Nay, tis not, Madam, that our Goods can be put out of Countenance by the most glaring Light—as for that matter—

Lesb. Nay, pry'thee, Fellow, have done.

[*Diomedes goes out, and returns with* Agyrtes.

Ulys. I wou'd not offer you these Pearls, Ladies, if the World cou'd produce such another Pair.

Phil. A Pair, Fellow—Dost thou think that Jewels pair like Men and Women because they were never made to agree ?   40

Diom. Now, Ladies, here is all that Art can shew you.—Open the Packet.

Lesb. This very individual Pattern, in a blue Pink, had been infinitely charming.

Phil. Don't you think it pretty, *Deidamia ?*

Lesb. For Heaven's sake, Lady *Pyrrha*.—Nay, dear Child, how can any Creature have so little Curiosity !

Ulys. Look upon it again, Madam.—Never was so delightful a Mixture !

Diom. So soft ! so mellow !

Ulys. So advantageous for the Complexion !

Lesb. I can't bear it, Man ; the Colour is frightful.   50

Phil. I hate our own tame home-bred Fancy.—I own I like the Design—but take it away, Man.

Art. There must be something pretty in every thing that is foreign.

[*Ulysses shews another Piece.*

Deid. I am sure, Madam, this must convince you to the contrary.—Never was any thing so detestable !

Lesb. For Heavens sake, Sir, open that other Packet ; and take away this hideous Trumpery.

Ulys. How coud'st thou make this Mistake ?—Never was such an eternal Blunderer.   [*Opens the Armour.*

Phil. How ridiculous is this Accident !   60

Diom. Pardon the Mistake, Ladies.

Lesb. A Suit of Armour !—You see, *Philoe*, they can at least equip us for the Camp.

Phil. Nay, *Lesbia*, for that Matter it might serve many a stiff awkward Creature that we see every Day in the Drawing-room ; for their Dress is every way as absurd and preposterous.   [*Another Packet open'd.*

Ulys. If your Expectations, Ladies, are not now answer'd, let Fancy own herself at a stand. 'Tis inimitable ! 'Tis irresistible !

[*As the Ladies are employ'd in examining the Stuffs,* Achilles *is handling and poising the Armour,* Ulysses *observing him.*

Ach. The Workmanship is curious ; and so justly mounted ! This very Sword seems fitted to my Hand.—The Shield too is so little cumbersome ; so very easy !—Was *Hector* here, the Fate of *Troy* shou'd this Instant be decided.—How my Heart burns to meet him !   72

Ulys. [*Aside to* Diom.] That intrepid Air ! That Godlike Look ! It must he He ! His Nature, his Disposition shews him through the Disguise. [*To* Achilles.] Son of *Thetis*, I know thee, *Greece* demands thee, and now, *Achilles*, the House of *Priam* shakes.

Ach.   But what are you, Friend, who thus presume to know me ?

Ulys.   You cannot be a Stranger, Sir, to the Name of *Ulysses*.

Ach.   As I have long honour'd, I shall now endeavour, Sir, to emulate your Fame.   80

Ulys.   Know, Sir, *Diomedes* ; He too is ambitious to attend you, and partake your Glory.

Diom.   Come, *Agyrtes* ; with him we carry Conquest to the Confederates.

[*Agyrtes takes a Trumpet, which lay amongst the Armour, and sounds.*

A I R   X L V I I.   My Dame hath a lame tame Crane.

Ulys.	*Thy Fate then, O* Troy, *is decreed.*
Diom.	*How I pant !*
Ach.	*How I burn for the Fight.*
Diom.	*Hark, Glory calls.*
Ach.	*Now great* Hector *shall bleed.*
Agyr.	*Fame shall our Deeds requite.* 90

[*As* Achilles *is going off, he turns and looks on* Deidamia.

A I R   X L V I I I.   *Geminiani's* Minuet.

Ach.   *Beauty weeps.—Ah, why that Languish ?*
        See she calls and bids me stay.
        How can I leave her ? my Heart feels her Anguish.
        Hence, Fame and Glory.   Love wins the Day.

[He drops the Sword and Shield, Trumpet sounds, and he takes 'em up again.

A I R   My Dame hath a lame, *&c.* as before, Sung in Four Parts
as a Catch.

Ulys.	*Thy Fate then, O* Troy, *is decreed.*
Ach.	*How I pant ! How I burn for the Fight !*
Diom.	*Hark, Glory calls. Now great* Hector *shall bleed.*
Agyr.	*Fame shall our Deeds requite.*

[*As they are going ;* Achilles *stops with his eyes fix'd on* Deidamia.

Art.   For Heaven's sake, Ladies, support *Deidamia*.   100

Phil.   Never was any thing so astonishing !

Lesb.   Run then, *Artemona*, and acquaint the King and Queen with what hath happen'd.

Scene XI.

Philoe, Lesbia, Deidamia, Achilles, Diomedes, Ulysses, Agyrtes.

Phil.   Ah Sister, Sister, the Mystery then of that particular intimacy between you and *Pyrrha* is at last unravell'd.

Les.   Now if it had not been a Man of this prodigious Consequence, it had been the same thing.——Sure never unguarded Woman was so unaccountably lucky !

Deid. Can you leave me, *Achilles* ?—Can you ?
Ulys. Consider your own Glory, Sir.

AIR XLIX.　Gavotte of *Corelli.*

Ach.

> *Why this Pain ?*
> *Love adieu,*
> *Break thy Chain,*　　　　　　10
> *Fame pursue.*
> *Ah, false Heart,*
> *Can'st thou part ?*
> *Oaths and Vows have bound me.*
> *Fame cries, Go ;*
> *Love says, No.*
> *Why d'ye thus confound me ?*

Deid. Think of my Condition.—Save my Honour.
Ulys. Think of the Honour of *Greece.*
Deid. Think of your solemn Oaths and Promises.　　　20
Ulys. Nations depend upon you.—Victory, Sir, calls you hence.
Deid. Can you, *Achilles*, be perfidious ?
Ulys. Can you lose your Glory in the Arms of a Woman ?
Deid. Can you sacrifice the Fame of your faithful *Deidamia ?*

AIR L.　The Scheme.

Ach.　　*O, what a Conflict's in my Breast !*
Ulys.　　*What, still in suspence ? bid Fame adieu.*
Deid.　　*See me with Shame opprest :*
　　　　I curse, yet I love thee too.
Ulys.　　*Let not her Sighs unman your Heart.*
Deid.　　*Can you then go, and Faith resign ?*　　　30
Ach.　　*Shou'd I !——How can.I part ?*
Deid.　　*Your Honour is link'd with mine.*

SCENE. *The Last.*

Philoe, Lesbia, Deidamia, Achilles, Ulysses, Artemona, Diomedes, Agyrtes, Lycomedes, Theaspe, Diphilus, Periphas, Ajax.

Lycom. Hence, *Diphilus* ; and presume no more to come into my Presence. 'Twas your paltry Flattery that made me ridiculous.—Such a Genius can never be at a loss for Employment, for I have found you qualified for the very meanest Offices.　　　　　　　　　　　　　　　[*Exit* Diphilus.
Theas. My Daughter, Sir, I hope, hath put Confidence in a Man of Honour.
Ach. My Word, Madam, is as sacred as the most religious Ceremony. ——Yet (though we are already solemnly betroth'd to each other) 'tis my Request, Madam, that before I leave the Court the Priest may confirm the Marriage.　　　　　　　　　[Theaspe *whispers* Artemona, *who goes out.*
Theas. This might have prov'd a scurvy Affair, *Deidamia* ; for a Woman can never depend upon a Man's Honour after she hath lost her own to him.
　　　　　　　　　　　　　[Achilles *talks apart to* Ulysses, Periphas, *&c.*

Lycom. You must own, Madam, that 'twas your own Jealousies that were
the occasion of *Deidamia*'s Disgrace.   13
Theas. How can you have the Assurance to name it? Does it not put
you in mind of your own?—Let her marriage to *Achilles* make us forget every
thing past.
Ach. As you was so furiously in Love, Lord *Ajax*, I hope I shall still retain
your Friendship.
Ajax. No joking I beg you, young Man.—But pr'ythee, how came you
here? and in a Woman's Dress too!—Your setting out, Stripling, did not
seem to promise much.   21
Ach. The Adventure wou'd be too long to tell you.——I shall reserve the
Story for the Camp.   [*Artemona returns with the Priests.*
Art. The Priest, Sir, is ready.
Lycom. The Ceremony waits you.
Ach. It shall be my Study, *Lycomedes*, to deserve this Alliance.
Lycom. May you be happy!
Theas. Let the Priest then join your Hands.   28
        [Achilles, Deidamia, Lycomedes, Theaspe, Lesbia, Philoe, Artemona,
            retire to the back part of the Stage. The Priest performs the Ceremony.
Per. Our Duel, *Ajax*, had made a much better Figure if there had been
a Woman in the Case.——But you know, like Men of violent Honour, we were
so very valiant that we did not know what we were fighting for.
Ajax. If you are too free with your Wit, *Periphas*, perhaps we may know
what we quarrel about.   35
Ulys. What testy, *Ajax!* Petticoats have led many a Man into an Error.
How lucky was the Discovery! for had you found a real complying Woman,
you had irretrievably been married.——The Presence of *Achilles* shall now
animate the War.

              A I R L 1.   The Man that is drunk, *&c.*

Per.   *Was ever a Lover so happily freed!*   40
Ajax.   *Try me no more; and mention it never.*
Ulys.   *Suppose you had found her a Woman indeed.*
Ajax.   *Must I be teaz'd and worried for ever!*

Diom.   *By Conquest in Battle we finish the Strife;*
Per.   *But Marriage had kept you in Quarrels for Life.*
Ajax.   *Must you be fleering?*
                 Truce with your jeering.
            Know that you Wits oft' paid for your sneering.

Per. If you had been deceiv'd by a Woman—'tis what we are all liable to.
Diom. But *Ajax* is a Man of warm Imagination.   50
Ajax. After this Day let me hear no more of this ridiculous Affair.
Per. Nay for that matter any Man might have been deceiv'd; for Love,
you know, is blind.
Ajax. With my Sword I can answer any Man.——I tell you, I hate joking.
                                   [Lycomedes, *&c. come forwards.*

    36 What testy, *Ajax!*] 1733 and 1777 What, testy *Ajax* 1760.

Lycom. I have the common Cause so much at Heart, that I wou'd not, son, detain you from the Siege.

         A I R L I I.   There liv'd long ago in a Country Place.

Deid.   *How short was my Calm ! in a Moment 'tis past ;*
            Fresh Sorrows arise, and my Day is o'ercast.
            But since 'tis decreed.——Let me stifle this Tear.
            Be bold, yet be cautious ; my Life is thy Care ;   60
            On thine it depends ; 'tis for thee that I fear.

Lycom. As both her Country and your Glory are concern'd, *Deidamia* must learn to bear your Absence.—In the mean time, *Achilles,* she shall be our Care.——As the Marriage is confirm'd ; let the Dancers, who were preparing for th' approaching Festival, celebrate the Wedding.

    Ajax. But hearkee, young Fellow,——This is the old Soldier's Play ; for we seldom leave Quarters but the Landlord's Daughter is the better for us.—
Hah !   [To Achilles.

D A N C E.

Ulys. We may for a while put on a feign'd Character, but Nature is so often unguarded that it will shew itself.——'Tis to the Armour we owe *Achilles.* 70

         A I R L I I I.   Minuet of *Corelli.*

Single.   *Nature breaks forth at the Moment unguarded ;*
Chorus.   *Through all Disguise she her self must betray.*
Single.   *Heav'n with Success hath our Labours rewarded.*
Chorus.   *Let's with* Achilles *our Genius obey.*

         A I R L I V.   Saraband of *Corelli.*

Ulys.   *Thus when the Cat had once all Woman's Graces ;*
           Courtship, Marriage won her Embraces :
           Forth leapt a Mouse ; she, forgetting Enjoyment,
           Quits her fond Spouse for her former Employment.

C H O R U S.

            Minuet of *Corelli.*

Nature breaks forth at the Moment unguarded ;
   Through all Disguise she her self must betray.   80
Heav'n with Success hath our Labours rewarded ;
   Let's with Achilles *our Genius obey.*

THE DISTRESS'D WIFE

[*Editions* :
1. *The Distress'd Wife.* A Comedy. By the late Mr. Gay, Author of the Beggar's Opera. London : Printed for Thomas Astley, at the Rose in St. Paul's Church-Yard. 1743.

8vo. The Advertisement says : 'This Comedy was finished by Mr. Gay, and intended for the Stage before his Death ; when it was left with his other Papers to the Care of his Noble Friend and Patron the Duke of Queensberry : His Grace has accordingly permitted it to the Press, as it is here printed from the Original in the Author's own Hand-writing.'

2. The same. Second Edition. 1750.
3. *Plays*, 1760.]

Fragments

Sir *Thomas Willit* (*speaks*.)

'Tis then our selves who, by implicit Trust,
Tempt Servants, Friends and Wives to be Unjust.

End of Act I.

Lady *Frankair* (*speaks*)

Man knows us not ; we trifle with their Art :
Woman can only Judge of Woman's Heart.

End of Act II.

Miss *Sprightly* (*speaks*)

Am I to be terrified with *Shakespear* ? Let *Shakespear* then thus answer you.

Of all the Wonders that I yet have heard,
It seems to me most strange Women should fear ;
Since Marriage is a necessary Ill,
And will come when it will come.

Act III. Scene iv.

Pert (*speaks*)

How sweet, though short, would be the nuptial Life !
If 'twas no longer Love, no longer Wife.

End of Act III.

Barter (*speaks*)

Honour alone supports a noble Name ;
Without it, Title but sets off the Shame.

End of Act IV.

Barter (*speaks*)

Those, who the Gifts of Fortune truly rate,
Find and secure the independant State.
How much we hazard by superfluous Cost !
In ev'ry Debt some Liberty is lost.
He then, whose Fortune and Expence agree,
Is wise and great ; for he alone is free.

End of Act V.

THE REHEARSAL AT GOATHAM

[*Editions :*
1. *The Rehearsal at Goatham.*—Ole quid ad te ? Martial. By the late Mr. Gay,
Author of the Beggar's Opera. London : Printed for T. Astley ; And Sold by
R. Baldwin, jun. at the Rose in Pater-Noster-Row ; and R. and J. Dodsley in Pall-
Mall. 1754.
2. *Plays*, 1760.]

Fragments

SCENE IX. SCENE THE LAST.

Pickle (*speaks the Prologue to the Puppet-Shew*)
> Courteous Spectators, see with your own Eyes,
> Hear with your Ears ; and there's an end of Lies.

Pickle (*beginning the Shew*)
> At Tables, Don ! was ever such a Sot !
> His Money squander'd, and his Wife forgot !
> Haste, rise, reclaim thy poor distressed Beauty :
> This Cudgel else shall ding thee into Duty.

     .   .   .   .

Now listen Gallants. 'Tis Don *Gayferos* that speaks.

> Thus clad in Steel I go to risk my Life.

To which his Servant says,

> To bring home Peace, Sir ?

No, replies Don *Gayferos*

> To bring home my Wife.

     .   .   .   .

The next Figure, Ladies, is his Cousin *Roldan*, who offers to assist him,
and in these Words encourages him to the Undertaking :

> Do, Cousin, what all worthy Knights should do ;
> Pride, Av'rice, Rapine, every Vice subdue.

Peter (*speaks*)
> The Drift of Plays, by *Aristotle*'s Rules,
> Is, what you've seen—Exposing Knaves and Fools.

End of Play.

APPENDIX I.

POEMS OF DOUBTFUL AUTHENTICITY

Horace, Epod. IV.

IMITATED

By Sir *James Baker*, Kt.

TO

Lord Cad——n.

[Both the British Museum and Bodleian Catalogues treat 'Sir James Baker, Kt.' as a pseudonym of John Gay's—I do not know on what authority. The Libel was published as a Broadside together with 'An Excellent New Ballad' beginning 'Of all the days in the Year'. The latter, a coarse and clumsy Jacobite Ballad, is certainly not Gay's composition.

The pseudonym was attached to two other productions; one a pamphlet, dated 1717, and entitled *An Admonition Merry and Wise To the Famous Mr. Tr-p, on His Late Encomiums upon the Bishop of Bangor. For the Use of Young Divines. By Sir James Baker, Kt. and Bart.* A mock-contribution to a violent contemporary debate.

The other was a Broadsheet, dated 1716, and entitled *God's Revenge against Punning. Shewing the miserable Fates of Persons addicted to this Crying Sin, in Court and Town.* The latter is now, in the British Museum Catalogue, ascribed to Alexander Pope, as well as to Gay. But a contemporary hand has written the words *By Gay* below the title. [*Vide* Brit. Mus., C 70 h. 4.] A reference to a 'Devonshire Man of Wit' in the Broad-side may be thought to support the ascription to Gay. It is to be observed that the *same* contemporary hand has written the same words *By Gay* on the British Museum copy of the *Argument Proving . . . That the Present Mohocks and Hawkubites are the Gog and Magog* &c. See p. 211.

On the whole I believe the following piece to be Gay's, for the reasons given on page xxxi. It has (so far as I know) not been included in any edition of Gay's poems.]

As tender Lambs with Wolves agree,
Or as thy *Holland*-Spouse with
   thee,
  (Which is but ill they tell us);
So, Baron, does it raise my Spleen
To see thy bloated Pride and
   Mien;
  We Quality are Jealous.

Thou dar'st not surely plead thy
   Blood,
It runs thro' such *Plebeian* Mud,
  No Titles can refine it:
It had, my Friend, been much more
   wise,   10
To wear thy coarse paternal Frize,
  Than thus in Robes to shine it.

Thy modest kindred can aspire
In their ambitious Thoughts no
    higher,
  Than to thy Footman's Wages :
St. *Andrew*'s doubly Crucify'd,
Dangling inglorious by thy Side,
  Whilst they wear Parish-badges.

Now, when conspicuous from afar,
Thy Diamond, Cockade and Star, 20
  Set all *Pall-Mall* a Staring :
Thy Chariot new, and nothing yet
(Except thy Arms and Coronet)
  A jot the worse for Wearing.

How swift, they cry, the Noble
    runs
Escap'd from uncompounding Duns,
  Swift as a Hare new Started :

His dear Mamma's not far behind,
But Justice, Oh ! is now stark Blind ;
  Ah, Sirs, she ne'er was Carted !   30

Slaves think thee an important Lord,
In Senate and at Council-Board,
  In Camps a Son of Thunder ;
But sure, as I'm a valiant Knight,
If *Marlb'rough* taught thee not to
    Fight,
  He taught thee how to Plunder.

Tho' fierce in Scarlet Sash and Plume,
Yet shou'd the needy Clans presume
  To re-unite their Forces :
They yet might see their KING re-
    stor'd   40
Without much Blood : The Baron's
    Sword
  Is best at cutting Purses.

AN

EPISTLE

To the most LEARNED

Doctor W — — d — — — — d.

[An | EPISTLE | to the most LEARNED | Doctor W — — d — — — — d ; | FROM A | P R U D E,
That was unfortunately metamorphos'd on *Saturday* | *December* 29, 1722. | ——

—Jam, quæ
Fœmina nuper eras, puer es—
Ovid. Metam.
The latent Parts at length reveal'd, began
To shoot, and spread, and burnish into Man :
The Maid becomes a Youth——

Dryden.

LONDON

| —— | | London : | Printed by *T.W.* and Sold by *J. Roberts* in *Warwick-
lane* ; | *B. Creak* in *Jermyn-street* ; and *S. Chapman* in *Pall-Mall.* | M DCC XXIII.
Price 6*d*
Probably by Arbuthnot. See pages xxxi–xxxii.]

O Son of *Galen*, lend your friendly Aid,
To veil the Blushes of an undone Maid ;
A Maid !—alas !—whilst I your Help implore,
I downwards look—and sigh !—a Maid no more !

Your Patients Lives for some few Moments save,
And let my Griefs reprieve 'em from the Grave:
A while let all your curious Fossils rest;
Each scaly Fish, and each four-footed Beast:
On Nature's wond'rous Trifles do not dwell,
The beauteous Butterfly, or shining Shell;   10
Your pretious Time, oh! throw not now away,
The various Dyes of Feathers to display;
Let not old *Egypt*'s Monarchs plague your Head,
For what's a Mummy to a Modern Maid?
Since Animals amphibious you pursue,
A doubtful Sex to fix, belongs to you:
If searching into Nature can prevail,
O Heav'n!—such Secrets!—but attend my Tale.

  Last *Saturday*,—oh fatal *Op'ra* Night!
What has thy horrid Darkness brought to Light?   20
Malicious Planets! oh, why did you join?
What had the Stars to do with Me or Mine?
Alas! too late I to my Sorrow find
That these Astrologers ar'n't always blind;
What Depths they search? What Mysteries unfold?
Annus Mirabilis—this Change foretold:
I read it thrice—and cry'd—there's nothing in't,
Grubstreet all o'er—the Paper—Stile—and Print.

  For this Conjunction's Influence prepar'd,
To lulling Crispo I that Night repair'd: 30
Just to the Time the fatal Song is sung,
And the whole House, with—*Se vedete*—rung;
The Aire scarce ended, with Surprize, we view'd
Chast *Senesino* turn'd into a *Prude*:
Poor Innocent!—what hast thou felt before?
Sure Nature's self can change thee now no more.

  With this prepost'rous turn whilst I'm amaz'd,
Prodigious Laughter the whole Audience seiz'd;
Which I suppress'd—scarce breath'd I all the while,—
For *Prudes*—(the thing I was)—do never smile: 40
Those airy Particles in *Hippo*' pent,
Try'd ev'ry Hole, resolv'd to find a Vent;
Their Exit I forbid;—a rumbling Sound
From Vapours thus confin'd began it's hollow Round,
In restless Torments I the *Op'ra* pass'd,
Dreading some frightful Squeak or horrid Blast:
My guarded Tongue its Silence did not break,
Lest in undecent Terms the Wind shou'd speak.

  My Chairmen trotted home;—poor I Half dead,
With equal Speed undress'd, am put to Bed: 50

The Vapours (that I fear'd before wou'd stray)
Nor upwards now, nor downwards take their Way;
Restless they roll and bounce—that, tho' a Maid,
Of matrimonial Pangs I seem'd afraid;
Till all at once they burst with dreadful Roar,
And force out something—I ne'er felt before.

Thus when an Earthquake shakes the trembling Ground,
First, from below, strange bellowing Noises sound;
Inward Convulsions torture Mother Earth,
She seems prepar'd to give some Monster Birth;   60
All Nature's sick—but whilst she lab'ring heaves,
A gaping hideous Chasm her Bosom cleaves;
Some Mountain she thrusts forth, to ease her Pain,
Which sprouts at once, and tow'rs it o'er the Plain.

Have I for this so long the Wonder stood
Of either Sex?—in rigid Virtue proud,
I wag'd immortal Wars with half the Town,
And few escap'd my Censure or my Frown:
Love to my Breast durst never yet intrude; ⎫
But in my Nurse's Arms to Man most rude, ⎬   70
I e'en in leading-Strings commenc'd a *Prude*: ⎭
On Footmen's Backs I ne'er wou'd get astride,
Or on my Brother's Hobby-Horses ride:
No Romps cou'd on my Conduct e'er prevail,
Nor cou'd I bear a Baby, if a Male;
The Sight of Breeches shook my very Frame,
And sooner wou'd I starve, than Cod-fish name:
E'en now my poor Heart pants—do what I can,
Convulsions sieze me at the Thoughts of Man;
Yet I'm that odious Thing—which I abhor—   80
What cou'd the Malice of my Stars do more?

Where shall I run? Where shall I Comfort find?
I cannot leave one Inch of Woe behind;
No!—let me travel Earth, or Seas, or Sky,
I cannot drop the Cause for which I fly.

Some truant School-boy thus, in Mischief wise,
To a poor Mastiffs Tail a Bottle ties:
The frighten'd Cur his alter'd State does wail,
And mourning wonders at his length'ned Tail;
Now runs, now stops, now turns, but still he views ⎫   90
His Foe fast clung; his Fear his Flight renews; ⎬
But all in vain he flies; the Bottle still pursues. ⎭

Haste to my Aid, thou *Esculapian* Sage,
By Physick's mystick Arts my Pains asswage;
From filthy Fame my Reputation save,
And in return I'll give—oh!—All I have.

* Y

In Nature's Secrets you're her eldest Son;
Tell me but what I am, or what is done:
Whilst both Hands I employ to screen my Face,
Put on your Spectacles,—and view my Case:　　　　　100
Your Judgment so profound, can best decide,
If I in Love must Bridegroom prove or Bride:
I dare not view this Guest, so new, so strange,
I scarce have Courage yet to feel the Change;
Somewhat there is—(a Badge of my Disgrace)—
Impertinently perks up in my Face:
By Female Dress it's Boldness I oppose,　　　⎫
In Petticoats the Monster bolder grows,　　　⎬
And bears aloft my Hoop—'spite of my Nose—⎭

These horrid Pangs no longer I'll endure,　　　　　110
Oh! cut it off—or bring some other Cure;
Till when—(as undetermin'd what I am)
I venture to subscribe my Maiden Name—

　　　　　　　　　　PRUDENTIA.

BALLAD.

[*Miscellanies in Verse*, 1727 and 1747. See page 177. On the question of
authorship see pages xxiv–xxv. The Ballad is generally ascribed to Arbuthnot.]

OF all the Girls that e'er were seen,
　There 's none so fine as *Nelly*,
For charming Face, and Shape, and
　Mien,
　And what 's not fit to tell ye:
Oh! the turn'd Neck, and smooth
　white Skin
　Of lovely dearest *Nelly*!
For many a Swain it well had been
　Had she ne'er past by *Calai-*.

For when as *Nelly* came to *France*,
　(Invited by her Cosins)　　10
Across the *Tuilleries* each Glance
　Kill'd *Frenchmen* by whole Dozens.
The King, as he at Dinner sate,
　Did beckon to his *Hussar*,
And bid him bring his Tabby Cat,
　For charming *Nell* to buss her.

The Ladies were with Rage provok'd,
　To see her so respected;
The Men look'd arch, as *Nelly* strok'd,
　And Puss her Tail erected.　　20
But not a Man did Look imploy,
　Except on pretty *Nelly*;
Then said the Duke *de Villeroy*
　Ah! qu'elle est bien jolie!

But who 's that grave Philosopher,
　That carefully looks a'ter?
By his Concern it should appear,
　The Fair One is his Daughter.
Ma foy! (quoth then a Courtier
　sly,)
　He on his Child does leer too:　　30
I wish he has no Mind to try
　What some Papa 's will here do.

1 were] was *1747*　　　8 Calai-.] Calai. *1747*　　　10 Cosins] Cousins *1747*
21 imploy] employ *1747*　　27 should] shou'd *1747*

The Courtiers all, with one Accord,
  Broke out in *Nelly*'s Praises,
Admir'd her *Rose*, and *Lys sans farde*,
  (Which are your *Termes Françoises*).
Then might you see a painted Ring
  Of Dames that stood by *Nelly* ;
She like the Pride of all the Spring,
  And they, like *Fleurs du Palais*. 40

In *Marli*'s Gardens, and *St. Clou*,
  I saw this charming *Nelly*,
Where shameless Nymphs, expos'd to
    view,
  Stand naked in each *Allee* :

            40 *du*] *de* 1747

But *Venus* had a Brazen Face
  Both at *Versailles* and *Meudon*,
Or else she had resign'd her Place,
  And left the Stone she stood on.

Were *Nelly*'s Figure mounted there,
  'Twould put down all th' *Italian* : 50
Lord ! how those Foreigners would
    stare !
But I shou'd turn *Pygmalion* :
For spite of Lips, and Eyes, and Mien,
  Me, nothing can delight so,
As does that Part that lies between
  Her Left Toe, and her Right Toe.

       44 *Allee*] *Alley* 1747

A

B A L L A D

O N

Q U A D R I L L E.

[*Miscellanies in Verse*, 1727 and 1747. See page 177. Also in Watts's *Musical Miscellany*, vol. v, 1731. On the question of authorship see pages xxiv–xxv. The Ballad is ascribed to Congreve by Scott.]

I.

WHEN as Corruption hence did go,
  And left the Nation free ;
When *Ay* said *Ay*, and *No* said *No*,
  Without or Place or Fee ;
Then *Satan*, thinking Things went ill,
Sent forth his Spirit call'd *Quadrille*.
    Quadrille, *Quadrille*, &c.

II.

Kings, Queens and Knaves, made up
    his Pack,
  And four fair Sutes he wore ;

His Troops they were with red and
    black   10
  All blotch'd and spotted o're ;
And ev'ry House, go where you will,
Is haunted by this Imp *Quadrille, &c.*

III.

Sure Cards he has for ev'ry Thing,
  Which well *Court-cards* they name,
And Statesman-like, calls in the King,
  To help out a bad Game ;
But if the Parties manage ill,
The King is forc'd to lose *Codille, &c.*

    8 Sutes] Suit *1731*, *1747*   11 o're] o'er *1731*, *1747*   13 this] the *1747*

IV.

When two and two were met of old,   20
  Tho' they ne'er meant to marry,
They were in *Cupid*'s Books enroll'd,
  And call'd a *Party Quarree;*
But now, meet when and where you
    will,
A *Party Quarree* is *Quadrille, &c.*

V.

The Commoner, the Knight, and Peer,
  Men of all Ranks and Fame,
Leave to their Wives the only Care
  To propagate their Name;
And well that Duty they fulfil,   30
When the good Husband's at *Quad-*
  rille, &c.

VI.

When Patients lie in piteous Case,
  In comes the *Apothecary;*
And to the Doctor cries, Alas!
  Non debes Quadrillare:
The patient dies without a Pill,
For why? the Doctor's at *Quadrille,*
  &c.

VII.

Should *France* and *Spain* again grow
    loud,
  The *Muscovite* grow louder;   39
Britain to curb her Neighbours proud,
  Would want both Ball and Powder;

Must want both Sword and Gun to
    kill;
For why? The General's at *Quadrille,*
  &c.

VIII.

The King of late drew forth his Sword,
  (Thank God 'twas not in Wrath)
And made, of many a Squire and
    Lord,
  An unwash'd Knight of *Bath*:
What are their Feats of Arms and
    Skill?
They're but nine Parties at *Quadrille,*
  &c.

IX.

A Party late at *Cambray* met,   50
  Which drew all *Europe*'s Eyes
'Twas call'd in *Post-Boy* and *Gazette*
  The *Quadruple Allies*;
But some-body took something ill,
So broke this Party at *Quadrille, &c.*

X.

And now, God save this noble Realm,
And God save eke *Hanover*;
And God save those who hold the
    Helm,
  When as the King goes over;
But let the King go where he will,   60
His Subjects must play at *Quadrille.*
  Quadrille, Quadrille, &c.

26 the ... and] and ... the *1747*   31 When] While *1731.*

A NEW

SONG

OF NEW

SIMILIES.

[*Miscellanies in Verse* 1727 and 1747. See page 177. Also in Watts's *Musical Miscellany*, vol. iv, 1730. On the question of Gay's authorship see pages xxiv–xxv.]

My Passion is as Mustard strong ;
  I sit, all sober sad ;
Drunk as a Piper all day long,
  Or like a *March*-Hare mad.

Round as a Hoop the Bumpers flow ;
  I drink, yet can't forget her ;
For tho' as drunk as *David*'s Sow,
  I love her still the better.

Pert as a Pear-Monger I'd be,
  If *Molly* were but kind ;   10
Cool as a Cucumber could see
  The rest of Womankind.

Like a stuck Pig I gaping stare,
  And eye her o'er and o'er ;
Lean as a Rake with Sighs and Care,
  Sleek as a Mouse before.

Plump as a Partridge was I known,
  And soft as Silk my Skin,
My Cheeks as fat as Butter grown ;
  But as a Groat now thin !   20

I melancholy, as a Cat,
  Am kept awake to weep ;
But she insensible of that,
  Sound as a Top can sleep.

Hard is her Heart as Flint or Stone,
  She laughs to see me pale,
And merry as a Grig is grown,
  And brisk as Bottled-Ale.

The God of Love at her Approach
  Is busy as a Bee,   30
Hearts sound as any Bell or Roach,
  Are smit and sigh like me.

Ay me, as thick as Hops or Hail,
  The fine Men crowd about her ;
But soon as dead as a Door-Nail
  Shall I be if without her.

Strait as my Leg her Shape appears ;
  O were we join'd together !
My Heart would be scot-free from
    Cares,
  And lighter than a Feather.   40

As fine as Five-pence is her Mien,
  No Drum was ever tighter ;
Her Glance is as the Razor keen,
  And not the Sun is brighter.

As soft as Pap her Kisses are,
  Methinks I taste them yet.
Brown as a Berry is her Hair,
  Her Eyes as black as Jet ;

As smooth as Glass, as white as Curds,
  Her pretty Hand invites ;   50
Sharp as a Needle are her Words,
  Her Wit, like Pepper, bites :

Brisk as a Body-Louse she trips,
  Clean as a Penny drest ;
Sweet as a Rose her Breath and Lips,
  Round as the Globe her Breast.

Full as an Egg was I with Glee ;
　And happy as a King.
Good Lord ! how all Men envy'd me !
　She lov'd like any thing.　　60

But false as Hell, she, like the Wind,
　Chang'd, as her Sex must do.
Tho' seeming as the Turtle kind,
　And like the Gospel true ;

If I and *Molly* could agree,
　Let who would take *Peru !*
Great as an Emp'ror should I be,
　And richer than a *Jew* ;

Till you grow tender as a Chick,
　I'm dull as any Post ;　　70
Let us, like Burs, together stick,
　And warm as any Toast.

You'll know me truer than a Dye,
　And wish me better sped ;
Flat as a Flounder when I lie,
　And as a Herring dead.

Sure as a Gun, she'll drop a Tear
　And sigh perhaps, and wish,
When I am rotten as a Pear,
　And mute as any fish.　　80

AY and NO:

A

FABLE.

[*Miscellanies in Verse*, 1727 and 1747.　See page 177.　On the question of Gay's authorship see pages xxiv–xxv.]

In Fable all things hold Discourse ;
Then *Words*, no doubt, must talk of
　course.
　Once on a Time, near *Channel-Row*,
Two hostile Adverbs, *Ay* and *No*,
Were hast'ning to the Field of Fight,
And Front to Front stood opposite.
Before each Gen'ral join'd the Van,
Ay, the more courteous Knight, began.
　Stop, peevish Particle, beware !
I'm told you are not such a Bear, 10
But sometimes *yield*, when *offer'd*
　fair.
Suffer yon' Folks awhile to tattle ;·
'Tis *We* who must decide the Battle.
Whene'er we war on yonder Stage,
With various Fate, and equal Rage,

The Nation trembles at each Blow
That *No* gives *Ay*, and *Ay* gives *No* ;
Yet in expensive long Contention,
We gain nor Office, Grant, or Pension.
Why then shou'd Kinsfolks quarrel
　thus ?　　20
(For, *Two* of *You* make *One* of *Us*.)
To some wise Statesman let us go,
Where each his *proper Use* may know.
He may admit two such Commanders,
And make those wait, who serv'd in
　Flanders.
　Let's quarter on a Great-Man's
　Tongue,
A Treas'ry Lord, not Maister Y——g.
Obsequious at his high Command,
Ay shall march forth to Tax the Land:

3 *In* The Works of Dr. Jonathan Swift 1754 vol. vi *the following note is given* (*it does not occur in earlier editions of the* Miscellanies) :
　' *Channel-row* is a dirty street near the parliament-house, *Westminster*.'
　The late addition of this note suggests that the piece was not Gay's.

Impeachments, *No* can best resist, 30
And *Ay* support the Civil List :
Ay ! quick as *Caesar*, wins the Day ;
And *No*, like *Fabius*, by Delay.
Sometimes, in mutual sly Disguise,
Let *Ay's* seem *No's*, and *No's* seem
    Ay's ;

35 *Ay's* ;] *I's* ; *1727 and 1747.*

Ay's be in Courts Denials meant,
And *No's* in Bishops give Consent.
    Thus *Ay* propos'd—And for Reply,
No, for the first time, answer'd *Ay*.
They parted with a Thousand Kisses,
And fight e'er since, for *Pay*, like
    Swisses.   41

39 *Ay.*] *I. 1727 and 1747.*

THE

Q U I D N U N C K I ' S :

A

T A L E.

Occasion'd by the DEATH of the Duke Regent of *France*.

[*Editions :*
  1. A | POEM | ADDRESS'D to the | QUIDNUNC'S, | AT | St. *JAMES*'s *Coffee-House LONDON*. | Occasion'd by the Death of the | *Duke of* ORLEANS. | —*Nec deficit Alter.*   Virg. | . . . [Follows the Poem.] . . . PRINTED in the YEAR, MDCCXXIV.
      Broad-side.   Single-sheet Folio.
  2. *Miscellanies in Verse*, 1727.   See page 177.
  3. *Miscellanies. The Fourth Volume*, 1747.
On the question of Gay's authorship see pages xxiv–xxvii.]

How vain are Mortal Man's Endea-
    vours !
(Said, at * Dame *Elliot's*, Master
    Tr——*s*)
Good *Orleans* dead ! in Truth 'tis
    hard :
Oh ! may all Statesmen die pre-
    par'd !

I do foresee (and for Fore-seeing
He equals any Man in being)
The Army ne'er can be disbanded.
——I wish the King were safely
    landed.
Ah Friends ! great Changes threat
    the Land !
All *France* and *England* at a stand ! 10

* *A Coffee-House near* St. James's.

2 Dame *Elliot*'s] St. *Jame*'s *1724*.   4 *O may all States-men die prepar'd !* 1724.
5 for] in *1724*.   9 the] this *1724*.
10 All *France* and *England*'s at a stand *1724*.

There 's *Meroweis*—mark !   strange Work !
And there 's the *Czar*, and there 's the *Turk*——
The *Pope*——An *India*-Merchant by,
Cut short the Speech with this Reply.
All at a Stand ?   You see great Changes ?
Ah, Sir ! you never saw the *Ganges*.
There dwells the Nations of *Quidnuncki's*
(So *Monomotapa* calls Monkies :)
On,either Bank, from Bough to Bough,
They meet and chat (as we may now.)
Whispers go round, they grin, they shrug,   21
They bow, they snarl, they scratch, they hug ;
And, just as Chance, or Whim provoke them,
They either bite their Friends, or stroke them.
There have I seen some active Prig,
To shew his Parts, bestride a Twig :
Lord ! how the chatt'ring Tribe admire,
Not that he 's wiser, but he 's higher :

All long to try the vent'rous thing,
(For Pow'r is but to have one's Swing.)
From Side to Side he springs, he spurns,   31
And bangs his Foes and Friends by turns.
Thus, as in giddy Freaks, he bounces,
Crack goes the Twig, and in he flounces !
Down the swift Stream the Wretch is born ;
Never, ah never, to return !
Z—ds ! What a Fall had our dear Brother ?
Morblêu ! cries one, and *Damme*, t'other.
The Nations give a gen'ral Screech,
None cocks his Tail, none claws his Breech ;   40
Each trembles for the publick Weal,
And, for a while, forgets to steal.
A while all Eyes, intent and steddy,
Pursue him, whirling down the Eddy.
But out of Mind when out of View,
Some other mounts the Twig anew ;
And Business, on each Monkey Shore,
Runs the same Track it went before.

---

11 There 's *Miriweis*, d'ye mark ? Strange Work ! *1724*.
13 *Indian* Merchant] *1724*.
14 the] his *1724*.   15 Thing's at a Stand ! why dread such Changes ? *1724*.
17–18   There dwells a Race, we call them *Monkeys* ;
              Grave, Sober, Sage, like you *Quidnunc's*,   *1724*
20 may] do *1724*.   22 snarl] smile *1724*.
23–4 provoke 'em . . . Stroak 'em *1724*.
25 There have I seen, some active Prig *1727*.
28 he 's higher] is higher *1724*.
37 Hah, what a Fall has our dear Brother ! *1724*.
38 *Morbleau*, cries one, *Hela*, says t'other. *1724*.
40 Tail . . . Breech] *Tail . . . Breech 1724*.
43 A while all Eyes,] *1747* A while, all Eyes *1724, 1727*.
47–8   *And Business on each Monkey Shore,*
             Runs the same Track it ran before. 1724.

T H E

B A N I S H ' D

B E A U T Y.

[THE | BANISH'D | BEAUTY : | or, a | Fair FACE in *Disgrace,* | A | POEM. ——
Is She not Fair, as Painting can express,
Or youthful Poets fancy when they love ?
Rowe.

———

LONDON :

Printed for A. Moore, near St. *Paul*'s, and Sold by the Booksellers of London | and Westminster. 1729. | (Price Sixpence.)

On the question of authorship see page xxxi.]

Let jarring Realms, and *Europe's* doubtful State,
Of Politicians be the dull Debate,
Stocks, languish'd Trade, let such, their Subject make,
And plead, and bellow for their *Country's* Sake ;
A more important Theme demands the Muse,
A Theme, She neither can, nor dares refuse,

A Theme, from whence her fairest Lawrels spring,
Which first inspir'd, and taught her first to sing ;
'Tis Beauty calls her ; and in Beauty's Cause,
Her Lays are ready, and her Pen she draws ;　　　　10
Yet think *Clarissa* ! what her Pangs must be,
To Sing in Sorrow, when she sings of Thee.

　　In matchless Lustre lately did'st thou shine,
Nor knew the *Court* a brighter Name than Thine ?
Of Wit and Beauty had'st thou ev'ry Grace ?
(Thy *Mind* the only Rival of thy *Face* ;)
O'er thy own Sex triumphant did'st thou reign,
And bid them put forth all their Charms in vain ?
Was this thy Empire, till *Lorenzo*'s Ire,
Mean and inglorious, did thy Fall conspire ?　　　20
To his dread *Liege* thy keen Rebukes convey'd,
And gave thy weak despairing Sex his Aid ?
If so he thinks, *His* Triumph let it be,
And still new Cause of just Contempt from *Thee* ;
Thy wrongs, *bright Exile* ! like thy self endure,
And let the Muse thy injur'd Beauty cure ;

* Y 3

The Muse with faithful Service shall attend,
And be, at all Events, *Clarissa*'s Friend,
With joyful Pains Thy ev'ry Merit trace,
And shew Thee even bright'ned by *Disgrace*.   30

Nor think thy Beauty claims her Lays alone,
She has a Debt of Gratitude to own,
Since in her Cause, you wag'd a generous War,
And urg'd your *Stout* Antagonist so far,
That, thy superior Arguments to close,
He vengeful, made the *Court* and *Beauty*, Foes.

The Task be thine, at large, much envied *G—y* ?
Thy own, and ev'ry Muse's Debt to pay,
Nor let the *Fair*, who rose in the Defence
Of *Wit*, *just Satyr*, *Truth*, and *common Sense*,   40
In These her Moments of *Dishonour*, find,
Thy *pointed* Numbers, like the C—— unkind.

From bold *MACHEATH* awhile thy Rage withdraw,
And let him, still uncensur'd, brave the Law,
Attack, Despoil, with a rapacious Hand,
And deal to Tools the *Plunder* of a *Land* ;
Give him, *kind Bard* ! the Grace of *thy* Reprieve,
And to his own dark *Breast* the *Robber* leave ;
He'll find, when trembling late with Guilt and Fear,
No *Stings*, no *Satire* are excluded *There*.   50
Lorenzo be thy Satire's present View ;
'Tis a Resentment to *Clarissa* due :
Ask him, what Warmth could urge him to despise
The brightest *Judgment*, and the brightest *Eyes* ;
Could it arraign his *Prudence*, to submit,
When *Beauty* soft'ned the Attacks of *Wit* ?
Or could it taint his *Honour*, to be meek,
And, unresenting, hear a *Lady* speak ?

When *Greece* and *Troy*, as say Great *Homer*'s Strains,
With fierce embatt'led Numbers throng'd the Plains,   60
And when their clashing Arms, and Martial Rage
Did in their Contests all the *Gods* engage ;
Unaw'd, in Slaughter did *Tydides* move,
And wound with daring Arm the *Queen of Love* ?
Rough was *He* form'd, unfashion'd for a Court,
War was his *Feast*, and *Cruelty* his *Sport* :
From him, *Lorenzo*, would'st Thou Pattern take ?
In Courage, first, Thyself an equal make :
But 'twas Thy Merit to be train'd *Polite*,
And rather taught the Art to *Wooe*, than Fight.   70
At Beauty's Altar daily did'st thou vow ;
Then, whence a Carriage quite so diff'rent, *now* ?

Could'st Thou not use, for once, the *Courtier's* Guile,
Caress thy Foe, and tho' offended, Smile ?

Rallied by Woman, think it no Disgrace ?
And let her *Tongue* be pardon'd, for her *Face* ?
Such is the Conduct should *Lorenzo* boast ;
Were not *Lorenzo* in the *Statesman* lost.
Repent of *lovely Woman* thy Disdain,
And to thy *former Self* return again :   80
Make Thy Submission to the *Banish'd Fair,*
Confess her Beauty, and her Wrongs repair.

   No, no, *Lorenzo* is too proud to yield,
And when he once has gain'd, to quit the Field ;
The Sanction of his *Dignity* and *Post,*
With Insolence unparallell'd, He'll boast,
Facts charg'd upon him, nor deny, nor own,
But poorly fly for Shelter to the ——

   What ! by *Lorenzo* is That —— —— abus'd,
At which, his *ROYAL MASTER* stood accus'd ?   90
Fresh Charges does he still presume to bring,
And in the *injur'd PRINCE,* to court the *KING* ?
Whilst frantick Humours in his Brain prevail,
Trots He industrious on each *Gossip's* Tale ?
Does He at *Empire,* and at *Beauty* strike ?
And wound his *SOVEREIGN,* and the *Fair* alike ?

   Once more, disdain, *Clarissa* ! to repine,
And let the Muse assure the Conquest Thine ;
The Lustre of the *Court* impair'd we see,
(Impair'd indeed, —— —— because depriv'd of Thee ;)   100
In thy Disgrace the *First* does more than Share ;
The *Banishment* is *Thine* ; the *Loss* is *There.*

VERSES

To be placed under the Picture of England*'s Arch-Poet :
Containing a Compleat Catalogue of his Works.*

[*Editions* .
1. MISCELLANIES. | THE | THIRD VOLUME. | *LONDON :* | Printed for
BENJ. MOTTE at the *Middle* | *Temple-Gate,* and LAWTON GILLIVER | at *Homer's
Head,* against St. *Dunstan's* | Church in *Fleetstreet,* 1732.
2. *Miscellanies. The Fourth Volume,* 1747.
On the question of authorship see pages xxiv–xxv.]

SEE who ne'er was or will be half
    read !
Who first sung [1]*Arthur,* then sung
    [2]*Alfred,*
Prais'd great [3]*Eliza* in God's anger,
Till all true *Englishmen* cry'd, hang
    her !
Made *William's* Virtues wipe the
    bare A—
And hang'd up *Marlborough* in [4]*Arras:*
Then hiss'd from Earth, grew
    Heav'nly quite ;
Made ev'ry Reader curse the [5]*Light* ;
Maul'd human *Wit* in one thick
    [6]Satyr,
Next in three Books, sunk [7]human
    Nature,   10

Un-did [8]*Creation* at a Jerk,
And of [9]*Redemption* made damn'd
    Work.

Then took his Muse at once, and
    dipt her
Full in the Middle of the Scripture.
What Wonders there the Man grown
    old, did ?
Sternhold himself he *out-Sternholded,*
Made [10]*David* seem so mad and
    freakish,
All thought him just what thought
    king *Achiz.*
No mortal read his [11] Salomon,
But judg'd *Roboam* his own Son.   20

[1] Two Heroick Poems in Folio, twenty Books.   [2] Heroick Poem in twelve Books.
[3] Heroick Poem in Folio, ten Books.
[4] Instructions to *Vanberbank* a Tapestry-Weaver.   [5] Hymn to the *Light.*
[6] Satyr against *Wit.*   [7] Of the *Nature* of Man.
[8] *Creation,* a Poem in seven Books.
[9] The *Redeemer,* another Heroick Poem in six Books.
[10] Translation of all the *Psalms.*   [11] *Canticles* and *Ecclesiast.*

England's Arch-Poet] i.e. Sir Richard Blackmore. Like Arbuthnot, Blackmore
was a doctor as well as a man of letters, and with Arbuthnot attended Queen Anne
in her last illness. Arbuthnot, writing to Swift, December 11, 1718, says, ' Mr. Rowe,
the poet laureate, is dead, and has left a damned jade of a Pegasus. I'll answer
for it, he won't do as your mare did, having more need of Lucan's present than
Sir Richard Blackmore.'

10 sunk] sent *1747* spoil'd *1795.*

Moses[12] he serv'd as *Moses Pharaoh*,
And *Deborah*, as She *Sise-rah* :
Made [13]*Jeremy* full sore to cry,
And [14]*Job* himself curse God and die.

What Punishment all this must follow ?
Shall *Arthur* use him like king *Tollo*,
Shall *David* as *Uriah* slay him,

Or dex'trous *Deb'rah Sisera*-him ?
Or shall *Eliza* lay a Plot,
To treat him like her sister *Scot*, 30
Shall *William* dub his better * End,
Or *Marlb'rough* serve him like a Friend ?
No, none of these—Heav'n spare his Life !
But send him, honest *Job*, thy *Wife*.

[12] Paraphrase of the Canticles of *Moses* and *Deborah*, &c.
[13] The *Lamentations*.   [14] The whole book of *Job*, a Poem in Folio.
* Kick him on the Breech, not Knight him on the Shoulder.

E P I T A P H [*of By-Words*]

[Editions : *Miscellanies. The Third Volume*, 1732.
Miscellanies. The Fourth Volume, 1747.
On the question of authorship see pages xxiv–xxv.]

HERE lies a round Woman, who thought *mighty odd*
Every Word she e'er heard in this Church about God.
To convince her of *God* the good Dean did indeavour,
But still in her Heart she held *Nature* more *clever*.
Tho' he talk'd much of Virtue, her Head always run
Upon something or other, she found better *Fun*.
For the Dame, by her Skill in Affairs Astronomical,
Imagin'd, to live in the Clouds was but *comical*.
In this World, she despis'd ev'ry Soul she met here,
And now she 's in t'other, she thinks it but *Queer*.

AN ODE FOR THE NEW YEAR :

Written by Colley Cibber *Esq.   Poet Laureate.*

[*Notes and Queries*, 2nd series, x. l.   There seems very little evidence for the
ascription to Gay. See page xxxi.]

GOD prosper long our gracious King,
  Now sitting on the throne ;
Who leads this nation in a *String*,
  And governs all but *One*.

This is the day when right or wrong,
  I COLLEY BAYS, Esquire,
Must for my sack indite a song,
  And thrum my venal lyre.

Not he who ruled great Judah's realm,
  Y-clyped Solomon,   10
Was wiser than Our's at the helm,
  Or had a wiser Son.

He raked up wealth to glut his till,
  In drinking, w—s, and houses ;
Which wiser G—e can save to fill
  His pocket, and his spouse's.

His head with wisdom deep is fraught,
  His breast with courage glows ;
Alas, how mournful is the thought
  He ever should want foes !   20

For, in his heart he loves a drum,
  As children love a rattle ;
If not in field, in drawing-room,
  He daily sounds to battle.

The Q—n, I also pray, God save !
  His consort plump and dear ;
Who, just as he is *wise* and *brave*,
  Is *pious* and *sincere*.

She 's courteous, good, and charms
    all folks,
  Loves one as well as t'other ;   30
Of Arian and of Orthodox
  Alike the nursing-mother.

Oh ! may she always meet success
  In every scheme and job ;
And still continue to caress
  That honest statesman, BOB.

God send the P—, that babe of grace,
  A little w— and horse ;
A little meaning in his face,
  And money in his purse.   40

Heaven spread o'er all his family
  That broad illustrious glare ;
Which shines so flat in ev'ry eye,
  And makes them all *so stare*.

All many *gratis*, boy and miss,
  And still increase their store ;
As in beginning was, now is,
  And shall be ever more.

But oh ! ev'n Kings must die, of
    course,
  And to their heirs be civil ;   50
We poets, too, on winged-horse,
  Must soon post to the devil :

Then, since I have a son, like you,
  May he Parnassus rule ;
So shall the Crown and Laurel, too,
  Descend from F—l to F—l !

APPENDIX II.

Rural Sports : first version (1713).

RURAL SPORTS.

A

P O E M

To Mr. *POPE.*

You, who the Sweets of Rural Life have known,
Despise th' ungrateful Hurry of the Town ;
'Midst *Windsor* Groves your easie Hours employ,
And, undisturb'd, your self and Muse enjoy.
Soft flowing *Thames* his mazy Course retains,
And in suspence admires thy charming Strains ;
The River-Gods and Nymphs about thee throng,
To hear the *Syrens* warble in thy Song.
But I, who ne'er was bless'd from Fortune's Hand,
Nor brighten'd Plough-shares in Paternal Land,   10
Have long been in the noisie Town immur'd,
Respir'd it's Smoak, and all it's Toils endur'd,
Have courted Bus'ness with successless Pain,
And in Attendance wasted Years in vain ;
Where News and Politicks amuse Mankind,
And Schemes of State involve th' uneasie Mind ;
Faction embroils the World ; and ev'ry Tongue
Is fraught with Malice, and with Scandal hung :
Friendship, for Sylvan Shades, does Courts despise,
Where all must yield to Int'rest's dearer Ties ;   20
Each Rival *Machiavel* with Envy burns,
And Honesty forsakes them All by turns ;
Whilst Calumny upon each Party's thrown,
Which Both abhor, and Both alike disown.
Thus have I, 'midst the Brawls of factious Strife,
Long undergone the Drudgery of Life ;

The lines in the original are not numbered.

On Courtiers Promises I founded Schemes,
Which still deluded me, like golden Dreams;
Expectance wore the tedious Hours away,
And glimm'ring Hope roll'd on each lazy Day.   30
Resolv'd at last no more Fatigues to bear,
At once I both forsook the Town and Care;
At a kind Friend's a calm *Asylum* chose,
And bless'd my harass'd Mind with sweet Repose,
Where Fields and Shades, and the refreshing Clime,
Inspire the Sylvan Song, and prompt my Rhime.
My Muse shall rove through flow'ry Meads and Plains,
And Rural Sports adorn these homely Strains,
And the same Road ambitiously pursue,
Frequented by the *Mantuan* Swain, and You.   40
    Now did the Spring her Native Sweets diffuse,
And feed the chearful Plains with wholesome Dews;
A kindly Warmth th' approaching Sun bestows,
And o'er the Year a verdant Mantle throws;
The jocund Fields their gaudiest Liv'ry wear,
And breath fresh Odours through the wanton Air;
The gladsome Birds begin their various Lays,
And fill with warbling Songs the blooming Sprays;
No swelling Inundation hides the Grounds,
But crystal Currents glide within their Bounds;   50
The sporting Fish their wonted Haunts forsake,
And in the Rivers wide Excursions take;
They range with frequent Leaps the shallow Streams,
And their bright Scales reflect the daz'ling Beams,
The Fisherman does now his Toils prepare,
And Arms himself with ev'ry watry Snare,
He meditates new Methods to betray,
Threat'ning Destruction to the finny Prey.
    When floating Clouds their spongy Fleeces drain,
Troubling the Streams with swift-descending Rain, 60
And Waters, tumbling down the Mountain's Side,
Bear the loose Soil into the swelling Tide;
Then, soon as Vernal Gales begin to rise,
And drive the liquid Burthen through the Skies,
The Fisher strait his Taper Rod prepares,
And to the Neighb'ring Stream in haste repairs;
Upon a rising Border of the Brook
He sits him down, and ties the treach'rous Hook;
A twining Earth-worm he draws on with Care,
With which he neatly hides the pointed Snare.   70
Now Expectation chears his eager Thought,
His Bosom glows with Treasures yet uncaught,
Before his Eyes a Banquet seems to stand,
The kind Effects of his industrious Hand.
    Into the Stream the twisted Hair he throws,
Which gently down the murm'ring Current flows;

When if or Chance or Hunger's pow'rful Sway
Directs a ranging Trout this fatal way,
He greedily sucks in the tortur'd Bait,
And shoots away with the fallacious Meat.   80
The trembling Rod the joyful Angler eyes,
And the strait Line assures him of the Prize ;
With a quick Hand the nibbled Hook he draws,
And strikes the barbed Steel within his Jaws ;
The Fish now flounces with the startling Pain,
And, plunging, strives to free himself, in vain :
Into the thinner Element he 's cast,
And on the verdant Margin gasps his Last.

He must not ev'ry Worm promiscuous use,
Judgment will tell him proper Bait to chuse ;   90
The Worm that draws a long immod'rate Size
The Trout abhors, and the rank Morsel flies ;
But if too small, the naked Fraud 's in sight,
And Fear forbids, while Hunger does invite.
Their shining Tails when a deep Yellow stains,
That Bait will well reward the Fisher's Pains :
Cleanse them from Filth, to give a tempting Gloss,
Cherish the sully'd Animals with Moss ;
Where they rejoice, wreathing around in Play,
And from their Bodies wipe their native Clay.   100

But when the Sun displays his glorious Beams,
And falling Rivers flow with Silver Streams,
When no moist Clouds the radiant Air invest.
And *Flora* in her richest State is drest,
Then the disporting Fish the Cheat survey,
Bask in the Sun, and look into the Day.
You now a more delusive Art must try,
And tempt their Hunger with the Curious Fly ;
Your wary Steps must not advance too near,
Whilst all your Hope hangs on a single Hair ;   110
Upon the curling Surface let it glide,
With Nat'ral Motion from thy Hand supply'd,
Against the Stream now let it gently play,
Now in the rapid Eddy roll away ;
The sporting Fish leaps at the floating Bait,
And in the dainty Morsel seeks his Fate.
Thus the nice *Epicure*, whom Lux'ry sways,
Who ev'ry Craving of his Taste obeys,
Makes his false Appetite his only Care,
In poignant Sauce disguises all his Fare ;   120
And whilst he would his vicious Palate please,
In ev'ry Bit sucks in a new Disease ;
The Cook destroys with his compounding Art,
And dextrously performs the Doctor's Part.

To frame the little Animal, provide
All the gay Hues that wait on Female Pride,

Let Nature guide thee ; sometimes Golden Wire
The glitt'ring Bellies of the Fly require ;
The Peacock's Plumes thy Tackle must not fail,
Nor the dear Purchase of the Sable's Tail. 130
Each gaudy Bird some slender Tribute brings,
And lends the growing Insect proper Wings,
Silks of all Colours must their Aid impart,
And ev'ry Fur promote the Fisher's Art.
So the gay Lady, with Expensive Care,
Borrows the Pride of Land, of Sea, and Air ;
Furs, Pearls, and Plumes, the painted Thing displays,
Dazles our Eyes, and easie Hearts betrays.
 Mark well the various Seasons of the Year,
How the succeeding Insect Race appear ; 140
In this revolving Moon one Colour reigns,
Which in the next the fickle Trout disdains.
Oft' have I seen a skillful Angler try
The various Colours of the treach'rous Fly ;
When he with fruitless Pain hath skim'd the Brook,
And the coy Fish rejects the skipping Hook,
He shakes the Boughs that on the Margin grow,
Which o'er the Streams a waving Forrest throw ;
When if an Insect falls, (his certain Guide)
He gently takes him from the whirling Tide ; 150
Examines well his Form with curious Eyes,
His gaudy Colours, Wings, his Horns and Size,
Then round his Hook a proper Fur he winds,
And on the Back a speckled Feather binds,
So just the Properties in ev'ry part,
That even Nature's Hand revives in Art.
His new-form'd Creature on the Water moves,
The roving Trout th' inviting Snare approves,
Upon his Skill successful Sport attends,
The Rod, with the succeeding Burthen, bends ; 160
The Fishes sail along, and in Surprize
Behold their Fellows drawn into the Skies ;
When soon they rashly seize the deadly Bait,
And Lux'ry draws them to their Fellow's Fate.
 When a brisk Gale against the Current blows,
And all the watry Plain in Wrinkles flows,
Then let the Fisherman his Art repeat,
Where bubbling Eddys favour the Deceit.
If an huge scaly Salmon chance to spy
The wanton Errors of the swimming Fly, 170
He lifts his Silver Gills above the Flood,
And greedily sucks in th' unfaithful Food ;
Then plunges down with the deceitful Prey,
And bears with Joy the little Spoils away.
Soon in smart Pains he feels the dire Mistake,
Lashes the Waves, and beats the foamy Lake,

With sudden Rage he now aloft appears,
And in his Look convulsive Anguish bears ;
And now again, impatient of the Wound,
He rolls and wreathes his shining Body round ;   180
Then headlong shoots himself into the Tide,
And trembling Fins the boiling Waves divide ;
Now Hope and Fear the Fisher's Heart employ,
His smiling Looks glow with depending Joy,
He views the tumbling Fish with eager Eyes,
While his Line stretches with th' unwieldly Prize ;
Each Motion humours with his steady Hands,
And a slight Hair the mighty Bulk commands ;
Till tir'd at last, despoil'd of all his Strength,
The Fish athwart the Streams unfolds his Length.   190
He now, with Pleasure, views the gasping Prize
Gnash his sharp Teeth, and roll his Blood-shot Eyes,
Then draws him t'wards the Shore, with gentle Care,
And holds his Nostrils in the sick'ning Air :
Upon the burthen'd Stream he floating lies,
Stretches his quiv'ring Fins, and Panting dies.
So the Coquet th' unhappy Youth ensnares,
With artful Glances and affected Airs,
Baits him with Frowns, now lures him on with Smiles,
And in Disport employs her practis'd Wiles ;   200
The Boy at last, betray'd by borrow'd Charms,
A Victim falls in her enslaving Arms.
   If you'd preserve a num'rous finny Race,
Let your fierce Dogs the Rav'nous Otter chase ;
Th' amphibious Creature ranges all the Shores,
Shoots through the Waves, and ev'ry Haunt explores :
Or let the Gin his roving Steps betray,
And save from hostile Jaws the scaly Prey.
   Now, sporting Muse, draw in the flowing Reins,
Leave the clear Streams a-while for sunny Plains.   210
Should you the various Arms and Toils rehearse,
And all the Fisherman adorn thy Verse ;
Should you the wide encircling Net display,
And in it's spacious Arch enclose the Sea,
Then haul the plunging Load upon the Land,
And with the Soale and Turbet hide the Sand ;
It would extend the growing Theme too long,
And tire the Reader with the watry Song.
   Nor do such vacant Sports alone invite,
But all the grateful Country breaths Delight ;   220
Here blooming Health exerts her gentle Reign,
And strings the Sinews of th' industrious Swain.
Soon as the Morning Lark proclaims the Day,
Into the Fields I take my frequent Way,
Where I behold the Farmer's early Care,
In the revolving Labours of the Year.

When high Luxuriant Grass o'erspreads the Ground,
And the fresh Spring in all her State is Crown'd.
The Lab'rer with the bending Scythe is seen,
Shaving the Surface of the waving Green ;   230
Of all her Native Pride disrobes the Land,
And Meads lays waste before his sweeping Hand :
While with the mounting Sun the Meadows glows,
The fading Herbage round he loosely throws ;
From rip'ning Hay diffusive Odours rise,
Which breathing *Zephyrs* bear throughout the Skies :
But if some Sign portend a lasting Show'r,
Th' observing Swain foresees th' approaching Hour ;
He strait in haste the scatt'ring Fork forsakes
And cleanly Damsels ply the saving Rakes ;   240
In rising Hills the fragrant Harvest grows,
And spreads throughout the Plain in equal Rows.
    What Happiness the Rural Maid attends,
In chearful Labour while each Day she spends !
She gratefully receives what Heav'n has sent,
And, rich in Poverty, enjoys Content :
Upon her Cheek a pure Vermilion glows,
And all her Beauty she to Nature owes ;
(Such Happiness, and such a constant Frame,
Ne'er glads the Bosom of the Courtly Dame.)   250
She never feels the Spleen's imagin'd Pains,
Nor Melancholy stagnates in her Veins ;
She never loses Life in thoughtless Ease,
Nor on a downy Couch invites Disease ;
Her Dress in a clean simple Neatness lies,
No glaring Equipage excites her Sighs ;
Her Reputation, which she values most,
Is ne'er in a Malicious Visit lost :
No Midnight Masquerade her Beauty wears,
And Health, not Paint, the fading Bloom repairs.   260
If Love's soft Passions in her Bosom reign,
She meets Returns in an obliging Swain ;
Domestick Broils do ne'er her Peace controul,
Nor watchful Jealousie torments her Soul ;
With secret Joy she sees her little Race
Hang on her Breast, and her small Cottage grace ;
Thus flow her peaceful Hours, unknown to Strife,
'Till Age exhausts the latest Thread of Life.
    But when th' Ascent of Heav'n bright *Phoebus* gains
And scorches with fierce Rays the thirsty Plains ;   270
When sleeping Snakes bask in the sultry Sky,
And Swains with fainting Hand their Labours ply,
With naked Breast they court each welcome Breeze,
Nor know the Shelter of the shady Trees :
Then to some secret Covert I retreat,
To shun the Pressure of th' uneasie Heat ;

Where the tall Oak his spreading Arms entwines,
And with the Beech a mutual Shade combines;
Here on the Mossy Couch my Limbs I lay,
And taste an Ev'ning at the Noon of Day: 230
Beneath, a shallow Rivulet runs by,
Whose Silver Streams o'er the smooth Pebbles fly,
With gentle Falls it wanders through the Grounds,
And all the Wood the murm'ring Noise resounds.
In such a Shade was fair *Calisto* laid,
When am'rous *Jove* th' unwary Nymph betray'd:
The God, disguis'd in *Cynthia*'s borrow'd Charms,
Her Lips with more than Virgin Kisses Warms;
While she, surpriz'd, lay melting in his Arms.

Here I with *Virgil*'s Muse refresh my Mind,   290
And in his Numbers all the Country find;
I wander o'er the various Rural Toil,
And learn the Nature of each diff'rent Soil;
This fertile Field groans with a Load of Corn,
That spreading Trees with blushing Fruit adorn.
Here I survey the Purple Vintage grow,
Climb round the Poles, and rise in graceful Row,
Whilst *Bacchanalian* Bowls with the rich Nectar flow.
Here I behold the Steed curvet and bound,
And paw with restless Hoof the smoaking Ground.   300
The Dewlap'd Bull now scow'rs throughout the Plains,
While burning Love shoots through his raging Veins,
His well-arm'd Front against his Rival aims,
And by the Dint of War his Mistress claims.
His tuneful Muse the industrious Bee recites,
His Wars, his Government, and toilsome Flights;
The careful Insect 'midst his Works I view,
Now from the Flow'rs exhaust the fragrant Dew;
With golden Treasures load his little Thighs,
And steer his airy Journey through the Skies;   310
With liquid Sweets the waxen Cells distend,
While some 'gainst Hostile Drones their Cave defend;
Each in the Toil a proper Station bears,
And in the little Bulk a mighty Soul appears.
The Country all her native Charms displays,
And various Landscapes flourish in his Lays.
   Or when the Lab'rer leaves the Task of Day,
And trudging homewards whistles on the Way;
When the big udder'd Cows with Patience stand,
Waiting the Stroakings of the Damsel's Hand   320
No Warbling chears the Woods; the Feather'd Choir
To court kind Slumbers, to their Sprays retire;
When no rude Gale disturbs the sleeping Trees,
Nor Aspen Leaves confess the gentlest Breeze;
I sooth my Mind with an indulgent Walk,
And shun a-while the tiresome Noise of Talk,

Engag'd in Thought, to *Neptune's* Bounds I stray,
To take my Farewel of the parting Day;
The blushing Skies glow with the sinking Beams,
And a bright Glory mingles with the Streams:　　　330
A Golden Light upon the Surface plays,
And the wide Ocean smiles with trembling Rays;
Here Pensive I behold the fading Light,
And in the distant Billows lose my Sight.
　Now Night in silent State begins to rise,
And twinkling Orbs bestrow th' uncloudy Skies;
Her borrow'd Lustre growing *Cynthia* lends,
And o'er the Main a glitt'ring Path extends;
Millions of Worlds hang in the spacious Air,
Which round their Suns their Annual Circles steer.　　340
Sweet Contemplation elevates my Sense,
While I survey the Works of Providence.
Oh, could my Muse in loftier Strains rehearse
The Glorious Author of this Universe,
Who reins the Winds, gives the vast Ocean Bounds,
And circumscribes the floating Worlds their Rounds!
My Soul should overflow in Songs of Praise,
And my Creator's Name inspire my Lays.
　Now *Ceres* pours out Plenty from her Horn,
And cloaths the Fields with golden Ears of Corn;　　350
Let the keen Hunter from the Chase refrain,
Nor render all the Plowman's Labour vain.
The Reapers to their sweating Task repair,
To save the Product of the bounteous Year:
To the wide-gathering Hook long Furrows yield,
And rising Sheaves extend through all the Field.
　Oh happy Plains! remote from War's Alarms,
And all the Ravages of Hostile Arms;
And happy Shepherds who secure from Fear
On open Downs preserve your fleecy Care!　　360
Where no rude Soldier, bent on cruel Spoil,
Spreads Desolation o'er the fertile Soil;
No trampling Steed lays waste the rip'ning Grain,
Nor crackling Flames devour the promis'd Gain;
No flaming Beacons cast their Blaze afar,
The dreadful Signal of invasive War;
No Trumpet's Clangor wounds the Mother's Ear,
Nor calls the Lover from his swooning Fair;
But the fill'd Barns groan with th' encreasing Store,
And whirling Flails disjoint the cracking Floor:　　370
Let *Anna* then adorn your Rural Lays,
And ev'ry Wood resound with grateful Praise;
Anna, who binds the Tyrant War in Chains,
And Peace diffuses o'er the chearful Plains;
In whom again the bright *Astrea* Reigns.
　As in successive Toil the Seasons roll,
So various Pleasures recreate the Soul;

The setting Dog, instructed to betray,
Rewards the Fowler with the Feather'd Prey.
Soon as the lab'ring Horse with swelling Veins,   380
Hath safely hous'd the Farmer's doubtful Gains,
To sweet Repast th' unwary Partridge flies,
At Ease amidst the scatter'd Harvest lies,
Wandring in Plenty, Danger he forgets,
Nor dreads the Slav'ry of entangling Nets.
The subtle Dog now with sagacious Nose
Scowres through the Field, and snuffs each Breeze that blows,
Against the Wind he takes his prudent way,
While the strong Gale directs him to the Prey ;
Now the warm Scent assures the Covey near,   390
He treads with Caution, and he points with Fear ;
Then least some Sentry Fowl his Fraud descry,
And bid his Fellows from the Danger fly,
Close to the Ground in Expectation lies,
Till in the Snare the flutt'ring Covey rise.
Thus the sly Sharper sets the thoughtless 'Squire,
Who to the Town does aukwardly aspire :
Trick'd of his Gold, he Mortgages his Land,
And falls a Captive to the Bailiff's Hand.
Soon as the blushing Light begins to spread,   400
And rising *Phoebus* gilds the Mountain's Head,
His early Flight th' ill-fated Partridge takes,
And quits the friendly Shelter of the Brakes :
Or when the Sun casts a declining Ray,
And drives his Chariot down the Western way,
Let your obsequious Ranger search around,
Where the dry Stubble withers on the Ground :
Nor will the roving Spy direct in vain,
But num'rous Coveys gratifie thy Pain.
When the Meridian Sun contracts the Shade,   410
And frisking Heifers seek the cooling Glade ;
Or when the Country floats with sudden Rains,
Or driving Mists deface the moist'ned Plains ;
In vain his Toils th' unskillful Fowler tries,
Whilst in thick Woods the feeding Partridge lies.
    Nor must the sporting Verse the Gun forbear,
But what 's the Fowler's be the Muse's Care ;
The Birds that in the Thicket seek their Food,
Who love the Covert, and frequent the Wood,
Despise the Net : But still can never shun   420
The momentary Lightning of the Gun.
The Spaniel ranges all the Forrest round,
And with discerning Nostril snuffs the Ground
Now rusling on, with barking Noise alarms,
And bids his watchful Lord prepare to Arms ;
The dreadful Sound the springing Pheasant hears,
Leaves his close Haunt, and to some Tree repairs :
The Dog, aloft the painted Fowl, surveys,

Observes his Motions, and at distance Bays.
His noisie Foe the stooping Pheasant eyes,   430
Fear binds his Feet, and useless Pinions ties,
Till the sure Fowler, with a sudden Aim,
From the tall Bough precipitates the Game.
So the Pale Coward from the Battel flies,
Soon as a Rout the Victor Army cries ;
With clashing Weapons Fancy fills his Ear,
And Bullets whistle round his bristled Hair ;
Now from all Sides th' imagin'd Foe draws nigh,
He trembling stands, nor knows which Way to fly ;
'Till Fate behind aims a disgraceful Wound,   440
And throws his gasping Carcass to the Ground.
But if the Bird, to shun the dreadful Snare,
With quiv'ring Pinions cuts the liquid Air ;
The scatt'ring Lead pursues th' unerring Sight,
And Death in Thunder overtakes his flight.
    The tow'ring Hawk let future Poets sing,
Who Terror bears upon his soaring Wing :
Let him on high the frighted Horn survey,
And lofty Numbers paint their Airy Fray.
Nor shall the mounting Lark the Muse detain,   450
That greets the Morning with his early Strain ;
How, 'midst his Song, by the false Glass betray'd,
(That fatal Snare to the fantastick Maid,)
Pride lures the little Warbler from the Skies,
Where folding Nets the Captive Bird surprize.
    The Greyhound now pursues the tim'rous Hare,
And shoots along the Plain with swift Career ;
While the sly Game escapes beneath his Paws,
He snaps deceitful Air with empty Jaws ;
Enrag'd, upon his Foe he quickly gains,   460
And with wide Stretches measures o'er the Plains ;
Again the cunning Creature winds around,
While the fleet Dog o'ershoots, and loses ground ;
Now Speed he doubles to regain the Way,
And crushes in his Jaws the screaming Prey.
Thus does the Country various Sports afford,
And unbought Dainties heap the wholesome Board.
    But still the Chase, a pleasing Task, remains ;
The Hound must open in these rural Strains.
Soon as *Aurora* drives away the Night,   470
And edges Eastern Clouds with rosie Light,
The wakeful Huntsman, with the chearful Horn,
Summons the Dogs, and greets the rising Morn :
Th' enliven'd Hounds the welcome Accent hear,
Start from their Sleep, and for the Chase prepare.
Now o'er the Field a diff'rent Route they take,
Search ev'ry Bush, and force the thorny Brake
No bounding Hedge obstructs their eager Way,
While their sure Nostril leads them to the Prey ;

Now they with Joy th' encreasing Scent pursue,   430
And trace the Game along the tainted Dew ;
A sudden Clamour rings throughout the Plain,
And calls the Straglers from their fruitless Pain,
All swiftly to the welcome Sound repair,
And join their Force against the skulking Hare.
Thus when the Drum an idle Camp alarms,
And summons all the scatt'ring Troops to Arms ;
The Soldiers the commanding Thunder know,
And in one Body meet th' approaching Foe.
The tuneful Noise the sprightly Courser hears,   490
He paws the Turf, and pricks his rising Ears :
The list'ning Hare, unsafe in longer Stay,
With wary Caution steals unseen away ;
But soon his treach'rous Feet his Flight betray.
The distant Mountains eccho from afar,
And neighb'ring Woods resound the flying War ;
The slackned Rein admits the Horse's Speed,
And the swift Ground flies back beneath the Steed.
Now at a Fault the Dogs confus'dly stray,
And strive t' unravel his perplexing Way ;   500
They trace his artful Doubles o'er and o'er,
Smell ev'ry Shrub, and all the Plain explore,
'Till some stanch Hound summons the baffled Crew,
And strikes away his wily Steps anew.
Along the Fields they scow'r with jocund Voice,
The frighted Hare starts at the distant Noise ;
New Stratagems and various Shifts he tries,
Oft' he looks back, and dreads a close Surprise ;
Th' advancing. Dogs still haunt his list'ning Ear,
And ev'ry Breeze augments his growing Fear :   510
'Till tir'd at last, he pants, and heaves for Breath ;
Then lays him down, and waits approaching Death.
Nor should the Fox shun the pursuing Hound,
Nor the tall Stag with branching Antlers crown'd ;
But each revolving Sport the Year employ,
And fortifie the Mind with healthful Joy.
  Oh happy Fields, unknown to Noise and Strife,
The kind Rewarders of industrious Life ;
Ye shady Woods, where once I us'd to rove,
Alike indulgent to the Muse and Love ;   520
Ye murm'ring Streams that in *Maeanders* roll,
The sweet Composers of the peaceful Soul,
Farewel.——Now Business calls me from the Plains,
Confines my Fancy, and my Song restrains.

APPENDIX III.

To Charles Ford Esqʳ to be left at Sʳ Richard Chantillon's Banker in Paris

[A letter in Mr. R. B. Adam's collection, Buffalo, U.S.A. The lines are from *Trivia* (I. 83–104). See page 58.]

Sⁱʳ.

Not that I'll wander from my native home,
And tempting Dangers foreign Citys roam,
Let Paris be the Theme of Gallia's Muse,
Where Slav'ry treads the Streets in wooden shoes ;
Nor will I sing of Belgia's frozen Clime,
And teach the clumsy Boor to skate in Rhime ;
Where, if the warmer Clouds in Rain descend
No miry Ways industrious Steps offend,
The rushing Flood from sloping Pavements pours
And blackens the Canals with dirty show'rs.
Let others Naples' smoother Streets rehearse
Or with proud Roman Structures grace their Verse,
Where frequent Murders wake the Night with Groans,
And Blood in purple Torrents dyes the Stones.
Nor shall the Muse through narrow Venice stray,
Where Gondalas their painted Oars display.
Oh happy Streets, to rumbling wheels unknown,
No Carts or Coaches shake the floating Town.

Thus was of old Britannia's City blest
E'er Pride and Luxury her Sons possest ;
Coaches and chariots yet unfashion'd lay
Nor late invented chairs perplex'd the Way. &c.

That &c signifies near 300 Lines. so much for Poetry ; you may easily imagine by this progress, that I have not been interrupted by any Places at Court. Mr. Domville told me how to direct to you a day or two since as I accidentally met him in the Park. I have not heard any thing of Parnell or the Dean since you left England ; Pope has been in the Country, near (torn) but I expect him in Town this Week to forward the Printing of his Homer, which is already begun to be printed off ; he will publish his Temple of Fame as soon as he comes to Town ; Rowe hath finish'd his Play, and Lintot told me just now, that he was made Clerk of the Council to the Prince. There was a Ball at Somerset House last Tuesday, where I saw the Dutchess ; the Prince and Princess were there, and danc'd our English Country Dances. I have been studying these two or three Minutes for something (   ) to write to you, but I find myself at a Loss, and can't say any thing but that I am

Sir
Your most obedient
Humble Servt
J. Gay

London
Decemʳ. 30. 1714.

APPENDIX IV.

Alexander Pope

his safe return from

T R O Y

a Congratulatory Poem on
the compleating his Translation of Homer's Ilias.
in the manner of the beginning
of the last Canto of
Ariosto.

[This is among the MSS. in the British Museum. (Add. MSS. 6419 ff. 53, 54.) The same volume contains the translations from Ariosto given in this edition, and some papers of the Duchess of Queensberry's, in whose possession the Gay MSS. must have been. For the final version see page 164.]

1.

Long hast thou, Friend been absent from thy soil
    Like patient Ithacus at siege of Troy
I have been witness of thy six years toil
    Thy daily Labours and thy night's annoy,
Lost to thy native land; with great turmoil
    on the wide Sea, oft threatning to destroy.
Methinks with thee, I've trod Sigæan ground,
And heard hoarse Hellespontic shores resound.

2.

Did I not see thee when thou first setst sail
    To seek Adventures fair in Grecian Land   10
Did I not see thy sinking Spirits fail
    And wish thy Bark had never left the Strand?
Ev'n in mid Ocean often didst thou quail,
    And oft' lift up thy holy eye & hand,
Praying thy Virgin dear, and Saintly Choir
Back to the Port to speed thy Bark entire.

3.

Chear up, my friend ; thy dangers now are oer ;
    Methinks, nay sure the rising Coasts appear,
Hark how the Guns salute from either shore
    As thy trim Vessell cuts the Thames so fair ;   20
Shouts answ'ring Shouts from Kent & Essex roar
    And Bells break loud through ev'ry gust of Air :
Bonefires do blaze, and bones & Cleavers ring,
As at the coming of some mighty King.

4.

Now pass we Gravesend with a prosp'rous wind,
    And Tilbury's white Fort, & long Blackwall ;
Greenwich, where dwells the friend of Humankind
    More visited than or her Park or Hall,
Withers the good, and with him ever-join'd
    Facetious Disney greet thee first of all.   30
I see his Chimney smoak, & hear him say,
Duke, that's the room for Pope, & that for Gay.

5.

Come in, my Friends, here shall ye dine & lye,
    And here shall breakfast & here dine again,
And sup and breakfast on, if ye comply,
    For I have still one dozen of Champaigne.
His Voice still lessens, as the Ship saild by,
    He waves his hand to bring us back invain.
For now methinks I see proud London's spires,
Greenwich is lost, and Deptford Dock retires.   40

6.

O what a Concourse swarm on yonder Kay !
    The Sky re-ecchoes with new shouts of joy,
By all this Show, I ween, 'tis Lord Mayor's day,
    I hear the Voice of Trumpet & Haut-boy :
But now I see them near, Oh ! these are they
    Who come in Crouds to welcome thee from Troy :
Hail to the Bard, whom long as lost we mourn'd,
Safe from the Fights of Ten years War return'd !

On a torn fragment in the same volume of manuscripts is what appears to be the
rough copy of stanza 3 and part of stanza 2.   This agrees with the more complete
manuscript.   In line 14 the word *pious* is erased before *hand*, and in line 16 *speed*
is substituted for *bring*.   Line 18 ran first *Methinks I see the rising Coast appear*.
This is altered to *Methinks nay sure I see the Coast appear*.   Finally *I see* is erased and
rising reinstated.   On the back of this fragment is stanza 14.
    26 Gay first wrote *black W*, then altered *b* to *B*, then erased as far as he had written
and wrote *Blackwall*.

7.

Of Goodly Dames and Courteous Knights I view
The silken Petticoat, & broider'd Vest,   50
Yea Peers and mighty Dukes with ribbands blue,
True blue, fair emblem of unstained breast,
Others I see as noble and as true
     By no Court badge distinguish'd from the rest
There See I Pulteney, generous good & kind
And gallant Methuen of sincerest mind

8.

[This verse is scored through.]

What Lady's that to whom he gently bends ?
Who knows not her ? ah those are Howard's Eyes.
How art thou honour'd, number'd with her friends !
For She distinguishes the good & wise.   60
Harmonious Cowper near her side attends
     Now to my heart the glance of Howard flies ;
Now Pult'ney's gracefull air I mark full well
With thee, Youth's youngest daughter sweet Lepell.

9.

I see two lovely sisters hand in hand,
     The fair-hair'd Martha and Teresa brown,
One Bellenden, the bonniest of the Land
     And blue-ey'd Mary, soft & fair as Down ;
Yonder I see the cheerfull Dutchess stand
     For friendly Zeal & blithsome humour known,   70
Whence that loud Shout in such a hearty strain ?
Why, all the Hamiltons are in her train.

10.

See, see, the decent Scudamore advance
     With Winchelsea, still-meditating song
And Sophy How demure came there by chance
     Nor knows with whom, nor why she goes along ;
Far off from these fair Santlow fam'd for dance
     With frolick Bicknell & her Sister Young
With other names by me not to be named
Much lov'd in private, not in publick famed.   80

58 *Howard's* substituted for some obliterated name.
61 The first form of this line was *See sweet-tongu'd* [illegible name] *near her side
attends*. For *See* was substituted *There*, and for the deleted name *Cowper*, before the
final change.
67 *One* and *bonniest* substituted for two erased words, now illegible.
75 *And Sophy* substituted for *With her Miss*

11

But lo aloof the female Band retire ;
Now the shrill musick of their Voice is still'd.
Methinks I see fam'd Buckingham admire
That in Troys ruine thou hadst not been kill'd ;
Sheffield who knows to strike the living Lyre
With hand judicious, like thy Homer skill'd,
Bathurst impetuous hastens to the Coast,
Whom you & I strive who shall love the most.

The manuscript ends at this point. On a separate fragment of paper bearing on the other side Stanza 3 and part of Stanza 2, is Stanza 14, as below, followed by an asterisk.

14.

Harcourt I see, for eloquence renown'd,
The mouth of Justice, Oracle of Law   9⊃
Another Simon is beside him found
Another Simon like as Straw to Straw.
There Lansdown smiles whom ev'ry Muse has crown'd.
What miter'd Prelate there commands our awe ?
See Rochester approving nods his head
And ranks one modern with the mighty dead.

*

On a similar torn fragment, headed by an asterisk, and followed by the words *Carlton & Hanmer &c.* (which, in the published version, begin stanza xv), is the stanza which follows, not used in the poem as published in the *Additions to Pope's Works*. It is evident that the verse was written subsequently to the rest of the copy, and was meant to be inserted between stanzas xiv and xv.

*

See there two Brothers greet thee wth applause
Both for prevailing Eloquence renown'd
Argyll the brave and Islay learn'd in Laws
Than whom no truer friends were ever found.   100
Tom had been nigh you zealous in your Cause
But Tom alas, dear friend is underground
There see I Colman blithe as bird in May
In vast Surprize to see this happy day.

* 3 This was, at first, *Argyll the gracefull, Islay* etc. The word *graceful* is lightly scored through ; above it are written *brave*, then an illegible word scored through, followed by *and.*

APPENDIX V.

"THE POEMS FROM GAY'S CHAIR"

I.

THE problem presented by the pieces usually known as ' Poems from Gay's Chair ' has not, so far as I know, been seriously attacked, though their authenticity has, with reason, been suspected. In this Appendix I present what I believe to be the solution of the problem. A trick successfully practised on the reading public for over a hundred years deserves proper exposure, even though it has not appreciably damaged Gay's reputation. The detection of fraud has, too, an entertainment of its own, which I am not without hope of persuading the reader to share.

In 1820, when Gay's popularity was still at its height, appeared a slim f'cap 8vo volume, printed by W. Syle, Barnstaple, for Longman & Co., London, with the title-page : Gay's Chair. | Poems, | Never before printed, | written by | John Gay, | Author of the Beggar's Opera, Fables, &c. | with | A Sketch of his Life, | from the MSS. of | the Rev. Joseph Baller, | his nephew. | Edited by Henry Lee, | Author of Poetic Impressions, Caleb Quotem, &c. | To which are added, | Two New Tales, | The World, and Gossip, | by the Editor. | London : | Longman, Hurst, Rees, Orme, and Brown, | Paternoster Row, | 1820.

The way had already been prepared. In October of the previous year the *Gentleman's Magazine* published the following letter :

Exeter, Oct. 16.

MR. URBAN,
Most of your Readers are doubtless aware that the Poet Gay was a native of Barnstaple. A curiously formed *Chair* has lately been discovered there, which appears incontestably to have been his property : on examination of this piece of furniture, a private drawer was found which contained various documents and interesting papers, some of them in the handwriting of the Poet. The discovery was made by a Cabinet-maker of Barnstaple : the papers are the property of Mr. Henry Lee, who intends publishing some of them, under the title of " Gay's Chair ".
Mr. Lee is already known to the publick, as author of " Poetic Impressions " ; " Dash ", a tale ; " Caleb Quotem ", &c.
[There follows a print and a description of the chair.]
E. EDWARDS.

The volume of 1820 contains 147 pages. A print of the Chair is given as a frontispiece. The Chair has no arms, but the back is provided with elbow rests, so that a man straddling across the seat, and facing the back, could use it as a writing- or reading-desk. The contents of the book include a *Preface* ; a facsimile of Gay's handwriting ; a *Memoir* by the Rev. Joseph Baller, Gay's Nephew, ' taken from one of the manuscripts in the possession of the Editor ' ; a *Description* [of the Chair] headed by another and smaller cut ; and a *Nota Bene*.

Ten poems, said to be Gay's, occupy pp. 33–69. The remainder of the volume (pp. 71–147) is filled by the Editor's two poems *The World* and *Gossip*.

Before we give our attention to the poems themselves let us hear the story of their discovery. The Editor offers in the *Preface* ' a plain narrative of facts '.

> Many of the most respectable inhabitants of Barnstaple and its vicinity remember having often seen this Chair, several years ago, while it was in the possession of Gay's immediate descendants, who always spoke of it as having been the property of the Poet, and which, as his favorite Easy Chair, he highly valued. . . . About twelve years since, it was sold amongst some of the effects of the late Mrs. WILLIAMS, niece of the Rev. JOSEPH BALLER, and who by a previous marriage had been the wife of the Rev. HUGH FORTESCUE of Filleigh, near Barnstaple. Both families (the FORTESCUES and the BALLERS) were by marriage nearly related to GAY, whose property was, at his decease . . . equally divided betwixt his sisters, KATHERINE BALLER and JOANNA FORTESCUE.
>
> Since the period of Mrs. Williams's death, the Chair came into the hands of the late Mr. Clarke, of High-street, Barnstaple, and it was sold, with the rest of his household furniture, by public auction. The Editor happening to be then in Devonshire, heard of the above circumstance, and anxious to ascertain the particulars, applied to the auctioneer, who informed him that the Chair had been sold to a person of the name of Symonds, to whom the Editor immediately went, saw the Chair, and afterwards purchased it : orders were given that it should be sent to the house of Mr. Crook, a cabinet maker in the same street, to be repaired ; who, on removing the drawers, discovered the manuscripts from which the principal articles of this publication are taken.
>
> The following extract from Mr. Crook's letter to a Gentleman who made inquiries on the subject, will, it is presumed, be satisfactory.——" The Chair was bought " at an auction by Mr. Symonds of this town, from whose house it came to mine. " I was desired to repair it, and on taking out the drawer in front, which was " somewhat broken, I found at the back part of the Chair, a *concealed drawer*, " ingeniously fastened with a small wooden bolt. Those who have lately had " possession of the Chair never knew of this concealed drawer : it was full of " manuscript papers, some of which appeared to have slipped over, as I found " them stuck in the bottom or seat of the Chair.—A respectable tradesman of this " town was present when I made the discovery. The owner of the Chair was " immediately sent for, and the whole of the papers safely delivered into his hands.
>
> " I am, Sir, your humble servant,
" RICHARD CROOK,
" Cabinet-maker, Barnstaple."
>
> " March 21st, 1819."

After quoting the testimony of certain persons that the Chair was indeed Gay's, the Preface ends with a description of Gay's alleged money-box ' amongst the documents and relics of Gay and his family, which the Editor has become possessed of, (and which may, at some future time, be more particularly noticed) '.[1]

The *Description* runs as follows (the words in brackets are added from the similar description in the Letter to the *Gentleman's Magazine*) :

> UNDER the arms of the Chair are drawers, with the necessary implements for writing ; each drawer turns on a pivot, and has attached to it a brass candlestick. The wooden leaf [at the back] for reading or writing upon, may be raised or depressed, or entirely let down, at the student's pleasure. Under the seat [in front] is a drawer for books or paper[s], and behind it is the *concealed* [or private] *drawer*, in which were found the manuscripts : it is curiously fastened by a small [wooden]

This promise was not fulfilled.

bolt [connected with a rod in front], not perceivable till the larger drawer is removed. The Chair is made of very fine grained dark coloured mahogany ; the seat, back and arms stuffed, and covered with brown leather, ornamented with brass nails ; the whole, considering its antiquity, in pretty good repair, and (as may be seen from the preceding print) is admirably constructed for meditative ease and literary application.

Lastly, the remarkable *Nota Bene* must be given here in full :

THE "Ladies' Petition " is printed nearly verbatim from a manuscript in the hand-writing of the poet, and the style is decidedly his. A few alterations have been made, to render the poem more conciliatory to the refined taste of the present day.—The Editor is not aware of its having been before published. Reasons equally satisfactory cannot perhaps be offered with respect to all the other pieces, yet it may be confidently avowed, that there does not appear any cause to question their authenticity. The Editor's presumption in adding any attempts of his own, will, he trusts, be pardoned. The public have approved of some of his former effusions, and, while he feels grateful for the liberality he has been honored with, he trusts that the present volume will not be unacceptable.

II.

In the *Gentleman's Magazine* for April 1820 the book was reviewed at length.

Mr. LEE is already known to the public as the Author of that laughable character Caleb Quotem—Poetic Impressions—and some other Poems that exhibit considerable depth of thought on subjects connected with the human mind . . . quite sufficient evidence, we think, is given to satisfy the most suspicious that the Chair really was the property of the Poet Gay ;—that there was in it a concealed drawer, undiscovered till it came into the hands of the present possessor ; and that the little pieces now given to the world were found in that drawer. That these productions will brighten the lustre of Gay's reputation it might perhaps be too much to assert : we do not, however, think that they will tarnish it : and to the admirer of departed genius, this kind of literary resurrection is peculiarly pleasing.

The Reviewer goes on to say that ' *The Ladies' Petition* . . . is decidedly in the style of Gray's [*sic*] lighter productions ' ; he finds ' the equivoque ' in the concluding word of the lines *To Miss Jane Scott* ' very neat ' ; and ' a similar playfulness of fancy ' in *Absence*. But the larger portion of the Review is taken up with the poems of Lee himself, which the Reviewer considers ' that part most likely to be generally pleasing '.

A similar notice appeared in the *London Review and Literary Journal* for July 1820. The Reviewer thinks

these poems of Gay are the characteristic companions of an easy chair ; scribbled in a fit of laziness ; and thrown by, probably, without the slightest intention that they should ever be arranged in print.

A long and favourable review of Lee's own poems follows :

Mr. Lee is about the only humorous writer of the present day that keeps his muse within the bounds of propriety. He may not possess the wit and facetiousness of Coleman, but he has none of that *gentleman's vulgarity* and is therefore even with him.

The Reviewer hints, by the way, that the incident [1] of ' the boy marking the priest's back . . . is of too undoubted an origin to be mistaken . . . we

[1] See *infra*, p. 681.

* Z

are sure that he [Lee] is indebted to our mutual and ancient friend, Joe Miller, for his subject '.

Doubtless other notices appeared in other papers ; these are the only two I have been able to find in a rather brief search. To judge from them both, *Gay's Chair* was received with little or no suspicion ; and a more than kindly welcome was given to the poems which the Editor had thrown in to ballast his craft.

The Chair is, I believe, now in Barnstaple.[1] It would be interesting to know through whose hands it has passed. But a more important question is, What has become of the MSS. ? A Mr. Julian Marshall, writing in *Notes and Queries* (6th Series, v. 235, March 25, 1882), and asking for news of the Chair, continues :

As to the MSS. the memoir, in a villainously bad hand, by the Rev. J. Baller, and the MSS. of the *Maids' Petition* and *An Answer to a Predestinarian* came not very long ago into my possession. The former is the most important of the poems printed in the little volume called *Gay's Chair* ; the latter, strange to say, is not included in that Collection. The former beginning with the lines :—

> Sirs, we the Maids of Exon City,
> The Maids ! Good lack, the more 's the Pity !

and called in the printed copy the *Ladies' Petition*, is there given with very little fidelity to the MS. What has become of the other MSS. found with these in the chair ? and were any others found there which, like that of the *Answer to a Predestinarian*, have not been published ?

So far as I know, these inquiries were made in vain.

Scepticism was expressed by Mr. Underhill, in his edition of 1893. He prints the poems, but says they ' cannot with perfect certainty be ascribed to Gay. They were none of them printed in his life-time ; and the story of their discovery in a secret drawer nearly ninety years after his death is not in the highest degree convincing. . . . The verses . . . if really Gay's, may, we think, a great many of them, be safely regarded as the productions of his youth, written, perhaps, during the somewhat extended visit to Devonshire which preceded his introduction to the literary world and to Pope. The least doubtful piece, *The Ladies' Petition*, was possibly " thrown off " upon the occasion of his visit to Exeter in 1715 '. And Mr. Melville, premising that the poems are not certainly genuine, nevertheless deduces from them the course of two youthful love affairs.

III.

Something must now be said of Mr. Henry Lee, the ' Editor of *Gay's Chair* ', a man of sufficient eminence to come into the purview of the *Dictionary of National Biography*. He was born in 1765 at Nottingham, and before he was eighteen ' began to send verses and other articles to various periodical publications ', amongst others to Moore's Almanacks. Later he went to London, became an actor, and in partnership with his friend Shatford[2] toured the West of England. About 1789 he wrote the farce *Caleb Quotem*, which was produced at the Haymarket Theatre in 1798 under the title *Throw*

[1] Mr. Melville, in his recent *Life* of Gay refers to ' Sydney Harper, Esq., of Barnstaple, the happy possessor of Gay's chair '.
[2] Not *Stratford*, as the *D. N. B.* has it.

Physic to the Dogs. A revised version was refused by George Colman the younger, who coolly borrowed the character of Caleb Quotem for a play of his own. Lee, not unnaturally, made some capital out of this. He seems to have owned more than one West of England theatre ; but his interest in literature was not swamped by his profession. He published successively *Caleb Quotem and his wife ! or Paint, Poetry, and Putty !* An opera in three Acts (1809), *Poetic Impressions. A Pocket book, with Scraps and Memorandums* (1817), *Dash, A Tale* (in verse, 3rd edition, 1817), *Gay's Chair* (1820), *The Manager, A Melo-Dramatic Tale* (in verse, dedicated to Kean, 1822), and *Memoirs of a Manager ; or Life's Stage with New Scenery* (Taunton, 1830). Lee's death was recorded in the *Gentleman's Magazine* for May 1836.

March 30. In Long-acre, aged 71, Mr. Henry Lee, for many years the proprietor and manager of Theatres in the West of England, author of various poems, &c. including " Caleb Quotem and his Wife, an Opera ", 1810, 8vo.

Considerable light on his character, if not upon his career, is thrown by the rambling *Memoirs of a Manager.* They show him to us as a restless, ambitious, many-sided man ; anxious to stand in the limelight, yet conscious that he does not really deserve to be there ; full of the fact that he has been twice successfully married ; [1] and a born scribbler, if ever there was one. He begins his recollections by telling the reader that ' he has known no regularity . . . his journey has been, like the comet's—eccentric '. Here is a self-revealing passage :

I had imbibed early in life a taste of a romantic kind ;—a passion, perhaps common amongst young men whose minds are somewhat ardent, or in any degree enterprising. I had conceived a desire of notice, of notoriety of some kind or other. If not talented, so as to be capable of obtaining legitimate and genuine notoriety, I fancied that something of an adventurous or perilous nature, might supply the deficiency . . . I asked myself, can I contrive a method for jumping upwards instead of downwards ? . . . Alas ! I have been contriving ever since and am less likely to jump up than ever.

His reference to Gay's Chair is very jejune.

It may be remembered by some, if not by many, that a few years ago I discovered a curious old chair, which was traced to have once been the property of the poet Gay, who was a native of Barnstaple : and on my first going there, upwards of thirty years ago, several persons were living who knew something of his family. The finding of this chair, and the curiosity raised about it, created some interest in the minds of the parties most immediately concerned.
Besides the papers and memorandums originally found, several others were given me : some of which I have been deprived of in a manner very provoking, as may hereafter be explained.[2]

Space prevents me from dealing with Lee's literary qualifications at any length. The following four extracts from *Poetic Impressions*, chosen to illustrate his style and methods, must be given without comment, before we go on to consider the problem, Who wrote the poems in *Gay's Chair* ?

[1] The theme of marriage, as a desirable state, recurs in several of the ' Poems from Gay's Chair '. In his authentic poems and plays Gay too seldom speaks of marriage without a sneer.
[2] The explanation is that Lee decided to sell the Chair. Gay's relatives would not buy ; but the Chair was sold in Bath by Lee's family in Lee's absence. Apparently the purchaser left the country without paying for it.

CHOICE READING.

In sweet poetic chime
From Milton I learnt rhyme ;
From Pope I got blank verse ;
And could many a line rehearse,
With sprightly comic glee,
From Otway, Rowe and Lee !
While the tragic style I caught
From Gay and Congreve's thought ! [1]

and so on, through all the Poets.

THE LITTLE OLD WOMAN CUT SHORTER.

A Comic Song.

Sung at the Theatres London, &c.

When I was a maid I was bashful and shy,
  To all rudeness I made much resistance ;
If a youth caught a glance, then I cast down my eye,
  'Twas—" I beg, sir, you'll keep at a distance ! "
Tho' not very tall, yet I held myself high ;
  For my beauty made all their mouths water,
And now, as I pass, the folks titter and cry
  " There 's the little old woman cut shorter ! "

(A verse omitted.)

Six husbands I've had, but, poor souls ! they are gone ;
  I shall soon wed a seventh, my cozen ;
Egad, if at this rate, I keep going on,
  Ere I die, I shall make up the dozen !
I cared not a pin for their humours and airs ;
  At a scolding I never gave quarter ;
If they kick'd up a dust, why I kick'd 'em down stairs,
  Tho' " a little old woman grown shorter ! "

Three husbands I lost by the palsy and gout,
  I had two shovell'd off by a dropsy ;
My sixth was a tippler, for ever was out—
  And turn'd my affairs turvy topsy !
So I'll marry again, just to set all things right ;
  For I've match'd both my son and my daughter !
At their weddings I danced—at my *own* dance to-night—
  Like " a little old woman cut shorter ! "

REVENGE : OR FATHERLY KINDNESS.

A vixen wife, who felt the horsewhip's smart,
Ran to her Father—begg'd he'd take her part.
" What was your fault ? (said he) Come, state the case."
" I threw some coffee in my husband's face,
" For which he beat me ! "—" Beat you, did he ?—'S'life
" *He* beat my Daughter !—then I'll beat his Wife !

[1] *Tragic* style ? Gay wrote two tragedies *Dione,* a Pastoral Tragedy, and *The Captives,* a Tragedy in Blank Verse.

" If for such faults, he gives my dear *Child* pain,
" Come but his *Wife*, I'll flog her home again ! "
This said, most amply he revenged his daughter,
And stopt domestic squabbles ever after !

From THE FOP AND ECHO.

When cits on horseback take the air,
And wits to Rotten Row repair,
Saddles to *mules* compared have been,
As placed a horse and ass between ;
And others think the Fribble no man,
But something man between and woman.
Abroad Sir Fopling chanced to stray . .
Within a grove, unseen, unheard
Except by Echo, who each word
Promptly received, and then for sport
Return'd the same with sham retort.
Oft as he sigh'd " Sweet Venus ! Cupid ! "
Echo replied . . . *Between us—stupid* !
Now on a fish-pond's bank he stood,
His image viewing in the flood,
A while he look'd, the silly elf
Pretended not to know himself :
" That beauteous face (said he) and shape,
To whom can they belong ? "

ECHO . . . . . *An Ape !* (and so forth.)

Our picture of Mr. Henry Lee would not be quite complete, if it did not include the extracts from reviews which he selected for an advertisement of his previous works on the first page of *Gay's Chair*.

The author indeed forcibly reminds us of our witty friend George Colman.— Mr. Lee possesses no small fund of wit and humour, as well as genius. His versification is easy and correct ; his sentiments are just and good ; and he suffers no proper opportunity to escape him, for the inculcation of religious and moral principles. In his minor pieces there are at once a manliness of thought, and a neatness of expression, which is not excelled by any poetical writer of the present day.

Thus an *Anonymous Review*. The *Literary Gazette* adds this overwhelming recommendation :

The volume contains, with a good deal of playfulness and wit, no one line which a good man would, at a serious moment, wish to blot out.

IV.

The (external) evidence in support of the authenticity of the poems is rightly divided by Mr. Underhill into two parts ; first the circumstances of their discovery, second the fact (if it be a fact) ' that the Ladies' Petition was printed nearly verbatim from a manuscript in the handwriting of the poet '. The reader has now before him all the information relevant to the discovery and publication of the MSS. In so far as I can do so without the reproduction of facsimiles, I must now try to put him in the same advantage with regard to the handwriting.

There is, then, Lee's assertion in the *Nota Bene,* confirmed in some particulars by Mr. Julian Marshall's letter to *Notes and Queries* ; there is also the facsimile of the opening lines of the *Petition* :

> Sirs, we the Maids of Exon City
> The Maids ! Good lack, the more 's the Pity !
> Do humbly offer this Petition
> To represent our sad Condition ;
>
> J. Gay.

The first two lines agree in the use of capitals and stops with Mr. Marshall's quotation, rather than with the printed text, which runs thus :

> SIRS !
> We, the Maids of Exon City,
> The Maids ! Good lack, the more 's the pity !
> Do humbly offer this petition,
> To represent our sad condition ;

except for the fact that Mr. Marshall puts in the comma after *City*, which the facsimile lacks. I will not press this small point in favour of my argument that the facsimile is taken not from the original MS. but from a transcription ; for Mr. Marshall may well have not been at pains to copy his MS. accurately. From the differences between the facsimile and the printed text, it may be inferred that the typographical peculiarities found in the poems attributed to Gay, and so characteristic of Lee, e. g. *wo*-MEN, were not necessarily indicated in the MSS. The use of capital letters in the facsimile is also characteristic of Gay. Up to this point, then, the facsimile favours the case for the defence.

But how are we to explain the presence of Gay's signature in the facsimile ? Is the facsimile taken from two separate specimens of Gay's writing ? If so, why is this not explained, and why is the signature reproduced in so curious a position, for all the world as if it had been written there ? Perhaps the answer to these questions is that it *was* written there—by the same hand which wrote the original MS. and transcribed the first four lines for reproduction.

There are numerous documents in Gay's handwriting easily accessible in the British Museum. I have studied with some care the following speciméns of his writing. A portion of the *Welcome to Pope* ; a translation from Ariosto ; a letter to Tonson ; a Memorandum of a Conversation ; and a letter to Mrs. Howard. Some of these are written rapidly, others with extreme care and neatness, and they naturally differ in some respects. But some characteristics are constant ; and I shall only refer to these. In Gay's indubitable writing, for example, his *C* is looped above and curled below and dips below the line ; in the facsimile it is neither looped nor curled and rests on the line. His *D* always has a wide backward flourish ; the facsimile *D* has nothing that can be called a flourish. His *b* is always looped and clearly ' hitched ' to the following letter, even if that letter is an *l* ; the facsimile *b* is not looped, and has no ' hitch ', and stands distinct from the *l*. His *f* and *ff* are entirely different letters from those of the facsimile. His *h* is almost always looped, the facsimile *h* never. So too with *k* (a very odd letter in the facsimile). His *l* is also always looped ; the facsimile *l* is looped by its attachment to the preceding *d*, but has no loop when it follows *b*. His *p* is a curious letter, quite distinct from the facsimile *p* (also a curious letter). His long *s* is always looped above and below ; the facsimile long *s* (in *represent*) is not looped. His *t* is never crossed with a separate stroke, but always written in one piece either with a small crossing low down the letter attaching to it the following letter or frequently without any crossing at all ; the facsimile *t* is always plainly crossed half-way up with a separate stroke, except in the word *represent*, where the writer has made a bold cross on the right-hand side of the letter without taking his pen off the paper. His *w* (like his *b*) is always plainly ' hitched ' at the end ; the facsimile *w* has no hitch.

Such are the most striking differences between the facsimile and Gay's genuine handwriting. In using the words *always* and *never* I can of course only speak of those specimens which I have examined. It is open to any curious person to make the same examination for himself : and I do not doubt that whoever does so will conclude that the hand-writing of the facsimile is not that of Gay.

V.

Is this conclusion borne out by an examination of the poems ? The octo-syllabic measure of the *Petition* and some of the other pieces is used by Gay for the *Fables* and for several *Tales, Epistles*, and other shorter pieces. But Gay used it in two manners ; it is a quiet pedestrian measure in the *Fables* ; but in the shorter facetious pieces it is looser and livelier, and it is with the latter that the *Petition* must be compared. The proportion of double to single rhymes in the *Petition* is a great deal higher than Gay's average ; but it can be paralleled in *The Quidnunchi's* (not certainly by Gay), and is exceeded in the *Epistle to a Young Lady with some Lampreys*. I do not, however, know of a single instance in Gay of a triple rhyme ; [1] and in the *Petition* there are two, *boddices—goddesses, marrying—carrion*. Lee has many such. The freedom of the rhymes is perhaps rather beyond Gay's happy-go-luckiest manner. He has *fellow—pillow, sallad—palate, give t'ye—fifty, pity'd—remitted* ; but are these quite so violent as *compel us—fellows, pretences—consci-ences, proper—troop here, ten—wo-men, one day—John Gay* ? Lee, the reader may take it, is capable of all such licences.

Another method of comparison is to determine the proportion of lines which begin with a stressed syllable. The number of such lines in the *Petition* is only half Gay's average, and less by one-third than in the *Equivocation*, which approaches most nearly in this respect to the *Petition*.

If we turn the magnifying glass on to the vocabulary of the poems in *Gay's Chair*, and of Lee's contributions to the same volume, we observe some curious peculiarities and correspondences. Common to both are a great number of idiosyncratic words, such as *leisure, fluent, single* (unmarried), *confound, boon, spleen, sans, scandal, meek, grace* (verb and noun), *pry, treat* (noun), *prop, elves, Satan, prate, aptly, dame, Reason, piece, abject, sequel, bait, cell, musing, inheritance*. There are also a few suggestive parallelisms : *'bout, 'dorn : want expressing, not to be express'd : notice shares, notice claim : mutual love, mutual vows : vital air, vital powers : why a month—a week in ?*

---

[1] In the mysterious addition (of 12 lines) to *Bounce to Fop*, found in some late eighteenth-century edition, occurs the rhyme *Tory ones—Pythagoreans*. But *Bounce to Fop* was probably written by Pope. The addition was perhaps by another hand. In the Ballad on *Nelly* we have *Italian—Pygmalion* ; but *Nelly* is believed to have been written by Arbuthnot, and is moreover in a different metre.

pass the day—the week : mellow, mellow'd (i. e. by drink ; *one day* rhymed with
John Gay, one rhymed with *John.*

I cannot remember that Gay ever uses the words *sans* or *mellow* (in this
sense). Nor are such words as the following characteristic of Gay's vocabulary ;
volubility (Lee is fond of words in *-ility*), *speechify, gravitates, carriage* (taunting
carriage), *interlope, invective, genteel, contracted* (married), *parliamentary, waggish, megrims, unique.* Do not most of these words belong to the language of
1820 rather than that of 1720 ? The metaphorical use of the word *gravitates* is
particularly remarkable.

It must, of course, be remembered that if these poems are not Gay's, they
were written in deliberate imitation of Gay's manner ; in one instance the
imitator has sailed, I think, too close into the wind. Gay's tale *Work for
a Cooper* begins

> A man may lead a happy life,
> Without that needful thing, a wife.

The *Petition* has

> Not one in fifty would be led
> To Hymen's shrine, or, during life,
> Become that envied thing—a wife.

But it is the form only which is copied ; the sentiment—be it noted—is
reversed.

Mechanical tests, like these, yield some result—a result not altogether
favourable to the good name of Mr. Henry Lee—but they cannot carry us to
the heart of the poetic style, nor can they supply a wholly decisive answer
to the questions, Could Gay have written these pieces ? and, Did Lee write
them ? For one thing, we know that the printed version of the *Petition*
differed from the MS, and that whether the poem was written by Gay or Lee
it was worked over by Lee. But, if this be the explanation of its ' Lee-ishness ',
the revision was oddly thorough-going. The poems are not (*pace* Mr. Underhill, who says ' most of them are feeble and amateurish in a marked degree ')
contemptible pieces of writing. Nor have they, to my mind, the character of
Juvenilia. They are fluent, easy, at times witty—the work surely of a practised hand. But the fluency and the wit are not the fluency and the wit of
Gay. Gay rarely sustains a sentence for six or even four lines ; the *Petition*
has many sentences six, eight, or even twelve lines long. As for the quality of
the wit—there is a sprightliness, a jauntiness, about these poems, which tastes
very differently on the palate from the unobtrusive humour of Gay. Their
author flings up his heels a little too high. That, too, is a characteristic of Lee.
And was Gay, who hated walking, and spent all his money in coach hire, the
man to find himself nearer heaven at the top of a hill ? Gay, who wrote in
the *Epistle to Lord Burlington*

> On either side low fertile valleys lye,
> The distant prospects tire the trav'ling eye.

praising a hill ' for prospect extended and landscape most rare ' ! It seems
unlikely.

If Gay wrote these pieces, when and where did he write them ? Pope
looked upon the octosyllabic measure as Swift's peculiar property ; and
Gay's short pieces in it bear indications of having been written very much

under Swift's influence. Whether, in youthful seclusion at Barnstaple, Gay would have used this manner, is doubtful. That the pieces, if genuine, were all written in the Chair, and at Barnstaple, would seem to be certain. Four directly purport to be Devonshire pieces, and one to have been written in the Chair; all were hidden together, and presumably all belong to the same period. It is very unlikely that Gay ever had the Chair in London. Even Mr. Lee found it an intolerable nuisance to carry about.[1] Nor would it have escaped mention by Gay's friends.

Did Gay write these poems when staying in his uncle's house, before his return to London about 1706 ? Do they read like the verses of a youngster ? [2] According to Mr. Baller he was, on this occasion, only some months in Barnstaple. Could he have said to his chair after so short a visit

Days, months, and *years* I've musing sat in thee ?

When else could they have been written ? Mr. Underhill suggests that the *Petition* was ' thrown off ' upon the occasion of his visit to Exeter in 1715. But that visit (at Lord Burlington's expense) was a brief one, and neither then nor when repeated in 1716 could have justified the apostrophe to the Chair. And, whenever written, how improbable that they should have been so elaborately concealed, as to remain undiscovered for more than a hundred years !

VI.

The evidence, above set forth, seems to me quite conclusive. Gay did not write the ' poems from Gay's Chair '. Who, then, was their author ? Who other than Henry Lee himself ? If the reader will compare the extracts I have given from Lee's *Poetic Impressions* with the poems from the Chair, he cannot fail to be struck by a family likeness. Note the similarity of *A Devonshire Hill* and *The Little Old Woman Cut Shorter*, the same over-loaded metre, the same double rhyme in the alternate lines, the same repetition of the last line in each verse. Note, again, the management of dialogue in *Revenge* and *Prognostication*. Note the tendency to playing upon words. Note, finally, the unacknowledged plagiarism from Swift's poem *A gentle Echo on Woman*.[3] And, apart from all such comparative analysis, the more the poems are read the more irresistible does the impression of Lee's authorship become. The

[1] He says so, in *Memoirs of a Manager*.
[2] He was born in 1685. *Wine* (1708), his first published poem, is crude and involved.
[3] Published in the *Miscellanies* of Swift and Pope. Here are a few lines, for the sake of the comparison :

Shepherd ;
Echo ; I ween, will in the Woods reply,
And quaintly answer Question : shall I try ?
Echo : *Try.*
Shepherd ;
What must we do our Passion to express ?
Echo : *Press.*

. . . . . .

Shepherd ;
If Musick softens Rocks, Love tunes my Lyre,
Echo : *Lyar !*
Shepherd ;
Then teach me, Echo, how shall I come by her ?
Echo : *Buy her.*

poems which Lee added to *Gay's Chair* are sententious and long-winded, but facile, even vigorous. His picture of the curate, who would argue

> Till his *quid est*, in disquisition (fine as
> That of Dun Scotus, or old Tom Aquinas)
> Would come full bolt at Truth, and, point-blank, hit it!

sticks in the memory. Nor do his humorous strokes fail of their effect. The wordy parson on horseback, preaching to the lad whom he has taken up behind him on his way home, fresh from marking sheep with ' ruddle pitch and tar ', and punctuating his sermon with ' Mark, Ben, mark ! ' unconscious that the sly boy is taking him at his word and marking his Sunday suit all over with the mixture—the picture is amusing, and worthy of the author of the *Petition*. We have seen that it was probably not original. No more was the idea of the *Petition*.

In *Notes and Queries* (1st Series, vii. 594) an account is given of a petition by sixteen maids of Charleston, South Carolina, presented to the Governor of that province on March 1, 1733–4.

> To His Excellency Governor Johnson.
> The humble Petition of all the Maids whose names are under written :
> Whereas we the humble petitioners are at present in a very melancholy disposition of mind, considering how all the bachelors are blindly captivated by widows, and our more youthful charms thereby neglected : the consequence of this our request is, that your Excellency will for the future order that no widow shall presume to marry any young man till the maids are provided for ; or else to pay each of them a fine for satisfaction, for invading our liberties ; and likewise a fine to be laid on all such bachelors as shall be married to widows. The great disadvantage it is to maids, is, that the widows, by their forward carriages, do snap up the young men ; and have the vanity to think their merits beyond ours, which is a great imposition upon us who ought to have the preference.
> This is humbly recommended to your Excellency's consideration, and hope you will prevent any further insults.
>
> And we poor Maids as in duty bound will ever pray. P.S.—I, being the oldest Maid, and therefore most concerned, do think it proper to be the messenger to your Excellency in behalf of my fellow subscribers.

Here, without much doubt, is the germ of the *Maids' Petition*. The very phrase ' forward carriages ' is reproduced in the ' taunting carriage ' of the poem. Gay, who died in 1732, could not have utilized it ; and the *Petition*, if he had written it, could not have inspired the ladies of Charleston from its secret hiding-place. Lee was exactly the man to make use of it, if it had come (as it must have come) to his knowledge.[1]

No one else except Lee would have taken the trouble to forge the poems, for no one else stood to profit by their discovery. Deliberate forgeries they must have been, introducing Gay's name as they twice do. What Lee hoped to gain, and apparently did gain, by their publication, was a tow into notoriety. We have seen how, in his *Memoirs*, he confesses that he always hankered for publicity, and was always contriving to obtain it. Gay's Chair was, I suspect, the most ingenious and not the least rewarded, of all his contrivances.

Mere chance, we must suppose, put the brilliant idea into his head. I

---

[1] There are earlier *Maids' Petitions*. Mr. Wise kindly permitted me to examine two or three in his possession. But these have only the title in common with the Charleston petition ; they present the grievances of Maids against Mistresses, not of Virgins against Widows.

see no reason to regard the story he tells in the Preface as in any respect false. Lee was perhaps one of those not uncommon persons who will act a lie to any extent, but shrink from uttering it. Nowhere in the *Preface* or the *Nota Bene* does he say anything demonstrably untrue. ' In the handwriting of the poet ' means ' In a handwriting like the poet's ' ; ' there does not appear any cause to question their authenticity ' means ' I have covered up my tracks pretty carefully '. Even in the *Memoirs* it is remarkable that he only says ' I discovered a curious old *chair* '. His only reference there to the *poems* is in the odd sentence ' Besides the papers *and memorandums* originally found. . . .' He skates most carefully round the ice. But the old man's pen trips him up. What memorandums ? Nothing was said of any memorandums *found* anywhere. There was Mr. Baller's memoir ; but that was not concealed in the chair.

As for the discovery of the papers, the testimony of Crook, the cabinet-maker, is straightforward and convincing, and was open to contemporary proof or disproof. I imagine that everything occurred just as we are told. But what Lee has not told us is that he, by accident, found the hiding-place (not difficult to find, probably, by any one who took out the drawer under the seat), when he first went to Symonds' house or shop ; that he went away, wrote the *Ladies' Petition*, imitating Gay's handwriting as best he could ; came back, had another look at the chair, concealed the papers, bought the chair, and sent it to Crook to repair—knowing that the papers were bound to be discovered.[1]

For confirmation of this hypothesis, I ask the reader to consider carefully the very peculiar statement made by Lee in his *Nota Bene*. The *Petition*, he says, was in Gay's writing and style, but ' reasons equally satisfactory cannot perhaps be offered with respect to all the other pieces '. What does this mean ? If the other pieces were in Gay's writing, that was proof positive of their being Gay's ; if they were not it was *prima facie* proof that they were *not* Gay's. Since the writing must have proved them authentic or not, the question of style was (for Lee, who had the MSS.) secondary. Now on our hypothesis we can find an explanation. After the discovery, and after the ' papers ' had been handed over to the ' owner '˒ (Lee) by Crook, Lee may have decided that *one* poem by Gay would not float his volume so well as *ten* ; he therefore wrote nine further pieces, but shirked the labour of again imitating Gay's writing.

Such I believe to have been the true history of the Poems from Gay's Chair —a very ingenious and artistic piece of work, entitling Mr. Henry Lee to a special niche in the Gallery of Literary Forgers. What pleases me most in the affair, is the thought that the *Petition* needed amendment before it could be submitted to the public. It is a delicious touch. I wonder to what lengths the good man, in compensation for his ' more serious moments ', had permitted himself to go !

---

[1] ' The Editor . . . saw the Chair, and *afterwards* purchased it.'

POEMS.

THE LADIES' PETITION

to the

*HONORABLE THE HOUSE
OF COMMONS.*

SIRS!
WE, the Maids of Exon City,
The Maids! good lack, the more's the
  pity!
Do humbly offer this petition,
To represent our sad condition ;
Which once made known, our hope and
  trust is,
Your honored House will do us justice.
But lest our tender sense of wrong,
And volubility of tongue,
Should make us trespass on your leisure,
And speechify it out of measure,
To save our breath, and eke your time,
We clog our fluent speech with rhyme.
  First you shall hear—But cann't you
    guess
The reason of our sad distress ?—
(Plague on the Widows that compel us
Thus to petition 'bout young fellows !)
But we were saying—you must know,
Tho' blushing we declare our woe,
A maiden was designed by nature
A weakly and imperfect creature,
So liable to err or stray,
Her wants require a guide, a stay ;
And then so timorous of sprites,
She dreads to be alone at nights !
Say what she will, do what she can,
Her heart still gravitates to man ;
From whence 'tis evident as light
That marriage is a woman's right ;
And therefore 'tis prodigious hard
To be of such a right debarred :
Yet we, poor souls, cann't have the
  freedom
To get good husbands, tho' we need 'em !

The Widows, Sirs !—Their art denotes
Them *Machiavels* in petticoats !
  These plagues, with heads on mischief
    running,
Exceed by far the fox in cunning !
They cut us out, are still before us,
And leave no lovers to adore us !
' Adore us ! ' nay, 'tis ten times worse,
Deuce take 'em ! (but we should not
  curse)
For tho' our number is not small,
There's hardly one amongst us all,
Scarce one—'tis true as G—'s in Glo'ster,*
Can get a Strephon to accost her !
No single creature e'er is seen
With bearded chin and manly mien,
But what they have him in a minute !
Well ! sure there is some witchcraft in it ;
And all the elves are magic pimps
To aid and succour widow imps !
For when, by force of all our wits,
Kind looks, kind words, and fainting fits,
We've brought our beaus just to the lure,
And think the captives are secure—
When the ring glitters in our eye,
The lawyer called, the parson nigh,
Up starts a widow in the way,
And disappoints us of the prey ;
By some curst hocus pocus trick
The lover leaves us in the nick,
And our confusion to confound,
He's led directly to Lob's pound.†
Besides, what makes it more provoking,
The dames oft wound us by their joking,
Tho' they've a thousand times been told
They need not be so pert and bold ;
For could we have the chance to try,
We would be wives, or else know why !
And having welcomed wedlock's boon,
We might be widows, too, and soon !
Thank heaven, we want nor will nor
  breath
To plague or talk a man to death !
But then the spiteful troop upbraids,
Calling us, sneeringly, old maids !

* This proverb will remind the reader of another—" Sure as the D—l's in London ! " *Ed.* [Lee's note.]

  † " *Crowdero*, whom, in irons bound,
    " Thou basely threw'st into Lob's pound."
                                      Hudibras.

'Tis evident that in this couplet of Butler's, the stocks or some mean prison is referred to ; but in the present text, *Lob's pound* probably alludes to a bondage more dignified. *Ed.* [Lee's note.]

(The major part of us they mean.)
You well may think it moves our spleen,
When we must suffer such disgraces,
Or, what is worse, display our faces : *
The fair and timid sex esteem'd,
We should about fifteen be deem'd ;
Timid and fair are signs of youth ;
The widows cann't deny this truth.
If still they urge we are not young,
However glib or loud the tongue,
'Till we afford 'em more conviction,
E'en let them talk *sans* contradiction !
' Old maids indeed ! ' for goodness sake
Could they no likelier scandal make ?
When time's so much at our devotion,
They could not think to spread the notion.
In spite of registers and nurses,
(Whose blunders well deserve our curses)
Obsequious to a maiden's will,
Old Time turns backward or stands still.
However strange the thing appears,
Some have been twenty, twenty years !
And some that reckon just a score,
Were thirty, ten years since, or more !
Need any person now be told
That single ladies cann't grow old !
We should despise such taunting carriage,
Did we not quite despair of marriage ;
Nor about husbands make this fuss,
Were there enough for them and us.
But, tis the truth we represent t'ye,
Men are so scarce, and maids so plenty,
That were each man a maid to wed,
Not one in fifty would be led
To Hymen's shrine, or, during life,
Become that envied thing—a wife.
While thus the widows interlope,
How can we maidens live in hope ?
Your honored House will then debate
On our most lamentable state,
And after hearing this as fact,
Will guard our rights by legal act :
For if the widows be allowed
To taunt us thus, and be so proud,
We maidens must embrace the pillow,
Or cut a caper from a willow !
But lest your honors should surmise,
That we, more resolute than wise,
Make 'gainst the widows an invective,
When 'tis ourselves are most defective,
We state, (and thus for favor sue)
That ail that can be done, we do ;
We plot, devise, try every plan,
To win the fickle creature man ;
Contriving, or pursuing schemes,
Not more when waking than in dreams ;

At every moment, every place,
Our lures we're throwing with a grace,
In curtsying, smiling, nodding, talking,
In laughing, singing, dancing, walking,
In romping, frowning, ogling, dressing,
And fifty things that want expressing ;
At home, abroad, by night, by day,
We various stratagems display.
But sure the most becoming airs
Are those we practise at our prayers !
And therefore nothing can be fitter
Than frequent visits to St. Peter ! †
Which every maid more duly pays
Than Canons on refection days.
Ah ! Sirs, 'twould do you good to know
The nice demeanour there we show :
And sure such visits are enchanting—
Good company is never wanting !
The forms too, and the ordinances,
So suited to young ladies' fancies ;
For meekness grac'd by pure contrition,
To female beauty gives addition.
While turning round, to crave a blessing,
The figure 's seen, and taste in dressing !
There one may sit, the eye not idle,
Tho' our discretion hold the bridle,
And archly view, behind a fan,
Which is the smartest gentleman ;
And while we are his worth attesting,
He soon becomes more interesting,
Claims more respect, more notice shares,
And renders more devout our prayers !
If ever, as 'twill sometimes happen,
One cannot get one's hood or cap on,
So early as to be at church,
We never leave it in the lurch,
But with all possible regard
Wait in the consecrated yard :
Hindered by no profane pretences,
There we discharge our consci-ences !
Away we sail—if rough the weather,
It more directly drives us thither.
What tho' the wind disturb our clothes,
Why should the widows harm suppose ?
Surely there can be nothing shocking
In a neat ankle and silk stocking !
If coxcombs pry, and make a fuss,
The blame must lie with them, not us.
So far we trust we do our duty,
In setting off our wit and beauty.
But more, if Nature, on her part,
Leaves us the smallest room for art,
We say, and to our praise 'tis known,
We show more graces than our own ;
With stiffened stays, or iron boddices,
We are as finely shaped as goddesses.
If native colours are too faint,
It surely cann't be wrong to paint :

* Alluding to the fashion of wearing hoods or veils. *Ed.* [Lee's note.]
† The cathedral at Exeter is dedicated to this saint. *Ed.* [Lee's note.]

If too reveal'd the lily shows,
What harm to imitate the rose ?
A patch that hides a freckled place
May add a beauty to the face ;
Then as to faults—admit we've one,
It's name we change—the fault is gone :
For instance, if Miss looks awry,
Ha ! Miss has got an ogling eye !
Or if a lengthened heel she want,
Her step's genteel, 'tis elegant !
Yet, Sirs, in spite of all our cares,
Our melting eyes and plaintive airs,
We must allow, when pressed thus far,
Just where we were at first, we are ;
All means have failed—all tricks mis-
carried,
And we, alas ! are still unmarried !
Since, then, 'tis not our fault, but
fortune,
We take the freedom to importune
Your House will let it be enacted,
That not one widow be contracted,
Or, that it henceforth may be reckon'd,
" She killed the first who weds a second,"
'Till every maid is in the way
Of wedlock's treat, as well as they.
And yet in case (but heaven avert it !)
A luckless fair should be deserted,
She from that very hour may claim
A widow's privilege and name.
But since we plainly can foresee
The task will not more easy be
To keep the widow's host from marrying,
Than 'tis to keep the crows from carrion,
We think 'twill be extremely proper,
With all despatch to send a troop here
Of bold gallants to prop our cause,
Our rights maintain, and aid the laws !
But if you find it hard to muster
Of such like beaus sufficient cluster,
Rather than leave a single creature
Of our complacent, modest nature,
To bear the taunts of widow elves,
Take us, we pray you, to yourselves ;
For we imagine, and don't flatter,
You will not start at such a matter ;
For if 'tis rightly understood,
Our private weal is public good,
And public good, the wise ones say,
All real patriots should sway.
Then if you are not dead to beauty,
And know your parliamentary duty,
The question put—divide—and so,
When you say AY, we'll not say NO !
Come—make election—pick and
choose,
Welcome to take, but not refuse :
Here all your fancies may be suited,
With real maids and maids reputed.
From these proposals we expect
The best your judgment can effect·

Aid then our wishes—grant the boon,
And, we beseech you, grant it soon.
Old proverbs state, strike while you
may,
All men lose something by delay,
And maids in sunshine should make hay :
Grant then this suit, Exonian Spinsters
say,
And your petitioners will ever pray.

TO

MISS JANE SCOT.

THE WELCH girl is pretty,
    The ENGLISH girl fair,
The IRISH deem'd witty,
    The FRENCH *debonnaire* ;
Tho' all may invite me,
    I'd value them not ;
The charms that delight me
    I find in a SCOT.

PREDICTION.

DAME Doleful, as old stories say,
Foresaw th' events of every day,
And tho' to Satan no relation,
Dealt largely in prognostication :
Whatever accident befel,
She plainly could the cause foretell ;
A hundred reasons she could show,
And finish with—" I told you so ! "

One day her son (a waggish youth)
Put on the serious face of truth,
And feigning sorrow, to her ran—
He thus his wond'rous tale began :
' Oh mother !—mother !—What d'ye
    think ?
' Letting old Dobbin out to drink,
' Poor beast, he neigh'd, and shook his
    mane,
' And had such megrims in his brain,
' That I did fear.'——Dame stopp'd him
    short
Before half finished his report :
" Ay, ay ; thy mother all forsees—
" Dobbin hath fall'n and broke his knees
" I knew how 'twas ;—I told you so."
In vain her son replied, ' No, no ;
' Good mother, listen, hear me out—
' As Dobbin, hungry, smelt about,'——
" Boy, I foresee what thou would'st say,
" Dobbin hath eat—the rick of hay ! "
' O worse than that !—He paw'd the
    ground,
' And snorted, kick'd, and gallop'd round,

'Then, wildly staring, ran to find
  The stone on which our scythes we
    grind ;
'And knaw'd—and knaw'd—ah, woe
    betide !
' He ope'd his hungry chops so wide,
' And look'd so ravenous, d'ye see,
' I was afraid he'd swallow *me* !—
'At last '——" Ay, ay, I'm not sur-
    prised,
" 'Tis what I all along surmised,—
" I knew 'twould be—I heard him groan—
" Dobbin hath eat—the GRINDING-
    STONE ! "

COMPARISONS.

A LAMB and a Lion—a Fox and an Ass,
Resemble Mankind, as it were in a glass ;
Males are harmless as lambs 'till they're
    fourteen years old,
And 'till they are forty, as lions are bold ;
As foxes they're cunning 'till three-score
    and ten,
Then, silly as asses, no longer are men.

A Dove and a Sparrow—a Parrot and
    Crow,
The life of a Woman most aptly will
    show ;
Girls innocent doves are 'till fourteen
    years old,
And chirrup like sparrows, till forty are
    told ;
Like parrots they'll prate 'till they're
    three-score and ten,
And as crows often croak, so do most old
    wo-MEN !

ABSENCE.

AUGUSTUS, frowning, gave com-
    mand,
And OVID left his native land ;
From JULIA, as an exile sent,
He long with barbarous Goths was
    pent.

So Fortune frown'd on me, and I was
    driven
From friends, from home, from JANE,
    and happy Devon !
And JANE sore grieved when from me
    torn away ;—
I loved her sorrow, tho' I wish'd her—
    GAY !

FABLE.

A MILK-WHITE Swan, in Aesop's time,
Had got the knack of making rhyme ;
All other birds he did excel ;
Wrote verses,—yes,—and wrote them
    well :
Praised was his genius, and his parts—
All wondered how he reached the arts :
Except some Geese, in neighbouring
    brook ;
Yet even *they* admired his look,
And grudged each feather in his wing ;
But, envious, hiss'd whene'er he'd sing !
His sonnets they denounced as *satire*,
His lyric pleasantries, *ill-nature !*

One day these Geese most pertly
    squall'd,
" Cygnet ! "—for so the Swan was
    call'd—
" Cygnet,—why will you thus abuse
" Our patience with your doggerel
    muse ?
" Not only you offend our ears,
" But you assail our characters !
" Blush, and no longer do amiss."
The critics ended with a hiss.

Erect the Cygnet raised his crest,
And thus the silly Geese address'd :
' I know not any of your tribe—
' Why, then, d'ye feel my jest or gibe ?
' Fools ever—('tis a certain rule)
' Think they're the butts of ridicule ;
' As if they so important were,
' No other theme the muse could cheer.
' Begone ! you but yourselves expose,
' When thus your folly you disclose :
' Know this, and then your gabbling
    cease—
' Swans like my verse ; but YOU are—
    Geese ! '

CONGRATULATION

TO

A NEWLY MARRIED PAIR.

WHILE artful dames and gay coquettes
Catch fops and fools in cobweb nets ;
While giddy girls wed hoary swains,
And barter happiness for gains ;
While misers, anxious to be great,
With fortunes take the wives they hate ;
Your wiser plan has proved 'tis right
The heart should with the hand unite ;

And those who would their joys improve,
Must build their hopes on mutual love.
Whoe'er attend to Reason's voice;
Will thus with prudence make their
    choice;
On this hinge hangs the chance in life,
Of peace, or war, 'twixt man and wife;
And such as disregard this caution,
May shipwreck'd be on wedlock's ocean.

A DEVONSHIRE HILL.

OFT have shepherds enamoured, in
    pastoral lays,
  Sweetly sung of the grove, grot, or
    fountain,
No scene that is rural, but loudly it's
    praise
  They have echoed from mountain to
    mountain.
Some delighted have been with a meadow
    or vale,
  But with these my taste never could
    tally ;
The meadow is pleasant, enchanting the
    dale,
  But a hill I prefer to a valley.

For prospect extended, and landscape
    most rare,
  With health-breathing breezes invit-
    ing,
No daisy-pied mead with a hill can
    compare,
  No garden yield sweets more delight-
    ing ;
As a mole-heap's excell'd by a mound
    that 's rais'd high,
  As a street may exceed a small alley,
Even so to my mind, when these objects
    are nigh,
  Is the hill I prefer to a valley.

But the hill of all hills, the most pleasing
    to me,
  Is famed COTTON,* the pride of *North
    Devon ;*
When it's summit I climb, O, I then seem
    to be
  Just as if I approached nearer heaven !
When with troubles depress'd, to this
    hill I repair,
  My spirits then instantly rally ;
It was near this bless'd spot I first drew
    vital air,
  So—a hill I prefer to a valley.

LETTER

TO

A YOUNG LADY.

DEAR MADAM,
        I your mercy crave
For my poor namesake *John,* your slave,
Behold him abject at your feet ;
Now is your triumph most complete :
A helpless victim see he lies,
Half slain by your all-conquering eyes !
Those eyes which like the mid-day sun,
None can with safety look upon.

To you (oh ! take it in good part)
He gave the maid-hood of his heart,
Untouched by any former love ;
Sure some compassion this might move ;
His heart, which ne'er before was sway'd,
You like a cullender have made,
And 'less your power and mercy's equal,
Indeed, dear ma'am, I dread the sequel ;
For love, beyond all other ills,
Despises juleps, drops, and pills.

If wedlock may be deemed a pleasure,
You cann't too soon possess the treasure !
Consider then the loss of time,
And snatch the roses in their prime ;
Teaze not the man who'll grace your
    house,
As a young cat torments a mouse :
Seeming regardless of the prize,
Puss slily turns aside her eyes ;
But should he run—'tis all in vain,
For, snap ! she brings him back again !
Again the panting wretch she mumbles,
Again she tosses him, and tumbles !—

But have you, madam, never seen,
When in the wall a hole hath been,
The pris'ner seize a lucky minute,
And in a trice hath slipp'd within it,
Leaving behind the tyrant puss,
To purr and claw and make a fuss ?

Pardon, I pray, the facts I state,
Nor think I mean t' insinuate
Your captive *mouse* will run away,
And you the part of puss must play !
O, no such thing ! what I fear most,
Is, that the mouse, thus plagued and
    tost,

* Cotton Hill, near Barnstaple. [Lee's note.]

Should by such usage be quite wasted,
Before one morsel has been tasted ;
For what are all such tricks at last,
But schemes to heighten the repast ?
Or what avails it thus to treat,
And take him when there's nought to
    eat ?
Rather than hazard such mishap,
Entice him kindly to the trap :
You won't, I trust, the thought dispar-
    age,
I mean, dear ma'am, the trap of mar-
    riage !
A trap, I'm sure he cann't withstand,
If you but lay the bait—your hand !

As I've his welfare much at heart,
Don't blame me that I take his part ;
He my companion was, and chearful,
And not of any female fearful,
He joked at love, or seemed to doubt
    it,
And laughed at those who talk'd about
    it :
But hear him as a child now mutter ;
Like one that's lost its bread and
    butter !
Since thoughts of you first filled his head,
His heart as heavy is as lead,
And if, dear ma'am, you do'nt befriend
    him,
Love's fatal power will surely end him.

But fearing this may be intrusion,
I'll bring my subject to conclusion,
Begging you will not mock his sighing,
And keep him thus whole years a dying !
' Whole years ! '—Excuse my freely
    speaking,
Such torture, why a month—a week
    in ?
Caress, or kill him quite in one day,
Obliging thus your servant,

JOHN GAY.

TO MY CHAIR.

THOU faithful vassal to my wayward will.
Thou patient midwife to my labouring
    skill !
My pen and ink's choice cell ! my paper's
    pillow !
Thou steady friend, e'en were thy master
    mellow !
My seat !—I visit not the proud St.
    Stephen ;
St. Stephen knows not *me*—so we are
    even.
A seat, obtained not by a threat or
    bribe ;
But free, uninfluenced by an influenced
    tribe :
Thou'rt my inheritance—I boast no
    other ;
My throne, *unique !* for thou hast not
    a brother.

Surrounded by my friends, secure from
    foes,
By thee upheld, I calmly seek repose.
Soothed by thy comfort, my ideas
    spread—
Aerial forms assemble round my head !
Titles and honours court me—in the air !
A proof that I've been *building castles*
    there !

Days, months, and years I've musing
    sat in thee,
And when grown pettish, thou ne'er
    answered'st me ;
A quality this is, so rarely seen,
'Twould be a jewel might adorn a queen.

My study thou !—my favorite resting
    place !
My tabernacle where I pray for grace !
My spouse ! for in thy arms I oft recline,
And hope, tho' pleased with progeny of
    thine,
That no base offspring ever may be mine!

INDEX OF TITLES

INDEX OF FIRST LINES

(Other than First Lines of Songs in the Plays and Operas, which are indexed separately.)

INDEX OF FIRST LINES OF SONGS
IN THE PLAYS AND OPERAS

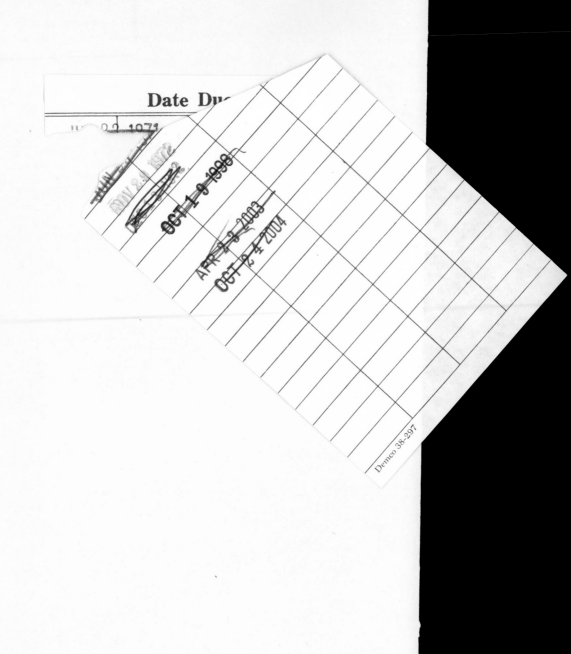